THE GAP YEAR BOOK

Charlotte Hindle, Joe Bindloss

Bradley Mayhew, Jolyon Attwooll, Heather Dickson, George Dunford,
Matt Fletcher, Anthony Ham, Andrew Dean Nystrom, China Williams

ROUND THE WORLD AIR ROUTES

Gap Year

San Francisco p229

Dubrovnik & Dalmatian Coast p109

Dogon Country p126

Machu Picchu p249

See the Round the World chapter in Part II for the lowdown on all routes shown here

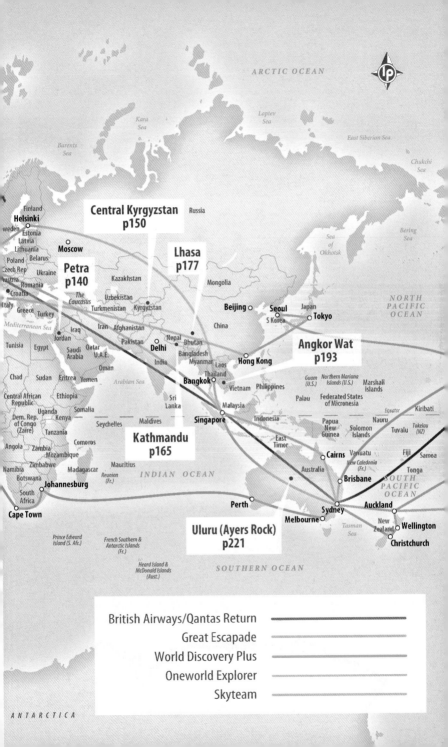

TOP TEN MUST-SEES IN THE WORLD

Our authors picked their favourite spots in their favourite regions and they are:

Angkor Wat (Cambodia) A world wonder of extensive temples built by the former Khmer empire, here pictured at sunrise.

Machu Picchu & the Inca Trail (Peru) This classic trek takes you to one of the wonders of the ancient world.

Lhasa (Tibet) The Potala Palace (pictured here engulfed in a dust storm), Jokhang Temple and bruised heart of Tibetan culture.

Uluru (Ayers Rock; Australia) The mystical red heart of the outback.

Dogon Country (Mali) A stunning escarpment forms the backdrop for a unique, animist culture. Pictured here is a traditional Dogon ceremony associated with the end of harvest in the village of Tirelli.

San Francisco (USA) The nation's most un-American city is also its most beautiful, outrageous and fun-loving.

Petra (Jordan) Spectacular, rose-coloured city hewn from the rock amid stunning scenery. The Treasury (pictured here) was built some time between 100 BC and AD 200.

Dubrovnik & Dalmatian Coast (Croatia) Jaw-droppingly beautiful coastline and a fabulous 1300-year-old walled city.

Central Kyrgyzstan (Kyrgyzstan) Gorgeous highland lakes and valleys, where you can visit the Tash Rabat caravanserai (pictured here), a 15th-century inn on the old Silk Road.

Kathmandu (Nepal) The ultimate backpacker hangout, with bars and temples, like the one pictured here in Durbar Square.

Foreword

So you're thinking about taking a gap year? Good idea. Universities encourage it, employers value it and you get a break from writing essays. It sounds like a cliché but you really do learn a whole new set of life skills along the way.

Also, you won't be alone – the number of people taking a gap year is growing every year with thousands of opportunities awaiting you.

A year out is the perfect time to try something new. Build schools in Africa, teach English in Japan, coach rugby in Fiji or work on a farm in the Australian outback. Seize the opportunity to give something back to the community with voluntary work or a conservation project. Set yourself a challenge like trekking the Himalaya. Whatever you do, revel in your personal achievement.

At STA Travel we send more than six million young people around the world every year – the gap year section on our website is one of the most popular as it includes comprehensive information to offer travellers a helping hand for that big trip. It even offers a route planner to help you plan your perfect year out. The majority of our consultants have taken a gap year themselves and loved it so much we now employ them to pass on their first-hand knowledge to you.

A gap year may seem slightly daunting, but this excellent Gap Year Book from Lonely Planet has all the advice and information you need to get on the road. All your questions are answered: Will my university mind if I take a gap year? Will I be left behind if I take time off? Even parents' concerns are addressed. The pre-trip planning advice is invaluable: how to budget for your trip and how to raise or save the cash; who to travel with or whether to explore alone; what to pack and where to buy it; how to keep in touch while you're away; how to stay safe and healthy on the road; what visas to get and which tickets to buy; and finally, advice on coming home (because you're bound to eventually).

Preparation is essential, so use all the tools at your fingertips. Read this guidebook, visit our website www.statravel.co.uk and talk to one of our experienced staff to ensure you get the most out of your trip.

Take The Gap Year Book with you – it's the essential travel companion.

Have fun and happy travels!

Litsa Constantinou
Managing Director – STA Travel

Contents

THE AUTHORS

CHARLOTTE HINDLE

After university, Charlotte worked in a coat-hanger factory to earn money for her gap year. She then worked as a waitress in a Swiss ski resort, and followed that with six months of travel through central and Eastern Europe, Turkey, Egypt and India to Australia. There she got a job temping as a foot courier in Melbourne before landing a job at Lonely Planet. She worked at Lonely Planet's head office for three years. In 1991 she returned to England to set up Lonely Planet's UK office, which she ran until June 2002. She then took a mini career break to spend the summer with her growing family and to consider more flexible, child-friendly working options. Charlotte is now a freelance travel writer, photographer and gap-year/career-break consultant. Over the years Charlotte has written for the following Lonely Planet titles: The Career Break Book, Travel Writing, Australia, Mediterranean Europe, Walking in Britain, England *and* Britain. *For this book she wrote Part I, the Round the World chapter of Part II and the following chapters in Part III: Volunteering, Conservation & Expeditions; Work Your Route; Au Pairing & Working with Kids; and Courses.*

JOE BINDLOSS

Joe was born in Cyprus, grew up in the UK and has since lived and worked in numerous countries around the world, including the Philippines, Australia, Thailand and India. Joe took his first extended gap year after university, working at a museum, and a rock-climbing gym and painting murals in the USA. Then he went backpacking for a year in Asia. Joe has since worked on more than 20 guidebooks for Lonely Planet. He wrote the Casual/Seasonal Work, Proper Jobs and Teaching chapters for this book.

CONTRIBUTING AUTHORS

Our Part II chapters were written by Lonely Planet regional experts. For information about them (and to take a peek at their mugshots), please see Part II.

Part I

WHY TAKE A GAP YEAR?

You are about to finish school or university. Big decisions are looming like belligerent gate-crashers at your end-of-term party. Now is the best opportunity you will ever have to chase a dream, to do something outrageous, extraordinary or fulfilling, and to explore the world. Louise Ellerton raves about her gap year, saying:

It was amazing. I saw things and did things that I never normally would have done. I went trekking through the Sahara on a camel, and slept out under the stars, on the roofs of houses and in bus shelters, I tried all sorts of foods and experienced the wonderful hospitality of locals, who always had time for me.

At this very moment there are around 200,000 pre-university and post-university students doing something different before getting back on the educational treadmill or thinking about a career. Gap years are not just the preserve of the Prince Harrys and Prince Williams of the world; more than half of the gappers out there come from state schools. Don't think just because the closest thing you have to a healthy bank account is a pig-shaped china object with a slit at the top that you need give up hope – raising money is much easier than you think and this book will give you advice on ways to do it.

A gap year is the perfect time to go out and meet people outside your local postcode. Leaping into a gap you will learn about different cultures, as Claire Loseby, who taught English in China, explains:

I got so much out of my gap year: the chance to learn about and live in a culture different to my own, the opportunity to make new friends, and unbelievable life experiences! I'd never imagined myself eating slugs before, but now I believe anything is possible!

Slugs aside (or on the side, perhaps with a salad garnish?), it'd be such a shame to look back and wish that you had done something when you had the opportunity. Edith Piaf was able to sing 'Non, je ne regrette rien' with such feeling because she did a season as an Alpine chalet cleaner. Well perhaps not, but you get the idea. Lucy Misch agrees:

I got so much out of my gap year it isn't even possible to write it all down! Friends, experiences, memories, passions for things I never thought possible, excitement, independence, and the travel bug more than ever.

People who take a gap year usually emerge more mature, self-confident and focussed, or at least with a bit more to talk about. This is certainly true of Amanda Akass, who had this to say about her gap year:

I got out of it a huge sense of achievement and confidence in myself. Once you have trekked through the Andes in the freezing cold, scared off muggers in Rio, or been lost in a jungle at night, you feel you can do anything! I have seen some of the world, and the incredible memories I have are definitely something to hold on to forever.

And this happened to Naomi Lisney too:

What I hadn't anticipated was how much of a boost to my self-confidence the year would be. I now know that I was actually capable of going out there on my own to make new friends; I also realised that I was free to be a whole person with these new friends, to reinvent myself, as it were. All of this and more really gave me the boost I needed to start uni in a happy, confident state of mind, more likely to make friends and also less likely to spend time worrying about what other people thought of me.

Sometimes your intended career or course, from Arabic to zoology, benefits from a stint of learning abroad. In Amanda Akass' case, this was something the university suggested:

I originally intended to travel after university, but I ended up having a gap year after school because the university said it would benefit me to broaden my experience before starting my English degree. I had been considering this option already; the idea of taking a year out to see the world rather than being stuck in an endless cycle of study and exams was very appealing.

For Sarah Bruce, her post-university gap-year experience helped her get the job she wanted:

I volunteered overseas for five months with Trekforce Expeditions. This really changed my perspective and my priorities and it opened a door for me to work in the charity sector, doing marketing. Having studied law at university, this was something that had never crossed my mind.

Otherwise, a gap year is an ideal time to learn a language properly – how do Spanish classes in Guatemala or Italian classes in Switzerland grab you? Or what about learning a new skill such as skiing, salsa dancing or sailing? Voluntary work is another way to gain valuable experience. You can learn a whole heap of stuff by living and working with new communities, cultures and people.

Then again, you may want to get a job during your gap year – either to save for those cruel variable top-up fees, or, if you've just finished university, to pay off debts you accrued while studying. Otherwise, you might want to get some work experience, like Jonathan Williams did. He explains:

I travelled abroad for six months and then sought relevant work experience to prepare for my degree. I intended to study politics and got a job working as an MP's assistant in the House of Commons.

Or perhaps you're just unsure what to do next. Away from the rigours of formal education you might discover what actually interests you. This is what happened to Ramone Param:

My main reason for taking a gap year was because I was undecided on my course and university choice. My gap year helped me to firm up my idea of what I wanted to achieve and what I wanted to do.

Perhaps your grades weren't high enough or you need to save up before you can go on to higher education. Your enforced gap might throw you at first, but you'll soon find out that there are thousands of ways to fill your time. This was Mark Ramsden's experience:

I never actually intended to take a gap year, but I didn't get the grades I needed for Durham. I also wasn't convinced I was doing the right degree for me; and now that I am on a different course, I know I was right. It was either jump into a university I didn't know anything about or take my time about it and make the most of what had happened.

Of course, you might just want a good, old-fashioned break and there's absolutely nothing wrong with that. Naomi Lisney says:

I'd had a really gruelling last year of school and really needed a break. I felt that going away, having a year to let my hair down, would be a good way of making sure I was refreshed and ready to study again when it came to starting my degree.

Having taken the decision to take a gap year, you are faced with an awesome but bewildering number of choices. Do you want to work abroad, or just travel around? Your friend's going to South Africa but you want to go to Australia. Your boy/girlfriend doesn't want to take a year off, so will it affect your relationship? Can you afford the photography course in Havana (Cuba) that will cost £769.42 more than you possess? And is crewing in the Caribbean better than jungle-trekking in Costa Rica, or can you do both?

With the information in this book, you can find out what opportunities are out there and how you decide which ones are right for you. Part I contains essential predeparture reading, Part II (written by Lonely Planet's country specialists) looks at different regions of the world, and Part III outlines all the various things you can do.

CONCERNS

Are you worrying that your gap year will be a gaping gap – a setback to higher education or the career ladder? If you are, here are some words of wisdom from two organisations that know a thing or two about gap years. Anthony McClaran, chief executive of the Universities & Colleges Admissions Service (UCAS), says:

A gap-year experience can be an excellent preparation for entry into higher education, alongside your formal qualifications. The key is to make sure it is well structured, with outcomes that are going to be of value to universities and colleges.

For post-university gappers or those intending to work after taking time off, this is what Neil Bentley, head of skills and employment at the Confederation of British Industry (CBI), has to say about gap years:

Employers look for a broad range of experience when recruiting. Taking a gap year can help broaden horizons and provide skills that firms seek, such as self-management, foreign languages and a positive attitude to work. Young people that spend a productive gap year developing these skills will appeal most to employers.

The key to how your gap year will be viewed, either by your university/college or by your prospective employers, is how you spend it. If you fritter your time away, perched bum downwards on a beach somewhere then no-one (not even your best mate) will think it has much value. If, however, you take a constructive approach, use your time well and can list your gap-year achievements and accomplishments on your CV, then this will distinguish you from the hoards of job-hungry graduates. By all means, build in some days to do nothing on the beach – you've earned a rest – but, at the end of your year, you'll be judged on whether you used or abused your time. Sophia Haque taught in Pakistan and says:

I haven't met anyone who has not been interested or full of admiration on hearing about my gap year. It is definitely something prospective employers like to talk about in an interview, which is great, as I love talking about it!

PERSUADING YOUR PARENTS

It's wise to get your parents' support and approval for your gap year. You might have no trouble with this if your parents did something similar when they were younger, or if you are a post-university gapper. Any younger, however, and it might be more difficult. Regardless of your age, here are some ways to make your parents feel better about waving you off into the sunset:

- Involve them in your planning and preparation. Get them to read this book and ask them for their ideas and advice. They'll feel better for having a say and a role in your plans.
- Show them that you're responsible by doing thorough research about the destinations you intend to visit. Read the guidebooks, search for information online and, most importantly, talk to returned gappers about their experiences.
- Surprise them with your commitment to fundraising. If they see you're trying, they'll be keener to help.
- If they don't have internet access at home, persuade them to get it. Email is going to be the best way of keeping in touch and they'll appreciate your thinking along these lines.
- Make a plan, with them, for keeping in touch. This shouldn't be too specific because there'll be times when you cannot make contact, and you don't want to worry them unnecessarily.
- If you can afford it, go on a gap-year survival course (see p444 for details). Even better, ask if they'll pay for one – perhaps for a birthday or Christmas present.
- Do a first-aid course. It could save your life, or someone else's. St John Ambulance (www.sja.org .uk) has some excellent ones.
- Make sure they have a copy of your rough itinerary and promise to let them know if it changes.
- Show them you're sensible and buy first-class travel insurance with adequate medical cover (see p30 for details).

If all else fails, rent the *Finding Nemo* DVD for them. This is basically a gap-year story (albeit an enforced gap year) about letting your children go and respecting their decisions and resourcefulness. It's also quite funny, especially the bit when...

If you have not been away from home for an extended period before this may be enough to keep you from deciding to go away. You will undoubtedly miss people and you may feel gripped with fear at the thought of being alone and lonely in an unfamiliar place. But there are ways to make the prospect a lot less intimidating – read on to find out about organisations, activities and approaches that will help you shake off these concerns. Bear in mind that keeping in good contact with your friends and family is an excellent way to combat homesickness (see the Keeping in Touch chapter, p86), and that people tend to cement strong friendships while living an intense existence abroad – most gappers point to this as one of the chief benefits they took away from their experience.

One of the most frightening things to face is the unknown – this is always the case, no matter how old you are. Once you get to a place, you will find that it's easy to adjust, to fit in, and to start enjoying yourself. This is a great confidence booster, as your butterflies disappear and you start to feel both at home and exhilarated by how different everything is.

There are other worries too. What if you spend all this money, time and effort, and then don't like it? Or it doesn't live up to your expectations? A good way to get around this one is to prepare well for your gap – think about what you want to get out of it and take the time to plan. If you research properly, you're less likely to have unrealistic expectations of your choices, and so will be less prone to disappointment.

And what if you run out of money when you're there? This nightmare scenario is usually easily avoided or addressed – see p48 for some solutions to keep you solvent.

It can also be daunting to think about what you'll return to (apart from a bank account bleaker than Scarborough in February). Well, give this some thought before you leave. Plan your gap year so that debts aren't weighing you down while you're starting university or looking for work. Avoid crashing down to earth on your homecoming by having a few things to look forward to when you return (see p8 and the Coming Home chapter, p97).

The prospect of jetting off into the unknown with your mate Mungo who, up till now, has found negotiating trolleys up supermarket aisles pretty challenging, probably should be a concern. Think carefully about whom you want to spend your gap year with (see the next chapter, p13, for more on this). It may be with one particular friend, perhaps a few, or maybe you want to go on your own. If this is the case, there are hundreds of organisations out there that can arrange for you to join a group, whether they're building a school in Nepal or studying art history in Florence (Italy).

Leaving someone behind can make you waver too. If you have a steady boy/girlfriend, you might feel bad about leaving them. Isabel Young had a serious boyfriend whom she left for a year:

The internet helped us keep in touch, and I loved my time away despite the separation. I was so relieved, as it was a real concern – I almost went for a shorter time because of it, but if I had I would've regretted it.

TIMING & PLANNING

Before or after university is the time when you have fewest ties – you won't have to leave a secure job, you're unlikely to have 2.4 kids and rarely – unless you're a millionaire – will you have mortgage payments to consider. Sarah Collinson says:

I chose to do a gap year because I thought that it provided the perfect opportunity to go out and see the world while I didn't have any commitments to keep me in the UK.

One worry is that you will fall behind your peers, as those not taking a gap year will be a year ahead on the education or work ladder. But does this matter? A year is actually a really short amount of time (as anyone over 30 will tell you) and, in all probability, what you get out of your gap year will be a hell of a lot more than your peers get out of an extra year working or studying. Mandy-Lee Trew says:

My year was absolutely amazing – I met so many wonderful people, saw places that held such beauty and did some really crazy stuff that I would not have ordinarily done. It certainly opened my eyes to the world and what's really out there.

And Gareth Potts agrees:

I had a feeling that it was important to see a bit of the world and encounter different cultures and ideas before settling down into a full-time job where opportunities to do a similar sort of thing would be more limited.

Some gappers start thinking about their time off as early as Easter in the lower sixth or in the second year at university. If you want to get onto some of the volunteering expeditions run by gap-year organisations (see the Volunteering, Conservation & Expeditions chapter, p264) then you need to get your applications in up to a year or 18 months in advance. In addition, many (though not all) volunteering programs or placements require you to raise a few thousand quid, so you'll need to give yourself a year (or more) to raise the money. Even if you're not going down this route then you'll need to save for international airfares and a travel budget, unless you plan to spend a portion of your gap year working at home to fund a portion travelling abroad. Many gap-year students do half-and-half (ie work for half a year and travel for half a year) or else work three jobs all summer and take off in October (exhausted but excited).

Otherwise, of course, you might be planning to work while you're travelling, in which case you won't need to save so much dosh and you won't have to start planning your gap year so early. Of course, you might not decide to go abroad at all, in which case there is a host of interesting and varied options open to you in the UK but, again, many of these can be arranged in a few weeks.

To plan or not to plan, that is the question. One of the beauties of taking a gap year is breaking away from the strictures of structure. And after all that education, perhaps the last thing you need is more training and another timetable. Jonathan Williams agrees:

Studying seems to be based around other people's deadlines, whether it be those set by the teachers or exam boards – I wanted some time when I could be in charge!

So, you need to decide whether you want a goal-led gap year with plenty of aims and objectives or a less-structured affair with more leeway to make decisions on the spur of the moment. The best option is probably a cuddly mix of the two. However, you footloose types, just remember it can be financially beneficial, if not exactly thrilling, to plan a bit to avoid blowing all your cash after two hedonistic months in Thailand and to help you get the most out of your time. You also want to bear in mind that universities and future employers are keener to see a well-structured gap year on your CV than a well-maintained, all-over suntan on your body. A little bit more planning might have helped Mark Ramsden, who very honestly says:

I tried to do as much as I could during my year. It wasn't something that I planned, so it ended up all a bit random…To be honest, I think it is fairly obvious that I don't really know what I got from my gap year.

Before Higher Education

Having been at school since the age of five, you might feel that you'd quite like to do something different. A gap year is welcomed by most universities. You will be less likely to drop out, will be more mature, and will have had a chance to become more worldly, whether that be through work, travel or both. It also means that you don't have to rush into a decision about your choice of university and course and can take time to think about what you want to do. Kate Wilkinson says:

I wanted to get more life experience before I went back to college because I hoped that it would make me more mature and responsible. I was also burnt out after my secondary education and didn't think that I would do as well at university if I didn't take a break.

Ramone Param agrees:

I took my gap year before university as an opportunity to reinforce my ideas about my course and to broaden my perspectives for university. I felt that a travelling and working experience before university would help me adapt to the different academic and social requirements of university life.

And so does Damien Rickwood, who explains:

I took a gap year before university because I needed a break from education and I wanted to do something really exciting before settling down again. Also, I didn't really feel like I was ready for university and I thought that a gap year would help me mature a bit (whether it did or not, I'm not sure!).

Debt is another big reason why many gap-year students choose to take time off pre-university rather than after. Hazel Sheard explains:

After university was less good because I felt that with the debt I would accumulate while studying I'd be unable to justify not getting a job as soon as possible.

This was also Louise Ellerton's thinking:

By taking a gap year before uni I knew I had the time to do it and the opportunity to save some money towards it. After uni there are all the loans and debts to pay off, which may lead to you not taking the gap year after all. Though after my great gap-year experience before uni I am now hoping for one afterwards too.

If you choose this option you do, as Louise says, have time. You'll have 15 months to play with, as you'll leave school in early July and start university in early October the next year. Taking a gap year before college also means that you have something very specific to return to, solving the pesky problem of what to do when you come home.

Coming home and looking forward to the prospect of becoming an impoverished student might be as appealing as a prawn-and-chocolate sandwich. But, despite what your parents say, it's more likely that your time-out will impress on you the joys and privilege of further education, rather than the reverse. There's not a lot of evidence to suggest that a gap year taken pre-university means that you won't come home or won't go to university or college at all.

If you're plumping for this option, you can make your UCAS application before you get your A-level results, but ask for deferred entry. This means that you should explain on your form what you will be doing with your time and be prepared to discuss this at an interview. Once you have submitted your UCAS forms you have six to eight months to plan your year.

Or you can sometimes defer after your results. In this case, you will have to contact the college directly. All universities are different but most are usually quite flexible. However, do remember that by this stage there is a mutual contract between you and your chosen university. You've agreed that if you get the grades you'll accept the place and the university has agreed that it will accept you if you have fulfilled the grade requirements.

If your results were worse than expected, you may have failed to gain entry to a course. Don't panic; contact your preferred university. You may be allowed to defer a year despite your grades. Otherwise, you'll have to go through Clearing or retake.

You can still take a gap year if you go through Clearing, as long as it's approved by the university. If you need to retake, you'll have a year off between school and university anyway. How much of that is spent studying depends on your circumstances. Sometimes you can retake quite quickly, go through the whole application process again and still end up with around nine months for a more traditional gap-year break. This is what happened to Tabitha Cook:

I had planned to go to university but once my results came out this didn't happen. I dropped a grade and the uni was unforgiving. I had to reapply to university, which meant that it was hard to plan the year until I was sure that I had a place at university. However, my gap year ended up being one of the best experiences of my life.

The other option, of course, is not to apply to university straight away but to get your application into UCAS before 15 January the following year (your parents will hate this one).

ON THE UCAS CASE

Some key dates provided by **UCAS Customer Services** (☎ 0870 112 2211; www.ucas.com):

15 October	Applications to Oxbridge, medicine, dentistry and veterinary medicine/science courses to be at UCAS.
15 January	Other applications should be at UCAS.
24 March	Route B Art & Design applications to be at UCAS.
30 June	Any applications received after this date go straight into Clearing.
Third week in August (A-level Day) First Clearing vacancies advertised.	
20 September	Closing dates for applications.

SAVING FOR VARIABLE TOP-UP FEES

Now that variable top-up fees (VTFs) are a reality from 2006, you might need to spend a year between school and university working in the UK to save for your student days. If so, there are still a number of UK courses (see p420) and voluntary-work programs (see p284) that you could undertake at the weekends or in the evenings. If this is your lot but you still want a few fantastic foreign experiences, then there are plenty of things you can do for a few months over the summer before starting to work and save for university in the autumn. In addition, some gap-year organisations are starting to run overseas 'mini-gap' programs specifically designed for the student who needs to spend the majority of their gap year working in the UK.

After Higher Education

There are plenty of reasons to take a gap year after higher education. Jane Williams, for instance, says:

I chose to take a gap year after university because I wanted to get my degree out of the way before I started travelling.

And, of course, there's no real time constraint if you take a gap year after university. Indeed, a gap year could quite easily turn into a gap year or two or three.

Justin Ward thought that his greater maturity meant he got more out of his gap year than he might have done if he'd been younger. He says:

I took a gap year after university – actually, I had a job for a while and then went on the VSO (Voluntary Service Overseas) World Youth program. I felt that I got more out of the program because I was more focussed than I might have been if I was a school leaver.

It might also mean that you have a better idea of what career you eventually want to pursue and so could tailor a gap year based upon getting some relevant experience. This could be anything from taking a film course in New York, or working with children in an American summer camp to volunteering in a local newspaper office in Ghana.

Alastair Fearn didn't take a year off between school and university but is now planning one. He says:

I feel it is my last chance to get away for a substantial period of time before I start work and become burdened with life in general, job, mortgage etc.

There are a number of issues that might worry you about taking a gap year after higher education. Perhaps you feel it will delay your launch into the job market and you're worried how future employers will react. However, the majority of employers look favourably on a well-spent gap year – it means you will have something more to offer them than just a degree. It will also mark you out as an interesting candidate with get-up-and-go (as long as it's not so much get-up-and-go that you drool at planes going overhead). In addition, a gap year after university gives you time to think seriously about your future career, while you're doing something exciting and constructive. This can only be good news for your new boss.

The biggest issue will be debt. According to the National Union of Students (NUS) and based on a report by Barclays, students graduating in 2006 will do so with debts of around £17,500. After that, students will be landed (from outer space – only aliens could have devised such a regressive scheme) with variable top-up fees and it is estimated that those graduating in 2010 will do so with £33,700 of debt. However, from April 2005 you don't have to pay off your student loan until your earnings reach £15,000 a year. Yes, all that sounds pretty horrible but it's going to be the same whether you take a gap year before or after university. If you choose not to take a gap year after uni because of this debt, what have you actually achieved? You're going to be working for the rest of your life, so is deferring any loan repayments (dependent on your earnings) for one measly year going to make that much difference? And, of course, if you can't save or fundraise to pay for your gap year, you can always work abroad.

Perhaps you're worried about missing out on graduate recruitment drives. During your final year, there will be numerous job fairs set up by universities and colleges (the main season is from October to March, but some take place in summer). Even if you are intending to take a gap year, these are still relevant to you. Talk to the companies that interest you. Tell them what you're planning on doing and see what they say. Make sure you find out when you need to apply for jobs. You can apply from anywhere in the world; it doesn't matter if you're on a jackaroo or jillaroo course in Australia's outback. However, if you're intending to do this, you must have access to your updated CV and references. And, more of a drawback, you'll need to be available for an interview. If you are a rare and exotic bird (ie the company really wants you), you may be able to apply for a job before you go but defer your starting date.

Don't skip the free careers advice at the end of your final year, as you won't be able to access it a year later. Talk to your careers advisors about your gap-year decision.

TRAVEL COMPANIONS

'Friends, Romans, countrymen, lend me your gap years'. Contrary to popular belief, this was Julius Caesar deciding on whom to go with on his year out. Yes, this thorny question has occupied many a fine mind through the ages. However, as Alastair Fearn points out:

It is more about the people you meet than the person you go with.

SOLO

Ask any seasoned traveller and they'll tell you that the *best* way to travel is on your own. Mandy-Lee Trew au-paired in America and then went travelling. She says:

Going on my own was not half as daunting and scary as I thought it would be. If anything, it was more liberating than anything else I've ever done.

Many gappers agree – you never have to ask anyone what they want to do, your plan is always the most popular and you never have to take anyone else's feelings into account. Jonathan Williams found:

During my time backpacking around Australia, New Zealand and Singapore, I liked to be on my own. Although it was sometimes lonely, I preferred to do the things I wanted to do, rather than worrying about compromising with other people. In cities, in particular, it was better being on my own, as it isn't great spending money (which you are short of) on things you don't really want to do.

Jonathan mentions money and this is sometimes an issue for single travellers because it can be more expensive to travel on your own. However, any traveller who has ever travelled alone knows that you never end up being on your own for very long (unless you want to be). Lucy Misch explains:

I can recommend travelling on your own to anyone. It is a great way to meet people. You are never on your own, and you always have someone else to help you look out for yourself.

As Lucy's experience shows, when you're on your own you make more of an effort to meet new people. You are more approachable and you often bond much more readily with local people who will often start up a conversation with you.

In addition, you don't have to worry about falling out with yourself (if you do, you may have hit a problem and should head back home). You'll also get a lot of people telling you how brave they think you are, so practise your self-deprecating it-was-nothing-but-I-am-very-brave look.

However, you are bound to feel lonely at times and that's when your book, your travel diary, your international phonecard, or the local internet café comes in handy. Having said that, being on your own and being ill isn't the greatest feeling on earth; it's the pits if you've got the shits. You have to look after yourself and make sound judgements about the seriousness of your condition. Are you too ill to travel? Should you see a doctor? These are questions that are much easier to answer with the help of someone else. See p75 for ways to cope if you do get sick.

Solo Women

There's no denying it, travelling on your own as a woman can be challenging. It can also be extremely rewarding. Lucy Misch travelled in Australia and Greece on her own and says:

I recommend travelling on your own to everyone. Even as a girl, it's just the best and most rewarding way of doing it.

Wherever you're going, it is important to establish the status and position of women in local society, noting how they behave and how they are expected to behave. In some cultures, drinking in bars (particularly on your own), smoking, wearing make-up and showing too much flesh may give off the wrong signs to the local male population. Changing the way you dress and behave will not only protect you from harassment but also shows respect to the people of your host country.

If you're on your own, you'll find that people are more likely to offer you hospitality – you are so much less threatening than a man alone. You are also perceived as much more vulnerable and people will fall over themselves to offer you assistance. In some countries you can even take advantage of separate carriages, waiting rooms and queues for women.

However, there is a down side. Depending on where you travel, you probably will get hassled. Often it is pretty harmless stuff – young men wanting to accompany you down the street to practise their English (or so they say) – but always pay attention to your common sense and instinct. If you start to feel uncomfortable in a situation, get yourself out of it. And, never put up with any invasive behaviour. If you're groped in a crowded place, make a scene and publicly embarrass the groping pond life. Do remember, though, that you've gone abroad to see and experience new cultures, and you can't do that if you're entirely protected and afraid to meet people's eyes.

For more tips on travelling safely as a solo woman traveller see p82. Marco Polo Travel Advisory Service (www.marcopolotravel.co.uk) in Bristol also runs one-hour consultancies (£40) for up to four women on safe travel for women (the opposite sex are welcome to come along too).

BOY/GIRLFRIEND

If you've got it going on, going away together can be great. You're with the person you're closest to, sharing excellent experiences, and you don't have to leave them behind. As for the economics, two people can't travel as cheaply as one but depending on the destination they can travel as cheaply as one-and-a-half.

However, travelling with your partner will really test the strength of your relationship. Travelling can be stressful – think of those long, uncomfortable bus rides and cockroach-infested bathrooms. You'll spend more time in each other's company than you normally do and you won't have the support network of your usual friends to have a good moan with. In addition, being in a couple will make it more difficult to make new friends. If you are living, working or travelling abroad, there's not the same drive to go out and meet new people, and other people don't find you so approachable. If you bear this in mind, though, you can overcompensate with openness and friendliness and then you'll meet loads of fellow travellers despite your loved-up status.

Another issue to consider is money. On the road, more couples argue about every baht, rouble and zloty than anything else. If you're going away with your soul mate discuss your budget carefully. If you have a joint kitty it's a good idea to allocate a certain amount each week for both of you to spend on whatever you want.

Alastair Fearn has travelled all sorts of ways and says:

I have travelled with my best friend, girlfriend and for a short time on my own. Going with my friend was excellent as we were young single men in Europe and made the most of things! This obviously wasn't going to happen with my girlfriend but we still had an excellent time.

FRIENDS

It's often the greatest thing on earth to go away with a good friend. Kate Wilkinson travelled to Cuba and on to Central America:

I travelled with my best friend. It was a good pairing because while my friend is an organiser and knew what there was to see and do, I was the one who would find out how to get there and which buses to take. This meant that she chose where we went and I got us there. There were so many pros in going with Immy; she was outgoing, organised, adventurous and really up for a laugh. This meant that I was never bored and always had someone to talk to and we gave each other support.

Molly Bird agrees:

I went with my best friend from school. This was one of the best decisions I made. Sharing a problem with another person means that the problem is more than halved, and sharing a great experience makes that experience all the more exciting. When we took our first look at the Taj Mahal we were able to say, 'Look at that!' and 'I know!' and 'Isn't it amazing?'. It was so exciting because we were experiencing it together. It's so great when you get home too – just to be able to say, 'Do you remember when…'.

Hazel Sheard had an amazing experience travelling for part of her time in India with her grandfather:

He was born and brought up in India and came out to show me where our family lived, went to school, worked, fought and died. This was a fascinating journey from one coast of the Subcontinent to the other, travelling along railway lines that my great-grandfather had engineered. We even had coffee with the maharajah of Jaipur, as my great-grandfather ran the Jaipur state railway, and my grandfather had photos of him as a boy.

But Kate Wilkinson rounds off her tale by saying:

After living with someone for such a long time it did mean that we knew each other very well and little things started to niggle. We had two arguments, but they were just to let off steam and then we got on fine again.

So, like everything else there are pros and cons. Before you set off round the world with someone, do ask yourself if there's anything that has always annoyed you about them. Is it their grumpiness at breakfast? Their tuneless whistling? Or the way they always manage to be late for everything – especially planes? Foibles are charming in small doses but can really get on your nerves after a while.

And then there's travelling with a group of friends. This can be a lot of fun, and not as intense as the one-on-one scenario. You're bound to come back with brilliant memories of funny times, but it does make it more difficult to make decisions, and can be more restrictive than going with just one other person or on your own. You can always get around this by breaking away from the group as well – getting the best of both worlds. Paul Walker travelled with two other friends and says:

It can be difficult as people want to do different things and go to different places, so pleasing everyone can be a bit stressful. For this reason I went off on my own but after a few days found I wanted the company of my close friends again.

Sharing a trip with a friend or a group can save you money. It's cheaper to share a room than get a single, and sharing a flat abroad works out even less expensive. It's also best if you're quite evenly matched financially. If you've got a lot more money, it'll feel weird as you tuck into your king prawns while they chew on the cardboard drink coasters, and you'll both feel agitated by the imbalance.

TRAVEL M8S

Got a burning ambition to visit Baffin Island (very northern Canada) or Spitsbergen (a Norwegian island in the middle of the Arctic Ocean) and no-one wants to come with you? Funny that. Well, there are various ways you can advertise or search for a like-minded travel m8 (mate) or travel group. Of course, it can be a bit of a risky business: what will this random character be like? (Presumably as mad as you.) But finding someone can be an adventure in itself, and at least you're starting off with a major interest in common. If you do get together and it doesn't work out, you'll have someone to accompany you in those difficult first few weeks, and you can always ditch each other once you find your feet.

To meet potential travel companions, you can advertise in the Connections page of *Wanderlust* magazine (www.wanderlust.co.uk) or in *Globe,* the magazine of the Globetrotters Club (www.globetrotters.co.uk). The www.gapyear.com website has a message-board section, with a specific strand called 'Find a travel mate'. On the Lonely Planet website (www.lonelyplanet.com) people often use the Thorn Tree (the travellers' notice board) to find people going the same way.

Another great way to bump into travellers before you go is at your local travel club (there's a list of these on the Wanderlust website), at slide nights and at travel talks in bookshops. There are also notice boards at the spring travel fairs, such as the Daily Telegraph Travel Adventure & Sports Show (www.adventureshow.co.uk) or Destinations (www.destinations show.com), which are full of travellers who WLTM (ie 'would like to meet' – get with the lingo) other travellers.

GAP-YEAR ORGANISATIONS

If you'd still prefer to eat dinner with cannibals than travel alone, then consider beginning your travels with a gap-year organisation or course. As Sarah Collinson says:

I went with VentureCo and worked on an aid project, did a Spanish course and then did two months of overlanding. I did not know anyone in the group beforehand and it was very nerve-racking meeting them all for the first time. However, we all got on very well; we were all interested in similar things and just got on with enjoying ourselves. It worked out really well for us as we all wanted to travel on afterwards and we just split into smaller groups and went off together. I can't think of any negatives.

And this is what Tabitha Cook decided to do too:

I went out with an organisation called Travellers Worldwide. You could go with friends or partners with this group but I didn't, I went on my own and met some amazing friends who I'll keep in touch with for the rest of my life.

For more information on the range of gap-year organisations see the Volunteering, Conservation & Expeditions chapter on p264; for courses catering to the gap-year market, see p429, p432, p437 and p444.

ADVENTURE TOUR OPERATORS

If heading off on your own with no safety net is as unappealing as a mussel-topped meringue, you might want to kick off your gap year with an organised tour. These are a good way of meeting like-minded travellers and an exciting way of getting used to life as an international nomad. They're a sort of halfway house between true independent travel and a package tour. You will feel quite like an independent traveller but your tickets, accommodation, food and adventure activities will be pre-booked and you'll travel on a pre-arranged route in a group with a leader or guide. For example, going with one of the overland companies, such as Encounter Overland (www.encounter.co.uk) or Exodus (www.exodus.co.uk), in a huge 4WD truck is a great introduction to travel in many of the world's less-developed continents. In addition, Encounter Overland has a few trips where you can combine travelling with volunteering on aid projects.

Of course, going with a tour operator will be considerably more expensive than going it alone. Depending on what you're doing, where you're going, and how you're travelling, a one-week trip might start from £300. This excludes international flights, travel insurance, visas and vaccinations but usually includes accommodation, food and in-country travel.

The range of organised tours you could take is mind-boggling. There are cycling, walking, trekking, horse-riding, swimming, white-water rafting, cultural, historical and culinary tours. You can go anywhere in the world for as little as one week to as long as one year. There's a small list of tour operators, including overland companies, on p393 and p394; otherwise, for more information, consult the Association of Independent Tour Operators (AITO) directory at www.aito.co.uk, look at the classified ads in *Wanderlust* magazine (www.wanderlust.co.uk) or get along to one of the Daily Telegraph Adventure Travel & Sports Shows (www.adventureshow.co.uk).

MEETING OTHER TRAVELLERS ON THE ROAD

Common spots where this multicoloured, multifaceted species gather are backpacker hostels, cafés (especially if they do a good breakfast), bars, beaches, internet cafés, long-distance bus terminals and adventure activity centres. Sometimes they are spotted in self-contained, less-approachable packs, sometimes in more serene gatherings of two or three. The solo ones are furiously concentrating on a book, their demeanour shouting, 'I look like I'm loving my book but actually I'd be pleased to talk to you'.

Most travellers are interested in chatting to other travellers – you all have something in common. You can make great friends while on the road and meet some really interesting people. You will find out good places to stay and cool things to do. Never underestimate the travellers' grapevine; it is one of the most powerful in the world.

Sometimes, though, you'll meet travellers who do nothing but complain about the locals or complain about the cost of everything. Or you meet someone whom you think is very nice, amusing and laid-back and then later find out that they're not so fun and they've attached themselves to you like a leech. So how do you get away from people if they begin to irritate you? Well, people generally get the message if you refuse to answer to your name, wear a disguise and affect amazement when they approach…There are simpler ways though. All you need to do is change your plans – decide to leave a place, or stay on a bit longer if they're heading off. Travelling is usually so flexible that you won't have any problem escaping if that's what you want to do. Avoid situations of close-proximity to a new pal, unless you've really hit it off. For example, going on a 10-day, or even a four-day, trek or safari with someone you've only just met might prove to be one of life's longer journeys, if they start to irritate you after the first kilometre.

ALONE WITH A GOOD BOOK

When you're dining alone and want to look frantically interested in a book, here are 20 travel literature classics to consider. These are the favourites of staff at Stanford Bookshop, London:

- *Arabian Sands* by Wilfred Thesiger
- *Arabia Through the Looking Glass* by Jonathan Raban
- *Frontiers of Heaven: A Journey to the End of China* by Stanley Stewart
- *Full Tilt: Ireland to India with a Bicycle* by Dervla Murphy
- *From the Holy Mountain: A Journey Among the Christians of the Middle East* by William Dalrymple
- *I Came, I Saw: An Autobiography* by Norman Lewis
- *Into the Heart of Borneo* by Redmond O'Hanlon
- *Journey into Cyprus* by Colin Thubron
- *In Patagonia* by Bruce Chatwin
- *A Pattern of Islands* by Arthur Grimble
- *The Road to Oxiana* by Robert Byron
- *A Season in Heaven* by David Tomory
- *A Short Walk in the Hindu Kush* by Eric Newby
- *South from Granada* by Gerald Brenan
- *Southern Gates of Arabia: A Journey in the Hadhramaut* by Freya Stark
- *Terra Incognita: Travels in Antarctica* by Sara Wheeler
- *A Time of Gifts* by Patrick Leigh-Fermor
- *An Unexpected Light: Travels in Afghanistan* by Jason Elliot
- *Venice* by Jan Morris
- *The Worst Journey in the World* by Apsley Cherry-Garrard

PASSPORTS, VISAS, TICKETS & INSURANCE

PASSPORTS

Even though their colour might be a constant reminder of your school uniform, you'll need one of these EU beauties. Your passport is proof of your nationality and you'll need it for border crossings (even in some parts of the EU). Abroad, it is also your main means of identification and shows (via entry stamps and visas or papers) that you have the legal right to be in a country. Always keep your passport on you and avoid handing it over to anyone for any length of time – although sometimes you'll be required to leave it at a hotel or hostel desk. As a precaution, photocopy the back page with your mug-shot and vital statistics on it and all pages with prearranged visa stamps on them. Carry these separately from your passport.

If you've already got a passport, check its expiry date. If it's going to peter out within six months of arriving home from your gap year, get a new one. Some foreign governments require that your passport is valid for a period of time after you leave their country (usually three months beyond the date of departure), so the longer the validity of your passport, the better. Most passports are valid for 10 years.

Also check how many blank pages you have left. You might need quite a few for visas and entry and exit stamps, and many officials will refuse to issue a visa or stamp your passport unless it's on a clean page. It would be a real drag to run out of spare pages when you've just spent three days getting to the Mongolian border.

If you don't have a passport – get one. Apart from the fact that you won't be going anywhere without one, you often hand over your passport for visa applications. New passports usually take only two weeks to be issued. However, some visas can take up to one month to obtain, so try to apply for a new passport six months before you travel.

In the UK, passports are issued by the **UK Passport Service** (UKPS; ☎ 0870 521 0410; www.passport.gov.uk). Amazingly, this telephone number works 24 hours a day, seven days a week, so if you wake up from a passport-related bad dream in the middle of the night you can get on the phone and receive nocturnal passport therapy.

One reason why your nights might be disturbed by passport nightmares is that from late 2005 or early 2006 new UK passports will include a facial biometric identifier that will comply with standards established by the International Civil Aviation Organisation (ICAO). This will be stored on a paper-thin computer chip and inserted into new passports. If you've heard the term 'biometric passport' or 'smart passport' then this is what it refers to. At a later date a second biometric – either a fingerprint or an iris pattern – will be incorporated. The timing is important because US Congress is demanding that anyone hoping to enter America under the Visa Waiver Program (VWP) with a passport issued after 26 October 2005 must have a 'smart passport'. If yours is issued before this date, then you don't need to worry – assuming it is 'machine-readable'. Most UK passports are but some older ones aren't. (Does your passport have two lines of print, including lots of chevrons, on the white strip at the foot of the personal data page? If so, you're readable.)

These requirements may change, so for up-to-date information on entry requirements to the USA check the US embassy website at www.usembassy.org.uk/cons_web/visa/niv/mrp.htm.

So, do you need to have disturbed nights about all of this? Well, at the time of writing it seems unlikely. If you're applying for your first passport, no change is planned to the usual paperwork needed to prove your British nationality. Your facial biometric is obtained by scanning the passport-sized photos you get from any old photo booth. What you may need to do if you're a passport virgin is attend an interview. If you're simply renewing, the situation should be unchanged: you can just apply by post. And, don't feel you need to rush out to get a snazzy new biometric number immediately because these will be phased in over a period of time.

You can apply for a new passport online, via a post office or through a Worldchoice travel agent. Along with a completed application form, you'll need the following:

Payment A standard adult passport with the minimum number of pages will set you back around £42, if it's issued within the usual processing time. If you apply through a post office or Worldchoice travel agent there'll be an extra £6 handling charge.

Photographs Two recent, identical, head-and-shoulder shots taken against a white, cream or light-grey background are required. Your expression has to be neutral and your mouth must be closed (no toothy grins please!). One of these photos needs to be validated by the professional person who signed section 10 of your application form. See the UK Passport Service website for the precise wording.

Proof of any name change You'll need to provide proof of any name change, such as a marriage certificate or a deed poll.

Proof of citizenship A birth, naturalisation or registration certificate is required as proof of citizenship. If you were born after 1 January 1983 and are applying for the first time you'll need to provide a 'long' birth certificate, ie one that includes names and place of birth of both parents.

Proof of identity Your application needs to be counter-signed by a British or Irish passport holder who has known you for two years (but is unrelated to you) and has professional standing in the community. This is someone like an accountant, lawyer, doctor or journalist. There's a full list of acceptable people on the UK Passport Service website.

The UK Passport Service website is really comprehensive and covers everything you could ever wish to know about you and your little red book.

Issuing Period & Rush Jobs

Applications made through the post office or Worldchoice are given priority and normally take two weeks. If you apply by post directly to the UK Passport Service it will take longer. However, if you've left your application until the last moment or – oh no! – have lost your passport, then you might need to get a new or replacement passport in a hurry. To do this, apply in person to a UK Passport Service office and use the one-week Fast Track service. There's a faster one-day Premium service if you're simply renewing in a hurry, but you can't use it if you're applying for a first passport or need to replace a lost, stolen or damaged one. Of course, you have to pay extra for this – £89 for the Premium service or £70 for the Fast Track service – and your application must be properly completed and submitted with everything they need.

Lost or Stolen Passports

If your passport is lost or stolen while you're still in the UK you need to report it immediately to the UK Passport Service and fill out a lost/stolen report. If you lose it abroad, this will catapult you into a Kafkaesque realm of bureaucratic hassles. But, hey, it's not the end of the world.

If you lose your passport, contact the nearest British consulate, embassy or high commission. If your home country does not have diplomatic representation where you are, contact an embassy belonging to the nearest neighbouring country. Ask the staff whether you need to notify the local government of the loss, and how to handle it if you do. If your passport is stolen, inform the local police and get a police report before heading to your consulate.

You'll need some form of identification (a driver's licence, student card, old passport, birth certificate etc – preferably something with your photo on it) to satisfy the consular staff before they'll issue a replacement. This is your passport photocopy's big moment.

Your consulate should be able to issue an emergency passport within a couple of days but you may pay extra for the privilege. If you had visas in the passport that need replacing, you'll have to go to the nearest consulate of that country to reapply – and pay the visa fee again.

Dual Citizenship

If you've got two passports then you're a jammy dodger. Seriously, though, visa fees and the amount of time you're allowed to stay in one country depend on your nationality. If you've got two passports you can choose to use the one that gets you the best deal. For instance, Poppy Little has an Australian and a UK passport and used this to her advantage in Jordan:

I chose to use my Australian passport in Jordan because the visa cost me so much less than if I'd fessed up to being a UK passport-holder. My boyfriend's only got one passport and was spitting chips at the difference in price.

However, if you do decide to travel with two passports, be wary: it's wise not to let on to immigration officials that you have dual citizenship. You should also try to stick to the same passport when travelling between neighbouring countries – if you've entered Thailand on your British passport then don't try to enter Malaysia on your Australian passport, otherwise officials might wonder how you got into the region.

VISAS

A visa is a stamp or document in your passport that says you may enter a country and stay there for a specific amount of time. You usually have to pay and visas can be pricey. Your first step is to find out whether you need one or not. The easiest way to do this is to check what it says on the **Thames Consular Services** (☎ 020 8996 2912; www.thamesconsular.com) website. It's a visa agency but the website is amazingly comprehensive. The slow route is to check with the country's embassy or consulate.

There are two ways of getting visas. You can get them from the country's local consulate before you go, or in the country upon entry – it all depends on your destination. It also depends on whether the country you're going to has representation in the UK.

Bear in mind the following when gearing up to apply for visas:

- Nine out of 10 visas are valid from date of issue, which means that you'll be getting most of them on the road. For instance, a Chinese tourist visa runs for three months from date of issue, so you'd only get one in advance if this was early in your itinerary. However, an Australian working-holiday visa lasts for 12 months from date of entry, so you can apply for one of these at home and still plan on visiting Australia late in your gap year.
- Visa requirements can sometimes be affected by the transport you've used to enter a country. For instance, if you fly into Cambodia or Laos you can get visas on arrival but if you go overland you must arrange them in advance (usually in Bangkok).
- In some instances you can get a longer visa if you apply before you travel. For instance, Romania will give you six months if you apply in your home country but only 30 days if you rock up at the border.
- If you've got an Israeli stamp in your passport from earlier travels then it can cause problems when entering countries such as Syria and Lebanon (Jordan and Egypt are OK). If you're travelling around the Middle East on this trip and you have evidence of a visit to Israel in your passport, then consider getting another passport.

- Some overland border crossings are open for relatively short times during the day, so try to find out the opening hours in advance. Also, they are often closed during religious holidays. Molly Bird fell foul of this one, even before she'd left home:

Jess and I were going to India. The week before we left we set off for the Indian consulate in London. We got there at 7am to ensure success. Having made such an effort to get there on time it turned out that the consulate was closed for an Indian holiday. This was a good introduction to India where offices are always closed for holidays!

- If you want to visit the USA and don't qualify for the Visa Waiver Program (VWP) then you'll have to book a personal interview in London or Belfast before you're given a visa (there could be as much as a three- to four-week delay before you get an interview date). See www.usembassy.org.uk/cons_web/visa/visaindex.htm for US visa requirements. Mandy-Lee Trew, who au-paired in the USA, tells us:

I was sitting in the waiting room of the US consulate waiting for my number to be called. The gentleman before me was denied and there ensued a screaming match. I was the lucky one to go in after him. I was as friendly and as genuine as I could be. The interviewer appreciated this and issued my visa – mine was the first issued that day, after six other applicants had their visa applications refused.

- Take lots of passport-sized photographs with you. Many countries require two to four photos to process a visa and it's a hassle finding local photo booths abroad.

Types of Visa

There are essentially five types of visa (but each can have varying categories such as length of stay, and single or multiple entry). They are transit, tourist, business, student and working-holiday visas. The ones you're most likely to be interested in are tourist, student or working-holiday visas.

A tourist visa allows you to stay in a country for a restricted period, usually between 30 and 90 days – but don't panic, they can often be extended once you're in the country. Amanda Akass says:

In Bolivia we forgot to ask for a 90-day visa rather than the standard 30-day one but didn't have a problem changing this later.

If you're planning on studying abroad or doing a course then you'll probably have to get a student visa. Check with the school before you sign up and with the relevant consulate.

Transit visas are valid for only one or two days: you need these if you're just overlanding through a particular visa-hungry country but you don't intend to stay there.

If you are under 30 years and 11 months and you want to work in Australia or New Zealand, you can apply for a working-holiday visa. This allows you to stay for 12 months from date of entry and to work for no more than three months for one employer on a casual basis. You can only apply online (or through an agency) for an Australian working-holiday visa – this means you'll need a fairly powerful computer and your brain in gear, as the form isn't as logical as it could be. You'll also need your passport and credit card at the ready before logging on to www.immi.gov.au. The fee is approximately £70. Applications are processed in two days if there are no complications and there's no need for a bank statement or proof of funds. However, you won't have a paper visa in your passport and you have to go into the local Department of Immigration and Multicultural & Indigenous Affairs (DIMIA) office on your arrival in Australia to get your passport stamped. For New Zealand you need to apply by post, in person or with an agency and this is done through the New Zealand high commission in the Haymarket, London. Since 2004, New Zealand has more than doubled the quota for working-holiday visas.

Of course, you may want to work in Europe and if you're a Brit you can do this in any European Economic Area (EEA) country for up to three months without restrictions, though you may need to register upon arrival. For more information, see p332.

Planning & Applying for Visas

Visa arrangements can seem almost wilfully complex. Sorting out what you need for which country and when to apply can have you reaching for the hangover remedy before you've even had a drink. Basically, though, all you need to do is get organised. Start by writing down all the countries you're going to visit, how you're going to enter each country, how long you'll be staying in each one and whether you need a visa or not. This last point is usually easy to establish but do consider Ramone Param's unlucky experience:

Before travelling to Ecuador I was told that British citizens do not require a visa. However, on the day of my departure I was not allowed to depart from the UK being told that members of the Sikh religion, regardless of nationality, need a visa to travel to Ecuador. This meant I had to travel to London to get a visa from the Ecuadorian Embassy and I had to delay my gap year by a fortnight.

However, most gappers are upbeat about the whole process. Jonathan Williams says:

I didn't have any problems at all with my visas. I used to compare immigration officials' friendliness at every destination I visited. The ones in New Zealand were great because they seemed mostly interested in telling me where to visit to get the best Lord of the Rings *photo.*

After you've got your list together, work out which visas it makes sense to get in advance and which you'll get upon arrival. Also ask yourself what type of visa you require – unlike Heinz baked beans, there are only the five different varieties – and establish whether you'll need a multiple- or single-entry visa. Armed with this list, check that there's diplomatic representation in the UK and then:

- Phone in advance (or look on the website) to find out the consulate's opening hours and requirements (photographs, identification and documents) and fees. Don't forget to ask how long it takes to process the type of visa you require. Also, leave yourself lots of time as your visa may not be processed on your first attempt.
- Arrive early and be prepared to queue. Bring a book to help pass the time (there's no better time to start reading your friendly travel guidebook). Hazel Sheard remembers:

It takes a while – looking back, queuing for a visa at India House was excellent preparation for Indian bureaucracy in the country itself.

- Have all your documentation in order and ready to present to the clerk, including your planned entry and departure dates. Make sure you have the correct fee in the appropriate currency – those granite-featured staff sometimes can't or won't provide change. Come armed with five passport-style photos.

- When you pick up your visa, make sure that the dates, length of stay and other details are all correct before you leave the consulate.

Getting your visas takes time and, no matter where you apply, you're likely to face short opening hours, long queues (especially in London) and surly staff. Your best bet is to get all your visas at once and plan on spending a week or so in London (like it or not this is where most diplomatic representation is based) doing this. Try to treat it as a mini-holiday and remember to budget not only for the actual visa costs but for your stay too (if you can, sofa-surf with friends). You can apply for most visas by post, so if the city-break option doesn't appeal give this a go – but expect long delays for each one. To date, the only visa you can apply for online is the Australian working-holiday visa or the Australian Electronic Travel Authority (ETA) – in other words, the three-month tourist visa. Otherwise, there are visa agencies who will arrange all your visas for you, such as **Trailfinders** (☎ 0845 050 5905; www.trailfinder.com), though this will be more expensive than DIY.

TICKETS
Air

Unless your year off involves unicycling around the world or not straying outside your local bus network, you'll probably travel by plane at some point. More than likely, your flights will be your biggest single expense (see p34 for more information about planning your budget) and there are a bewildering number of ticket options, fare structures, destination computations and pitfalls to negotiate. Even if you're travelling with a gap-year or year-out organisation that's taking care of your flights, it's still a good idea to understand how it all works and, chances are, you'll be travelling independently at some point during your time off anyway. All fares quoted in this section were for departures in November 2004.

A class in air-ticket management might go something like this:

Cancellation penalties These vary considerably, but cancelling your ticket once it's booked may mean you lose the entire value of your ticket. (Most travel-insurance policies will protect against cancellation fees but only if the reason for cancelling is one covered by the particular policy you took out.)

Change penalties The three main changes possible are name, dates and route. In terms of the first, it is very rare that a name change will be permitted, so don't book a ticket, dump your boyfriend or girlfriend and hope to replace them with your new squeeze. As regards to dates, there are usually restrictions about changing your departure date from the UK. However, the dates of onward flights can often be changed, subject to seat availability. Although in many cases date changes are permitted free, quite hefty fees could be charged, depending on the rules of the ticket (and the policy of the travel agency and airline concerned). In some cases, tickets will allow no date changes at all. Route changes may be possible but usually attract a fee and where they are permitted there is likely to be a stipulation as to how many route changes you're allowed (often only one).

Minimum or maximum time limits It is virtually impossible to find a ticket that allows you to be away for more than 12 months. If you want to travel for longer than a year you might decide not to use the last leg of your ticket. A round-the-world (RTW) ticket is still good value even if you only end up using three-quarters of it. Before you go down this route, do some research on the web to see how much it'll cost you to buy a ticket home from wherever you end up. Some tickets also state that you cannot return to the UK within a certain period of time.

Refund policy Despite what you might be told by the local airline office, it is unlikely that you'll get any money back if you don't use a certain sector or portion of your ticket. Airline staff in Bangkok, for example, rarely know all the rules of a discounted ticket sold by an agent in London. If you are entitled to a refund then this can usually only be arranged through the travel agency where your ticket was purchased. This isn't terribly useful if you're in the middle of nowhere having the time of your life.

Seasonal limits The price of your ticket will depend on your departure date. Avoid departing from the UK during the school holidays, as all airline fares are jacked up at this time. The cheapest months to leave for Australia or New Zealand tend to be May and June, followed by February and November.

Stopover limits Most fares restrict the number of stopovers permitted.

When to purchase Start looking for special or bargain fares eight to 12 months in advance of your departure date. Note that many of the best deals will require you to pay in full soon after booking. Special or bargain fares often carry stricter and heavier change penalties (and these changes are rarely covered by your travel insurance). You may get cheap tickets at the last minute if you're superflexible, but it is more likely that you'll end up delaying your departure date. Very rarely do long-haul airlines slash prices for imminent departures, even if all seats do not have bums on them.

TYPES OF TICKET
RTW Tickets
A RTW ticket is a series of coupons (in one or more tickets) that will take you around the globe on two or more airlines (you can't go around the world on a single airline). The most common RTW tickets are put together by members of the airline alliances. Their RTW ticket options are all different. The main RTW offerings are: Great Escapade, World Discovery, Star Alliance, oneworld Explorer, Global Explorer, Worldwide Journey and SkyTeam. Which RTW ticket is right for you will depend on your budget, how many kilometres you plan to cover, how many stops you require and where you're going (some RTW tickets are better for certain areas of the world). If all this sounds a bit complicated, Jonathan Williams offers some comfort:

I bought an RTW air ticket that was very good value. I was surprised at how easy it was to book, and how quickly everything was sorted out. The destinations were based around my four-month placement in Fiji. It made sense to visit countries like Australia and Singapore as they were on my way home to England. It would have been a bit silly to rush from the South Pacific without seeing just a few of the amazing destinations on the way.

For a full discussion of what's on offer, how to choose and the major differences between the alliances, see the Round-the-World chapter on p102 and the table on p104.

Discount Return Tickets
If you've got one main gap-year destination in mind – such as Australia – and you're not intending to fly to another country from there, then all you'll need is a humble return ticket. However, going to Australia and not stopping off either on the way or on the way back is a crying shame. The good news is that a standard return can be jazzed up to allow one or more stopovers. This traveller-friendly system is due to the fact that no airline flies nonstop between the UK and Australia, as well as to airline alliances or partnerships. It means you can disembark at any airport that your carrier and its friends fly to, as long as it is roughly between your starting and finishing points. In other words, you don't have to buy a relatively expensive RTW ticket in order to see a large chunk of the world. For instance, the following itineraries are both return tickets to Australia or New Zealand routed through cities in Africa and Asia:

- London–Maldives–Colombo–Bangkok overland to Singapore-Brisbane overland to Melbourne–Delhi overland to Mumbai (Bombay)–Dubai–London. This route flies with Emirates and SriLankan Airlines and costs £807, plus tax.
- London–Dubai–Brisbane–Auckland–Brisbane overland to Sydney–Brunei–London. This route is with Royal Brunei and costs £697, plus tax.

In addition, if you want to fly domestically within your destination then it will probably be cheaper for you to purchase a return ticket to one city with a stopover in the other. For instance, a ticket to Sydney with a stopover in Perth is likely to be much cheaper than getting to Perth and then doing a side trip to Sydney.

Open-Jaw Tickets

With these snappy little numbers you fly to one destination and out of another. This allows you to revel in some good old-fashioned overland travel between your two points. For instance, flying into Bangkok and out of Singapore (£430–£650 plus taxes) means you can loop through Cambodia, Vietnam and Laos, travel down the southern gulf of Thailand (which is spectacular) and into Malaysia, before flying out of Singapore. Open-jaw tickets are rarely more expensive than standard return fares. They are also an excellent way of seeing a lot of Europe, in particular, as the UK's no-frills airlines always sell one-way tickets. A return on a no-frills airline is simply two one-way tickets, which means you could fly to Nice and out of Barcelona.

One-Way Tickets

If you're looking not so much at a gap year as a couple of gap years, or just don't know where you want to go next, you might purchase a one-way ticket to ride. Proportionally a one-way, long-haul ticket is very expensive, almost always costing a lot more than half the price of a return. In fact, they are sometimes even more expensive that a return. If you only want a single ticket, check in case a return is cheaper; if it is then buy the return and don't use the homeward part.

One drawback with one-way tickets is that often you have to show how you're going to get out of a country before you can get in (immigration officials may want to see an onward ticket). However, if you can prove that you've got sufficient funds for your stay and enough to purchase an exit ticket (whether by air, land or sea) you should be fine.

Also, bear in mind Kate Wilkinson's experiences:

Choosing Cuba as our first destination put a limit on where we could go afterwards because of the US embargo. Very few airlines fly out of Havana and this meant there were not that many places we could go to next. Originally we wanted to island hop around the Caribbean but because we couldn't find any cheap air flights we dropped that idea. However, once we'd found TACA, the Central American airline, it was easy to choose where to go and we flew to Costa Rica.

Air Passes

To explore a large country in depth (eg Brazil, India or Malaysia) ask your travel agent about air passes. These offer you a certain quota of flights within a single country. The flights are worked out either using a points system, a total distance limit or a number of flights within one region. They are usually valid for 30 days. Air passes are often very good value as long as journeys involving plane changes are not counted as two flights. You usually have to buy them in advance of your arrival in that country.

Circle Fares

Your UK travel agent will probably look blankly at you if you ask for one of these. Some circle fares are a bit like RTW tickets that don't actually go around the world; others allow you to fly to a region and then complete an itinerary with lots of stops (sometimes forming a rough circle) before returning to your point of departure. Basically, they are promoted for those starting their long-haul trips in countries such as Australia or the USA and are rarely used by travellers whose trips originate in the UK. The most popular circle fare is probably the Circle Pacific fare offered by the oneworld alliance. This, however, is only sold for travel commencing and terminating in Asia, Australasia or the Americas – not the UK.

Student & Youth Fares

Your International Student Identity Card (ISIC) and/or International Youth Travel Card (IYTC) could get you a significant discount on many airlines (both big and small) – see p38. You normally get a discount on the economy-class year-round fares, and specially negotiated conditions mean you can often avoid the restrictions that come with the cheapest fares open to anyone. Your specialist travel agency will have all the details and 95% of the airlines that STA Travel work with offer a student or youth fare.

No-Frills Flights

There are lots of no-frills carriers around the world and an increasing number in the UK and Europe (for a list of those on the continent, see p119). All the no-frills carriers operating in the UK only travel short haul. If you know how to play the game they can offer great value for money. Simon Calder, author of *No Frills: The Truth Behind the Low-Cost Revolution in the Skies*, tells you how:

- The key for getting a bargain is to book at the optimum time, be flexible, and try to travel when no-one else wants to: Tuesdays and Wednesdays are the best days, except when they coincide with a festival or big sporting event.
- Airlines usually panic about unsold seats between two months and two weeks before departure, which is when you are most likely to pick up a bargain flight. Top-up promotions are aimed at filling seats at marginal cost, typically around £15. Any earlier or any later and you're likely to pay substantially more. If you book at the last-minute you'll pay through the nose.
- You departure time is also critical; very early, very late or middle-of-the-day flights tend to be cheaper.
- Be flexible about where you fly from and where you fly into. For instance, several no-frills hubs might be in reach of your home town and several airports fairly close to your chosen destination. Some airports and destinations will be cheaper than others.

However, ensure that the savings you make on the flight aren't offset by the cost of travelling from an outlandishly rural airport to the city you want to end up in.

e-tickets

These days most airlines issue e-tickets instead of paper ones. You are given a computer reference number and are issued with (or invited to print out) a paper receipt/itinerary in order to show immigration officials that you have onward travel booked.

CHOOSING AN AIRLINE

Just like condoms, all airlines are different but basically do the same thing. Your choice of airline will probably depend on your budget and where you are going. Most likely you'll fly on some old bangers (although hopefully none will have holes in them) with prehistoric in-flight entertainment and cabin crew who think they're looking after inmates of a young-offenders institution. Beggars can't be choosers but before you book your tickets do log on to www.airsafe.com.

Chances are, you'll be interested in an airline's frequent-flyer program. Go to the airline's website or call their reservations' number to find out what is on offer. Although these programs are becoming less generous, the schemes are generally free to join and might end up benefiting you eventually. Unfortunately, most schemes won't register kilometres flown on discounted tickets towards your total, and it's often far from easy to find out who allows what. Rules of frequent-flyer programs often include phrases such as 'kilometres flown on all qualifying fares' and then don't define what they mean by 'qualifying fares'. If you ask your travel agent for clarification, they'll often refer you back to the airline.

If in-flight entertainment it going to be important to you, try to fly with British Airways, Emirates, Singapore Airlines or Virgin Atlantic.

BUYING TICKETS
Buying from Airlines
For short-haul flights it makes a lot of sense to buy direct from the airline. These flights are generally easy to book, so you don't really need the advice of an agent. Also, most no-frills and low-coast airlines flying to short-haul destinations only sell direct to the public.

For long-haul flights it's usually a daft idea to buy your ticket from the airline. For starters, airlines use travel agencies to sell tickets at less than you can buy direct. Next up, naturally enough airlines won't tell you about deals that their competitors are offering. And, finally, it is the travel agent's job to compare the best deals on different airlines for you.

Buying from Specialist Travel Agents
There are basically two types of travel agent. The 'bucket and spade' High Street ones (such as Thomson or Going Places), who will happily sell you an all-inclusive week in Benidorm, and the specialists. To work out a gap-year itinerary you need to go through the latter. A good specialist travel agent will be familiar with all routes that airlines fly, will have up-to-the-minute information on discounted fares, and may well have visited many of the places you want to go. If you're booking a RTW fare they will tell you which destinations are pushing up the price of your ticket and if there's anywhere else you could include in your itinerary without increasing the price. They can suggest the most efficient order in which to visit your destinations to take advantage of the best value fares. They'll also have a view on how long you'll need at each destination and advise you on any compulsory visas that you'll need to obtain in advance of travel.

Using the services of a travel agent is a safe method of purchasing tickets. Of course, your airline might still go bust when you're halfway around the world, but for the last five years or so most travel agencies have added a charge of £2 to £5 per person for 'Scheduled Airline Failure Insurance'. This will protect you if your airline goes belly up, as Ansett, Sabena and Swissair have done. If you hear that an airline you're flying with is in financial difficulties, check with your travel agent that you're covered.

On the whole, all the specialist travel agents have access to the same fares, so there isn't much to be gained by talking to a long list of them. Where there might be a difference is in how quickly they react to new fares on the market. However, for some under-26 and student-only deals that other specialist travel agents can't match, the favourite agency with gappers is **STA Travel** (☎ 0870 160 6070; www.statravel.co.uk).

Hazel Sheard says:

I bought my tickets from STA Travel – they were very helpful and looked for the cheapest and simplest way a first-time gapper like myself could get to where I wanted to go. Walking into the travel agent was certainly simpler than trying to do it myself online and it meant that I got a really good deal.

Other specialist travel agencies include:
- **Airline Network** (☎ 0870 241 0011, 0870 234 0729; www.airlinenetwork.co.uk)
- **Austravel** (☎ 0870 166 2020; www.austravel.com)
- **Bridge the World** (☎ 0870 443 2399; www.bridgetheworld.com)
- **Flight Centre** (☎ 0870 890 8099; www.flightcentre.co.uk)
- **Quest Travel** (☎ 0870 442 3542; www.questtravel.com)
- **Trailfinders** (☎ 020 7938 3939; www.trailfinders.com)
- **Travel Mood** (☎ 0870 066 0004; www.travelmood.com)
- **TravelBag** (☎ 0870 890 1456; www.travelbag.co.uk)

For long-haul or RTW itineraries, by all means try out some possible itineraries using a RTW route planner. There is a good one on the STA Travel website (www.statravel.co.uk) – there's a box to tick if you're over 26. However, for these more complicated fares there's nothing like talking it through with an experienced, real-life travel agent.

Buying Online
For point-to-point travel you can find some great bargains online. Clementine Patrick-Brown says:

I did a little shopping around on the internet, about an hour and a half of research, all in all, and ended up with a great deal on Singapore Airlines. The tickets arrived well in advance and I had no troubles at all.

Have a look at any of these and you might find yourself blowing your gap-year savings right now:
- ebookers (www.ebookers.com)
- Expedia (www.expedia.co.uk)
- Opodo (www.opodo.co.uk)
- Travelocity (www.travelocity.co.uk)

Or, for travel to/from airports that are supposed to be near Europe's major cities (but are usually built in muddy fields many kilometres away) try the UK no-frills airlines (for a list of the European ones, see p119):
- Bmibaby (www.bmibaby.com)
- easyJet (www.easyjet.com)
- EUjet (www.eujet.com)
- Flybe (www.flybe.com)
- Jet2 (www.jet2.com)
- MyTravelLite (www.mytravellite.com)
- Thomsonfly (www.thomsonfly.com)
- Ryanair (www.ryanair.com)

Boat, Train & Coach
Being surrounded by water, it's a good job Britain has some of the best ferry connections in the world. If you're hopping across the channel there are endless options on www.ferry booker.com and www.ferrysavers.com. Otherwise, Speedferries (www.speedferries.com) is the boat equivalent of the no-frills airlines and whizzes between Dover and Boulogne (50 minutes on a good day).

If you want to see more of a country, then get your brain around a train. If you're under 26 a month's InterRail ticket (www.interrail.com) will give you practically unlimited travel in Europe from £295. And don't discount train travel on other continents – the Trans-Siberian and Trans-Mongolian are amazing ways to see Russia and/or China (book through www .regent-holidays.co.uk), and the classic travel route in Canada is by rail between Vancouver and Toronto with Via Rail Canada (www.viarail.ca).

For cheap coach travel there's Eurolines (www.eurolines.com), which connects to over 500 destinations in Europe. If you're aged 25 or under then you qualify for their youth fares and a 30-day pass will cost you £235. Otherwise, a lot of fun can be had on Busabout (www .busabout.co.uk), a hop-on, hop-off travel network between 41 European cities.

For more information on boat, train and coach options in other countries, see the Travel Around sections in Part II.

TRAVEL INSURANCE

Don't you just hate travel insurance? All that money and you may never need to make a claim; what a waste. But there are no certainties in life: something could go wrong, you could get really sick or you could have a serious accident and need to be evacuated. In these circumstances travel insurance could save your life. It could also save you from being in debt for the rest of your life – the cost of airlifting you out of any country will run into the tens of thousands of pounds.

If you're a UK citizen and travelling in the EEA you qualify for free or reduced-cost emergency medical treatment. All you need is a completed E111 form, stamped and signed by a post office. You can download a form from the Department of Health website (www .dh.gov.uk) or pick one up from a post office. You must then remember to take it abroad with you. This form is valid until 31 December 2005, when the UK is adopting the European Health Insurance Card (EHIC). If you depart after 31 December 2005, you will need an EHIC. However, you still need to get additional travel insurance because an E111 or EHIC will not cover you for many costs that you might incur.

Buying Your Insurance

Travel insurance policies are offered by travel agencies, student-travel organisations and general insurance companies. Scour the fine print before handing over your hard-earned cash. And remember that travel insurance costs are usually reasonable for Europe, Australasia and worldwide excluding North America. Premiums go way up when you want to visit Canada and the USA.

At the risk of boring the pants off you, here are some important points to bear in mind when you're buying your travel insurance:

- Buy a policy with medical cover up to £5,000,000, at least. Make sure that it covers repatriation – you really don't want a policy that only covers evacuation to the nearest regional medical facility rather than back to your home country. While you're at it, check how large your medical excess will be (ie how much you have to pay before your insurance company will pick up the tab) – good policies will only charge around £50, but some try to get away with up to £200.
- Carefully study the list of activities you're covered for. Often you'll be allowed one or two bungee jumps within a policy but will have to pay twice as much if you want to go gliding, for instance. If you want to try snowboarding or scuba diving then ask about these activities because often they're not included. Also, look at the list of sports you're allowed to play.

- Check whether your policy obliges you to pay on the spot and redeem the money later, or whether the company will pay the providers direct. If you have to claim later, make sure you keep all documentation. If you have a medical problem, some policies will ask you to call back (reverse charges) to a centre in your home country where an immediate assessment of your problem will be made.
- Ensure you know what is meant by repatriation. Is this being flown home or to the country where you bought the travel insurance?
- If you've got high blood pressure, diabetes, asthma or any other pre-existing conditions, then make sure you are covered. Usually you're OK if your condition is diagnosed and stable, but all policies vary.
- In case you suddenly decide to stay away for longer, ensure that you can extend your policy while you're away and only pay for the difference in cost between the two periods rather than having to take out a fresh policy for your additional time away.
- Keep receipts at home for anything you might lose on your travels.
- Make sure you and your insurance company are talking the same language when it comes to geography. Exactly which countries are included in the continents you'll be covered for? What do they understand by Europe, for instance? Are Turkey and Russia included?
- No-one will give you cover for nuclear, chemical or biological warfare but some policies do insure you against acts of terrorism.

With any travel insurance policy, it is also very important that you do not visit a country that the Foreign & Commonwealth Office (FCO) has advised against travelling to – if you do, it will usually invalidate your travel insurance. Make sure you understand your insurance company's exact policy on this. Some insurance policies will still pay out if your visit is within seven days of your destination being named and others won't. This means that you need to check the FCO website (www.fco.gov.uk) regularly when you're away, as you might have to make alternative travel arrangements.

Also, try out your travel insurance company's 24-hour emergency hotline before you go just to make sure that it is working.

You might want to insure your credit and debit cards with a company such as Card Protection Plan (www.cpp.co.uk) – remembering which cards you've got and cancelling them from abroad can be as much of a nightmare as having your bag stolen in the first place.

KNOW BEFORE YOU GO

Around eight million of us leave home without travel insurance and around a quarter of us will have a serious problem when we're overseas. The Know Before You Go campaign, run by the Foreign & Commonwealth Office (FCO), provides information to help you prepare before you go overseas. It's fairly simple and basically all travellers are being asked to:

- get comprehensive travel insurance
- check the FCO travel advice before going away
- be properly prepared for their trip

You can visit the website at www.fco.gov.uk for more information. Also, it lists the five locations where you're most likely to come to grief. They are: on the roads; at the beach; at hotels (falling off balconies or diving into the wrong end of the swimming pool); in remote locations; and on ski slopes. Don't become one of their statistics!

For more advice about your gap year from the FCO visit www.gogapyear.com.

There are hundreds of insurance companies out there. Here are a few with packages aimed at the backpacker or gapper:

Columbus Travel Insurance (☎ 0800 074 4558; www.columbusdirect.com) This company offers a policy called the 'Backpacker', which gives you worldwide 12-month cover for only £149. In addition, there's a 10% discount for YHA members. However, the medical cover is only up to £1,000,000.

Endsleigh (☎ 0800 028 3571; www.endsleigh.co.uk) This company has three interesting policies. The 'Backpacker' gives worldwide 12-month cover with medical insurance up to £2,000,000; it costs £275. The 'Globetrotter' costs £526 for worldwide 12-month cover with unlimited medical insurance. The 'Category Two Activity Policy' (ie cover for the world's most extreme sports) costs £890 for worldwide 12-month cover with unlimited medical insurance.

STA Travel (☎ 0870 160 6070; www.statravel.co.uk) STA's 'Premier' policy allows for unlimited medical expenses and costs £379 for worldwide 12-month cover. Otherwise, the 'Standard' policy is £275 for worldwide 12-month cover and medical expenses up to £2,000,000.

MONEY & COSTS

PLANNING YOUR BUDGET

There is no magical mathematical formula that works out how much money to budget for travelling. Despite this, Mark Ramsden says:

I work out how much I think I'll need and then add about 10% + £100. Usually that works, but whatever happens you will always spend as much money as you go away with.

Basically, your costs fall into two camps – what you'll spend pre-departure and what you'll spend on the road. Your pre-departure costs will be flights, visas, immunisations, medical kit, travel insurance, equipment and gap-year organisation or course fees (if you're going down this route). Many of these costs are fairly easy to estimate – see the following sections. Also, check out the money side of volunteering (p270) and studying (p420). However, flights, equipment and course or gap-year organisation costs aside, you'll probably spend around £450 on your pre-departure items.

Estimating what you'll need while you're away depends on many factors. For instance, are you going to supplement your funds by doing any work? Will you be travelling on your own or with someone? Travelling on your tod will be more expensive than in a group or in a pair. As Molly Bird says:

Things are definitely cheaper the more people you share them with.

Are you intending to spend long periods of time in one place, or will you be whizzing fairly quickly through a region? One rule of thumb is that every day on the road can cost twice as much as a day in one place. Claire Loseby says:

I did a month of travelling around China and that is where all my money went. If you stay in one place I'm sure you spend much less.

Where you intend to go will have the greatest impact on your budget. Some countries are relatively more expensive than others. Laurence Gale is very upfront about this and advises:

Go to a cheap country like Ghana – £200 lasted nearly three months and it was still more than enough!

Parts of the world where your pounds can be stretched include Southeast Asia, the Indian Subcontinent, China, Mexico and Latin America. Parts where they can't be stretched include Australia, New Zealand, the Pacific, Europe, Russia, Japan, North America and much of the Caribbean. Africa can be cheap, but some countries, such as those using the West African CFA currency (eg Senegal and Mali), are surprisingly costly. For an estimate of what you'll spend on accommodation and food in various countries, visit Lonely Planet's Worldguide at www.lonelyplanet.com/destinations.

Of course, how long you intend to be away is rather critical to the whole equation. So, when you know this you can start doing your sums. This is best done using Excel spreadsheets (but you can also do it on the back of an envelope, using your fingers and toes to add up). Write down where you are going, how long you're going to spend there and, using Lonely Planet's Worldguide, your average daily spend. Don't forget to budget for emergencies and for the odd day or night when you might want to splurge out. Having done this you will probably find that you'll need a budget of £5000 to £6000 for 12 months' travel. Jonathan Williams agrees:

I saved about £3000 for my six-month trip around the world.

Obviously, you can sometimes spend more than this like Amanda Akass:

Altogether I saved about £5500. Of that, £3500 went to my gap-year organisation but then that was everything paid for three months, and £1000 went on flights and equipment etc. The final £1000 was for travelling afterwards for a month. I was staying for this month in Rio and Buenos Aires. Rio, in particular, was more expensive than anywhere else we went. In Bolivia and Peru I could have got by on about £200 or £300 for the month if I'd been careful. I hadn't spent everything by the time I got back, and I could have spent even less, but I would recommend having more money than you are likely to need, if possible. You feel more secure knowing you do have the money in case of emergencies and it helps you make the most of your experience.

While you're working out your budget, don't ignore the budgeting. You don't want to spend uncontrollably in your first four weeks and then be living off rice and peas for the next 48 weeks. Or, as Amanda Akass puts it:

I have friends who spent their last weeks living on bread and water as they had run out of money.

Plane Tickets

A good proportion of your pre-departure budget will go on air tickets. Trying to generalise how much you might spend is like guessing the weight of a cake at a village fête. It all depends on where you are going, when you are going, and what ticket you'll be purchasing. However, your cheapest, most basic round-the-world (RTW) air ticket, going London–Bangkok/Singapore–Sydney–Los Angeles–London will start in the region of £890, plus tax. A more comprehensive ticket with lots of interesting stops will cost around £1000 to £1500, plus tax. Areas such as the Caribbean, some European cities, Russia or Central Asia might make your RTW fare too expensive. In addition, wanting to visit certain places (or certain combinations of destinations) can prove very costly on your RTW trip. For instance, going to South Africa instead of Southeast Asia might not push the price up much but going to South Africa *and* Southeast Asia might. The same applies to South America and North America. In addition, RTW tickets that don't include Australia or New Zealand are generally more expensive.

Don't forget that the price of any ticket will depend on your departure date. For bargain fares it often pays to start shopping around eight to 12 months in advance of your intended departure date. For plenty of tips for keeping the costs of air travel to the minimum see p24 and the Round the World chapter (p102).

TAX

While we're on the subject of planes, a word about tax. Airport tax is normally added to the cost of your ticket. However, this is not always the case and you might need to pay for it in cash (local currency) at the airport. It's not usually a lot of money, around £15, but if you don't have the cash you won't be allowed to leave (not always a bad thing). To avoid this, contact the airline you're flying with a day or two before you leave to check the situation.

Visas

Don't omit these when working out your expenses. They're sometimes free but if you've got a few hefty charges, they might mount up and take an unexpected bite out of your budget. For example, a tourist visa for Mozambique costs £40 and for Vietnam it is £38.

Travel Insurance

Don't yawn. And don't skimp on insurance. A cheap policy is a real waste of money and isn't worth the paper it's written on. Pay a little more for a decent one and if you need to use it, at least it won't let you down. Expect to pay between £149 and £379 for 12 months of worldwide cover. Try to buy a policy that covers you for up to £5,000,000 in medical expenses. If you're a member of the YHA, you can get a 10% discount on travel insurance booked with Columbus.

Immunisations

Go to your local travel clinic six to eight weeks before you depart to discuss what vaccinations you need. Ask which ones you can get for free on the NHS with your local GP and which you can't. Most travellers end up paying around £100 at a travel clinic for their vaccinations and malaria tablets. It is a good idea to visit a travel clinic first, as opposed to your local GP, because the doctors there are specialists in this area and have the most up-to-date information.

Equipment

For the complete low-down on equipment, rummage through the recesses of the Packing chapter (p50). Your equipment or kit is one place where you might be able to scrimp a little. For example, you could borrow some items. Or you can cleverly use equipment to save you money – buy a tent and save on accommodation costs, for example. A lightweight, two-person tent will set you back £120 but if you're using it for six months you'll be more than grateful that you spent the money. Otherwise, if you're travelling with a friend you can choose to share some items to save on space, money and weight you'll carry.

However, there's a lot of equipment that is worth splashing out on. For example, you need a good backpack that won't split at the seams as you land in foreign climes. Expect to pay between £80 and £120 for a decent, sturdy specimen. Another item worth paying more for is a pair of comfortable boots. These will cost around £60 to £80 and remember to wear them in *before* you travel, not on your first trek of the season where the pain from your blisters might blast you off the mountainside. And, don't make cuts on your medical kit – a good one will cost in the region of £30.

If you're going to Asia or the USA, you can save money by buying clothes there (it's usually cheaper). In Asia you need to be under 6ft and less than a shoe 10. Simon Marshall says:

I took enough clothes for three days with me, and then when I arrived in New York I went to charity shops and bought clothes that I didn't care about ruining.

He then adds:

Coming home was a delight after wearing charity shop clothes for three months. I was able to wear a T-shirt that wasn't printed with Mickey Mouse, and jeans that actually fitted me.

Cost of Living

In some parts of the world you can get by on £10 a day, while in others this would just about pay for a tube of toothpaste. To check out the cost of living destination by destination, see the continent chapters in Part II. Also log on to Lonely Planet's Worldguide. There are lots of ways you can keep a lid on your spending while away – the following sheds some light on ways to be tight.

ACCOMMODATION

Where you stay will have a huge impact on your budget and there are lots of ways to cut down on the cost of where you kip. Jonathan Williams backpacked around Australia, New Zealand and Singapore and says:

To keep costs down I avoided staying in the big hostels that are advertised everywhere. Although they do have marginally better facilities than the smaller hostels, they tend to charge much higher prices.

Simon Marshall went to the USA and says:

Staying in motels that cost £40 to £50 can work out cheaper if there is a big group of you. Draw straws for who gets to sleep in the bed and who gets to sleep in the bath.

Jane Williams told us:

A great site for booking accommodation is www.hostelworld.com, and travelling out of peak season will save you heaps on accommodation. In Venice and Florence I paid half as much in October as I would have done in August.

Other interesting accommodation sites include www.globalfreeloaders.com and www.sleep inginairports.net. Alastair Fearn adds:

I always tried to get night trains or buses as it saved on accommodation.

And there's always the canvas option, if you've brought the tent.

FOOD & DRINK

There are tons of ways to save money here. Damien Rickwood found:

Food can be really cheap if you eat where the locals eat – street vendors and markets. This way, you also get to try out all the weird and wonderful things that restaurants might not have.

He's right. If there's ever going to be an expensive place to eat it will be a restaurant in the touristy part of town. However, eating out will always be more expensive than buying a picnic or self-catering. Paul Walker explains:

Cook your own food. I spent a fortune eating out. Also, a 4L box of dodgy Australian wine at £4 does the trick.

Kate Wilkinson makes a valuable point about the expense of buying bottled water:

We brought purification tablets to decontaminate the water. These were the best money-savers because it meant that we could drink tap water and not have to buy any bottled water throughout most of our travels.

This option is also good, of course, for the environment.

SIGHTSEEING
In lots of places, museums and galleries are free or cheaper on certain days or at certain times of day. Where there is an admission fee, your student or discount card will almost always get you a discount.

ENTERTAINMENT
It is amazing how much free entertainment there is when you really look for it – many cities have free concerts, cultural events, guided tours, ceremonies, roller-blading parks or firework displays. Ask at the local tourist office and check the town for flyers and posters. Otherwise, look out for specials at bars or nightclubs, or for places with no cover charge. Clubs and bars are often cheaper midweek, and in some cities cinemas have cheap days.

SHOPPING
Lots of things cost less if you buy them abroad. In Iceland, for instance, with many items you 'buy one, get one free' (ha, ha, got you; that's the supermarket, not the country). More seriously, almost anywhere outside Europe (except perhaps Japan and Hong Kong) you'll find that toiletries, clothes and shoes are usually cheaper. In the USA and Russia CDs are a real bargain. Plus, certain regions of the world specialise in certain trades, so things made in leather or wood will cost less in some parts of the world than in others. You could, in principle, save by buying on arrival – particularly items such as sandals. What's more *likely* to happen is that you'll take what you need, then buy more stuff when you're there.

COMMUNICATION
Email will be the cheapest way to communicate with friends and family. Internet cafés generally charge by the hour or in shorter blocks of time, so work out which is best for you. Phonecards and calling cards work out much cheaper than any other type of phone call, and texting on your mobile phone is significantly cheaper than making a normal call. If you've got your mobile and are hanging around in one place for a period of time, consider buying a local SIM card. For more details see the Keeping in Touch chapter (p86).

LAUNDRY
Laundromats might be a good place to meet the locals but, by the time you've paid for the machine, the powder and the dryer, they can be costly. Think about saving cash by hand washing your clothes in the hostel sink and only giving them a machine wash when they really need one.

TRANSPORT
Getting from A to B can be costly. However, there are ways of minimising the expense. Kate Wilkinson advises:

Work out the local transport routes, especially buses, to cut a lot of money off the cost of transport. In Costa Rica I travelled halfway across the country on £2. Granted, it took nearly 11 hours, but we got there and we weren't delayed. In the USA, we used the Greyhound bus to get from San Diego all the way up to Vancouver in Canada. That cost us about £70.

It almost goes without saying, but taxis will be more expensive than public transport and the number 11 bus (ie walking) is one of the best ways to see a new place. Cycling is usually cheap and fun too.

Also, take a look at the Work Your Route chapter (p388) for information on getting from A to B without it costing the earth.

CHANGING MONEY
See Carrying Your Money (p44) for the best-value options on taking and exchanging money abroad. Also, think about this one from Kate Wilkinson:

Use the local currency if you're in a country where there's a dual currency as that really saves you money. In both Cuba and Costa Rica, the American dollar is the accepted tourist currency, but by using pesos and calones I saved a lot of money.

Activities
There will always be something really expensive and really active that you want to do, whether it is white-water rafting down the Zambezi or camel-trekking through the Sahara. Where possible, do it and hang the expense – this is what gap years are all about. However, there are cheaper ways of taking part in costly activities. For instance, if you're interested in skiing you could apply to work a season as chalet or hotel staff or even as a nanny. You'll usually get a free lift pass, reduced ski hire and a portion of the day free to ski to your heart's content. If you want to get some more serious skiing in, take a ski instructor's course – it might be more expensive but you'll have a qualification that will mean many more years of fun in the white stuff. And, of course, there are instructor courses in all sorts of activities, from diving to kite-surfing. There are also seasonal jobs available for all kinds of activity instructors around the world. For more information, see the Casual/Seasonal Work (p363) and Courses (p416) chapters.

If you're interested in sailing, take a look at the Work Your Route chapter (p388) for details on how to get crewing work around the world. This is a cost-effective way of indulging a passion for 'messing around on boats' as well as an interesting way of travelling around the world.

DISCOUNT & MEMBERSHIP CARDS
There are three main student or under-26 cards on the market: the International Student Identity Card (ISIC), the International Youth Travel Card (IYTC) and the Euro<26 youth card. The ISIC and IYTC can significantly cut your travel costs and save you money at your destination.

These days there are good deals to be had on international flights regardless of your age; however, these cards can often secure you better ones. All the cards will also get you discounts at museums, restaurants and hostels. They are all very cheap and you'll probably save the cost of your card the first time you use it.

There is a thriving black market in these cards in such places as Bangkok and Cairo. As such, it is as well to travel with your home student card as supplementary proof of your status.

IT'S COOL TO TREAT YOURSELF

Are you obsessed with how much money you're saving and how many months this means you can travel for? If you're like this now, beware. It can get much worse when you're on the road, not earning, and simply spending. There'll be times when you count your coins, dividing them by what you expect to spend each day to see how many months you have left abroad. Then you end up planning to spend less and less each day in order to spend longer and longer on the road. It's a mug's game and a traveller's trap. This is not how it should be. If you fall into a routine of constant scrimping and saving, it will get you down. From time to time, it is good for body and soul to have a splurge. When you're fed up with cheap, dimly lit basement rooms in crummy hostels, arrange to spend a night at a comfy hotel. When you've had your absolute fill of rice with gravy, decide to eat in a fancy restaurant beside the port. Treating yourself when you're away should be an integral part of life on the road. It'll lift your spirits, it'll be good fun and it'll recharge your batteries.

Related to this, is the question of spending money on extraordinary experiences. It's fine to do things cheaply but not to the extent where you miss out on amazing activities or sights because you won't spend the money. For instance, it costs to go white-water rafting down the Zambezi, but do you really want to miss out on this opportunity? Emily Simms dithered between taking a boat along the Niger to Timbuktu or the cheaper bus option and was so pleased to spend the extra money:

It was an extraordinary journey – the river is edged by sand dunes and we kept seeing hippos. I would have really missed out if I had taken the bus and saved about the equivalent of £5.

So, don't choke the life out of your trip. You need to preserve your sanity and health as much as your money, and you will probably have a far more enjoyable time if you're not too hard on yourself. Budget travel shouldn't be an endurance contest – there's no moral superiority in surviving on the least money, so plan your budget with the occasional treat in mind.

International Student Identity Card (ISIC)

The ISIC (www.isiccard.com) is the Elvis of student cards. It entitles the holder to 35,000 discounts in over 106 countries, including the UK. The availability and level of discounts varies from country to country. To find out what you can save where, log on to the website, type a country and city, then choose from the following categories: transport, accommodation, entertainment, museums and culture, food and retail shopping.

The ISIC card lasts for 16 months (September to the following December), is available only to full-time students (there's no age limit) and costs £7. You can download an application form from the website or apply through a travel agency such as STA Travel. You'll need to prove you're a full-time student – a NUS card or a letter from your school or college on headed notepaper will do.

This card is the most forged (like the King, the ISIC has lots of imitators), so don't be surprised if it is heavily scrutinised when used.

International Youth Travel Card (IYTC)

The IYTC is more of a Barry White, not as widely recognised as the ISIC card but still worth having. You'll want one of these if you are not a full-time student but are under 26. To apply, download an application form from the ISIC card website or from STA Travel (both the ISIC and IYTC are issued by the International Student Travel Confederation, or ISTC). An IYTC costs £7 and lasts 12 months.

Euro<26

The Euro<26 youth card (www.euro26.org) is only accepted in Europe, albeit in 35 of Europe's countries. It is available to anyone under 26 and lasts for 12 months. Wherever you see the Euro<26 logo (a juggling pixie) marks the places offering advantages and discounts. It costs £7 and can be ordered in the UK from the Youth Information Service (www.yis.org.uk).

YHA Membership Card

A Youth Hostels Association (YHA) membership card entitles you to stay at any of the 4500 youth hostels around the world. To search for a hostel, log on to the Hostelling International website (www.hihostels.com). To join, contact your home association (note the membership fee is for life but does vary):

England & Wales – YHA (☎ 0870 770 8868, fax 0870 770 6127; customerservices@yha.org.uk; www.yha.org.uk; Trevelyan House, Dimple Rd, Matlock, Derbyshire DE4 3YH) It costs £14 to join.

Northern Ireland – Hostelling International NI (☎ 028 903 24733, fax 028 904 39699; info@hini.org.uk; www.hini .org.uk; 22-32 Donegall Rd, Belfast BT12 5JN) It costs £13 to join.

Scotland – YHA (☎ 01786 891 400; fax 01786 891 336; reservations@syha.org.uk; www.syha.org.uk; 7 Glebe Crescent, Stirling FK8 2JA) It costs £6 to join.

Ireland – Irish Youth Hostel Association (An Óige; ☎ 00 353 1 830 4555; fax 00 353 1 830 5808; mailbox@anoige.ie; www.irelandyha.org; 61 Mountjoy St, Dublin 7, Ireland) It costs €20 to join.

If you don't manage to join before you go abroad, you can usually sign up with a youth hostel overseas when you arrive. YHA membership not only entitles you to some good-value accommodation it also means you get discounts on other goods and services – see www .hihostels.com for details. In addition, there's a scheme running in the majority of hostels worldwide where you earn points for each stay until you qualify for a free night.

GETTING YOUR CASH

Now you've done your sums and worked out how much your gap year will cost, all you need to do is find the money. Sometimes it falls in your lap, as was the case with Claire Loseby:

I used money I'd inherited from my grandparents.

If you haven't had a windfall, read on.

Saving Up

The most obvious option is to work. Some gappers work weekends or evenings during the sixth form or while at uni, but many spend anything up to six months after school or higher education working during their gap year in order to pay for the adventurous bit of it. Jonathan Williams says:

It took me two years of working in a supermarket on a Saturday, whilst studying for my A-levels at school. To be perfectly honest, it wasn't actually that hard to accumulate the money.

Amanda Akass advises:

Fundraising I found fairly fruitless and very time-consuming. Unless you have big plans, and a lot of generous friends and family, I would advise just spending your efforts on attempting to get yourself a well-paid job and working for six months or so.

Hazel Sheard agrees about the well-paid job:

I worked for five months before I went and saved during this period. I was fortunate enough to get a job working for KPMG Accounts Payable, which paid me very well considering I was an 18-year-old school leaver.

Kate Wilkinson also managed to earn a decent wage:

I earned my money working as a nursing auxiliary in a geriatric ward of the hospital. Not only was the pay good, but it was such an experience working there. I learnt so much about life and death that it was a valuable part of my gap year, not a means to an end. I loved working there as well, because it was so different and no day was the same.

Kate makes a really good point here. If you're going to spend part of your gap year working to save money, try to see it as an experience you can learn from. Mark Ramsden says:

I earned £3000 for the travelling part and it was all well spent. The earning of it was as much a part of my gap year as the spending.

If possible, try to find something that will be relevant to your career or to your degree, as Amanda Akass did:

Through a London temping agency I worked for an international bank in the Docklands, which was an excellent experience in itself. I felt I had learnt a lot about the workplace, and it helped me to focus on my own goals in life beyond university.

And, Amanda's case highlights another good place to look for a decent hourly wage – the temping agencies. It's often easy to pick up clerical or reception work and you're always paid overtime. It's helpful if you're good at typing and/or know lots of computer packages, but temping agencies don't only offer office employment. Sarah Bruce says:

I had a temping job that paid great overtime, so I worked as many hours as they would give me. This was usually 50 hours a week.

However, the easiest places to find work are in supermarkets, bars, restaurants, shops and factories where the pay leaves much to be desired. Damien Rickwood says:

After finishing my A-levels I started full-time work at Tesco for six months. I can't say this was the most enjoyable experience of my life, but it was definitely worth doing.

What you end up doing in this case is working mad hours, as Mandy-Lee Trew explains:

I saved my money for my trip by working some really crazy hours. Some days I'd work double shifts, pulling in 15 hours at a time – almost killing myself – but it was worth every cent.

Don't forget, though, while you're working you're not spending, and that's good. This also holds true for any night-shift work you may get – not only do you earn a higher wage in the small hours but the only shops open when you're awake are the all-night garages so, unless you develop a voracious passion for soggy pasties, your savings are safe.

Of course, saving goes hand-in-hand with not spending, so you'll need to cut out extravagances – the quickest way to drain your bank account is to go out drinking, eating and shopping. This doesn't mean you have to stay in all the time but be very careful how much you spend if you do venture into a social situation. Allow yourself a certain amount of money and then stop spending. Find things to do in the evening that don't involve spending too much money – even better, offer your services as a baby-sitter. Keep your goal in mind and building up that inviting glittering pile will help you deal with being broke. Quite a few of your friends should be in the same boat, so why not all pitch in and rent a DVD rather than go to the cinema, or take turns to cook each other meals rather than go out to eat.

Another tip is to open a high-interest savings account especially for your going-away fund (check the interest rate at ING Direct; www.ingdirect.co.uk). Then do as Alastair Fearn did:

I had a direct debit out of my account to a savings account for a fixed amount every month.

Finally, what most gappers who work to pay for their gap year agree upon is that they're proud of having saved. Molly Bird says:

I worked as a cook during the first six months of my gap year and I had a great time doing it. It was with a real sense of achievement that I set off from Heathrow with a plane ticket in my pocket that I knew I had worked for.

Fundraising for a Good Cause

Another way to get the money together is to fundraise for a volunteer project by thinking of ingenious ways to sell your time, energy and skills. If you're travelling with a gap-year or year-out organisation then you'll get some help with the fundraising element of your gap-year experience (the Daneford Trust is particularly good at this.) However, truth be told, many gappers these days just get a job or combine a proper job with a few fundraising activities. Sarah Bruce says:

I organised a raffle and a sponsored event that raised over £1000. I also used my birthday and Christmas to get bits of kit that I needed for my trip.

Justin Ward says:

I wrote to organisations asking for sponsorship, completed a skydive and carried out a collection at my local theatre.

Damien Rickwood explains:

I asked for sponsorship from local schools and companies and held a few events like a BBQ and a raffle.

With a bit of resourcefulness there are many things that you could do to help pay your way. You could wash cars, walk dogs, sell home-made cakes and biscuits or do the neighbours' gardens. You could collect all the junk in the house (ask first) and sell it at a car-boot sale – you'll not only raise money but also be amazed at the tat people will buy.

You could also auction stuff on eBay (www.ebay.co.uk) – you can sell almost anything here, even your little brother's favourite teddy bear.

You could hold an event. Organise a concert, hold a fashion show or set up a cinema night. If you can think of an original way to pitch your mission, this'll capture people's imagination and attract attention. Sian Robertson hired a cinema for a private screening of *Romancing the Stone* to raise money for her trip with Raleigh to Costa Rica and Nicaragua. Remember, any event you do needs to be well publicised, so put up posters and give out leaflets. Also, clearly set out why you want the money, giving details of your project.

A good way to raise money is to hold a party. Get a venue for free (some places won't charge if they're going to win out on the bar, and they might even give you a cut if they feel it's for a good cause), charge a fee to get in, and once you have your guests trapped in an alcoholic, generous-spirited haze, hit them with a raffle. Sarah Collinson did this:

When I was still at school I organised a ball with two of my friends and from that we raised about £300 each.

Get your friends and relatives to help. Catherine Bruzzone has been through the fundraising process with two daughters:

It was pretty exhausting for all of us, especially as it was the A-level year but now (looking back!) it was enjoyable and represented the last year our daughters were fully part of the family. So it was good that we could all work together and have happy memories of the parties, sponsored cycle rides, car-boot sales etc.

If you ask for money from relatives or businesses, offer to give something in return. For example, you might supply regular reports about the project, work for their company for a week for a donation, or set up an exhibition about the project when you get back. It's also worth approaching your old school and local organisations. Hazel Sheard says:

I was lucky enough to win a £500 bursary from my school to go travelling with, which helped a lot.

You could also get hold of the *Directory of Grantmaking Trusts,* which lists companies that give out funds for projects, and write to any appropriate ones (your local library should hold a copy or will help you track one down – it's rather expensive to buy). But, be warned, these trusts rarely sponsor individuals, so you might not hit gold. From such letters you might expect about a one-in-20 success rate. When sending them off, avoid the mass mail-out look; it won't do you any favours.

Various gap-year organisations have bursary schemes to help well-deserving candidates without funds. Gap Activity Projects (GAP), Blue Ventures and the Nepal Kingdom Foundation are good examples. In addition, some courses have grants available to help with funds, like those run by the Arvon Foundation or the Peter Kirk Memorial Scholarships. Where grants, bursaries or help with funding is given by an educational or gap-year organisation, this is detailed in the contacts section of the relevant chapters – see Part III for more info.

Loans

A loan may seem the easiest solution to your cash conundrum, but think carefully about it. If you're a school leaver, do you really want to start higher education with a loan from a gap year hanging over you? In this educational climate you're going to leave university with some hefty debts to pay off anyway. It's an even worse idea if you're a post-university gapper, since you'll have even more money to pay off. About the only circumstance where a loan might make a modicum of sense is if you're a school leaver intending to start a career after your gap year.

If you want to do some vocational education (something directly related to a job) at home or abroad, you can apply for a career-development loan – but you must be a UK citizen. You also need to make sure that the provider of the course is registered with the career-development loan system. This will pay a large proportion of your course fees, and your living expenses if you're studying full time. Call ☎ 0800 585 505, or check the fine print at www.lifelonglearning.co.uk.

The best place to find a loan is through your bank or building society. When choosing a loan, think about how large your repayments will be, how long you will have to pay them for, and how you will manage your repayments.

You could also approach your parents for a loan: the more professional you are about this the more success you'll have. Be fair to both parties; draw up an agreement of the amount you need, when you'll pay it back, and what interest you'll give them.

Working on the Road

If you haven't saved enough before you go, then you can always work while you're there. If you have a good balance of spending and earning, you should end up breaking even, or even coming out richer. See the Work Your Route (p388) chapter for information and inspiration about what you might do, as well as the Proper Jobs (p325) and Casual/Seasonal Work (p363) chapters.

CARRYING MONEY

Now you've got all this lovely money in a UK bank account, how are you going access it when you're away? Well, the best approach is to take a good mixture of credit and debit cards, travellers cheques and old-fashioned bank notes. Sarah Bruce says:

I took most of my money in travellers cheques and then I also took a debit card and a credit card as well. I made sure I had emergency numbers for both my banks and I kept these separately from my cards so that if (when, in my case…) my wallet was stolen I could cancel them straight away and order replacements.

Claire Loseby advises:

I'd recommend gappers check out how advanced the country is in terms of banking before they go. I took mostly cash and travellers cheques with me, as well as credit and debit cards, which were practically useless in China.

Molly Bird says:

We took a card and some travellers cheques with us. This gives you flexibility and allows you to play along with some good exchange rates – sometimes exchanging travellers cheques will be horrendously expensive and sometimes using a card will be. You just have to investigate. If you are travelling with a friend, it's a good idea if one of you takes out a lot of money, enough for both, each time. Then you can alternate. In the long run it will save you money, as you're usually charged each time you take your money out abroad.

A combination of cash, travellers cheques and credit/debit cards should ensure that you're rarely stuck without any funds (unless you've already spent all your money). Do remember to keep your exchange receipts in case they're needed as proof of legal exchanges either within a country or when leaving. Also, if you're travelling with a mate or group of friends, divide your money up, just in case one of you is robbed or you're separated.

Debit Cards

Most gappers get cash on the road by using their debit card in automatic teller machines (ATMs). With debit cards the money you withdraw comes straight from your UK account. As long as you've got enough money in there, it's simple. Look for your debit card network logo (ie Visa or MasterCard) on the outside of ATMs abroad and away you go.

There can be drawbacks to this system. As Claire Loseby points out, some countries have way fewer ATMs than others, so check the MasterCard ATM locator (www.mastercard.com/atm locator/index.jsp) and the one for Visa (http://visa.via.infonow.net/locator/global/) before you go. In addition, ATMs sometimes break down and for mysterious reasons only known to themselves sometimes refuse to accept your card, even though in theory they should.

The rate of exchange for cash withdrawals from ATMs is often pretty good but that's offset by costly transaction charges. Jonathan Williams went to Australia, New Zealand, Fiji and Singapore. He says:

I didn't really use travellers cheques at all because I could use my debit card in ATM machines all around the world. However, I was stung by the charges that the big banks impose for withdrawing cash. A few banks actually absorb the cost of the transaction themselves, so I would strongly recommend opening an account with such banks and building societies.

Sarah Collinson provides the solution:

I used my debit card. I recommend the Nationwide FlexAccount Visa debit card, as the band doesn't charge you for taking money out abroad and also gives a very good rate of exchange. It also has an excellent internet banking website, which you can use anywhere to check your balance or move money around.

In addition, this Nationwide (www.nationwide.co.uk) card option allows you to keep your savings in a relatively high interest-bearing current account. The only problem with this card is that it cannot be replaced when you're abroad – so, don't lose it. Another plus belonging to a debit card is outlined by Sarah Bruce, who says:

It is really good to take a debit card particularly if you have parents in the UK who might be able to lend you money if you get stuck. Make sure they have your bank details handy so that they can transfer money to your account if you get into a difficult situation.

If you're travelling with a debit card or, indeed, a credit card (see the next section) then do bear in mind the following:

Communication Tell your credit card company or bank that you're going travelling and that your user pattern will change. If you don't do this, your card might be blocked by a well-meaning employee who thinks it may have been stolen.

Demagnetisation If the magnetic strip on the back of your card is scratched it might not work when swiped, so get a new one. Some travellers replace all their cards before they travel, just to be on the safe side. (This problem will hopefully be solved shortly by the new 'contactless' cards.)

Expiration Check when your cards expire and make sure they're not going to turn up their toes when you're on the road. **PIN** The best option is to remember it. If you can't then pop the number into a secure online travel vault, like the one at www.lonelyplanet.ekit.com. If you do write it down in your diary, you must make sure that it isn't obviously your PIN number. And, whatever you do, don't tell anyone but your teddy bear what the number is.

As in Britain, many ATMs abroad are located outside banks. However, handling largish sums of cash on the street in a foreign country is more risky than in the mall of your hometown (or perhaps it's not…). Also, bear in mind that most travellers are robbed on the day they get money out. This is no coincidence, so be wary of being tailed when you've just made a transaction.

Credit Cards

These bits of plastic are very useful in an emergency or to pay for unexpected big-ticket items. You can also use them to get cash from ATMs in the same way as the debit card. However, the catch is in the name – the money you spend doesn't come out of your account; it goes onto a bill that you need to pay off promptly to avoid being hit by exorbitant interest rates on your loan. If you're going to use a credit card you need to think about how you're going to pay off your credit card bill and arrange this before you leave home. You could ask a friend who has access to one of your accounts to pay it off; you could set up a direct debit that covers either the minimum payment or the full payment or a fixed amount; or you could pay the bills online yourself through an internet bank.

Travellers Cheques

Don't these just get on your nerves? You're charged a commission when you buy them, a commission when you convert them, and to cap it all you get a pea-sized rate of exchange. Regardless, it's still a good idea to take a few of these. As Hazel Sheard says:

I did take some travellers cheques for emergencies – it's worth doing in case you lose your cards or find yourself somewhere with no cash machines.

Amanda Akass agrees:

Travellers cheques were quite a performance compared to cash in many places, so I don't think it is a good idea to rely upon them absolutely. But they are extremely handy to have as an emergency back up.

The main advantage with travellers cheques is that if they get lost or stolen they'll be replaced by the issuing bank within a few days. But the only way this can happen is if you've recorded the serial numbers of the cheques as you cash them. This means you can tell the bank which ones have gone walkies. Also, remember to sign them immediately but not to counter-sign until you're using them.

In the UK you can buy American Express travellers cheques free of charge from the post office (www.postoffice.co.uk), as long as you don't want them in UK pounds. This is fine, as you probably want them in American dollars anyway. You can also exchange American Express travellers cheques commission free at most American Express offices when you're abroad. Commission-free travellers cheques can also be bought online from the Nationwide (www.nationwide.co.uk), although there is a £3.50 delivery charge and a cash advance charge of 1% unless you pay with your FlexAccount debit card. These are

Travelex travellers cheques and that means you can change them without commission at most Travelex offices worldwide.

Obviously, you're going to want to change your travellers cheques at a bank or bureau de change where it's commission free. Sometimes, though, this won't be possible. At these times, ask the locals or other travellers where the best place is to go. Get an idea of the current exchange rate from a local newspaper so you can compare rates. If you're caught short out of office hours then remember you can usually change travellers cheques at fancy hotels, though the rate of exchange will be poor and the commission high.

Always count the bills carefully after you change your money to ensure you haven't been short-changed – it pays to be particularly vigilant the first few times when you're unfamiliar with the local currency. Most instances of short-changing happen at airports when travellers have just arrived in a new country.

Cash

Sarah Collinson told us:

I took the equivalent of £100 in emergency American dollars. In South America this was really helpful, as sometimes we would go places where there were no cash machines or places to exchange travellers cheques. Everyone in South America will change dollars even if they do give you a fairly bad rate of exchange.

Mark Ramsden admits:

I carry cash because I'm stupid.

Well, let's not go that far. It isn't stupid to carry a little cash. Obviously, you don't want to carry a big wad around – if it's stolen or lost you'll never see it again. But some 'readies' in US dollars can be very useful (yes, it's really got to be dollars, not pounds). Keep your notes in a very safe place, perhaps carrying some in your money belt and stashing some away as emergency money (for example, inside a backpack frame).

In some countries, it's possible to change cash on the black market, though this is illegal and may leave you vulnerable to arrest or bribery attempts. All sorts of scams exist that are designed specifically to short-change you and, if you're ripped off, you'll have no legal recourse. If you have no option, ask other travellers for advice about a trustworthy person to change money with, and keep your wits about you, especially if you're changing at border crossings.

International Money Transfers

If at all possible, don't go down this route as there's often a hefty fee for wiring (isn't that a quaint word?) money overseas. If you run out of money on the road your best option is to ask mum and dad (or your favourite fairy godmother) to deposit some in your bank account and you can then access it using your debit card. Otherwise, use your credit card and ensure the bill is paid on time.

However, if the world turns to shit, everything is stolen and you don't have a penny to your name then you will need to get money transferred. One of the cheapest and fastest (it only takes 10 minutes) ways of doing this is with the UK post office's MoneyGram service (www.postoffice.co.uk), which can send money to over 160 countries. Check their website to see if the countries you're visiting are included on its list. Otherwise, you can go through a company like Western Union (www.westernunion.co.uk), which has 170,000 agents worldwide. When collecting transferred money you'll always need some form of government-issued photo ID, such as a passport or driving licence. The money will be ready for you in cash, usually in local currency.

In both cases, you'll have to arrange for someone in your home country to transfer money to one of their offices before they'll send it on to you.

If you intend to spend a lot of time in a particular country, enquire with your bank about having money transferred directly into an account in a bank of that country.

RUNNING OUT OF MONEY

If you're budgeting properly this shouldn't happen. Travelling is like running a business – you need to forecast your spending and manage your cash flow.

If you realise you are getting skint, do something before you go flat broke. Most gappers in this position get themselves a casual job real quick. See the Casual/Seasonal Work chapter (p363) in Part III. Obviously, you'll have to consider visa restrictions but, caught between a rock and a hard place, you're going to choose to put food in your mouth. To tide yourself over, be resourceful and inventive. Your first problem will be paying for accommodation, so see if you can do some work for free at your hostel or hotel in exchange for board. Next, think about selling a few possessions – from jewellery to guidebooks – to boost your funds.

Broke gappers who are talented could also try busking or selling artwork to get by. Other things to consider are babysitting (for all those travellers, or even locals, with children), hair-braiding or giving massages (as long as you know how). If you're a hairdresser and have packed your scissors, you can offer haircuts. Writing letters or emails for local people may be worth a try, as well as offering computer training or English lessons.

OBSESSED WITH HAGGLING

Haggling is not a vicious contest. Are you about to walk away in disgust because you couldn't knock the vendor's price down by...10p? It's small change to you but a significant sum of money to the vendor.

Many countries across the world lack government-funded social-security systems and charity-run support services and it's every person for themselves – especially in the cities where they might be separated from the family or village-based networks that would normally look after them during difficult times.

In these countries, even the poorest foreign visitor is loaded. Your clothes, backpack, watch, and spending on food, accommodation and souvenirs mark you as a person of wealth. The fact that you have done time at the local pork-pie factory to get here and own nothing of value at home is not going to register with the locals. The mere fact that you can afford to go abroad or take any time off means you are in a different league.

The envy this can produce is often aggravated by the never-ending flow of tourists who are often demanding, rude and heedless of local customs. It is also caused by changes that the tourist industry has on local cultures, from inappropriate redevelopment to the breakdown of family and social values. Your gap year might do wonders for your confidence and self-esteem but take time to think about what you are doing for your destination.

Being 'ripped off' can leave you feeling a noodle, especially if the amount is significant, but beware of adopting a siege mentality. There is, as yet, no awards system for the traveller who got by on the least money. Keep it in perspective and empathise with the other person's circumstances. They'll be happier and your blood pressure will remain steadier.

BARGAINING

If you've grown up in the UK, you might have only haggled over a piece of junk jewellery in a second-hand market. This is not the best preparation for going up against people who have been at it their whole lives. You'll save yourself a lot of anguish by accepting that you'll pay more than the locals. And in most cases this is fair. The best you can hope for is a price reasonably close to what locals pay. There's nothing more pathetic than those travellers who are obsessed with paying only the 'local price', and whose trip has been reduced to a series of bitter and humourless head-to-heads. You should also have a feel for where it's appropriate to bargain (don't try it at a US gas station or the Louvre ticket office, for example); this usually will be clear in your guidebook.

There are also lots of implicit bargaining rules. Most important is to conduct the procedure in a friendly, polite, good-natured way – getting angry won't make it any cheaper; it is also offensive and will usually bring the negotiations to a halt. Also, never offer a price unless you're willing to go through with the transaction if that price is accepted – bargaining for sport is cruel (the vendors are trying to earn a living) and can even lead to violence.

And never lose a sense of how much money you're haggling over. You should pay what's fair: don't take advantage of poor and desperate traders by forcing them to sell too low.

TIPPING

The custom of tipping varies from country to country. In some countries (eg the USA) a 15% tip is expected whenever you've been served by someone (and however small their service). In others (eg Japan) it is considered rude to tip. In many countries a discretionary service charge will be added to your bill (check to see whether it has been). In others it's left up to you. In almost all countries porters and guides expect a tip and their wages are set accordingly.

There's an interesting tipping table at www.tramex.com/tips/tipping.htm but it only covers 28 countries. In general, though, if you feel that someone has done you a good service, then leave them some cash. If service has been really lousy then skip the tip (in the US make a run for it, as restaurant staff have been known to chase after non-tipping clients).

PACKING

Everyone's got a packing tip. Molly Bird's advice is similar to an old travel saying that goes: 'Pack it and halve it; time it and double it.' She says:

Only take half of what you originally pack. You can always get stuff when you're away and a heavy backpack will become the bane of your life. Limit yourself to a smaller bag. If you give yourself space you'll fill it. Remember you can always send stuff home. And, don't forget that even if everything fits in your backpack when you're packing meticulously at home with mum, it will be more difficult when you're packing in a rush and running late for that train.

Jonathan Williams agrees:

I know everybody always says 'pack light' when you go backpacking, but this cliché is really essential to remember. I ended up sending 15kg of things home, at great expense to myself, because I simply packed too many clothes. One tip I would pass on is to pack all your clothes in large freezer bags that can be sealed, thus allowing all the excess air to be squeezed out. Once everything is sealed, you will have a lot more space to play around with. The bags are also handy for when your clothes are wet, dirty or smelly, as they protect everything else.

Clementine Patrick-Brown advises:

Pack less than you need. Unless you're going somewhere extremely remote, things will be readily available and cheaper at your destination. However, there are specific things that may be hard to find; for instance, deodorant and tampons are difficult to locate in China, so take enough to last.

Some travellers leave home with their backpack only half full. Louise Ellerton reminds everyone:

Don't forget, you will always want to bring back souvenirs, so do leave space for them!

Another packing tip is to roll all your clothes up, that way they'll crease less and they'll take up less space. Amanda Akass suggests loading yourself up rather than your suitcase:

I would advise wearing the most bulky items when you are on the move – hiking boots, fleece etc, to avoid taking up space.

Obviously, you might look a real Wally striding along the beach to the train station in your winter woollies but…

Whatever you choose to take, you'll want a versatile range of clothes, particularly if you're flitting from climate to climate. You might also want to pack some presentable clothes for job interviews or any dealings you may have with officialdom. What you won't want to pack are any precious items – whether this is jewels or things of personal value that couldn't be replaced if stolen.

THAT'S NOT MY BAG

There are three main luggage options: travel packs, top-loading backpacks, and wheelie bags.

Backpacks

If you're going to be a backpacker, you'll need a backpack. Snails aren't stupid: it's the most practical way to carry stuff, even if you're not constantly on the move. It's also worth buying the right one so that you don't end up dragging it, cursing, over wild terrain and cobbled streets. You'll be eternally grateful that it's comfortable, doesn't fall apart when you sneeze, and fits nicely down your spine. Buy one that will last and you'll use it over and over again, now that you've got the travel bag – I mean, travel bug!

Whatever you do, don't leave this purchase until the last minute. Buy your backpack six weeks in advance, pack it and use it as much as you can before you go. Keep the receipt. Don't worry about the weird looks you'll get in the local nightclub as you and your backpack dance the night away; using it is the only way of knowing if it's got a manufacturing fault. If your personal belongings end up all over the dance floor, take it back to the shop (along with the receipt).

TRAVEL PACKS

Eight out of 10 gappers will choose a travel pack. A travel pack is a backpack with a secret weapon – a zip that runs all the way around the edge and top, allowing you to open up the main compartment completely. This is what Alistair Fearn bought and recommends:

Get a rucksack that zips all the way down the side so it's more like a suitcase. This means you can access your stuff easier.

As he says, it is easy to pack, easy to unpack and easy to live out of. A travel pack also has a zippered flap (stowed at the base of the back) that hides and protects the harness when necessary. There are also side handles and a detachable shoulder strap, making it easy to carry in cramped spaces. This is something that Jonathan Williams appreciated:

I recommend a backpack that allows you to zip away the shoulder straps, because this prevents them getting caught during transit – particularly when using planes.

A travel pack also looks fairly respectable if you have to deal with officialdom, and it is easy to lock up (because you can lock the zips together).

Another reason to buy a travel pack is that most have a detachable day pack (see p52 for why you might want one of these). The advantage of having a day pack attached to your main piece of luggage is that when you're on the move you only have one item to watch, remember and keep safe. Also, when you're carrying your travel pack but need access to your day pack, it can very easily clip onto the travel pack's front strap. Try this manoeuvre with a top-loading backpack and separate day pack and the crossing of straps will make you feel like an extra in a bondage movie.

TOP LOADERS

A top loader is a traditional backpack – basically a long tube with access through the top. It is more watertight than a travel pack because it doesn't have a great big zip running around the outside. Top loaders are also better for trekking and expeditions because they balance well. However, top loaders can be less convenient to use because sod's law dictates that anything you want to find will be at the bottom (so you have to either play lucky dip or chuck everything out on the floor). Top loaders also have at least three useful outside pockets for water, waterproofs, food etc, while travel packs and wheelie bags rarely have pockets.

FITTING & FINE-TUNING YOUR BACKPACK

Having decided which type to go for, now consider:

Fit All backs are different. You can only tell if a backpack is comfortable and right for you by trying it on. The key, though, is to try it on with weight inside (this doesn't mean you go shopping with bricks in your handbag; any good equipment supplier will hoist a 10kg weight into the backpack for you). Most decent packs have an adjustable internal frame that can be fitted to the length of your back and these are useful for getting the fitting exactly right. In addition, most companies now have male- and female-specific models (basically 'long' and 'short' ones) – if you're a tall lass don't be put off trying a male model and vice versa.

Size The short answer is: unless you're camping, 65L is big enough. Sarah Collinson agrees:

My backpack was 65L and I managed for six months out of it – I just got better and better at packing it.

Strength You need to be led by price with this one – a cheaper model probably won't be as strong as a more expensive one. It is not always obvious from examining a backpack how durable it will be. Some of today's materials seem light but are actually much more durable than heavy-weight canvas.

Backpacks are priced from around £60 to £200. For durability and comfort go for one in the £80–120 price range. In the backpack trade they always say that a £60 model will 'wear out' after a year, and a £120 model will start to 'wear in' after this period of time. You'll need to factor your pack price into your budget (see the Money & Costs chapter, p33).

Wheelie Bags

A wheelie bag is a suitcase with wheels and a retractable handle. Nobody wants to look like their parents. However, if you're not on a big, off-the-beaten-track trip where there's no option but to carry everything on your back, it's worth taking a look at the new generation of wheelie bags. These resemble travel packs, with soft sides, a detachable day pack and hideaway straps that mean you can wear the bag on your back when needed. These bags are a popular alternative to the more traditional travel packs or top-loading backpacks and many gappers are choosing this option. However, they are not for everyone. Claire Loseby explains:

If people are planning to do a lot of moving about I'd definitely say take a big backpack because I learnt my lesson the hard way – trying to wheel a big holdall down a dirt track is never the fastest or most convenient thing in the world.

Day Packs & Shoulder Bags

When you're stationary and have a base, you won't want to take your backpack out with you (can you imagine lumping it around for a 12-hour stretch?). Instead, you will want to carry a smaller bag for things like your guidebook, camera, map, water bottle, medical kit and sunscreen. Tabitha Cook tells us:

I was lucky in that the organisation I went away with had a house where all the volunteers lived, so I could leave my large backpack there and carry a small day pack that would do a weekend away. If you go by public transport, space is often an issue as is weight. Also, there are not many places where you can leave heavy backpacks if you want to go off and do some shopping in the day.

If you've bought a travel pack then you've probably already got a day pack. If not, you will have to make a separate purchase. If you intend to do a lot of walking then look for a strong, well-padded day pack but remember this is yet another item to carry when travelling. If you're not a great trekker then a lightweight foldaway day pack is the way to go. Also, a day pack is what you'll use as carry-on baggage when you're on flights. A day pack will set you back from around £15 to £30 and is another cost to add to your list (see Money & Costs chapter, p33).

Of course, a shoulder bag is another alternative for outings. This has the main advantage of being easily accessible – it's a pain having to take a day pack off every time you want to consult your map or take a photo. Sometimes it can also be safer – a day pack can be easily knifed at the bottom and you might be none the wiser because it's on your back. However, if you do use a shoulder bag, don't forget to watch out for bag-snatchers...

WHAT TO PACK

Basically, your packing list can be broken down into the following nine sections: security, sleeping, eating and drinking, hygiene, health, travel essentials, clothing, footwear and luxuries.

Security

Money belt A money belt is vital – it's the safest way to carry debit/credit cards, travellers cheques, cash, passport, ticket and other important items. You want one that can be worn unobtrusively beneath whatever you're wearing. Keeping your stuff in a bumbag over your clothes is like wearing a sign saying 'This is where I keep my valuables: come take your pick'. The most common types of money belt are worn either around the waist or the neck. Neither design is particularly easy to access, so don't keep your ready cash in it or you'll be delving under your clothes every five minutes and attracting attention. The fabric is important too. Plastic sweats, while leather is heavy and will get stinky. Cotton is the best bet as it's washable and the most comfortable. If you use a cotton money belt, put your ticket, passport and other documents in a plastic bag so they don't get damaged by too much 'glowing' (ie sweat). Check out the belt's clasp or attachment. You'll want to keep your money belt secure at all times.

Padlock & chain Apart from securing your backpack, a padlock can be used to fasten the door of a hostel room. A chain is useful for attaching your backpack to the roof rack of a bus or the luggage rack on trains.

Personal security There are loads of personal-security items on the market, such as personal alarms, internal door guards, Pacsafe for your backpack (metal gridwork which covers your backpack to make it unslashable), and packable safes for your room (attach them to a radiator). Check out what's on offer at your local travel specialist.

Waterproof pouch Consider taking one of these for your documents and money; it can be worn when swimming, diving or snorkelling.

Sleeping

Alarm clock You'll need an alarm for early morning trains, planes and buses, unless you're using the one on your mobile phone.

Mosquito net Malaria is no joke. In risky places, many cheap hotels provide mosquito nets, but it's good to have your own because it is crucial that your net is treated with a mosquito killer (permethrin) and that, like condoms, there are no holes in it.

Pillow There are three types: inflatable head and neck pillows; inflatable neck cushions; and compact pillows. The inflatable ones can get punctured easily. Compact ones don't take up that much more room and there's no risk of them deflating. If you're not taking a pillow with you, at least nab a pillow case from home.

Sleeping bag/liner A lightweight sleeping bag is a must if you want to be totally independent and travel around a lot. These days they are not big and bulky. A reasonable sleeping bag ranges from £40 to £90 – the lighter they are the more expensive they become. A sleeping bag liner is absolutely essential. You'll use this all the time, either as a sheet in dubious hotels and hostels or to keep your sleeping bag clean.

Tea lights If you're not keen on being left in the dark during power cuts, these are safer than regular candles.

Torch A torch is essential for finding stuff late at night in a dorm, for avoiding nocturnal mishaps on the way to outside toilets and for when the electricity packs in. It will also come in handy for exploring caves and ruins. The Maglite is the toughest, but the bulbs and batteries run out quickly. The new LED (light emitting diodes) torches are good because the bulbs don't blow and the batteries last much longer. You can get an LED Petzl miner-style lamp that straps to your forehead and frees up both your hands (and is slightly less comic than light-up slippers).

Eating & Drinking

Cup & spoon Though you're probably not taking a cooker and cooking utensils, your own cup and spoon is still handy and helps to avoid catching and spreading disease.

Water bottle Most water bottles hold 1L, but a 2L bottle is what you need for travelling. Buy the collapsible bladder type of water bottle because they take up very little room in your backpack when not in use. You can save money and just keep refilling a standard plastic bottle, but something sturdier will last longer and be more suitable for purifying water on a regular basis.

Water purification See the Health chapter (p59) for details of what to take.

Health & Hygiene

Bath plug The humble bath plug is a rare commodity in some cheaper accommodation. Double-sided rubber or plastic plugs will fit most bath and basin plugholes.

Contraception Condoms are sold in most countries, but the quality can be variable (always check the use-by date). It's safer and easier to bring a supply with you. If you use the pill then bring enough to cover your whole trip, as it is difficult to obtain in many countries.

Medical kit See the Health chapter (p59) for gory details.

Tampons or pads Depending on your destination, these might be hard to find.

Toilet paper It's best to learn how to use your hand and water because toilet paper often blocks sewage systems in developing countries. Otherwise, take toilet paper but think about how you're going to dispose of it. When you pack it, squash the roll down and put it in a plastic bag.

Toiletries Most items are widely available – and often cheaper – but take any speciality products with you. Shower gels travel much better than soap and will often do hair as well as body. Decamp large bottles into smaller ones. Plus, you can now get concentrated travel soaps, which will keep both you and your clothes clean. Make sure your travel soaps are biodegradable.

Towel Your favourite, fluffy cotton towel will take up too much space in your backpack and never dry out. There are two types of travel towels – one made from chamois (works wet and packs down to the size of a small tin of beans) and the other from microfibre (works dry and packs down to a large can of beans). Which sort you take will depend your bathing routine. If you love wrapping up in your towel after your shower then the microfibre one is for you, but if you want pure towelling performance and don't mind something real weenie then take a chamois.

Washing line A piece of string, or even dental floss, will do the job but there are relatively cheap lines on the market that don't need pegs but have suckers, hooks or both on each end making them more versatile.

Wet wipes & no-water washes Both are handy where clean water is in short-supply (eating on the street or on a trek).

Travel Essentials

Address book, travel journal & pens You'll want these so that you can keep in touch with friends, family and all the people you'll meet, and to write your best-selling travelogue.

Batteries Bring spares for all your equipment and put new batteries in everything before you depart.

Calculator This is good for currency conversions and other exciting sums. Forget gimmicky electronic converters; a calculator is better (use the one on your mobile if you have one).

Compass Get a basic one from a reputable company (eg Silva, Recter or Suunto), not a fancy map-reading one, and make sure you know how to use it.

Earplugs You'll never regret taking these if you spend a lot of time in cities or take a 10-hour ride in a bus with a blaring stereo.

Eye wear Take your glasses (in a hard case) and contact lenses. Sunglasses are indispensable for both comfort and protection. If you wear prescription glasses or contact lenses, take the prescription with you, along with extras such as a case and contact-lens solution. Contact-lens wearers should also take a supply of dailies, which are really useful in an emergency. Also consider taking swimming goggles.

Gaffer tape Need a belt for your jeans? Got a hole in your tent? Does your backpack need repairing? Gaffer tape can save your life in the most unexpected situations.

Glue stick The glue on stamps and envelopes can be remarkably unsticky. Glue is also useful for sticking tickets etc into your journal.

Guidebooks, maps & phrasebooks These are essential for reading up on your destination and knowing what to expect.

Lighter/matches You'll need something to light your camp fire, mosquito coils, candles and fags. Don't bring your favourite Zippo lighter, as the fuel evaporates in the heat of the tropics.

Pocketknife A Swiss army knife (or good-quality equivalent) has loads of useful tools: scissors, bottle opener (the most useful item), can opener and straight blade, as well as all those strange ones. You don't need a huge one unless you're going camping. Remember not to keep this in your in-flight luggage, as it'll be confiscated.

Sewing kit Needle, thread, a few buttons and safety pins to mend clothing, mosquito net, tent or sunglasses will come in handy.

Clothing

Keeping cool If you're travelling in hot climates you'll need a lightweight, loose-fitting wardrobe (not the wooden variety). Cotton clothing will absorb sweat and help keep you cool. Synthetic clothing doesn't get so creased and dries out quickly, but it can sometimes make you feel clammy. Take a couple of long-sleeved tops with you as they'll give protection from the sun and biting insects. They can also be more appropriate to wear at religious sites. Trousers that convert into shorts are good because you get two for the price of one. Take a hat and make sure it protects the back of your neck from sunburn.

Keeping warm Several layers, topped by a good-quality jacket, will give you the versatility you need. For starters, pack some thermal underwear. If you're not into granny gear, take the lightweight, cycling-style, base-layer T-shirts or merino wool vests. Both will allow your body to breathe while offering good insulation. Then you need a fleece or pile-jacket (yes, this goes directly over your underwear), which is lighter and less bulky than a thick jumper. Most fleeces and pile-jackets are not fully water or windproof, so you'll also need a lightweight, breathable waterproof jacket. If you're travelling in an extremely cold environment then consider the more expensive Gore-Tex mountain jackets. Take some synthetic or merino wool long johns (yes, you're going to look really sexy) and then wear your usual travel trousers. Don't forget your gloves and hat.

Waterproof poncho Whether you're going hot or cold, think about taking one. You can use it to cover you and your pack, as a ground-sheet or sleeping-bag cover, on your bed as a barrier between you and a mouldy mattress, or as a sun-awning.

Footwear

Boots/shoes You've got three options: a full-on, high-leg hiking boot; a mid-boot (a cross between a shoe and a boot); and normal shoes or trainers. Unless you're doing lots of trekking, you probably don't need a full-on boot. If you want versatility then the mid-boot is good because it gives you a modicum of ankle support. Whatever you choose, non-waterproof is better than waterproof (unless you're going somewhere real cold), as your feet will always breathe better. However, at the end of the day, buy what your feet feel most comfortable wearing. And, remember to break in your footwear well before you travel so that you can deal with any blisters and rubbing in the comfort of your own home.

Watersport sandals These are ideal for day-to-day wear in warm climates, even if you're doing a lot of walking. You can also wear them in dodgy showers or in the sea and leave them on your feet to dry out. If you buy a more-expensive pair (eg Teva) they'll last forever and you'll become more attached to them than your best friend.

Luxuries

Binoculars These are handy for wildlife spotting and spying on your neighbours.

Books Take a couple of decent-sized books. You can swap them later on and they'll help pass endless hours waiting for trains and planes.

Camera See p56 for details.

Camping gear Only lug this around if you're really going to do the tent thing properly. It's bulky, heavy stuff. However, think about a small brew kit (for coffee, not beer) if you need a caffeine shot to get you going in the morning.

Family photos You might want to take some of pics of your nearest and dearest.

Games Cards and backgammon are the best games, as they are known worldwide – you can play either with the locals or with other travellers.

Gifts If you are going to stay with a family, you'll want to take a few of these.

Mobile phone See p88 for the pros and cons of taking your mobile.

Personal stereo/radio This is good for keeping up with news and views while away but can cut you off from the culture you're there to experience.

WHERE TO BUY YOUR EQUIPMENT

The best place to buy your equipment is specialised outdoor shops where the staff have a keen interest in travel. It's pretty easy to judge whether staff members have been there, done that and got the knowledge. Branches to look out for include Nomad Travel & Outdoor (www.nomadtravel.co.uk), with shops in London, Bristol and Southampton that include immunisation clinics; Itchy Feet (www.itchyfeet.com), with stores in London and Bath; Cotswold (www.cotswold-outdoor.com), with 15 stores nationally; and Blacks (www.blacks .co.uk), with 74 shops. All these shops sell online too.

If possible, try to buy your equipment in person so you can soak up advice from the experts and try everything on for comfort. However, there are three useful online equipment sites: www.safariquip.com, www.gear-zone.co.uk and www.travelwithcare.com.

Good brands across a whole range of kit include Berghaus (www.berghaus.com), Eagle Creek (www.eaglecreek.com), the North Face (www.thenorthface.com) and Lowe Alpine (www.lowealpine.com).

CAMERAS

Some gappers choose not to travel with a camera. Apart from being another expense, it can be a pain if you keep worrying about whether it will be stolen, lost or damaged. And it might become a barrier between you and the places you're visiting if you're constantly taking shots rather than just enjoying the view.

However, a gap-year photo album can be a source of constant pleasure in years to come. Sure, you'll have the memories but they're more difficult to share with your friends, family and, perhaps, your own children when they're heading off on their gap year.

If you're wavering, consider sharing a camera with a travelling companion. Susie Clements and Maria Duncan shared a camera on their travels:

We thought it a good way of saving space, especially as we were likely to be taking photos of the same scenes. We often had different ideas on what makes a good photo and who was going to take the shot but a little diplomacy, violence and a lot of film eased the way.

If you want your own camera, you'll need to think about what type you need. This will very much depend on the sort of photos you want to take. You could write a whole book on this subject and, oh yes, someone has. For the full picture, check out Lonely Planet's *Travel Photography* book by Richard I'Anson. And, in the meantime, here's a quick overview.

Digital Cameras

Sometimes it feels like no-one travels with anything else these days. Digital cameras do have a lot of advantages – they're affordable, small and light; there are no film or processing costs; you get immediate gratification; you can delete your rubbishy shots immediately; they usually have a video option; and, best of all for gappers, images can be emailed or posted to a website at once. And you can make prints of your digital images if you later want to make up your gap-year photo album.

So, what are the disadvantages? Well, there are more for the long-term traveller than for the average two-weeks-in-the-sun tourist. The main question is how you're going to store your images. There are four options: download them on to a laptop; take enough memory cards to cover your entire trip; carry a portable storage device; or get photographic retailers to transfer your images on to CD while you're travelling. Another key issue to think about is batteries. These power-hungry little items need constant recharging on a digital camera and you can't plug your charger (and adapter) into a tree trunk in the jungle to siphon off electricity.

Like anything there are pros and cons. A digital camera can be more hard work than a traditional one and might not be so convenient in out-of-the-way places. However, if you're a keen photographer and want to take a digital camera along with either a point-and-shoot or an SLR then you'll have the best of all worlds.

Point-and-Shoot Cameras

These compact 35mm cameras are just the ticket if all you want to do is take snaps to show your friends and family with the minimum of fuss. They are small, light and easy to use; there are no accessories to worry about, and most have built-in flash and zoom lenses. They work best using colour print film but you're probably not going to want to use slide film unless you're an aspiring semi-professional. A point-and-shoot beaut is what most gappers go for, and if you happen to lose it en route then you'll probably be more upset about losing the photos on the half-used film rather than the camera itself.

Single Lens Reflex (SLR) Cameras

If you're a keen amateur photographer then you'll have one of these. A 35mm SLR camera allows you to get all creative by shooting with the camera on its manual setting and by using different lenses. Many SLRs also have automatic settings, which are handy for when you want to take a quick snap. A downside of taking your SLR on a gap year is that it'll be relatively heavy and, even if you've only got the minimum number of lenses and filters, relatively bulky. The minimum kit with an SLR is as follows:

- Two lenses: a standard 28–80mm and then an 80–200mm zoom. Obviously, you might want to add a wide-angle lens and a zoomier zoom but then we're really talking weight, as well as more costly items that you won't want to lose or have stolen. Some people prefer travelling with just one lens, in which case go for a 28–105mm.
- A Skylight or UV (ultraviolet) filter for each of your lenses. These protect your lenses and screen out excess UV light (which makes pictures look dull). Also consider taking a polarising (PL) filter, which eliminates reflections and improves photos taken in strong, bland sunlight (if you have no option but to take them at high noon).

Film

If you're taking an SLR then you'll probably be using good-quality or professional film. You might be taking slides. In some places decent film stored at the right temperature can be hard to find, so bring some from home. Remember it has a shorter lifespan than your standard, all-purpose film; likes to be kept cold; and prefers to be developed as soon as possible.

Print film for your point-and-shoot can be found everywhere and lasts for ages. Choose a 200 ISO for sunny conditions and 400 ISO for when the light's not so good.

Heat can damage film – a day in a car's hot glove compartment is usually enough to toast a roll. Store your film in as cool a place as possible, and always out of direct sunlight.

When flying, put film in your hand luggage to protect it from the high-energy X-ray machines used in some airports to inspect baggage. The metal detectors used to check your carry-on baggage are usually film-safe. However, if you've got professional aspirations ask for it to be hand-checked – some airport security staff will readily agree, though many will not take the risk and insist it goes through the detectors.

DEVELOPING FILM

If you want your pictures to look like you spent your gap year in a spotted cloud, develop all your film when you get back from your trip. The smarter option is to get it developed as soon as you can. You can do this on the road but results will vary widely, so ask other travellers for recommendations. Otherwise, send it back to your family and get them to do the needful. If you're developing abroad, consider sending the slides or prints back home, as they will get mashed up in your pack and are heavy.

Video Cameras

Do you really want to look like your parents?

DOCUMENTS

All important documents (passport data and visa pages, credit card numbers, travel insurance policy, driving licence, air/train/bus tickets, vaccination certificates etc) should be photo copied before you depart for foreign shores. Leave one set of copies with someone at home and take one set with you (keep it separate from the originals). You can also store this information electronically, either in your email account, or in an online travel vault (www.lonelyplanet.ekit.com). You may think you'll never need it, and you might not, but Gareth Potts says:

I had to carry a photocopy of my visa in Madagascar as, apparently, the police periodically do checks on this and do 'round ups' of foreigners without copies, which lead to a night in the police cells for those concerned.

If you're planning to look for work abroad, you'll need to access copies of an up-to-date CV, primed for the type of thing you're after. References will be essential in some places too, so sort these out before you go.

WHAT NOT TO PACK

No, this is not the title of Trinny and Susannah's new TV show. If it was, however, they'd tell you not to pack anything you couldn't bear to lose (this includes jewellery with sentimental value). You also won't want your hair dryer and three different types of hair gel. Aftershave and perfume often change their scent in a hot climate, and, wherever you're headed, will just clutter up your bag. Aim to buy things when you get to your destination so you're not taking coals to Newcastle.

You'll need to do a couple of dry runs at packing before you get it right. Your first attempt will put the frighteners on your mum as it will look as if you're emigrating forever. On your second attempt, try to cut in half what you packed first time around. By your third go you'll probably have got it just about right.

HEALTH

Feeling unwell when you're travelling is the pits, and you'll probably get the odd bout of Delhi belly or Montezuma's revenge (ie the squits) unless you've got a super-hardy stomach like Clementine Patrick-Brown:

A few of my friends found the food change a struggle, with tummy upsets and the like, but I seem to have an iron constitution, or my mum fed me really dirty food when I was a child.

The good news is that there's heaps you can do before you go away and while you're on the road to minimise the risk of catching anything more serious. For instance, of the many diseases travellers worry about most can be prevented by basic eating, drinking and hygiene precautions. The ones that are transmitted by insects, including malaria, can be prevented by practising bite-avoidance and the ones you get from other human beings, well, you just need to be careful what you do with your bodily fluids. Read on for more details.

Be aware, though, that if you do catch something serious, it isn't always easy to tell from how you're feeling. Flu-like symptoms or diarrhoea and vomiting are the initial symptoms of many of the world's tropical diseases.

Also, to get things into perspective, remember that by far the biggest risk to your health when abroad is being involved in a traffic, drowning or skiing accident.

This chapter was written with advice and help from Nomad Travel Clinics (www.nomad travel.co.uk) in the UK.

IMMUNISATIONS

One of the best ways to prevent catching something bigger and potentially more dangerous than the number 12 bus is by getting yourself an armful of jabs. Go along to your nearest travel clinic six to eight weeks before travel. Which immunisations you need depends on where and when you're going and what you plan to do when you get there. It's also influenced by what you've had in the past and your medical history. After a consultation, ask which vaccinations you should be able to have free on the NHS and pop along to your local GP for these (beware, not all GPs are aware of the latest guidelines on this). For all others, you'll need to stick out your arm but not your arse.

The reason you need to give so much notice when getting your jabs is that sometimes a course of vaccinations is required over a period of weeks. For example, a full course of rabies vaccine takes a month. Or sometimes, you might need to wait one or two weeks after a booster or the last dose of a course before you are fully protected. If you have left it to the last minute, immunisation schedules can be rushed if necessary and squeezed into a couple of weeks. This is likely to mean that you will have less cover, particularly in the first week or two of your trip.

The reason you visit a travel clinic before your local GP is that they are the experts in travel health. Travel medicine is a complicated area and you need to speak to someone who has bang up-to-the-minute advice and information. MASTA (www.masta.org) has travel clinics all over Britain; Nomad Travel Clinics (www.nomadtravel.co.uk) has clinics in London, Bristol and Southampton; and there are loads of other travel clinics in the London area.

Vaccines can sometimes cause side effects but usually nothing more annoying than a sore arm or fever for half a day. Very occasionally serious allergic reactions can occur. Think about what you might be doing on the days you get your jabs. Juliet Browning didn't and says:

As part of saving to go away I worked in a pub three nights a week. I had my first lot of jabs in the afternoon (in my right arm) and then was using it in the pub that night to pull pints. At first I wondered why my arm was aching, I didn't make the connection and then I remembered. Still, I felt fine in the morning and glad of the extra money I'd earned the night before.

Cholera

This is a diarrhoeal disease that you can catch from contaminated food and water. For ages there wasn't a vaccine but now there is, and it's oral. It will also give reasonable protection from general travellers' diarrhoea. You need two doses and it takes a week to come into effect after your last dose.

Hepatitis A

This acute viral infection of the liver is spread by contaminated food and water. All travellers to Latin America, Africa, Asia (apart from Japan), the Pacific Islands and off the beaten track in Eastern, central or southern Europe and Turkey should be protected with a hepatitis A vaccine. This will give good protection for at least a year (and a further injection boosts immunity for 10 years).

There is a combined hepatitis A and typhoid vaccine and a combined hepatitis A and hepatitis B vaccine – good news if you're not keen on needles.

Hepatitis B

This is a serious liver infection, passed via bodily fluids – theoretically, you can even get it from snogging the wrong person. Protection is recommended for long-term travellers to Latin America, Asia, Africa, Eastern Europe and Turkey. It is recommended you get one of these if you intend to work as a medic or nurse, or if needle sharing or sexual contact with a local person is a possibility. There's a course of three injections over six months, so you have to sort this one out earlier than your other jabs. You can combine it with a vaccine against hepatitis A.

Japanese Encephalitis

Mosquitoes have a lot to answer for. This is a disease passed by mosquito, but a different one to the malaria mozzie. A vaccination is often needed if you're planning a long stay in some rural areas of Papua New Guinea, the far north of Australia (mainly Torres Strait Islands and Cape York) or rural, rice-growing areas of Asia.

Meningococcal Meningitis

This is a serious brain infection passed from person to person, usually by coughing and sneezing. There are occasional outbreaks in some areas of Latin America (eg around São Paulo in Brazil). In Africa, epidemics occur periodically, mainly in the Sahel area in the dry season, although the so-called 'meningitis belt' extends as far south as Zambia and Malawi. Pilgrims travelling to the Haj in Saudi are asked for a certificate showing immunisation against meningitis ACWY. Immunisation is usually recommended if you are travelling to risk areas in the dry season. Meningitis outbreaks can occur in many parts of the world, so if you're a long-term traveller check with your travel expert.

Rabies

This is a virus spread by contact with a rabid-seeming beast. You don't have to be bitten; you could just be licked or scratched. The animal could be anything from a dog out in the midday sun to a monkey making off with your day pack. Rabies hotspots include Africa, the Indian subcontinent, Thailand, the Philippines and Latin America. Although rare, it does exist in many European countries, with the exception of the UK, Ireland, Portugal, Monaco and Malta. A vaccination is recommended for travel off the beaten track or for those handling wild animals in high-risk areas.

You can be immunised before you go, or after you've been in contact with the suspected animal. A pre-trip immunisation means a course of three injections over a month, and gives you some (but not complete) protection against the disease. Whether you have been immunised or not, you need to have booster injections within 24 hours of contact – you will need more if you haven't been immunised. This vaccine doesn't prevent rabies totally, but it does give you more time to get medical help.

Tick-Borne Encephalitis (TBE)

This disease is passed by the bite of infected ticks. It can occur in most forest and rural areas of Europe, especially in Austria, Germany, Hungary and the Czech Republic. Consider a vaccination against this tick-transmitted disease if you plan to play Goldilocks and the Three Bears in the woods between May and September or if you are doing some extensive hiking. The vaccine is available as a series of two or three injections; it takes about 28 days to get the three shots.

Typhoid

This disease is transmitted by food and water that has been in contact with infected poo. You'll need protection if you're travelling for longer than two weeks in Latin America, Africa, the Pacific Islands or most parts of Asia (except Japan). It is also wise to be vaccinated if you intend to rough it in remote areas of Turkey and Eastern European countries, including Albania, Croatia and Romania. A vaccination is available as an injection or as tablets (oral form). You can have it as a combined vaccine with hepatitis A.

Yellow Fever

It's a mozzie again that is responsible for this disease that occurs in tropical parts of South America and Africa. Proof of immunisation against yellow fever is a statutory requirement for entry into all Latin American and African countries if you are coming from a yellow-fever infected country in South America or the African continent. A yellow-fever vaccination lasts for 10 years. It's not recommended if you have a severe egg allergy or if your immunity is lowered for some reason (for example, you are HIV-positive).

Boosters for Childhood Vaccinations

Read on: this section is not for kids; it's for adults. You probably can't remember it, but you had a set of childhood immunisations at two, three and four months old and then at various intervals until you were a teenager. Many childhood vaccinations need boosting after 10 years or, in the case of tetanus, after a cut or an injury. Make sure you're up to date with these childhood immunisations and particularly with:

- measles, mumps and rubella (MMR)
- polio, diphtheria, tetanus and meningitis C
- tuberculosis (BCG)

Vaccination Certificate

Make sure your immunisations are recorded on an official certificate. This is useful for your own information and, if necessary, you will be able to show it to any doctor treating you. Take this certificate on your travels – maybe attach it inside your passport with an elastic band.

MOSQUITO-BORNE DISEASES
Malaria

Malaria is a potentially fatal mosquito-borne disease and to date there is no vaccination. Malarial risks and antimalarial drug-resistance patterns change constantly. If you're going to a malarial area, you need to get expert advice from your travel clinic on how to prevent catching this potentially fatal mosquito-borne disease.

There are a number of antimalarial medicines on the market and they all have their pros and cons. (For a clear, no-nonsense discussion, see www.fitfortravel.scot.nhs.uk.) Your friendly travel clinic will discuss these with you and come up with the best solution for you and the type of trip you're planning. Remember, if you need to take malaria pills, they generally have to be started at least one week before you head into a malarial area. This is so they have a chance to reach maximum protective levels in your body before you arrive in a malarial zone. If you're popping your pills in the UK a week before you depart and you're going directly to a malarial area, it also gives any side effects a chance to show themselves so you can change medication before you go, if necessary. Very importantly, most malarial pills need to be continued for four weeks after you depart a malarial area. This means that if you're a pre-university gapper you could still be carrying your pills around during Freshers' Week at university (luckily, you don't have to abstain from drinking while you take them). Don't be tempted to stop taking your malaria pills as soon as you leave a malarial area or you may get malaria from parasites you picked up in the last few days of your trip.

One of the most important things to remember about antimalarials is that they do not stop you getting malaria, they just suppress it if you do get it. This means that you always need to combine antimalarials with proper precautions against being bitten in the first place. For a list of these, see p71.

So, what happens if you do get bitten? How do you know if you've caught malaria? You'd think this would be an easy question to answer, but it isn't. Any flulike symptom could be malaria. If you're feeling off-colour in a malarial area then you must go to a local hospital and ask for a blood test. If you're feeling off-colour in a malarial area then you must go to a local hospital and ask for a blood test. Yes, you did read that twice. No, it isn't a printing mistake. Just like writing lines on the blackboard, now you'll remember it. For instance, in Thailand, most hospitals will test you on the spot – it takes 20 minutes and costs 20p. Molly Bird writes:

When I was living in a remote village in India I became feverous and was worried that I had malaria. I feel very lucky that I had a friend there to look after me. When you're in a different culture it's very nice to have someone else who understands. I had my own needles so all I had to do was get to a doctor and have a blood test. Luckily, I was fine. Really look after yourself when you are ill and away from home.

If you do catch malaria, it is important that you give yourself time to recover and rest afterwards before you get back on to that adventure treadmill. Gareth Potts says:

One of the girls I was with had malaria. Initially it was no problem – she took the medication and was just about fine. The rest of us were cycling to one of the national parks, and she went with us. With hindsight, she hadn't completely recovered, and we started cycling at about noon when it was incredibly hot. By the time we got there we were all exhausted and the girl in question started vomiting quite badly during the night, and started getting ill again. The place where we were camping wasn't near a road and one of us had to go out and arrange a lift in the morning to take her back to civilisation quickly.

Dengue Fever

Another insect-borne disease, this one is on the increase. It is carried by a mozzie that bites during the day and there is no vaccination or tablet that prevents it. It is especially prevalent in Central America, Malaysia and Queensland (Australia) and most malarial areas. Dengue fever is also known as 'break-bone disease' because you get extreme joint pain, along with flu-like symptoms. The best way to avoid catching dengue fever is to practice bite-avoidance (see p71). If you do think you've picked it up then you'll need to get to hospital and it'll take about three weeks to get over.

PRE-TRAVEL CHECKUPS
Medical

In addition to finding out about vaccinations, it may be worth making an appointment with your doctor before you go, for the following reasons:

- If you suffer from any ongoing conditions such as asthma, hay fever or dermatitis, try to clarify any specific problems travelling may cause and what to do about them.
- To get supplies of prescription medicines you might need and to discuss taking emergency treatment for diarrhoea or chest infections, especially if you will be travelling in remote areas.
- To discuss problems that travel may pose to any contraceptives you are using, or to discuss options if you want to start contraception.
- If you're planning on doing any diving while you are away, remember to get a specific diving medical checkup before you go as, in theory at least, you'll need a certificate of fitness before any dive centre will let you dive.

Dental

Now is also the time to stop putting off going to your favourite place. You don't want to find you need a filling when you're in a remote area far from the nearest pain-killing injection. Your teeth can take quite a battering when you're abroad because you can end up drinking gallons of sweet drinks, and inadequate water supplies may mean you can't keep up your usual highly vigilant dental-health routine.

Optical

If you wear contact lenses, your optometrist can advise you about hygiene on the road. You'll either want to take a plentiful supply of cleaning solutions or consider daily contact lenses. 'Dailies' can be expensive for long trips but you won't have to faff about cleaning them as you'll have a new sterile pair each day. If you wear contact lenses and hate your glasses, don't be tempted not to pack them. There will be days when your eyes will need a rest. If you wear glasses, consider taking a replacement pair or take your prescription with you. In many countries you can have prescription lenses made up quite cheaply.

FIRST-AID & SURVIVAL TRAINING

You might not be accident-prone, but you're bound to bump into someone who is, so it's smart to have basic first-aid knowledge. First-aiders can save lives and even if you don't use your skills while you're away you might use them one day walking the dog in your local park. Consider doing a basic course before you leave. A group like St John Ambulance (www.sja.org.uk) runs a number of excellent courses. Otherwise, more specialised ones include:

- Adventure Lifesigns (www.adventurelifesigns.co.uk)
- Wilderness Expertise (www.wilderness-expertise.co.uk)
- Wilderness Medical Training (www.wildernessmedicaltraining.co.uk)

See p444 for more information.

STAYING HEALTHY

Guess what? Avoiding illness and injury can help make your trip a lot better. Staying healthy becomes even more important if you're planning to spend some time in a remote location where medical help is a couple of days away. It's also vital if you're doing outdoor activities such as trekking that rely on your physical – and mental – fitness. If you're aware of potential health hazards and take some basic steps to avoid them, you shouldn't find it too tricky to stay safe and healthy.

Medical Kit

You'll need a good one of these. Many travel clinics sell a range of prepared medical kits to suit all types of traveller (overland, expedition, independent etc). They usually cost between £25 and £45. If you're travelling with a gap-year organisation they will often prescribe the one they want you to buy (often it is one that's specifically made up for them) and let you know of stockists. Otherwise, what you'll pack will depend on where you're going and what you plan to do.

Following is a list of your basic requirements:

- antidiarrhoeals – loperamide is probably the most effective, or the preventative Pepto-Bismol
- antifungal cream
- antihistamine tablets for hay fever and other allergies or itching
- any prescription medicines, including antibiotics and antimalarials
- calamine cream or aloe vera for sunburn and other skin rashes
- cough and cold remedies, and sore-throat lozenges
- eye drops
- indigestion remedies such as antacid tablets or liquids
- insect repellent (DEET or plant-based) and permethrin (for treating mosquito nets and clothes)

- laxatives (particularly if you're headed to an area such as Mongolia where there's little fibre in the diet)
- oral-rehydration sachets and a measuring spoon for making up your own solution
- over-the-counter cystitis treatment (if you're prone to this)
- painkillers such as paracetamol and aspirin for pain and fever and an anti-inflammatory such as ibuprofen
- sting-relief spray or hydrocortisone cream for insect bites
- sunscreen and lip salve with sunblock
- water-purifying tablets or water filter/purifier

First-Aid Equipment
Remember to stow this in your luggage when flying because anything sharp will get confiscated if it's packed in your hand luggage:

- antiseptic powder or solution (eg povidone-iodine) and/or antiseptic wipes
- bandages and safety pins
- digital thermometer (not mercury – can you imagine what would happen if it broke?)
- gauze swabs and adhesive tape
- nonadhesive dressings
- scissors
- sticking plasters
- syringes and needles – ask your doctor for a note explaining why you have them
- tweezers to remove splinters, cactus needles and ticks
- wound-closure strips

If you're really going remote then you'll also need:

- antibiotic cream or powder
- antibiotic eye and ear drops
- dental first-aid kit (either a commercial kit, or make up your own – ask your dentist to advise you)
- elasticated support bandage
- emergency splints (eg SamSplints)
- triangular bandage for making an arm sling

If you're allergic to any drugs (such as penicillin), it's a good idea to carry information about that on you at all times.

Acclimatisation
Always allow yourself time to adjust physically and mentally to a new place. You'll probably need time to recover from jet lag, catch up on sleep and perhaps missed meals, so aim to settle into your new venue slowly.

FEELING HOT HOT HOT
If you've gone from a cool climate to a baking one, make sure you give yourself a chance to get used to the heat. Your body has an amazing capacity to adjust to temperature changes but it doesn't happen overnight.

It takes about a week for your body to make initial adjustments to deal with the temperature change. After this, you'll probably find you can cope with the heat much better, and your capacity for activity gets back to normal.

If you want to avoid serious problems such as heat exhaustion and heatstroke, it's vital to drink like a fish (not booze though) to replace the amount you're sweating out. Cool water is best. Don't wait until you feel thirsty before drinking; thirst is a very bad indicator of your fluid needs, and if you're thirsty, you're already dehydrated. You should keep a supply of water with you and drink it regularly. Remember that tea, coffee and alcohol all have a diuretic effect (ie they make you lose fluid), so it's best to go easy on these. If you sweat a lot, you may need to supplement your drinking with rehydration salts.

Physical activity generates heat, which means that your body has to work even harder to stay cool if you're exercising. If you're getting busy in a tropical climate, plan to take it easy during the first week, building up slowly as you acclimatise.

Avoid overexerting yourself (and this includes eating loads of food) during the hottest part of the day; it's the perfect time for a siesta. As far as clothing is concerned, you need to choose clothes that will protect your skin from the sun (and insects) but that won't make you too darn hot. Sunburn makes your body less able to cope with the heat. So, sorry to disappoint but skin-tight lycra outfits are probably out, at least off the beach; loose, light-coloured clothing made of natural fibres like cotton are in. (Dark colours will absorb the heat more.) You'll need to consider any local cultural considerations when deciding what to wear – see your travel guidebook for more details.

If you're so white that people don shades as you pass, it can be hard to resist the temptation to stretch out in the sun. If you're determined to tan, then at least take some damage-control measures. Make sure you allow your skin to brown slowly without burning, starting with 15 or 20 minutes exposure a day. As soon as your skin starts to feel sore or look red, and preferably long beforehand, head for the shade. Remember that freckles may be cute but they're also a sign of skin damage.

Sunlight or solar energy is made up of radiation of many different wavelengths, including ultraviolet-A (UVA) rays, the bad guys. UVA rays used to be thought to be less harmful than UVB (ultraviolet-B rays) but there's plenty of evidence that they are just as bad, so you need to look for sunscreen products that protect against both types. In the short term, ultraviolet radiation causes redness, blisters and soreness – sunburn. If you've ever frazzled yourself, you'll know how painful this can be but the long-term effects are even scarier. Skin changes like wrinkles, broken veins and pigmented patches ('liver spots') are due to sun damage rather than old age. Worst of all, UV rays can damage the metabolism of skin cells, leading to skin cancer.

A suntan is a layer of skin pigment (melanin) that forms in response to sunlight falling on your skin. It can protect against sunburn but not against the ageing or cancer-inducing effects of UV radiation. In any case, it takes two to three weeks before a suntan can provide good protection against sunburn.

If you're somewhere where the sun is almost always shining and you're spending a lot of your time outdoors, it can be hard to be on your guard all the time. It takes a bit of effort but protection against the sun should become part of your daily routine. Sun intensity is greatly increased at altitude and by reflection off water and snow, so you need to take particular care in these situations. The state of the protective ozone layer is another good reason to take care, especially in Australia and New Zealand. Unless you're a mad dog (in which case, why are you reading this?), keep out of the sun in the middle of the day.

Do the Aussie slip, slop, slap thing:

Slip on a shirt Covering up with clothing of a reasonable thickness provides by far the best protection from harmful rays; special protective sunsuits are available for wearing on the beach, and are ideal if you're doing watersports; sun does just as much damage to your eyes, so slip on some shades too.

Slop on sunscreen Use liberal amounts of high-protection factor (SPF 60 is currently the highest available), broad-spectrum sunscreen on any exposed bits of skin; apply 30 minutes before going into the sun and splash it on frequently, especially after swimming.

Slap on a hat A wide-brimmed hat or a cap with a neck protector will help to keep damaging rays off your face and ears and the back of your neck.

Remember:

- The ambient temperature doesn't make any difference to the burning power of the sun – you can still get burnt on a cold day if the sun is shining.
- You can also fry on a cloudy day (because clouds let through some UV radiation) and in the shade (from reflected light, often off water).
- You can get sunburnt through water (snorkelling can leave you smouldering), so take care to cover up with a T-shirt and use plenty of water-resistant sunscreen.

COLD COMFORT

You may be exposed to the extreme cold, especially if you are trekking or just travelling through highland areas. In the desert, it can get nippy at night as there is nothing to retain the heat. Clare Hall got chilly in Australia:

I've never been so cold as when I was sleeping out in the desert near Ayers Rock in Australia. The days were boiling but the nights freezing. In the morning we'd all find frost on our sleeping bags and it didn't matter how close we tried to get to the camp fire, my friends and I shivered all night.

Your body is fairly limited in what it can do to stay warm – saying 'brrr' and shivering are just about the only things in the short term – so it's up to you to minimise the dangers by wearing lots of warm clothes and avoiding temperature extremes (unless you're well prepared). Food equals heat, so make sure you eat regularly and get sufficient calories in cold climates.

Other chilling problems are dehydration (cold makes you urinate more) and so, like in a hot climate, you should drink as much as you can. The cold can also give you constipation and sunburn (especially at altitude). Worse problems are general body cooling (hypothermia) or localised cooling, usually affecting hands and feet, called frostnip or frostbite.

GETTING HIGH

The lack of oxygen at altitude (usually over 2400m) affects people to varying degrees, but is common if you fly straight to a high place. One of the highest airports in the world is La Paz (3658m). Other high travel spots include: Cochabamba (2500m) in Bolivia; Quito (2879m) in Ecuador; Cusco (3225m) in Peru; and Lhasa (3685m) in Tibet.

Symptoms of mild altitude sickness are common when you first arrive at altitude and include headache, nausea and loss of appetite; difficulty sleeping; and lack of energy. Jack Hall and Janey Smith even had a few problems in San Cristóbal in Mexico (2100m):

You can do a tour of the town and surrounding area on mountain bikes and we thought that'd be a really interesting introduction to the place. We couldn't work out, though, why we struggled to keep up with the guide and felt so breathless, as we're both keen cyclists at home. Then someone mentioned that it would be the lack of oxygen and we didn't feel so unfit. At night we dreamt really vividly and someone else said that this was a side-effect of our altitude.

Mild symptoms of altitude sickness respond to rest. More serious forms of altitude sickness are less common but can be fatal.

To get advice on preventing acute mountain sickness (AMS) consult with your travel health clinic or expedition organiser, or read up about it in your guidebook. An authoritative website with a good section about AMS is www.fitfortravel.scot.nhs.uk.

Before you leave, it's a good idea to check that your travel insurance covers altitude sickness. If you have any ongoing illnesses such as asthma or diabetes, or you're taking the oral contraceptive pill, discuss with your doctor the possible effects altitude may have.

If you are trekking or climbing, the best way to prevent AMS is to ascend slowly. Try to sleep at a lower altitude than the greatest height you reached during the day, and make sure you allow extra time in your schedule for rest days. Drugs such as acetazolamide (trade name Diamox) are sometimes used to prevent AMS. However, taking drugs is no substitute for proper acclimatisation. If symptoms persist or increase you must descend. You must never continue to climb if you have symptoms of AMS.

Food, Water & Hygiene

Food, rather than water, is the most common source of gastro problems. Unfriendly fauna can contaminate your snack at any stage of the production chain, including during harvesting, transportation, handling, washing and preparation. Many forms of diarrhoea and dysentery (bloody diarrhoea) are transmitted in this way, as well as other diseases such as hepatitis A (common in travellers) and typhoid (uncommon).

You can get sick from dodgy food anywhere, but it's more likely when you're living in a less-developed country or travelling. This can be because sewage-disposal systems may be inadequate or there's a higher level of disease in some parts of the population, meaning there's an increased likelihood that your food will have a not-so-tantalising topping of disease-causing microorganisms.

In foreign countries you may eat out a lot more and have to rely on other people to prepare your food safely. This is always a risk and, even in countries with supposedly high food-safety standards such as Australia, outbreaks of food poisoning still occur with alarming regularity.

Eating safely is about taking simple precautions to minimise your risk of getting something nasty – you don't need to live in a germ-free bubble. Some common sense and background knowledge are the ideal accompaniments to your meal. Here are some food-and-drink guidelines:

- Always wash your hands prior to eating.
- Avoid food that has been peeled, sliced or nicely arranged, as this means it has been handled a lot – you might have washed your hands but did the head cook and the head bottle washer?
- Avoid ice cubes in drinks; they may have been made from contaminated water.
- Be wary of ice cream and seafood – though for totally different reasons.
- Drink bottled water or canned drinks where possible.
- Eat only food that's freshly prepared and piping hot – avoid the hotel buffet like the plague.
- Raw fruit and vegetables are hard to clean. Only eat them if you know they've been washed in clean water or if you can safely peel them yourself. Bananas and papayas are good fruits to eat in the tropics.
- Remember that food can get contaminated from dirty dishes, cutlery, utensils and cups, and blenders or pulpers used for fruit juices are often suspect. Bring your own cup or spoon or clean the restaurant's with a wet wipe.

- The simplest way of purifying water is to bring it to a 'roaring' boil for a couple of minutes, otherwise use chlorine, iodine or a water purifier.
- Think twice before you drink water from the tap or brush your teeth with it.

Despite taking all these precautions, you probably will succumb to the odd stomach upset.

SAFE DRINKING WATER
Water, water everywhere but not a drop to drink…Whatever the weather, you need to drink lots of water to stay in sparkling health. Although contaminated food is the most common source of bad belly when you're travelling, water can also bring on nasty illnesses, including diarrhoea, dysentery, hepatitis A and typhoid.

In countries with good infrastructure and resources, communal water supplies are generally safe from contamination, but you can't rely on this in nations with fewer resources. Contamination of the water supply can occur at any point, usually from human or animal sewage. Unless you are sure that the water is safe, it's best to err on the side of caution.

Ice is only as safe as the water it's made from, so it's best avoided if you're unsure. Paul Benson says:

One of the first phrases I learned in Hindi was 'no ice please'. Sometimes I felt like I was being rude if I were offered a drink and refused it but I weighed it up: a minute's awkwardness versus four days of hell.

Drinking bottled water is an obvious answer to the water question. As a general rule, it's best to stick to major brands of bottled water, and make sure the seal on the lid is not broken (this means the bottle can't have been refilled with any old dodgy water). If you're in any doubt, choose carbonated water (for example plain soda water), as this is harder to counterfeit.

The cost of bottled water can add up over a long trip and the millions of discarded and unrecycled plastic bottles are having a severe environmental impact in many countries. If you're trekking or travelling off the beaten track, bottled water is just not practical and may not be available in remote areas. In these situations, you'll have to have some means with you of making water safe to drink. Make sure you have more than one means of purifying water in case one method fails (for example, take some iodine as well as a pump-action purifier).

The simplest and most effective way of making water safe to drink is bring it to a 'roaring' boil for a minute or two – prolonged boiling is not necessary. If boiling is not practical, it's relatively easy to disinfect clear water with chemicals. Chlorine and iodine are the chemicals most widely used, and at optimal concentrations both kill bacteria, viruses and most parasites (one exception is cryptosporidium). Iodine and chlorine are both available as tablets or liquids ('tincture' of iodine), and iodine is also available as crystals. You can usually buy them from good pharmacies, travel health clinics and outdoor-equipment suppliers.

Factors that affect the ability of these chemicals to disinfect water include concentration, how long you leave the water to stand after adding the chemical, water temperature (the colder the water, the longer it needs to be left to stand before use) and any particulate matter in the water.

Make sure you follow the manufacturer's dosage and contact time if you're using tablets, but as a rule you'll need to leave the water for at least 20 minutes before drinking it. If the water is really cold, you will need to leave it for longer, sometimes an hour or two; alternatively, you could add the chemicals the night before and leave it to stand overnight. With 2% tincture of iodine you need to add five drops to every litre of water to be purified.

Iodine should not be used continuously to purify water over a long period of time (more than six weeks) as it can cause thyroid problems. Unsurprisingly enough, it should be avoided if you already have thyroid problems. Chlorine is considered less reliable than iodine, as it is more likely to be affected by factors such as water alkalinity.

Chemically treated water – mmm, how nice. But there are ways of neutralising its grim taste. Charcoal resins or a carbon filter can remove the taste and smell of chemicals, or you can add ascorbic acid (vitamin C) or flavouring. These need to be added after the treated water has been allowed to stand for the required length of time.

If the water is cloudy, chemicals won't be effective because organic matter tends to neutralise the chemical. This problem will only arise if you're going off the beaten track and taking water from a surface source (ie river, puddle or lake), not from a tap. In this case you'll need a filter/purifier. There are tons of different types on the market, and they can be expensive (up to £200) and break down easily. As a consequence, if you're going down this route you really need to get advice from your specialist outdoor retailer.

DIARRHOEA
Many globetrotters will get the trots at some point. Just in case you've led a sheltered life: diarrhoea means the passing of loose, frequent faeces and is often associated with vomiting.

Although there are many causes of travellers' diarrhoea, your risk of getting ill mainly depends on how likely it is that the food and drink you are consuming is contaminated with disease-causing nasties. The risks vary with your destination but diarrhoea affects about 50% of travellers to developing countries. Even if it's relatively mild you're probably going to feel sorry for yourself for a day or so as the bug passes through your system, so it's worth building a few rest days into your travel schedule to allow for this. Taking basic precautions with food and drink and paying attention to your personal hygiene (washing your hands before eating) are the most important preventive strategies.

Travellers' diarrhoea usually strikes about the third day after you arrive and lasts about three to five days. It's caused by many factors, including jet lag, new food, a new lifestyle and new bugs. It can come back again in the second week, though you do build up immunity to some of the causes.

The most important aspect of treatment is to prevent dehydration by replacing lost fluid – and to rest. You can drink most liquids, except alcohol, very sugary drinks, and dairy products. Oral rehydration sachets can be useful but aren't essential if you're usually healthy. Starchy foods such as potatoes, plain rice or bread are thought to help fluid replacement, and you need to stick to a bland diet as you start to feel better.

Antidiarrhoeal tablets are of limited use, as they prevent your system from clearing out the toxin and can make certain types of diarrhoea worse – though they can be useful as a temporary stopping measure if you have to go on a long bus journey, for example.

Sometimes diarrhoea can be more serious, with blood, a high fever and cramps (bacterial dysentery), or it can be persistent and bloody (amoebic dysentery) or persistent, explosive and gassy (giardia). All need treatment with specific antibiotics. Jonathan Williams remembers:

I caught gastroenteritis whilst I was in Fiji, which basically meant I had to sit on a toilet with a bowl in front of me for three days. It was really unpleasant and was made worse by the fact that the awful little hostel I was staying in had no water or electricity for most of the day.

If you're going to a remote area far from medical help, you may want to consider taking antibiotics with you for self-treating diarrhoea. However, it's generally better to seek medical advice to diagnose which type of diarrhoea you have and to decide which antibiotics you should be taking.

Insect Bites

Insect bites can be brain-scramblingly itchy as well as a health hazard. It isn't only malaria that is transmitted by mosquito but also diseases such as yellow fever, Japanese encephalitis and dengue fever.

The best way to minimise your risk of contracting diseases caused by the little blighters is to avoid getting bitten. Even if you're taking antimalarials, you must also practise bite avoidance, as antimalarials don't stop you getting malaria – they just suppress it.

As with protecting yourself against the sun, insect-bite prevention should become part of your daily routine. And in some areas of the world you'll have to concentrate on bite avoidance 24 hours a day. The mozzie responsible for dengue fever, especially prevalent in Central America, Malaysia and Queensland (Australia), is a daytime biting mosquito.

Biting insects are attracted by many variables: body heat, body odour, chemicals in your sweat, perfumes, soap and types of clothing. The following simple precautions are effective ways of avoiding bites:

- Changing into permethrin-treated long-sleeved tops, long trousers and socks at dusk (mosquitoes don't just bite at night).
- Using a DEET-based inspect repellent on any exposed skin.
- Using electric insecticide vaporisers or burning mosquito coils in your room or under restaurant tables.
- Spraying your room, tent or campervan with a knock-down insect spray before you bed down for the night.
- Sleeping under a permethrin-treated mosquito net.
- Travelling in the height of the dry season – the risk of being bitten and therefore catching malaria is far less at this time.

INSECT REPELLENTS

There are many repellent products out there but the most effective are those containing the compound DEET (diethyltoluamide) – check the label or ask your pharmacist to tell you which brands contain DEET.

DEET is very effective against mosquitoes, midges, ticks, bedbugs and leeches, and slightly less effective against flies. One application should last up to four hours, although if it's very humid or you're very sweaty it may not last as long. Different formulations have different concentrations of DEET. The higher the concentration, the longer it will last, with around 50% being the optimal concentration, although there are some longer-acting formulations with lower strengths of DEET. It's a good idea to try a test dose before you leave to check for any allergy or skin irritation.

You may prefer to use one of the new lemon eucalyptus–based natural products, which have been shown to be an effective alternative to DEET (although DEET is probably still your best bet in high-risk areas). Other natural repellents include citronella but these tend to be less effective and to have a short action (up to an hour), making them less practical.

Cotton bands soaked well in insect repellent can be useful to wear around your wrists and ankles – a prime target for mosquitoes – and the repellent will not rub off quite as easily.

If you're using sunscreen or other lotions, apply insect repellent last, and reapply it after swimming; also note that insect repellent may reduce the protection of a sunscreen. Don't apply insect repellents before going to bed as this can cause irritation.

INSECTICIDES

Permethrin is a pyrethrum-like compound that can be applied to clothes and mosquito nets (but not on your skin). It repels mosquitoes, fleas, ticks, mites, bedbugs, cockroaches, flies, crocodiles, lions and swooping pterodactyls (only joking about the last three). If you're planning on trekking through potentially tick-infested areas, it's probably worth treating your clothes, particularly your trousers and socks, with permethrin before you go.

You get the best protection against insect bites if you apply a DEET-based product on your skin and use permethrin-treated clothes and nets.

MOSQUITO NETS

If you're going to a malarial area you'll need your own mosquito net. They don't weigh much and don't take up much room. Get one that has been soaked in permethrin, or you can treat your own net if necessary.

Freestanding nets are on the market but they are still quite costly, more bulky and not fit for coupling.

Accidents & Injury

Although travellers tend to worry about getting a tropical illness that will make their head shrivel up, you're actually at far greater risk from accident and injury than from any exotic infection.

Accidents are the most common cause of death in young travellers, especially road accidents. These are the main reason for travellers needing emergency medical treatment, including the possibility of a blood transfusion – risky in less-developed countries. Road accidents are closely followed by water-related accidents such as drowning at the beach or in the swimming pool. Then you've got hotel/hostel-style injuries, the most popular of which is falling off a balcony (no prizes for guessing why this happens so much).

When you're in a foreign place, don't take risks you wouldn't dream of taking at home. Just because you're abroad, it doesn't mean you've suddenly become death-defying. So, while you're at the travel clinic getting your vaccinations, remember to get a common-sense booster, as well (get the one that lasts for 10 years). This should kick in whenever you consider riding a bicycle, moped or motorbike without a helmet or sensible clothing, or when you ponder going paddling on a coastline known for its rip currents even though you don't know what to do if you get caught in one.

While we don't want to rain on your beach party, just be aware that alcohol and other mind-altering substances are major factors in accidents of all types in travellers, from dignity-challenging falls to life-threatening road accidents. And, obviously, the risk of having an accident increases if you're doing potentially risky outdoor activities such as white-water rafting or mountaineering. This is something to take into account when you're planning your trip and taking out your travel insurance.

Accidents are preventable to a great extent. Awareness of potential risks, together with good planning for outdoor activities and a few sensible precautions, especially if you are driving or swimming, should keep you relatively safe. And don't sit under a coconut tree…

Drugs & Alcohol

Always be careful when you're out drinking abroad. This is when you're at your most vulnerable. Also, beware of the local brew, which might be a lot stronger than you think. Charlotte Graham and Simon Mathews were in a bar in Turkey:

A couple of lads approached us and insisted on paying for drinks. We had found the Turkish people so hospitable everywhere we went that we didn't find this particularly unusual. They were nice blokes; we spent the evening with them and then we all took a taxi back to our hostel. They went off home (or so I thought) and we went to bed. Simon fell asleep immediately. Suddenly there was a knock at the door and it was one of the guys we'd been with. He said he'd lost the keys to his house and had nowhere to sleep, and he asked if he could kip on our floor. I didn't see any harm in letting him in; after all, Simon was there and I felt I owed him something because he'd been so generous at the bar. When he was in the room he started to try it on with me. And I just couldn't wake Simon. I didn't understand it. Simon never slept this soundly. Whatever I did, I couldn't wake him up. Anyway, I was lucky – the Turkish guy was obviously quite new to this game and I managed to fend him off with a mixture of good humour and a tiny bit of force. In the end he left. I still couldn't wake Simon. In the morning he came around and we worked out that someone had slipped something in his drink that evening, which is why he crashed out so completely when he got home.

And, this funnier incident (as long as you weren't the friend) from Paul Walker:

On the way out to Venezuela my friend got drunk in Lisbon airport waiting for our connecting flight and supposedly had his passport stolen. He wasn't allowed on the plane and spent five days on his own in Lisbon, where he got mugged. His passport later turned up in an airport bin where he had left it!

Other mind-altering substances are readily available throughout much of the world, and in tourist haunts especially you may be offered drugs at every opportunity. If you decide to use drugs, be aware that there's no guarantee of quality, and locally available drugs can be unexpectedly strong or mixed with other harmful substances. Acute anxiety and panic attacks are common with many drugs, especially if you're taking them for the first time under stressful conditions. Acute paranoia can occur with cocaine, amphetamines, ecstasy, LSD and mushrooms and is very frightening. Drugs can accentuate or trigger a mentally fragile state. If you take drugs intravenously, remember that needle-sharing carries the risk of HIV and hepatitis B and C infection. Because unexpected reactions can occur, never take drugs when you are on your tod.

If you're taking Larium as an antimalarial, be very careful about what else you take in terms of recreational drugs and alcohol, as Larium itself has some characteristics of a mind-altering drug.

Safe Sex

While it's true that sexually transmitted infections (STIs) are a risk anywhere if you're having casual sex, it seems that you're more likely to meet casual partners and be careless when you are away from home. Added to this, levels of STIs in the countries you are visiting may be higher. Of course, abstaining from shagging strangers is the safest option; otherwise, remember to use condoms. They will protect you against HIV, hepatitis B and C, gonorrhoea, chlamydia and syphilis but won't stop you getting any of the charming trio: genital herpes, genital warts or pubic lice. Take a familiar, reliable brand of condoms with you. Rubber condoms disintegrate in the heat, so take care to store them deep in your pack and to check them carefully before use.

WOMEN'S HEALTH
Periods
Most women have few period problems when on the road. You might find that your cycle is affected by time changes and the newness of travelling, but in most cases it will soon settle down. You may find that your periods stop altogether when you're away – affected by your change of routine and having different stresses (but do a pregnancy test if you think you may be pregnant). Or they might become heavier. If you suffer from PMT, be prepared for it to be worse while you are away and take plentiful supplies of any remedy you find helpful.

If you think you may need contraception, you could consider starting the pill before you leave – it can reduce PMT and gives lighter and regular periods.

Vaginal Infections
Hot weather and limited washing facilities make thrush (yeast infection) more likely when you're travelling. If you know you are prone to thrush, it's worth taking a supply of medication with you.

A new partner could mean you acquire an STI. Get any symptoms like an abnormal vaginal discharge or genital sores checked out as soon as possible. Some STIs don't cause any symptoms, even though they can cause infertility and other problems, so if you have unprotected intercourse while you're away, be sure to have a checkup when you return home.

The Pill
If you think you'll need this while you are away, see your doctor, a family-planning clinic or your local women's health organisation before you leave. The Marie Stopes website at www.mariestopes.org.uk has useful information on your options.

The timing of pill-taking can be tricky if you're crossing time zones, and diarrhoea, vomiting and antibiotics used to treat common infections can all reduce its effectiveness. Take a plentiful supply of your medication with you, as it may be difficult to get your brand. In some countries, oral contraceptives may not be readily available.

TRAVELLING WITH A DISABILITY
The key to travelling with a disability is to realise that everything will be different and to be well prepared. This means you need to know what to expect at your destination and, where possible, to have notified in advance travel services such as airports, airlines, bus companies and hotels, of any special needs. Some tourist offices have quite good information for travellers with disabilities, so it is worth contacting them before you travel. Airlines are usually quite helpful. They'll give you assistance getting to the plane and on board – although some airlines in Africa, Asia and South America offer less assistance. Many hotels in Europe, North America, Australia and New Zealand are geared for travellers with a disability but, not surprisingly, this isn't the case in the developing world (although people here are usually keen to help you and this can make up for the lack of facilities). The same

can be said for your transport options – in the USA, for instance, if you call the Greyhound Customers with Disabilities Travel Assistance Line (☎ 0800 752 4841) at least 48 hours before you want to travel they'll make any necessary arrangements for you. And there's good news about French railways – they are much more accessible than they used to be. Wherever you're going, you'll also have to think carefully about travel insurance and how your disability will impact on that.

There are a number of travel operators specialising in travel for disabled travellers but, to be honest, they're mostly for older people. For the younger market there are a few options, including the Jubilee Sailing Trust (JST; www.jst.org.uk) and Epic-Enabled (www.epic-enabled.com), which is a South African overland company specialising in wildlife and cultural tours for travellers with disabilities. The JST runs sailing adventures abroad on tall ships for both able-bodied and disabled people. For full details see p440. Keira Procter joined one of their voyages:

In March 2002 I was a passenger in a car accident which left me paralysed from the waist down and I'm wheelchair bound. I was a keen sailor before my accident and ecstatic when I heard about the JST's boats for mixed-ability crew. I was not disappointed when I joined the Tenacious. I had few difficulties but when I did the permanent crew did everything to assist me.

There's a lot of information about travelling with special needs on the net. Two excellent sites are Global Access: disabled travel network (www.geocities.com/paris/1502) and Access-Able Travel Source (www.access-able.com). In addition, there's a Travellers with Disabilities section on Lonely Planet's Thorn Tree (www.lonelyplanet.com). In terms of guidebooks, there ain't a lot. However, RADAR (www.radar.org.uk) publishes the well-known, annual *Holidays in Britain & Ireland* guidebook.

DIABETIC TRAVELLERS
Being a type-1 diabetic shouldn't stop you from having your gap year. Yes, there'll be many more things for you to think about but it is do-able. Your first step is to discuss your plans with your doctor or specialist. Then you need to find out what to expect at your destinations. National diabetic associations are usually the best source of information on local diabetic care:

American Diabetes Association (☎ 00 1 800-342 2383; www.diabetes.org; National Call Center, 1701 North Beauregard St, Alexandria, VA 22311, USA)

Diabetes Australia (☎ 00 61 8-8222 6821; www.diabetes.org.au; Queen Elizabeth Hospital, 28 Woodville Rd, Woodville South, South Australia)

Diabetes UK (Careline; ☎ 0845 120 2960; www.diabetes.org.uk; 10 Queen Anne St, London W1M 0BD) Produces a useful leaflet on travel with diabetes, as well as a number of specific country guides for people with diabetes.

International Diabetes Federation (☎ 00 32 2-538 5511; www.idf.org; Av Emile de Mot 19, B-1000 Brussels, Belgium) Maintains a listing of diabetic associations in different countries around the world, as well as other information on diabetes.

Alternatively, check out the information on diabetes and travel at www.fitfortravel.scot.nhs .uk. It is also a very good idea to wear a medical bracelet showing that you are diabetic.

IF YOU GET ILL ON THE ROAD
Self-diagnosis is not a good idea, even if you're a trained doctor, but when you get ill abroad you need to know when to sit it out and when to get help. In the UK you can call **NHS Direct** (☎ 0845 4647) 24-hours a day, tell them your symptoms and they'll either advise you on what to do or advise you to go to a doctor. Unfortunately, this is a system that

doesn't work worldwide. Of course, if you're travelling with a gap-year company then you will either be accompanied by doctors or there'll be good local help at hand to sort out any medical emergencies. Damien Rickwood remembers:

Trekforce provides two trained medics on each expedition. However, some things are unavoidable and when one of my friends contracted an unknown tropical disease, she was swiftly evacuated by plane to the best hospital in Belize, where she recovered quickly.

Louise Ellerton was in Ghana when she became unwell:

Me and the three girls I lived with all became very ill at once. We were weak, exhausted and had sickness, diarrhoea and high temperatures. The gap-year company were always nearby and we had been made to register with the hospital as soon as we had entered the country. This made life much easier when we were admitted and we knew we were at the best hospital possible.

If you're on your own then err on the side of caution and go to see a doctor. Before you do this, ring your travel insurance company's 24-hour hotline number. It's a good idea to keep them informed if you've got a medical problem and they should be able to provide you with names of English-speaking doctors. Otherwise, the local people are a good source of information, and most hostels or hotels will know how to contact a decent doctor (or even an English-speaking doctor). There are also lists of English-speaking doctors on many foreign British embassy websites.

Sometimes, though, you'll have to go straight to a hospital, as was the case with Amanda Akass:

In Bolivia I managed to somersault off a mountain bike and gashed my arm quite badly and needed stitches. I was taken to a clean and bright hospital where I was the only person in casualty. I was treated immediately by about six doctors. They were very friendly and professional and the whole procedure cost me less than £3. Some of my other friends had less satisfactory encounters with South American provincial doctors who seem to prescribe antibiotics for any ailment, accompanied by their favourite cure-all, the arse-injection.

Amanda brings up a good point. How do you know which hospitals abroad are good and which aren't? It isn't wise to put off going to one just because you fear what you might find, as Paul Walker did:

I broke a bone in my foot in Thailand on Ko Samui and foolishly didn't go to the hospital due to fear of dodgy Thai doctors on the islands. So it took about three months to heal properly and I still have a large lump on the side of my foot. It occurred at the full moon party – too many Thai rums and Red Bull buckets with dodgy mushroom milkshakes.

Well, again, this is where your travel insurance comes in. Your 24-hour hotline should be able to arrange referral to a hospital and guarantee payment if you need to pay upfront. You will often have to pay cash for medical treatment and be reimbursed later, so it's a good idea to have an emergency stash just in case (your insurance provider may be able to provide a guarantee of payment that will be accepted instead but don't count on it). Always keep any receipts in case you need to present them later to be reimbursed.

Of course, if you've got a medical emergency on your hands then your travel insurance will arrange for you to repatriated or for you to be evacuated to the best hospital nearby. If you're travelling in the European Economic Area (EEA) and have an E111 then you'll qualify for reduced emergency-care costs – see p30.

The number for emergency services in Europe (including Britain) is ☎ 112 and in the USA, ☎ 911.

HEALTH-RELATED DOCUMENTS

When you're travelling, it's a good idea to keep the following information (where applicable) in your day pack:

- blood group
- contact details of the nearest embassy
- contact details of your doctor back home
- copy of the prescription for any medication you take regularly
- details of any serious allergies
- E111 form or equivalent (see p30)
- letter from your doctor explaining why you're carrying syringes in a medical kit
- prescription for glasses or contact lenses
- proof of yellow fever immunisation
- summary of any important medical condition you have
- travel insurance emergency number and serial number of your policy
- vaccination certificate

SOURCES OF HEALTH INFORMATION & ADVICE

The Department of Health publishes a good, free leaflet called *Health Advice for Travellers*. You can get a copy by calling ☎ 0800 555 777, or online at www.dh.gov.uk/PolicyAnd Guidance/HealthAdviceForTravellers. It has a useful section on countries that Britain has health-care agreements with (as well as those with which it doesn't) – where emergency treatment will be either free or at reduced cost, as long as you've got your E111. However, at all times, you should be covered by your own travel insurance anyway.

There are loads of books on the market about travel health. The bible is considered to be *Travellers' Health: How to Stay Healthy Abroad*, by Dr Richard Dawood. However, it is quite heavy to take with you on the road. Lonely Planet has a range of mini health guides broken down by continent, which means you only have to pack the ones relevant to where you're going. If you do a first-aid course with someone such as the St John Ambulance (www.sja .org.uk) then you'll be given a booklet containing all the vital information you've just learned on your course. This can be really useful to take with you, just in case you need to keep someone alive long enough for the emergency services to get there. Otherwise, there are lots of good health sites on the web:

- Centers for Disease Control & Prevention (www.cdc.gov/travel)
- Department of Health (www.dh.gov.uk)
- Diabetes UK Careline (www.diabetes.org.uk/help/careline.htm)
- Diving Medicine Online (www.scuba-doc.com)
- fitfortravel (www.fitfortravel.scot.nhs.uk)
- Hospital for Tropical Diseases (www.uclh.org/services/htd/advice.shtml)
- International Society of Travel Medicine (www.istm.org)
- Malaria Foundation International (www.malaria.org)
- MASTA (www.masta.org)

- Nomad Travel Clinics (www.nomadtravel.co.uk)
- Shoreland – Travel Health Online (www.tripprep.com)
- The Travel Doctor TMVC (www.tmvc.com.au)
- Travel Doctor Site (www.traveldoctor.co.uk)
- World Health Organisation (www.who.int)

Advice for travellers can vary from country to country, so it's best to follow the advice given by your home country.

SAFETY

Safe travel is about being sensible and being aware of what's happening around you. There are a number of basic precautions you can take to ensure you don't come home with too many eventful stories to tell. However, as Louise Ellerton points out:

You have to be aware that travellers do stand out and make easy targets, so this should make you more careful. Always guard your property.

You need to keep everything in perspective, though. Mandy-Lee Trew says:

I felt pretty safe during my time in the States. I was actually more afraid of the weather than crime.

And, Thomas Law, who taught in Sudan, explains:

To be honest, I feel far safer walking around at night in Sudan than I do at home in London; indeed, statistically, Khartoum is supposed to be the safest capital city in the whole of Africa.

However, read up on your destination before you go – your guidebook can warn you of any potential dangers. In addition, you may want to do a gap-year safety course, like the ones held by Planet Wise (www.planetwise.net) to increase your confidence and teach you how to behave in certain situations. See p444 for more details. Above all, stay out of the way of cars – more travellers come to grief on the roads than they ever do in a darkened alleyway.

THEFT/MUGGING

Now, here's an idea: you want to avoid being robbed. And you pretty much can, as long as you're not careless and try to keep your wits about you all the time. Sarah Collinson was and didn't, she says:

I was robbed while I was away. However, it was completely my own fault and at the time I was angry with myself for being so silly. I was in Cusco, Peru, and had had a couple of drinks and was lagging behind the back of the group when we walked across the main square. A group of boys kind of surrounded us and were being very friendly and chatty. However, while my attention was being distracted, one of them pickpocketed me. I knew instantly what had happened, however; because I had had a bit to drink, I did not react fast enough. Luckily, because I had been warned never to take out more money than I could afford to lose, I only lost around US$15. But the experience did make me more careful in future.

And, remember not to get complacent. Lucy Misch advises:

Don't get sloppy, no matter how long you have been travelling for. I left my mobile phone in a communal locked room in my handbag. When I came back it was gone. I spent the evening at the police station.

The following tips should help you to avoid donating your belongings to a crafty thief:
- Be careful of unregistered taxis and never fall asleep in the back of a taxi.
- Be especially careful when boarding and riding buses and trains. You're at your most vulnerable to pickpockets at these times. If the bus or train is really crowded, try to keep your hands unobtrusively over your wallet and money belt. Hazel Sheard says:

I regularly got people feeling in my pockets at railway stations but made sure I never kept anything valuable in them so this wasn't a problem.

- Divide and conquer – you should never keep all your valuables (passports, tickets, debit and credit cards, cash, travellers cheques, important travel documents etc) in one place. If you trust the hostel or hotel where you are staying, use their safety-deposit boxes. Undoubtedly, this will be the safest place for anything you don't need when you're out and about. Again, depending on where you are staying, you can hide some valuables in your room but not if you think they'll have pilfering staff. The next safest place for your belongings is your money belt. Your money belt should never see the light of day. If you're constantly diving under your clothes to find it then you'll be attracting unwanted attention. Always carry a second wallet or purse where you keep a form of ID and your ready cash – the amount of money you think you'll need that day. At night, put everything that isn't in a safety-deposit box in your money belt and slip it *into* your pillow case (this is safer than under your pillow).
- Don't accept drinks or food from strangers. In some countries, thieves have been known to put drugs in drinks (even into your water bottle) or food and then rob the unconscious victim.
- Don't close the door of a taxi or pay the driver until your baggage has been unloaded.
- Don't give the name of your hotel or room number to strangers, as they might follow you back and try to rob you.
- Don't walk alone at night or in unfamiliar areas. If you find yourself in an unsavoury spot, flag down a taxi or tuk-tuk. Amanda Akass says:

I was mugged in Rio, which was quite scary, but my assailant wasn't armed and ran off empty-handed after I screeched at him very loudly. You should be on your guard in the cities. In Rio it is worth noting that locals will always take a taxi and never walk around the streets at night.

- If you are mugged, just give them what they want. There's no point putting yourself at risk for the sake of material possessions – they can be replaced but you can't.
- If you're getting your cash out of ATMs with your debit card, take particular care while the transaction takes place and for the rest of the day. Not by chance, most travellers are mugged on the day they have most money on them.
- It's difficult to keep your wits about you when you're drinking. Always be careful in these circumstances.
- Keep an eye on your backpack when on long bus trips. If it is on the roof or in a luggage compartment, make sure it's secure (add your own lock if possible). During rest stops, make sure no-one tries to walk off with it. Molly Bird says:

Jess and I boarded the bus for Kathmandu from India at 4.30am and got off hot, tired and hungry at 9pm the following night. This was the moment that we realised that Jess's back-pack had been stolen. It was one of the most unpleasant experiences of the whole trip.

- Keep photocopies of all your important travel documents in a separate place from your money belt. The best place for this is in an online travel vault (see www.lonelyplanet .ekit.com for details).
- Look after your valuables while you're taking a shower. If you're not sure that your room is safe, bring them into the bathroom with you.
- Never flash your cash, valuables or camera around. If possible, do not let people see that you are wearing a money belt.
- Pickpockets usually work in teams. If you feel that people are jostling or crowding you for no reason, stand back and check discreetly to see that your valuables are still on you. As Amanda Akass says:

Beware of gangs of small children swamping you (especially in tourist spots like Cusco). They are not as cute as they look.

- Remember that it's not just locals who may steal your belongings – there are quite a few unscrupulous travellers around who pay for their trips by ripping off other travellers. Elizabeth Hawkins remembers:

I lent my alarm clock to a fellow traveller in the Greek islands who had to get up early the next morning to catch a ferry. The next morning, he was nowhere to be seen and neither was my alarm clock.

- Take a small padlock to secure your room door, and to lock your luggage to overhead racks on long-distance buses or trains.
- To avoid having your bags slashed and belongings fall out, think about buying a Pacsafe – a stainless-steel net that fits around the outside of a backpack or bag and is almost impossible to slash through. Most travel stores stock them.
- When swimming, diving or snorkelling, bring your important documents and money with you in a waterproof pouch, or leave them in a safety-deposit box (if you're confident it's safe).
- When you're in a restaurant or bar, secure your pack with a lock to your chair or wrap the strap around your leg so that you'll know if someone is trying to take it.
- You will be at your most vulnerable at the start of your trip because you won't yet have got into your stride and it might take a few near misses to switch your danger antennae on completely.

SCAMS

Scams prey on gullible travellers, often those who trust and want to think the best of people. At the end of the day, scams are all about money and relieving you of yours. There are scams that appeal to your greed – you are persuaded that you'll make some money out of a certain venture or game. There are scams that play on your good nature and desire to help, and, in a way, these are the worst kind of all. Perhaps you've stopped to help someone in the street and while you do this, their friend is helping themselves to your daypack. Whatever, you will encounter scams, so travel with a healthy dose of scepticism but don't let this come between you and the country you're travelling in. And, don't suspect everybody – many people you meet are being nice to you because they are nice people.

Scammers will usually try to win you over; often the scammer is a charming man (rarely a woman) who speaks good English, is very friendly, and goes out of his way to be helpful.

TIPS FOR WOMEN TRAVELLERS

Women can be more vulnerable when travelling. Keep these safety tips up your sleeve (you know, the long sleeves you'll be wearing from now on instead of those flesh-bearing, vesty little numbers):

- Act confidently, walk purposefully, and look as if you know what you're doing and where you're going. If you look like a target you're more likely to become one.
- Avoid arriving in a new place late at night; if you can't avoid arriving late, book your first night's accommodation.
- Be informed about where you are going so that you have a rough idea of a town's layout and of any areas that might be unsafe.
- Carry a wedding-style ring with you, just in case you need it for respectability or to fend off persistent advances. Some women even go as far as carrying photos of their imaginary children (borrow pics of your nephews or nieces).
- If you feel like having a few too many drinks then do so at your hotel or hostel bar.
- If you're getting a lot of hassle in a particular place then put on your sunglasses – if you make less eye contact you'll get fewer approaches.
- If you're going out at night on your own, tell someone (hotel or hostel staff or perhaps that nice couple down the hall) where you're going and what time you expect to be back.
- If you're travelling on an overnight train or ferry, always choose the top bunk of a sleeping compartment. You'll be out of sight and out of mind.
- Instead of going out at night on your own, think of getting up really early in the morning instead. You'll still make the most of your waking hours.
- Pack your common sense. Just because you feel like you're on holiday don't do anything abroad that you wouldn't dream of doing at home (eg walking down a deserted, dark alley on your own).
- Pay a bit extra for accommodation in a good part of town, with safer streets in the vicinity and more security, eg decent locks on the doors.
- Pay attention to what you wear, and cover up. In many regions of the world, skimpy shorts and T-shirts relay a very different message to what you're used to at home.
- Pay close attention to your instincts. If you're in a situation that feels wrong, even if you don't know why, get out and go somewhere safe.
- Take a taxi more frequently than you might at home but do make sure it is bone fide. If you're unsure, get staff from the nearest up-market hotel to call one for you. Ensure that you always have enough cash on you to get home this way if you need to.
- Take care in hotel lifts and never go down to the basement in one on your own or at night.

If it'll make you feel safer, think about carrying a personal alarm. Hazel Sheard did this and says:

I carried a rape alarm, though I was more worried about activating it by accident and causing a huge scene than actually having to use it to protect myself.

They will lull you into a false sense of security and trust. At some point your new friend will gently suggest something that, under normal circumstances, you would not do. Many scams take the form of an offer from a businessperson or local who befriends you. Perpetrators can be enormously charming and convincing, with testimonials from previous happy business partners.

However, the bottom line is this: if what you're being offered is too good to be true then it probably is. Scams change all the time, and your guidebook will point out the most common and up-to-date tricks tried at your destination. But, as a general rule of thumb, a few things to sprint a mile from are:

Card games for money with friendly locals Even though the games might look simple, the locals will be a lot better at them than you.

Changing money on the black market There's a very good chance that you'll get ripped off here. Often, notes will be counted in front of you, possibly several times, but you've actually been conned and don't have half of what you've converted. Or, you might hand over the money to be changed and then an imaginary policeman will appear, followed by a bit of a commotion, and the money-changer running off with your cash.

Fake police In Africa, India, Central and South America, men in official-looking outfits might demand to see your passport and then order you to pay a fee for some fabricated reason. Never hand over your passport, or the money, and always ask to see ID. If they are for real then they won't mind walking with you to the local police station to sort out the, er, problem.

Friendly strangers on the street The person who is pointing to your shoes or offering to wipe bird shit or some other concoction (possibly something they've just spilled) off your coat or shoulder is actually trying to distract you while an accomplice helps themselves to your handbag or backpack. Otherwise, a local will approach you and seem mortally offended that you do not recognise them – they'll say they're from your hotel, or you met them on the bus etc. You'll feel guilty, get all matey and off-your-guard and then any number of scams can start. Any of these things can happen anywhere, as Mark Ramsden points out:

I've heard a few stories. The best was from a friend who went to Colombia – on a bus one guy talks to you while another cuts open your bag and empties it out. You're none the wiser until you get off at your stop and find your rucksack seems a lot lighter.

Gem or carpet deals Someone might suggest you carry valuables home for them, or buy some items to sell at enormous profits back home – these are most commonly spotted in India and Morocco. Of course, you may just buy some expensive gems or carpets and then find that they're actually pretty much worthless. This is what happened to Charlotte Graham:

We were in Agra, India. There was a carpet-dealer there who claimed to be the architect of the Lotus Temple (Bahá'í Temple) – I thought this structure was amazing and I was impressed to have met the man who was behind it. His wife worked with local disadvantaged children to weave carpets and he told us that if we bought some we could sell them at a big profit to his dealers in the UK. He showed us a book with the names and addresses of the dealers and also of the British travellers who had made money in this way. I noticed that one of the dealers appeared to live next door to one of the travellers who had written a testament. He shrugged this off as a coincidence. My boyfriend and I were very sceptical but we did keep on talking about how we wouldn't have any money when we got home. Eventually, we decided to buy with our credit cards. We were given the names of the dealers and off we went. I cannot believe how stupid we were. We just didn't listen to our instincts. There was something fishy about the whole thing from the beginning but we put this out of our minds because we wanted to believe that we could avoid being broke when we got home. As it turned out, the carpets were sent to us. It cost a fortune to get them out of customs. The dealer addresses were all false and the carpet shops in London that we showed the carpets to were not interested in buying them at all. It was all so predictable.

Letting your credit card out of your sight Credit-card fraud is on the increase. Carefully watch what is done with your card and try not to let it out of your sight. If you go online and find charges on your card that aren't yours, you'll have to inform your credit-card company immediately.

Offers of food & drink from friendly strangers Whether you're on a bus, in someone's home, in a bar or restaurant, be careful about sharing a drink or a snack with someone you don't know. Travellers can be drugged and their possessions stolen. This can happen pretty much anywhere in the world but is particularly prevalent in the Philippines.

Transporting packages Obviously, you should never take anything for anyone across a border for any reason.

You get left holding the baby A mother hands you a small child and while your attention is momentarily distracted and your hands are full, something is stolen – your camera, your bag, anything.

OK, it seems a long list but it is just to give you a flavour of what is out there. Don't be paranoid, and don't cut yourself off from the people you meet, most of whom are interested in striking up a genuine friendship. Trust your instincts, know when to do a runner and don't let a sense of obligation make you go along with things when you have a bad feeling about them. Also, whether you're man or mouse, have a read of the Tips for Women Travellers, p82, because there's a lot of good advice there, no matter what model you are.

NATURAL DISASTERS, POLITICAL UNREST & WILD ANIMALS

Horrific events such as the Indian Ocean tsunami in 2004 occasionally remind us that the world is not wrapped up in cotton wool. That said, natural disasters, political unrest and marauding wild beasts are much less of a risk than you might suppose (especially in Crawley). Keep up to date with what's happening in the world online, on TV (you can get BBC World and CNN almost anywhere these days) and by reading the local English-language and international newspapers and magazines. Read your guidebook, which should have a detailed section on dangers and how to avoid them. If you are anywhere that is hit by something natural – a flood, hurricane, avalanche etc, contact home immediately and tell your family you're all right as news travels fast and your mum will be frantic as soon as she hears the six o'clock news.

TRAVEL HOTSPOTS

It is absolutely essential when travelling to check the UK Foreign & Commonwealth Office (FCO) website at www.fco.gov.uk. The officials in Whitehall are continually updating its travel advice and if you go to a country that the FCO advises against then it can make your travel insurance invalid. Yes, it's been said before, but it is surprising how much of a secret this fact appears to be.

It is also worth reading through advice put out by other governments. Try the Bureau of Consular Affairs at the US Department of State (www.travel.state.gov) and the Australian Department of Foreign Affairs and Trade (www.dfat.gov.au/travel).

TERRORISM

You could be in the wrong place at the wrong time anywhere in the world, including London, Manchester or Edinburgh. As such, there's no real point in worrying about acts of terrorism when you're travelling. However, the FCO website (www.fco.gov.uk) warns against visiting countries where there is a heightened risk of terrorism, so this is another good reason to log on to this site regularly when you're on the road.

DRUGS

Many countries, such as Thailand, Singapore, Malaysia and India, have exceedingly strict laws on drugs, ranging from long sentences to the death penalty, and grim jails worldwide have their share of travellers frittering away time inside. Just because other people are openly taking drugs doesn't mean that it's OK to do so, and you might find your time away turns into time inside if you get caught. It's not just your own safety you should think about before building a bong or popping a pill; consider also the effect you are having on your surroundings. Travellers' drug use can have a detrimental impact on the local economy and society as people get caught up in this lucrative industry.

In certain countries, particularly where the drug trade is a powerful force, such as in parts of South and Central America, Thailand and Jamaica, other travellers or locals may try to use you as a 'mule' to carry drugs or other illegal items across international borders. People may approach you with an opportunity or they may just hide parcels of drugs in your pack. Do not accept packages from anyone, and check your bag carefully before boarding planes or crossing borders in countries where this might be a risk.

In addition, when you buy drugs abroad you might unwittingly be buying from the police or a police informer. Of course, you might just be ripped off, which is a much more appealing thought.

Still not convinced? Log onto www.prisonersabroad.org.uk and check out the inmates. If you can, go and visit them when you're there.

HITCHHIKING

Hitchhiking is not usually recommended and a woman should never hitch alone. However, in certain parts of the world hitching is commonplace. Simon Calder, travel editor of the *Independent*, says one rule has helped him to stay safe in more than 30 years of hitchhiking:

If in any doubt, turn down a lift. If the driver screeches to a halt across three lanes of traffic, or you can smell alcohol on their breath or you don't like the look of the occupants, don't get in. That applies even if you have been standing in the rain for seven hours and night is falling. There are enough good people around that you will get a ride…eventually.

IF YOU DO GET INTO TROUBLE

If you are about to be mugged, shout out, call for help, or do something unexpected like pretending to see your friend across the street. This might make your assailant think twice about picking on you, or it might buy you some time to think. Don't get violent, as this rarely helps. Do give a mugger what they want, if you cannot easily get rid of them.

If you want to make an insurance claim or if travellers cheques need replacing then you'll have to report whatever has been stolen to the police. If there's a fellow traveller who can accompany you to do this then it'll make you feel better. Someone at the police station will probably speak English; otherwise there might be an interpreter.

In the case of a lost or stolen passport, you should report it to the police then go to your embassy, consulate or high commission where a new passport can be issued. The diplomatic staff will also advise you about local laws, put you in touch with English-speaking lawyers or doctors, and contact friends or relatives back home in the case of an emergency. They will not, however, lend you money, get you out of jail or pay to fly you home.

If you divided up your valuables (as advised) then you won't have lost everything – if you've lost your credit card then you've still got your debit one; if you've lost your cash then you've still got your travellers cheques. However, if you have lost everything then you're going to need some money from home. See p44 for details of what to do. If you're seriously hurt then you will need to get in contact with your travel insurance company. See p75 for more details.

To end on a bright note, Damien Rickwood says:

I managed to go my whole trip without any such problems. I found that if you read the guidebooks to find out which areas to stay away from, and if you use reputable tour companies, you are generally OK. It is also important to be aware of the current political and social situations in the countries or areas where you are travelling. Other than that, a bit of common sense goes a long way.

KEEPING IN TOUCH

While you're on the other side of the world having rip-roaring adventures, you can sometimes forget that there are people at home hanging on your every email or phone call. The folks back home will want to hear from you regularly. You know you're having an amazing time but they don't. Perhaps not all of us would want to do what Mark Ramsden did to his poor mum:

I wrote home once I think. Just saying I am still alive, see you soon. There was little point in much more; I figured my mum would panic whatever I did, so I just let her stew for a little while!

OK, let's all write to Mark Ramsden's mum as well as our own, just to make up for everything. Seriously, though, it's only fair to ease the minds of those at home with the occasional email and phone call and to let your friends know you're still thinking about them (lie through your teeth). Also, there's no better way of appreciating the experiences you're having than by relating them to someone at home. They'll be the best and most interested listeners you'll ever have. And, if something goes wrong or you feel down, the best way to pick yourself up is to hear a few comforting words from the people who care about you most.

Most gappers keep in touch using a combination of methods. Justin Ward even discovered the delights of snail mail:

I mainly wrote and received letters, but I did write the occasional email.

Staying in touch via email is cheap but phoning will cost a little more, so do some budgeting. Here are some top staying-in-touch tips:

- When you're on the road, give those at home a rough itinerary. Agree to let them know if it changes dramatically.
- If heading out on long treks or trips into remote areas where you may be out of touch for a while, let your family and friends know. When you're safely back again, let them know that too.
- Ask someone at home to save the emails or letters you send them. This is almost as good as keeping a diary and they make great reading when you get home.
- If you're not going to do all your communication by email, work out ideal times to call family and friends to minimise the chance of calling when they're out. Don't make definite calling times or schedules, in case you forget to make that call or for some reason can't – your not calling when you said you would is the surest way to panic everyone back home. If you've got the ekit communications package (see Integrated Communications Packages, p91), then your friends and family can leave a free message for you on your personal voicemail service, which you can pick up when the time suits.
- The round-robin email is a good way to keep in touch with a group of friends, especially as you'll probably get bored writing the same news and views to everyone.
- If your personal stereo has a record function, you can send some sounds of where you are back home – the market, the local steel band, interviews with your new friends, etc – these are particularly fun if you're giving a running commentary while out and about, and, again, are a great reminder when you're back home.
- Upload some photos to a web journal for your friends and family to access – it's a great way to illustrate what you're describing and gives people a feel for the place.

THE INTERNET

As we all know, the internet is absolutely fabulous for travellers and has revolutionised the way they keep in touch.

Email

It's official: this is how the majority of gappers communicate with home and other friends on a gap year. Kate Wilkinson says:

Using email was the easiest and cheapest way to keep in touch with my family.

Sarah Collinson agrees:

I kept in touch with home by email. This worked out very well as I emailed every four to five days about what I had been up to and where I had been. The internet in South America was so cheap to use and even in the smallest place they seemed to have access. I then called home on special occasions.

Of course, a country's internet (and email) access will only be as good as its phone lines. Also, access to the net in some countries may be limited to the larger cities or towns and often the fewer internet resources there are, the more expensive and slower access will be. The best places to access email worldwide are internet cafés, libraries and hotels.

FREE EMAIL

As you probably know, it's a breeze to set up a free email account! You can do it at home or when you're abroad, from your own computer or from one in an internet café. If you can, set up one of these before you leave because you'll be able to build up your electronic address book, making sure you've got all your friends' email addresses safely stored away.

There are lots of free email services out there but they don't all offer the same storage space and, just like your backpack, it's space you're after. Currently there's a bit of a storage war going on amongst free email service providers, which is good news for travellers. At the time of writing, Hotmail (www.hotmail.co.uk) was offering 250MB; Yahoo! (www.yahoo .co.uk) 100MB; and, the new kid on the block, Google's GMail (www.gmail.com) 1000MB. Check all of this out before you go – it's the hostess with the mostest that you want. After all, you'll want to save a lot of the messages you send or receive, plus your mail box will get inundated with spam that takes up space before you have time to delete it.

If you've already got an internet connection at home then many internet service providers (ISPs) will allow you check email via webmail.

Internet Cafés

These handy little numbers are getting more and more prevalent all over the world, ranging from glitzy giants to joints the size of a jellybean. These cafés usually charge in blocks of 15 minutes or by the hour. Sometimes there's a minimum fee and sometimes not. To find out if your destinations have a gigabyte or a megabyte of internet cafés log on to www .cybercafe.com.

Net to Phone

An increasing number of internet cafés are offering net phone technology, which allows you to place calls over the internet via a headset. It's cheap, very cheap, and sometimes the technology is so advanced that all you do is go into a booth, dial the number – often using the US international access code (011) – and, hey presto, you're through. The reason you dial a US access code is that many of these systems use a telecom company based in America. The internet café pays the firm a set rate per minute to route the call to its final destination, and adds its profit margin. Amanda Akass sometimes used these on her travels:

I kept in touch by email. There is guaranteed to be at least one internet café in any town in South America, and it is cheap and relatively fast. I phoned home every few weeks, which was expensive, except in the bigger cities which had internet phones.

Web Journals

A 'weblog', or 'blog', is a web journal where you write about your experiences and upload your photos – some even have fancy mapping facilities so you can display your route. It's a really effective, if sometimes time-consuming, way to keep in touch with your loved ones. There are quite a number of web journal services available now – some are free, some you have to pay for; some offer you a private service and others make your website public; some will even send an email to your friends and family when you've added new information to your travelogue. Lonely Planet's Personal Trip Website (www.lonelyplanet.com; look under Travel Services) costs £33 for a year. You can write as much as you like in your journal, add maps, and upload a maximum of 60 photos a month. You choose whether it is public or private, and everyone's told when you've updated it.

TELEPHONE

When we're away we particularly like to hear the voice of our loved ones. However, tele phoning can be a costly business abroad, although there are ways of making it cheaper. There are a couple of basic numerical details you're going to have to negotiate. For instance, you'll need to know the international call prefix of the country you're in (ie the number you need to dial out of the country) and the international country code of the country you're calling (eg Britain is 44, Australia is 61). Then you usually leave the '0' off any regional code. For a list of all these numbers see www.countrycallingcodes.com. Oh, and then it's quite useful to know what time it is at the other end so that you're not waking the wrinklies in the middle of the night. For this see www.timeanddate.com/worldclock.

So, now to your calling options. Whatever you choose, remember that the biggest no-no is using the phone in a hotel room (this could set you back more than you saved for your whole trip).

Your Beloved Mobile

Do you feel surgically attached to your mobile? Do you wonder if your thumbs would ever recover if you didn't take it with you?

There are pros and cons of taking your mobile. The major drawback is cost. Alastair Fearn says:

The first time I went away I used my mobile but racked up a huge bill.

Tabitha Cook agrees:

I knew people that took mobiles, and of those that phoned home a lot, their costs mounted up.

However, you can always use your mobile phone to make calls on your calling card, which works out much cheaper (see the following section) than using your home network.

However, this isn't much use if there's no network coverage. Damien Rickwood went to Central America and says:

I didn't take a mobile phone because I didn't think I'd get much of a signal in the remote rainforests of Central America. I found that email was a reliable and cheap way to keep in touch.

Molly Bird also has something to say about mobile phones and remote locations:

I didn't take a mobile phone with me but my friend Jess did. Although it didn't work most of the time, when it did it was really nice to be able to text home and just say hi.

Jonathan Williams had a different reason for not taking his phone:

I chose to keep in touch with my friends and family mainly by email. I thought it wasn't worth taking a mobile phone with me because if it got lost or stolen, it would only add unnecessary hassle to my trip.

Most gappers choose not to take their mobile phone with them on their gap year, and this is mainly due to cost. However, in an emergency it can be helpful to have your mobile on you. If you're going to take your phone but keep it switched off for most of the time, then don't forget to turn voicemail off too; otherwise you could get a nasty bill.

If you're going to Europe, Africa and Asia then a dual-band phone will work in most areas. For a round-the-world trip what you really need is a tri-band GSM handset, as it can be used in parts of North America as well. For more detailed information on where your phone will and won't work check GSM World at www.gsmworld.com/roaming/gsminfo /roa_cucc.shtml. It will also tell you if the countries you're going to visit have a GSM roaming agreement with your service provider.

If you're going mobile with your mobile you'll have to ask your provider to activate your 'international roaming'; otherwise your phone won't work anywhere south of Dover, let alone Dubai. While you're at it, think about the call plan you're currently on and whether it is the most appropriate for your trip (probably not). As your call pattern will change, it might be best to switch to pay-as-you-go.

If you're planning to stay in one country for a decent period of time then you will be able to cut the cost of calls on your mobile phone by using a local, prepaid SIM card. A SIM card will allow you to access the local network for calls instead of your home network, making calls much cheaper. You can buy local SIM cards almost everywhere from telephone or service-provider shops. However, some mobile phones are 'simlocked' (which means you can't swap SIM cards). Check the status of your phone with your provider and if it is locked then get the code to unlock it. If you use a local SIM card then your phone will be allocated a new number – think about whether this will be a drawback or not. Alastair Fearn says:

When I lived in Rhodes for six weeks I bought a Greek SIM card which was excellent, as I could call home at reasonable rates.

Also, if you're not taking a camera, a phone with a camera can be a good compromise.

New marketing ploys from companies like O2 and Vodafone allow you to turn your mobile phone photos into postcards that can be sent with your messages to anyone in the UK.

Despite all the benefits of taking your phone, Alastair Fearn goes on to say:

I do feel that having your mobile on you ruins a trip anyway. I think half the idea is to get away from that stuff.

If you do take your mobile phone, don't forget the charger and plug adaptor and, yes, this means you will be carrying some extra weight.

2 TXT OR NOT 2 TXT

Obviously, if u don't have your mobile then you u can't txt. Txting internationally is a relatively cheap way to keep in contact but still way more expensive than email. Claire Loseby recalls:

I took my mobile phone to text home but it still worked out quite expensive. I recommend people find internet cafés and a good phonecard to keep in contact.

If u r addicted, however, then give it a go. There are gappers who swear by it. And, again, if you're in one place for any length of time, cut the cost of txting by swapping to a local SIM card.

Prepaid Phonecards & Other Ways to Call Home

In recent years the cost of making international phone calls has dropped dramatically – and, for travellers in many countries the low cost of using a prepaid phonecard can make calling home daily a real possibility. In most countries, newsagencies and other shops are plastered with garish posters advertising prepaid phonecards of various descriptions. Often these will show a list of countries with the per-minute rate, eg UK 2.8p per minute. You pay a flat fee – typically £5 or £10 – for a flimsy plastic scratchcard that shows the freephone access number, and when you scrape away the foil you find another code number. Dial the access number, tap in your code and you will be instructed (possibly in a foreign language) to start dialling. The way these work is that telecom companies bulk-buy space on international phone lines, which they sell off cheaply. You benefit from rates much lower than you would get from shovelling coins into a payphone, using a hotel phone or buying an official phonecard from the local telecom provider – the sort of card you actually place in the slot in the phone.

Many gappers use prepaid phonecards. Mandy Lee-Trew says:

To stay in touch with family and friends I called home on a monthly basis using a phonecard, and I was in email contact almost every day.

And Jonathan Williams writes:

My family called me from England relatively cheaply by purchasing international calling cards, which work out to be far better value than simply picking up the phone and dialling.

Because of the savings to be made, not all countries allow prepaid phonecards; France Telecom insists you buy a card that costs you around 60p a minute to phone the UK. In other cases you may have to pay for a local call to gain access to the network. In addition, the amount of time you get varies from one brand of card to another; ask experienced travellers (they're the ones spending half the night chatting on the hostel phone) for the current best buy.

If you are crossing a lot of borders, you may want a more sophisticated system. With a charge card you set up an account in advance in your home country, eg with BT. A good example of an international telecom company with a calling card facility is ekit (www.lonelyplanet.ekit.com). The company provides you with a list of free access numbers for each country. You dial the appropriate number, punch in your account number and dial the number you want. Apart from cheap rates, the advantage of using a charge card is that you can call from any phone (eg in someone's house, in a hotel, in a phone box, and even from your mobile where you're only charged for the local call).

The most expensive way to make a call is to reverse the charges (ie the recipient of the call pays). This is known in North America, and increasingly worldwide, as 'calling collect'. You dial the local operator, who places the call for you and asks the person who answers whether they will accept a call from, say, Ulaan Baatar. There is usually a three-minute minimum charge, typically £20, for the privilege.

Public phones where you can swipe your credit card and have the call billed to it are becoming more common in places such as Europe, the USA, Hong Kong and Singapore. These calls may be charged at a higher rate, so beware. Often the phones accept both credit cards and phonecards.

Integrated Communications Package

If you want everything from one place then you should consider looking at the ekit's phonecard package available through Lonely Planet (www.lonelyplanet.ekit.com). You get a global calling card, a voicemail service (family and friends can leave you messages no matter where you are), email, text messaging, text message alerts, faxmail, 24-hour travel assistance, a travel vault for storing details of your travel documents, and 24-hour customer service in six languages (English, German, Spanish, Italian, French and Portuguese). In addition, there is also a global mobile service. You can purchase a tri-band mobile including a global SIM card, which will save you money on global roaming costs from 80 countries, or buy either the global SIM card or a domestic SIM card (available in the UK, Australia or USA) if you intend to stay long term. These are all pay-as-you-go and recharge-as-you-go services.

POST

Sometimes it is nice to write a letter – it's different to an email and somehow more personal. Sometimes you'll find just the right postcard to send to someone and decide to pop that in the post instead of clicking a mouse. In fact, the nicest thing about writing letters or postcards when you're travelling is that you can do it outside in the sun at your favourite café without a computer in sight.

However, this all means that from time to time you're going to have to negotiate the dim interior of foreign post offices. It also means that whatever you choose to send might not get there for weeks and weeks, depending on the quality of the postal service you're using. Those in South America and the Indian Subcontinent are notorious for being slower than a boat to China. If you've got something important to send, you'd better do it with an international express delivery service such as DHL or FedEx.

Receiving Mail

There are three main ways to receiving mail on the road: c/o poste restante at post offices in cities, poste restante at American Express offices (which you can use if you're a card member), or you can ask for mail to be sent to your accommodation. Most post offices hold poste restante mail for no longer than a month or so before discarding it. Mail is usually filed under your surname but mistakes are often made. When you pick up a poste restante letter (or package) you will usually have to present your passport.

Shipping Items Home

Everyone ends up sending stuff back home, whether it be winter clothes when you're looking forward to a season of summer or all those items you knew you shouldn't have packed but did. Post offices are particular about sending packages and there will usually be weight and size limits and packaging requirements. Plus, everything has to be inspected by customs. Still, sending things home is a superb way to lighten your pack.

In some countries you will have the choice of sending your package by air or surface mail. Airmail is always more expensive but is faster and probably more reliable. Surface mail may be your very cheapest option, with packages may arriving up to four to six months later. Skip all these options, though, if you couldn't bear to lose what you're sending. Instead, go with the international express delivery companies or with a shipping service.

If you have lots of stuff to ship or a few heavy items, you may save some money by using a shipping agent. These companies charge by space rather than weight. One cubic metre is usually the minimum amount, so you may want to team up with friends to maximise your savings. Shipping agents usually offer door-to-door service – you don't want a service where you'll have to pick up your goods from the port nearest your destination address because you ain't going to be there. All goods that are shipped must pass through customs and you may have to pay duty on them.

MEDIA

You'll probably be monitoring the international and local news to keep an eye on any events that may impact on your travels. After all, you don't really want to turn up in Florida when it's directly in the path of a devastating hurricane or in Bangladesh when it's awash with floods. You'll also want to keep up with what's happening in the world so that you don't feel as if you're travelling around in a bubble.

Internet

The internet is one of the best ways to keep yourself informed of world events. Before or after you check your emails at your favourite internet café, you can log on to any number of current affairs websites. You can read your favourite paper online (www.timesonline.co.uk or www.guardian.co.uk) or log on to BBC News (http://news.bbc.co.uk). You could also catch up with events from your home town and impress all those at home by how much you know about their world, as well as yours. And you can keep tabs on your local soccer team.

Press

Many countries have either an English-language daily or weekly newspaper. In cities, you will often find the *International Herald Tribune* and copies of *Time* and *Newsweek*. Airports are sometimes the best places to find international newspapers and magazines, though top-end hotels, bookshops and newsstands may also stock them.

Radio & TV

The three most accessible English-language stations worldwide are the soothing tones of the BBC World Service, the Voice of America and ABC Radio Australia. For scheduling and frequency information, visit their websites: www.bbc.co.uk/worldservice, www.voanews.com and www.abc.net.au/ra. These services often also broadcast features and music.

Hotels and guesthouses often have TVs, and many hostels have TV rooms. These will invariably have cable or satellite connections, but you may have to get familiar with the local stations. CNN and BBC World are the stations most commonly picked up globally. Bars worldwide often screen major sporting events, which can be unforgettable to watch if there's a good crowd, particularly if your host country is winning.

BEING A GOOD TRAVELLER

RESPECTING LOCAL CULTURES

Culture shock does exist – it's when you arrive in a totally new environment and feel disorientated, displaced and sometimes ill at ease. This is because for a while you feel like a fish out of water. You might find a new city too noisy, the streets too crowded, the pollution too heavy or the way you're stared at disconcerting. Naomi Lisney volunteered in India and says:

It took me a while to get used to there being no privacy in India. There were only two rooms in the school where I lived: I was in one of them, the family shared the other (the principal, his brother, his wife and son). Their room turned into a makeshift library/storeroom during the day. And my room was the perfect place for people to have their lunch, or to stretch out for a nap. Whereas I was used to closing my door on the world whenever I felt like it, they equate being alone with being lonely. Soon, though, I no longer minded having people coming and going. I was also less shy about seeking out other people's company.

Culture shock is an inevitable part of travelling and the point that Naomi makes here is that you will adjust to your new surroundings over time and get used to a different way of living. Molly Bird says:

There were cultural differences in every single place we visited and that's probably what made travelling so exciting. I think it is important to remember that you're in someone else's country and so you should show respect for the way they do things. This doesn't mean compromising yourself or your identity, but if you're not prepared to compromise on how you act when you're on someone else's turf then stay at home. Being aware of a culture and respecting it is how you're going to really learn about it.

Culture shock and homesickness often go hand in hand: the confusion you feel over a foreign culture can evoke a desire for the familiar. However, just ease into it; there's no good reason to tuck into fried guinea pig on your first day. Do as much research as you can before you go, to gain an understanding of and respect for local culture and to avoid shocking people yourself. Tourists can have a detrimental impact on the places they visit if they are careless about behaving appropriately. And, remember why you're travelling. Sarah Collinson points out:

There were large cultural differences, but that was all part of the experience of travelling and that was what I was there to see.

Avoiding Offence

Remember, one culture's horror is another's norm. Read up about how you're expected to behave before you land in a new country. If you're travelling with a gap-year organisation, they will inform you of cultural do's and don'ts. For instance, Gareth Potts travelled to Madagascar and says:

There were a wide variety of cultural differences to be aware of; eg the Malagasy were very uncomfortable with people touching their hair or head, can't remember quite why. The staff at the organisation we were with, Azafady, told us all about these things.

Most behavioural taboos are usually related to:

Dress You need to dress appropriately – looking at the locals is a good way to gauge what to wear. In some countries – particularly Muslim ones, and in the Indian Subcontinent – it is offensive to flash your flesh, particularly if you're a women. If you do, you'll just be confirming suspect ideas about Western women, as well as attracting unwanted attention. In Latin America, even the poorest people strive to look neat and clean, so grubby or torn clothing is considered disrespectful. Also, in some places there you should be careful about wearing indigenous clothing while you're still in that country. For example, in Guatemala is considered in poor taste to wear the beautiful *huipiles* (blouses) for which the country is known.

Hospitality Make sure you know what is considered polite and what is rude if you are eating and drinking with local people. Claire Loseby travelled to China and says:

I never imagined that I'd have to eat gross things like chicken feet, sea slugs and animal intestines so as not to offend my hosts.

Religion You must always be respectful in a place of worship such as a church, mosque or temple. This means dressing respectfully – long trousers for men and long skirts or trousers for women. You may be required to remove your hat at some temples, while at mosques you should cover your head. At both temples and mosques, remove your shoes. At Hindu temples, you will sometimes have to remove leather objects such as belts before entering. Remember also not to point at Buddha images, especially with your feet. If you sit in front of a Buddha image, sit with your feet pointing away.

Showing emotion In many parts of the world it is really uncool to lose your cool – getting angry in Southeast Asia or Japan, for instance, is a real no-no. In addition, in many parts of the world it is just not on for couples to show any emotion towards each other in public – if you can't keep your hands, lips and tongues off each other then you'll have to stay in your room until you can bear to walk down the street together in compatible isolation.

Women Like it or not, in many countries women travellers are expected to behave in a certain fashion and local women expect to be treated in a particular way. For example, women are usually not allowed in the main prayer hall of a mosque. In many countries it is also inappropriate for women to drink alone in a bar or restaurant (or if you do then it is considered that you are 'working', not at leisure).

TAKING PHOTOS

Don't let the temptation to get that shot get the better of you. Treat locals with respect when taking pictures. The following are some basic tips to make sure that both you and your subject come away happy:

- Do not take photographs inside religious structures such as temples or shrines, unless you are sure it is OK.
- Do not take photos of private or sacred events unless you have asked permission. Just imagine if a stranger burst in on a funeral in your home country and started taking pictures. Crazy as it sounds, this is pretty much what lots of foreign travellers do at the ritual cremations performed on the banks of the Ganges in Varanasi, India.
- If you are taking a picture of a person, ask their permission. Do not treat people like zoo animals. Some people enjoy having their picture taken and some do not.
- People whose pictures you take may sometimes ask you to send them copies; do not promise to do so unless you really intend to follow through.
- Some locals might charge money to have their photo taken. There is no need to regard this as a detrimental effect of tourism: it is a way of supplementing what is often a meagre existence, and when people allow themselves to be used as subjects for your photography they are providing you with a service.

SUSTAINABLE TOURISM

Tourism is the world's largest industry, with around 700 million people travelling internationally each year. (This number is probably only exceeded by the number of parties you've been to in the last 12 months.) With such numbers travelling, however, it is crucial that travel and tourism should strive towards protecting and conserving natural and social environments, rather than destroying them.

As a foreign visitor, you should ensure that you are helping to protect and support the environment and communities of the areas you visit. The following tips will go a long way to ensure that your gap year is beneficial to the world and won't cost the earth:

Be informed Read up about the countries you intend to visit so that you arrive with an understanding of their political, economical and cultural diversity.

Benefit the local communities Make sure that what you spend contributes to the local economy. Stay in locally run hostels, B&Bs or houses; eat from street stalls and family-run restaurants; shop in markets; drink the local beer (not the imported stuff); use public transport; and hire local or indigenous guides. Also, be fair when bargaining.

Conserve resources & protect the environment Be considerate when using water, electricity or fuel. Instead of hiring a car, think about walking, cycling or using public transport. Minimise your contribution to pollution – use biodegradable products and take your packaging home, especially used batteries. Ask your hotel or hostel if it has a green policy or what it does about recycling and minimising waste and pollution.

Respect local culture & traditions Don't cause offence by gesture or dress, whether you're at the beach or in a place of worship. Learn a few words of the local language.

Ethical Travel Resources

Climate Care (www.co2.org) This organisation encourages people to become 'carbon neutral' by planting trees to counter the effects of CO_2 emissions. Enter the number of kilometres you intend to fly by plane into their air travel calculator and get ready for a shock. There's also a list of companies, some of them tour operators, who've signed up to offset the emissions from clients' flights.

responsibletravel.com (www.responsibletravel.com) UK internet site selling holidays from companies that fulfil strict responsible-travel criteria.

Tourism Concern (www.tourismconcern.org.uk) UK's leading organisation dealing with fair-trade tourism; its book, *The Good Alternative Travel Guide* by Mark Mann, lists loads of 'ethical' holidays.

COMING HOME

CULTURE SHOCK

Yes, you're right, you've just read about culture shock in the last chapter but, guess what, you can get culture shock when you come home too. Being immersed in a foreign way of life casts your own into a new light. Sarah Collinson explains:

I found coming home very hard. It was difficult leaving the country and the people I had been travelling with. I felt really strange and kind of uncomfortable at home as it felt so foreign compared to what I had become used to.

Naomi Lisney agrees:

I think people often find that the biggest culture shock is coming home. Everyone commented on how much I had changed, whereas I didn't necessarily realise I had.

Amanda Akass found it hard to adapt to life back home too:

Coming back home was a huge culture shock. It was wonderful to see my friends and family again, be greeted as a returning adventurer, give exotic presents, develop my photos and tell all and sundry about my experiences. However, I found it very strange trying to fit back into the old mundane cycle of life.

And, Damien Rickwood had butterflies in his stomach after six months away:

On the plane home I felt really nervous. I kept telling myself that I didn't need to be nervous about seeing my family but it had been such a long time. Coming out of the arrivals gate was an amazing experience in itself – being pounced upon by my whole family. But I'd been away for such a long time that I didn't even recognise my little brother!

The best way to fight feeling forlorn is to plunge back into life at home. Jonathan Williams advises:

The best way to re-integrate into 'normal' life is to not to allow yourself to get bored. Stay busy as much as possible.

Molly Bird agrees:

I think it's really important to have something fixed for when you come home, whether university or a job; sort something out. Otherwise you could easily end up feeling lost or at a loose end.

Preparing for university or looking for a new job will be new and exciting. At the same time, don't let your trip evaporate. Amanda Akass says:

Two months on, my gap year feels like a dream, but I would go back at the drop of a hat and do the whole thing again if I could.

So, now's the time to pin your experiences down. Make a photo album, refresh your web journal, or re-read your personal diary. And, says Claire Loseby:

I think the most important thing when you get back home is to make sure you keep in touch with the friends you've made because they share all your memories.

Also, if you promised to send photos to people, do it now. Write thank-you letters and emails. You'll find continuity of contact will help keep your memories vivid.

Coming home might, of course, be a totally positive experience, making you appreciate what you've got, as Gareth Potts found:

It was good to come home, especially as we had been in tents for nearly three months. I had no real problems integrating back in. I found returning home one of the best things about the whole trip, and that is by no means being negative about it. When you return home you appreciate everything so much more, things like listening to your own music or sleeping in your own bed.

WHAT AM I GOING TO DO NOW?

If you've come home to go to college then you've got loads to prepare for and look forward to. Tabitha Cook says:

I wanted to be back with enough time to get uni stuff sorted. It's a good idea to fill out all the forms, get your back account sorted and qualify for their 'rewards' which sometimes end really early.

Also, get on the university website and plan what societies you're going to join and what sports you're going to take up – you know you've always wanted to be a synchronised swimmer. Perhaps you've had a rethink about what you want to do. If you've left making a decision about a course till you get back, then make sure you time your homecoming right so you can sort out an application with the Universities & Colleges Admissions Service (UCAS; www.ucas.ac.uk).

If you've finished college, then it's time to think about a proper job. Check out the ads in local and national newspapers. The *Guardian* (www.guardian.co.uk) still has the best jobs section but you'll be wanting to scan them all. Don't discount the High Street recruitment agencies like Adecco (www.adecco.co.uk) or Hays Personnel (www.hayspersonnel.co.uk). Also, think about online agencies like www.monster.co.uk (a good website to check out for information, anyway).

Finding the right job can take time – don't get dispirited but *do* get solvent and think about temping in the meantime. Sarah Bruce, a post-university gapper, found:

I had no plans for the rest of my life when I stepped off the plane from Mexico but I went straight into doing some temporary work until I found a suitable job a few weeks later.

If you're not sure of which career path to take, then try some work experience to enhance your CV and to help you with your choices. If you're flat broke this may not be an attractive financial option, but if you target the companies or organisations that you're really interested in working for then you might just happen to be in the right place at the right time and be able to apply for any permanent positions that come up. If you don't have the right experience for what you want to do then perhaps you can get it doing some voluntary work (see the Volunteering, Conservation & Expeditions chapter, p264, for more information). Maybe you need a bit more training, in which case a short course might be right for you (see the Courses chapter, p416, for details). You can always go back to your school or university for contact numbers and advice.

To ease yourself into life back home, it helps to give the end of your trip some serious thought while you're still on the road. Your time away will have recharged your batteries, given you a new perspective on the world and realigned your priorities. Instead of suffering from post–gap-year blues, go out with bling and zing and get started on your new life as quickly as possible.

ITCHY FEET

When you come back, you usually have a brief excited phase when it's thrilling to have returned. The familiar looks strange, everyone wants to hear about your trip, and you can indulge in some deliciously novel home comforts. This phase lasts three-quarters of a day, max. By the next day, your feet are so goddamn itchy you can't wear socks. You want to go back to experiencing things intensely. Life at home seems half-hearted after all the colour, thrills and spills of your time away. And, for some, more travel is the answer. Laurence Gale says:

My tip is to go away again immediately. For example, my girlfriend and I went snowboarding in Italy for two weeks straight after getting back – the gold coast of Africa to the cold snow-capped mountains of Italy. That helped get over the withdrawal symptoms, and the empty bank account emphasised the need to get back to work.

Kate Wilkinson made a promise to herself:

I promised that I'd go away for a week a month after I arrived back, so I bought tickets to Madrid and that gave me something to look forward to.

Of course, many don't have the time or money to go away again so soon. However, coming home doesn't mean: game over, you've used up all your travel points for this lifetime. Your newly acquired taste for travel will drive you to create more opportunities to do it. Long live your itchy feet and your stinky socks.

TALKING ABOUT IT (BUT NOT A LOT)

The reality is that the world you experienced is so far removed from the daily lives of your friends and family that it's difficult for them to get engaged hearing your stories. What is so vivid to you doesn't have the same resonance for them. There may also be an element of jealousy floating around about the good times you've had, and it's unpleasant for your friends to feel you're looking down on them for not having experienced them. And refusing to answer to anything but your Tibetan name is *really* annoying. Jonathan Williams says:

When you get home it is worth remembering that whilst you have been off having a brilliant time, everybody at home has done relatively little in comparison. Therefore, whilst people like to hear about your travelling experiences, don't rub it in too much that you have done so much and they have done so little.

And Amanda admits:

After a week I was ritually beaten up by my friends if I started too many sentences with 'When I was in South America…'

However, Louise Ellerton urges:

Talk to people about your experience; it will bring back pleasurable memories for you and at the same time you can entertain everyone with your wonderful stories.

One way to keep your memories alive and to see them in print is to write some articles for your university or local newspaper. Another way is to write to Lonely Planet – we always want to hear about your experiences and views. And, who knows, you might be contacted to talk about your experiences in more detail than you ever dreamed for the next edition of *The Gap Year Book.*

Part II

ROUND THE WORLD (RTW)

CHARLOTTE HINDLE
Charlotte is the coordinating author of The Gap Year Book. *Her main biography appears on p2. She has flown to and from Australia 13 times but only once around the world.*

Molly Bird proudly says:

I am the only person in my family who's actually been all around the world!

In a way, that says it all. Despite the fact that RTW tickets have been in existence for decades there is still a certain cache about being able to say you've circumnavigated the globe. If you get a kick out of this, however, just wait until you've bought the tickets and you're actually doing it for real. Where will you decide to go? What will you decide to do? The world is literally at your fingertips waiting to be explored. Will you choose to sample the earth's greatest tourist highlights, from the Taj Mahal to the Grand Canyon, will you track down some of the world's best trekking, skiing, surfing or scuba-diving? Or is it the diversity of the people and their cultures that really turns you on? How cool is this, you get to decide.

HOW DO RTW TICKETS WORK?

As daft as it may sound, you can't actually buy a ticket on a single airline that goes around the world. Instead, you buy a ticket that is a series of coupons (in one or more tickets) that will take you around the globe on two or more airlines. This is all possible due to those nice people at British Airways (BA) and Qantas who joined forces in the mid-90s and took the concept of 'alliance building' in the airline industry to new heights, allowing them to offer RTW tickets at competitive prices.

An 'alliance' is basically a group of airlines who decide to work together and pool their routes in order to give their customers as much choice and variety of destination as possible. This means that almost anywhere you might wish to visit can be folded into your RTW ticket. If your destinations are on mainstream routes then your RTW ticket will be relatively cheap, if not then flying to and from certain places may well push the price up.

If you're travelling around the world then you'll need to decide which alliance to fly with. They all have a RTW ticket offering but different rules and regulations. Having said that, most RTW tickets have the following in common:

Frequent-flyer points Some RTW deals allow you to collect FFPs (particularly Oneworld Explorer, Global Explorer and Star Alliance). With many of the others restrictions apply.

Maximum time limit You've usually got up to one year to get around the globe.

Mileage allowance Most RTW tickets give you a distance allowance, which means that your trip can't be longer than a certain amount of kilometres. This is typically between 40,000km and 46,000km (London–Singapore–Sydney–Los Angeles–London is 38,000km). You may be allowed to backtrack, as long as you can still meet this criterion. Some fares allow you to pay a surcharge to buy more kilometres. (The Oneworld Explorer ticket is an exception to this general model as its cost is based on the number of continents that you fly through.)

Stopover limit Most deals restrict you to a set number of stopovers although you can often pay higher fares that allow more. Many fares only allow you to stop in a particular city once, at other times you're allowed to change planes in that city but not actually break your journey there more than once.

To compare what's on offer you need to make up a table showing the mileage allowances and stopover limits of each RTW ticket. On top of that, some RTW tickets are particularly good for certain parts of the world and, conversely, pretty shite for others. So, add this information to your table too. If that all sounds a little daunting, don't worry, we've done it for you – see the table on the next page (all fares correct as of December 2004, excluding pre-payable taxes – usually between £100 and £170 depending on each routing).

But Where do I Start?

OK, make a list of everywhere you want to go and then prioritise under three headings: 'must see', 'would like to see', and 'nice to see but could drop if too expensive'. Be aware that one or more of your chosen destinations might be better visited on a separate trip from the UK. Areas such as the Caribbean, some European cities, Russia or Central Asia might make your RTW fare too expensive. If, for instance, you're looking at Prague (Czech Republic), Hong Kong, Singapore, Australia, New Zealand (NZ), Tahiti and Los Angeles (LA) you might have to drop Prague. This is because at certain times of the year all except Prague can be visited for £843 (plus tax). Having Prague on your itinerary, however, pushes the price of your RTW ticket up to £1249 plus tax. So, forget it, go there another time and take advantage of a low no frills airline fare (around £80 return).

In addition, though there are almost limitless possible RTW routes, wanting to visit certain places (or certain combinations of destinations) can prove very costly. For instance, going to South Africa instead of Southeast Asia might not push the price up much, but going to South Africa *and* Southeast Asia might. The same applies to South America and North America. In addition, RTW tickets that don't include Australia or NZ are generally more expensive.

When you've decided where you want to go, think about the order in which to visit your destinations. Are you visiting friends or family and need to fit in with their dates? Do you want to be in a particular city for a festival or special event? You also need to work out how long you want to spend in each area. Think about what you want to see and do when you're there. Remember that you probably don't want to fly everywhere because many parts of your itinerary will lend themselves perfectly to a 'surface sector' (p106). Rather annoyingly, though, the kilometres you cover overland will still count as part of your total mileage package on most tickets (the main exception is Oneworld Explorer, which uses a different system based on the number of continents you fly through rather than the total distance flown.)

Classic Routes

Your cheapest, most basic RTW fare goes London–Singapore–Sydney–LA–London. Actually, this isn't a proper RTW ticket but a BA/Qantas return fare where you get one stop-over on the way out to Australia in one hemisphere and one on the way back in the other. A return

(Continued on page 106)

Fare	Major Airlines	Max Distance	Distance Surcharges
Great Escapade	Air New Zealand Singapore Airlines Virgin	46,670km	Up to 49,085km for £75 Up to 51,500km for £145 Up to 53,915km for £215
World Discovery	Air Pacific Australian Airlines BA Qantas	46,670km	Up to 52,300km for £275
World Discovery Plus	Air Pacific Australian Airlines BA Cathay Pacific Qantas	46,670km	Up to 52,300km for £275
Star Alliance	Air Canada Air New Zealand All Nippon Airlines Austrian Airlines Lufthansa SAS Singapore Airlines Thai United Airlines US Airways Varig	46,670km	Three fare levels based on distance: 46,670km for £1249 54,720km for £1549 62,765km for £1749
Oneworld Explorer	American Airlines BA Cathay Pacific Finnair Iberia Lan Chile Qantas	Unlimited; based on continents	NA – but extra sectors can be bought
Global Explorer	Air Pacific American Airlines BA Cathay Pacific Finnair Gulf Air Iberia Lan Chile Qantas	46,670km	Based on two fare levels and the season; so you can buy up to 54,720km
Worldwide Journey	Air Pacific Continental Emirates KLM Malaysian Northwest South African Airways SriLankan (Plus lots of smaller airlines)	40,230km	Four fare levels based on distance: 40,235km for £1019 48,280km for £1299 56,330km for £1599 64,375km for £1799
Skyteam	AeroMexico Air France Alitalia Czech Delta Korean Air	41,850km	Four fare levels based on distance: 41,845km for £1099 46,470km for £1299 54,720km for £1549 62,765km for £1749

Max Stops	Good For...	Bad For...	Reroute Fees	Cost Range
Unlimited – max of 3 stops in NZ. Must go RTW.	Asia, NZ and Pacific Islands	Australia (domestic flights), Africa, South America and USA	£75 before departure and £50 after departure from the UK	£843-£1403
4 free stops in more restricted destinations. Only one stop in Australia and one in NZ. Must go RTW.	SE Asia, Australia, NZ	South America, Australia (domestic flights), Africa	£75 for the first change before departure and £50 after departure from the UK	£783-£1463 (includes two fare levels depending on availability)
7 stops	Africa, South America, Australia, USA and Asia	Only bad thing is the max stops	£50 before and after departure from the UK	£891-£1733 (includes two fare levels depending on availability)
Max of 15 but restrictions in certain regions, no more than: 5 in US and Canada, 3 in Japan, 5 in Europe and 5 in Australasia.	USA and Canada, Australia, NZ, Asia, Pacific	Not great for Africa. If South America is your destination after Australia/NZ then you'll be in the highest distance bracket.	£55 but not permitted to change the first intercontinental sector or any sectors up to the first intercontinental. So if stopping in Europe before going on then these dates or destinations cannot be changed.	£1299-£1799
Unlimited but restrictions within continents. No more than: 4 flight sectors in each of Europe and Middle East, Africa, Asia, South America and 6 flight sectors in North America. Extra sectors can be purchased per continent.	Everywhere – if you want to see it all then this is the fare – price goes up based on the number of continents travelled to but must count Europe as the first continent.		£40 en route but £55 before departure	£1169-£2199
10 stops with 46,670km and 15 stops with 54,720km	Everywhere – but limited by stop allowance; max 3 in each continent on 46,670km or 4 on 54,720km.		£40 en route but £55 before departure from the UK	£1319-£1919
10 stops plus extra stops for £55. Max of 5 in each region: North America, Central America, South America, Europe, Asia, Africa, Middle East, Southwest Pacific.	USA, Asia, Australia, Pacific Islands, NZ, Africa	South America	£95 before departure or $150 en route	£1019-£1799
5 stops on 41,845km tickets but up to 15 on 46,670km plus max of 5 in Australia, US and Canada, and Europe	USA, Asia, Europe, Central America	South America, Africa	Around £55	£1099-£1749

(Continued from page 103)

ticket like this can be picked up for around £827, if you depart the UK outside of the school holidays. If you spend more money on your ticket, then you'll get more stops and more choice of stops.

For instance, you could get a little fancier and take in NZ and some Pacific islands with this routing from the Great Escapade for around £843: London–Singapore–Sydney–Christchurch–Wellington–Auckland–Rarotonga–Papeete (Tahiti)–LA–London.

If you're aching to visit Africa then take a look at this route with World Discovery Plus for around £973: London–Cape Town–Johannesburg–Perth–Melbourne–Brisbane–LA–New York–London.

Otherwise, if it's South America and the home of Paddington Bear that really turns you on then you could travel with Oneworld Explorer for £1319 and go: London–Helsinki–Bangkok–Singapore–Cairns–Sydney–Auckland–Santiago–Lima–Buenos Aires–London.

Or, for something with a Tex Mex flavour featuring jugfuls of margarita and a popular backpacker hang-out, here's an interesting Skyteam RTW ticket for around £1299: London–Rome–Hong Kong–Tokyo–Seoul–Honolulu–San Francisco–New Orleans–Atlanta–Cancun–Mexico City–Paris–London.

All these fares depend on your departure date from the UK and appropriate availability. Each fare is quoted excluding tax. In addition, many of these fares can accommodate surface or overland sectors so read the following section and then ask your travel agent what's available. And, for those of you who like pretty colours, lots of dotted lines and want to get your travel juices running, all of these fares are illustrated on the RTW Airfares map at the beginning of this book.

Popular Surface Sectors

Even if flying makes you feel as high as a kite, you really don't want to experience too many countries from 30,000 ft. Flying into one city and travelling overland to fly out of another is something you want to experience at least once on your RTW ticket. In airline parlance, the bit of land you traverse by bus/camel/Rollerblade is called a 'surface sector'. The most popular ones in each region are:

Africa Nairobi (Kenya) and Johannesburg (South Africa); Johannesburg and Cape Town (South Africa)

Asia Bangkok (Thailand) and Singapore; Bangkok and Bali (Indonesia); Beijing and Hong Kong (China)

Australia & NZ Sydney and Melbourne (Oz); Perth and Brisbane (Oz); Cairns and Sydney/Melbourne (Oz); Adelaide and Darwin (Oz); Auckland and Christchurch (NZ)

Indian Subcontinent Delhi and Mumbai (India); Delhi and Kathmandu (Nepal)

North America LA and New York (USA); San Francisco and LA (USA); Vancouver and Toronto (Canada)

South America Rio de Janeiro (Brazil) and Buenos Aires (Argentina); Quito (Ecuador) and La Paz (Bolivia); Lima (Peru) and Santiago (Chile)

What Happens Next?

Now you've got a good grasp of the basics, you're ready to speak to your friendly, specialist travel agent – see p24 for details. Try to make a visit in person because talking everything through face-to-face will be much easier and more enjoyable. Plus, if your plans are still quite vague, they'll have brochures with maps of possible RTW routings, which means they might already have found exactly what you're looking for. When discussing your requirements, remember to bear in mind the following:

- Ask to be put on your travel agent's mailing list. Although you'll receive a lot of information you don't want, you'll also be the first to hear about the fares that do interest you.

- Don't stopover in too many places, you won't be able to do justice to them. Every travel agent will tell you that most travellers cram too much into their itinerary.
- If you live a long way from the capital, ask about flying out of your local airport as well as a London one. Many fares allow provincial departures at little or no extra cost.
- If you're travelling through a lot of different regions you might not fit them all in during the so-called 'best time to visit'. Don't spend too much time and effort trying to achieve the impossible.
- In general, the best RTW fares tend to be for departures just after Easter until mid-June. Next best is February until Easter, and November. The fortnight before Christmas is the worst of all.
- Remember, the least expensive routes take in Australia and NZ. However, you don't have to visit Australasia. There are numerous routing possibilities across the North Pacific. For starters, try London–Delhi–Singapore–Beijing overland to Hong Kong–San Francisco overland to New York–London for £843 plus tax with the Great Escapade.
- Think about your visas when choosing dates. Touching down in Thailand with a 60-day visa and a ticket that says you'll be flying out in four months will not endear you to immigration officials.
- When booking a ticket, your travel agent will ask you to give exact dates for all the flights on your ticket, even though you may be unsure of the timing on some. Don't worry, apart from your departure date from the UK, all other dates are usually 'provisional'. Before handing over any money, check the agency's policy about changing these dates before you depart. After you take off, date changes are often free but some airline offices will charge you a small administration fee. Again, be sure to check the rules before handing over your cash.

Remember, if you want to go around the world then a RTW ticket is the way to go. Buying tickets as you travel according to whim and fancy may sound appealingly nonprescriptive but will cost a fortune. In addition, you'll always have the 'onward ticket problem' when entering new countries.

However, as an alternative to a RTW ticket, your specialist travel agent may cobble together two separate 'one way' tickets on two different airlines as a more economical option for you.

GOING OVERLAND

There's no denying it. Flying means you miss out on what's going on below. If you can't stand the thought of this then you can either travel around the world by land and sea or do the bare minimum of flying. For instance, how about travelling overland to Moscow (Russia), taking the Trans-Mongolian railway between Moscow and Beijing. From there you're within easy reach of Southeast Asia from where a well-worn trail leads to Bali and a short flight to Australia. Unless you can hitch a lift on a yacht (see p388) from here, you can fly to somewhere such as Santiago and head north up the Gringo Trail from South America to the USA. Once there, take your pick of fantastic road trips leading to New York and a cheap ticket home.

In fact, STA Travel currently sells the flights for this type of RTW trip. It's called the Overland Odyssey and costs just under £1050 (some of the fares on it are only for students or those under 26). Yes, a bit expensive huh? Overlanding actually is more expensive than flying, so be warned, all those bus and train tickets could add up to a great deal more than a cheap RTW ticket where you fly almost everywhere.

For more information on amazing overland journeys see the continent sections that make up the rest of Part II.

EUROPE

HEATHER DICKSON
Heather first fell in love with continental Europe when her mother bought her a pair of stylish French shoes after a rather rough ferry crossing from Ramsgate to Dunkerque. Since then Heather has explored many European countries and is happiest eating tapas in Spain, walking in Scandinavia and drinking beer anywhere in central Europe. Heather has worked for Lonely Planet since 2000 and is the commissioning editor for Europe on a shoestring. *She has also written for Lonely Planet's* Andalucía *and* Out to Eat London.

INTRODUCTION

Packing in more than 30 national cultures on a modest landmass, Europe frequently even dazzles Europeans. It is dubbed a living museum for the way its past and present coexist, with modern architecture sprouting up alongside Roman ruins, and fairytale cities such as Prague a short hop from metropolises such as Berlin. And just as the European Union (EU) has expanded east, with 10 new countries in May 2004, so too has the gappers' itinerary. Many formerly communist countries – even those outside the EU – are opening up to tourism, and no-frills flights now reach as far as Ljubljana (Slovenia), Bratislava (Slovakia) and Tallinn (Estonia). As an extra bonus, these hot locations are among the continent's cheapest, which means that a trip to pricey Scandinavia or Switzerland can easily be evened out by sunbathing for a month in Croatia or Turkey. So, with public transport ready to whisk you off to every corner, it's time to experience the continent on our doorstep.

WHY EUROPE?

Europe is at once chic and gritty, exhilarating and slow-placed, built-up and wild. It boasts some of the best transport, food, scenery and mix of cultures on the planet, and offers gappers the chance to do what gappers love to do: learn a language. No, not just that! It offers gappers the chance to explore world-famous cities, hop on a train in Rome, get off in a town that isn't listed in a guidebook, pour beers in a Spanish resort, learn to ski in the Alps, go clubbing in Greece, teach children in Poland. A gap year in Europe also provides you with a good excuse for getting to know the neighbours and gaining a better understanding of the continent that has shaped us so much.

Indeed, because of this closeness, Europe has never been an exotic choice for gappers, but depending on where you spend your time, you can have an original trip. Thanks to the extensive airline, rail, bus and ferry networks it's possible to branch off in any direction or jet from one hub to the next rather than follow a well-worn route. It means that you can tour Spain and Italy, add on a no-frills flight to Eastern Europe, which has burst open with new destinations with the help of budget airlines, and head back home via Scandinavia. Or, if you simply want to get ahead of the pack, visit the Carpathian Mountains (Romania), Triglav National Park

(Slovenia) and Belgrade (Serbia) – a selection of the hottest up-and-coming destinations in Europe. Alternatively, you can immerse yourself in the underground art, culture and music scenes of Paris, Berlin and Madrid or dive into Europe's staggering history by visiting Neolithic tombs in Sweden or Byzantine monasteries in Macedonia. Either way, you'll be off the beaten track in no time, wondering why you ever thought you knew Europe.

However, dreamers will be stirred by the Europe that they've read about in books and there's nothing more satisfying than seeing a well-loved monument or eating a national dish that everyone raves about. You can even skirt the crowds if you pick the right season. So, whether you want to climb the Eiffel Tower in Paris, check out Gaudí's architecture in Barcelona or ride a sleigh in Lapland, you're bound to be impressed.

That being said, you'll only be impressed if you can afford it and, as the saying goes, a gapper and their money are soon parted in Europe. With transport tickets and museum passes to purchase, beer and food to sample, it won't be long before funds run dry. Thankfully, though, this is Europe, which means should you blow half your travel money in one crazy weekend there's bound to be seasonal work, such as fruit picking or table waiting, somewhere on the continent that will stave off a premature journey home. And you wouldn't want to leave until you'd let your hair down in Ibiza, Madrid, Barcelona, Amsterdam or Berlin.

Overall, Europe might need a little more ingenuity when it comes to planning and minding the 'gap', but get the cheap/pricey, work/play mixes right and you'll have a tasty gap-year cocktail.

WHAT TO DO?

Apart from learning a few languages, most gappers in Europe work for a few months, travel for a few months, top up the bank account again and continue travelling. Others have pre-arranged jobs or the intention to work, study or learn a skill in a specific place, which forms the focus of the gap year – but it's common for gappers to take a month out to travel at the end. For some, work is a fallback proposition, to be considered only in emergencies. Certainly it's possible to stretch your funds by camping, living on pasta and spending a lot of time in Eastern Europe.

Happily, Brits can work in any other EU member state, there are organisations set up for heaps of activities (eg, skiing, surfing, climbing) and infrastructure is in place for learning languages, finding placements and meeting similar-minded people. Resort work and au pairing are some popular job options and, although the wages are minimal, at least you'll learn a language if you opt for the latter. See Part III for more information on overseas jobs, volunteer work and courses.

TOP 10 MUST-SEES

Paris (France) One of the world's most romantic cities, with its Gothic cathedral, twisting old streets and relaxing cafés.

Český Krumlov (Czech Republic) Cool backpacker magnet, topped off with a fairytale castle and medieval townscape.

Sognefjorden (Norway) The longest (204km), deepest (1308m) and most breathtaking of Norway's fjords.

Ibiza (Spain) Spanish party island where breakbeats and bongos meet the beach.

Istanbul (Turkey) Mystical and magnificent city with Ottoman mosques and a chaotic Grand Bazaar.

Dubrovnik & Dalmatian Coast (Croatia) Jaw-droppingly beautiful coastline and a fabulous 1300-year-old city.

Berlin (Germany) Best European capital for late-night drinking and contemporary architecture.

Scotland's Highlands & Islands A wild and enchanting region, from its deep lochs to its soaring peaks.

Rome Italy's Eternal City and home to the awe-inspiring Vatican, Colosseum and Sistine Chapel.

Andalucía Spain's passionate south, with beaches, cities and the rugged Sierra Nevada mountains.

EUROPE

LEGEND

★ Top 10 Must-Sees

CLASSIC ROUTES

A Mediterranean Meander
Northern Lights
Central Europe to the Coast

Get Active

Europe might not boast like brasher destinations, but its geography and climate support the full range of outdoor pursuits, including windsurfing, skiing, trekking, cycling, mountaineering, dog-sledding and adventure sports ranging from bungee jumping to zorbing.

CYCLING & MOUNTAIN BIKING

Europe is a cyclist's fantasy: flashy hybrid road bikes meet squeaking boneshakers and bubblegum-pink cruisers in cities such as Amsterdam, Copenhagen and Berlin; mountainbikers pump their calf muscles through the Alps; and pannier-laden tourers breeze through southern France. Among the best cycling regions (with huge cycle-path networks) are the Netherlands, the Belgian Ardennes, Scandinavia, the west of Ireland, the upper reaches of the Danube in southern Germany, and Provence and the Dordogne (France).

As a foot passenger you won't be charged extra for taking a bike on most cross-channel ferries (see p120) and you can take bikes on many trains, just look for the bike symbol on the timetable. This makes cycling an attractive option in Europe's pricier regions, such as Scandinavia and some of central Europe, where the cost of transport and accommodation can easily be lessened with two wheels and a tent.

For more information on cycling in Europe, contact the **Cycling Touring Club** (CTC; ☎ 0870 873 0060; www.ctc.org.uk). Membership for students aged under 26 costs £12 annually.

European Bike Express (☎ 01642 308 800; www.bike-express.co.uk) is a UK-based service that offers coach travel across Europe for cyclists and their bikes. It runs in the summer from northeastern England to France, Italy and Spain with pick-up/drop-off points en route. The maximum return fare is £194 (with a £10 discount for CTC members).

Hassle-free bike hire is also widely available throughout Europe and in bike-friendly Copenhagen you can rent one for free.

SKIING & SNOWBOARDING

The ski season runs from December to April and the Alps are the best and most popular ski destination in Europe. Well-known resorts include Chamonix (France), Interlaken (Switzerland) and Val d'Aosta (Italy). The best skiing in the Pyrenees can be found at Soldeu-El Tarter and Pas de la Casa-Grau Roig in eastern Andorra. These are among the cheapest ski resorts in Europe in terms of equipment hire, lift passes, accommodation and après-ski, and therefore a good option for gappers. The Sierra Nevada (southern Spain), a handful of Eastern European countries (Romania, Slovakia, Czech Republic and Poland) and Norway and Sweden (very cold) all have limited ski facilities.

One of the most attractive Alpine resorts for snowboarders is the Stubai Glacier, which is south of Innsbruck in Austria.

Cross-country skiing is very popular in Scandinavia and the Alps, while snow shoeing (a great alternative to winter walking) is also possible – these activities are more popular from February to April.

TREKKING & MOUNTAINEERING

There are thousands of trekking and mountaineering opportunities in Europe, ranging from full-on crampon adventures to gentle low-land walks. The Alps and Dolomites (Italy) offer the greatest variety to mountaineers, while trekkers may opt for Spain's national parks or France's rolling countryside. Alternatively, escape the crowds by heading to the Carpathian Mountains (Romania), the High Tatras Mountains (Slovakia) or a quiet island off the coast of Norway (Osterøy is a good choice).

For long-distance walkers there are a number of transcontinental routes, known as GR – Gran Recorrido – in Spain and France. A famous trek worth undertaking is the Camino de Santiago pilgrim's route, which starts in France and ends in Santiago de Compostela (Spain).

One trend that has been sweeping Alpine countries such as Austria and Switzerland is so-called 'Nordic walking', which is basically skiing without the snow. So, if you see people rhythmically swinging themselves between two walking poles, don't be taken aback; they're simply working their upper bodies and giving themselves a better cardio workout. You might even want to try it yourself.

Via Ferrata (www.viaferrata.org) is another high-adrenalin activity, popular in southern France. It consists of being roped up and climbing with the aid of steel rope bridges and pre-attached cables.

Those interested in developing their hill-walking and mountaineering skills before they head off should opt for a course at Plas y Brenin, The National Mountain Centre (www.pyb .co.uk) – see p437 for details.

For good climbing and walking maps visit www.stanfords.co.uk.

WATERSPORTS & DIVING
There are some good surf breaks on the Atlantic coasts of southern France, Portugal and Spain. Tarifa (Spain) is one of the best windsurfing locations in Europe. For details on other hot windsurfing spots in Europe visit www.windlords.com.

Canoeing and kayaking is possible on rivers and lakes across Europe and sea kayaking around the Greek islands and the fractured Scandinavian coast is popular. More extreme white-water rafting can be found in the Alps, Norway, the Pyrenees, Slovenia and Turkey.

Great sailing locations include the Greek and Balearic Islands, Croatia, southern France, Ireland and Turkey. Look out for crewing along the Côte d'Azur (France) and Europe's wealthier sailing centres. (See the Work your Route chapter on p388.)

There are dive centres all around the Mediterranean. Croatia, Malta and the Balearics can be particularly recommended along with Turkey and Greece if you want to dive among antiquities.

ADVENTURE SPORTS
At Interlaken in Switzerland you can try bungee jumping, canyoning, dog-sledding, ice climbing, paragliding and sky diving, and once you've done all that, you might fancy zorbing (where you're strapped inside an inflated ball, in another inflated ball, and pushed head-over-heels down a hill) or hydrospeed (where you get to ride the wild river, wearing a helmet and wetsuit, and lying flat on a specially designed 'raft').

Bovec in Slovenia is another burgeoning and more reasonably priced adventure-sports destination.

Work a Little
Europe is a dream for gappers thanks to the fact that it's legal for British citizens to work in all of the EU countries. That means if you're thinking about fruit-picking in southern Europe, cleaning chalets in the Alps, working behind a bar in the Greek islands or au pairing in Germany, you'll be able to pick up work with little hassle. To get a 'proper' job (ie office work) you'll need excellent language skills, but British expat communities can sometimes provide more diverse employment for those who only speak English. Wherever you work, wages will usually be lower than back home.

See the Casual/Seasonal Work chapter (p363) for information on work permits and other Part III chapters for information on organisations that can help find work.

Travel Around

Transport in the UK might have a lot of bad press but that doesn't mean the rest of Europe hasn't got it right. There are train, bus, ferry and flight networks galore and you only have to check out the *Thomas Cook European Rail Timetable*, the *Thomas Cook Rail Map of Europe* or an Inter-Railing map at www.raileurope.co.uk to see how well-connected and highly serviced places are. Eastern Europe isn't quite so blessed but it's catching up slowly.

If you're looking to blast through cities, then invest in an Inter-Rail pass (either for 16 days, 22 days or one month of travel), which is available from **Rail Europe** (☎ 0870 837 1371; www.raileurope.co.uk). City to city coach passes valid for up to 60 days are available from **Eurolines** (☎ 0870 580 8080; www.nationalexpress.com) or if you'd prefer a hop-on, hop-off tour then try Busabout (www.busabout.com).

If you're planning on taking to the high seas, including the Mediterranean and Baltic, then www.ferryto.com is a good booking and planning resource. Otherwise, check out the information on crewing a yacht on p388.

Having a vehicle (and knowing how to fix it) allows total freedom and flexibility. A camper van is ideal but security can be a headache and your metal bubble can put more 'distance' between you and the places you're travelling through.

Hitching around Europe is possible but never 100% safe and can't be recommended. However, if you are considering it then check out www.bugeurope.com and www.hitch hikers.org. Alternatively, there are also a few lift-sharing organisations in France (Allostop Provoya and Auto-Partage) and Germany (Mitfahrzentrale). These organisations remove the hassle and inevitable, despondent road-side waits to provide one of the cheapest ways to get around Europe.

With no-frills routes increasing all the time, flying around Europe is now more feasible. In some instances it's cheaper than the train.

As for visas and border crossings, British nationals don't need to worry when heading into Europe. If you're travelling beyond Europe and into Russia or other former Russian states then you will need to organise visas (see p21 for general visa details).

CLASSIC ROUTES

Europe is one of those destinations where you can plan your own classic route just by looking at a map. However, concentrate your efforts and don't try to cram in too much. The following route suggestions may help.

A Mediterranean Meander

Paris is a poetic start to a tour of southern Europe and the Med, which takes in some of the hottest hangouts. From Paris head southwest to Bayonne, hop over the border into Spain's Basque country, visit San Sebastián and travel south to Madrid. Catch a train from Madrid to Lisbon and continue south to Faro and the Algarve. Make your way east to Seville, before checking out Tarifa and Málaga on the coast. From there continue on to Granada, Córdoba and Valencia before hitting Barcelona. Cut back into France and visit Marseille and nice Nice before stepping into Italy. No Italian tour would be complete without a visit to Pisa, Florence and Rome. Reach Greece by boat from Brindisi (Italy), check out Athens and spend the last leg relaxing in the Greek islands.

Northern Lights
Lounge around in Amsterdam and save some cash before striking Scandinavia on this arctic adventure. From Amsterdam, head to Hamburg and on to Copenhagen. Continue north to Gothenburg and Stockholm in Sweden before veering west to Oslo in Norway. Experience the enchanting train journey from Oslo to Bergen and then wend your way north to Trondheim and the Artic Circle. Bus it north to Bodo and Nordkapp before returning south through Karasjok and Rovaniemi (Finland). Throw snowballs in Lapland. Continue south through Kemi, Oulu and Tampere, the 'Manchester of Finland'. Finally, snuggle up in Helsinki.

Central Europe to the Coast
A central European tour starts in Berlin from where you can head east to Warsaw (Poland) and cut back to the fairytale city of Prague. Travelling southeast from there you can visit Vienna (Austria), Bratislava (Slovakia) and Budapest (Hungary). Take the train from Budapest to Zagreb (Croatia), hop over to Ljubljana (Slovenia) and then take a trip down the beautiful coast from Trieste (Italy) to Piran, Zadar, Split and the splendid city of Dubrovnik in Croatia. Lastly, laze on Montenegrin beaches at Budva and Bar. (If you want to get into Italy from here, ferries go from Bar to Bari.)

WHEN TO GO?
A European adventure can start at any time but it's a good idea to go to the right place in the right season or you may need an umbrella on every leg of the trip. If you can, travel in the south or check out cities (Madrid, Barcelona, Paris, Berlin, Rome are some options) between April and June, then move to Scandinavia for the height of summer (the midnight sun on 21 June is a great experience), then visit central or Eastern Europe in July and August before catching the last rays of Mediterranean sun in September and October. The ski season runs from December and April but you'll need to be there by November if you're looking for work. Alternatively, if you're not worried about weather or work, you can get better deals on accommodation by travelling out of season.

The Arctic Circle and the region's high mountains are amazing places to visit during winter, while alpine flowers carpet high valleys in spring. The great forests of central and Eastern Europe are beautiful in autumn, and at the height of summer when tourists overwhelm many popular tourist destinations, Eastern Europe and Scandinavia can be pleasant and quiet. If you don't want quiet, the clubbing season in Ibiza and the Greek islands of Mykonos, Ios and Santorini is between June and September.

France, Italy and Germany are essentially on holiday during August, the time to avoid Mediterranean beaches that are blisteringly hot in any case. Conversely, from October to May some coastal resorts can be desolate places.

Climate
The seasons in the rest of Europe are similar to Britain. Winters in southern Europe are mild, with Andalucía, the Greek islands, Malta, the Canary Islands and Cyprus the warmest places to visit (temperatures rise to the mid-teens). In central and northern Europe (and central Spain) temperatures in winter are low (below freezing at night) and snowfalls common (although snow doesn't linger long in the west). Scandinavian winters are extremely harsh but the aurora borealis (northern lights) are some compensation between December and March.

Generally speaking, spring and autumn are wetter and windier across the continent. Spring occurs first in the south. Winter lingers longer in Eastern and northern Europe and arrives earlier in upland and mountainous areas, which tend to experience extremes of climate.

Autumn may bring the occasional 'Indian summer' (mild, sunny and warm weather) in the south. The temperate Atlantic Coast is steadily wet throughout the year.

Festivals

With Finland's Air Guitar Championships, Spain's Running of the Bulls and the Netherlands' Cannabis Cup, it's clear to see why, in Europe, anything can be (and generally is) made a spectacle of. Here are a few of the major festivals:

Venice Carnevale (Italy) Held in the 10 days leading up to Ash Wednesday (January/February). Venetians don masks and costumes for a continuous street party.

Las Fallas (Spain) Week-long party in Valencia held in mid-March. All-night drinking, dancing and fireworks feature heavily.

Sumardagurinn Fyrsti (Iceland) Celebrates the first day of summer in Reykjavík on the third Thursday in April. There is much merriment.

Athens Festival (Greece) A feast of opera, ballet and classical music lasting from mid-June to November. Other Greek festivals take place at Easter (March/April).

Bastille Day (France) 14 July is a national holiday and celebrations take place across the country but the biggest celebration is in Paris (check out the fireworks at the Eiffel Tower).

Fiesta de Sanfermines (Spain) A non-stop eight-day party and bull-fighting celebration in early July that begins each day with the famous Running of the Bulls through the streets of Pamplona.

Festival of Avignon (France) Held between early July and early August and features some 300 shows of music, drama and dance. There's also a fringe festival.

Il Palio (Italy) An extraordinary horse race held in the main piazza of Siena on 2 July and 16 August. Get to it if you can.

Baltica International Folk Festival (Estonia, Latvia & Lithuania) Week-long celebration of Baltic music, dance and parades, held in mid-July.

Oktoberfest (Germany) Munich's legendary beer-drinking festival starts in late September and lasts two heady weeks.

TOP FIVE FESTIVALS WITH A TWIST

Wife Carrying Championships (Finland) www.sonkajarvi.fi
Castle Party (Poland) www.castleparty.com
La Tomatina (Spain) www.sanfermin.com
Cannabis Cup (the Netherlands) www.cannabiscup.com
International Festival of Fantastic Film (Belgium) www.bifff.org

---

WHAT TO EXPECT?
Travellers

Pinning down exactly who is going where in Europe isn't easy but Spain is currently the number one destination in the world for British travellers, so you know who'll be lazing on the beach there. Eastern Europe and the Balkans are now becoming more popular with British travellers and continue to be heavily visited by Germans, Austrians and Scandinavians. Antipodeans and, to a lesser extent, Americans and Canadians can be found all over the place.

Travellers congregate in cities such as Barcelona, Amsterdam and Berlin and are most likely to be playing cards or banging a drum in dull transport hubs, such as Brindisi in Italy, too. Backpacker hostels are also a good place to find, well, backpackers. Check out a good string of them online at www.europefamoushostels.com.

Locals

One of the great delights of travelling in Europe is the way so many cultures live shoulder to shoulder. The differences can make your head spin – especially as you enter countries like Bulgaria where they nod their heads up and down to say 'no'. And just by watching a little local interaction you'll see that, by and large, Europe is a friendly place where kissing and shaking hands is common. Be careful to get the gestures right though. In some countries it's rude to raise your fingers when ordering two beers at the bar, even with your palm facing the bar staff.

There are a huge variety of traditions across Europe but common traits are a little more respect for elders, politeness and a less-hurried attitude. In the east, a sprinkling of Islam becomes a blanket of belief in Turkey, while in much of southern, Western and Eastern Europe Christian traditions still dominate cultural life. Attitudes and practices also vary within countries. The industrial north of Italy and Spain show all the outward signs of chic Western capitalism but in remote rural southern areas farmers still ride donkeys. These rural areas are more conservative and often considerably poorer than cities, and you are more likely to experience traditional practices.

Europeans are among the planet's most dedicated followers of fashion and scruffy clothing will give you away as a tourist, and won't do you any favours when dealing with officialdom or looking for work. Also take care with dress (long sleeves, and trousers or skirts below the knee) when visiting religious buildings and show respect in rural towns. A bikini top and hotpants will not go down well. In cities, normal urban-wear such as jeans and trainers is, thankfully, fine.

Language

English is the most widely understood second language on the continent, but speaking it loudly and slowly isn't going to cut it. Other than in Scandinavia and the Netherlands, where most people are happy to speak in English, don't expect a warm welcome if you haven't tried learning the basics. A little French, Spanish, German and Italian will go a long way. In rural areas and Eastern Europe you will certainly need a phrasebook.

See p425 for information on language courses. Reading Material, p121, gives information on Lonely Planet's useful phrasebooks.

Health Risks

Europe is, on the whole, a pretty healthy place. A change of diet may upset your stomach but other than getting sunburned or heatstroke, being bitten by insects or giving yourself the devil's own hangover, there's little to worry about. That said, it's worth bearing in mind that HIV and sexually transmitted infections are on the rise in Europe and a typhoid vaccination is recommended for some southeastern countries. Tuberculosis is becoming more common, especially in the east, and there is the odd case of rabies. Tick-Borne encephalitis (TBE) – a disease passed on by the bite of infected ticks – can occur in most forest and rural areas of Europe, especially in Austria, Germany, Hungary and the Czech Republic. Consider a vaccination against this tick-transmitted disease if you're in the woods between May and September or if you are doing some extensive hiking.

Consult the Health chapter (p59) and seek professional medical advice for more travel health information. Read the information about E111 forms and the new European Health Insurance Card on p30.

Time & Flight Time

Three time zones cover the continent, starting with Greenwich Mean Time (GMT) in the UK, Portugal and Iceland. The vast majority of the continent is one hour ahead, while Sweden, Eastern Europe, Greece and Turkey are two hours ahead. Between the end of

March and end of October many European countries push their clocks forward one hour for summer daylight savings.

From London, Paris is just a 1¼-hour flight away, while Madrid is 2½ hours away and Istanbul 3¾ hours.

Issues

There are no visa issues for British passport holders travelling in Europe. However, it's always worth considering onward travel especially if you're heading to Russia, Kaliningrad, Ukraine or other former Russian states (for general visa information see p21). EU citizens are allowed to remain in Romania for 90 days without a visa but check the Ministry of Foreign Affairs website (www.mae.ro) for the latest information. If taking the Bucharest–St Petersburg train, be advised that you will need a Ukrainian and Belarusian transit visa on top of the Russian visa.

PKK activity in southeastern Turkey has largely faded out, making the area much safer to travel, but with the situation in Iraq still volatile we wouldn't recommend going anywhere near the borders.

In parts of Croatia, Bosnia and Hercegovina and around Kosovo unexploded ordnance and landmines remain a problem. Sarajevo's **Mine Action Centre** (☎ 00 387 33 253 860; www.bhmac.org) has valuable mine awareness information.

Border guards, police, train conductors and other low-level bureaucrats in Eastern Europe may ask you for a bribe to oil their creaking bureaucratic machines but more common are rip-offs, scams and petty thefts in popular tourist destinations – you need to keep your wits about you on overnight trains and at bus stations.

For further information on travel hotspots, general safety issues and governmental travel advice see the Safety chapter (p79).

Internet & Communications

There are internet café's in towns and cities all over Europe and usually they're very reasonably priced.

Affordable pay-as-you-go mobile services are available across the continent and worth considering if you're spending a considerable amount of time in one country. Your UK mobile will cost you a fortune to use unless you are just accepting text messages.

DAILY SPEND

Eastern Europe, Greece, Portugal, southern Spain and Turkey are the cheapest destinations, while Iceland (followed closely by Scandinavia where two beers can cost you your daily budget) is the most expensive. Switzerland, Austria and southern Germany are also going to drain your finances before you've even set foot outside the hostel.

Long-time travellers wanting to keep costs below £14–21 per day will have to stay in cheap (and sometimes free) campsites, self-cater and not move around too quickly. Fun for a while, especially when camping out in the wilds, but the novelty soon wears off, particularly when you realise that a night out partying is going to mean two nights sleeping under a hedge to balance the books.

A little more cash (say £24–35) allows for a more varied diet (no more noodles), the odd good meal out, a bed to sleep in (usually in a dormitory from £7 to £10 a night) and less tramplike behaviour. This isn't five-star travel though, and in Europe's most expensive countries you'll struggle to get by on this. For £38–52 you'll be able to use nicer guesthouses, have a room to yourself and not think twice before ordering a dessert or a second gin and tonic.

It's still possible to get a good three-course meal for £6–8 in Mediterranean Europe and for much less in the east. In northern Europe you're looking at £5–8 a course.

Visa or MasterCard credit cards are widely accepted and European automatic teller machines (ATMs) accept a huge variety of debit cards.

GETTING THERE

The best ways of getting to the continent from the UK are by plane, train and ferry – in that order if you want to get there fast. Cheap flights to destinations all over the continent are booming, so it's never been easier to travel to Europe.

Air

No-frills airlines are quite literally taking off all over the place, so as well as flying there and back you could live a jet-set life while you're in Europe too (see No Frills Please, We're British, p119). Frillier major carriers, such as British Airways (BA), also offer flights to a bewildering number of destinations across the continent but, as you'd expect, they are not necessarily the cheapest.

TICKET COSTS

To get the best flight deals you first need to master the world of online booking and be prepared to scream as the £13 flight to Oslo you checked out yesterday turns into a £130 flight today. The cheapest no-frills deals (the £1 ones) come as part of brief online promotions and an average no-frills ticket costs around £50 one way and is almost always the cheapest option for one-way flights. One-way standby tickets on charter flights coming back from southern Europe cost around £100.

Currently you can book a flight, departing in a week's time, from one of London's airports to: Madrid for £49; Copenhagen for £43; Berlin for £27; Warsaw for £17; Rome for £15; and Tallinn for £43 (all prices listed are inclusive of tax). However, you should note that these are the lowest fares; the highest one-way fares for some of these flights are over £100. For that reason, it is often better to book months in advance when there are more seats available and a wider choice of budget deals. However, if you want to change your date of travel then you'll have to pay a charge plus the difference between the price of your ticket when you bought it and the price on the day you now want to travel, which could be a whopping difference.

Nearer the time of departure, and often giving more flexibility, are under-26 return tickets on established airlines such as Air France (via Paris; www.airfrance.com), KLM (via Amsterdam; www.klm.com), Lufthansa (via Munich and Frankfurt; www.lufthansa.com) and Swiss (via Zurich; www.swiss.com). You must book through a youth/student travel agent but £150–200 for a return ticket is easily achievable. Flexible 'open-jaw' tickets (flying into one city and out of another) are available for the same sort of money and most are valid for a year. However, in reality, it's cheaper to go no-frills unless you really miss airline food.

NO FRILLS PLEASE, WE'RE BRITISH

Flying has never been cheaper and with budget airlines continuously adding new routes, it's easy to plan a whole European itinerary around dirt-cheap fares. Plus, with the help of web-based, cheap-flight search engines such as www.skyscanner.net, it's simple to compare prices and find the best deals. However, always factor the cost of getting to and from the airport into your trip: you might find that flying BA from an airport closer to home is cheaper than flying no frills.

Also remember that some budget carriers are notorious for delays to flights because of their tight turnaround times. If you're taking an evening flight, it's a good idea to check when local transport stops running should the airline let you down. In addition, there is a high attrition rate among low-cost airlines (several went bust during the writing of this book), so you could lose the cash you have paid in advance. Oh, and in general, be prepared for antisocial flying times and a tight squeeze on the plane.

Here is a list of European no-frills airlines that offer some good deals (see p29 for UK-based no frills airlines):

Aer Lingus (☎ 0845 084 4444; www.aerlingus.com) Has turned itself from a traditional airline into a low-cost carrier and flies from Dublin, Shannon and Cork to destinations throughout Europe, including Copenhagen, Frankfurt and Faro.

Air Berlin (☎ 0870 738 8880; www.airberlin.com) Operates a wide network of flights from Germany to destinations around Europe, including services to London, Manchester and Southampton.

Basiq Air (☎ 0207 365 4997; www.basiqair.com) Flies from Amsterdam and Rotterdam to 19 destinations in Europe, including London Stansted.

Germanwings (☎ 020 8321 7255; www.germanwings.com) Has flights from its hub in Cologne to Stansted, Gatwick and Edinburgh, plus destinations across Europe.

Hapag-Lloyd Express (☎ 0870 606 0519; www.hlx.com) Flies into Coventry, Newcastle, Edinburgh and Manchester from Cologne and operates around 15 other European routes from its other German hub in Hanover.

helvetic (☎ 0207 026 3464; www.helvetic.com) Flies to 18 European destinations, including London Gatwick, from its hub in Zurich.

Iceland Express (☎ 0870 240 5600; www.icelandexpress.com) Flies from Reykjavík to Stansted and Copenhagen.

SkyEurope Airlines (☎ 0207 365 0365; www.skyeurope.com) This central European airline based in Slovakia connects London with Budapest, Kosice, Krakow, Warsaw and Bratislava (with a bus connection to and from Vienna).

snowflake (☎ 00 45 77 66 10 05; www.flysnowflake.com) The low-cost offshoot of SAS Scandinavian Airlines; sells seats on selected flights from London Heathrow to Copenhagen and Stockholm.

Wizz Air (☎ 00 48 22 500 9499; www.wizzair.com) A central and Eastern European no-frills operator (registered in London) that connects London Luton and Liverpool with Budapest, Katowice and Warsaw.

Sea & Overland

There are numerous options for crossing the channel by ferry to France, Belgium, the Netherlands and Scandinavia. Calais in France is one of the busiest ports and a main gateway into Europe. Following is a list of ferries with routes from the UK (unless otherwise stated it is free to take a bike onboard as a foot passenger):

Brittany Ferries (☎ 0870 366 5333; www.brittany-ferries.com) Offers a number of routes including Poole to Cherbourg and Plymouth to Santander (Spain).

DFDS Seaways (☎ 0870 533 3111; www.dfdsseaways.com) Routes between the UK and Scandinavia include Newcastle to Gothenburg (Sweden) and Harwich to Kristiansand (Norway).

P&O Ferries (☎ 0870 600 0613; www.poferries.com) Sea crossings include Portsmouth to Bilbao, Hull to Rotterdam and Dover to Calais.

Sea France (☎ 0870 571 1711; www.seafrance.fr) Ferries run from Dover to Calais.

Speedferries.com (☎ 0870 220 0570; www.speedferries.com) New low-cost, 50-minute ferry service from Dover to Boulogne.

Stena Line (☎ 0870 570 7070; www.stenaline.com) Serves Britain, Ireland, Scandinavia and the Netherlands. A popular route is Harwich to the Hook of Holland. Taking a bike costs a further £9.

For a quicker trip catch the Eurostar train from London to the heart of Paris (via the Eurotunnel) for £40 one way for those aged 25 or under. The Eurostar also stops in Brussels and Lille.

It is also possible to get into Europe from Central and Eastern Asia, though count on spending at least eight days doing it. Routes include the Trans-Siberian, Trans-Mongolian, Trans-Manchurian and Trans-Kazakhstan. For more information see the chapter on Russia, Central Asia and the Caucasus (p149).

Specialist Tour Operators

There are hundreds of tour operators running specialist activity and sightseeing tours in Europe. A few European specialists that particularly appeal to gappers include:

Contiki Holidays for 18-35s (☎ 020 8290 6777; www.contiki.com; travel@contiki.co.uk; fax 020 8225 4246; Wells House, 15 Elmfield Rd, Bromley, Kent BR1 1LS) Offers various group trips across the continent for between three and 48 days.

Top Deck Travel Ltd (☎ 020 8879 6789, www.topdecktravel.co.uk; res@topdecktravel.co.uk; fax 020 8944 9474; William House, 14 Worple Rd, London SW19 4DD) Plugs similar adventures, plus a few short trips that coincide with festivals.

EUROPE & BEYOND

Classic overland routes from Europe include journeys across Russia on the Trans-Siberian Railway (see p155 for details), from Gibraltar to Morocco and on to the rest of Africa, or from Denmark and Iceland on to Greenland. Routes from Istanbul to Cairo are also very popular, though travel from Turkey to Iran, Iraq and Syria is not currently recommended.

FURTHER INFORMATION
Reading Material

Lonely Planet publishes over 80 guides to Europe alone, covering cities, countries, regions and multi-regions (such as *Western Europe* and *Eastern Europe*). *Europe on a shoestring* is the most comprehensive guide to Europe, covering 40 countries. As well as travel guides, Lonely Planet produces 14 pocket phrasebooks for Europe's major languages.

Every aspect of Europe is covered in print. Whether you want to read up on architecture in Spain, fashion in Italy or reindeer herding in Norway there's always a specialist book to be found. A particularly good history book is Norman Davies' international bestseller *Europe: A History*, which is impressive in size, scope and balance.

Rev up your wanderlust with Bill Bryson's humorous take on Europe, *Neither Here Nor There*, Tim Moore's similar *Continental Drifter* or Mark Twain's classic, *A Tramp Abroad*. Paul Theroux's *The Pillars of Hercules* documents his contemporary grand tour, while Eric Newby concentrates on coastal delights in *On the Shores of the Mediterranean*.

George Orwell's *Down and Out in Paris and London* and *Homage to Catalonia* give a tramp's view of travel and war in Europe. *Through the Embers of Chaos: Balkan Journeys*, by Dervla Murphy, details a sober cycle ride through the Balkans, while *Driving Over Lemons* and *A Parrot in the Pepper Tree*, by Chris Stewart, provide an optimist's view of expat life. Among the best classic European novels are *Don Quixote* by Miguel de Cervantes (1605), *Madame Bovary* by Gustave Flaubert (1857) and *The Trial* by Franz Kafka (1925). Alternatively, mull over the meaning of it all with pop philosopher Alain de Botton's *The Art of Travel*.

Good quality newspapers such as the *Independent* (www.independent.co.uk), the *Guardian* (www.guardian.co.uk), *The Times* (www.timesonline.co.uk) and the *Telegraph* (www .telegraph.co.uk) all have travel supplements in their weekend papers. These contain some good tips, deals and flight listings. The online versions are a great way to keep up with home news while on the road.

Useful Information Sources

For specific country overviews, the low-down on travel in the region and hundreds of useful links head first to Lonely Planet's website (www.lonelyplanet.com).

The following portals and useful websites should help you chase down any aspect of interest in Europe:

http://europa.eu.int/index_en.htm Official website for the EU.

www.alliancefr.org Website of the French cultural and language teaching institute Alliance Française.

www.cervantes.es Instituto Cervantes website for those wanting to learn Spanish.

www.goethe.de Learn *Deutsch* all over Europe, including in Germany itself.

www.guideforeurope.com Backpackers guide to Europe including hostel reviews.

www.jobs-in-europe.net Includes links to job websites and agencies in Europe.

www.wwoof.org Links volunteers to organic farms in Europe.

www.youthinformation.com UK's National Youth Agency website with information on working in Europe.

BEEN THERE, DONE THAT

Puffing my way to the top of La Sagrada Família in Barcelona, I wondered whether I'd ever complete my grand tour of Europe. The cities were draining my cash and all I had to show for the trip was a cheap umbrella and a flashing, light-up Santa hat from Copenhagen. However, as the cathedral's megaphone bells peeled in my ear, I awoke from my daydream and was evermore eager to continue, even if it meant less food, less sleep and less beer.

I artfully checked out night trains (to save the cost of accommodation) and inexpensive early flights, which are a good option if you don't mind feeling cranky and jetlagged. I also kept an eye out for happy hours and other assorted deals, and found tourist offices that could fix me up in a swanky hotel for less than the price of a dorm bed. And so, with a more frugal outlook, I started to appreciate the beauty and quirks of Europe: the icy backstreets of Montmartre in Paris; an orange sunset over the haunting remains of the Berlin wall; suave gitanos in Madrid's underground flamenco bars; the Oslo–Bergen railway in Norway; cross little dogs in Seville. I even tenderly fondled my light-up Santa hat and remembered being in Copenhagen, freezing, waiting for the Carlsberg and Tuborg breweries to release their 'Christmas beers'. After that, I hazily recall singing along to Danish pop and feeling very attractive in my hat.

The trip ended with pretzels and snow in Munich but the snapshots of Europe still flip round in my mind like a badly edited version of a Bridget Jones movie – but with cooler locations and a much better cast.

Heather Dickson

AFRICA

MATT FLETCHER

Duped into not taking a gap year after school, Matt had to put up with an under-funded 'beer and train station' tour of Europe and summers in Spain and Morocco until, emerging from art college with a 'sportsman's degree', he left for east and southern Africa. This year-long trip kick-started a writing career and enabled him to embark upon a 'gap life' during which he has so far contributed to Lonely Planet's Walking in Spain, Walking in Australia, Africa, Morocco, Kenya, West Africa *and* Tonga *guides. In order to contribute to the company's* Unpacked *and* Unpacked Again *titles he got stranded in a Madagascan swamp and had a dingo steal his breakfast.*

INTRODUCTION

Africa will give your senses a slap. This is a continent with a legacy of ancient civilisations and with diverse cultures that demand your attention. It's a place of majestic landscapes, stunning wildlife and adventurous travel. Africa remains a largely rural continent; a place of wonderful, intoxicating, overland journeys; a land of exotic coastal hideaways and natural marvels. Africa will challenge you. You've got to be up for the odd hard journey, and there are a few ugly and frantic cities. Africa is also home to the poorest people on earth, but from the medinas of Mediterranean cities (see the Middle East chapter on p137 for in-depth coverage of Libya and Egypt) to Soweto in South Africa, the honesty and vitality of the African people is second to none. Africa is a kick-ass travel destination – enlightening, surprising and intriguing – and the rewards for the gapper are as huge as the continent itself.

WHY AFRICA?

Africa is a travel destination known to strike fear into the hearts of parents, but to hell with that. Don't believe the hype; when travelling to Africa bring only the baggage strapped to your back. Wildlife wonders are certainly a trump card (and wildlife havens actually exist across Africa), but Africa is so diverse it can provide almost any sort of travel experience. Want to cruise palm-fringed beaches? Fine. Fancy living with local people out in the African savanna? That's possible. Want to jump out of aeroplanes, ride quad bikes through the desert, then party till dawn? Absolutely no problem. And if you want to spend months checking out the continent's vibrant cultural life, exploring off the beaten track and being stunned by the sheer scale and diversity of a unique continent, then Africa is definitely your bag.

Africa is not known for its high-quality tourist offices. It's just not the kind of place where great experiences are always advertised on flyers. Africa is a place you need to explore, work at, and put something into in order to get the maximum out. Only in isolated pockets is it a place of conveyor-belt tourism or a trawl around 'must see' tourist sites. God knows, Africa is not shy about partying, and it has its fair share of backpacker havens and party towns, but when people experience Africa they really experience its communities, not a string of tourist sites. Travelling around Africa is often about experiencing the place for its own sake. It's also about the adventure of travel, for this is a continent where an eight-hour bus ride can turn into a two-day epic. Sure, there are tremendous problems (see p132), but the vast majority of this continent's 30 million sq km are trouble-free, relaxed and safe, and Africans are, by and large, hospitable, ceaselessly cheerful and gregarious (traits that are certainly not dependent on material wealth).

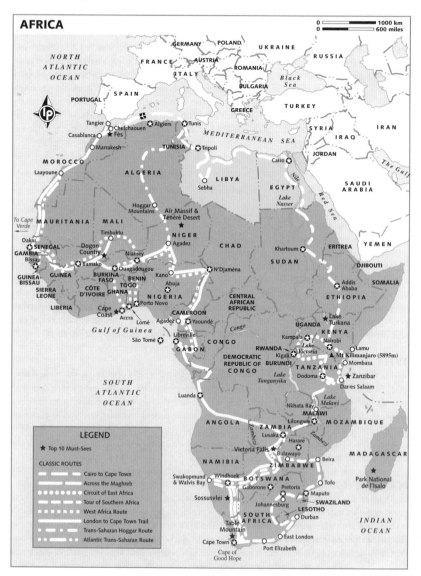

Remains of the world's oldest empires are found in northeast Africa, and great civilisations rose and fell across the continent while Britons were still scrabbling around in the mud. For the most part, physical remains are rare, with this great history manifesting itself more readily in a diverse range of evolving cultures and tribal identities, through music, poetry and the traditions of everyday life – Africa is a great place to people-watch. West Africa, home to over half the continent's people, is culturally and musically rich (the capitals of Senegal and Mali are positively jumping). British Africa virgins who speak little French often overlook West Africa, but this is a huge mistake.

You'll be begging to get off the bus and explore the wild geography of Africa. The Aïr Massif and Ténéré Desert in Niger (connected by charter flights from France), Victoria Falls, Namibia's Skeleton Coast (lined with shipwrecks) and the Great Rift Valley attract herds of tourists, and rightly so, but once you've drunk your fill of those places there are more adventurous options. What about the tropical islands of Guinea Bissau (West Africa); the highlands and monasteries of Ethiopia; Togo; or the remote national parks of northeast Zambia?

As you'll soon find out, things are done differently in Africa. Occasionally the simplest tasks can take an age, and gappers in Africa certainly need time. It's not as cheap as you'd think to travel in this continent, and sadly a few countries are out of bounds (see p132) unless you work for Médecins Sans Frontières. But in Africa there are always signs of hope, even if the leaders of some countries seem intent to flush their people's future down the toilet. Sierra Leone, Mozambique and Rwanda, all recent war zones, are now seeing a steady flow of backpackers. Africa is the sort of place where opportunities and surprises wait around every corner.

WHAT TO DO?

Many gappers undertake a little pre-planned voluntary work and then travel. A few folks just wing it and pick up voluntary work if the opportunity arises and it fits in with their travels. Many travellers simply jump in with both feet and spend a year exploring the vast continent; huge overland challenges (dozens of companies run overland truck tours; see p128) and remarkable, remote regions await the bold and adventurous.

What's for sure is that Africa is the don in terms of the volume and variety of volunteer opportunities. All sorts of organisations offer gap placements in Africa, many of which focus on health, education, teaching English and social-development projects. Prepaid gap placements are very common. You could find yourself a placement as a self-supporting volunteer with a local voluntary organisation or international non-governmental organisation (NGO). You should make enquires and arrangements well in advance. Approaching schools directly could save you money, but do your homework. Major humanitarian disasters do attract more adventurous volunteers, but paid work is rare, specialists are often required and locals are obviously employed in preference to foreigners.

You have, alas, little chance of finding paid work in Africa to subsidise your gap year, but there are a few opportunities. See Part III for more information on overseas jobs, volunteer work and courses.

Get Active

Possibilities abound for the active gapper. Activities can be arranged by local companies or by hiring individual guides.

TREKKING & CLIMBING

The desire to get away from Africa's noisy, vibrant and often chaotic towns and cities hits all gappers. There is no better way to do this than to take off on foot. For some gappers trekking becomes the focus of their trip (how many of Africa's 3000m-plus peaks can you conquer?), and no wonder. From the Drakensberg and Transkei in South Africa to the Atlas Mountains in Morocco there are many fabulous trekking regions, and who in walking boots could resist the magical allure of Uganda's 'Mountains of the Moon'? Mt Kilimanjaro (5895m), the continent's highest peak, is a tremendous challenge, but more often than not trekking in Africa is more than just peak bagging. Places like the Fouta Djalon Highlands (Guinea), animist Dogon Country (Mali), and the Fish River Canyon and Namib-Naukluft National Parks (Namibia) offer easy-going trekking. The continent has many curious little corners where you can pick up a guide, shoulder a pack, and walk through beautiful countryside and meet, and learn about, local people on their own terms. Donkeys, horses or camels will extend your range (or could be your sole means of transport if you're feeling truly adventurous) and in many places (eg the fringes of the Sahara) organised treks using beasts of burden are possible.

TOP 10 MUST-SEES

Victoria Falls (Zambia & Zimbabwe) Stunning scenery and some seriously adventurous white-water rafting.
Table Mountain (South Africa) A magnificent site above a magnificent city.
Aïr Massif & Ténéré Desert (Niger) Rock art, camel trains and fabulous Saharan landscapes.
Park National de l'Isalo (Madagascar) Special scenery, trekking and wildlife.
Fès (Morocco) One of the most incredible and complex North African cities.
Sossusvlei (Namibia) Giant red dunes in one of the driest ecosystems on earth.
Dogon Country (Mali) A stunning escarpment forms the backdrop for a unique, animist culture.
Cape Coast (Ghana) The famed colonial fort in this lively town is just one of many along the West African coast.
Zanzibar (Tanzania) The exotic spice island; all winding streets, ancient minarets and paradise beaches.
Lake Turkana (Kenya) The stunning, arid and inhospitable cradle of mankind.

WILDLIFE WATCHING

Going on safari (Swahili for 'journey') is undoubtedly an African highlight for many a gapper. East and southern Africa have the highest density of the 'big five' (buffalos, elephants, lions, leopards and rhinoceroses), showcased in a series of excellent parks. The wildebeest migration (July, August and October) between the Serengeti and Masai Mara reserves on the Tanzanian-Kenyan border is one of the world's great wildlife spectacles. Safaris are possible year-round, but best at the end of the dry season when animals are concentrated around dwindling water sources. At the end of the rains the grass can be just too darn high to see much. Budget camping safaris are easily arranged for £50 a day, but going cheap often means fewer smiles per mile.

Don't focus all your attention on eastern and southern Africa; you can mix it with wildlife across the continent. There's the wondrous weirdness of Madagascar's wildlife; lions in Benin; great white sharks off South Africa; mountain gorillas in Uganda's Bwindi Impenetrable Forest; desert elephants in Burkina Faso and Mali; and chimpanzees in Guinea and Tanzania. And there are wildlife-rich countries you wouldn't immediately think of: Burkina Faso, Cameroon, Ghana, Senegal and the prosperous, stable (but expensive) Gabon, where 11% of the country has been declared national park in the hope it'll become an ecotourism paradise.

Old hands at Africa often get more into Africa's bird life, than its big beasts – great birding spots include Nigeria, Senegal, The Gambia, Ethiopia, Kenya and South Africa. Binoculars are an essential accessory in Africa.

OTHER ACTIVITIES

Arguably Africa's best diving and snorkelling is found in the Red Sea. Charter packages to Egypt are the cheapest way to go (see the Middle East chapter, p137), but nearby Eritrea and Sudan also have some superb reefs (but see Issues on p132). The whole east coast of Africa is peppered with great dive locations (people rave about Mozambique). Bring your own mask and snorkel if you plan on exploring the east coast where local dhow (traditional sailing vessel) captains offer rides to offshore reefs. São Tomé and Príncipe is an expensive place to dive, while the shores of Lake Malawi are cheap.

White-water rafting on the Zambezi River below Victoria Falls (Zambia/Zimbabwe) is simply incredible (it's the hardest commercially run rapid in the world) and you can also raft in Ethiopia, Kenya, Namibia, Swaziland and at the Nile's source in Uganda. The Okavango Delta in Botswana and the Zambezi River in Zambia/Zimbabwe are the ultimate locations for multi-day kayak safaris, while Lake Malawi is a good place for renting canoes. Pole-propelled pirogues (dugout canoes) can give you a taste of local life on the continent's waterways – exploring the thatched huts of Ganvié, perched on stilts above Lake Nokoué in Benin, is a classic experience – and you could always bring your own canoe (buy a flat-pack craft) and paddle the great rivers of Africa at your own pace.

Between April and July there's world-class surfing to be had in South Africa (notably at Jeffrey's Bay) and there are also good breaks in Madagascar, Mozambique, Senegal and Namibia. The Cape Verde Islands and Morocco are emerging as strong windsurfing (and surfing) destinations.

You can ski in Morocco (January–March) and South Africa (mid-May to September); ride horses in Lesotho, Swaziland, Malawi, South Africa, Zambia and Zimbabwe; go deep-sea game fishing around the coast; and mountain-bike across the continent. South Africa is one, big adventure playground.

STRIKING OUT

One of the joys of travelling through the vastness of Africa is exploring off the beaten track. People are often warm and welcoming in these places and it's often much easier to connect with local people and get a proper insight to a country. Africa is a fantastic place for an expedition (there's just so much wilderness to choose from) and it's relatively easy to join a Saharan camel caravan leaving from Timbuktu (Mali) or Agadez (Niger), to reach the source of the Niger River (Guinea/Sierra Leone), or to retrace the first, struggling footsteps of European explorers.

If that sounds a bit much, simply look into places covered sparsely (or not covered at all) by your guidebook. Think northern Mozambique, eastern Zambia and the back roads of Transkei (South Africa) rather than the big backpacker draws. How about tackling a country like Chad, Eritrea or Togo – places that would never get on BBC1's *Holiday* program?

HANGING OUT

Africa is not the coin-op party paradise that Australia is, but there are a few hangouts dotted around the continent (often on the coasts) where travellers seem to congregate, kickback and let the good times roll. You'll rarely be short of a buddy or two in the following spots:

Cape Maclear & Nkhata Bay (Malawi) Classic, bleary, 'beach' hangouts.

Casamance (Senegal) Beach-side chill outs a plenty.

Chefchaouen (Morocco) Chilled-out town where weeks pass unnoticed.

Cintsa (South Africa) You can be as active, or inactive, as you like at Buccaneers Backpackers.

Kokrobite (Ghana) Great seafood, palm-fringed beaches and drumming lessons.

Lamu (Kenya) Unique, historic, small-scale Swahili island.

Swakopmund (Namibia) Desert 'n' coast party town for adrenalin junkies.

Tofo (Mozambique) Surf, dive, relax and party.

You can add to this list classic party capitals such as Dakar (Senegal; arguably top of the pops for African live music), Bamako (Mali), Maputo (Mozambique), Kampala (Uganda), Kigali (Rwanda) and Cape Town (South Africa). But of course, in Africa parties often find you.

Work a Little

For those without specialist skills and training, getting paid work in Africa is hard, and usually you'll need to spend a lot of time chatting up the expat community. A few travellers get lucky and land tourist-industry jobs (tour guiding, bar work, etc) in eastern and southern Africa's Western-orientated backpacker destinations, but don't expect great (if any) wages. Travellers with a degree can sometimes get teaching work, most commonly in private schools.

Travel Around

Travelling around much of Africa is simply a matter of catching a bus or shared taxi between villages, towns and cities. In remote country, transport is more circumspect and unreliable. Time, patience and stamina are needed for travel around Africa. Roads (many of which are dirt or fractured tarmac) can be truly terrible, especially during the rainy season. Vehicles can be unreliable and uncomfortable, especially on remote routes, and apart from the most expensive buses (intercity services are usually the most together) vehicles are often fully packed with people, goods and livestock. Bus stations, too, can be chaotic and taxing places. Buses, minibuses, pick-up trucks and shared taxis (often Peugeot 505s following fixed routes to no set timetable) all serve as road transport. In rough, remote areas flatbed trucks converted to carry passengers are used, though you may find yourself at the roadside effectively hitchhiking.

Many of the traits displayed by road transportation also apply to African train travel, which can be crowded and run very, very late. Security is occasionally a problem. That said, train travel can be a wonderful way to get around Africa, and some journeys are simply stunning (see p128); the landscapes alone are worth the fare.

Think about travelling by train from Dakar (Senegal) to Bamako (Mali), Nairobi to Mombasa (Kenya) and Harare (Zimbabwe) to Pretoria (South Africa) via Victoria Falls (a great trip in itself).

Old ferries ply routes on Lakes Malawi, Tanganyika and Victoria in East Africa, and Lakes Volta (Ghana) and Nasser (Sudan-Egypt). Liberally mixed cargos of people and goods move along The Gambia, Niger and Senegal Rivers in West Africa, plus the Nile (Egypt) and Congo (in the Democratic Republic of Congo and Congo), in barges, ferries and traditional wooden vessels. Big ferries and freighters operate along some sections of West Africa's coast but only Tanzania has a coastal ferry service. You'll struggle to catch a freighter along the east coast, but dhows can be caught for short coastal hops or to get to outlying islands.

The ferry trip up Lake Malawi (taking in Chizumulu and Likoma Islands) is a classic African travel experience, as is gliding up the Niger River to legendary Timbuktu (Mali).

Africa's internal air network is pretty comprehensive, can save time and hardship and has a better safety record than it used to. Some airlines (like South African, Ethiopian and Air Kenya) are first-class operations; others are about as reliable as a chocolate fireguard. Check flight details carefully but be prepared for delays, cancellations and bureaucratic pantomimes.

The transport infrastructure of southern and northern Africa is the best, and going third class is usually an 'experience'. Little of the transport would pass a safety inspection in Europe and most only *sometimes* leaves/arrives roughly on time, but the trick to coping with African transport is not to fight against it. Let go, accept the odd chaotic journey, bond with your fellow passengers (sharing your food is a good idea) and enjoy the ride.

CLASSIC ROUTES
Cairo to Cape Town & Circuit of East Africa
Cairo (Egypt) to Cape Town (South Africa), via Botswana and Namibia, is a classic overland trail, though most travellers cut out the tricky (but highly rewarding!) first bit and start in Nairobi (Kenya). A good bolt-on is a circuit of East Africa (Kenya, Uganda, Rwanda and Tanzania), and some folks tackle the adventurous Tanzania-Mozambique border to cross into northern Mozambique and skip down the India Ocean coast to South Africa.

Tour of Southern Africa
Many gappers tour South Africa, Botswana and Namibia as part of one trip (countries packed with possibilities for adventurous activities), but you could easily add Zambia, Zimbabwe and Mozambique to this cluster.

Across the Maghreb
A continuous trip across the Maghreb (North Africa) is scuppered by the continued closure of the Morocco-Algeria border (see p132). Nevertheless, it's highly recommended, and you can start with the ancient glories of Egypt and Libya (see the Middle East chapter, p137), move into Tunisia, hit Algeria (with a trip south to the Hoggar Mountains) and then fly to the marvels of Morocco.

Tour of West Africa
French-speaking West Africa offers some fantastic travelling. Start in Senegal and head southeast, avoiding Côte d'Ivoire, but not skimping on the magic of Mali or the remarkable cultures of Togo and Benin. English-speaking Ghana is a common finishing point, but consider crossing Nigeria then continuing to Cameroon and Gabon.

London to Cape Town Trail
Transcontinental routes are regularly upset by African conflicts. War in Darfur (on the Chad–Sudan border) has blocked the difficult (but once popular) link to East Africa for those travelling from Morocco and West Africa on the London to Cape Town trail. This route gave gappers a comprehensive slice of Africa, but adventurous overland truck companies (see p134) have not given up and are already blazing an Atlantic coast trail that runs south through Congo, the Democratic Republic of Congo, Angola and Gabon and then cuts into Zambia (taking seven months, all in all). When one door closes in Africa another often opens, but it has to be said that despite various peace agreements the volatility of some of these countries can't be underestimated (see p132), and travel is likely to be very difficult even with your own vehicle.

Travelling from extreme north to south across Africa (Cap Blanc in Tunisia to Cape Agulhas in South Africa) is an easier overland challenge – take the Italian ferry to Tunisia and cross Libya to join the classic Cairo to Cape Town route.

Trans-Saharan Hoggar Route & Atlantic Trans-Saharan Route
There are several adventurous trans-Saharan 4WD routes linking North and West Africa. The classic *piste* (desert trail) leads through the Hoggar Mountains of southern Algeria to the excellent desert town of Agadez, Niger (see p132 for information on security concerns). If that seems all too much, take note: the popular Atlantic trans-Saharan route (which follows the coast from Morocco to Senegal) *should* be sealed by the end of 2005, creating a network of tarmac roads stretching from Nigeria to Europe. This gives gappers the amazing possibility of taking a 2WD vehicle to explore Africa!

WHEN TO GO?

The equator cuts through the middle of Africa and the continent enjoys a huge variety of climates, so there's never a bad time to visit – the weather is always perfect somewhere. The British winter is a great time to visit the fringes of the Sahara or to enjoy the warm summer days of southern Africa. And when it's spring in the UK, North Africa's usually arid lands are green and fresh. When it's winter or early spring in Britain, conditions are ideal for coastal West and East Africa. Transcontinental trips are best begun in October/November.

Climate

The rains in West Africa begin between March and June and finish between September and October – their exact timing is influenced by distance from the coast. Temperatures are generally higher just before the torrential downpours begin.

North Africa has seasons similar to southern Europe, but summer is terribly hot, even in the High Atlas. Winters can be cold, grey and nasty.

In East Africa the 'long rains' occur between March and May, while the 'short rains' are between October and December. June and July are the coolest months, with temperatures and rainfall varying less along the coast. The best time to visit is between June and October. From November to March northern and eastern Madagascar get nailed by the occasional cyclone (which can cause problems in Mozambique) and some hot, very wet weather – visit between April and October.

The southern African summer (that's November to March) is hot and wet, while winter can be surprisingly cold. Not all areas experience spring, and a reverse of Britain's four-season pattern is most pronounced in South Africa.

Festivals

Festivals take place across the continent and almost every nation hosts a handful of religious and cultural events. Here are some of the highlights:

Leddet & Timkat (Ethiopia) The Ethiopian Christian Orthodox festivals are celebrated in grand style in Gondar. They mark the birth and baptism of Jesus on 7 and 19 January respectively.

Festival Pan-Africain du Cinema (Fespaco or Pan-African Film Festival; Burkina Faso; www.fespaco.bf) This festival is held over nine days in Ougadougou during late February/early March in odd-numbered years. Fespaco's Oscar equivalent is the Étalon de Yennenga.

Dogon festivals (Mali) Agguet, Ondonfile and Boulo (the rain-welcoming festival) include complex masked dances and take place in April and May. The Sigui takes place roughly every 60 years in Dogon Country, depending on the position of the star known as Sirius.

Grahamstown Festival (South Africa) A 10-day celebration of arts and crafts with an associated fringe festival in June/July.

Festival of the Dhow Countries (Zanzibar; www.ziff.or.tz) East Africa's largest cultural event showcases the film, literature, music, culture and art of coastal countries and is held in July. Numerous open-air gigs make it quite a party.

Maralal International Camel Derby (Kenya; www.yaresafaris.com/camelderby.htm) Held in August/September, this raucous event is held in the 'wild west' of northern Kenya. Anyone can enter and there's a cycle race too.

Umhlanga (Reed Dance; Swaziland) This is a week-long debutante ball for marriageable young women held in August/September. The reed dance, when reeds are presented to the Swazi queen mother, is the finale.

/Ae//Gams Arts & Cultural Festival (Namibia; www.windhoekcc.org.na) Windhoek's extravaganza of music, dance and ethnic dress takes place in September.

Cure Salée (Niger) Held in late September, the most famous version of this celebration is the Gerewol festival, which includes the male beauty contest of the Woodaabé people (Fula cattle herders).

Odwira (Ghana) Held in Kumasi, this is a huge Ashanti purification festival taking place in the ninth month (or Adae) of the Ashanti calendar (usually December or January).

Islamic festivals (see the Middle East chapter, p137, for details) are widely celebrated in the north, west and coastal regions of East Africa. The end of Ramadan and Eid al-Adha are celebrated big style in Foumban (Cameroon) – expect horse racing and all-night parties. Christian festivals are common elsewhere in Africa.

WHAT TO EXPECT?
Travellers
Africa attracts a huge cross section of nationalities, though French-speaking nationals are more prevalent in West and northwest Africa (where French is an official language). East and southern Africa's huge tourist profile ensures the widest variety (and number) of nationalities, including the most English-speakers.

Morocco gives many gappers their first taste of Africa (if you can survive getting off the ferry in Tangier you can survive anything), but post-apartheid South Africa has seen a huge surge in visitors, many of them new to Africa. It's probably true that East and southern Africa make quite an easy introduction to Africa (certainly more so than rocking up in Lagos, or certain central African nations). English is spoken and the infrastructure is better than elsewhere.

Locals
By and large, Africans are easy-going and polite. Good manners are respected and many people will think you most rude if you do not say hello and inquire after their health before asking them when the bus is going to leave. In some African societies greetings can go on for minutes. Elders in African societies receive a good deal of respect, so try to find an elder and introduce yourself when entering small communities or when asking permission for anything in remote areas.

Hospitality to travellers is common – occasionally it's overwhelming – but in a few (and this is an exception rather than the rule) tourist hot spots hospitality sometimes comes with a catch and travellers are exploited for income rather then genuine friendship.

It's hard to generalise about appropriate behaviour, given Africa's diversity of cultures. Certainly traditional cultural values remain strong and vibrant across the continent, even when they are masked with a veneer of Westernisation or Christianity/Islam. It's common in Kenya to see a Masai *moran* (warrior) dressed in trousers and shirt in town and then in traditional Masai garb once he's home.

Africans are generally conservative in their outlook. It's inappropriate to wear revealing clothes and display affection in public. There are few queues in Africa, just scrums, and people (many of whom are used to sleeping eight to a room) have a different perception of personal space. Travellers in some remote areas are treated pretty much as curiosities and their habits and dress are often a source of considerable amusement.

Language
Africa is a place of, quite literally, thousands of languages, but happily for gappers English is widely spoken except in swaths of West and northwest Africa where French is the most common second language. Portuguese is good for Angola, Mozambique and São Tomé & Príncipe, while Swahili is the trading language of East Africa, just as Hausa is in West Africa and Arabic in North Africa. Creole (a mixture of West African and European languages) is spoken on the coast of West Africa.

See p420 for information on language courses and p134 for information on Lonely Planet's Africa phrasebooks.

Health Risks

All the great world diseases are found in Africa. Malaria is a problem from the southern fringes of the Sahara down to the South African border. Yellow fever is a problem across a similar area but not endemic south of Namibia and Zambia – you'll need to show a Yellow Fever Vaccination Certificate when applying for some visas. It's impossible to overstate the disaster wrought by HIV/AIDS in sub-Saharan Africa. Infection rates of over 20% of the adult population aren't uncommon in southern Africa and there are an estimated 8000 new infections per day, the huge majority from heterosexual intercourse (see www.unaids. org for more information).

Schistosomiasis (bilharziasis) is sadly present in many beautiful (and inviting) lakes and waterways, including the ever-popular Lake Malawi. The risk to tourists is pretty low, but if you do get wet (especially after tramping through standing water on reedy shorelines) dry off quickly and dry your clothes well.

Dirty water is a common source of infection, but tap water is safe in many countries. Bring water purification equipment – bottled water is expensive and the bottles are a pollution problem.

Consult the Health chapter (p59) and seek professional medical advice for more travel health information.

Time & Flight Time

Four time zones cover Africa, starting with Greenwich Mean Time (GMT) in the far west of the continent.

Casablanca is just a short hop away from London (3½ hours flying time). Cairo is a little further (five hours), and Nairobi (eight hours) and Cape Town (11½ hours) are long hauls.

Issues

Crossing between countries in Africa is relatively easy and usually straightforward, especially in the most popular and stable countries. West African borders are generally okay, but some frontiers and remote borders, as well as at government roadblocks in rarely visited countries, all kinds of bureaucratic obstacles and hassle can be thrown your way, along with demands for 'fines'. At other borders you'll receive nothing but welcome and curiosity.

Corruption is common in Africa, where leaders have looted billions of dollars, further impoverishing their people. Dangerous and tricky regions include the fringes of the Sahara, central Sierra Leone, Côte d'Ivoire, Liberia, parts of Nigeria, northern Algeria, northern Chad and eastern/southern Sudan, the Central African Republic, Congo, the Democratic Republic of Congo, and Somalia. Rebel activity continues in parts of Burundi, Rwanda and Uganda; there are pockets of banditry and general looseness in northern Kenya and southern Ethiopia, plus eastern Eritrea – travel permits are required here, in Sudan and Libya. Normally safe and stable countries bordering the above states occasionally import problems. Sierra Leone and Angola are getting better, but there are huge problems with unexploded ordnance and banditry.

Zimbabwe, once a fantastic travel destination, is beset by political and social unrest and commodity shortages. However, travellers have not been targeted and some parts are still attracting tourists. Check the situation carefully before travelling.

For further information on travel hotspots, general safety issues and governmental travel advice see the Safety chapter (p79).

Internet & Communications

Cheap internet cafés are available in major towns and cities from Transkei to Timbuktu. Connections vary in speed and quality but almost all allow you to access web-based email servers such as Yahoo! and Hotmail.

Mobile phone technology is changing telecommunications in Africa. Unreliable land-line networks are being usurped by affordable pay-as-you-go mobile services in countries from Morocco to Uganda, so buying a SIM card and/or mobile phone can be a good idea if you're spending a long time in one country. Using your UK mobile in Africa will cost a fortune.

DAILY SPEND

Compared with most of the developing world Africa is expensive. Budget travellers can scrape around for £10 per day but for a degree of luxury, like a toilet in your room (although this can be a mixed blessing), you're looking at £20. Cities are obviously more expensive than the sticks and some countries (such as Zambia) have a policy of low-impact, high-cost tourism. Accommodation in national parks commonly costs over £80 per person per night. The actual cost of living (food, transport etc) varies only a little around the continent (North, East and southern Africa are the most expensive) but some things are better value in some countries than in others – for example, accommodation in Mozambique and Mali is poor value.

Travellers commonly blow big chunks of their wedge on car/4WD hire (£60 per day on average), internal flights and partying. Try to save some cash for some of the following: going on safari; taking a course in Swahili, Hausa or another useful African language; camel trekking; doing a PADI open-water dive course; climbing a big impressive mountain; quad-biking; taking a 4WD desert trip; sailing; or learning to surf. Of course, you could get to Africa and buy yourself a cheap motorbike, camel, donkey or dhow to get around!

GETTING THERE

You could hitch to Africa or even take the train via Spain. Driving down the continent via Morocco, Tunisia or Egypt is a fantastic experience, but most travellers pick up a cheap airfare and head straight into the heart of Africa.

Air

The UK has air connections with almost all African countries, some directly, others via a European hub. The main gateway into East Africa is Nairobi, though Dar es Salaam (Tanzania) is also busy. Johannesburg is by far the busiest hub in southern Africa but there's also plenty of traffic into Cape Town (South Africa). In West Africa, Accra (Ghana) and Lagos (Nigeria) are the busiest gateways but considerable traffic heads into Dakar (Senegal) as well. Casablanca (Morocco) and Cairo (Egypt) are the busiest gateways in North Africa.

Many major European airlines offer open-jaw tickets that allow you to fly into, say, Cairo and out of Nairobi, Harare or Cape Town. Air France even allows gappers attempting one the world's great overland journeys to fly into Dakar and out of Cape Town! Shorter overland routes include flying into Dakar and out of Ouagadougou (Burkina Faso) or Accra, and into Nairobi and out of Harare, Cape Town or Johannesburg.

Africa features on a few round-the-world (RTW) tickets. Nairobi and Johannesburg are the usual options. Sadly, putting Africa onto your ticket can cut down options elsewhere (Australia is often the only next available destination).

Air France has some of the best connections to French-speaking West and Central Africa but SN Brussels Airlines provides stiff competition. British Airways (BA) has good connections across Africa and offers some flexibility, though not always the cheapest fares. KLM has a huge African network and cheap fares. Lufthansa, Ethiopian Airlines, South African Airways and Kenya Airways are all good bets for flights to Africa.

TICKET COSTS
The best available student/under-26 fares are quoted here. See the Passports, Visas, Tickets & Insurance chapter (p19) for more information on how to get the best, most flexible deal.

For around £250 you can get a return flight to Cairo or Casablanca, while flights into Dakar, Cape Town and Nairobi should cost around £450. Return flights into places such as Douala (Cameroon) cost between £650 and £900.

A standard open-jaw ticket into Nairobi and out of Johannesburg should cost around £550, while anything using Cairo is often around £100 cheaper. Into Dakar and out of Cape Town costs around £650.

It's sometimes possible to pick up cheap charter flights (and some one-way fares) into Morocco, The Gambia, Kenya and airports across Egypt. If you can get to Paris first, cheap, one-way charter flights into Saharan West Africa are possible during winter (see p134).

Sea & Overland
The days of working your way to Africa aboard a cargo ship are, alas, over, but ferries link Spain and France with Morocco, France with Algeria and Tunisia, Italy with Tunisia, Malta with Libya, and Egypt with Jordan and Saudi Arabia (which also has a ferry to Sudan and Eritrea).

The only land access is across the Sinai from Israel to Egypt (cross at the Taba–Eilat boarder post and not at Rafah in the troubled Gaza Strip).

Specialist Tour Operators
Dozens of tour operators run trips in Africa. Region-specific operators include:
African Trails (☎ 01772 330907; www.africantrails.co.uk; sales@africantrails.co.uk; fax 01772 628281) Offers truck tours through East Africa plus a trans-African route.
Point Afrique (☎ 00 33 4 75 97 20 40; www.point-afrique.com) Offers cheap charter flights to, and French-speaking tours around, Saharan West Africa.
Truck Africa (☎ 01772 462638; www.truckafrica.com; sales@truckafrica.com) Runs overland-truck safaris from London to Cape Town and shorter tours around East Africa.

AFRICA & BEYOND
From Cape Town at the bottom of the continent, flying is your only option and there are occasionally good deals to Australia, India and South America. If you're doing it the other way around then it's easy to continue (by bus) into the Middle East before heading east into Asia or northeast towards Russia. You could also go by rail through China or Europe. Cheap flights to India are often found in Nairobi and Dar es Salaam.

FURTHER INFORMATION
Reading Material
Useful Lonely Planet guides include *Africa on a shoestring*, *Healthy Travel Africa* and regional guides to southern, eastern and western Africa. There are also over a dozen individual country guides, as well as *Trekking in East Africa*, *Watching Wildlife: East Africa* and phrasebooks to *Moroccan Arabic*, *Swahili* and the complex *Ethiopian Amharic* language.

A History of Africa, by JD Fage, is comprehensive and digestible. *Africa: Dispatches from a Fragile Continent*, by Blaine Harden, is insightful and critical, while Michela Wrong's *In the Footsteps of Mr Kurtz* tells the long, sorry tale of Mobutu's reign in the Democratic Republic of Congo (formerly Zaïre). *My Traitor's Heart* is the excellent autobiography of Rian Malan, an Afrikaner in the 'new' South Africa.

Paul Theroux weaves pessimism and anger into a trans-African tale in *Dark Star Safari* while *Travels in West Africa*, by Mary Kingsley, is a remarkable account of a woman's travels in 19th-century West Africa. It's worth reading anything by Wilfred Thesiger for an insight into adventuring in colonial and post-colonial Africa, while *Shadows Across the Sahara* tells the tale of John Hare's remarkable trans-Saharan camel trek.

For African literature check out *Africa: A Traveller's Literary Companion* by Oona Strathern. Nigerian authors are big in the African literature scene, and many use African folklore in their novels – check out *The Palm Wine Drunkard* by Amos Tutuola and the classic *Things Fall Apart* by Chinua Achebe.

Africa by Road, by Bob Swain and Paula Snyder, and *Sahara Overland*, by Chris Scott, are invaluable reading for those driving around the continent.

The New African is probably the best magazine for politics and economics, although *Focus on Africa* is not far behind and is better on culture. *Africa Today* can also be recommended. *Travel Africa* is a quarterly subscription magazine with great up-to-date travel information.

Useful Information Sources

For specific country overviews, the lowdown on travel in the region and hundreds of useful links, head to Lonely Planet's website (www.lonelyplanet.com).

For African news and background www.bbc.co.uk, www.newsafrica.net and www.all africa.com, http://afrika.no and www.justiceafrica.org (which campaigns for human rights in Africa) are all good starting points. Many universities have enormous African academic resources. Stanford University (http://library.stanford.edu/depts/ssrg/africa/guide.html) and the University of London's **School of Oriental and African Studies** (SOAS; ☎ 020 7637 2388; www .soas.ac.uk; Thornhaugh St, Russell Square, London WC1H 0XG) are just two. The later has an incredible library you can access (students get discounted entry and the catalogue can be searched online) and numerous events/talks are held at the school. Also take a look at the **Africa Centre** (☎ 020 7836 1973; www.africacentre.org.uk; 38 King St, Covent Garden, London WC2E), which is a cultural centre, gig venue and education resource for all things African. It also houses the African Book Centre.

BEEN THERE, DONE THAT

When I made the short journey across the Rovuma River and into northern Mozambique in a dugout canoe I felt like a trailblazer. This is what I'd come to Africa for – crossing remote, slightly sketchy borders and exploring countries well off the beaten track (Mozambique had been at war 18 months earlier). A rotting hippo carcass and a couple of backpackers coming the other way didn't dampen my spirits and, passport stamped (in a mud hut), I boarded a beaten up Land Rover and sped towards the coast.

I had known my journey south from Dar es Salaam was going to be bad when my bus window fell out in the city's bus station just as the heavens opened. It was 32 hours later before I reached Mtwara, the border town. 'Recovering' in a ramshackle bar, I was befriended by a bunch of second-hand clothing dealers, and, bemused by my ramblings about white-sand beaches and 'undiscovered' northern Mozambique, they helped me reach the remote border trail.

Pangane fulfilled my wildest dreams. The village was built amongst coconut palms on a long, sandy spit that arched out from the mainland. Coral reefs were visible below the warm turquoise sea, and fishing dhows lined the shore. At the spit's narrowest point sat Gondwana Lodge, property of Gavin – a South African travel buddy who had drunkenly sold me the idea of his slice of paradise some months before. I was in paradise, the ninth person to visit the lodge (though Gavin was in Johannesburg).

I fell in love with the place and the days flew by. I remember doing quite a lot of snorkelling, wandering about the village trying to buy beer and local biscuits, and catching a dhow out to a tiny off-shore coral island where the remains of a 16th-century Portuguese fort stood. Although the region had been isolated and improvised, my corner of Mozambique seemed untouched by war. Nowhere in Africa have I had such a warm, local welcome or enjoyed such an exciting, guidebook-free travel experience. I never wanted to see the beaten track again.

Matt Fletcher

THE MIDDLE EAST

ANTHONY HAM

Anthony Ham's gap year started with a one-way ticket to Bang-kok and ended with a motorcycle accident in Turkey. En route, he experienced a life-changing moment of clarity while sitting on the running boards of a Thai train and decided to become a writer. He also fell irretrievably in love with Damascus. He now lives in Madrid and has a master's degree in Middle Eastern politics under his belt. He keeps returning to the Arab world whenever he can and has written Lonely Planet's Libya *and* Saudi Arabia *guides and contributed to, among others,* Jordan, Iran *and* Middle East.

INTRODUCTION

The Middle East, where Africa, Asia and Europe meet, is the place to let your imagination roam free. Across the region, the great civilisations have left their mark in an astonishing open-air museum of ancient cities and historic buildings carved from a remarkable landscape. This is a land once home to the Seven Wonders of the World and it was the birthplace of the three great monotheistic religions – Judaism, Christianity and Islam – which remain at the forefront of everyday life. It all adds up to a rich tapestry of cultures, an intriguing modern story and one of the few places on earth where the ancient world lives and breathes.

The Middle East stretches from the Sahara Desert in Libya to the peaks of Central Asia in Iran (ancient Persia). Within its boundaries fall Egypt, Jordan, Israel & the Palestinian Territories, Lebanon, Syria, Iraq and the countries of the Arabian Peninsula. In this book, Turkey is covered in the Europe chapter.

WHY THE MIDDLE EAST?

Quite simply, the Middle East is an extraordinary place.

The region's landscapes of surprising natural beauty serve as landmarks to the great moments in history. From the summit of Mt Sinai and across the Red Sea to the hills of Jordan, Moses – a prophet in all three religions – left a trail of religious signposts that still resonate with the faithful. It was amid the shifting sand dunes and palm-fringed oases of Arabia that Islam was born. And from Damascus, down through Wadi Rum (Jordan) and then deep into the Arabian Peninsula, one of history's most controversial figures, Lawrence of Arabia, would write the story that would become legend.

Many of the great cities of antiquity – Cairo (Egypt), Damascus (Syria), Baghdad (Iraq) and Jerusalem (Israel & the Palestinian Territories) – are also to be found here, now transformed into fascinating modern metropolises. And then there are the ancient monuments – those of Egypt and Petra (Jordan) among them – which are among the world's top attractions.

However, so overwhelming is the rich historical heritage of the region and the bad press that many of its countries receive that many would-be travellers overlook the Middle East's greatest treasure: its people. Whether you meet them in bazaars evocative of *A Thousand*

and One Nights, or challenge them to a game of backgammon in the teahouses that are a regional institution, their welcome and adherence to the ancient tradition of hospitality will live long in your memory.

Tourism across the region is diverse. The United Arab Emirates (UAE) is an exotic and upmarket travel destination with lavish, state-of-the-art hotels. It fuses 21st-century sophistication with roots planted deeply in the desert soil. Jordan, Egypt and Israel are the most geared up for tourists, while Iraq and Saudi Arabia remain largely off-limits to travellers.

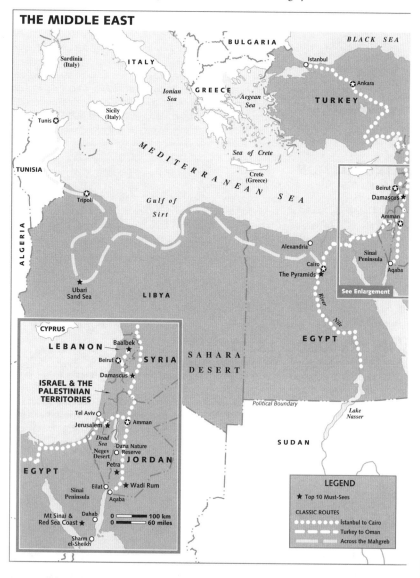

THE MIDDLE EAST

- BULGARIA
- BLACK SEA
- Sardinia (Italy)
- ITALY
- Istanbul
- Ankara
- Ionian Sea
- GREECE
- Aegean Sea
- TURKEY
- Tunis
- Sicily (Italy)
- Sea of Crete
- MEDITERRANEAN SEA
- TUNISIA
- Crete (Greece)
- Beirut
- Damascus ★
- Tripoli
- Gulf of Sirt
- Amman
- ALGERIA
- Alexandria
- Sinai Peninsula
- Aqaba
- Cairo
- The Pyramids ★
- See Enlargement
- Ubari Sand Sea ★
- LIBYA
- River Nile
- CYPRUS
- EGYPT
- LEBANON
- Baalbek ★
- Beirut
- SYRIA
- SAHARA DESERT
- Damascus ★
- ISRAEL & THE PALESTINIAN TERRITORIES
- Tel Aviv
- Jerusalem ★
- Amman
- Political Boundary
- Lake Nasser
- Dead Sea
- Negev Desert
- Dana Nature Reserve
- JORDAN
- SUDAN
- Petra ★
- EGYPT
- Eilat
- ★ Wadi Rum
- Sinai Peninsula
- Aqaba
- Mt Sinai & Red Sea Coast ★
- Dahab
- 0 — 100 km
- 0 — 60 miles
- Sharm el-Sheikh

LEGEND
- ★ Top 10 Must-Sees
- CLASSIC ROUTES
- ○○○○ Istanbul to Cairo
- - - - Turkey to Oman
- ─ ─ Across the Mahgreb

Accommodation along the Gulf coast can be fiercely expensive, but further west, from Syria south to Egypt, you'll find hostels that will make your bank manager smile. In Libya, most visas require some sort of tour, which can mean escalating costs, but they're a great way to see this vast country in a compressed period of time.

Travel here is more about experiencing a completely different culture than it is a gap-year cocktail of beaches and all-night partying. Opportunities for partying 'Western style' do exist, particularly in the clubs of Tel Aviv (Israel). Dubai (UAE) can get lively, while Beirut (Lebanon)

has been reborn as a vibrant and cosmopolitan city. Elsewhere, traditional celebrations, majestic deserts, wonderful mountain landscapes and the joy of simply travelling through an ever-changing physical and cultural landscape more than compensate for the absence of nightlife.

One final thing to remember: don't believe everything you read about the Middle East. Yes, there are regions that travellers would be ill-advised to visit. But alongside the sometimes disturbing hard facts is a vast corpus of exaggeration, stereotyping and downright misrepresentation. The region's problems are invariably highly localised, meaning that most countries remain safe to visit.

This is a region for the discerning traveller, for those looking for the real story behind the headline, and for those drawn to places where history is daily being made and where the bridges between ancient and modern civilisations are everywhere evident. If you let the scaremongering put you off, you'll be missing out on the journey of a lifetime.

WHAT TO DO?

Although there are exceptions, the Middle East is the sort of place where you'll keep your CV stashed somewhere safe for a rainy day and get down to the serious business of travelling. For more information on overseas jobs, volunteer work and courses, see Part III of this book.

The Middle East is a full-immersion experience, offering the chance to wander through aromatic bazaars, soak up the silence of the world's greatest deserts or explore the underwater wonders of the Red Sea.

It's easy to get drawn into the web of Middle Eastern history. With so much to see, the only problem is choosing where to start.

TOP 10 MUST-SEES

Petra (Jordan) Spectacular, rose-coloured city hewn from the rock amid stunning scenery.
Wadi Rum (Jordan) Unrivalled desert landscape synonymous with Lawrence of Arabia.
The Pyramids (Egypt) The premier wonder of the ancient world.
Mt Sinai & Red Sea coast (Egypt) Mountain scenery immortalised by Moses and breathtaking underwater geography.
Esfahan (Iran) Blue-tiled evocation of Islam's sublime aesthetic vision.
Damascus (Syria) Evocative old city that travellers never want to leave.
Jerusalem (Israel & Palestinian Territories) Old city at the intersection of Islam, Christianity and Judaism.
Baalbek (Lebanon) Splendid Phoenician and Roman ruins replete with temples to the gods.
San'a (Yemen) Fairytale, labyrinthine 2500-year-old walled city.
Ubari Sand Sea (Libya) Saharan landscape at its best with dunes and palm-fringed lakes.

Get Active
CAMEL TREKKING & 4WD SAFARIS
When most people think of the Middle East, they think of deserts (and with good reason) – the deserts of Wadi Rum (Jordan), Sinai (Egypt), the Sahara (Libya) and the Empty Quarter (Saudi Arabia and Oman) are among the most spectacular on earth. In Egypt and Jordan, travel by camel is the perfect vehicle for desert contemplation. Although camel trekking is also possible in Libya you're more likely to travel by 4WD, which is more expensive but allows you to cover far greater distances. Saudi Arabian and Omani deserts are almost entirely the preserve of 4WD enthusiasts.

CYCLING & MOUNTAIN-BIKING
The Middle East offers some fantastic, if largely undeveloped, opportunities for cyclists and mountain-bikers. Unlike in Europe, you're likely to have many of the trails to yourself.

However, the heat can be a killer (avoid June to September) and you'll need to be pretty self-sufficient as spare parts can be extremely scarce. Mountain-biking is popular in Israel, Jordan and to some extent in Lebanon (eg in the Mt Lebanon Range). Many people particularly enjoy cycling the flatter roads of Syria. One of the highlights of travelling in this way is that locals in more out-of-the-way places will wonder what on earth you're doing – an ideal way to break the ice and meet new friends.

SKIING & SNOWBOARDING

Although snow sports hardly spring to mind when considering the Middle East, there are some places where they're possible. In the 1970s, Beirut was famous for the fact that you could swim in the Mediterranean waters of the Lebanese capital in the morning and then ski on the slopes of Mt Makmal, northeast of Beirut, in the afternoon. This is possible again as Beirut continues to regain its sophisticated soul. A somewhat different, but no less improbable, experience awaits in the Alborz Mountains north of Tehran where Iran's slowly re-emerging middle class takes to the slopes and invites you to join them.

TREKKING, MOUNTAINEERING & CLIMBING

Jordan is a trekkers' and climbers' paradise, most notably in the spectacular landscapes around Wadi Rum, Petra and the precipitous valleys of Dana Nature Reserve. Maktesh Ramon (the world's largest crater) and the canyons and pools of Ein Avdat in Israel's Negev Desert are great trekking areas, but those who don sturdy boots and head to the higher, cooler Upper Galilee and Golan regions of the country will also be amply rewarded.

North of Tehran, it's possible to climb Mt Damavand (5671m), the highest peak in the Middle East. The surrounding Alborz Mountains also offer some marvellous trekking and mountaineering.

Oman is probably the most accessible trekking destination in the southern Arabian Peninsula, with climbing also a possibility. The challenges of reaching the ancient, fortified mountain settlements around Manakhah and Al-Mahwit in Yemen are also well worth the effort.

If your trekking route takes you into the desert, as many trails do, don't even think of setting out from May to September.

WATERSPORTS

The Red Sea – particularly along the Sinai coast of Egypt and the coast of Saudi Arabia (if you can get in) and at Eilat (Israel) and Aqaba (Jordan) – has astonishing world-class coral reefs. Snorkelling and scuba diving is a major tourist industry and everyone from beginners to experienced divers can easily access the best sites; dive courses are available at each of these places. At any Red Sea coast resort worth its salt – from the expensive package-tour resorts of Sharm el-Sheikh (Egypt) to the chilled, backpacker-friendly Dahab (Egypt) – you can also indulge your passion for a variety of watersports from sailing to water-skiing. On Egypt's Sinai coast, Moon Beach is a renowned windsurfing destination. The UAE is also geared up for watersports, though it's more about high-adrenaline jet skis than underwater contemplation. For something completely different, you might want to try your hand at pearl diving in Bahrain.

Work a Little

It's pretty unlikely, nay downright impossible, that gappers will cruise into a tax-free, expat job in the Middle East. Nor will you find volunteer opportunities in abundance.

Job possibilities, such as they are, are limited to teaching English and working in the occasional backpackers hostel (especially Israel) and in the kibbutz or moshav systems (see p279) in Israel. If you have specific vocational skills and considerable professional experience and are prepared to plan months ahead, you may be able to join the massive expat workforce in the Gulf States.

If you're an archaeology buff, joining a dig, especially in Israel and Jordan between May and September, won't feel like work, but volunteer opportunities also require months of advance planning.

For more information about where to start your search for work, see p264 and p363 for details.

Travel Around

Travelling around the Middle East is one of the region's great experiences.

Buses traverse much of the region and do so relatively efficiently. Minibuses and shared taxis, the great workhorses of Middle Eastern roads, tend to be more chaotic and 'local' experiences. Being squeezed into a shared taxi full of Syrians or a minibus clamouring with Egyptians is a great way to meet people. Many minibuses and almost all shared taxis leave when full. On busy routes this can mean departures at regular intervals. If you're heading out to a village on a road to nowhere else, you can expect a long wait (unless, of course, you're willing to pay for the empty seats). Shared taxis and minibuses run to fixed routes and, though a touch more expensive than buses, they're often quicker. In the wealthy Gulf States, expect your shared taxi to be a Mercedes minibus.

Iran, Egypt and Israel all offer comfortable train services, though what you gain in comfort is usually lost in time. There are also rail services connecting Amman (Jordan) with Damascus and Aleppo (Syria), and Tehran (Iran) with Istanbul (Turkey).

Flying can be a good option for long journeys and to skip over Iraq and Saudi Arabia. Emirates and Gulf Air both have extensive regional networks. Iran has domestic flights at prices not much in excess of the equivalent bus fare, while Egypt and Libya also have domestic air services.

There are ferries from Oman and the UAE to Iran and from the UAE to Iraq but surprisingly few other ferry services around the Gulf. Ferries also operate from Egypt to Jordan or Saudi Arabia.

Hitchhiking is never safe and is not recommended. However, if you find yourself stranded, wave your down-turned, flattened palm up and down. A raised thumb is an obscene gesture in the Middle East.

CLASSIC ROUTES

There are three stumbling blocks to overland travel in the Middle East: Iraq, for obvious reasons; Saudi Arabia, thanks to the near impossibility of getting a visa; and Israel, as an Israeli stamp in your passport prevents entry into Iran, Lebanon, Libya, Syria and all Arabian Peninsula states.

Istanbul to Cairo

This itinerary, one of the great overland journeys, enables you to ease your way through Turkey (see p108 for information on Turkey) and make a gentle transition from European to Middle Eastern worlds. Aleppo (Syria) is a wonderful city and from Damascus, a detour to Beirut and Baalbek (Lebanon) is easy and not to be missed. Jordan is compact and rich in sights, offering the chance to float in the Dead Sea and to see the wonders of Petra and

Wadi Rum. You can dip into Israel or sail from Aqaba (Jordan) to Egypt's Sinai Peninsula, where the clamour of incomparable Cairo is not far away – not to mention the sophistication of Alexandria or the antiquities of the Nile Valley (see p128 for the Across the Maghreb route, which continues across Libya to Tunisia). If you're planning to continue from the Middle East to Asia, this route can be done in reverse, by flying to Tunisia (see p123) and then crossing Libya to Egypt to join the trail.

Turkey to Oman
Crossing Turkey's border (the nearest large town in Turkey is Dogubayazit) with Iran takes you down onto the old Silk Road, from which many of the great historical cities – Tabriz, Esfahan, Yazd and Shiraz – survive. From Iran, ferries cross the Gulf to the UAE, from where it's an easy trip across the border to the deserts and tranquil ports of Oman.

WHEN TO GO?
The best times to visit the Middle East are spring and autumn. Summer is way too hot, especially in desert regions and along the Gulf and Red Sea coasts. Winter can bring some surprisingly miserable weather to the northern Middle East – yes, you will need to pack the winter woollies if you're travelling at this time.

You may also want to avoid Ramadan (see Festivals below) when the whole region is on a go-slow – everyone can seem grumpy (as would you be if you hadn't eaten all day) and most restaurants and cafés are closed during daylight hours. This can be especially wearisome in those years when Ramadan falls in summer and the days are long.

Climate
A snapshot of the Middle East's geographical diversity can be seen in its climate. The coasts of the Red Sea, Arabian Sea and the Gulf range from hot to damn hot, often with 70% humidity – strolling through Jeddah or Dubai at 3pm on a July afternoon is not for the faint-hearted. Summer daytime temperatures can exceed 50°C, while in winter 30°C is not uncommon.

The shores of the Mediterranean enjoy a milder, more European climate. Much of Iran and Yemen are above 1000m and, together with highland areas in Lebanon, northern Israel and the Hajar Mountains of Oman, experience very cold winters with snow on some peaks.

Many parts of the Middle East rarely receives more than 100mm of rainfall annually. The notable exceptions are along the Mediterranean coast, southeastern Iran, Yemen and southern Oman. The latter three areas are affected by Indian monsoonal systems from March to May and July to August.

Festivals
Major festivals in the Middle East tend to be religious. The Islamic ones are celebrated according to the Hegira year or Muslim calendar, which is based on the lunar cycle just like the Jewish calendar around which all Jewish religious festivals are based. The Christian or Gregorian calendar is used for secular events across the region and is based on the solar cycle, making it 10 or 11 days longer than the Jewish and Muslim calendars. So when it is 2005 in the UK, it is 5766 in Israel and 1426 in Oman (www.soultospirit.com/calendar/holiday_by_religion.asp lists the dates of many religious festivals). Some of the region's most important festivals include:
Islamic New Year (Ras as-Sana) A family celebration throughout the region.
Eid al-Moulid (Moulid an-Nabi) Commemorates the Prophet Mohammed's birthday with the usual mix of feasting and religious observance.

Ramadan Falls at the end of the ninth month of the Islamic calendar. Muslims fast during daylight hours and eat till they drop after sunset.

Eid al-Fitr Marks the end of Ramadan with a three-day eating extravaganza.

Eid al-Adha The time that Muslims make the Haj pilgrimage to Mecca; again, family feasts are a feature.

Eid al-Kebir (Tabaski) Commemorates Abraham's willingness to sacrifice his son on God's command, and the last-minute substitution of a ram. Rams are admired across the region and then slaughtered before a big feast.

No Ruz (Persian New Year) Celebrated in Iran and occurs around 21 March with much merriment but also massive transport and accommodation problems.

Dubai World Cup The world's richest horse race is held in the UAE at the end of March.

Easter & Christmas Very important times in Israel because of the influx of pilgrims to the holy sites.

Pesah (Passover) Honours the exodus of the Jews from Egypt and lasts a week. All shops in Israel are closed.

Purim (Feast of Lots) One of the happiest of all Jewish festivals, honouring how the Jewish people living in Persia were saved from massacre.

WHAT TO EXPECT?
Travellers

Historic links mean that British travellers are fairly common in the region, but they're joined by plenty of Aussies, Kiwis, French and other Europeans. The more prominent a country's military is in the region (eg US, UK and Australian forces in Iraq), the less likely you are to see travellers from these countries.

Anywhere along, or just off the corridor that runs from Istanbul to Cairo, you'll find more than enough fellow journeyers, especially in Wadi Musa (around Petra in Jordan) and Cairo. Damascus, with its slow pace and abundant hospitality, and Dahab, Egypt's Red Sea magnet for those resting from life on the Middle Eastern road, are two places in particular where travellers always seem to stay longer than they planned.

Locals

The Middle East (Israel aside) is dominated by two very Islamic characteristics: conservative codes of social behaviour and an honouring of guests with boundless hospitality.

The social conservatism can manifest itself in frustrating ways that require careful adherence to local norms. Women tend to take the back seat in public to men in almost all matters and are required to dress conservatively – travellers should opt for baggy, loose-fitting clothes and always keep a headscarf handy. In Saudi Arabia and Iran all women are required to wear Islamic dress. Many Middle Eastern men, fed on a satellite-TV diet of Hollywood movies, see Western women, particularly solo travellers, as creatures of loose morals and are genuinely surprised that you don't want to sleep with them. However, Islamic prohibitions mean that persistent comments are infinitely more likely than physical harassment. In stricter Islamic societies, such as Iran and Saudi Arabia, you may be treated as a second-class citizen but you're probably safer than in Egypt or Israel. It's a far from universal picture, however. You'll see young, mini-skirted Lebanese women rollerblading along the Corniche in Beirut, while in the Tuareg societies of southern Libya it is the men who frequently wear head and face coverings.

Other forms of behaviour to avoid include public displays of affection or using your left hand unless absolutely unavoidable. Saudi Arabia is probably the strictest Muslim country – women are not permitted to drive, and pork, alcohol, cinemas, theatres and Bibles are all banned.

If all of this sounds like a minefield, it is and it isn't. Egypt, Jordan, Syria, Lebanon and Israel are quite liberal societies, at least as they're experienced by travellers. And where cultural and political differences do emerge, they're far more likely to result in an invitation to tea and a good deal of discussion, rather than aggression.

Language

Arabic is the official language everywhere accept Iran and Israel, where Farsi (Persian) and Hebrew, respectively, are spoken. English is widely spoken in the region and some older Syrians and Lebanese still speak a little French as both were former French colonies, but you're well advised to learn a little of the local language (possible in the Middle East; see p416 for information on language courses) if you're travelling off the beaten track.

Health Risks

The Middle East poses few health risks compared with, say, the heart of Africa or deepest Asia. Nevertheless, malaria is endemic in a few rural areas outside Israel, some Gulf States and some of Egypt's desert oases (eg Siwa). Waterborne diseases are also common.

For more information on health matters, see the Health chapter (p59) and seek professional medical advice for more travel health information.

Time & Flight Time

The Middle East is divided into three main time zones. Libya, Egypt, Israel, Jordan, Lebanon and Syria are two hours ahead of Greenwich Mean Time (GMT). Bahrain, Iraq, Kuwait, Qatar, Saudi Arabia and Yemen are three hours ahead of GMT and Oman is four hours ahead. Iran is the odd one out; it's 3½ hours ahead of GMT.

Tel Aviv is a 4¾-hour flight from London, while Tehran is 6½ hours away and Muscat (Oman) is eight hours.

Issues

For further information on travel hotspots, general safety issues and governmental travel advice, see the Safety chapter (p79).

ANTI-WESTERN SENTIMENTS

Hostility towards Western countries, particularly against America, is certainly increasing in the Middle East, largely because of the conflicts in Iraq and the Palestinian Territories (Israel). However, the region remains one of the most hospitable and generous in the world (especially Syria, Jordan and Iran) and most locals will argue vociferously on matters of foreign policy and then invite you home to dinner to continue the discussions over a banquet of mint tea and bountiful food. Be careful with whom and where you talk politics – repression is common in the Middle East and public political dissent can lead to unpleasant consequences for locals.

Acts of terrorism against Western targets in the Middle East are possible and you should always check out the latest security warnings before travelling. We wouldn't recommend a fortnight in Nablus or Gaza (the Palestinian Territories), camping out anywhere near the Iraqi or Afghan borders or a scientific exchange program with Baghdad University (Iraq). Likewise, rambling around the Israel-Lebanon border is not a smart move and you're well advised to stay away from political demonstrations.

BORDER CROSSINGS

The most user-friendly land border is between Turkey and Syria or Iran, provided of course that your papers are in order and you possess the requisite visas. In the east, Iran has land borders with Turkmenistan, Pakistan and (problematically) Afghanistan. To the west, Libya borders Tunisia, with little-used deep-desert frontier outposts with Algeria, Niger and Chad. Egypt also shares a border with Sudan in the south.

PERSONAL SAFETY
Isolated acts of terrorism aside, personal safety is not too much of an issue in the region. You're far less likely to be mugged on the streets of Damascus, Tehran or Tripoli than you are in London.

WOMEN'S RIGHTS
For women travellers, the confronting situation of women in many Middle Eastern countries, when combined with the limitations placed upon your own freedom, will be a recurring theme of your visit. One thing to remember, however, is that the Middle East is not a monolithic block and there are great differences across the region. Even within countries, the situation is rarely black and white. Iran, for example, is renowned for its strict interpretation of Islamic dress codes, yet there are more female than male students in Iranian schools and universities and many Iranian women serve in parliament and play a role in public life. Women travellers will also be uniquely placed to speak to women themselves.

Internet & Communications
The internet is widely accessible throughout the region, even in formerly recidivist states like Syria and Saudi Arabia. In these and other countries (eg Iran) where information is strictly controlled by government censors, many political and other websites are blocked. However, you shouldn't encounter any problems logging on to your Yahoo! or Hotmail account.

Mobile phone networks now cover much of the region. Lebanon and the UAE regularly figure among those countries with the highest number of mobile phones per capita in the world.

DAILY SPEND
Costs vary greatly. The region's surfeit of oil, and government subsidies, mean that transport costs are generally low, while the basic necessities remain quite reasonable. In Syria it's possible to sleep comfortably for around £3.50, but in some parts of the Gulf you can struggle to find anything habitable under £20. The cheapest places are Syria, Egypt and Iran, where you can easily get by on £10-15 per day. In Lebanon, Jordan and Yemen, those on a tight budget can keep below £20-25 without the need for a starvation diet. Israel, Oman, Qatar and the UAE are certainly not budget destinations (allow £30-40 a day). The most expensive place (with arguably the least to see) is Kuwait, where you'll need £45 per day as a bare minimum.

GETTING THERE
You can cycle, drive, fly, get the bus or take the train to the Middle East from Europe.

Air
The region's major air hubs are Cairo, Tel Aviv, Beirut, Dubai and, to a lesser extent, Amman (Jordan). Dubai is a popular stopover on many round-the-world (RTW) tickets.

Many European carriers offer flights to the Middle East. Alitalia (via Rome), British Airways (BA), Olympic Airways (via Athens) and Lufthansa (via Frankfurt) offer some of the cheapest deals, while Gulf Air and Emirates offer competitive prices and have good connections throughout the region.

TICKET COSTS
The best available student/under-26 fares are quoted here. See p19 for more information on how to get the best, most flexible deal.

Return fares to Beirut (£225), Cairo (£230), Tel Aviv (£250) and Dubai (£275) are the cheapest, while Muscat (£415) tends to be the most expensive destination. In these days of no-frills airlines, you may also find cheap deals to the beach resorts along Egypt's Sinai Red Sea coast. The cheapest open-jaw options are those flying into Cairo and out of Dubai (around £280), but fares don't rise too steeply should you want to fly into Amman and out of Tehran (around £350), or a dozen other similar combinations.

Sea & Overland

Ferries to Israel sometimes leave from mainland Greece, Crete and Rhodes. However, these services were suspended at the time of writing. Also, remember that any evidence of time spent in Israel will mean that you will be denied entry to most countries in the Middle East, with Egypt and Jordan the only notable exceptions.

Most overland travellers enter the Middle East at the Turkey-Syria or Pakistan-Iran border; cross-border transport services operate from nearby towns and further afield.

Specialist Tour Operators

Dozens of British tour companies operate trips in the Middle East. Some of the region-specific operators include:

Caravanserai Tours (☎ 020 8855 6373; www.caravanserai-tours.com; info@caravanserai-tours.com; 1–3 Love Lane, Woolwich, London SE18 6QT) Libya specialist.

Magic Carpet Travel (☎ 01344 622832; www.magiccarpettravel.co.uk; info@magiccarpettravel.co.uk; 1 Field House Close, Ascot, Berkshire, SL5 9LT) Specialises in Iran.

Wind, Sand & Stars (☎ 020 7359 7551; www.windsandstars.co.uk; office@windsandstars.co.uk; 6 Tyndale Terrace, London N1 2AT) Expeditions to Egypt's Sinai region, including gap-year itineraries.

The Middle East & Beyond

Standing as it does at the crossroads of three continents, the Middle East can be a launch pad for an epic overland journey. Egypt, and to a lesser extent Libya, enable you to travel south into the heart of Africa and on to Cape Town. The most popular route heads south from Egypt into Sudan. Desert routes from Libya to Algeria, Chad or Niger are strictly for the intrepid and extremely well prepared and aren't always possible. An alternative is the classic Asian overland route, the so-called Hippy Trail, running from Turkey to Iran, the Indian Subcontinent and on to Kathmandu. If you're flying, Dubai is good for cheap deals to the Indian Subcontinent. A final option is to wind your way back home through southern and eastern Europe.

FURTHER INFORMATION
Reading Material

Lonely Planet publishes a single guide to the *Middle East,* a guide to the *Arabian Peninsula,* plus individual guides to many of the countries in the region. There are also *Farsi* (Persian) and *Arabic* phrasebooks.

For a highly readable, balanced overview of the Israel-Palestine issue, *The Arab World: Forty Years of Change,* by Elizabeth Fernea and Robert Warnock, is hard to beat. Similarly essential reading is the encyclopaedic *A History of the Arab Peoples* by Albert Hourani. *A Peace to End All Peace: Creating the Modern Middle East, 1914-1922,* by David Fromkin, is an intriguing account of how the map of the modern Middle East was drawn arbitrarily by European colonial governments.

Pity the Nation: Lebanon at War, by Robert Fisk, is a classic account of the issues that resonate throughout the region. *Mezzoterra,* by the Egyptian writer Ahdaf Soueif, challenges

Western stereotypes about the region, while *Jerusalem: One City, Three Faiths,* by Karen Armstrong, is comprehensive and without prejudice.

The situation for women in the Middle East is nowhere better covered than in Geraldine Brooks' *Nine Parts of Desire,* or *The Hidden Face of Eve: Women in the Arab World* by Egyptian psychiatrist Nawal el-Sadaawi. *Black on Black,* by Ana M Briongos, thoroughly dismantles many prejudices about Iran, while *Gates of Damascus,* by Lieve Joris, delivers a woman's inside look into the Syrian capital.

Lovers of picaresque will devour *Seven Pillars of Wisdom* by TE Lawrence. Wilfred Thesiger's *Arabian Sands,* describing his crossing of the Empty Quarter of Saudi Arabia and Oman, is an all-time classic of desert travel.

And in what could be an emblem for your own journey, William Dalrymple's *From the Holy Mountain* skips lightly across the region's landscape of sacred and profane.

Useful Information Sources

For specific country overviews, the low-down on travel in the region and hundreds of useful links, head to Lonely Planet's website (www.lonelyplanet.com).

The following websites are an excellent way to get information about the Middle East:

Al Mashriq (http://almashriq.hiof.no) Terrific gateway to the cultures of the eastern Mediterranean (Israel, Jordan, Lebanon, Palestine and Syria).

al-bab.com (www.al-bab.com) Encyclopaedic site for all things Arab.

Al Bawaba (www.albawaba.com) Good mix of news, entertainment and Yellow Pages directories.

arab.net (www.arab.net) Comprehensive Middle Eastern site with news, history, culture and useful links.

BEEN THERE, DONE THAT

It had been a difficult day. In the morning, in all innocence, I had wandered into the police station in the Iranian city of Yazd, ready to research how travellers could obtain visa extensions. By virtue of a simple wrong turn, I found myself standing to attention in front of a visibly angry, many-starred general. He closed the door. While my local interpreter and friend stood sweating alongside me, I laid out my questions with a sense of impending doom. The general never took his eyes off me, even when my friend was speaking. And then, while I was in mid-sentence, it came: 'You are under arrest. Your friend will stay here. You will return to your hotel to collect your passport.' It was the longest hour of my life. By the time I returned, the old general had grown bored with his game and passed us on to a colleague (in a room across the hall clearly marked 'visa extensions') who was the epitome of politeness. We were free to leave.

Nonetheless, I nearly jumped through the roof when the phone rang in my hotel room a few hours later. A female voice said: 'I hope you don't mind, but my friend and I are English students and we'd like to practise our English. Can you spend some time with us?' I had been warned not to approach Iranian women because Iran's strict codes of social behaviour forbade such male-female interaction. But I hadn't been told what to do if they approached me. For the remainder of the afternoon, two young Iranian women, dressed in the full-length black chador (Islamic cloak covering the whole body) showed me the sights of Yazd. We stopped at teahouses, they introduced me to their friends, and all the while they chatted about their lives and what it was like to be a woman in Iran. Near the end of this enjoyable but entirely unexpected afternoon, we encountered the father of one of the women. He wasn't happy at this public breach of Iranian protocol. He eyed me suspiciously. Then, although still with some evident misgivings, he smiled benevolently at his daughter and waved us on our way. One of the women turned to me and said, 'Iran is changing. Here most things are possible. You just have to be discreet.'

Anthony Ham

RUSSIA, CENTRAL ASIA & THE CAUCASUS

BRADLEY MAYHEW
Bradley started exploring the world while studying Chinese at Oxford and in Taiwan. He travelled to Tibet and took the Trans-Siberian railway back home, arriving in Berlin the morning of reunification. Since then he's managed to shrug off any kind of formal employment, instead learning Spanish in Central America, leading adventure tours along the Silk Road, and working in Beijing and across Central Asia and Ladakh. His first guidebook was the Odyssey *guide to Uzbekistan and since then he's written for Lonely Planet's* Tibet, Southwest China, Central Asia, Shanghai, Mongolia, Yellowstone National Park *and others. He's very proud of the fact that he's never worn a suit to work and doesn't own an alarm clock.*

INTRODUCTION

The area described in this chapter is bigger than Africa and Australasia put together. Central Asia alone (Kazakhstan, Uzbekistan, Kyrgyzstan, Tajikistan, Turkmenistan and Afghanistan) is about the size of Europe; Russia itself spans half the globe. Together with Belarus, the Caucasus and Ukraine this creates a region of huge contrasts, covering everything from permanently frozen tundra to baking desert, and embracing Christianity, Islam and Buddhism. For travellers the echoes of great empires still remain in historic centres from St Petersburg (Russia) to Samarkand (Uzbekistan), and outside the cities there are enough blanks in the maps, enough wildness and wilderness, to keep you exploring for years.

You'll need patience, tolerance and a good sense of humour for travel in this unique and sometimes challenging region, but the former realm of the communist bogeyman, off-limits to foreigners for most of the 20th century, offers a world of opportunities for the adventurous gapper.

WHY RUSSIA, CENTRAL ASIA & THE CAUCASUS?

The collapse of the Soviet Union in 1989 opened up a huge brave new world to backpackers. Thailand or Goa it is not, but history, mystery and the opportunity to take a voyeuristic peek at the outcome of the failed Soviet experiment lures thousands of travellers to the region. Rarely visited mountains, remote wilderness and the general quirkiness of the region drag in many more. Some people are drawn to the sheer mystique of places like Altay and Tuva (Russia), Siberia and Samarkand, and come here simply because no-one else does.

If you want your gap year to be filled with fine food, sensual delights and a frolic on the beach, then this region may not be for you. The changes since 1989 have been incredible but only slowly is the generosity and interest locals show to travellers manifesting itself in the region's previously grey and humourless tourist and service industries. Capitalism has

---

TOP 10 MUST-SEES

St Petersburg & Moscow (Russia) Home to Russia's greatest museums and cultural masterpieces.

Yaroslavl, Suzdal & Nizhny Novgorod (Russia) Classic old Russia is found in the atmospheric choirs and cathedrals of these Golden Ring towns.

Lake Baikal (Russia) The Pearl of Siberia is crystal clear, packed with wildlife and ringed by mountains.

Kamchatka Peninsula (Russia) An otherworldly string of live volcanoes, black-sand beaches and reindeer; the downside is that it's difficult (and pricey) to get to.

Bukhara & Samarkand (Uzbekistan) Respectively Central Asia's most extravagant and densest collection of Islamic monuments; about as Silk Road as it gets.

Pamir Highway (Tajikistan) Awe-inspiring mountain scenery and views into Afghanistan's Wakhan corridor; you'll most likely have the place to yourself.

Central Kyrgyzstan (Kyrgyzstan) Bargain-priced horse treks to gorgeous highland lakes and valleys where you can stay in a yurt with local Kyrgyz nomads.

Kazbegi & the Caucasus (Georgia) Picturesque Orthodox church in superb mountain scenery.

Odessa (Ukraine) Viennese-inspired opera houses, cathedrals and funky nightlife next to the Black Sea.

Minsk (Belarus) Seriously odd, Soviet-style city belonging to another era.

---

been embraced with a big, warm-hearted Russian bear hug in the west, most notably in Moscow where every tourist is cheerfully overcharged just as they would be in London or Paris. Outside the capital, businesses gear themselves towards local people (who are probably not earning more than £30 per month) and prices plummet.

So, what's on offer? Well, in the west you could comfortably spend your time checking out some of Europe's classiest museums and historical sites then hang out in cafés when the sheer weight of culture wears you down. Cultured St Petersburg and bustling Moscow are filled with museums, palaces and monuments (St Petersburg's Hermitage is one of the world's great museums). The Bolshoi, Red Square and the Kremlin all offer wonderful doses of high culture, which are happily offset by some of the wildest, most hedonistic clubbing in the world.

Central Asia offers a completely different travel experience. The Eurasian steppe quickly turns to untamed jagged mountains, expansive deserts, and lush alpine valleys populated by Mongolian-looking horsemen and their yurts. Down in the plains and valleys lies a string of ancient Silk Road cities and Islamic architectural treasures that stretches from Tbilisi (Georgia) to the China. Reality may not quite gel with romantic images of camel caravans, caravanserais (buildings that acted as pit stops for trade caravans as they travelled across the Silk Road) and turbaned Silk Road merchants, but in places you can definitely get the sense that you are travelling directly in the footsteps of Marco Polo.

Halfway across Russia is Lake Baikal, the deepest freshwater lake in the world, a magnificent place to explore and an essential stop on the famed Trans-Siberian Railway. The Trans-Sib (actually divided into the Trans-Siberian to Vladivostok, and the Trans-Mongolian and Trans-Manchurian routes to Beijing) offers one of the great rail journeys of the world and is a springboard to exploring not only the Siberian wilderness but also Mongolia (Trans-Mongolian route) and northern China (trans-Manchurian route).

The lands beyond the old Iron Curtain still feel like a recently rediscovered country. Occasionally you get a full dose of Soviet weirdness, like in Minsk (Belarus), parts of Kazakhstan and pretty much the whole of bizarre Turkmenistan – places that still give you a feel for what life under communism must have been like. At other times the problems thrown up by the collapse of the Soviet Union are only too evident; encounters with poorly paid border guards or corrupt police; the logistical difficulty of travelling; poor accommodation; and shocking food.

But there are more positives than negatives in this addictive region. The fledgling countries of Kyrgyzstan, Tajikistan and Kazakhstan are world leaders in community-based tourism, a system that allows you to stay in a network of family homes or horse trek from yurt to yurt for around £10 per day. These unrivalled opportunities for an on-the-cheap Central Asian adventure are limited only by your imagination.

Share your sleeping space with a nomadic family in a remote yurt, take in the sacred beauty of an Orthodox Christian choir in one of Russia's great churches, watch Siberia pass by though a train window or go eagle hunting with a Kyrgyz nomad – the region has it all.

WHAT TO DO?

There are a few voluntary options in this region, often working in children's summer camps, otherwise there's not much doing on this front. If you want to learn the lingo then there are some excellent language schools in Moscow and St Petersburg. Otherwise, most gappers content themselves with travel, often including a trip along the Trans-Mongolian Railway and ending up in China.

Get Active

Outdoor activities are embraced with enthusiasm in the region. Local inquiries may well turn up a group participating in an activity you're interested in. New adventure-travel possibilities are cropping up all the time and there are numerous opportunities for expeditions into the Arctic, Siberian wilderness and mountains of Central Asia.

CYCLING & MOUNTAIN-BIKING

Fairly extreme mountain-biking is organised by local and international companies in many areas also recommended for walking and trekking. A few hardy people set off to cross continental-sized Russia by bike, but spares are rare and there's a lot to be said for putting the wheels on the train across much of Siberia.

HORSE & CAMEL TRIPS

You can immerse yourself in Central Asia's rich culture of nomadic horsemanship in lovely Kyrgyzstan from as little as £10 a day, which must one of the world's great travel bargains. Trips vary from a couple of days to three-week-long expeditions. For a touch of the Silk Road take an overnight camel trek into the deserts of northern Uzbekistan or even the high Pamirs (Tajikistan).

SKIING & SNOWBOARDING

Ski facilities are found outside Almaty in Kazakhstan and in the central Caucasus region around Elbrus (5642m). For the ultimate downhill rush join a group for some high-altitude heli-skiing in both areas.

The Kola Peninsula north of Moscow, the Altay Mountains on the Kazakhstan-Russia border and the Carpathians in Ukraine provide cross-country skiing par excellence, and reasonable locally made gear is readily available.

TREKKING, MOUNTAINEERING & CLIMBING

Mountainous and wild, Central Asia is a fantastic walking and trekking destination. Some great treks start right at city limits, notably in Almaty in Kazakhstan and Bishkek and Karakol in Kyrgyzstan. Further afield, the alpine valleys of the Fan Mountains in Tajikistan and the gorgeous pyramid peaks of Khan Tengri and the Tian Shan range in eastern Kyrgyzstan

RUSSIA, CENTRAL ASIA & CAUCASUS

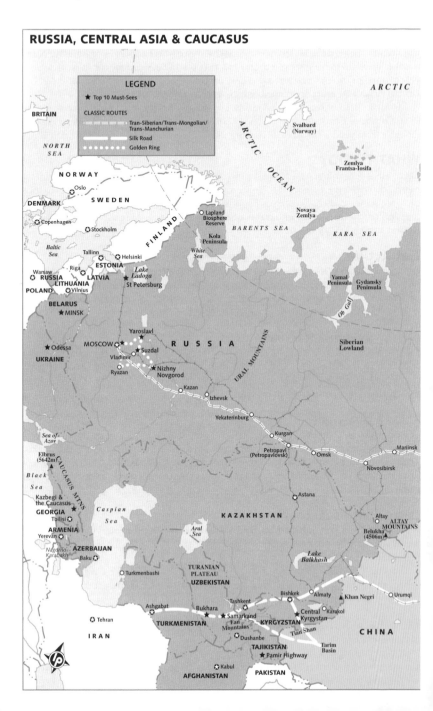

LEGEND

★ Top 10 Must-Sees

CLASSIC ROUTES

▬▬▬▬ Tran-Siberian/Trans-Mongolian/
Trans-Manchurian

━━━━ Silk Road

•••••• Golden Ring

ARCTIC

ARCTIC OCEAN

BRITAIN

NORTH SEA

NORWAY
Oslo

DENMARK
Copenhagen

SWEDEN
Stockholm

Svalbard
(Norway)

Zemlya
Frantsa-Iosifa

Lapland
Biosphere
Reserve

Novaya
Zemlya

BARENTS SEA

KARA SEA

FINLAND

Kola
Peninsula

White
Sea

Yamal
Peninsula

Gydansky
Peninsula

Baltic
Sea

Tallinn
ESTONIA
Helsinki

Lake
Ladoga
St Petersburg

Warsaw
Riga
RUSSIA
LATVIA

LITHUANIA
Vilnius

POLAND

BELARUS
★ MINSK

★ Odessa

UKRAINE

MOSCOW

Yaroslavl
★
★ Suzdal
Vladimir
Ryazan
★ Nizhny
Novgorod

RUSSIA

Kazan

Izhevsk

Yekaterinburg

Ob Gulf

URAL MOUNTAINS

Siberian
Lowland

Sea of
Azov

Elbrus
(5642m)

Black
Sea

Kazbegi &
the Caucasus
GEORGIA ★
Tbilisi

ARMENIA
Yerevan

CAUCASUS MTS

AZERBAIJAN
Baku

Nagorno-
Karabakh

Caspian
Sea

Aral
Sea

Kurgan

Petropavl
(Petropavlovsk)

Omsk

Mariinsk

Novosibirsk

Astana

KAZAKHSTAN

Lake
Balkhash

Altay
ALTAY
MOUNTAINS

Belukha
(4506m)

Turkmenbashi

TURANIAN
PLATEAU

UZBEKISTAN

Tashkent

Bishkek

Almaty

Khan Negri

Urumqi

Ashgabat

Bukhara
★

Samarkand
★ Fan
Mountains

Central
Kyrgystan

Karakol

CHINA

Tehran

TURKMENISTAN

KYRGYZSTAN

Tian Shan

Tarim
Basin

IRAN

Dushanbe

TAJIKISTAN
★ Pamir Highway

Kabul

AFGHANISTAN

PAKISTAN

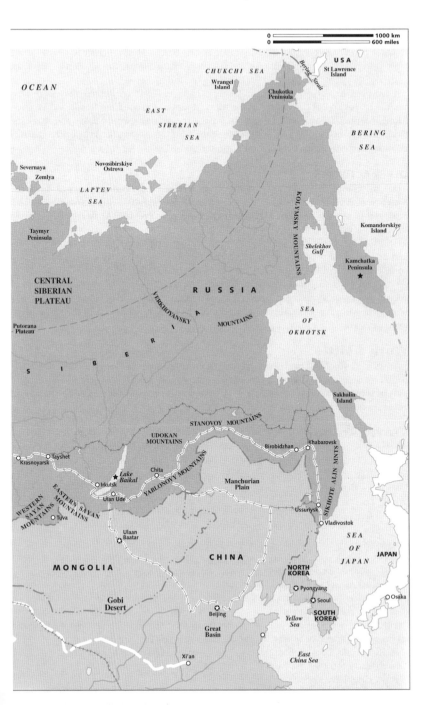

provide impressive goals for climbers, trekkers and mountaineers. Eastern Tajikistan and remoter parts of Kyrgyzstan offer more ambitious treks and never-climbed peaks for the truly intrepid. Plenty of local agencies offer logistical support, though don't expect the convenient system of lodges and porters that you find in Nepal.

Elsewhere the Carpathian range in Ukraine, Lapland Biosphere Reserve in western Russia, the Elbrus area of the Caucasus, the Altay Mountains in southern Russia and Western Mongolia, the Ural Mountains in central Russia (the divide between Europe and Asia), the Sayan Mountains on the border with Mongolia, and the volcanic and surreal Kamchatka Peninsula all offer fantastic scope for adventure.

OTHER ACTIVITIES
You can explore Siberia by ferry on the Irtysh, Yenisey and Ob rivers, or float down the Volga from Nizhny Novgord to Volgograd (former Stalingrad). Boating around the Black Sea coast is popular between May and mid-October. The remote Altay area has some of the region's most intense white-water rafting.

Jeep tours are becoming popular in Central Asia, particularly in Kyrgyzstan and Tajikistan, and don't discount the region's wildlife, which includes Siberian tigers in the far east and some fantastic bird life in the southern Caucasus and Kaliningrad (Russia).

You can go caving in Kyrgyzstan, Kazakhstan and Armenia, where the speleological society takes guided hiking, caving and mountain expeditions. In Siberia a Russian sauna (complete with the optional beating with birch twigs and naked roll in the snow) is an experience you won't forget in a rush.

Work a Little
Few gappers find any paid work in the region other than teaching English, but many people participate in voluntary student exchanges and English-teaching programs with kids in summer camps on Lake Baikal. Other volunteer opportunities need sorting out in advance.

Travel Around
Air travel has been tightened up somewhat since 1994 when the passengers and crew of an Aeroflot Airbus A310 were killed after the pilot let his kids have a go on the controls, but on less popular internal routes there are still overloaded crates held together with little more than cable ties and gaffer tape. Aeroflot (www.aeroflot.co.uk or www.aeroflot .com), Transaero (www.transaero.ru) and Uzbekistan Airways (www.uzairways.com) are up to international safety standards – but treat the other 'baby-flots' with care, especially in Siberia.

Train travel is the best way to get around the region and offers a cultural experience all of its own. Pack a Dostoyevsky-sized novel for the epic rides and expect anything under second class to be cramped, uncomfortable and insecure.

Buses service a huge network cheaply, slowly and with less bureaucratic insanity. Shared *(marshrutnoe)* taxis are normally the best bet; wait for all four seats to fill up or pay for them all for a touch of luxury.

Hitching is never entirely safe but it is common and the distinction between hitching and taking a taxi (shared or otherwise) is often blurred – you pay either way.

In Russia and the west, boat travel on canals, rivers and lakes is a great way to get about. There's also a ferry service from Baku (Azerbaijan) to Turkmenbashi (Turkmenistan).

Most cities have a good public-transport system.

CLASSIC ROUTES
Trans-Siberian Railway
The seven-day Trans-Siberian Railway links Moscow in the west to Vladivostok (Russia) on the Pacific coast, clanking through eight time zones and across 9289km of mountain, steppe, forest and desert.

The most popular route is actually the Trans-Mongolian, which branches south two-thirds along the route, passing through Mongolia en route to Beijing. If you don't plan to stop in Mongolia to or from Beijing then you can take the Trans-Manchurian route, which cuts through northern China instead of Mongolia. Another alternative is the BAM spur line, which can act as a springboard for exploration of the Siberian wilderness. Some travellers do a route nonstop. Others break their trip en route, though this means having to buy separate tickets, either at local train stations or in the UK before you leave through specialist travel agencies such as Regent Holidays (see Specialist Tour Operators on p159).

An interesting Central Asian alternative (the Silk Road by rail) detours through Kazakhstan and western China, along old trade routes to Xi'an and Beijing.

Golden Ring
The Golden Ring (Zolotoe Koltso) allows the exploration of historic old towns (such as Suzdal and Yaroslavl), Russian Orthodox churches and magnificent monasteries northeast of Moscow. It's not going to take months (a week would take in the highlights) but will give a real taste of what old Russia must have been like.

Silk Road
The Silk Road is not so much one trail as a network of trade routes linking Xi'an in China with the Mediterranean. This fantastic, difficult route leads from China into Kyrgyzstan via the Torugart or Irkeshtam Passes, and is still in use today. Travellers can continue northwest across central Kyrgyzstan to Bishkek and then southwest down to Uzbekistan and the delights of Samarkand and the winding back streets and stunning Islamic architecture of Bukhara. From there you can cross Turkmenistan on a transit visa to Iran (or take a boat to Azerbaijan in the Caucasus) to continue the Silk Road into the Middle East. You could transit across Central Asia in a week or two, though a month or even two would be much better if you want to explore the great sights en route.

WHEN TO GO?
If you like snow, ice, ludicrous temperatures and extravagantly silly fur hats then travel in winter. Siberia is at its best in February, apparently. Not convinced? Then choose spring or autumn but avoid the April spring thaw. The deserts in Central Asia become a riot of colour in April. Summer is the essential time to explore the mountains of Central Asia or cross the Torugart or Irkeshtam Passes to China (snowbound November to May) and provides rain and nice temperatures for western Russia and the Black Sea coast. During June and July you'll be plagued by biting insects in northern Russia and Siberia (August and September are a better bet) and this is also a resoundingly duff time to visit Central Asia's deserts.

Climate
Generally the region has an extreme continental European climate. Summers are very warm but Russia's long, dark, very cold winters are truly extreme – much of the country is well below freezing for over four months of the year (November to March). In February

and March the sun shines, there's a lack of humidity and it doesn't feel so cold. The coast bordering the Sea of Japan experiences a northern monsoonal climate, which means there's a 30–40% chance of rain each day between May and September.

Festivals

There are plenty of festivals in the region and a number of national celebrations and obscure anniversaries disrupt bureaucratic life – much of Russia shuts down for the first half of May.

Christian holidays and festivals are widely (and wildly) celebrated by members of the Russian Orthodox Church.

Islamic holidays (see p143) are mildly celebrated in Central Asia.

Rozhdestvo (Russia) Russian Orthodox Christmas is held on 7 January and begins with midnight church services.

Maslenitsa (Russia) The Goodbye Russian Winter festival is held across eastern Russia in late February/early March and features folk shows and various games.

Navrus (New Days) This is a huge two-day festival and Islamic celebration of the spring equinox in Central Asia (normally fixed on 21 March). Banned until 1989, it involves traditional food, music, drama, art and colourful fairs.

Festival of the North (Russia) Held in eastern Russia in the last week of March – Murmansk and other northern towns hold reindeer races, ski marathons etc.

International Labour Day & Spring Festival (Russia) Celebrated on 1 May and 2 May, traditionally with a huge military parade in Moscow.

Victory Day (Russia) Offers more impressive parades on 9 May, centred around the epic Soviet-style WWII memorials common across the former Soviet Union.

St Petersburg White Nights (Russia) Takes place in the last 10 days of June and involves cultural events, merry-making and late-night partying. Many other northern towns have their own version.

Naadym Mongolian-style festival featuring horse racing, wrestling and throat singing. Held in Tuva (Russia) in July.

National Days Celebrate independence with the shiny new Central Asian nations of Kyrgyzstan (31 August), Uzbekistan (1 September), Tajikistan (9 September), Turkmenistan (27 October) and Kazakhstan (16 December).

WHAT TO EXPECT?
Travellers

While the tourist trail in western Russia is well trodden, the rest of the country and Central Asia are the preserve of hardy travellers that mostly hail from Europe.

Tourist hangouts are difficult to determine. The region has no Ibiza or idyllic Thai islands but you'll find plenty of travellers in Russia's Golden Ring, on the Trans-Siberian Railway and, to a lesser extent, around Lake Baikal and the Black Sea coast, and in the Central Asian towns of Bukhara, Samarkand and Bishkek.

Locals

Despite the often dull, grey face and downright rudeness of the bureaucracy and service industry, friendliness and unconditional hospitality are common and sometimes overwhelming. Respond with a small gift and be careful not to take advantage of others' generosity. Vodka is often forced upon guests, even in Muslim Central Asia. 'Vodka terrorism' is also common on train journeys and during other chance social encounters. Saying 'well, just a small one then' puts you on the slippery slope to hangover oblivion; 'I'm an alcoholic' is a plausible excuse.

Immigrants from former colonies make up 20% of Russia's population, and Central Asian states all have an ethnic majority bearing their names. The millions of Russians and Ukrainians living in Central Asia are referred to as Slavs.

Generally attitudes are conservative, particularly in Central Asia where care should be taken around religious sites – skimpy clothing is a definite cultural gaff in the Fergana Valley of Uzbekistan. A neat appearance goes far in the region and polite, gentlemanly behaviour is expected by female Russians.

The Russian Orthodox Church is enjoying a revival in Russia, Georgia and Armenia (which have some of the world's oldest and most spectacularly located churches). Central Asia is staunchly Muslim but suffers from almost no religious extremism (Chechnya is a different story, however). Buddhism and Judaism exist in small pockets, although there has been a mass emigration of Jews in recent years.

Food
The food in the former Soviet Union is almost exclusively awful, almost everywhere. Bland Russian dumplings, beetroot borscht and black bread are all washed down with vodka and sausage. Then there's *kvas,* the local beerlike beverage that's made from…bread. No wonder Russians are so stoic. Central Asian cuisine has been likewise dismissed, not entirely unfairly, as a bleak choice between mutton fat in a bowl *(shorpa)*, mutton fat on a stick *(shashlyk* kebabs) or mutton fat in rice *(plov,* or pilau).

Still, it's not all that bad. The wonderful markets groan with fruit in summer, and the region's melons, grapes and nuts (not to mention the caviar) are the best in the world. Most towns have Turkish, Korean, Chinese and Western restaurants, so you won't starve.

Language
Russian is the second language of most people in Central Asia, where numerous Turkic (and occasionally Persian) ethnic languages are used locally. Learning the Cyrillic alphabet is a huge help, not only for Russian but for deciphering Central Asian, Ukrainian and Belarusian languages too. English is not widely spoken. In Central Asia you'll gain a lot of friends by learning a few words of the local language.

See p421 for details on language courses in the region and the UK. The School of Oriental and African Languages (SOAS) in London is particularly strong on Central Asian languages. Check out p160 for information on Lonely Planet's useful phrasebooks.

Health Risks
Travellers require the usual armful of jabs and there are a few other health issues to consider. Tick-borne encephalitis, Lyme disease and Japanese encephalitis (spread by mosquitoes) are major problems in eastern Siberia during the summer, especially for trekkers. Cholera is not uncommon in southern regions and you can catch malaria in southern Tajikistan. Diphtheria is on the increase in Ukraine.

Short-term visitors are at little risk from the region's well-known nuclear pollution – you can even take a tour of radioactive Chernobyl in the Ukraine or the disappearing Aral Sea in Uzbekistan and Kazakhstan!

Consult the Health chapter (p59) and seek professional medical advice for more travel health information.

Time & Flight Time
Central Asia is divided into three time zones and Russia has 10! Moscow and most of western Russia is three hours ahead of Greenwich Mean Time (GMT). Many countries in the region change to daylight savings time (moving their clocks one hour forward) in summer.

From London, Almaty (Kazakhstan) is an 8½-hour flight away, while Moscow is 3½ hours away. Vladivostok is 12 hours from London – you fly over the Arctic – while Baku (Azerbaijan) is a relatively short hop in comparison (5¾ hours).

Issues

Getting visas for the region can be a big hassle, so leave at least three months to organise it all prior to departure – getting them on the road will draw you into a huge web of bureaucratic nastiness. Clusters of countries, snakelike borders, complicated regulations and fixed visa dates demand more pre-trip planning than most regions.

That said, the visa situation has improved greatly in recent years. Only Turkmenistan remains a significant problem, requiring that you book a tour and guide before offering a visa. Tajikistan requires a visa invitation from a travel agency.

Some Central Asian states (Turkmenistan, Tajikistan and Kazakhstan) insist that you register with the police upon arrival in the country. This is a pain but irregularities with registration and visas can cause expensive problems – officials have a reputation for shaking down travellers. That said, many states are clamping down on corruption and easing visa regulations. Most travellers these days find their trip relatively hassle-free.

At the time of writing the following were danger zones and essentially out of bounds to travellers: Afghanistan, the borders of Azerbaijan and Armenia, Ngorno Karabakh and surrounding borders, parts of Georgia (including Abkhazia, South Ossetia and Svaneti) and some regions within Russia (Chechnya, Dagestan, North Ossetia, Ingushetia, Karachai-Cherkassia and Kabardino-Balkaria, and the surrounding borders).

Afghanistan remains an unstable place, particularly the southeast, which is still haunted by the ghosts of the Taliban.

Repression of human rights, lack of press freedom, massive corruption and occasional acts of terrorism all feature in the colourful life of the region but it's only the sporadic violent drunk (including the occasional policeman) that you are likely to come face to face with.

For further information on travel hotspots, general safety issues and governmental travel advice see the Safety chapter (p79).

Internet & Communications

You'll find plenty of internet cafés but good connections are scarce in Central Asia. The same holds true for mobile communication (don't bother taking your mobile to Kyrgyzstan), the use of which is spreading out of big cities in Russia and Ukraine and into the boondocks.

DAILY SPEND

In Russia, Ukraine and Belarus a two-tier pricing policy exists, which means tourists pay more for many hotels, museums and attractions, though not for train and air tickets.

Moscow is pretty much as expensive as your average European city and a dorm bed is going to cost you at least £10. St Petersburg and Kiev (Kyiv; Ukraine) are only a little better, but away from these cities prices plummet. Budget for £20–25 a day in Russia, Belarus and Ukraine and you'll have a fine time.

In Central Asia budget on spending £15–25 a day if you're not living on caviar and hiring 4WDs. A half-decent hotel bed costs around £8 but homestay accommodation out in the countryside is a quarter of that. US dollars are the currency to carry. You'll get the best from your buck in bargain-priced Tajikistan and Kyrgyzstan. Turkmenistan remains the most expensive Central Asian destination as you need to book a tour and guide in order to get a visa.

GETTING THERE

You can arrive by road and rail from Iran, China and Europe. Or you can just fly, which given the taxing nature of the region's borders and visa regulations is not a bad way to start your trip.

Air

The region's major hubs, in ascending order of flight expense, are Kiev, Moscow, Almaty and Baku. Sadly the region is rarely included in round-the-world (RTW) tickets but open-jaw tickets are offered between a number of major cities.

Moscow is serviced by dozens of airlines but in Central Asia your options are limited – often it's Lufthansa (who have great connections and alliances in the region) and BMED (part of British Airways; www.flybmed.com) who offer the best deals, though KLM and Turkish Airlines are worth checking out. Aeroflot occasionally comes out with some top deals via Moscow and is the only airline servicing Vladivostok.

TICKET COSTS

The best available student/under-26 fares are quoted here. See the Passports, Visas, Tickets & Insurance chapter (p19) for more information on tickets and how to get the best deal.

You can often find return tickets to Kiev for under £200, while flying into Moscow is only a little more expensive. If you're flying into Almaty or Tashkent you can stumble across tickets for £450, but £550 is more likely. Ashgabat (Turkmenistan) and Dushanbe (Tajikistan) are two expensive destinations (don't be surprised by a £800 price tag); for these you are better off taking a local flight once you get to Central Asia.

Of the open-jaw options, flying into Almaty or Baku and out of Kiev or Moscow comes out cheapest (about £400). Flying to/from more obscure destinations will cost closer to £550.

Vladivostok and destinations in far-eastern Russia are better served from China and South Korea.

Sea & Overland

Despite the amazing network of ship canals and sea ports there are only a few scheduled services into Russia (from Japan) and only a little traffic across the Black and Caspian Seas.

By land there are hundreds of routes into the region from east, west, north and south. Trains are the easiest option into the region and are available from all directions.

Before you make any plans, check out the border crossings you want to use carefully.

Specialist Tour Operators

Dozens of British tour operators run trips in Russia and Central Asia. Here are a few regional specialists:

Hinterland Travel (☎ 01883 743584; hinterland@tinyworld.cu.uk; 2 Ivy Hill Lane, Godstone, Surrey RH9 8WH) Tours to Afghanistan.

Monkey Business (☎ 00 86 10 6591 6519; www.monkeyshrine.com; Hidden Tree Bar, 12 Dongdaqiao Xie Street, Nan Sanlitun, Chaoyang District, Beijing) Good for Trans-Mongolian or Trans-Manchurion rail tickets (if you're travelling east to west).

Moonsky Star (☎ 00 852 2723 1376; Chungking Mansion, E-block, 4th floor, FSlat 6, Nathan Road 36-44, Kowloon, Hong Kong) Ditto.

Regent Holidays (☎ 0117 921 1711; www.regent-holidays.co.uk; 14 John St, Bristol BS1 2HR) Offers tours and independent travel, including Trans-Siberian routes.

Russian Travel (☎ 0870 366 5454; www.russiantravel.co.uk; fax 0366 5453; Premier House, 11 Marlborough Place, Brighton, East Sussex BN1 1UB)

The Russia Experience (☎ 020 8566 8846; www.trans-siberian.co.uk; fax 020 8566 8843; Research House, Frasier Rd, Perivale, Middlesex UB6 7AQ) Can organise transport, tours and all-inclusive adventures, for individuals or groups, in Russia, Central Asia and China.

Ukrainian Travel (☎ 0161 652 5050; www.ukraine.co.uk; fax 0161 633 0825; Falcon House, Victoria St, Chadderton, Oldham, OL9OBH) The UK's leading Ukraine specialist, also known as Bob Sopel's.

You can also contact the following reliable local agencies direct:
Ayan Travel (Ashgabat) www.ayan-travel.com
Celestial Mountains (Bishkek) www.celestial.com.kg
Great Game Travel (Dushanbe) www.greatgametravel.co.uk
Lenalptours (St Petersburg) www.russia-climbing.com
Salom Travel (Bukhara) www.salomtravel.com
Stantours (Almaty) www.stantours.com
Wild Russia (St Petersburg) www.wildrussia.spb.ru

RUSSIA, CENTRAL ASIA, THE CAUCASUS & BEYOND

The world's your oyster from Russia and Central Asia. Overland routes back to Blighty could take in the best of the Middle East or rarely explored parts of Eastern Europe. If you move into western China you could follow the Karakoram Highway (one of the most breathtaking overland trips in the world) down into the Indian Subcontinent. Just as easy would be an exploration of China, ending in Southeast Asia, from where Australia is a short plane ride away.

FURTHER INFORMATION
Reading Material

Lonely Planet publishes *Central Asia*; *Georgia, Armenia & Azerbaijan*; *Russia & Belarus*; *Moscow*; *St Petersburg*; and *Trans-Siberian Railway*. Travellers will also find Lonely Planet's *Central Asia, Russian* and *Ukrainian* phrasebooks invaluable.

For good background information consult Benson Bobrick's *East of the Sun: the Epic Conquest and Tragic History of Siberia*. Also good are *The Rise and Fall of the Soviet Empire*, by Stephen Dalziel, and the highly recommended *The Great Game*, by Peter Hopkirk.

Mission to Tashkent is the autobiography of British intelligence officer FM Bailey. His greatest tale recounts how after the Russian revolution he was employed as a Bolshevik agent tasked with tracking down himself!

Journey into Russia, by Laurens van der Post, is a classic travelogue from the 1960s that offers many insights into the Russian psyche.

A tough river journey is recalled by Frederick Kempe in *Siberian Odyssey: A Voyage into the Russian Soul*. Colin Thubron's *Among the Russians* is a precise and eloquent account of travelling before the Iron Curtain fell; Thubron's more recent *In Siberia* is probably the single best book on that region. For something a bit more humorous try *USSR: From an Original Idea by Karl Marx*, by Marc Polonsky and Russell Taylor.

Journey to Khiva, by Philip Glazebrook, and *Apples in the Snow*, by Geoffrey Moorhouse, both describe journeys in Central Asia in the early 1990s.

Trekking in Russia and Central Asia, by Frith Maier, provides a great background for anyone wanting to trek and climb in the region, though it's dated now (1997).

For inspiration on Afghanistan try *Danziger's Travels*, by Nick Danziger, a contemporary tale of derring-do; the classic *A Short Walk in the Hindu Kush*, by Eric Newby; and the wonderful *An Unexpected Light* by Jason Elliot, written in 2001.

Useful Information Sources

For specific country overviews, the lowdown on travel in the region and hundreds of useful links head to Lonely Planet's website (www.lonelyplanet.com).

Useful starting points for web searches include:
Baikal Explorer (www.baikalex.com) Travel agency site full of ideas for exploring the Lake Baikal area.
Virtual Guide to Belarus (www.belarusguide.com) A good start for Belarus.

Brama Gateway Ukraine (www.brama.com) Click on 'Travel' for Ukraine travel info.
Kyrgyz Community Based Tourism Association (www.cbtkyrgzstan.kg) Community-based tourism projects in Kyrgyzstan.
Bucknell Russian Program (www.departments.bucknell.edu/russian) Academic look at aspects of Russian culture.
eurasianet.org (www.eurasianet.org) Good news source and portal for Central Asia.
Kabul Caravan (www.kabulcaravan.com) Afghan-heads will appreciate this site.
Pamirs (www.pamirs.org) Excellent travel info for exploring the Pamirs in Tajikistan.
Siberian Nomads (www.siberianomad.com) Good travel info from a travel agency in Yakutsk.
Trans-Siberian Railway (www.transsib.ru/Eng) Trans-Siberian info.
Trans-Siberia.com (www.trans-siberia.com) Personal web page full of route overviews and travel advice.
East Russia Travel Market (www.traveleastrussia.com) Travel info on eastern Siberia and beyond.
UA Zone.net (www.uazone.net) Ukrainian information.
Visit Russia (www.visitrussia.org.uk) Government tourist site.
Russian National Group (www.russia-travel.com) Another government tourist site.
waytorussia.net (www.waytorussia.net) Good travel agency guide.

BEEN THERE, DONE THAT

Travel in the former Soviet Union is an intriguing mix of the exotic and banal. Sure, there are some world-beating sights, but what really makes travel here such a riot are the daily eccentricities of the region. There's something about Russia and the ex-Soviet republics that is just so deliciously, well…weird.

Local newspapers are full of wacky stories that hint at the weirdness to come, from yeti hunters scouring the hills of Kyrgyzstan to the army of termites that apparently ate a town of 3000 homes in western Uzbekistan.

Travel in the region reveals equally weird Twilight Zone–*style encounters. I particularly admired the sheep who boarded the local bus in Tajikistan, alone, and then got off two stops later, without paying. Or the old man on a bus, also in Tajikistan, who handed me a light bulb and absolutely refused to take it back until he got off the bus eight hours later.*

For those who like their trips to have a bit more edge, I wholeheartedly recommend the one-legged taxi driver who drove me to Ala-Archa in Kyrgyzstan (where was that brake…?). And don't even think about wearing your seat belt in Uzbekistan – I almost made that fatal mistake but then the driver told me in a panic 'people will think we're rebels from Tajikistan!'. Of course they will…

My favourite moment on my last trip was being driven across Kyrgyzstan, crammed in the back seat of an ancient Volga, squashed between three giant Kyrgyz women, drinking kymyz *(fermented mare's milk) and listening to a scratchy recording of a local bard called* Manas *on the stereo. But the moment that summed up Central Asia for me was when the driver suddenly turned off the road in the middle of nowhere, parked the car hurriedly and, suddenly, and without any warning at all (not even a yawn), fell asleep…along with all the other passengers in the car.*

I sat there for a little while, temporarily at a loss, smashed in between a comatose, many-cardiganed granny and the side window.

Twenty minutes later I checked my watch.

Someone started snoring.

I went for a walk…

Bradley Mayhew

INDIAN SUBCONTINENT

JOE BINDLOSS
Joe is one of the authors of The Gap Year Book. *His main biography appears on p2. Joe has visited India seven times, has updated the last three editions of Lonely Planet's* India *and was a co-author of its* North India *guidebook.*

INTRODUCTION

Someone once said that there are two types of people in the world, those who have been to India, and those who haven't. That may be laying it on a bit strong, but the Indian Subcontinent is magnificent and squalid, enchanting and tormenting in equal measures, and no-one leaves the region without being affected in some way.

There are few places in the world that offer quite such an intense travelling experience. The region includes the highest, the most remote, and the most populated areas on earth and the variety of sights and experiences on offer is breathtaking – temples and tigers, mystic rivers and snowy mountains, snake-charmers and Buddhist lamas…the list goes on and on.

Some people fall instantly in love with the place, returning time and again to sip chai (Indian-style tea) on the steps of Indian trains or listen to the wind stirring temple bells in remote Himalayan valleys. Other people find it all too much. Every year there are travellers who leave within a few days, overwhelmed by the crush of humanity, the endless scams and the notorious stomach upsets.

Tragically parts of India, Sri Lanka and the Maldives were devastated in the Indian Ocean tsunami on 26 December 2004. These areas are rebuilding and for many, tourism remains an important part of their economy. For up-to-date information on the status of these regions, see www.lonelyplanet.com/tsunami and www.fco.gov.uk.

WHY THE INDIAN SUBCONTINENT?

When backpacking was first invented in the 1960s, India was where everyone wanted to go. The Beatles came here to find their Maharishi and Led Zeppelin sought inspiration in the Kashmir valley. Travellers still come here by the thousand in search of mystic experiences, iconic monuments, weird and wonderful wildlife and possibly the greatest food on the planet.

For those who love it, the noise, the bustle and the energy are intoxicating and addictive. After you've spent time in India, other countries can feel like they have the sound turned down. For those who hate it, India is a place where foreigners pay twice as much as locals, where cleanliness is a dirty word, and where your personal space stops a few millimetres from your body.

Which group you fall into will largely be determined by whether you are content to give up control and just roll with whatever experiences the region throws at you, or whether you are a stickler for itineraries and punctuality. Although the Subcontinent is modernising in leaps and bounds, hotel rooms are damp and musty, trains are routinely delayed and the electricity supply fails with monotonous regularity.

In spite of this, there are few places that come close to India in terms of cultural depth and intensity. The region is home to Hindus, Buddhists, Muslims, Jains, Sikhs and Christians – learning the rituals and traditions of the different faiths is an integral part of a trip to the Subcontinent.

Because of these rich religious traditions, there is something to see in every town, be it a temple, a holy lake, a historic mosque or a Buddhist monastery. Festivals in the region are incredible spectacles, with singing, dancing, exotic foods and sometimes animal sacrifices and bizarre acts of masochism. During the Hindu festival of Holi, people throw around huge amounts of coloured powder and India becomes quite literally the most colourful place on earth.

Most people in the region are incredibly friendly, though they can be very in your face. It will probably take a few days to get used to the endless questions and shaking everyone's hand. Unfortunately, single women can expect a fair bit of unwanted attention throughout the region, except in Bhutan.

India's other trump card is its incredible variety of scenery and landscapes. If you take a train from north to south, you could start at the foot of snow-capped mountains, cross dusty plains and deserts, weave through dense jungles and terraced rice fields and emerge on a picture-postcard beach backed by swaying palm trees.

And then there are the monuments. The Taj Mahal is probably the most identifiable building on the planet, and there are ancient temples and mosques throughout the Subcontinent. The far north is dotted with serene Buddhist monasteries, with fabulous murals showing scenes from the life of the Buddha.

On top of all this, India is probably the cheapest place in the world to travel. Thali meals (a selection of curries and rice served on a single plate) can cost pennies and a basic hotel room can be had for just a few pounds. Souvenirs and long distance transport are also cheap as chapattis.

Those are the perks. The flip side of travel in India is the hardship, the endless delays and the stomach bugs. The hassle can be unrelenting, and there are plenty of con men out there waiting to take you for a ride. Try to maintain a sensible level of alertness and don't judge everyone by the standards of these bad apples.

The Subcontinent can be divided into several distinct regions. The mountainous areas in the far north – including Bhutan, Nepal and the Indian states of Sikkim, Arunachal Pradesh and the Leh valley – are centres for Buddhist culture, with incredible landscapes and magnificent monasteries and stupas. Nepal is probably the best choice for first-time visitors – Kathmandu is jam-packed with medieval temples and budget hotels and you can trek independently into the Himalaya without having to join an expensive tour. However, the current Maoist uprising is making travel a little dicey in some parts of the country. In the far northeast, Bhutan can only be entered on an expensive tour arranged through a Bhutanese travel agent.

The area immediately south – comprising the central plains and the arid highlands in the northeast – was the heartland of the Muslim Mughal Empire. Here you'll find many of India's most famous monuments – including the Taj Mahal – and the most intense mix of religions and cultures. This region stretches from Bangladesh to Pakistan, passing right through the middle of India.

The plains of India are probably the most interesting area to visit, though Bangladesh sees remarkably few tourists and is delightfully laid-back as a result. Pakistan has largely dropped off the backpacker circuit because of the increasing risk to foreigners from armed fundamentalist groups.

The south of India is different again. This increasingly lush and tropical area is the heartland of Dravidian Hindu culture. The people of the south were never conquered by the Mughal Empire, so the religious architecture, traditions and cuisine are quite different from the north. The states of Kerala and Goa are home to India's tiny Christian population, who were originally converted by St Thomas the Apostle.

Off the southern tip of India is the paradise island of Sri Lanka, which boasts tropical beaches, Buddhist temples and fantastic, spicy food. However, some areas are off-limits due to separatist violence. East of Sri Lanka, the idyllic Maldives are primarily a package tourism destination.

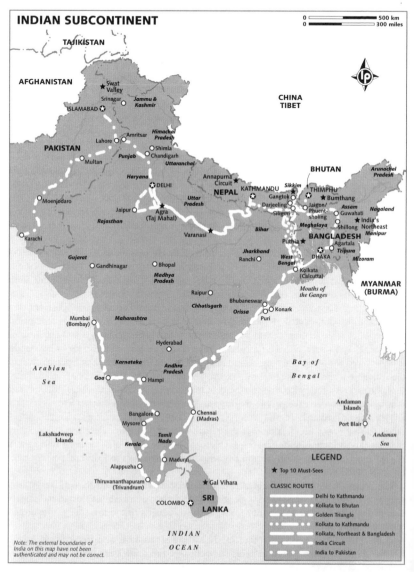

WHAT TO DO?

India is packed with interesting things to see and do. Many people come here specifically to study yoga, or go trekking, or spot tigers and elephants in their natural habitat. There are also fantastic opportunities for volunteering and adventure sports.

Some of the main activities in the region are covered here. See Part III for more information on overseas jobs, volunteer work and courses available in the region.

TOP TEN MUST-SEES

Kathmandu (Nepal) The ultimate backpacker hangout, with backpacker bars and tremendous temples.
Taj Mahal (India) Because no other monument comes close…
Varanasi (India) The most Indian of all Indian cities, perched beside the holy River Ganges.
Annapurna Circuit (Nepal) The most famous trek in the Himalaya.
Sikkim (India) Serene Himalayan Shangri-la with monasteries, mountains and treks.
Gal Vihara (Sri Lanka) Just big, beautiful Buddhas.
Puthia (Bangladesh) The finest temples in Bangladesh.
Swat Valley (Pakistan) Ancient Sufi architecture and the remains of a Buddhist kingdom.
India's Northeast (India) Rarely seen tribes, wild rhinos and magnificent monasteries.
Bumthang (Bhutan) Strange name but wonderful valley, with monasteries, temples and palaces.

Get Active

There are loads of ways to get active in the Subcontinent – here are some of the most popular options.

RUINS & TEMPLES

A good starting point for temple buffs is the Kathmandu Valley in Nepal, which is littered with medieval temples and shrines. In India, tops spots include the Sun Temple at Konark, the Shore Temple at Mahabalipuram, the Sri Meenakshi temple at Madurai, the erotic temples of Khajuraho and the ruins and temples at Hampi.

For Mughal architecture, you can't beat the glorious Taj Mahal at Agra in India. There are more Mughal wonders in Fatehpur Sikri, Delhi and most of the towns in Rajasthan. Pakistan is also famous for its Mughal architecture, particularly around Multan and Lahore.

Gompas (Buddhist monasteries) can be found all over north India, in Nepal and Bhutan and also – surprisingly – in Pakistan and Bangladesh (both areas were Buddhist before the arrival of the Mughals). The most impressive monasteries are in Nepal, Bhutan, and in Sikkim, Arunachal Pradesh and Leh in India.

A slightly different kind of Buddhist architecture is found in Sri Lanka, which follows the original Indian form of Buddhism, rather than the mystical Tibetan form practiced in the north. The most famous monuments in Sri Lanka are the giant Buddha statues at Gal Vihara and the Sri Dalada Maligwara temple in Kandy.

SPIRITUAL JOURNEYS

India is the source of most of the alternative therapies currently practiced in the West. Yoga was invented here in around 500 BC, and Siddhartha Gautama (the historical Buddha) achieved enlightenment near Bodhgaya at around the same time.

For modern day spiritual travellers, the best place to study yoga is Rishikesh in India. There are dozens of yoga ashrams where you can take daily classes, but most expect you to follow strict rules regarding silence, diet and behaviour. Those in search of inner peace can study Buddhist meditation in Bodhgaya and Dharamsala in India and Kathmandu in Nepal.

For a total immersion spiritual experience, you might consider staying at a famous ashram, such as Aurobindo near Pondicherry (www.sriaurobindosociety.org.in). However, some of these organisations have a strong proselytising agenda and there are regular reports of dodgy goings on at Indian spiritual communities.

ELEPHANTS & TIGERS
India is one of the so-called 'megadiversity countries' that account for 70% of the world's biodiversity. In India the big stars are tigers and elephants, but you can also see rare one-horned rhinos in northeast India and Nepal and snow leopards in parts of the Himalaya.

The most famous places to see tigers are the Ranthambhore, Kanha, Corbett and Sunderbans national parks in India. Wild elephants can be seen in Periyar National Park and many of the national parks in Assam. For rhinos, head to Royal Chitwan National Park in Nepal or Kaziranga National Park in India. Conventional leopards can be seen in many national parks in Sri Lanka.

Other animals you may encounter in the region include lions, bears, crocodiles and numerous species of deer and birds. Monkeys are so common as to barely qualify as wildlife. Be very wary of carrying bananas anywhere in the Subcontinent. A hungry rhesus macaque – the cheekiest of all the apes – may be waiting to pounce at any moment!

At most national parks, visitors are driven around in 4WD jeeps but some parks offer safaris on elephant back – a much more exciting and intimate way to explore the jungle. A few parks can also be explored by boat, including Sunderbans National Park in West Bengal. Most parks have cheap, government-run or private accommodation.

TREKKING & MOUNTAINEERING
Compared to the Himalaya, other mountain ranges aren't really trying. The world's highest mountains stretch all the way across the Subcontinent from southern China to Afghanistan. As you might expect, this fantastic region of snowy mountains and high altitude valleys offers some of the best trekking on the planet.

Nepal is by far the easiest place to trek. No permits are required for the most popular trekking routes – including the Annapurna Circuit and the Everest Base Camp trek – and there are basic hotels and restaurants along the main trails, so you can just turn up and trek, without having to join an organised tour.

The scenery on these trekking routes is truly jaw-dropping, but don't underestimate the effort involved in trekking in the Himalaya. Days of thumping up and down steep mountain paths will turn your knees to jelly and you need to be wary of altitude sickness, which can be fatal. With the recent upsurge in Maoist rebel violence in Nepal, it's wise to check the security situation before setting off on any trek.

India is also well set up for Himalayan trekking – Sikkim has some of the best trekking in India, but you have to be part of an organised group for high-altitude routes. Himachal Pradesh and Uttaranchal offer wonderful treks to remote temples and holy lakes, but you may need a permit and guide and most routes are camping all the way.

Be very cautious trekking in the Kullu and Parvati Valleys in Himachal Pradesh – a number of backpackers have been murdered here in recent years. There is more trekking in Ladakh in the east and around Darjeeling in the West.

If you can afford to visit Bhutan, it offers some fantastic trekking routes. Mountain trekking is also possible in Pakistan, but most of the trekking areas are currently considered unsafe. There are a few interesting low-altitude treks in Sri Lanka, including the ascent to Adam's Peak (2224m).

Many companies offer organised mountaineering expeditions in the Himalaya in both India and Nepal, but the 'mountain fees' – on top of the cost of the expedition – range from £180 for small peaks to £26,000 for Mt Everest.

For more information on trekking in any of these areas, consult the relevant Lonely Planet country or trekking guide. See When to Go (p169) for the best trekking times.

WHITE-WATER RAFTING
The rushing rivers that flow down from the Himalaya offer some fantastic white-water rafting. Again, Nepal is the best place to organise a rafting trip – dozens of rafting companies offer trips on the Trisuli River near Kathmandu and the Sun Kosi River in east Nepal.

In India, you can go rafting on the Teesta and Rangeet Rivers in Sikkim and West Bengal, and the Beas, Ganges, Indus, Spiti and Kanskar Rivers in Himachal Pradesh. Rafting is also possible in Pakistan and Bhutan, but the rafting industry is only just getting off the ground.

MOUNTAIN BIKING
The Subcontinent attracts loads of mountain bikers. Most people bring their own bikes as locally made bikes aren't really up to the rugged terrain. Popular spots include the Kathmandu Valley in Nepal and Sikkim and Himachal Pradesh in India. There are more challenging routes along the Thimphu and Paro Valleys in Bhutan and the Karakoram Hwy in Pakistan.

Lowland cycling is also popular in central and southern India and Bangladesh, but you'll have to share the roads with wandering cows, speeding trucks and drivers with a death wish. Expect regular punctures, long days under the beating sun and endless questions from locals about your flashy foreign bike.

DIVING, SNORKELLING & WATERSPORTS
As a major beach destination, Sri Lanka has the usual beachfront watersports and there are decent surf breaks at Hikkaduwa, Unawatuna and Arugam Bay. Although India is surrounded by sea, the only decent scuba diving and snorkelling is in Sri Lanka (at Hikkaduwa and Unawatuna), on the touristy Maldives, or on India's Andaman and Nicobar Islands. A variety of watersports are on offer in Goa. Unfortunately all of these coastal places were badly hit by the 2004 tsunami and at the time of writing were in different stages of recovery with some places already receiving travellers and others taking longer to rebuild.

OTHER ACTIVITIES
Adventure sports are incredibly cheap in India, but tread carefully as safety standards aren't always as good as they should be. Himachal Pradesh, Goa and Maharashtra are the main centres for paragliding and hang-gliding, but there have been some tragic mishaps over the years.

Indian skiing has a better record and prices are possibly the lowest in the world. The main resorts are Solang Nullah in Himachal Pradesh and Auli in Uttar Pradesh. The season runs from January to March and a day's skiing can cost you less than £5.

Spectator sports are a popular diversion across the Subcontinent and there are opportunities to cheer on the local team at football matches, cricket tournaments and even kabaddi games (traditional Indian-team game). Cricket is an Indian obsession and the whole region grinds to a halt during international matches.

The region also offers some unusual tours, from jeep trips to visiting tribal villages in the far northeast of India, to camel and horse safaris through the deserts of Rajasthan (particularly from Jaisalmer and Pushkar). Cowboys who prefer steel horses can join motorcycling tours in Sikkim, Nepal and Bhutan.

Work a Little

There isn't much in the way of paying work for gappers in the region, but there are loads of opportunities for volunteers. India, Nepal and Sri Lanka have hundreds of humanitarian and conservation projects that need teachers, researchers, healthcare staff and other support workers.

Some accept direct applications from volunteers, but most get their staff through international volunteering organisations – see p264 for some suggestions.

Travel Around

Getting around inside the Indian Subcontinent is easy and inexpensive. Domestic flights are possible within India, Pakistan, Bangladesh and Nepal and fares are comparatively cheap considering the distances.

India has the most options – you have a choice of the huge network (but cranky aircraft) of government-owned Indian Airlines (www.indian-airlines.nic.in) or flashier Jet Airways (www.jetairways.com) and Air Sahara (www.airsahara.net), which both fly on to Colombo (Sri Lanka). Jet also has flights between India and Nepal.

The best way to travel around India, Pakistan and Bangladesh is by train. Indian trains are legendary and there are classes to suit all budgets from cheap wooden bench seats to air-conditioned berths. The computerised reservations system is remarkably efficient and even when trains are booked solid, travellers can avail of special 'tourist quotas' on popular routes. The Indian Railways website (www.indianrail.gov.in) has up-to-the-minute timetables, route information and fare lists.

Interesting train journeys include 'palace on wheels' trips in the carriages of former Maharajas and the World Heritage–listed metre-gauge service from Siliguri to Darjeeling. A single international rail line runs from Pakistan to India, but you must change trains at the border and services are frequently suspended due to political tensions between the two countries.

The trains are supplemented by an incredible network of bus routes, but drivers have a devil-may-care attitude to safety. The cheapest buses are the non-air conditioned government buses, but they can be crowded and uncomfortable and there is rarely anywhere to put your bags. On long routes, it's worth paying a bit extra for an air-con bus with a proper luggage locker. Long distance routes connect India to Nepal, Pakistan, Bangladesh and Bhutan, sometimes with a change of bus at the border.

Boat transport is possible along the Brahmaputra River in Assam, around the backwaters of Kerala, and along the coast from Mumbai to Goa in India. Ferries also run to the Andaman Islands from Chennai and Kolkata. Bangladesh has the famous and charming 'Rocket' paddle wheel steamer between Dhaka and Khulna.

In mountainous areas, 4WD jeeps act as shared taxis, providing a cramped but efficient way of getting around. You can hire a vehicle and driver for day tours and longer trips throughout the Subcontinent. Motorcycling around India and Nepal is great fun but the roads are lethal. Inexperienced riders are best off renting bikes for local trips around Hampi and Mahabalipuram in India and Kathmandu in Nepal.

Taxis, trams, auto-rickshaws, cycle-rickshaws and tongas (horse-drawn carriages) all serve as transport in urban areas, but you normally have to agree a price before you set off.

CLASSIC ROUTES

There are numerous well-worn backpacker circuits though the region, and while you may be loath to follow the beaten path, these take in some of the most interesting and impressive places in the Subcontinent.

Delhi to Kathmandu
The most famous route is the overland trip from Delhi to Agra, Varanasi and Kathmandu. This will let you visit the Taj Mahal and Fatehpur Sikri near Agra, take a boat trip on the holy River Ganges in Varanasi and finish off among the temples and travellers in Kathmandu.

Golden Triangle
An alternative version starts off in Delhi, and continues to Agra and then Jaipur, the gateway to Rajasthan. This is the so-called Golden Triangle, and there's loads to see, including the medieval fortress at Jaisalmer and the Lake Palace in Udaipur. However, it's also the most touristy part of the Subcontinent.

India Circuit
Quite a few people do the grand circuit of India, from Mumbai to Kolkata or Kolkata to Mumbai. This route mostly follows the coast – beginning in Mumbai, you can visit the temples and caves of Maharashtra, the beaches of Goa, the fabulous ruins of Hampi in Karnataka, the backwaters of Kerala, the Dravidian monuments of Tamil Nadu, mighty Chennai, the Sun Temple at Konark and Puri in Orissa and, finally, India's cultural and artistic capital, Kolkata.

Kolkata to Bhutan & Kolkata, Northeast & Bangladesh
An interesting, little-followed route, begins in Kolkata and winds up through West Bengal to Sikkim, then on to the northeast, passing through Assam, Meghalaya and Tripura and returning to Kolkata overland through Bangladesh. Alternatively you can head from Kolkata to Darjeeling and on to western Nepal, continuing by bus to Kathmandu. Kolkata is also the stepping off point for overland trips to Bhutan, via the land border at Jaigon/Phuentsholing.

India to Pakistan
It's easy to tag Sri Lanka onto any loop through south India (there are flights from Chennai, Trivandrum and Bangalore) and most people find time to tour around the entire island. Crossing into Pakistan is more tricky, but you can head from Amritsar to Lahore by train and then continue to Islamabad or head south through Multan and Moenjodaro to Karachi. The famous Karakoram Hwy passes through Pakistan's risky Northwest Frontier Province. You should obtain up-to-date travel advice before travelling through this lawless area.

WHEN TO GO?
India has a distinct wet season and dry season. Most travellers choose to visit between November and February, when the mountain views are clearest and the weather is cool and dry for trekking. From February, the heat begins to build up on the plains. Travel can become unbearable until the monsoon arrives to cool everything off in June.

However, there are disadvantages to visiting during the peak season. Prices are higher, and there is more competition for rooms and seats on public transport. You also have to deal with the chill winter fog, which can close airports on the plains for days at a time. Some high-altitude areas – including Ladakh, Spiti and Lahaul in India and the Karakoram Hwy in Pakistan – are only accessible by road from June to September.

Climate
The Indian Subcontinent has a classic monsoon climate, with clear wet and dry seasons. The year can broken down into the 'hot' season from February to May; the 'wet' (monsoon) season from June to October and the 'cool' season from October to February.

During the monsoon, the region is lashed by incredible amounts of rain. Rivers flood, landslides block roads and the mountains vanish behind swirls of cloud. There is also a smaller second monsoon on the southeast coast from October to December.

The cool season is the best time for tourism. Mountain views are excellent and the weather is mostly cool and dry, though it can get quite chilly on higher ground and in the central plains. From February, the heat starts to rise and plains bake – expect to sweat buckets until June when the first rains arrive.

Of course, there are big regional variations. Meghalaya in India is the wettest place on earth, while the deserts of Pakistan and Rajasthan and areas that fall under the rain-shadow of the Himalaya can be incredibly parched and dry. Much of southern India, Bangladesh and Sri Lanka are tropical and subtropical and cyclones are a risk in coastal areas from April to May and October to December.

Festivals

Festivals in the Indian Subcontinent tend to be spectacular affairs and many people plan their trip to coincide with festival season. The following are the largest nationwide and regional festivals:

Holi Festival (India) Held in February/March, Hindus celebrate the arrival of spring and the defeat of the demon Holika by throwing tons of water and coloured powder over as many people as possible, including foreign visitors!

Losar (all Tibetan Buddhist areas) Buddhists celebrate the Tibetan new year (in February/March) with masked dances and processions.

Shivaratri (India & Nepal) Hindus fast in February/March in honour of the cosmic dance performed by the god Shiva. Sadhus (holy men) make pilgrimages to Nepal and bathe in the Bagmati River in Kathmandu.

Rath Yatra (India) Held in June/July, Hindus commemorate the journey of Krishna from Gokul to Mathura with processions of gigantic temple 'chariots' pulled by thousands of eager devotees. The most famous procession takes place at Puri in Orissa.

Esala Perahera (Sri Lanka) Kandy holds this huge and important pageant, with 10 days of candle-lit processions and elephants lit up like giant birthday cakes. Held in July/August.

Kataragama (Sri Lanka) Hindu pilgrims visit the shrine at Kataragama and put themselves through the whole gamut of ritual masochism. Held in July/August.

Durga Puja (West Bengal, Northeast India & Bangladesh) Held in October. Hindus make thousands of colourful statues of the goddess Durga and ritually immerse them in rivers and streams. At the same, Nepal celebrates the Dasain festival with animal sacrifices and central parts of India hold the Dussehra festival to celebrate the defeat of the demon king Ravana.

Diwali (India & Nepal) During October/November Hindus across the Subcontinent light oil lamps and let off firecrackers for five days to show the god Rama the way home from his period in exile. The festival is known as Deepavali in some parts of India and Tihar in Nepal.

There are also the following festivals that either move each year or take place at different times in different locations:

Ramadan (Pakistan, Bangladesh) In Muslim areas, people fast throughout the holy month of Ramadan and many shops and restaurants stay closed until the fast is broken for the feast of Eid al-Fitr. The festival moves with the lunar calendar, advancing 10 or 11 days each year.

Tsechus (Bhutan) In spring and autumn, Buddhist monasteries across Bhutan hold five days of masked dances in honour of Guru Rinpoche.

Kumbh Mela (India) Every three years, the world's largest festival takes place at either Allahabad, Haridwar, Nasik or Ujjain to commemorate an ancient battle between gods and demons. The Mela attracts tens of millions of Hindu pilgrims and each of these cities hosts the festival once every 12 years.

WHAT TO EXPECT?
Travellers
Some commentators have described India as the greatest show on earth, and that's just the travellers. You'll probably never meet such a broad selection of freaks, do-gooders, adventurers, enlightenment seekers, beach bums, drug fiends, obsessive trekkers and barstool philosophers. Numerous traveller centres have grown up to cater to this curious demographic, offering Indian versions of Western meals, cold beers and various things to inhale. Be careful if you follow this last avenue – drugs are illegal throughout the region and the penalties can be severe.

The main traveller centres around the Subcontinent are:

Dharamsala (India) The seat of Tibetan government in exile, with hundreds of backpackers seeking inner peace and *momos* (Tibetan dumplings).

Goa (India) Once famous for wild rave parties, but now making an impact on the package tourist scene.

Hampi (India) Ruins, temples, cheap food and accommodation and loads of travellers to pass the time of day with.

Kathmandu (Nepal) The famous end of the Hippy Trail, with backpacker bars, cheap cafés, budget hotels and more temples than you can shake a stick at.

Kullu Valley (India) Mountain valley with trekking and rafting, cheap digs and dope dealers, but risky for hiking.

Pushkar (India) Hugely popular holy hang-out but famous for hassle during the Camel Fair.

Unawatuna & Mirissa (Sri Lanka) Laid-back villages with beaches and clear blue waters.

Varanasi (India) Hindu pilgrim centre and most culturally interesting traveller stop on the north India circuit.

Locals
The vast majority of people are hospitable and friendly, but privacy doesn't have quite the same meaning as it does in the West. On an average day, you might have to tell your life story to a dozen people, pose for a couple of photographs with newly-weds and shake hands with an entire school group. It's a bit like being David Beckham for the day.

Needless to say, it can be overwhelming when you first arrive, but most people get used to it after a few days. Be prepared for lots of inquiries about permissive sexual practices in the West – this is something of a national obsession in India.

Harder to deal with are the attentions of touts, hawkers and con merchants, who hang around the main travellers' haunts in alarming numbers. Quite a few travellers make the mistake of assuming all Indians are like this, only to be humbled by some random act of kindness later in their travels.

The important thing is to keep your sense of humour – prices are almost always elevated for foreigners but you can usually bargain down to something more reasonable. At the same time, it's probably not worth haggling for hours over a few rupees!

Of course, there are some real *badmashes* (the Indian term for villains). Theft is a risk in some areas – often through the use of drugged food and drink on trains. Pakistan is becoming increasingly lawless and kidnapping of foreigners for ransom is on the increase. In all Muslim areas, keep a low profile during public demonstrations and flash points of religious conflict.

Poverty is a fact of life in the Subcontinent and beggars hassle travellers throughout the region. Whether you give or not is a very personal decision – most people end up giving something, if only to gain a few moments of peace. If you really want to make a difference to the lives of local people, consider making a donation to a charity or development organisation.

You can also expect regular demands for baksheesh (tips) from officials and bureaucrats. It's corruption by another name, but it can open doors and make problems go away. Of course, if someone is just taking the mickey, you're quite within your rights to tell them where to get off!

Religion

After the demise of the British Empire the region was chopped up along broadly faith lines, so India and Nepal are mainly Hindu, Pakistan and Bangladesh are mainly Muslim and Bhutan is almost entirely Buddhist.

Hinduism is practised by more than 80% of Indians and Nepalis. Hindus believe in reincarnation, karma (the consequences of good and bad actions) and dharma (station in life). These last two factors affect how you'll be reincarnated – behave badly and you may come back as a cockroach. Be good and you may return in a higher caste. Caste plays an important role in the social structure of the region, but it doesn't usually affect relations between locals and travellers.

Other, less familiar faiths in India include Sikhism, a branch of Hinduism created in response to persecution by the Mughals in the Punjab, and Jainism, possibly the most peaceful faith in the Subcontinent – Jains believe strongly in non-violence and devout followers sweep the ground before them to avoid stepping on any living creatures.

Nepal, Sri Lanka, Bhutan and parts of north India have a strong Buddhist tradition. Sri Lanka follows a similar form of Buddhism to Myanmar (Burma), while Nepal, Bhutan and northern India look towards Tibet.

Pakistan and Bangladesh are predominantly Sunni Muslim and religious minorities have quite a tough time of it in both countries. While people are friendlier than the media would have you believe, anti-Western sentiments run high in many areas. In both countries, you should follow the standard codes of behaviour for Islamic countries – see the Middle East chapter (p137) for more advice. Many travellers adopt native clothing to break down some of the barriers.

Language

English is widely spoken throughout the region, but each country has its own dialects and regional languages. In India, Hindi is the official language but 80% of the population speak other Indian languages. Urdu is spoken by the Muslim population (especially in Pakistan) and Tamil and Sinhala are the official languages of Sri Lanka. Bengali is spoken in Bangladesh, Nepali in Nepal and Dzongkha (which is related to Tibetan) in Bhutan.

There are loads of language courses in the region and the UK. Lonely Planet's *Hindu & Urdu*, *Nepali* and *Bengali* phrasebooks will help you get your tongue round the local languages.

Health Risks

OK, time to come clean. You will have a few days of loose movements at some time during your stay, and we aren't talking about Michael Jackson's dance steps. Hygiene standards are lax throughout the region and even if you avoid unwashed fruit and vegetables, drink purified water and only eat food that is cooked fresh in front of you, the odd bug can still get through. It still makes sense to follow these precautions to minimise the chances.

Most bugs are self-limiting and short-lived – if you have a long journey ahead, Imodium can ease the symptoms temporarily. If things aren't back to normal after a couple of days, go to a local doctor as it could be something more serious.

It's also important to get the right vaccinations before you travel – your local travel clinic can advise you on which shots you need. Anti-malarial medication is a sensible precaution if you are travelling in lowland areas. Other health problems include cholera, dysentery, giardiasis and altitude sickness, which kills a handful of travellers each year.

Consult the Health chapter (p59) and seek professional medical advice for more travel health information.

Time & Flight Time

Pakistan is five hours ahead of Greenwich Mean Time (GMT), India and Sri Lanka are 5½ hours ahead, Nepal is 5¾ hours ahead and Bangladesh and Bhutan are six hours ahead. These slight odd-sounding time differences are designed to avoid the need for daylight saving time in this vast area.

Islamabad is an 8¼-hour flight away from London, Delhi nine hours away, Dhaka 9½ hours and Colombo 10½ hours away. You must fly via the Gulf or India from London to Kathmandu (about 11 hours in total).

Issues

Almost all of the conflicts in the Indian Subcontinent have been going on since Independence and most are intractable. India and Pakistan still hover on the edge of war over the disputed region of Kashmir, and Pakistan faces growing problems with violent Islamic radicals. The Foreign and Commonwealth Office (www.fco.gov.uk) currently warns against all but essential travel to Pakistan.

In the northeast of India, hundreds of insurgent armies are fighting for independent tribal states and the tribal people of Chittagong are fighting persecution by the Muslim majority in Bangladesh. Sri Lanka is still embroiled in a civil war between the Sinhalese majority and the Tamil minority.

Maoists rebels are fighting the government of Nepal, with violence occasionally threatening Kathmandu and the main trekking routes. Only Bhutan is an island of calm. All these situations flare up and die down with monotonous regularity – to stay safe, check the security situation before and while you travel.

These conflicts affect overland travel between all the countries of the region. There is only one open border crossing between India and Pakistan (the Wagah-Attari border) and foreigners are only permitted to cross between India and Bhutan at Jaigon/Phuentsholing. You can cross from India to Nepal and Bangladesh at numerous locations, but you cannot cross into Myanmar overland. The only overland route to China is the Karakoram Hwy through Pakistan.

For further information on travel hot spots, general safety issues and governmental travel advice see the Safety chapter (p79).

Internet & Communications

Cybercafés are very popular in the Indian Subcontinent and connection speeds are getting faster by the day. However, the Indian power supply is notoriously unreliable. There are public call offices in every town, village and hamlet where you can make cheap international calls. Travellers with roaming-activated mobile phones will find a signal in lowland areas but not in the mountains.

DAILY SPEND

With the exception of Bhutan, travel is cheap throughout the Indian Subcontinent. The cheapest country in the region is Bangladesh, followed closely by India and Pakistan. In all three countries, you can get by on £10 per day, and eat in the best restaurants and stay in comfortable hotels with TVs and hot showers for £15–20 per day. Rooms in Maharaja's palaces and travel by first class train come at international prices.

Nepal is slightly more expensive but you can still get by on £15 per day. You'll need more in Kathmandu because there are more things to spend money on. Living costs in Sri Lanka are about the same, though you'll need to budget extra for activities like scuba diving.

Bhutan can only be visited on an organised tour, and all travellers must pay £85–103 per day, which covers transport, meals and accommodation. Sadly, this puts Bhutan out of reach of all but the wealthiest gappers.

The Maldives is primarily a package tour destination and most resorts charge upwards of £80 per day including meals.

GETTING THERE

Numerous airlines travel between Britain and India, Bangladesh and Pakistan so fares are fairly competitive. To reach Nepal or Bhutan, you must change planes and/or airlines, so getting to these places is slightly more expensive. It's also possible to travel from Europe to India overland, but this is becoming increasingly difficult due to the security situation in Pakistan.

Air

India is the cheapest place to fly into and many people start here and continue overland into other countries in the region. Flights to Delhi and Mumbai are cheaper than flights to Kolkata or Chennai, but you can often find cheap charter flights to Goa and Kerala in the south.

There are also direct flights to Pakistan (Karachi, Islamabad and Lahore), Bangladesh (Dhaka) and Sri Lanka (Colombo). Getting to Kathmandu in Nepal involves a change in India or the Middle East. To reach Paro in Bhutan you must change to a Druk Air (www .drukair.com.bt) flight in India, Nepal, Bangladesh, Myanmar or Thailand. It is also possible to include Delhi, Mumbai and Colombo as part of a round-the-world (RTW) ticket.

Often, the cheapest flights from Britain to the Indian Subcontinent are with British Airways (BA), but you can also find cheap deals with KLM Royal Dutch Airlines, Austrian Airlines and most of the Middle Eastern airlines. Qatar Airways, Gulf Air, Austrian Airlines and Indian Airlines have flights into Kathmandu. Several carriers have flights on to Southeast Asia from Delhi and Kolkata.

TICKET COSTS

The best available economy fares are quoted here, but students and people under 26 may be eligible for extra discounts. Karachi, Delhi and Mumbai are the cheapest places on the Indian Subcontinent to fly into (about £400 return) but flights to Chennai, Kolkata, Dhaka and Islamabad are more expensive (£500 or more). Flights into Colombo and Kathmandu cost £400–500 depending on when you need to fly. Open-jaw flights – where you fly into one city and out of another – are only slightly more expensive.

Overland & Sea

The most common overland route is along the old Hippy Trail from London to India, via Turkey, Iran and Pakistan, and on to Nepal. Trains run most of the way, but a few audacious travellers do the whole journey by car or motorbike. However, this route is dependent on good relations between India and Pakistan.

An alternative route cuts down through Russia and Central Asia to Iran and then Pakistan or from Kyrgyzstan to China and down the legendary Karakoram Hwy into Pakistan, but again, these routes pass through politically volatile areas. Check locally to see if the proposed ferry route from India to Sri Lanka has started operating.

Specialist Tour Operators

Heaps of British tour operators run trips to and within the Indian Subcontinent – some big region-specific operators include:

Essential India (☎ /fax 01225 868544; www.essential-india.co.uk; 106a Upper Westwood, Bradford-on-Avon, Wiltshire BA15 2DS) Runs trips across the country including some focusing on arts and crafts.
Exodus Travels (☎ 0870 240 5550; www.exodus.co.uk; Grange Mills, Weir Road, London SW12 0NE) Offers trips throughout the region.
Imaginative Traveller (☎ 0800 316 2717; www.imaginative-traveller.com; 1 Betts Ave, Martlesham Heath, Suffolk IP5 7RH) Offers trips through India, Nepal, Sri Lanka and Bhutan.
Indian Encounters (☎ 01929 481421; www.indianencounters.com; Creech Barrow, East Creech, Wareham, Dorset BH20 5AP) Offers focused, tailor-made trips to India.

THE INDIAN SUBCONTINENT & BEYOND
It is possible to head overland from the Indian Subcontinent to China (via Pakistan) and the Middle East, and on to Europe, Northeast Asia and Russia. To get to Southeast Asia, you have no choice but to fly, or take a very circuitous route through China. There are no useful international ferry routes to the region.

FURTHER INFORMATION
Reading Material
Lonely Planet publishes guides to numerous countries, regions and cities in the Indian Subcontinent plus a guide to the route from *Istanbul to Kathmandu*. *Healthy Travel Asia & India* and *World Food India* are solid background reading, while *Trekking in the Indian Himalaya*, *Trekking in the Nepal Himalaya* and *Trekking in the Karakoram & Hindukush* are indispensable for trekkers. *Sacred India* is a beautifully photographed exploration of beliefs in India.

Recommended background reading on India includes *No Full Stops in India* and *India in Slow Motion* by BBC correspondent Mark Tully, *May You Be the Mother of a Hundred Sons* by Elisabeth Bumiller, *City of Djinns*, *White Mughals* and *Age of Kali* by William Dalrymple, *Plain Tales from the Hills* by Rudyard Kipling, and the novel *Midnight's Children* by Salman Rushdie. Top travelogues include *The Great Railway Bazaar* by Paul Theroux, *Chasing the Monsoon* by Alexander Frater, and *Travels on my Elephant* and *River Dog* by Mark Shand.

There are thousands of books on Buddhism, Hinduism and Islam – too many to list here. Several books on Buddhism have been written by the Dalai Lama himself. To understand Hinduism and Islam, start off by reading the *Ramayana*, the *Mahabharata* and the *Quran*. Gita Mehta's witty *Karma Cola* is an interesting exploration of the spiritual collision between India and the West.

Solid reading for Pakistan and Bangladesh includes *To the Frontier* by Geoffrey Moorhouse, *Bangladesh: Reflections on the Water* by James J Novak, *The Golden Peak: Travels in Northern Pakistan* by Kathleen Jamie, and *Full Tilt* by Dervla Murphy. For Sri Lanka, try *Running in the Family* by Michael Ondaatje, or *Only Man is Vile: The Tragedy of Sri Lanka* by William McGowan.

Interesting books on Nepal include Peter Somerville-Large's engagingly dotty *To the Navel of the World*, and *The Waiting Land: A Spell in Nepal* by Dervla Murphy. *Into Thin Air*, by Jon Krakauer, is an incredible account of the disastrous 1996 expeditions on Mt Everest. *So Close to Heaven* by Barbara Crossette deals with Bhutan and other vanishing Himalayan kingdoms.

Useful Information Sources
For specific country overviews, the low-down on travel in the region and hundreds of useful links head first to Lonely Planet's website (www.lonelyplanet.com).

The following portals and useful websites should help you chase down any aspect of interest on the Indian Subcontinent:

http://in.rediff.com Leading Indian news site.

www.123india.com Reliable India portal.

www.discoverybangladesh.com Good private Bangladesh tourism site.

www.info-nepal.com Great Nepalese travel site.

www.khoj.com Good portal for things Indian.

www.lanka.net Broad portal into all things Sri Lankan.

www.srilankatourism.org Sri Lanka government tourism site.

www.tourism.gov.bt Bhutan government tourism site.

www.tourism.gov.pk Pakistan government tourism site.

www.tourismofindia.com Indian government tourism site.

www.trekinfo.com Solid Nepal trekking portal.

www.welcomenepal.com Nepal government tourism site.

BEEN THERE, DONE THAT

Nothing matches your first trip to India. I can still remember touching down in New Delhi airport and feeling a pang of panic as I looked out through the doors and saw the waiting crowds of taxi drivers, rickshaw wallahs and assorted hangers-on. Thunder and lightning were cracking in the sky overhead and the air was full of the smell of earth after the first rains of the monsoon.

Fortunately, there were half a dozen other travellers in a similar state, so we all banded together to share a taxi into town. We were scammed rotten: the driver stopped on the wrong side of New Delhi railway station and told us we had to take an auto-rickshaw from there, which involved an 8km journey to a point 100m from where we started! But the rest of the trip was amazing.

The following morning I walked out into a street full of holy cows, street hawkers, ox-carts, food stalls, rickshaws, holy men, elephants, palm-readers, contortionists, mosques and temples, with monkeys running along the power lines and everywhere, noise, colour and confusion. It was like walking out into a giant open-air circus. I've made numerous trips to India since, but I still get that same buzz when I step out in the street and realise that, yes, I am back in India.

Too many things happened on that first trip to recount here. Highlights include being shot 'dead' as a movie extra in a Hindi gangster film, free climbing granite outcrops to meditate in my own private temple at Hampi, and riding around southern India – and periodically crashing – on a clapped-out Enfield motorcycle.

After six months in India, I headed up to Nepal and followed my own trekking route through the mountains, sleeping under the stars or in the porches of temples and barns at remote farms. Although I spoke no Nepali, and none of the locals spoke English, we somehow managed to communicate. Everyone I met showed me incredible hospitality. At one point, villagers even sent out a rescue party for me after a gang of bandits killed a local farmer and were last seen heading in my direction. The phrase 'the kindness of strangers' has never had so much meaning!

Joe Bindloss

NORTHEAST ASIA

BRADLEY MAYHEW
For Bradley's biography, see p149.

INTRODUCTION

Northeast Asia includes China, Japan, Hong Kong, Korea (North and South), Mongolia, Taiwan and Tibet. This is the land of Confucius, kung fu and karaoke, and its inhabitants' beliefs, traditions and cultures have captivated and perplexed Europeans for centuries.

The region is home to some of the world's most (Japan) and least (Mongolia) technologically obsessed nations. Yet beneath the fascinating gilded modernity of Japan, South Korea and Taiwan you'll find ancient cultures, traditions and ways of life that reward the time required to understand them. China is busily reinventing and reasserting itself with seemingly unstoppable economic momentum but still offers almost endless scope for adventure. Much is changing in this increasingly important part of the world but, along with the fantastic food, incredible temples and shrines, unsurpassed architectural monuments and beautiful landscapes, an undeniable Eastern magic remains.

Sleep in a Mongolian yurt or a Japanese capsule hotel; fill up on Chinese dim sum or Korean kimchi; learn Chinese in Taiwan or teach English in Tokyo – earn or spend a fortune; it's up to you.

TOP 10 MUST-SEES

Great Wall (China) Still essential viewing on any trip, even if you can't actually see it from space.
Lhasa (Tibet) The Potala Palace, Jokhang Temple and bruised heart of Tibetan culture.
Kakunodate (Japan) 17th-century samurai houses and cherry trees.
Tokyo & Shanghai (Japan & China) Welcome to the metropolises of the future, where *Blade Runner* meets *Lost in Translation*.
Gyeongju (South Korea) An important historic and religious former capital of tombs, pagodas and temples.
Naadam Festival (Mongolia) Horse racing, wrestling and archery reveal the ancient warrior traits of the Mongols. The biggest festivities are in the capital, Ulaan Baatar.
Beijing (China) Once you've checked out the impressive Forbidden City and Summer Palace, rent a bike and explore the winding *hutong* (alleyways).
Kyoto & Nara (Japan) Ancient capitals packed with shrines, temples and culture.
Kashgar (China) A medieval Central Asian city of mosques, shrines and lamb kebabs, with Asia's greatest market.
Hong Kong (China) The view at night from Victoria Peak may well be the world's most beautiful urban landscape.

WHY NORTHEAST ASIA?

Don't pack your preconceptions when coming to Northeast Asia. It's not a uniform place. The economic gap between nations may be getting smaller but the austere temples, serene Zen gardens and futuristic cityscapes of Tokyo are still a mighty contrast to the deserts of remote western China or the nomad camps of Mongolia, where the culture shock comes with a mutton fat dinner and a morning wash in the local river. Backpackers on the cheap will find plenty to explore in China and Mongolia (the 'Timbuktu' of Asia); those headed to Japan, Taiwan and Korea are generally looking for an opportunity to study or a chance to earn back some funds.

Travelling through Japan, South Korea and Taiwan is (language aside) pretty easy going, and you can still satisfy your desires for stunning Buddhist temples, sacred mist-shrouded peaks and cultural experiences.

China is the region's Goliath and you could easily spend your entire year here without even spotting a panda. Now is a fascinating time to visit China as the yin of Mao's fading revolutionary zeal is eclipsed by the yang of economic pragmatism, and there's a physical (in building and infrastructure) and social reincarnation under way. Gauge the pace of modernisation and shop till you drop in Beijing and glitzy Shanghai, before seeking out the soul of China in the countryside.

Most travellers' favourite is the southwest, which serves up China at its most colourful and enjoyable. Guizhou offers timeless villages of local 'minority' groups, who would be called hill tribes anywhere else in the world. The quintessential Chinese landscapes around Yangshuo (Guangxi province) are China's backpacking mecca. Yunnan province is most peoples' favourite province, from the gorgeous villages of Lijiang to the subtropical border areas next to Burma, Vietnam and Laos. Sichuan is a very diverse province, as the east is Chinese, and the west is Tibetan. Its attractions include pandas, the world's largest Buddha, several sacred Chinese Buddhist peaks in the east, and wild mountains dotted with Tibetan monasteries in the west.

Elsewhere in China you'll find deserts, Buddhist grottos, traditional villages, terracotta warriors and the magic of the Silk Road – the ancient trade route that for centuries connected China with the rest of the world. Much of China's colour comes from its fascinating ethnic groups, which range from Central Asian Uyghurs and nomadic Kazakhs to Mongolians and matriarchal groups such as the Naxi.

Tibet is another world completely and is still one of Asia's most amazing destinations. Give yourself a couple of days to learn how to breath at altitudes over 3700m and then head out to explore monasteries, pilgrim paths and Himalayan views. In Tibet, as in Xinjiang, the imposition of Han Chinese culture has been as brutal as the crushing of student demonstrations in Tiananmen Square in 1989. Chinese travel restrictions require some initiative to circumvent but once there you'll be surprised at how free you are to explore.

North Korea, though, is a totally different bag of travel treats, where entry to the very weird, totalitarian Marxist dictatorship is heavily restricted to tour groups. You could add on a tour of Libya and Iran for your very own 'Axis of Evil' tour extravaganza.

Mongolia is far more open and lives up to the hype as one of the last great adventure destinations in Asia. Ulaan Baatar (the capital of Mongolia) may no longer feel like the end of the earth but it's definitely the gateway. Travel here, as in Tibet, is a grade wilder than elsewhere in the region. Hire a minivan with some other travellers, bring a tent and cruise across the grasslands. After the teeming cities of China you'll get a rush from the intoxicating sense of space.

Japan, South Korea and Taiwan perhaps provide examples of where China is headed. In these countries modernity sits neatly alongside unique ancient cultures, and between the sanitised shopping malls there are sometimes incomprehensible traditions and unexpected rural festivals. Everyone creates his or her own impression of these countries. Many people will appreciate Japan's many Zen gardens and stunning Shinto shrines but whether you end up trekking the high peaks or immersing yourself in Buddhism, you'd better come with an open mind and prepare to be surprised. Japan in particular is a wonderfully wacky place that requires an extended stay for a deeper understanding. And it isn't all tea ceremonies, strict etiquette and raw fish; Japan has kinky 'love hotels' and even public vending machines that dispense magic mushrooms.

Travel in Northwest Asia, especially China, is not without its problems. Language and script can cause serious confusion, and cultural differences and an entrenched party bureaucracy also rear their head frequently. Get over this and you'll quickly find the sublime tastes, vibrant colours and amazing sights of the region second to none, whether you savour the high life in Asia's most exciting cities or head off the map into unrivalled opportunities for adventure.

WHAT TO DO?

Work in Northeast Asia is definitely on the cards but the region is not necessarily a great place for voluntary work (especially if you don't speak a local language).

A number of travellers specifically study the local beliefs. In Japan, Zen Buddhism is taught through exceedingly strict (both mentally and physically) courses. Tibetan Buddhism is less austere but restrictions in Tibet make retreats and courses very difficult if not impossible – you're better off heading to Kathmandu (Nepal) or Dharamsala (India) for these.

Other courses in regional culture include cooking, language, pottery, traditional medicine, martial arts, music, dance and craft. Kyoto (Japan) is particularly renowned for courses in Japanese arts, and you can learn t'ai chi in parks across China. Language courses are widespread throughout the region and in Japan a cultural visa may let you work too.

Learning Mandarin Chinese is becoming an increasingly popular option, as China's economy continues to boom. Taipei and Beijing are particularly popular places to study, though other cities such as Kunming and Chengdu also offer university courses.

See Part III for more information on overseas jobs, volunteer work and courses in the region.

Get Active

In Japan, Korea and Taiwan outdoor activities are pursued with passion. China has incredible scope for adventure sports, though much if this is do-it-yourself at the moment. Most Chinese would rather go shopping than hiking, but a new generation of adventurous Chinese travellers are trying on the Gore-Tex in affluent cities such as Beijing, Shanghai and Guangzhou.

CYCLING & MOUNTAIN-BIKING

Biking is a great way to get to parts of China (300 million Chinese cyclists can't be wrong…). You can hire clunky bikes in most towns in China and a few places offer mountain bikes for rural exploration; cycling around the wondrous peaks of Yangshuo is one of China's real highlights. The physically demanding run from Lhasa to Kathmandu is one of the world's great mountain-biking routes, as is the downhill run along the Karakorum Hwy from Kashgar to Gilgit in Pakistan.

The mountains of Japan, South Korea and Taiwan offer numerous mountain-bike trails. Japan's backroads, especially in the coastal regions, are particularly popular with cycle tourists.

SKIING & SNOWBOARDING

South Korea has some reasonable skiing and Japan has more than 300 (pricey) ski resorts, which get some great powder from December to April. Cross-country skiing is very popular and cheaper. Skiing in China is possible but pretty average.

NORTHEAST ASIA

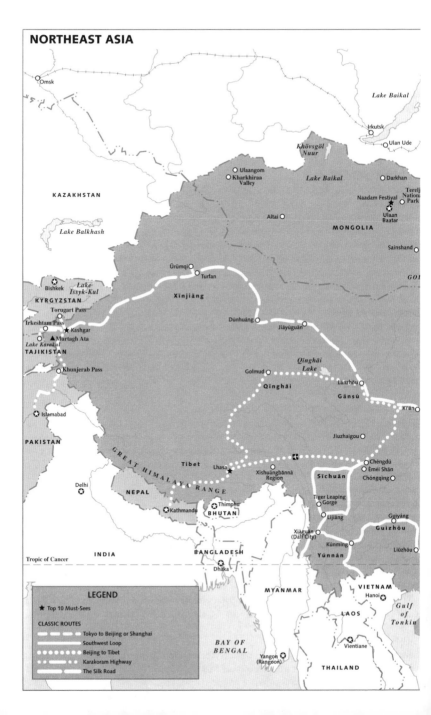

LEGEND

★ Top 10 Must-Sees

CLASSIC ROUTES

- Tokyo to Beijing or Shanghai
- Southwest Loop
- Beijing to Tibet
- Karakoram Highway
- The Silk Road

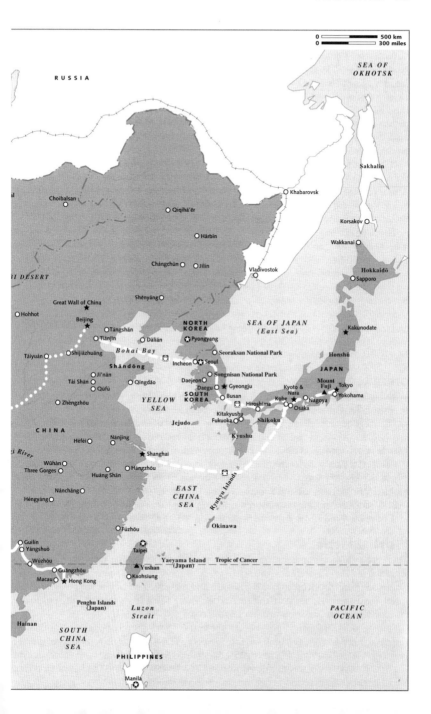

0 — 500 km
0 — 300 miles

SEA OF OKHOTSK

RUSSIA

Sakhalin

Choibalsan

Qiqihá'ér

Khabarovsk

Korsakov

Hárbin

Wakkanai

Chángchún   Jílín

Hokkaidō

Vladivostok

Sapporo

Shēnyáng

SEA OF JAPAN (East Sea)

Great Wall of China

Hohhot

Beijing

NORTH KOREA

Kakunodate

Tángshān

Pyongyang

Tiānjīn   Dàlián

Seoraksan National Park

Honshū

Bohai Bay

Tàiyuán   Shíjiāzhuāng

Incheon   Seoul

Shāndōng

JAPAN

Daejeon   Songnisan National Park

Jǐ'nán

Mount Fuji

Tài Shān   Qùfū   Qingdāo

Daegu   Gyeongju

Kyoto & Nara   Tokyo

Busan

Nagoya   Yokohama

Zhèngzhōu

YELLOW SEA

SOUTH KOREA

Hiroshima   Kōbe   Ōsaka

CHINA

Kitakyushu

Héféi   Nánjing

Jejudo   Fukuoka

Shikoku

Kyushu

Wūhàn   Hángzhōu

Shanghai

Three Gorges

Huáng Shān

Nánchāng

Héngyáng

EAST CHINA SEA

Ryukyu Islands

Fúzhōu

Okinawa

Guilin

Yángshuó

Taipei

Yaeyama Island (Japan)   Tropic of Cancer

Wūzhōu

Guǎngzhōu   Yushan

Macau   Hong Kong

Kāohsiung

Penghu Islands (Japan)

Luzon Strait

PACIFIC OCEAN

Hainan

SOUTH CHINA SEA

PHILIPPINES

Manila

TREKKING & MOUNTAINEERING

Scaling sacred mountains provides the highpoint of most people's walking experience in Northeast Asia. The trek up Mt Fuji (3776m) is a must-do overnight pilgrimage for many Japanese. Likewise, a trek up one of China's sacred mountains offers a great cultural experience (though not a lot of peace and solitude!). At Emei Shan, Huang Shan and Tai Shan thousands of stone steps lead up to a network of Buddhist monasteries linked by mountain paths thronged with pilgrims. Huang Shan in particular offers the quintessential Chinese landscape of swirling mist, craggy peaks and twisted pines, familiar from Chinese landscape painting – very *Crouching Tiger, Hidden Dragon*!

Other parts of the region have some classic, very accessible walking areas, particularly in the mountains of Japan, South Korea and Taiwan. Try the 3000m-plus peaks of the Japanese Alps on Honshū and in the heart of Hokkaidō; Songnisan and Seoraksan National Parks in South Korea; and Yangmingshan National Park and Yushan (3952m) and Xueshan (3883m) mountains in Taiwan. Many routes have camp sites and mountain huts.

The most exciting vertical terrain lies in the huge Himalayan peaks of western China and Tibet (where you can just about get away with some do-it-yourself trekking). The astonishingly beautiful forested alpine valleys of Jiuzhaigou (Sichuan), dramatic Tiger Leaping Gorge, and the jungles of Xishuangbanna in Yunnan offer a rare chance to explore places on foot. The remote mountains of western Sichuan offer challenging treks and horse treks but there are none of the lodges or trekking agencies that you find in Nepal.

Mongolia's mountains and deserts are the place for remote, adventurous mountaineering and trekking. Khövsgöl Nuur (a stunning lake near the border with Russia), the Kharkhiraa Valley, Terelj National Park and the Gobi Desert also offer great trekking. Extreme western Mongolia offers the best options for mountaineering around Tavanbogd Uul (4374m).

OTHER ACTIVITIES

With big mountains and no snow it was only a question of time before some fearless (and inventive) Taiwanese adrenaline junkie adopted grass skiing.

There's good scuba diving around the Japanese islands of Okinawa and Yaeyama; Jejudo in South Korea (a volcanic island and home of female pearl divers); and Kenting and the Pengh Islands in Taiwan (the cheapest place to learn). Golf is big in Japan but costs a fortune.

Camel rides are popular in Inner Mongolia and the deserts around Dunhuang (China). Horse riding is *the* way to travel across the steppes of Mongolia, and you can join cheap multi-day horse treks around Songpan (China).

Bird-watching in China is most rewarding on Qinghai Lake near Xining, Qinghai province (rare black-necked cranes can be seen from March to June).

Work a Little

There are a growing number of employment opportunities in China, particularly in Beijing and Shanghai, but theoretically you need a work visa and probably some Mandarin Chinese. Common openings include teaching English and marketing and there are possibilities for travel agents, writers, bar staff and secretaries. Hong Kong is another definite possibility, especially given its background as an English colony.

Finding work in Japan is possible but the costs of setting up house can be prohibitive (expect to need £3000). Teaching English comes top of the pops again – for information on Japan Exchange Teaching (JET), see p355. Bartending, hostessing (keep your wits about you – a British backpacker was murdered working as a hostess in Tokyo) and even modelling are all possibilities here and in South Korea and Taiwan.

Travel Around

Air travel can be a good-value way to cover huge distances in this region. In Japan it's not much more expensive than the train, and discounted flights in China are very good value. Regional flights are numerous but note that you usually can't fly between mainland China and Taiwan (unless you go via Hong Kong).

A good rail network covers the region. Japan's super-fast bullet trains are an essential experience, and rail passes are available (you must purchase these outside Japan). Chinese long-distance trains are a culture unto themselves and will give you some of your most memorable travel experiences. The overnight train from Beijing to Ulaan Baatar is the best way to get to Mongolia.

Buses throughout the region offer good value and huge coverage; in Japan overnight services are a way of saving on hotel bills.

In sparsely populated Mongolia and Tibet 4WD vehicles and trucks can be the only way to get around. Hiring a 4WD is common in both places; it gives you unparalleled freedom and won't require you to mortgage your rucksack if you split the costs between a small group. Otherwise you'll have to rely on hitching, which can be a long, frustrating business.

In South Korea and Taiwan, long-distance shared taxis known as bullet taxis travel between major destinations; negotiate a price before setting off.

There are daily ferries from Japan to South Korea and regular services to Taiwan and various parts of China. There are also ferries from Incheon in South Korea to several coastal towns in northern China. The 40-hour boat journey between Shanghai and Osaka is quite popular with travellers.

Within China, coastal and river ferry services are decreasing rapidly but you can still get to Macao and Hong Kong from southern China. The boat trip down the Yangtze River gets mixed reviews now that the Three Gorges have been dammed. The boat trip on the Li River in Guilin is touristy but still offers superb scenery.

CLASSIC ROUTES
Tokyo to Beijing or Shanghai

With a region so broad and diverse, classic routes are tricky to pin down. Many people start in Japan, explore between Tokyo and Kyoto (which contains a load of attractions in a small area) and then take the ferry from western Honshū to Busan in South Korea. From Incheon near Seoul there's a ferry to Tianjin in China where there's so much to explore you may not get the chance to see Mongolia, though you'd be missing out. Alternatively Korea could be cut out entirely by taking the ferry from Osaka in Japan to Shanghai (China).

Southwest Loop

The southwest loop route, from Hong Kong to Chengdu via Guilin, Kunming and Lijiang, is a favourite backpacker route across southwest China. Yunnan province is a particularly exotic and scenically stunning place that's rich in Chinese culture, and access to the delights of Southeast Asia (there are land crossings to Vietnam and Laos) is easy from Kunming. Head south as the weather cools.

Beijing to Tibet

Beijing to Tibet via Xi'an or Chengdu is another popular Chinese route. The train line to Lhasa opens in 2007; until then take the overnight bus from Golmud or fly in from Chengdu for much the same price. From Lhasa, the capital of Tibet, the wonderful overland trip across the Himalaya to Kathmandu in Nepal takes in many of Tibet's highlights.

Karakoram Highway

The Karakoram Hwy from Kashgar (China) as far as Gilgit (Pakistan) is another breath-taking mountain route into the Indian Subcontinent. It's probably the most stunning road in Asia, rivalled only by the Pamir Hwy in Tajikistan. Stop en route at the beautiful turquoise Karakul Lake at the foot of huge Muztagh-Ata (7546m). The 4730m Khunjerab Pass that forms the border is officially open from 1 May to 30 November. Check up-to-date travel advice before travelling in troubled northern Pakistan.

The Silk Road

Following the Silk Road from Beijing offers bucket loads of history, desert and remote adventure. The trail takes in the terracotta warriors and archaeological delights of Xi'an (the road's historical starting point), past the Silk Road Buddhist cave grottos of Dunhuang, the end-of-the-world fort at Jiayuguan and on into the deserts of Xinjiang. Stop off at backpacker-friendly Turfan before taking the train on to medieval Kashgar, a Central Asian city of Turkic-speaking Uyghurs that buzzes with one of the world's greatest bazaars. From here exciting options head over the Irkeshtam or Torugart mountain passes into Central Asia or down the Karakoram Hwy to Pakistan.

WHEN TO GO?

Given the range of climate (see next section) and attractions, you could visit Northeast Asia whenever you want and have a good time. That said, March to May (spring) and September to October (autumn) are generally considered to be the best times to visit.

Hanami, a celebration of the arrival of plum, peach and cherry blossoms from February to April, is a good but crowded time to visit Japan. June and September are probably the best months to visit Tibet and Mongolia, and September to October the time to consider entering the Gobi Desert. Planes, trains and hotels in China get booked solid in the weeks around the national holidays of 1 October and 1 May.

Climate

Northeast Asia stretches from sub-Siberian Mongolia down past the tropic of Cancer. Generally speaking, it experiences four seasons at the same times as in Britain, but temperatures are much more extreme. Humidity can be unpleasantly high in summer, when Japan, southeast China and South Korea are hit by the odd typhoon. The deserts of the Silk Road sizzle in August.

Spring and autumn (when the foliage is spectacular and skies are clear) are the best times to travel in China, though you have to be prepared for any weather at this time. In Mongolia and north of the Great Wall of China it gets incredibly cold in winter (how's minus 40°C for ya?), while the central Yangtze River valley experiences fiercely hot temperatures during long, hot summers. Summer is the only time it's unlikely to rain in central China. Summer is the best time to visit Tibet, the mountains of western Sichuan and Mongolia, though the days can be hot in the Gobi. South China is pretty nice year-round and some travellers find winter the perfect time to visit (often in conjunction with parts of Southeast Asia) because temperatures are cool but not prohibitively cold and the crowds of tourists are absent.

Japan has the most diverse climate in the region (thanks to the length of the archipelago and high mountains down its spine), which means it can be snowing in northern Hokkaidō and positively balmy in southern, subtropical Okinawa. Western Japan receives a large amount of precipitation in winter, while the Pacific side is cold but less snowy. If you're travelling in summer or winter then try to focus on coastal and southern areas, which are more temperate than inland.

Festivals

The region's fascinating festivals are a varied and unusual mix. They can be exuberant or sombre, chaotic or choreographed. Travellers should be aware that major celebrations clog up accommodation and public transport, so make your bookings well in advance. Check out some of the following:

Tsagaan Sar (Mongolia) White Month is a pocket of merriment held in January and February. Booze and food feature heavily.

Yah-Yah Matsuri (Owase, Japan) An argument contest at the beginning of February. Competitors scream Samurai chants and try to look fearsome. Then they take off all their clothes and jump in the ocean. Very Japanese.

Sapporo Snow Festival (Japan) Held in February with ice sculpture, an illumination of the park's winter landscapes. A similar event is held in Harbin in China.

Losar (Tibet) A colourful new year festival of drama, pilgrimage and dressing up held in February/March.

Water-Splashing Festival (China) Held at Xishuangbanna in Yunnan around mid-April. It's about washing away the dirt and sorrow of the old year and bringing in the happiness of the new; prepare to get soaked.

Dragon Boat Festival (Hong Kong) Honours the poet Qu Yuan in June with boat races and lively festivities.

Naadam (Mongolia) Showcases the nomadic roots of Mongolia (namely horse racing, archery and wrestling) across the country on 11 and 12 July. The biggest events are in Ulaan Baatar; the most interesting celebrations are in the countryside.

Gion Matsuri (Japan) Renowned festival commemorating a 9th-century request to the gods for an end to the plague sweeping Kyoto. There's an incredible parade of massive man-dragged floats on 17 July.

O-Bon (Japan) The Buddhist Festival of the Dead. The celebration of ancestors takes place in July and August. There's much lantern lighting.

Chusoek (Harvest Moon) Festival (Korea) The most important lunar holiday on the peninsula falls in September. People return to their family homes to pay homage to their ancestors.

Birthday of Confucius (China) Celebrated on 28 September with a giant festival in Qufu, Shandong province, where the great sage was born and died.

WHAT TO EXPECT?
Travellers

American and British expat businesspeople continue to be lured to China like moths to a flame, especially in Beijing and Shanghai, and there are still loads of expats in Hong Kong, which retains much of its British flavour. Japan, South Korea and Taiwan are all well used to seeing American tourists, less so Europeans. Seoul and Tokyo have large English-speaking expat communities.

Surrounded by limestone pinnacles and wonderful scenery, Yangshuo (Guangxi province) is China's favourite banana-muesli hangout, while the beautiful old walled towns of Dali and Lijiang, in Yunnan, are also popular. In summer you'll meet a fair number of tourists in Ulaan Baatar but if you disappear into the countryside you won't see anyone for weeks. Elsewhere in the region it's pretty easy to escape to an island or into the mountains, away from the hectic crowds of the cities.

Locals

Northeast Asian systems of social etiquette and religious beliefs are way too complex to explain in detail here. However, a few generalisations will help: directness is not a common trait. In fact, people often tell you what they think you want to hear, especially in China, where a smile doesn't necessarily indicate happiness; sometimes just embarrassment or worry.

'Face' and the avoidance of losing it are very important throughout the region. Try not to make anyone back down directly or look stupid if something goes awry. Smiling negotiation is the order of the day; direct confrontation is a last resort. Flattery and self-deprecation are useful traits to polish.

In Japan you'll find people extremely friendly and courteous, shy and hospitable (there's even a tourist system of evening home visits). The Japanese are most forgiving of social gaffs but long-term residents complain that it's difficult to get beyond being treated as a foreigner and guest.

China has only been 'open' to foreigners for 20 years and many people have a curious or suspicious attitude to travellers, especially in remoter areas. Chinese people will stare unashamedly at hairy, big-nosed foreigners, and travellers often tire of the endless cries of *'laowai!'* (a reasonably polite term for foreigners) and the constant battles against overcharging.

The boundaries between religion and philosophy are often blurred in Northeast Asian religions. Shinto, Japan's widest-held religion, is a mix of myths and gods. It sits easily alongside Japanese Zen Buddhism, but Mahayana (in contrast to the Hinayana Buddhism of Southeast Asia) is Northeast Asia's most common form of Buddhism. In Tibet a more mystical form of Tantric Buddhism is practised – it's this branch that the Dalai Lama heads. Taoism, based on the harmony of man and nature, is China's only home-grown religion. Islam has many followers in China, particularly in the west. There are pockets of Christianity across the region and Judaism in China. Mongolia has a long history of shamanism, overlaid with Tibetan-style Buddhism.

Food

The food is absolutely fantastic almost everywhere in the region. You can get a cheap Chinese meal and a cold beer anywhere in China for a couple of quid, though you won't get the same dishes you'd find in your local takeaway. Regional cuisines vary from the sweet and sour of Canton to the fiery red chillies that pepper Sichuan cuisine. An afternoon of Hong Kong's famous dim sum (Chinese snacks) is a must.

Japanese and Korean cuisines are also a major joy of travelling through the region. Both are strong on seafood and pickled vegetables, but there's also *yakitori, teppanyaki,* sushi and sashimi in Japan, *bibambap* and *bulgogi* in Korea and hot pot and dumplings just about everywhere.

By contrast, Mongolian food is just awful. One to try (or not) is *boodog* – marmot roasted from the inside by hot stones, or from the outside using a blowtorch (making Mongolia the only country we know of where you can fix a jeep and cook dinner with the same utensil!).

Language

Chinese students and businesspeople may know a little English but the language is more widely understood in Japan, South Korea and Taiwan (and especially in Hong Kong). Portuguese is spoken in Macau.

China throws up a mixed bag of languages and dialects. Mandarin (Putonghua) is the official language, though Cantonese is dominant in the south and Hong Kong. There are at least half a dozen other Chinese dialects, as well as an equal number of languages in China, ranging from Turkic to Thai. Japanese and Korean are fairly uniform across their respective countries but there are a few obscure dialects. In July 2000 Korea adopted a new method of Romanising the Korean language and introduced a few new spellings. You may see some old spellings knocking around.

An increasing number of signs display names in the Latin alphabet as well as Northeast Asian characters, but you'll certainly need to understand a few characters in each language, especially Mandarin. Language courses are available in the UK and in the region (see the Courses chapter on p416 for more information).

Health Risks

A variety of jabs is required for travel in this part of the world. In addition, dengue fever and Japanese encephalitis occasionally occur on Taiwan and are present in rural China, which is a huge reservoir of hepatitis B and various forms of flu. SARS is currently under control but flu cases tend to flare up every winter. Schistosomiasis (bilharziasis) and typhoid are present in the central Yangtze River basin. However, probably the main health problem for visitors to China is the omnipresent pollution and local habit of spitting, which encourages a range of respiratory ailments.

Dicey food may bring on an emergency toilet dash in China but Japan and South Korea are very healthy places. Mongolia is pretty healthy, apart from the odd case of meningococcal meningitis and brucellosis from unboiled milk or home-made cheese. Oh yes, and the occasional outbreak of bubonic plague (the original Black Death) in the far west!

Blood banks in Northeast Asia don't stock Rh-negative blood. Consult the Health chapter (p59) and seek professional medical advice for more travel health information.

Time & Flight Time

Japan and Korea are both nine hours ahead of Greenwich Mean Time (GMT). The whole of China is eight hours ahead of GMT, which is ideal for Beijing but hopeless in the west, where working days and opening hours are adjusted to avoid starting work two hours before dawn.

From London it's a 12-hour direct flight to Tokyo and Hong Kong, 11 hours to Seoul and 10 hours to Beijing.

Issues

Officially you can only cross from China into Russia and Mongolia by train but it's possible to get a bus to various Russian borders.

The repression of human rights is common in China. The occupation of Tibet and brutal imposition of Chinese rule is the most well-known issue in the country but there is also continuing repression of the ethnic Uyghur Muslim minority in Xinjiang province.

Foreigners face travel restrictions in Tibet and you'll probably have to take some kind of minimal tour just to get to Lhasa. It's currently a lot easier to get to Tibet from inside China rather than from Nepal. Towns and monasteries off the beaten track require travel permits that you can only get when booking a tour, but most of the major sights are visitable without much hassle.

Petty crime is more of a problem in China than elsewhere in Northeast Asia but it's still fairly minimal. 'Hard seat' (essentially third-class) train carriages can be insecure at night. If you're planning to cycle bring a good bicycle lock.

Travellers staying longer than 30 days in Mongolia must register with the police in Ulaan Baatar.

For further information on travel hotspots, general safety issues and governmental travel advice see the Safety chapter (p79).

Internet & Communications

Northeast Asia is one of the most technologically advanced regions on earth, so mobile phone coverage and internet access are no problem, except in Mongolia and rural China.

DAILY SPEND

Northeast Asia is generally expensive compared to Southeast Asia, but there's a lot of regional variety. The dubious honour of most expensive country goes not to Japan but

North Korea, where the few tightly policed tour groups that are allowed in are charged a minimum of around £100 per day.

Coastal China is surprisingly expensive (at least £20 a day; more in pricey Hong Kong) but moving inland can slash your costs to £10 per day. Western and southwestern China are the cheapest (and luckily the most interesting) regions. Food is cheap everywhere in China, but you'll have to battle against unofficial 'tourist' prices.

A Japanese hostel bed costs at least £15, and more like £25, in Tokyo and you're looking at least £40–50 of expenditure every day. Rail passes (only available overseas), overnight buses and the ubiquitous noodle stalls can help cut costs, as does continuing deflation.

South Korea is steadily becoming more expensive. Sniffing out the bargains brings down daily costs to £20 a day but £30 would be more realistic.

You can spend £10 a day bumming around Mongolia's capital Ulaan Baatar but more like £15 out in the wilds, due to transport costs and expensive traditional *ger* camps (£15 plus per person). Camping keeps down costs; hiring a minivan (often essential to get off the beaten track) pushes them back up but is good value split between four or five other travellers.

Budget for £15 a day bumping along the bottom in Taiwan or £25 away from sweaty dormitories. Taipei can be fiercely expensive.

Changing money is easy throughout the region. Cash rules in Japan, where ATMs (automatic teller machines) that recognise foreign cards are rare.

GETTING THERE

Many travellers appear in the region as part of a round-the-world (RTW) trip or after trawling around Southeast Asia. The Trans-Mongolian and Trans-Manchurian railway lines from Russia can deposit travellers in Beijing, northeast China and Mongolia.

Air

Direct flights are possible into Northeast Asian hubs, including Beijing, Shanghai, Hong Kong, Seoul, Taipei, Tokyo and Osaka. Ticket prices are not that different between them.

It's no problem getting open-jaw tickets into the region, and Beijing, Hong Kong and Tokyo crop up on a number of RTW tickets. Stopovers to the latter two, plus Osaka and occasionally Seoul, are possible on some tickets into Sydney (Australia), with carriers such as Japan Airlines (JAL) and Korea Air.

Northeast Asian routes are highly competitive and there's usually a wide choice of fares. European airlines such as KLM, Air France and Lufthansa were offering cheap student fares to Northeast Asia at the time of writing. British Airways (BA), Air China, Cathay Pacific, Gulf Air and Virgin also turn out cheap deals.

TICKET COSTS

The best available student/under-26 fares are quoted here. See p19 for more information on how to get the best, most flexible deal.

Beijing is the cheapest destination (return is £400 to £450) but occasionally some good deals for South Korea pop up. Getting to Hong Kong costs £430 to £480 return, about the same as to Shanghai. Return fares to Seoul cost £440 to £500, to Tokyo £450 to £475 (Osaka is a little more expensive) and Taipei £530 to £575.

Return tickets to Australia, including a stop in Japan, cost between £550 and £800. An open-jaw ticket into Osaka and out of Shanghai costs between £450 and £475. Into Seoul and out of Beijing is cheaper (£410 to £440) but into Hong Kong and out of Beijing is the cheapest of the lot (£400 to £460).

Sea & Overland

Although there's plenty of sea transport between the countries in Northeast Asia, there are only three sea links out of the region, namely the ferries from Vladivostok (the terminus of the Trans-Siberian Railway) to Fushiki in Japan and Sokcho in South Korea, or the much shorter run from Korsakov (Sakhalin Island, Russia) to Wakkanai (Japan's Hokkaidō island).

You can cross overland from China to Vietnam, Laos, Nepal, Pakistan, Kyrgyzstan, Kazakhstan and Mongolia. Train routes lead in from Mongolia, Kazakhstan and (partially) Vietnam. There are fantastically scenic high road passes to Pakistan and Kyrgyzstan in the far west. You cannot cross into Afghanistan, Bhutan or India by land.

It's still almost impossible to take your own vehicle into China – the authorities don't allow non-resident foreigners to drive.

Specialist Tour Operators

The number of tour operators offering trips in China is increasing but foreign operators are rare in Korea, Taiwan and Japan. Here are some country specialists:

Haiwei Trails (Lijiang ☎ 00 86 888-512-4540, Zhongdian ☎ 00 86 887-687-8737; www.haiweitrails.com) US-British company that operates out of Lijiang (Yunnan province).

Karakorum Expeditions (☎ 00 976 11-315655; www.gomongolia.com; Jiguur Grand Hotel, Transport St, PO Box 542, Ulaan Baatar-46, Mongolia) Foreign-run company based in Mongolia.

Khampa Caravan (☎ 00 86 887-828 8648; www.khampacaravan.com; Beimen Jie, Zhongdian, Yunnan, China) Overland trips from Yunnan, including to Lhasa, with an emphasis on sustainable tourism and local communities. Contact Dakpa or Yeshi.

Koryo Group (☎ 00 86 10-6416 7544; www.koryogroup.com; Room 43, Red House Hotel, 10 Taipingzhuang, Chunxiao Lu, Dongzhimenwai, Chaoyang district, Beijing, China) North Korea specialists.

Regent Holidays (☎ 0117 921 1711; www.regent-holidays.co.uk; 14 John St, Bristol BS1 2HR) Offers tours and independent travel and is particularly good for China.

Wild China (☎ 00 86 10-6465 6602; www.wildchina.com; Room 801, Oriental Place, 9 Dongfang Donglu, North Dongsanhuan Rd, Chaoyang District, Beijing, China) Professionally run and adventurous trips in China's most interesting regions.

NORTHEAST ASIA & BEYOND

The region borders an enormous number of countries, and flights out of the region's hubs can take you anywhere in the world reasonably cheaply. Heading back home overland is one fabulous possibility: the Trans-Mongolian railway (see p155) offers a superb overland option and a chance to explore Mongolia en route. Train routes also lead west to Kazakhstan and Russia beyond. Then there's the mouth-watering possibility of crossing into Nepal from Tibet and following the old overland Hippy Trail from Kathmandu back through Iran and the Middle East.

Tropical Southeast Asia and the Indian Subcontinent also beckon, as do the toys and joys of Australasia and North America. Circle Pacific airfares (see p26) allow exploration of the great ocean's islands and coastlines and need not cost the earth.

FURTHER INFORMATION
Reading Material

Lonely Planet publishes guidebooks to all the countries in the region, as well as to a few cities. Also helpful are *Healthy Travel Asia*, *Hiking in Japan*, *World Food Hong Kong*, *World Food Japan* and phrasebooks for the region's major languages.

For some insight into the current process of change in China check out *The Chinese* by Jaspar Becker and *China Wakes* by Nicholas D Kristof and Sheryl Wudunn. *Japan: a Short Cultural History*, by George B Sansom, is among the best introductions to Japanese history and

Inside Japan, by Peter Tasker, is an excellent insight to contemporary Japan. *Korea, Tradition & Transformation*, by Andrew Nahm, provides a great up-to-date history of the peninsula.

Trespassers on the Roof of the World by Peter Hopkirk recreates European explorers' early attempts to enter forbidden Tibet and it makes superb reading.

More personal accounts of the region include *The Private Life of Chairman Mao*, written by the man's private physician, Zhisui Li, and the wildly popular family saga *Wild Swans*, by Jung Chang. *Fire Under Snow: Testimony of a Tibetan Prisoner*, by Palden Gyatso, is a moving autobiography that recounts the life of a Buddhist monk imprisoned for 33 years for refusing to denounce the Dalai Lama.

Cohn Thubron's *Behind the Wall* and Paul Theroux's *Riding the Iron Rooster* remain the two best recent travel books written about China, though both date from over 15 years ago. The more recent *River Town* by Peter Hesssler is a must-read for anyone considering teaching in the People's Republic.

To Dream of Pigs, by Clive Leatherdale, is an excellent travelogue of both North and South Korea.

Alan Booth's *The Roads to Sata* traces a four-month journey on foot across northern Japan. *Lost Japan*, by Alex Kerr, covers 30 years of the author's experiences in Japan, while Kare Taro Greenfield's *Speed Tribes* is an entertaining foray into the drug-peddling, computer-hacking underworld of the disaffected Japanese youth. *Memoirs of a Geisha*, by Arthur Golden, is a classic.

Films

Asian films have become *very* cool in recent years; track down the following in your local video store for some pre-trip inspiration.

Two must-sees for Mongolia are the recent *Story of the Weeping Camel* and *Urga* (also known as *Close to Eden*). *Lost in Translation* expertly conveys the weirdness of jetlag in Tokyo.

China has produced some of the most gorgeous art-house films in recent years. Check out anything by directors Chen Kaige or Zhang Yimou, including *Yellow Earth*, *Farewell to My Concubine* and *Raise the Red Lantern*. Hong Kong has its own unique film industry that spans classic kung fu to the art-house movies of Wong Kar-Wai (try his *Happy Together* or *Chungking Express*).

Useful Information Sources

For specific country overviews, the low-down on travel in the region and hundreds of useful links head first to Lonely Planet's website (www.lonelyplanet.com).

The following portals and websites should help you chase down any aspect of interest:

http://taiwan.8m.net Focus on studying Chinese and teaching English in Taiwan.

www.ChinaPage.com Covers Chinese art, poetry and language.

www.cnta.com/lyen The portal of the China National Tourism Administration.

www.discoverhongkong.com Hong Kong's Tourist Association website.

www.gaijinpot.com Jobs in Japan.

www.japantravelinfo.com Portal of the Japan National Tourist Board.

www.korea.net Good portal with lots of info.

www.outdoorjapan.com A light overview of the outdoor possibilities in Japan.

www.silk-road.com An insight into culture along the Silk Road – click on 'Travel'.

www.taiwanho.com Expat guide to life and travel in Taiwan.

www.tibet.org Examines Tibet's tragic occupation and repression.

www.tour2korea.com Stacks of Korean travel information and links.

BEEN THERE, DONE THAT

In China or Japan, just being a foreigner somehow confers an elevated status that automatically makes you seem infinitely more remarkable, talented or attractive than you are back home (where you are, after all, pretty much nobody). Knowledge of this, combined with an open mind, a good bluff and a pinch of luck can take you a long way in a short time.

The first job I ever scored in China was while squatting down in a line of stinky pit toilets (not what you think…). I was visiting a remote part of Sichuan province when I struck up a slightly bizarre conversation with the Chinese guy squatting in the doorless (and wall-less!) cubicle next to me. Two minutes later I had lined up my first teaching job – a weekly English conversation class with his wife in Taipei. We shook on it, but not before washing our hands.

But I've heard of even weirder job-related stories in Taiwan. One charmed friend of mine got a job teaching English to a one-year-old baby (!) and another taught a Taiwanese man who had somewhat controversially named himself Bacteria Wang (so, yes, he taught English to bacteria for US$20 per hour!)

My dream job was slower coming. A few years later, while I was working at the front desk of a hotel in Beijing, a manic-looking American businessman asked me to moonlight as his translator. Pretending that I was used to earning significantly more than I actually was, I agreed. Every day for a week I crept out of the back door of the hotel, making my excuses with a plague-like hack and cough that would send the hotel staff diving for their surgical masks. I then flew around town in a rented flame-red BMW, negotiating with TV studios and trying to flog them The Muppet Show *in Chinese (Gonzo was particularly difficult to translate), until creeping back in time for the night shift.*

After a week of such subterfuge the dangerously sleep-deprived American casually mentioned that he wanted me to set up his Beijing branch office, as he was flying home the next day. Three days later I was sprawling about in a US$200 a night hotel room, marvelling at the US$20,000 that had been wired into my bank account and wondering what the hell to do with a US$1000 'clothing allowance'. Being a natural cheapskate I still ate in the noodle stalls outside the hotel (30p a bowl!) before retiring nightly to my penthouse apartment. I was the backpacker businessman. My duties, as far as I could make out, were limited to plugging in the fax machine, looking like a foreigner (I was good at that) and working out in the hotel gym. It was excellent.

A month later the real office manager turned up, of course, and I was back on the streets. And that's China for you. Crazy money, crazy opportunities and a real rollercoaster ride for all concerned. A great place to be someone different.

And I've still got US$600 of that clothing allowance left…

Bradley Mayhew

SOUTHEAST ASIA

CHINA WILLIAMS
A late bloomer, China eventually got around to taking a gap at the age of 25 when she spent a year as an English teacher in Thailand, and then travelled around Southeast Asia. She can also boast the obligatory tour of Europe during a summer in college. Otherwise, she was a dedicated underachiever in the nine-to-five world before morphing into a 'free'-lancer for Lonely Planet. Now she zips off to Bangkok, Washington, DC, or New York to work on various guidebook projects. She now lives in San Francisco with her husband, Matt.

INTRODUCTION

Vibrant and exotic, Southeast Asia is a poetic interplay of convenience and inefficiency, spirituality and consumerism, determination and tolerance.

At the geographic centre of the region lies Thailand, with a culture that adores fun (*sanuk* in Thai). Off either coast, all the postcard stereotypes of paradise exist in jewel-toned, palm-fringed islands. Sliding south down the Malay Peninsula is a thickly spiced stew of cultural fusions that empties into authoritarian Singapore and Indonesia's thick jungles. Crowning the island chain is beautiful Bali, which supplements lazy beach days and stunning scenery with a beguiling culture.

Forming the rind of mainland Southeast Asia are the survivors of war and turmoil – Cambodia, Laos, Vietnam and now isolated Myanmar (Burma). History and perseverance are tangible forces in these mending countries, where the adventurous traveller can cut a dusty trail into far-flung Cambodia, peep at napping Laos and brave Vietnam's tireless ambitions. Sitting at the rarely used front door to Southeast Asia, the exuberant Philippines boasts soaring volcanoes, coral-fringed beaches and a full calendar of Spanish-inspired fiestas. East Timor, the world's youngest country, is an underdog in the region's greatest-hits list and has yet to graduate into the leisure travel set.

Wherever you decide to go, you'll join an illustrious list of Southeast Asian pilgrims: Indian merchants, Chinese mandarins, European colonisers and modern globetrotters.

Tragically parts of Indonesia and Thailand were devastated in the Indian Ocean tsunami on 26 December 2004. These areas are rebuilding and for many, tourism remains an important part of their economy. For up-to-date information on the status of these regions, see www.lonelyplanet.com/tsunami and www.fco.gov.uk.

WHY SOUTHEAST ASIA?

First you'll come to Southeast Asia because you've heard that it is a good-time place. Thailand's laid-back beaches and budget-friendly hedonism are the stuff of backpacker myth-making. Once you're here, though, you'll discover why people return, or why they never leave at all.

Southeast Asia achieves an inner peace that the Western world could never legislate. It is gentle and graceful, serene and content. An invisible harmony orchestrates the speeding traffic, and a meditative state infuses crowded temples littered with burning incense and gifts to appease the beyond. Even gravity seems to work differently here – motorcycles effortlessly balance on narrow beams spanning flooded rice fields, and acrobatic deck hands negotiate crowds and railings to collect fares from boat passengers. The obvious contradictions begin to appear uniquely congruous once you slip into the Southeast Asian state of mind.

Many travellers are disappointed to find that the modern world is here in all of its global familiarity – ATMs, Western fast-food franchises and well-developed infrastructures (in most countries). But modernity hasn't blotted out the region's authenticity, which propels the daily rhythms of the dusty villages along the Mekong River as well as the chaotic mega-cities suchas Bangkok (Thailand) and Kuala Lumpur (Malaysia).

You don't have to travel to the deepest, darkest corners to see 'untouched' Southeast Asia. What many first-time visitors overlook is that the beaten path isn't very wide. Within the con-fines of the most touristy towns are streets where only the locals go. Turn off the path, and the children will stare at you with wide-eyed amazement as if they had just spotted an elephant, or people will wave you over to their family picnic for a chance to show off their English skills.

TOP 10 MUST-SEES

Angkor Wat (Cambodia) A world wonder of extensive temples built by the former Khmer empire.
Bali (Indonesia) Synonymous with heaven on earth for its beaches and beauty.
Baliem Valley (Papua, Indonesia) The stuff of *National Geographic*, with amazing indigenous cultures and jungle trekking.
Banaue (Philippines) Stunning rice terraces carved out of the fertile volcanic slopes.
Borneo (Sarawak in Malaysia, and Kalimantan in Indonesia) Long houses, long boats and long river journeys.
Hanoi (Vietnam) Indochina's finest French-colonial architecture.
Hoi An (Vietnam) Narrow cobblestone streets lined with hand-tailored silk houses and scenic bike rides to sandy beaches.
Kyaiktiyo Paya (Myanmar) A remarkable, stupa-topped gilded boulder.
Luang Nam Tha (Laos) Unique hill country with extensive ecotourism treks.
Ko Pha-Ngan (Thailand) Laid-back beach bumming for the rain-weary.

WHAT TO DO?

Kicking back on beautiful tropical beaches, drinking whisky cocktails from a bucket and searching for the perfect banana pancake takes up a serious amount of gappers' time in Southeast Asia, no matter how pious their intentions seemed back home.

Should it, God forbid, cloud over on the coast, there are tons of opportunities for sightsee-ing – thick tropical jungles, the architectural wonders of Angkor (Cambodia), quaint colonial towns in the Philippines and Vietnam and tranquil backwater villages lining the Mekong River. If you tire of the leisure life, learn a little something about your host country through culture courses – Vietnamese-language classes, informal Thai-cooking courses or a primer in Balinese handicrafts are all options. To embrace the Buddhist precept of existing in the present, consider studying *vipassana* (insight) meditation. If inner peace seems overrated, flex your muscles at Thai-boxing camps. Classes range from one day to month-long commitments

Teaching English is also a viable commodity in the region and provides a real glimpse into the inner workings of a Southeast Asian community, especially if the commitment is three months or longer.

See Part III for more information on overseas jobs, volunteer work and courses available in the region.

SOUTHEAST ASIA

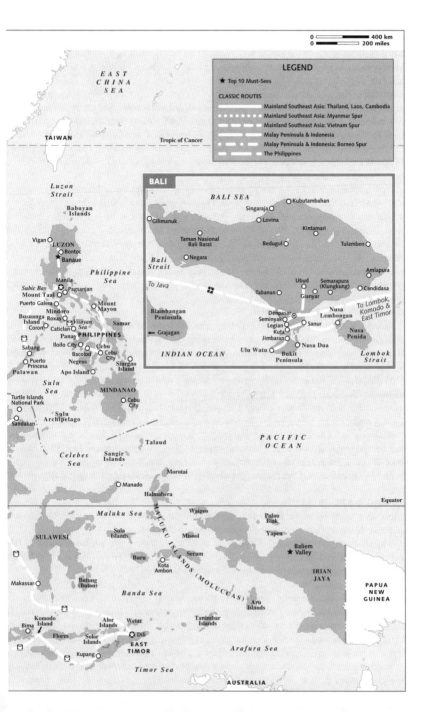

0 — 400 km
0 — 200 miles

LEGEND

★ Top 10 Must-Sees

CLASSIC ROUTES

——— Mainland Southeast Asia: Thailand, Laos, Cambodia
•••••• Mainland Southeast Asia: Myanmar Spur
— — Mainland Southeast Asia: Vietnam Spur
– – – Malay Peninsula & Indonesia
– · – Malay Peninsula & Indonesia: Borneo Spur
— — — The Philippines

*EAST
CHINA
SEA*

TAIWAN

Tropic of Cancer

*Luzon
Strait*

Babuyan
Islands

Vigan○
LUZON
○Bontoc
★ Banaue

*Philippine
Sea*

BALI

BALI SEA

○Kubutambahan

Singaraja○

○Gilimanuk

Lovina○

Kintamari○

Taman Nasional
Bali Barat

Bedugul○

Tulamben○

*Bali
Strait*

○Negara

Amlapura

To Java

Ubud
○

Semarapura
(Klungkung)

○Candidasa

Manila
Subic Bay ○Pagsanjan
Mount Taal○
Puerto Galera○
Mindoro
Busuanga ○Roxas
Island
Coron○ ○Caticlan
Mount
Mayon

Tabanan○

Gianyar
○

○

Nusa
Lembongan

To Lombok,
Komodo &
East Timor

*Blambangan
Peninsula*

Denpasar○
Seminyak○
Legian○
Kuta○
Jimbaran○

○Sanur

Nusa
Penida

← Grajagan

*Visayan
Sea*
Samar
PHILIPPINES

INDIAN OCEAN

Ulu Watu○
Bukit
Peninsula

○Nusa Dua

*Lombok
Strait*

Sabang○
○Puerto
Princesa
Palawan

Iloilo City○ ○Cebu
Bacolod○ ○Cebu
City
Negros ○
Panay
Apo Island○ Siargao
Island

*Sulu
Sea*

MINDANAO

○Cebu
City

Turtle Islands
National Park
○

*Sulu
Archipelago*

○Sandakan

*Celebes
Sea*

Sangir
Islands

Talaud

*PACIFIC
OCEAN*

○Manado

Morotai

Halmahera

Equator

Maluku Sea

Waigeo

Pulau
Biak

SULAWESI

Sula
Islands

MALUKU

Misool

Yapen

Baliem
★ Valley

Buru

Seram

**IRIAN
JAYA**

Makassar○

Butung
(Buton)

Kota
Ambon

ISLANDS

**PAPUA
NEW
GUINEA**

Banda Sea

(MOLUCCAS)

Aru
Islands

Komodo
Island
Bima○
Flores

Alor Wetar
Islands
Solor ✪Dili
Islands
Kupang○
**EAST
TIMOR**

Tanimbar
Islands

Arafura Sea

Timor Sea

AUSTRALIA

Get Active

Most of the activities in the region are available year round, although weather does affect tidal swells and ocean visibility, and monsoon rains can dampen a multi-day trekking trip.

CAVING

Gunung Mulu National Park in Malaysia is riddled with limestone caves, including the 51km-long Clearwater Cave, one of the longest in the world. Incidentally, the park is as big as Singapore and thick with green tangles of tropical vegetation and rainforests. And in the Philippines, Sabang's underground river on the island of Palawan sports an 8km-long meandering network of caves carved by water's supple handiwork. Adventure tours into both systems can be arranged at the destinations.

In Vietnam, spelunkers (cavers) should head for the spectacular Phong Nha (Fangs of the Wind) river caves, northwest of Dong Hoi, which ring with eerie echoes, allegedly the music of the mountain god. Examples of human ingenuity can be found in the network of tunnels at Cu Chi (35km from Ho Chi Minh City) and Vinh Moc (near the old border between North and South Vietnam), which were built during the American-Vietnam War (known as the American War in these parts). The Viet Cong transported and harboured people and weapons in these hand-dug tunnels. Modern-day visitors can crawl through the claustrophobic spaces on organised day trips.

CYCLING & MOUNTAIN BIKING

Touring the region by bicycle is becoming more widespread and many travellers combine cycling with buses for the boring or challenging stretches, or they take organised cycling tours. For long-distance touring, bring your own bike and gear, as bike shops aren't widespread or well stocked.

Hands down, Vietnam is the most spectacular country in the region for cycle-touring as the north–south highway predominately hugs the coast. Cycling is a great way to take advantage of the terrain in northern Vietnam (around Sapa) and Laos, and traffic is pretty light. Lonely Planet's *Cycling in Vietnam, Laos & Cambodia* covers these areas in detail.

Malaysia and Thailand also have viable touring routes, especially along the peninsula and the relatively flat terrain of the Mekong River. In the Philippines, areas around Moalboal on Cebu, and Guimaras Island, are other popular options.

In towns throughout the region, guesthouses rent out rickety bicycles for day trips.

DIVING & SNORKELLING

Clear seas, underwater gardens of coral reefs and affordable dive trips make the region a popular destination for scuba beginners and aquaholics.

Thailand sits at the diving helm, thanks to its accessibility, and budget-friendly PADI-certificate courses abound on the east coast island of Ko Tao. From Phuket, on the west coast, live-aboard trips go to the uninhabited Similan Islands.

Indonesia runs a close second in dive quality and variety, and the dive sites have been less crowded in recent years due to concerns over the country's political situation. Bali is ringed by a diversity of dives: on the northeast, near Tulamben, is an old WWII shipwreck. Advanced divers may prefer to battle the strong currents and cold waters of the southern coast (Nusa Penida and neighbouring islands). Live-aboards explore the marine park around Komodo and Flores. The sea gardens of Sulawesi, particularly around Manado, are legendary for sharks and turtles and even rare swimmers such as the ghost pipefish.

The Philippines has a wealth of underwater opportunities around Boracay, Alona Beach (Panglao Island, off the coast of Bohol), Puerto Princesa (Palawan) and the island of Apo. There is also some fantastic diving around the WWII shipwrecks in Subic Bay (Luzon) and Coron (Busuanga Island).

If you're new to the underwater world, snorkelling can be done at almost any beach destination, and most dive shops rent gear.

RAFTING & RIVER SPORTS
Rafting is offered on Java's Suyugai Citarak (Citarak River), bordering Gunung Halimun National Park near Bogor, and on the island of Bali. In Kalimantan, Sungai Mahakam is the province's superhighway and motorised canoes putter inland to stilt villages. Boatmen steer tourist-filled canoes through the rapids in Pagsanjan southeast of Manila in the Philippines. If it looks familiar in places, that's because Coppola filmed parts of *Apocalypse Now* here.

Rafting trips on large bamboo 'house rafts' can be taken on a number of rivers in northern Thailand around Pai, Fang and Tha Ton.

In Malaysia there's great fishing in Taman Negara National Park (which has wonderful bird-watching) and canoeing in beautiful Tasik Chini.

Kayaking and tubing are big fun on the white-water rivers around Vang Vieng, Laos.

ROCK-CLIMBING
Krabi in southern Thailand is a major rock-climbing destination because of the unbeatable scenery – craggy limestone teeth ring a shimmering sea beside a blond streak of sand. Experienced guides cater to all abilities, from novice to expert. Chiang Mai also has an emerging climbing scene, and guides lead one-day trips to jungle peaks and eroded caves. Towering over the rice-paddy landscape of Vang Vieng in Laos are several climbing sites accessible only with guides. Malaysia also has some scalable spots around Kuala Lumpur.

SURFING & WINDSURFING
Many of those sapphire-coloured, tubular walls caught on surf movies were filmed in Indonesia, one of the biggest surf destinations in the world. Renowned spots include the Bukit Peninsula in Bali, Java's G-Land (Grajagan on the southeastern tip), Pulau Nias in northern Sumatra and the Nusa Tenggara islands. Windsurfing is possible in the southern resorts of Bali. Accessible by yacht charter are the breaks off Pulau Panaitan, an uninhabited island.

The breaks off Siargao Island in the Philippines can reach Hawaiian scale between October and May. Boracay is the Philippine windsurfing mecca.

TREKKING & WILDLIFE WATCHING
Trekking in Southeast Asia is about scaling volcanoes, spotting jungle wildlife and visiting minority hill-tribe villages. For jungle treks, Indonesia is a world-renowned destination, thanks to its huge tracts of uninhabited rainforest, second in size to Brazil. Gunung Leuser National Park, on Sumatra, is home to the red-haired orang-utan ('forest man' in local parlance); trips into the park are organised in the towns of Berastagi and Bukit Lawang. The volcano that dominates Lombok, Gunung Rinjani (3726m), is a strenuous but worthwhile three-day jaunt. More adventurous jungle-trekking opportunities are available in Kalimantan and Papua (Irian Jaya). The prehistoric 'dragons' on the island of Komodo are the kings of Indonesian fauna.

Despite intense logging in Malaysia, Taman Negara National Park is a primal delight with deep, dark jungles; canopy walks; and lots of insects. Sabah's main event is a climb to the top of Mt Kinabalu (4101m), which is half the height of Mt Everest. Turtle Islands National Park, north of Sandakan, is composed of three protected islands visited by green sea turtles that come to nest between July and October.

When Mt Mayon (2450m), in the Philippines, isn't preparing to blow its top, it qualifies as one of the world's most beautiful active volcanoes. To see the destruction wrought by Mt Taal, a deadly little volcano, take a boat tour around the incongruously picturesque lake.

In the mountainous regions of northern Thailand (Chiang Mai, Mae Hong Son and Chiang Rai), Laos (Luang Nam Tha) and Vietnam (Sapa), minority hill-tribe communities are often visited by trekking tours. Choose guides who are sensitive in dealing with these fragile environments and cultures. In Laos, the Nam Ha Ecotourism Project is noteworthy being environmentally and culturally sensitive.

In southern Laos, Si Phan Don is an area of islands on the Mekong River where you can see Irrawaddy dolphins between December and May.

Work a Little

You've come to this international playground and want to work? You're not alone; many fall in love with the region's relaxed pace and survive off modest jobs teaching English. The pay is attractive only within the country, but teaching provides interaction with a community that you won't get as a tourist. Cambodia, Thailand, Vietnam and, to a lesser extent, Laos are all promising places to find teaching jobs. If you have organised a job before leaving home, you should file for the appropriate work visa in the UK, but many foreigners just arrive and arrange work visas once they find a job in the country. Some folks also pick up gigs working in bars on the Thai beaches or as dive instructors; the arrangements for these, from financial and visa angles, tend to be informal.

Travel Around

Air travel around Southeast Asia can be a real bargain, especially for trips between country capitals. With the rise of no-frills airlines, cheap air fares have gotten cheaper for provincial capitals as well as tourist hotspots. The best fares are found in Bangkok, Singapore and Penang (Malaysia). Indonesia and the Philippines also rely heavily on domestic flights for travel between islands. Check out these companies for budget fares: Air Andaman (www .airandaman.com), Air Asia (www.airasia.com), Dragon Air (www.dragonair.com), Nok Air (www.nokair.co.th) and Orient Thai (www.orient-thai.com).

Some carriers offer regional passes and discount options, most of which are available online. Be careful about buying tickets from untrustworthy agents in tourist centres and remember that most international airports charge a departure tax.

Within mainland Southeast Asia, travelling by land is the best way to see the different countries merge and retract from one another. By bus, Thailand and Malaysia are the easiest mainland countries to get around: the roads are in good shape and the bus systems reliable. In Cambodia, Laos and Myanmar, travel by bus is slow and the roads are narrow drainage ditches – allow yourself plenty of time to get around. Vietnam's hop-on/hop-off tourist buses (sometimes called 'open tour'), which are now shared with locals, ply a north–south route and provide a roomier alternative to the sardine-can local buses. Travel on the islands in Indonesia and the Philippines is usually by bus, and varies from cheap and cheerful to air-con luxury.

Thailand, Malaysia and Singapore are fused together by rail. Malaysia's internal train route travels the spine of the peninsula, while Thailand's fans out to the different corners of the country. Thailand's trains can also be used for border-hopping to Laos (through Nong Khai) and Cambodia (through Aranya Prathet).

Vietnam's communist crown is the *Reunification Express*, which links Ho Chi Minh City in the south with Hanoi in the north. Train travel is also an option within parts of Myanmar and Cambodia and on the Indonesian island of Java.

Former fishing vessels are often reconfigured to take tourists to offshore islands. Bigger vessels ply regular routes within the Indonesian and Philippine archipelagos. The Philippine archipelago is serviced by a flotilla of ferries, some of them little more than rickety tubs. Because fatal accidents do happen, take a good look at the boat to see if your gut deems it seaworthy. Speed boats between Sihanoukville and Krong Koh Kong in Cambodia are often used to avoid sloppy rainy-season roads. In the jungles of Kalimantan, Sarawak and Sabah there's plenty of river transport.

Local transport includes taxis, minibuses, pick-up trucks with rows of seats along each side, auto rickshaws, bicycle rickshaws and horse-drawn carts. Most are ridiculously cheap, but it's wise to agree on a fare in advance. Original to the Philippines are jeepneys – highly ornate, reconstructed jeeps.

CLASSIC ROUTES

Many travellers to Southeast Asia arrive in Bangkok and make a crucial decision – they'll either head north through Laos, Cambodia and Vietnam (see p199), or they'll head south through Malaysia, Singapore and Indonesia (see p199). Because they are on the geographic periphery, Myanmar and the Philippines are deliberate addendums to either subregional tour.

Mainland Southeast Asia

Start by following Thailand's culture trail from Bangkok to the former capitals of Ayuthaya and Sukhothai. From here most people hurry straight to Chiang Mai, but you could take the backdoor along the border with Myanmar through Mae Sai and Mae Hong Son.

The border crossing at Chiang Khong-Huay Xai will deliver you into Laos near the trekking base of Luang Nam Tha. Alternatively, you can follow the Mekong River on the Thai side to the charming town of Nong Khai and then cross into Laos at Vientiane.

If you stick with the Chiang Khong crossing, dip southeast to idyllic Luang Prabang and then scoot east to the Plain of Jars in Phonsavan (heading east are several border crossings into northern Vietnam). Continuing south toward the dusty capital of Vientiane, stop off in Vang Vieng to go kayaking or rock-climbing. You can also follow a laborious overland route to the southern river islands of Si Phan Don and cross at Voen Kham-Koh Chheuteal Tom into Cambodia. Boats ply the Mekong River to Phnom Penh.

From Phnom Phenh, fly or overland to Siem Reap and Angkor's magnificent temples. If you need to beat a trail back to Bangkok, follow the path through Sisophon to the Poipet–Aranya Prathet border crossing.

If you've got more time, head to Ho Chi Minh City (Vietnam). Vietnam's slim shape simplifies travel logistics. Either start in the south at cosmopolitan Ho Chi Minh City and work your way north to the wide avenues of Hanoi, or vice versa. Don't forget to diverge from Hanoi to Sapa or Halong Bay. In the northern reaches of Vietnam, you are on China's doorstep.

Malay Peninsula & Indonesia

From Bangkok, hightail it south to Ko Samui, Ko Pha-Ngan or Ko Tao – a string of islands that attract gappers – then bound across the peninsula to Krabi or Phuket. If the crowds become annoying, head further south to the undeveloped islands of Ko Tarutao National Marine Park.

Next, jump the Thai–Malaysian border to Penang. Head into the tranquil hill stations of the Cameron Highlands or the thick rainforest of Taman Negara National Park. From Kuala Lumpur, you could catch a cheap flight elsewhere, or bus to the historic port town of Melaka and wrap-up your trip in Chinese-influenced Singapore, another major air gateway. At the tip of the Malay Peninsula, you are poised for travel to Borneo. The Indonesian island of Sumatra can also be reached from Singapore by boat or air but at the time of writing northern and western parts of the island were off-limits following the tsunami.

To reach Borneo, fly into Bandar Seri Begawan, the capital of oil-rich Brunei and then bound over to Kota Kinabalu, from where buses speed to towering Mt Kinabalu and to Sandakan, the jumping-off point to the Turtle Islands National Park. Alternatively, take a bus to Miri in Malaysian Sarawak and then a boat to Gunung Mulu National Park. Flights also serve this route.

If your trip focuses on Indonesia, it is best to fly to Jakarta and head east. You can pick up the islands of Borneo and Sumatra if you need to make a visa run to extend your stay or if you're headed up the Malay Peninsula.

Jakarta charms few, but dropping south is Bogor, the gateway to Gunung Halimun National Park, and to the east is Yogyakarta, the cultural heart of the island and a good base for exploring the temple complex at Borobudur.

By air you can skip over to the southern side of Bali for the resort towns of Kuta and Sanur, surfing meccas off Bukit Peninsula and the diving hotspot of Nusa Lembongan. Ubud is the island's cultural centre and the capital, Denpasar, serves as a regional air hub for further flung islands, such as Komodo, Sulawesi, Flores, Maluku and East Timor.

The fast-disappearing forest of Kalimantan state on the island of Borneo can be accessed by air or sea from Sulawesi. In the base city of Samarinda, river trips stab into the lands of the indigenous Dayak tribes.

The Philippines

From any Southeast Asian capital you can fly to Manila and bus north to the hand-hewn rice terraces of Banaue and Bontoc or colonial-era Vigan, or bus south to the Mt Taal volcano. The limestone peaks and quiet beaches of far-flung Palawan are a quick flight from Manila. You can boat south to the island of Mindoro to hit Puerto Galera and nearby scuba sites. From the port town of Roxas, take a ferry to Caticlan on the island of Panay, the jumping off point for the beach at Boracay. Cebu is dead centre in the archipelago and a transport hub to the southern islands in the Visayan Sea. Many people buy an open-jaw ticket in order to fly in or out of Cebu. If you have to return to Manila, follow the eastern arc of islands to southern Luzon, which is graced with the Mt Mayon volcano and river rafting in Pagsanjan.

Myanmar

Regulations on entering Myanmar change frequently, so count on the most traditional method and fly from Bangkok or the Indian Subcontinent to Yangoon. From the capital, bus to the ancient capital of Mandalay, and then hop a ferry to the ruins of Bagan. Return to Mandalay to catch a bus to the floating gardens and island monasteries of Inle Lake.

WHEN TO GO?

There are few really bad times to visit Southeast Asia. Even during the monsoon, downpours are sudden, torrential, short and usually followed by sunshine. They're rarely an impediment to travel except in remote areas (Cambodia and Indonesia are most susceptible to washed-out roads) or certain island destinations.

As a rule of thumb, hit mainland Southeast Asia in the cool and dry months of November to March, then escape to the archipelagos of the Philippines and Indonesia between April and October. The region's peak tourist season coincidentally overlaps with its best season and with Europe's worst (November to March). Around Christmas and the Easter holidays, international airfares tend to inflate and accommodation becomes scarcer, though this scenario has been more friendly to travellers in recent years as tourism to the region has decreased slightly.

Along the Malay Peninsula (where many of the region's famous beaches are located), a monsoon hits the east coast from November to February and the west coast from May to October. Alternating between coasts often saves a rained-out beach vacation.

If you're hitting the trail from March to May, the hill stations of Myanmar, Malaysia and Vietnam, and the highlands of Laos, can be pleasant when everywhere else is boiling.

Ramadan causes disruption in the Muslim countries of Indonesia, Brunei and Malaysia. For more information on Islamic festivals, see p143.

Buddhist countries, such as Thailand, Laos and Cambodia, share many religious holidays (below), which typically affect accommodation and transport rather than daily business operations.

Climate

With the exception of northern Myanmar, all of Southeast Asia lies within the tropics. Warm or downright hot weather with high humidity is common in lowland areas.

Mainland Southeast Asia (Thailand, Laos, Myanmar, Cambodia and Vietnam) experiences a three-season climate – cool and dry from November to March (average temperature 25–30°C), followed by hot and dry from March to May (average temperature 30–35°C), and hot and rainy from June to October (average temperature 25–30°C). Highland areas are significantly cooler than the lowlands; for example, Hanoi is five to 10 degrees Celsius cooler than Bangkok.

Oceanic Southeast Asia (southern Thailand, Myanmar, Brunei, Indonesia, Malaysia and Singapore) experiences two monsoons yearly: one from the northeast (usually between October and April) and one from the southwest (between May and September). Rain is usually heavier during the northeast monsoon. Often you'll find better weather simply by crossing from one side of the island or country to the other.

The climates of the Philippines and Maluku (Indonesia) are more complex and share aspects of both mainland and oceanic climates. Typhoons occasionally strike the Philippines and north and central Vietnam between June and early October.

Festivals

The region is jam-packed with religious festivals (Buddhist and Muslim mostly, but also Chinese and Christian) and wild celebrations of a more irreligious nature. In Brunei, Indonesia and Malaysia, Islamic festivals are widely celebrated (see p143).

Black Nazarene Procession (Philippines) Involves the transporting of a life-size statue of Jesus through the streets of Manila's Quiapo district on January 9.

Ati-Atihan (Philippines) A three-day Filipino Mardi Gras celebrated on Panay in the third week of January.

Chinese New Year Widely celebrated in January/February with fireworks and parades in Hat Yai (Thailand), Kuala Lumpur, Singapore and other Chinese communities throughout the region.

Tet (Vietnam) Celebrates the lunar new year with large family gatherings and prolonged business closings.

Lunar New Year Celebrated in the spring by Thailand (where it is known as Songkran), Cambodia, Laos and Myanmar. It is mainly a water festival where revellers douse each other with buckets full, balloons or water guns. Bangkok and Chiang Mai are known for their Songkran festivities.

Tamu Besar (Malaysian Borneo) A huge tribal gathering in Kota Belud featuring a massive market, ornately decorated horsemen and medicine men. It's held in Kota Belud in Sabah.

Bun Bang Fai (Laos) The rocket festival is an irreverent animist celebration with processions, merriment and firing of bamboo rockets to prompt the rains for the new rice season. A similar festival is held in Yasothon in northern Thailand.

Tiet Doan Ngo (Vietnam) Summer Solstice Day in June sees the burning of human effigies to satisfy the need for souls to serve in the army of the god of death.

Trung Nguyen (Vietnam) Wandering Souls Day is held on the 15th day of the seventh moon (August); offerings are given to the wandering souls of the forgotten dead.

Independence Day (Indonesia) Marks the archipelago's release from colonialism on August 17; fireworks and parades light up across the country.

MassKara (Philippines) Many Faces Festival is held in mid-October in Bacolod on Negros, filling the streets with parades of oversized, smiling masked faces and dancing.

Festival of Light (Myanmar) Celebrates the end of Buddhist lent by illuminating the streets and houses with electric lights and paper lanterns.

Bon Om Tuk (Cambodia) The most important Khmer festival and celebrates the end of the wet season in early November.

Loi Krathong (Thailand) Honours the water goddess with miniature handmade bamboo boats decorated with flowers and candles; Chiang Mai is a scenic spot to float a *krathong*.

That Luang Festival (Laos) Centres around Vientiane's great golden stupa and features firework displays, candlelit processions and music.

Elephant Roundup (Thailand) Held in Surin during November; lumbering pachyderms indulge in races, tugs-of-war and football.

WHAT TO EXPECT?
Travellers

Southeast Asia is an almost compulsory stop on many round-the-world (RTW) routings from the UK, so there are a lot of Brits in the region, along with Europeans of all shapes and sizes (particularly Scandinavians, Dutch and Germans). Many French travellers pay homage to the former colonies of Vietnam, Laos and Cambodia. Israelis have a strong presence in Thailand.

Southeast Asia attracts everyone from gappers to retirees. More and more honeymooners are arriving in Thailand, and package tourists love Angkor Wat and the upscale resort beaches across the region.

The most important factor in choosing a beach spot isn't the idyllic scenery (they all have that), but the personalities sharing the sand and surf with you. The east coast islands of Thailand, especially Ko Tao and Ko Pha-Ngan, rank high with the 20-somethings. Ko Pha-Ngan hosts the trippy full-moon raves that your partying mates have bragged about. While stunningly beautiful, Phuket and Ko Phi Phi attract crowds of older, fatter bellies (and wallets). In Indonesia, fresh-faced candidates will find the Gili Islands and Bali to be suitable sunbathing spots. In the Philippines, check out Boracay and Puerto Galera. Be aware of the obvious: the beaches are for fun and sun, not for getting to know the culture or for making friends with the locals (who will be outnumbered by tourists).

The region's cultural destinations tend to attract people who are smitten with foreign traditions and customs. Some visitors might be able to speak the language, while others are there to appreciate and adore. You are more likely to interact with the local community in such places than in the beach resorts. Culture-trippers should check out, Yogyakarta (Java, Indonesia), Chiang Mai (Thailand), Luang Prabang (Laos), Angkor Wat (Cambodia) and Bagan (Myanmar).

Locals

Southeast Asians typically exude contentment. They are friendly, open and unhurried. By and large, locals are curious about travellers and will ask a laundry list of questions if a common language is available. People will want to know your age, marriage status and country of origin. While the questions may seem nosey, these are measures for placing outsiders into the highly hierarchical society. Your status (primarily your age, but also your wealth) determines how much deference should be afforded to you. Also, chit-chat is a well-practised art in the region and those who take the time to talk to you are extending their famed hospitality.

The concept of 'face' – avoiding embarrassment for yourself or others – is another guiding principle in social interactions. This translates into a host of baffling behaviours – sometimes locals will give incorrect information just to avoid admitting that they don't know something. Often the vaguer the answer, the closer you are treading to a face game. Although it is considered healthy in Western cultures, showing anger is a sure-fire way to make everyone lose face and is avoided at all costs. A more commonly employed tool is a smile, which will be used when the bus breaks down and as a gracious excuse for minor cultural snafus (like putting your feet on chairs or tables, a no-no in this foot-phobic culture). A smile will endear you to market ladies, children and water buffalo equally, but don't use it on those stray dogs.

In these accommodating countries, what will cause your hosts' smiles to turn upside down? The answer is easy, but the application is tricky. Most importantly you should remember to respect the 'sacred cows': the government, religion and monarchy (in Thailand). Any negative opinions should be kept to yourself, even if you think no-one around understands English. Pay special attention to the proper attire and behaviour required in the various temples and mosques.

Dress is an often overlooked cause of offence. Many people equate the hot temperatures with skimpy clothing, but Southeast Asians frown upon exposing their bodies. Wear clothes that cover to your elbows and knees, or further in Muslim countries. This is especially important for women, who may even consider covering their heads in rural Muslim regions. Think you'll be too hot? It is a little-known phenomenon that long sleeves actually help cool the body in tropical climates. Standards are relaxed on the beaches due to inundation, but avoid sunbathing topless – this will encourage a crowd of unabashed, gawking men.

Attitudes towards women vary greatly across the region. Gender equality is reasonable in Thailand and the Philippines but Indonesia is an almost 'pre-feminist' state. In Buddhist Indochina, women travellers are often perceived as a little odd, though this doesn't lead to hassles. In Indonesia the sight of solo women travellers can be seen as provocative, and Western women are often perceived as 'loose'.

Language

With an estimated 1000 spoken languages, Southeast Asia is one of the world's most linguistically diverse regions. This also means that very few visitors know how to speak the host country's language. Even the most basic pleasantries in the local parlance can garner excessive compliments. Try to learn how to say 'hello', 'thank you' and 'please' in every country visited. Learning how to count is also helpful for bargaining.

Bahasa Indonesian/Malaysian is fairly easy to pick up because the alphabet has been Romanised and there are no tones. Thai, Lao, Burmese and Khmer have their own script, which is based on Sanskrit, and are tonal languages. Vietnamese is a tonal language, but it has been Romanised, meaning street signs are readable if not pronounceable. Mandarin and Cantonese will also come in handy for conversing with ethnic Chinese across the region.

A great game to play with children is to exchange the different noises that animals make in different languages. In English, the rooster says 'cock-a-doodle-do', but in Thai it says 'ekey-ek-ek'.

Health Risks

The World Health Organization recommends quite a few jabs before travel to Southeast Asia. Start planning for the vaccines eight weeks in advance and check with your travel clinic on current recommendations. At the time of writing the following made the list: diphtheria and tetanus; hepatitis A and B; measles, mumps and rubella; and typhoid. Other vaccinations are recommended for travellers remaining in the region for longer than one month. Mosquito-borne diseases, like dengue fever, Japanese B encephalitis and malaria, are a problem in certain rural areas. Amoebic dysentery, giardiasis and travellers' diarrhoea often have the same initial symptoms – rushed trips to the bathroom. Rabies is a concern in the region as well.

HIV/AIDS is now one of the most common causes of death in people under the age of 50 in Thailand. The epidemic is worsening in Cambodia, Myanmar and Vietnam. Heterosexual sex is the primary method of transmission, and most of these countries have unregulated sex industries.

Recent outbreaks of avian flu have affected Vietnam and Thailand. Travellers should avoid exposure to raw poultry or live birds.

Consult the Health chapter (p59) and seek professional medical advice for more travel health information.

Time & Flight Time

Cambodia, Laos, Thailand and Vietnam are seven hours ahead of Greenwich Mean Time (GMT); Brunei, Malaysia, the Philippines and Singapore are eight hours ahead and Myanmar, slightly awkwardly, is 6½ hours ahead. Indonesia is divided into three time zones that are seven, eight and nine hours ahead of GMT.

Bangkok is 11½ hours' flying time from London. Singapore (12¾ hours) and Kuala Lumpur (12½ hours) also have nonstop flights from London, but destinations such as Manila (16 hours) and Jakarta (17 hours) require a change of planes.

Issues

There are hotspots in this region that require a nose for news in order to make intelligent, rather than reactionary, decisions. Most Western governments issue travel advisories that are overly cautious, perhaps to counter backpacking nationals who are overly optimistic. Be informed but don't be paranoid.

For the last few years, the UK Foreign Commonwealth Office has advised against visiting the province of Aceh (on Sumatra) in Indonesia because of rebel insurgency. The area was also devastated by the 2004 tsunami, and at the time of writing the situation was still critical and Aceh off-limits to foreigners.

Be aware that Westerners and Western establishments, including hotels and clubs on Bali and embassies in Jakarta, have been targeted by terrorist attacks. Bombings of Western targets have averaged one per year since 2002, and it is believed that Jemaah Islamiah, an Islamic radical group with ties to Al-Qaeda, is responsible for these attacks. Separatist movements generate civil unrest and clashes with the central Indonesian government in central Sulawesi, Aceh, Papua and Maluku. East Timor has been relatively stable, although militia activity does occur along the border with West Timor.

Travellers are advised not to travel to the Philippine island of Mindanao, especially the Zamboanga peninsula and the Sulu archipelago. Philippines-based Abu Sayyaf militants have claimed responsibility for bombings and kidnappings (including foreigners). Most of their activities centre on Mindanao, but they've also struck in Sipadan and Pandanan, which lie off the eastern coast of Sabah (Malaysian Borneo). A real risk of kidnap remains in this area and in the Mindanao and Sulu archipelagos. Kidnappings and bombings have occurred elsewhere in the Philippines too.

Cambodia is still prone to sporadic, often random, violence and petty street crime. It is also one of the world's most heavily mined countries. Stay on marked roads in rural areas and even in Angkor, and use taxis to get around Phnom Penh.

Sleepy Laos can woo travellers into a false sense of security, but banditry is still a problem. Ask around in Vientiane or Luang Prabang to check security before travelling the western portion of Rte 7 in Xieng Khuang province (Plain of Jars), between Muang Phu Khun and Phonsavan, or Rte 13 from Vang Viang north to Muang Phu Khun through to south of Luang Prabang. Small bombings and attempted bombings in Vientiane continue sporadically. The Saisombun Special Zone, considered a 'troubled' area, is definitely not safe. Permits, required for all visits to the zone, are not being issued.

The debate on whether or not to visit Myanmar is one of geo-philosophy rather than safety. The country is ruled by an oppressive military dictatorship, and many human rights and pro-democracy groups discourage supporting the government through tourism. The opposite side of the argument is that tourism, in the absence of a free press, can expose the regime's abuses to the world. Many also believe that supporting non-government businesses empowers a populace that would otherwise suffer destitution. Read more on this debate on Lonely Planet's website (www.lonelyplanet.com). You should monitor the current political situation carefully, as the government periodically changes regulations regarding tourism.

In the remote southern provinces of Thailand, bombings and targeted murders are part of the ongoing resistance from Muslim-separatist militias. The areas affected by violence don't usually appear on a traveller's itinerary, but you should be cautious and monitor the situation as you travel. It is also wise to avoid remote areas along Thailand's borders with Myanmar and Cambodia, where banditry and land mines are likely to be encountered.

Internet & Communications
You can now send and receive email in Myanmar, but surfing the internet is still off limits and the government may read your messages. The other countries, however, are well wired and internet access is inexpensive. Mobile communications in Thailand and Malaysia are up to speed with the rest of the world.

DAILY SPEND
If you live like an ascetic backpacker, you can survive on £5–8 per day in most Southeast Asian countries. In cities and resorts, the daily spend will bounce up to around £12 per day.

This involves opting for a guesthouse without air-con, hot-water shower and sometimes even cleanliness. Another cost saver is an iron stomach that can devour all those UFOs (unidentified floating objects) served by the street vendors. Because beer is comparatively expensive, a night of heavy-weight sloshing might be the day's biggest expense.

Laos and Cambodia are the budget beauties of the region. Lodging costs hang out around £1.50–4, restaurant meals £3–4 and long-distance transport is usually about £2.

Malaysia, Thailand and Vietnam are a tad more expensive: lodging is £2–10, restaurant meals are £3–5 and long-distance transport is £3–12 (for Vietnam's hop-on/hop-off bus). The capital cities and beach resorts are more expensive than the small towns. Sabah and Sarawak are about 30% more expensive than Peninsular Malaysia.

Prices bloat once you start floating between the archipelagos of the Philippines and Indonesia. Ferry trips can start at a pittance and climb up to £11, while flights start at £27. Lodging tends to be more expensive in the Philippines, starting at £4 and creeping up to £13 for budget digs.

With a likely daily spend of £13–16 a day, Singapore looks like a bargain beside pricey Brunei, which rings in at £21–27.

The regional currencies have recovered from the roller coaster ride of the 1990s. The most stable currencies are the Thai baht (B), Singapore dollar (S), Malaysian ringgit (RM), Indonesian rupiah (Rp) and Philippine peso (P). The local currencies of Vietnam (dong), Cambodia (riel), Laos (kip) and Myanmar (kyat) are used for small purchases on the street, but US dollars act as the second currency and are required for larger purchases (lodging and transport). East Timor's official currency is the US dollar.

GETTING THERE
There's a huge amount of traffic between London and Southeast Asia but only fares into the major hubs are cheap. Many travellers bound for Australia arrive on cheap RTW tickets or stopovers, but there are also some fantastic, if taxing, overland routes worth considering (see Southeast Asia & Beyond, p207).

Air
The major air hubs are Bangkok, Kuala Lumpur and Singapore. Direct flights into these cities are possible from the UK but if you're heading to Manila (Philippines), Jakarta or Bali (Indonesia), Hanoi (Vietnam) or Phnom Penh (Cambodia), you'll have to change planes at least once, most likely at one of the region's three hubs or in Hong Kong.

Singapore Airlines and Cathay Pacific are the region's major carriers and a joy to fly with. Other major players servicing the region include British Airways (BA), Qantas, Malaysia Airlines and Thai Airways International. Garuda Indonesia is perhaps not the world's favourite airline. A host of Middle Eastern and European carriers regularly offer cheap deals, usually via a hub somewhere else. Don't forget about the ubiquitous budget carriers such as Air Asia that pop up every season.

TICKET COSTS
The best available student/under-26 fares are quoted here. See p24 for more information on how to get the best, most flexible deal.

One-way tickets from London into the region's major hubs (Bangkok, Kuala Lumpur, Singapore and Jakarta) start at £250 to £300. Fares to Hanoi, Phnom Penh and Vientiane are £100 to £150 more. Open-jaw tickets into Bangkok and out of a Southeast Asian city like Manila or Singapore can be found for under £700, roughly the same amount as a ticket into and out of another capital city. Open-jaw fares including Hanoi or Phnom Penh aren't particularly cost effective, especially with the rise of regional discount carriers (see p198).

Sea
There are no ferries to or from the region, which means you'll have to fly between Southeast Asia and Australia. Occasionally gappers pick up berths on yachts heading to Southeast Asia from Darwin and elsewhere in Australia. The Darwin to Bali Yacht Race in July/August is a good time to look around.

Specialist Tour Operators
Heaps of British tour operators run trips within Southeast Asia. Specialists include:

Symbiosis (☎ 0845 123 2844, fax 0845 123 2845; www.symbiosis-travel.com; 3B Wilmot Place; London NW1 9JS) Offers tailor-made trips that are 'something beyond the normal package tour'.

Spice Roads (☎ 66 2 712 5305; fax 66 2 712 5306; www.spiceroads.com; 14/1-B Soi Promsi 2, Sukhumvit 39, Bangkok, Thailand) Bicycle tours of mainland Southeast Asia.

SOUTHEAST ASIA & BEYOND
Of the land borders that Southeast Asia shares with other regions, only two crossings are open to foreigners: Laos to China, and Vietnam to China. Once you cross into China all roads lead west towards Europe – the Trans-Mongolian railway is just one possibility. Although the Indian Subcontinent is geographically near, Myanmar's closed borders impede land passage between the two regions. Like spawning salmon, many travellers are running the Mekong River from mouth to source (or at least as close as officials will allow) through Vietnam, Cambodia and Laos and into China. You can also skip across the Indonesian islands to East Timor to arrive at Australia's backdoor.

FURTHER INFORMATION
Reading Material
Lonely Planet publishes a huge number of guides to countries, sub-regions and cities within the region. Add to this dozens of phrasebooks, books on the region's cuisine, diving guides and *Healthy Travel: Asia & India* and you have comprehensive background reading.

Book swaps are common on the Southeast Asian trail and it is rare that you'll be without the printed word. This region has been muse to historians, philosophers and travel writers for decades, especially during the tragic American–Vietnam War.

For an excavation of the USA's secret wars in Indochina, read *Sideshow: Kissinger, Nixon & the Destruction of Cambodia*, by William Shawcross. *Dispatches*, by war correspondent Michael Herr, is a brutal but vivid memoir of the American–Vietnam War. Bao Ninh gives a North Vietnamese perspective in the touching *The Sorrow of War*.

Norman Lewis' *A Dragon Apparent* is a classic tale set in 1950s Indochina that inspired Graham Greene to go to Vietnam and subsequently write *The Quiet American*, a legend in its own right. Flirting with the colonial and 'native' divide is George Orwell's heartbreaking novel, *Burmese Days*. Thai writer SP Somtow spins a charming coming-of-age tale in *Jasmine Nights*, which is about an eccentric upper-middle-class family in 1960s Bangkok. Close to 100 years of Indonesia's colonial period is poetically captured in Pramoedya Ananta Toer's novels, beginning with *This Earth of Mankind*. Although banned in Indonesia the series is recognised as a literary awakening for modern Indonesia.

A marvellously fun read, Redmond O'Hanlon's *Into the Heart of Borneo* follows the balding, out-of-shape author on a demanding jungle trek through Borneo. Paul Theroux, the undisputed king of travelogues, has published many titles to Southeast Asia and beyond, including *The Great Railway Bazaar: By Train Through Asia*. W Somerset Maugham recorded his aristocratic globetrotting from Rangoon to Haipong in *The Gentleman in the Parlour*.

The Culture Shock! series, with individual titles to Thailand, Vietnam and the Philippines, is especially helpful for explaining the daily oddities and customs of these very foreign cultures.

Useful Information Sources

For specific country overviews, the low-down on travel in the region, and hundreds of useful links, head first to Lonely Planet's website (www.lonelyplanet.com), especially the site's online bulletin board, the Thorn Tree.

The following portals and websites should help you chase down any aspect of interest in Southeast Asia:

Cambodian Information Center (www.cambodia.org) Comprehensive list of links on culture, government and current events.

indonesia.elga.net.id Billed as the 'Indonesian homepage', with a great introduction to Indonesian culture, food and citizens' web pages.

Visit-Mekong.com (www.visit-mekong.com) General site on touring the Mekong River, the region's lifeblood.

VientianeTimes.com (www.vientianetimes.com) Not the official government mouthpiece that it first appears to be.

Tanikalang Ginto (www.filipinolinks.com) Largest web directory of Philippines-related online sites.

thailand.com (www.thailand.com) General information on interesting Thai towns, festivals and customs.

Vietnam Adventures (www.vietnamadventures.com) Practical information on adventure travel.

ThingsAsian (www.thingsasian.com) Good portal to the whole of the region.

BEEN THERE, DONE THAT

As a popular border crossing between Thailand and Laos, the charming hamlet of Nong Khai, alongside the muddy Mekong River, often casts a spell of inertia on headstrong travellers. Even with a morning jolt of thick Thai coffee spiked with a layer of sweetened condensed milk, I found it hard to leave the riverside guesthouse for a trip to the town's main attraction: a bizarre sculpture garden based on Buddhist and Hindu mythology. Urged on by the possibility that the steamy day could reach a boil, I plunged into the humidity with a map and a squeaky bicycle. For any proper thîaw *(Thai for 'outing'), one must be armed with snacks in case hunger should strike. So I stopped by a roadside stand where a sarong-clad woman was toasting fingerling banana. Scrawny chickens, which would surely be lunch someday, danced around her stall. A foreigner always causes a bit of a stir in these parts, eliciting curiosity, bravado, kindness and mischievousness. Today, my ghostlike presence caught the attention of another bicycle-riding customer, who decided to play honorary salesman, ambassador and joker.*

'Hey, what do you want there?' he asked me coyly.

'I'd like toasted bananas. Five baht, please.' I responded more to the vendor than to him.

'Are you sure you don't want 10 baht?' he asked.

'Oh no, 10 baht is too much for me; I'm afraid of getting fat.' I answered.

'No need to worry about being fat,' the man replied. The Thai word for 'fat' also means 'perfect' and is rarely considered an insult. After he'd sugar-coated our exchange with a compliment, the teasing could begin.

'How about one of these?' he pointed to quarters of sweet potatoes, which were toasting alongside the bananas. A pun was in progress; I could smell it, so I played along.

'What are those?' I asked innocently.

'Mon faràng,' *he beamed. Literally 'a thing from the West', the word for potato signals its foreign origins, just like me (the word for a person from the West is 'faràng'). Do you see where this was going? Since the pun only packs a punch line in Thai, it will appear here untranslated: '*faràng gin [eats] mon faràng,' he said and we all laughed (some harder than others). The vendor then handed the old guy a plastic bag of Thai iced tea tied shut with a rubber band. He slung the bag of bright orange liquid over the handlebars of his bicycle and rode away giggling to himself. The vendor smiled apologetically and handed me a warm packet of bananas wrapped in recycled paper that a Thai student had once used for English homework. Funny, but the rest of the day doesn't stand out in my memory as clearly. I guess that is the power of a punch line.*

China Williams

AUSTRALIA, NEW ZEALAND & THE PACIFIC

GEORGE DUNFORD
A gap year to the UK had almost become three when George Dunford headed home to Australia after adventures cooking haggis in Scotland, kid-wrangling in Cleveland (Ohio) and taking too many saunas in Finland. Settling into life back home was difficult until he fell in with Lonely Planet, working on several top-secret in-house projects. He currently works as a freelance writer and has contributed to projects for Lonely Planet including The Travel Book, Australia & New Zealand on a shoestring, Adelaide & South Australia *and* Southeast Asia on a shoestring.

INTRODUCTION

Sun-soaked beaches, real island paradises and plenty of partying – could there be a better destination than Australasia? Beyond the clichés, the array of experiences is what attracts so many gappers to the great southern lands. Ever thought about skiing in New Zealand or diving on WWII wrecks in the south Pacific? You may not be the first to discover Australia and New Zealand, which means you can expect an industry geared towards packing in as much fun and new experiences as you can stand. Gappers have been making the trip to Australia and New Zealand since the first episode of *Neighbours*, so you'll never be short of travel companions.

WHY AUSTRALIA, NEW ZEALAND & THE PACIFIC?

The flight path from Heathrow to Sydney is well worn for a reason – Australasia is a genuinely stunning place. Think vast red-dust expanses of the outback or the fantastic *Lord of the Rings*-tinged vistas of New Zealand. Now imagine a laid-back lifestyle that revels in the sunny weather, plus friendly people, and you'll soon be wondering why you've waited this long.

If you're after musty museums or crusty culture, you've come to the wrong place (though Australasia has its fair share of both – they do use that opera house for something, you know), because the lure of the outdoors is too great. You'll have heard of the big names such as Uluru (Ayers Rock) and New Zealand's Rotorua, but away from the easy icons there's a surprising range of land, from volcanic islands to freezing ski fields. Australasians aren't shy about enjoying their region, with strange and spectacular activities available at almost every turn.

With a common British history, Australia and New Zealand are very doable destinations for gappers – the culture is familiar enough to be fun, but different enough to give you an occasional laugh. If you want to test your school French, venture into the Pacific, with a colonial heritage that includes France among its many influences. And you can still uncover the richer history of Aboriginal Australia, Maori Aotearoa (as its indigenous people call New Zealand) and the precolonial Pacific islands – all have survived colonisation and are exciting pieces in the Australasian puzzle.

Australia and New Zealand both have well-developed backpacker industries in places such as Sydney, Cairns, Auckland and Rotorua, which can be a great boon to your trip as well as your chances of getting a holiday job. You'll have plenty of other gappers as company, and loads of tours and activities geared specifically to your budget and lifestyle in towns such as Byron Bay and Queenstown. Both countries appreciate the influx of keen young workers who only want to earn enough to keep exploring, so there won't be any strings attached when you decide to move on.

The vastness of the Pacific Ocean usually intimidates gappers, as it is as big as the all of the world's other oceans put together. But if you take it in slow sips like a perfect cocktail you can avoid it all blurring into paradise island stereotypes. Mixed into this drink are three distinctive flavours – Polynesia (from the Greek for 'many islands'), Melanesia ('black islands') and Micronesia ('small islands') – that should be enjoyed responsibly. While some of the paradise myths are true, you'll also find that the Pacific islands are all about diversity – customs that are *de rigueur* in one nation are no-nos in another. Packing a little cultural sensitivity with the tanning lotion is certainly advised. Though it's not all banana daiquiris or mango smoothies, the blend of coral reefs, dreamy beaches and ever-smiling people can be so intoxicating you may be in too much of a stupor ever to leave.

WHAT TO DO?

Most gappers find that a year just isn't long enough to explore Australia, New Zealand and the Pacific. The trick is to score some cash by getting a job, and to then get out there and see some of the world. Even so, you'll find that experiencing the great outdoors can really drain the cash – you'll need to prioritise your activities. Will it be bungee jumping in New Zealand, scuba diving on the Great Barrier Reef or hiking through the rugged mountains of Rarotonga?

See Part III for more information on overseas jobs, volunteer work and courses available in the region.

Get Active

With bungee jumping, jet-boating and zorbing all on offer it can seem as though Australia and New Zealand are competing to be the world's most extreme destinations. The enthusiasm has spread to parts of the Pacific, though on many Christian islands it's still taboo (illegal in Tonga) for sports to be played on Sundays. Many countries in Australasia and the Pacific are committed to conservation, so national parks are epicentres for outdoor fun.

TOP 10 MUST-SEES

Sydney (Australia) The glitzy glamour queen of Australasia.

Great Barrier Reef (Australia) The world's largest reef, teeming with dazzling fish and spectacular corals.

Kakadu National Park (Australia) Outstanding Aboriginal art in a magnificent landscape packed with wildlife.

Uluru (Ayers Rock; Australia) The mystical red heart of the outback.

Flinders Ranges (Australia) Majestic mountains, Aboriginal culture and endearing country towns.

Rotorua (New Zealand) Maori culture on display amid geysers and percolating mud pools.

Tongariro National Park (New Zealand) A World Heritage–listed volcanic landscape with great snowboarding and tramping.

Waitomo Caves (New Zealand) Spooky limestone caves lit by glow worms, perfect for black-water rafting on underground rivers.

Rarotonga (Cook Islands) Idyllic beaches and friendly people.

Pape'ete (Tahiti) The essential island paradise, with a cosmopolitan combo of French culture and beach bumming.

AUSTRALIA, NEW ZEALAND & THE PACIFIC

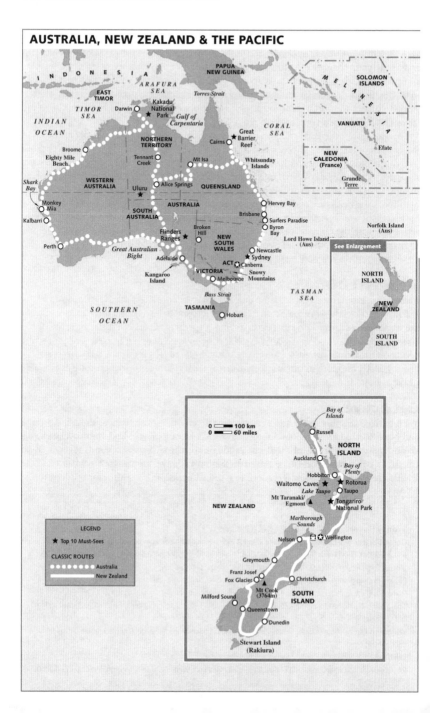

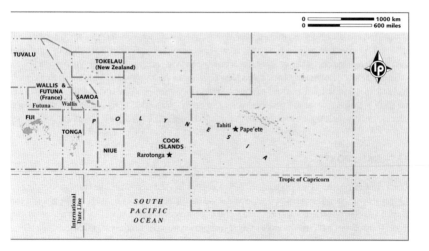

CYCLING & MOUNTAIN-BIKING

Light traffic and good bike tracks mean Australasia and the Pacific is a great destination to see on two wheels. On smaller Pacific islands it's possible to traverse a whole country by bike, rather than hiring a car. Even in bigger cities such as Melbourne, Canberra and Auckland there are excellent networks of cycle tracks, some of which can make picturesque day trips. Coastal routes – the east coast in Australia and around the North Island in New Zealand – can be a scenic pedal for beginners. The more adventurous can take on longer trips, such as the Otago Central Rail Trail (following an old rail line through the gold region), and the experienced can try heading out from Alice Springs along the Todd River. If that all sounds a bit tame you can hurtle down rough roads on a mountain bike – many wilderness areas have good trails, including Australia's Blue and Snowy Mountains, and New Zealand's Queen Charlotte Track.

Both Australia and New Zealand are easy cycling – relatively flat, uncrowded and unspoiled, with plenty of camp sites or other cheap accommodation. Bicycle rental is affordable and can be daily, weekly or monthly, though it's also cheap to buy a bike when you arrive if you plan on doing a lot of cycling. While laws in the Pacific are pretty forgiving, Australia and New Zealand both slap fines on cyclists for not wearing helmets and for riding under the influence, so lay off the drinks if you're cycling home.

DIVING & SNORKELLING

Divers are in for a real treat in the Pacific Ocean with clear waters, unique marine life, impressive wrecks and absolutely heaps of places to grab a snorkel and explore. Most gappers float over Queensland's Great Barrier Reef, but there are impressive dives at South Australia's shipwreck-strewn Kangaroo Island, and at Esperance, Rottnest Island, Ningaloo Reef and Carnarvon all in Western Australia. Diving in the southern waters around Melbourne, Adelaide, Perth and Tasmania showcases shipwrecks, seals and dolphins. Australia is a great place to learn to dive, and courses typically cost between £140 and £240.

Some of New Zealand's best aqua action is at Poor Knights Islands near Whangarei (North Island); Marlborough Sounds also has some excellent diving, including the largest diveable cruise ship in the world. Good diving can also be had in the Bay of Islands Maritime & Historic Park and Hauraki Gulf Maritime Park in the North Island.

The really exciting dives are found off the Pacific islands. Stunning coral, jaw-dropping drop-offs and an undersea museum of WWII wrecks all act as a magnet for international divers. Operators vary greatly in this area, from some bloke with a boat to fully qualified PADI masters, so check the credentials of anyone before you climb aboard. Rarotonga (Cook Islands), French Polynesia, Tonga and New Caledonia are all popular spots for diving. Don't forget tiny islands such as the Federated States of Micronesia, Guam and the Marshall Islands, which have coral-encrusted wrecks and are less crowded than the more resort-based places. For something a bit different try 'muck diving' off Papua New Guinea – the murky water offers limited visibility but creates the perfect habitat for rare sea life.

EXTREME SPORTS
New Zealand takes the biscuit when it comes to adrenaline-enhanced extreme sports, but Australia tries to be just as action packed. New Zealand has the easy stuff like bungee jumping in Queenstown, Hanmer Springs, Taupo and Auckland, and jet-boating at Queenstown and the Bay of Islands, but there's also zorbing – the Kiwi-invented sport of rolling down a slope in a giant transparent ball. In Australia bungee jumping is popular on the Gold Coast, which along with Byron Bay and Townsville, also makes an awesome spot for parachuting. Plus there's paragliding on thermal winds at spots such as Rainbow Beach (Australia), Bright (Australia) and Taupo (New Zealand). If all that hasn't got your heart racing, then try kite-boarding, a combination of surfing and paragliding usually practiced at windy spots such as Newcastle (Australia), Melbourne (Australia) and the Bay of Islands (New Zealand). Look out, though, as most of the world champs of this new sport have as many scars as trophies.

KAYAKING & RAFTING
Surrounded by expanses of ocean and often blessed with calm conditions, the Pacific islands are a great spot for sea kayaking. Countries such as Fiji, Tonga, New Caledonia and Samoa rent out kayaks and sometimes offer multi-day trips. Papua New Guinea's turbulent mountain rivers offer some extreme kayaking opportunities.

Australia's best white-water rafting trips are probably on the upper Murray and Nymboida Rivers in New South Wales and Tully River in Queensland. There's great canoeing in Katherine Gorge in Nitmiluk National Park (Northern Territory), the Ord and Blackwood Rivers (Western Australia), Murray River National Park (South Australia) and the Franklin River (Tasmania).

New Zealand's best rafting is on Rangitata River, but the Shotover Canyon and Kawarau River are both strong contenders for the title. On the North Island, there's black-water rafting – wetsuit-wearing journeys through underground rivers – at Waitomo. If that doesn't sound dangerous enough then you could try river sledging – darting down rivers on modified boogie boards with a helmet – at Wanaka and Rotorua. Sea kayaking at the Bay of Islands, Marlborough Sound, Abel Tasman National Park, Milford Sound and Coromandel offers slower-paced enjoyment.

SAILING
With Australia and New Zealand regularly vying for supremacy in the America's Cup, it's no wonder that sailing is a major way of getting around the region. Sailing cities such as Auckland (the so-called City of Sails), Sydney and Hobart, as well as Vava'u (Tonga) and Fiji, are all good places to get shanghaied as a crew member.

There are also sailing cruises from spots including Cairns (Queensland), the Bay of Islands (New Zealand) and Dunedin (New Zealand), which take in impressive vistas.

SKIING & SNOWBOARDING
From June to November, New Zealand boasts some of the best downhill skiing in the southern hemisphere, particularly on the South Island around Queenstown, Wanaka and Arthur's Pass. The North Island, while being blessed with slightly fewer slopes, offers the chance to ski on volcanoes – both Mt Ruapehu and Mt Taranaki are popular resorts. Australia's resorts are limited to New South Wales and Victoria, with resorts at Thredbo and Perisher in New South Wales' Snowy Mountains, and Falls Creek, Mt Hotham and Mt Buller in Victoria, all of which have brief seasons from mid-June to early September. Apart from downhill skiing, there's world-class cross-country skiing, ski touring and ski mountaineering on New Zealand's Southern Alps and in Australia's Snowy Mountains. If you're keen to add some extra altitude to your skiing, try heli-skiing at New Zealand's Mt Hutt.

SURFING & WINDSURFING
Wherever there's a beach in Australasia, someone will be trying to cut the curl of waves. Pacific islands attract waxheads from across the globe with surfing destinations such as American Samoa, the Cook Islands, Guam, Tonga, French Polynesia and Fiji. Many islanders make decent money in summer by renting out cheap beach huts to surfers.

Surf culture is deeply rooted in Australia, with classic breaks all along the coast at Bells Beach (Victoria), Byron Bay (New South Wales), Margaret River (Western Australia) and Fleurieu (South Australia). Geraldton (Western Australia) is a blustery windsurfing mecca.

New Zealand surfers are used to year-round wetsuits, particularly on the South Island, and if you don't mind zipping up there's always somewhere to break out the board. There are awesome breaks at Ragland (including the famous Waikato break), Marlborough Sounds and even around Wellington.

TREKKING & MOUNTAINEERING
Australians call it bush walking, while in New Zealand it's known as tramping; whatever name you give it, there are plenty of opportunities to explore the wilderness on foot. While many of the Pacific islands are too small to offer really challenging walks, Papua New Guinea has a network of trails (including the famous Kokoda Trail) that take several days to cover. Paths such as Rarotonga's Cross-Island Track – a hike of a few hours through some beautiful scenery – are common on the islands.

Australia and New Zealand will give you better chances to stretch your legs. Tiny Tasmania, in Australia, boasts the magnificent Overland Track (plus plenty of other walks in Cradle Mountain–Lake St Clair National Park) while South Australia has the impressive Mawson Trail in the Flinders Ranges. The Blue and Snowy Mountains (New South Wales) both have well-trafficked trails, but less beaten tracks include Western Australia's Bibbulmun Track and central Australia's challenging Larapinta Trail.

Many of these regions also offer fantastic rock climbing; don't forget to check out Mt Arapiles and the high country around Mt Buffalo (Victoria), Warrumbungle National Park (New South Wales), the Hazards (Tasmania) and Karijini National Park (Western Australia). The best places for caving in New Zealand are around Auckland, Wellington and Waitomo (which offers a spectacular 100m abseil into the Lost World cave). In Australia, the Blue and Snowy Mountains both have intriguing cave complexes.

New Zealand is criss-crossed with thousands of kilometres of marked tracks, many serviced by well-maintained huts. The South Island has wonderful walking trails through majestic national parks, including the Abel Tasman Coastal, Heaphy, Milford and Kepler Tracks. The North Island offers the Tongariro Northern Circuit and Whanganui Journey.

The walking season follows the good weather from January to March but tracks are useable any time from November to April.

Mt Cook has New Zealand's most outstanding mountaineering and climbing areas; others are Mt Aspiring National Park, Lake Taupo and Fjordland.

WILDLIFE WATCHING

Australasia's wildlife is not only unique but, thanks to centuries of isolation, remains plentiful. Migrating humpback and southern right whales pass Australia's southern shores between May and November. Popular whale-watching spots include Warrnambool (Victoria), Head of Bight (South Australia), Albany (Western Australia), and Hervey Bay and Fraser Island in Queensland. Dolphins are ubiquitous and can be seen year-round along the east coast (Jervis Bay, Port Stephens, Byron Bay) and Western Australia (Bunbury, Rockingham, Esperance, Monkey Mia). Kangaroo Island (South Australia) is another great wildlife-watching destination, with koalas and kangaroos in abundance.

Kaikoura on New Zealand's South Island is the centre for marine-mammal watching, with dolphin and seal swims year-round, while sperm whales are visible October to August. Whakatane, Paihia and Tau are other good spots to swim with dolphins in New Zealand. If all that isn't quite thrilling enough, you can cage-dive with sharks at Kaikoura. Shark-diving is also popular in Australia, with whale sharks (and other species) at Ningaloo Reef (Western Australia) and great white sharks along the Eyre Peninsula (South Australia), where scenes from *Jaws* were filmed.

OTHER ACTIVITIES

In Australia there's excellent horse riding in the Snowy Mountains and Upper Hunter Valley (New South Wales). There are also extended horse treks out of Alice Springs (Northern Territory) and in the Kimberley (Western Australia), where supported multi-day treks are possible. New Zealand's great horse-trekking destinations include Taupo, Coromandel Peninsula, Pakiri, Kaikoura, Mt Cook, Dunedin and west coast national parks. Camels provide alternative transport in Australia, with treks out of Alice Springs plus shorter trips from Broome (Western Australia).

Fraser Island is just one of the many places in Australia where you can test your 4WD driving skills on self-drive tours through stretches of beach and rainforest.

Work a Little

Getting a job can be a great way to extend your stay and, thanks to the working holiday visa (see p22), you can easily and legally find work in Australia and/or New Zealand. Although many gappers use Australia and New Zealand as a place to work, jobs don't have to be a drudge – there are opportunities in ski resorts (sample the slopes on your day off) and in the outback as a jackeroo/jillaroo. In French Polynesia you could mix drinks poolside at a resort. You might not find a career, but the skills and experiences you'll acquire will be some of the best souvenirs.

At the time of writing, employment prospects in Australia were good, with plenty of causal work on offer. Casual work includes fruit picking (poor pay, but days outdoors from January to April in New Zealand, and year-round in Australia) and the hospitality industry (bar/restaurant work). Hostels are often good places to start your job hunt, with many gappers working on the reception desk or finding other opportunities on notice boards. If you've got some basic computer skills, temping in office jobs is another option; several temp agencies find employment specifically for working-visa holders.

While the working holiday visa prevents you from working in your professional field (though this is difficult to police), you can gain good career-building experience by volunteering. Australia and New Zealand have loads of volunteer gigs, including working on organic farms or helping conserve the environment.

Employment in the Pacific is a more difficult prospect. You could try working on a resort – many recruit activities trainers and hospitality staff from Australia or the UK – though it's probably every physical education teacher's retirement plan to work in the Pacific.

Travel Around

Air travel is the only way to get around all of Australasia and the Pacific as there are massive distances to cover between destinations. Fortunately there's a lot of competition between the airlines, so prices are often very affordable. Qantas (www.qantas.com.au) is the major player and offers the Boomerang Pass – a deal that gives you so many kilometres of travel, depending on the price, and can include the south Pacific. The new kid on the block, Virgin Blue (www.virginblue.com.au), does budget flights both domestically in Australia and into New Zealand, Fiji and Vanuatu. Small airlines also offer good value – Qantas has a cut-price arm called Jet Star (www.jetstar.com), but Rex (Regional Express; www.regionalexpress.com.au) offers the best backpacker pass, with a month's unlimited travel for £210 including some more out-of-the-way destinations. Air New Zealand dominates the Pacific international and Kiwi domestic markets but Origin Pacific (www.originpacific.co.nz) sometimes offers cheaper fares, including its Wing It pass that allows five flights for £115. Polynesian Airlines (www.polynesianairlines.com) and Air New Zealand serve most Pacific destinations with several handy passes. Other national airlines cover smaller islands and can often be very pricey.

The major long-distance bus company in Australia is Greyhound (www.greyhound.com.au). Hop-on/hop-off buses specialising in the major tourist attractions are another good way to see Australia at your own pace, and you'll have loads of other gappers for company. Two good companies are the Wayward Bus (www.waywardbus.com.au) and Oz Experience (www.ozexperience.com), which also run buses in New Zealand with Kiwi Experience and in Fiji with FeeJee Experience. InterCity (www.intercitycoach.co.nz) is New Zealand's national bus company and offers good passes to gappers, but smaller shuttle operations run everywhere on both the North and South Islands.

The relaxed island life has definitely created a laid-back style of bus travel in the south Pacific, with timetables often flexible and operations little more than family-run minibuses. Small distances mean that rail journeys are rare and bus trips relatively brief.

Rail networks in Australia and New Zealand connect most major destinations, though Australian trains are usually more expensive than buses. In New Zealand, trains are modern, quick and expensive. Rail passes (including the Backtracker Pass, which allows unlimited travel for a month for £105) are available in Australia. Special routes – such as the classic *Ghan* train between Adelaide and Darwin – may not be included in some passes but are often well worth shelling out extra for.

Many gappers hit the roads in hire cars or buy their own camper van or 4WD to drive into Australia's outback. Big backpacker centres such as Sydney, Cairns and Auckland will all have a ready trade in vehicles between gappers, but beware of shysters when buying your own vehicle. Hire-car companies run cheap 'drive away' vehicle-delivery services, which can be an economical way of getting from A to B. Check out hostel notice boards for lift sharing, which is safer than hitching. In New Zealand, travellers report that hitching is a good way to cover the country's smaller distances.

Apart from the odd pleasure cruise, ferries from Melbourne and Sydney to Tasmania, and between New Zealand's North and South Islands are the only organised boating options in Australasia. Passenger ships, freighters, charters, outboard dinghies and canoes are used to get around Papua New Guinea and individual Pacific islands. Boat travel between south Pacific island groups is surprisingly rare, and passages on freighters are expensive (about the same, if not more, than flying). If you're set on boat travel around the Pacific, try crewing on a yacht by asking around at marinas and ports. From May to October, experienced sailors can crew in Samoa, Fiji, Tonga and Auckland. Scout around Sydney in April. Whenever you're looking at a crewing job beware of dodgy male sailors who are looking for single female crew members only. See p388 for more about crewing on yachts.

CLASSIC ROUTES

Aside from long trips, you should consider a few jaunts of a week or so, as major transport hubs, such as Sydney, Cairns and Auckland, are all good jumping-off points for brief return trips to the Pacific islands. Regular deals include flights to Fiji, the Cook Islands, Vanuatu or New Caledonia – check the internet or browse the newspapers for budget-friendly breaks. Alternatively you can get a taste of the Pacific by island-hopping across major destinations such as New Caledonia, Samoa and Fiji (and beyond to Hawaii or Easter Island, which make great gateways into North or South America – see p225). A round-the-world (RTW) ticket is handy for this, but you can organise individual hops.

Australia

The east coast of Australia is definitely the most popular area with travellers, who usually start from Melbourne or Sydney and meander up to the rainforest beyond Cairns. The route is sprinkled with excellent beaches and destinations such as Byron Bay, Port Douglas and Newcastle, but don't be shy of side trips. You can veer off to see Victoria's scenic Great Ocean Road, slip even further south with a trip to Tasmania, or head way out west to the outback mining town of Broken Hill (New South Wales). Unmissable points along the route include sparkling Sydney, the chilled-out Blue Mountains and the very diveable Great Barrier Reef. Then you can stretch the trip (and your budget) even further by heading north further to Fraser Island, the Whitsunday Islands or the truly remarkable rainforest of Cape Tribulation.

The outback has timeless appeal and many gappers want to get straight into the red heart of Australia by cutting west through Mount Isa to Alice Springs via Tennant Creek (Northern Territory). From the Alice you can explore Uluru (Ayers Rock) before heading down to Adelaide on the *Ghan*. Alternatively you can head up to Darwin and check out Kakadu National Park or stop off at Katherine Gorge.

The comprehensive way to 'do' Australia is to make a figure of eight around the country in an extension of the east coast route. Once you've tackled the east coast, headed into the Alice and made it to Adelaide, you can enjoy the long lonely expanse of the Nullarbor Plain before checking out the far-western city of Perth. From here you can cling to the coast, past Shark Bay (stop off for a dip with dolphins at Monkey Mia). Drift north along Eighty Mile Beach to stunning Broome, then cut across to Darwin with some exploration of Kakadu. From here you can head south to Adelaide and then across to Melbourne. You can now continue on the east coast route or take the ferry across to outdoorsy Tasmania.

New Zealand

Getting to New Zealand from Australia is cheap with competitive airlines (£150 return) but you might consider building it into a RTW ticket to save cash. Pocket-sized New Zealand is more manageable than Australia, but if you're short of time concentrate on either the North or South Island. Cosmopolitan Auckland is a good place to start, and you can stop off at idyllic Matamata, which stood in for Hobbiton in Peter Jackson's blockbuster. Head north to the spectacular Bay of Islands before looping south through the North Island's centre, making sure to include Rotorua, Lake Taupo and Tongariro National Park before striking windy Wellington. From here the South Island is very accessible by ferry and can be easily explored in a large loop. Visit Nelson and Abel Tasman National Park before following the west coast to Franz Josef Glacier and diverting inland to Mt Cook. Continue southward for kayaking and outdoor sports at Milford or to Queenstown for more extreme adrenaline-pumping fun. The remote southern coast is worth a detour and Otago Peninsula boasts some impressive wildlife, but all too soon you'll have to head up to Christchurch and then back north again.

Consider getting an open-jaw style plane ticket that lets you fly into one destination and out of another. You could, for example, fly into Perth, exploring your way overland to Sydney where you catch your return flight, or fly into Wellington, catch a ferry across to the South Island, then work your way north again to fly out of Auckland.

WHEN TO GO?
When isn't a good time to go to Australasia? Southern Australia and New Zealand's South Island are not at their best in winter, but temperatures still compare favourably with the UK. Events may be a good way to plan your trip (see p219). Overall, spring (September to October) and autumn (April to May) are probably the best times to travel – the weather is reasonably mild everywhere and spring brings out the outback's wild flowers. Some parts of the outback will be extremely hot from November to February, so you may want to plan around these unbearable temperatures.

The wet seasons in far-northern Queensland and around Darwin (November to December and April to May) and Papua New Guinea (December to March) can make travel difficult, with dirt roads often closed in Papua New Guinea. Heading into the Pacific during shoulder seasons – October and May – will reward you with smaller crowds and lower prices. Christmas is difficult everywhere, with many expat islanders returning home – flights can be booked out months in advance.

Climate
New Zealand greets summer (December to February) with warm pleasant weather, while Australia sizzles (particularly central Australia). In far-northern Australia the wet season (November to December and April to May) heralds humid weather and brings out the venomous box jellyfish on northern beaches. New Zealand's North Island is pleasant year-round, although the west of the country is generally wetter than the east, and Wellington cops the windy weather. New Zealand has harsh winters (June to August) but snow is seldom seen on the coast. Australian winters can be quite miserable in southern New South Wales, Victoria and Tasmania but this is the perfect time to visit Queensland, the Northern Territory and the outback.

In the south Pacific, south of the equator the dry season runs from May to October and the wet season from November to April. To the north of the equator, Micronesia has opposite seasons. It's always hot but the wet season is hot, humid and subject to rain, which can make things uncomfortable, with a rare risk of cyclones.

Festivals
There's no shortage of festivals, sporting events and general partying in Australasia and the Pacific. Here's just a sample of what you can get up to:

Festival of Sydney (Australia) The metropolis' high-art showcase, with open-air concerts, street theatre and fireworks in January.

Rugby Sevens Tournaments (Fiji, Samoa & the Cook Islands) A massive Pacific rugby competition (January/March) that includes much dancing, feasting and celebrating as well as the odd game of rugby.

World Buskers Festival (New Zealand) Sees the streets of Christchurch alive in January as international performers have their eyes on the trophy.

Big Day Out (Australia & New Zealand) A hard-rocking, roving music festival in late January that features local and international acts in several Australian cities and in Auckland.

Aotearoa Maori Performing Arts Festival (New Zealand) A rare opportunity to see the living Maori culture. Held every January in Auckland.

Summer City Programme (New Zealand) A fabulous series of festivals in and around Wellington in January/February.

Marlborough Food & Wine Festival (New Zealand) Gives you the chance to gobble great quantities of gourmet food and booze in mid-February in Blenheim.

International Festival of the Arts (New Zealand) Brings an entire month of national and international culture to Wellington in February (even-numbered years only).

Gay & Lesbian Mardi Gras (Australia) Sydney's massive, outlandish celebration in February/March. Melbourne's Midsumma Festival in January/February is also big.

Commonwealth Games (Australia) Will play again in Melbourne in March 2006.

Golden Shears Sheep-Shearing Contest (New Zealand) A must for lovers of sheep, scat and sweat. It's held in Masterton in March.

Henley-on-Todd (Australia) Alice Spring's unusual boat race 'run' on a dry river bed in September.

Festival of Pacific Arts A celebration of rare art, crafts, dance and song held in October every four years (the next is 2008) in a different Pacific country each time.

Hawaiki Nui Va'a (French Polynesia) Attracts canoes from many Pacific nations to race between the islands of Huahine, Rai'atea, Taha'a and Bora Bora in October.

Melbourne Cup (Australia) The country-stopping horse race held on the first Tuesday in November.

Canterbury Show Week (New Zealand) Held in Christchurch during November with agricultural exhibits, rides and local entertainment.

South Pacific Games Held every four years in a different location around the Pacific with the next competition scheduled for 2007.

Schoolies Week (Australia) A drunken and debauched end-of-school party for Australian high-school students that occurs from mid-November to mid-December, depending on the school and the state, usually around Queensland's Gold Coast.

Christian festivals are a big deal in the south Pacific, so if you're around for Christmas or Easter prepare for much merriment.

WHAT TO EXPECT?
Travellers

The gapper trail is fairly well established in both Australia and New Zealand, so if you stick to the main areas you're bound to make plenty of friends, particularly in the centres mentioned below. Wandering Canadians, backpacking South Africans and even the odd holidaying Kiwi and Aussie also take advantage of these destinations.

Airlie Beach, Magnetic Island & Mission Beach (Australia) Renowned traveller hangouts in glorious north Queensland.

Auckland (New Zealand) The biggest Kiwi city boasts its fair share of adventure sports as well as plenty of vacancies for job seekers.

Byron Bay (Australia) Expect dreadlocks and diamond rocks at this alternative centre that's seeing the moneyed creep up from Sydney.

Cairns (Australia) A humid, buzzing and gregarious place and launching point for so much activity.

Cape Tribulation (Australia) A tranquil rainforest paradise in northern Queensland.

Melbourne (Australia) Known for dining and culture, this metropolis fancies itself as the Paris of the southern hemisphere.

Nadi (Fiji) A well-kitted-out town offering blissful accommodation options for every budget.

Queenstown (New Zealand) The South Island's adventure/party town, with heaps of high-octane fun.

Rarotonga (Cook Islands) A chilled-out slice of heaven that's just a quick plane hop from New Zealand.

Sydney (Australia) Big, brash and unavoidable, every gapper will spend some time in Sydney, whether looking for work or beach bumming.

Wellington (New Zealand) A major good-time town and a good spot to start exploring the scenic 'sets' of *Lord of the Rings*.

Locals

Waves of immigration have made Australia and New Zealand essentially multicultural societies. After WWII, Australians received refugees from Greece, Italy, Yugoslavia, Lebanon and Turkey to increase its population. New Zealand sees its fair share of immigrants from Polynesia, with pockets of Samoan and Tongan communities co-existing with the Maori and Europeans, as well as Chinese and Indian immigrants. Australia has also received recent Asian immigration, including families from Vietnam and Indonesia. Of the traditional people of both countries, about 380,000 Aborigines and Torres Strait Islanders remain in Australia and 530,000 Maori in New Zealand.

Australia has large and proud gay and lesbian communities (8% of the adult population), particularly in larger cities such as Sydney and Melbourne, so sexuality isn't usually an issue. Australia and New Zealand both have macho, 'blokey' cultures that embrace sport as a religion, with Saturdays given over to worship 'footy' players in winter.

Many Australians and Kiwis occasionally describe Brits as Poms and rib them especially about British sporting failings, but it's light-hearted as both Aussies and Kiwis have cultures of harmless teasing. People are generally friendly and gregarious and will often go out of their way to help you (especially in New Zealand). The clichéd picture of Australasian beach bums is exaggerated, but certainly life outside of work is important to Australasians, with flexible hours in many jobs. When they're not working nine to five-ish, Australians like to drink (in cities wine is becoming as standard a tipple as the traditional beer) and party, though they also enjoy getting into the wilderness on weekends.

Pacific islanders are a diverse bunch with common links in European colonial histories that brought Christianity to many islands. After WWII, many islands gained independence from European colonial masters (notably not New Caledonia, which is still administratively part of France), but religion remained a strong influence. Holiday islands such as Tahiti are usually fairly relaxed, but more conservative islands such as Tonga frown on nakedness. The family remains important in many Pacific cultures and remnants of the 'big man' culture of strong leaders rather than consultative democracies remain in islands such as Fiji and the Solomons. Rugby is played by many islanders and runs a close second to church in terms of devotion. The peoples of the south Pacific are proud and nationalistic, though many are forced to leave their islands for work – Tuvaluans, for example, are well-respected sailors who crew on international ships. A few islands face problems such as pollution, economic hardship and poor diet, often associated with decolonisation. Some islanders are ambivalent about travellers, though many see tourism as crucial to their economy.

Language

Despite fairly thick accents, the English language is spoken throughout Australasia. Both Australian and New Zealand English abbreviate many terms, so you can expect to eat brekky (breakfast) after a night of slapping mozzies (mosquitos) and downing tinnies (tins of beer), before heading out to look for freshies (freshwater crocodiles). For insider's slang and a smattering of Aboriginal languages, Lonely Planet's *Australian* phrasebook is a good backgrounder.

New Zealand has two official languages – English and Maori, both of which are taught in schools, so you'll find that even *pakehas* (non-Maori New Zealanders) will use a little Maori in their daily conversation. You'll really only need English, though learning Maori will make your trip more interesting and the language is surprisingly easy to pronounce. You'll also come home with a very genuine souvenir.

While Papua New Guinea has created its fair share of linguistic theses (there are over 750 languages spoken, about 30% of the world's indigenous languages), pidgin (or Neo-Melanesian) will get you by in most tourist areas. Pidgin (covered in a Lonely Planet's *Pidgin* phrasebook) is a mashing together of English and German with a total vocabulary of just over 1300 words. Many educated people prefer to speak English. The south Pacific is a similarly confusing mass of languages, but most islanders also speak either French or English. Unless you're having an extended stay (anyone for a gap decade?) you probably won't need to learn any more of the Pacific languages than are covered in Lonely Planet's *South Pacific* phrasebook, which also includes Maori.

Health Risks

Despite exaggerated reports of sharks, snakes, spiders, box jellyfish and other scary critters, Australia and New Zealand are generally very safe and free of health risks. A few cases of mosquito-borne diseases (such as dengue fever, Ross River fever, malaria, and Murray Valley encephalitis) have been reported in northern Australia. You can get amoebic meningitis from bathing in New Zealand's geothermic pools, and a few unclean lakes and rivers have been known to transmit giardia.

The biggest health risks in the region occur in Papua New Guinea, the Solomon Islands and Vanuatu, where malaria is endemic and a raft of vaccinations are required. Check with your doctor before heading to any Pacific islands to see if shots are required.

The weather poses the greatest risk to health in the region. The sun can be fierce, especially if you're not used to it, so heat exhaustion, dehydration and sunburn pose a constant threat. Most Aussies pack sunscreen and a bottle of water with them before facing summer days, and sun hats are also helpful. With an expanding hole in the ozone layer above much of Australia and New Zealand, skin cancer is an all-too-real threat. In New Zealand, exposure and hypothermia are dangers for unprepared trekkers at high altitude; also be aware of the strength of the sun (you can burn in as little as six minutes in some places).

For more travel health information consult the Health chapter (p59) and seek professional medical advice.

Time & Flight Time

Australia is divided into Eastern Standard Time, which is 10 hours ahead of Greenwich Mean Time (GMT), Central Time (9½ hours ahead of GMT) and Western Time (eight hours ahead of GMT). New Zealand is 12 hours ahead of GMT. Both Kiwi and Australian clocks are put forward one hour between October and March, with Queensland the notable exception – apparently they don't want to confuse their cows about milking times. South Pacific nations are split by the International Date Line, which puts Tonga 13 hours ahead of GMT while Samoa, a short hop to the north, is 11 hours behind GMT and therefore exactly one day behind.

There are no direct flights into the region from the UK: all aircraft stop at least once, usually in either Singapore or Bangkok. This means that Sydney is a 22-hour flight away from London. Darwin (19 hours) and Perth (21 hours) are closer, while Auckland is further away (26½ hours). Beware of cheap tickets to Pacific destinations such as Nadi (Fiji), which can involve 35 hours of travelling and two stops.

Issues

Generally Australasia has few border conflicts or places of civil unrest to avoid. At the time of writing there had been no terrorist attacks within Australasia; however, the region is wary after Australians were targeted in the Bali bombings of 2002 and the 2004 bombing of the Australian Embassy in Jakarta, Indonesia.

Papua New Guinea is a continued cause for concern, and outbreaks of violence in Port Moresby and the highlands area are not uncommon. The Solomon Islands has quietened down with the injection of peacekeepers, but violence still occurs. The beleaguered island of Nauru is in financial trouble now that its guano (phosphate-rich bird droppings sold as fertiliser) profits have been frittered away. Several areas such as Tuvalu and Kiribati have been impacted by rising tides that have reduced their land, with plucky Kiribati going so far as to sue the US government for refusing to sign the Kyoto Protocol, which aims to reduce global warming. Other environmental catastrophes in the area include cyclones. In 2004 Cyclone Heta devastated large areas of Niue along with other nearby islands.

For further information on travel hotspots, general safety issues and governmental travel advice see the Safety chapter (p79). The Australian government also has a website dedicated to travel warnings (www.smartraveller.gov.au) that gives sound advice.

Internet & Communications

Internet access, pay-as-you-go mobile phones and cheap-as phonecards (you can call the UK for less than 5p a minute!) are widely available in Australia and New Zealand's bigger cities. For speedy downloads, look out for internet cafés with broadband. The Pacific is less teched-up but you'll be able to check your email on most islands, and mobile phone networks are spreading.

DAILY SPEND

Bringing pounds or euros into Australasia will give you a good rate of exchange with the Australian and New Zealand dollar. Food, in particular, is great value (a food-court feed costs around £3, while a sit-down meal is around £8) and £8 will get a reasonable dorm bed. Conceivably you could scrape by on £25 a day, but to enjoy yourself and do a few activities and sink a few drinks (a pot, or half-pint, of beer costs about £1) you could allow almost double that. Prices are generally cheaper in regional Australia, but budget accommodation is often limited, so you may find yourself splurging on hotels more. New Zealand is approximately the same in terms of prices, though more touristed areas – Rotorua and Queenstown, for example – are a little more expensive.

Camping can be a good budget beater, with sites costing around £3 in some national parks. Self-catering and enjoying free activities (such as walking, swimming, bird-watching or lazing on a beach) can help average out the days when you might be forking out a lot of cash for high-end activities such as bungee jumping (usually around £50) or scuba diving (£60 for a day's diving). Buying a car or motorcycle can save on the price of transport, but repair costs may set you back even more if you buy a dodgy vehicle. Petrol in outback areas can be very pricy, as can hire-car rates.

The establishment of big resorts in the Pacific has pushed prices up, but if you find quieter places you can live well for £20 a day. A few Pacific islands – such as the Cook Islands –

operate as tax havens, so they have expensive facilities to cater to high-end business visitors (who like to claim these trips as tax deductions). Here you can lose some serious currency, with luxury resorts charging anything from £250. Other resort islands – French Polynesia and New Caledonia among them – are similarly expensive. Eating local food (avoid hotel feasts and room service) can make this a little more affordable.

GETTING THERE
Air
Catching a plane is definitely the most popular way into the region. With a RTW ticket you can grab a couple of stopovers, though even basic return fares will offer stopovers in South America, the Middle East and, more commonly, Asia. More than one stopover is permitted by some airlines (see the Round the World chapter for details) and some airlines offer more open-jaw options and general flexibility on this route than others.

The main international hubs are Sydney, Melbourne, Perth and Auckland, though some airlines offer connections into Brisbane, Darwin, Wellington, Hobart, Cairns, Canberra and Adelaide. In the south Pacific, Nadi (Fiji), Pape'ete (French Polynesia) and Apia (Samoa) are regular stopovers for jets coming from the USA (Air New Zealand flights from Los Angeles stop in a number of south Pacific islands) but many south Pacific destinations are serviced via Sydney or Auckland.

The major airlines servicing the long haul from Britain are Qantas, British Airways (BA), Singapore Airlines, Cathay Pacific, Emirates, Malaysian Airlines, Royal Brunei, Korean Airlines, Virgin, Thai Airways and Air New Zealand. Shop around; this is a highly competitive route.

TICKET COSTS
The best available student/under-26 fares are quoted here. See p24 for information on how to get the best, most flexible deal.

At the time of writing the cheapest return fare into Sydney (£504) was with Qantas. Flying into Perth (£490) will save you a few pounds with Cathay Pacific and an Asian stopover is possible. The cheapest flights into Melbourne (£540) are with Singapore Airlines, with the chance of a stopover in Singapore.

Open-jaw tickets to/from cities cost around £560, though the more obscure cities will cost more.

The cheapest fares to Auckland were with Air New Zealand (£525), which allows a stop in Los Angeles and the possibility of additional stops in the Cook Islands or Singapore. It's also possible to travel with Air New Zealand from London to Sydney via Auckland for £585, which may work out cheaper than doing a separate side trip to New Zealand from Australia. Tickets to Nadi (Fiji) cost £925 with Air New Zealand.

Sea & Overland
If you're after a real challenge, then heading to Australasia by land should give you plenty of adventure. You'll pass through the Middle East and Southeast Asia on what was once called the Hippy Trail, partly because of the easy narcotics that were said to be available to travellers in the 1960s (maybe even your parents!). There are no ferries linking Southeast Asia to Australia, so crewing a yacht or hitching a ride on a cargo boat are the only options.

If you love the Pacific life, island-hopping your way from Hawaii or Easter Island is another good option, though boat transport between islands is often by small operators and can be difficult to coordinate.

Specialist Tour Operators

There's a plethora of British tour operators who offer a variety of different trips, including specialist trips based on adventure activities or sports like cricket or rugby.

Local companies (all of which are listed in Lonely Planet's guidebooks) mean that you can be more flexible with your plans once you arrive and can often be a bit cheaper. Here are a few good local tour companies:

Intrepid Travel (www.intrepidtravel.com) A Melbourne-based company that explores Australia, New Zealand and Fiji, as well as Southeast Asia, Latin America and Europe. It now has an office in the UK too.

Peregrine Adventures (www.peregrine.net.au) This company with offices in the UK offers tours to Papua New Guinea.

AUSTRALIA, NEW ZEALAND, THE PACIFIC & BEYOND

Flights on to Africa, South America, North America and Asia are all reasonably priced from Australia and New Zealand. It's definitely cheaper, however, to use a RTW ticket bought in the UK to travel on to these countries. You can also extend Pacific island-hopping from major destinations such as New Caledonia, Samoa and Fiji to Hawaii or Easter Island, which make great gateways into North or South America. Again, a RTW ticket is handy for this, but you can organise individual hops.

With a one-way ticket to Australia you can go on some brilliant overland trips to get back home. You could head through East Timor and fly to Indonesia (there are no ferries linking the two countries) to follow the old Hippy Trail. Or head north to China and take the Trans-Mongolian railway from Beijing to Moscow. Taking a more wandering route, you could head on to North or South America, maybe even with a few stops in the Pacific along the way there.

FURTHER INFORMATION
Reading Material

Lonely Planet's guides to Australasia are known for their local knowledge and authority. The new *Australia & New Zealand on a shoestring* title aims to save your pennies so you can stay longer. *East Coast Australia* is another gapper favourite. There are also excellent companion guides: *Aboriginal Australia & the Torres Strait Islands* (with an insight into indigenous Australia), *Healthy Travel Australia, New Zealand & the Pacific* and *Watching Wildlife: Australia* plus a number of walking, diving and cycling guides.

A fascinating (and frightening) Aboriginal view of Australia's history is explored in Henry Reynold's *The Other Side of the Frontier*, while *Te Ao Hurihuri: Aspects of Maoritanga*, by Michael King, explores Maori culture. *Once Were Warriors* by Alan Duff is a gritty fictional take on modern Maori life. *My Place*, by Sally Morgan, is a disturbing account of the stolen generation of Aboriginal children in Australia. Another politically charged book is Lonely Planet's *From Nothing to Zero: Letters from Refugees in Australia's Detention Centres*.

Sean & David's Long Drive, by Sean Condon, is the tale of two ill-equipped urban Australians faced with the vastness of their own country. Bill Bryson has his own hilarious take on Australia with *Down Under*, while *Songlines*, by Bruce Chatwin, is a classic travelogue about Australia. David Astle takes a look at all that is weird and wonderful about Australia in his *Cassowary Crossing,* a curiosity guide to the country. Tony Horwitz's *One for the Road* is an older gapper story of a journalist who quits his job in Sydney to explore the outback, while Roff Smith tries to make it even harder for himself in *Cold Beer and Crocodiles: A Bicycle Journey into Australia*. Across the Tasman, Polly Evans jumps on a motorbike in *Kiwis Might Fly: Around New Zealand on Two Big Wheels* and creates a rip-snorting travelogue. A great account of travels through the South Seas is *Slow Boats Home*, by Gavin

Young, the sequel to *Slow Boats to China*. Paul Theroux's *The Happy Isles of Oceania: Paddling the Pacific* is a downbeat account of his travels through the region. *The Kon-Tiki Expedition*, by Thor Heyerdahl, is a classic yarn about a re-enacted voyage on a raft through Polynesia. For a story of life in Papua New Guinea, Isabella Tree's *Islands in the Clouds* is an entertaining read. Sia Fiegel gives a gripping account of a Samoan girl's rite of passage in *Where We Once Belonged*.

Useful Information Sources

For the lowdown on specific countries, check out the Worldguide on Lonely Planet's website (www.lonelyplanet.com).

The following portals and websites should help your planning:

aboriginalaustralia.com (www.aboriginalaustralia.com) Aboriginal-owned, community-run website covering culture, art and tourism.

Australia Online (www.australiaonline.com.au) Information on accommodation, attractions, tours and activities.

BUG (www.backpackersultimateguide.com) An excellent guide to Australia, the Pacific and Europe.

Bushwise Women (www.bushwise.co.nz) Information about accommodation and activities in New Zealand and elsewhere tailored especially for women.

Department of Conservation (www.doc.govt.nz) New Zealand Department of Conservation site with news and information about tracks, parks and conservation.

Department of the Environment & Heritage (www.deh.gov.au/parks) The portal for Australia's national parks.

Guide to Australia (www.csu.edu.au/education/australia.html) A mine of useful information, with links to government organisations.

Kiwi NewZ (www.kiwinewz.com) Up-to-date site packed with information about Queenstown and the southern lakes.

Pacific Regional Environment Programme (www.sidsnet.org/pacific/sprep) Detailed information on environmental issues in the Pacific.

PacificIslands.com (www.pacificislands.com) Useful travel information.

Study in Australia (www.studyinaustralia.gov.au) A government site with the lowdown on studying in Australia.

Walkabout Australian Travel Guide (www.walkabout.com.au) A good information site for Australia that includes flights and accommodation.

BEEN THERE, DONE THAT

'You must have the best job in the world,' the desk-bound sergeant smiled at me as I filled out the occupation question on the police report.

'It has its days,' I tell him. This has definitely been one of them.

After years of religiously padlocking my backpack in Russian hostels, fumbling to get lira from my money belt in Italy and avoiding scammers on a train in southern Thailand, I get a crappy hire bike stolen when I'm writing a guidebook in my own country. What's worse, it happens in the supposedly laid-back beach town of Wollongong, where I should be checking out the best beaches to get a tan.

I'm still ticked off after seeing the thieves drive away in the van that they'd wheeled the bike into as I was coming out of a café. They left me lamely holding a cut bike chain as their van screeched away. I'd even had time to futilely run after them so they could give me the finger as they drove away. With only a few hours left before I had to catch the train to Sydney, I was left with a bike helmet and a distinct lack of bike.

And you know how they always say in Hollywood movies that you should get the licence plate so the police can bust the perpetrators? Yeah, well according to the desk sergeant, that was only going to be useful if I identified the thieves in a line-up – near impossible in a township of identical scruffy blond surfer dudes. I'd have to call the hire place to see if insurance would cover it, then get to the train station in time and, even worse, Hollywood had lied to me. This was a nightmare.

The sergeant was too busy minding the desk to complete the report, so I had to be 'written up' in an interview room, which would take at least an hour. There was no way I'd get that train. At least being 'written up' sounded like a genuine cop-show experience to tell the folks about back home.

And maybe that's the best way to look at this sort of experience – a story to tell people when I got back, rather than a few hours of paperwork that made me miss my train. Sure, I could have been lying on a beach like everyone else who came here, but this was a genuine travel experience and I'd never been 'written up' before.

The interview itself was a lot like a crime show – there were two police officers but instead of interrogating me they seemed to be playing 'good cop, better cop' – the latter got me a cup of tea. We even had a bit of a chat about the best places to eat in town. Sure, I missed the train and had to stay longer, but if you're a little flexible and go with it you'll have a 'non-tourist' experience with the odd free cuppa into the bargain.

George Dunford

NORTH AMERICA & THE CARIBBEAN

ANDREW DEAN NYSTROM
Highlights of US native Andrew Dean Nystrom's pre-university sab-
batical included a professional football trial in Scotland, cooking
at a B&B in rural Tipperary and learning how to milk a cow while
reclaiming a derelict farmstead in County Cork. His writing has
been translated into a dozen languages and he has contributed
text and images to a baker's dozen of Lonely Planet titles, including
Best of Las Vegas, Bolivia, The Career Break Book, Experimen-
tal Travel, Mexico, Out to Eat San Francisco, Rocky Mountains,
South America on a shoestring, Yellowstone & Grand Teton
National Parks, USA *and* USA & Canada on a shoestring.

INTRODUCTION

North America may seem familiar, thanks to cinema and TV, but the scale of the place
and the scope of possibilities will stagger you. There's so much space, such a diversity of
landscapes – and a formidable number of fast-food outlets waiting to supersize you. Love
it or loathe it, North America has left its mark on the world. To understand the place
better, forget what you think you know and instead immerse yourself in it. The continent
is a huge, wonder-full and diverse playground for those who can afford the entrance fee.
Current exchange rates make it as good a time as ever to visit.

The Caribbean is a different kettle of fish – unique in atmosphere and attitude but, for
better or worse, influenced strongly by its great neighbour. Greenland and the Ultima Thule
add otherworldly frosting to the region's already-sweet cake.

WHY NORTH AMERICA & THE CARIBBEAN?

The US of A is the greatest success story of the modern world – a nation fashioned from
an incredibly disparate population whose desire to choose their own paths to wealth or
heaven forged the richest, most inventive and powerful nation on earth. It's quite a story,
with Canada contributing a pretty hefty subplot. It can be hard work dismantling your preconceptions about North America. So much of the region has been filmed, photographed,
painted and written about that you need to peel back multiple layers of representation to
keep it all from feeling like a wonderful stage set.

Rambling around America and Canada is the antithesis of travelling in India. It's not
even like touring Europe. There aren't heaps of architecturally stunning monuments or
relics of ancient cultures to visit. Instead, historical sites often relate to the pioneers of a
great continent and the monuments focus on triumph over a new, harsh land. However,
arguably it's the natural wonders that are the real highlights: Niagara Falls; Yellowstone
National Park; the Grand Canyon; Utah's red-rock deserts; the vast swamps of the Florida

Everglades; Hawaii's volcanoes; and the fjords, islands and glaciers of Alaska's sublime Inside Passage. What's more, there's virtually no activity you can't partake in. Looking to devote your gap year to activism or turntablism? Yearning to become a skateboard guru or nude free-fall parachutist? Go right ahead, you won't be alone and plenty of experts will be only too happy to show you the ropes.

Despite polemicists who justly cite the destruction of Native American cultures, racism and imperialism at the top of a long list of wrong-doings, much of the world still remains in love with the idea of America, a land blessed with some of the world's most vibrant cities and mind-blowing landscapes, and, indeed, the place where anything is possible.

Most foreigners' concept of Canada goes little beyond appreciating its vastness and recognising its flag, but this nation has a complex three-dimensional character influenced by English, French (Québec is definitely more about croissants than hamburgers) and Native American culture. Those expecting the country to the north to be a blander version of the USA should check their preconceptions at the door. Canada's wild northern frontier has etched itself into the national psyche, and its distinct patchwork of peoples has created a country that is decidedly different from its southern neighbour.

What both nations have in common is a strong sense of regionalism, a trenchant mythology, more history than you can slap a hockey puck at and some of the most approachable natives (and wildlife!) in the world.

The march of time has not flattened the myths about Greenland. The aurora borealis (northern lights), the vast tundra, the monstrous glaciers and glittering columns of ice are one part of the frosty picture; igloos, dogsleds and proverbially tight-lipped Inuit are another.

The Caribbean vibe is the perfect antidote to North American go-getting. Laid-back was invented here, but it is not all package-tourist purgatory. The Dominican Republic is a picture-postcard Caribbean paradise (white-sand beaches, impressive mountains, exotic fish and enigmatic wildlife), while Jamaica caters to all comers with empty beaches, party-hearty resorts and the three Rs – reggae, rum and reefers. Communist Cuba struggles on and you pay for the privilege of seeing this intriguing island nation with the currency of the oppressor, the US dollar. Due to political instability, Haiti is out of the gapper's loop. Much of the Eastern Caribbean (the string of islands stretching from St Martin/Sint Maarten to Trinidad and Tobago), where private beaches and £500-a-night resorts are par for the course, will also be out of bounds.

WHAT TO DO?

Many gappers start their North American adventures working at a summer camp, as an au pair, training to be a ski instructor on the Canadian slopes or on a student work program

---

TOP 10 MUST-SEES

San Francisco (USA) The nation's most un-American city is also its most beautiful, outrageous and fun-loving.
New Orleans (USA) Soulful music, Mardi Gras and bonzer Creole and Cajun cuisine.
Grand Canyon (USA) Ditch your preconceptions; the Big Hole will blow you away.
Havana (Cuba) Faded glory, '50s American cars and Spanish-colonial architecture.
Kingston (Jamaica) Smokin' reggae, cultural vibrancy and great cricket.
Alaska's Inside Passage (USA) Some of the continent's most stunning scenery.
Niagara Falls (Canada) Premier Canadian tourist attraction; marvellous and garish.
Vancouver Island (Canada) Fantastic wilderness, natural beauty and adventure activities galore.
Hawaii Volcanoes National Park (USA) An active lava landscape where you can witness – and feel – the earth expanding.
Monument Valley (USA) The southwest's expansive desert parks and uncanny natural landscapes never cease to stun.

NORTH AMERICA & THE CARIBBEAN

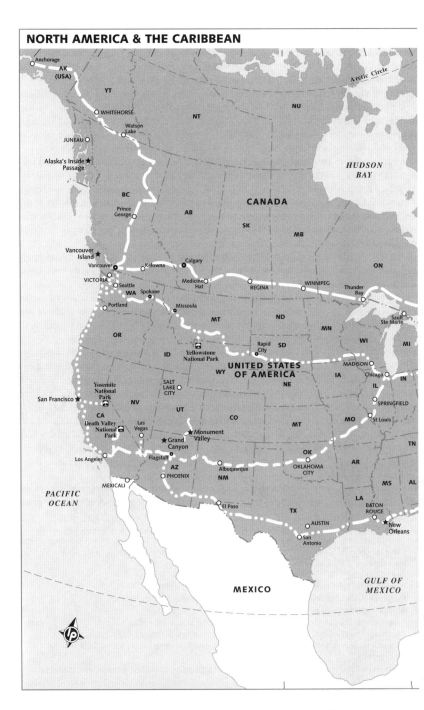

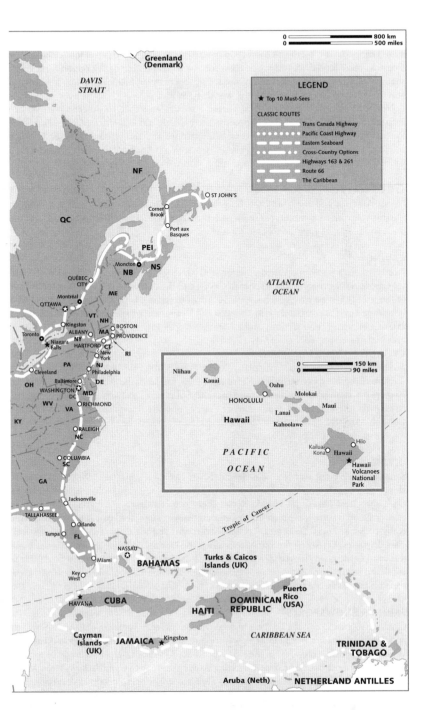

0 ⊏━━━━━━━━━━ 800 km
0 ▅▅▅▅▅━━━━ 500 miles

Greenland
(Denmark)

DAVIS
STRAIT

LEGEND

★ Top 10 Must-Sees

CLASSIC ROUTES

━━━ Trans Canada Highway
●●●●● Pacific Coast Highway
▬ ▬ ▬ Eastern Seaboard
●● ▬ ●● Cross-Country Options
▬▬ ▬▬ Highways 163 & 261
▬ Route 66
● ▬ ● ▬ The Caribbean

NF

QC

○ ST JOHN'S

Corner ○
Brook

○ Port aux
Basques

PEI

Moncton ◉
NB   NS

QUÉBEC ○
CITY

Montréal ◉
OTTAWA ✪

ME

ATLANTIC
OCEAN

VT
○ Kingston   NH
Toronto ◉ ALBANY ○ ○ BOSTON
Niagara ★ NY MA ○ PROVIDENCE
Falls   HARTFORD ○ CT
          ○ New   RI
PA   York
○ Cleveland   ○ NJ
              ○ Philadelphia   Niihau
OH Baltimore ○ DE
WASHINGTON ✪   Kauai
          DC MD
WV   Oahu
VA ○ RICHMOND   Molokai
KY   HONOLULU   Maui
                  Lanai
○ RALEIGH   Hawaii   Kahoolawe
NC

○ COLUMBIA
SC   PACIFIC
                Kailua- ○ Hilo
GA   OCEAN   Kona ○ Hawaii
○ Jacksonville   ★
○   Hawaii
TALLAHASSEE   Volcanoes
                        National
○ Orlando   Park
Tampa ○ FL
        Tropic of Cancer
○ Miami
NASSAU
○   Turks & Caicos
Key ◉   Islands (UK)
West ○ BAHAMAS

            Puerto
            Rico
★   Turks & Caicos   DOMINICAN (USA)
HAVANA CUBA   REPUBLIC
        HAITI

Cayman   Kingston
Islands JAMAICA ★   CARIBBEAN SEA
(UK)   TRINIDAD &
                TOBAGO

Aruba (Neth) NETHERLAND ANTILLES

0 ⊏━━━━━━━ 150 km
0 ▅▅▅▅━━━ 90 miles

Hawaii

before spending a few months exploring independently. Others go for it big style by buying a used car and roaming the highways and byways for as long as the petrol money holds out. Coast-to-coast auto driveaways (see p396) can be a good budget-savvy option for a group that's pooling expenses while linking surface sectors between major stops – eg Los Angeles (LA) and New York – on a round-the-world (RTW) ticket.

North America is a great place to pursue a particular activity or interest – if you can secure the proper visa, which has become increasingly difficult since September 11. See Part III for more information on overseas internships and course opportunities. If you're interested in volunteering or doing charity work, you'll find many more openings and a more welcoming reception in the developing world.

Get Active

North America and the Caribbean have world-class terrain for just about any outdoor pursuit you care to mention. No matter what makes you tick, you'll find a perfect spot to do it and plenty of gung-ho folks to do it with.

CAVING

North America is vast and varied underground. Caving is possible in New Mexico's beautiful Carlsbad Caverns, Nevada's Lehman Caves, and the Mammoth Cave in Kentucky (one of the world's largest cave systems, with 540km of passages). Jamaica is honeycombed with limestone caverns, particularly in the west, and experienced spelunkers can explore the extensive underground sections of the Camuy River in Puerto Rico.

CYCLING & MOUNTAIN-BIKING

Mountain biking is huge, particularly in northern California (where it was invented). Cycle-touring hotspots include the forests of New England, the Atlantic coast's offshore islands, the swamps of southern Louisiana, and California's west coast and wine country. In Canada, the Laurentian Mountains of Québec and the Rockies of Alberta and British Columbia are prime mountain-biking destinations. Cycling is the most budget-friendly way to get around the Caribbean islands.

DIVING

Scuba diving is good year-round in Hawaii, where caves, canyons, lava tubes, vertical walls, shipwrecks and the sunken volcanic crater of Molokini await exploration. Elsewhere in the USA, the Great Lakes, the Florida Keys (where you can dive with sharks) and southern California all feature top-notch underwater ambiance. The Caribbean is where the diving really rocks: St Lucia, Dominica, Tobago, St Vincent and the Grenadines all boast world-class dive sites. Exploring the shipwrecks along the Dominican Republic's north coast and the coral gardens on the warmer southern coast is deservedly popular. Haiti boasts black coral and stunning underwater geology and there are hundreds of picture-postcard coral reefs off islands in the Eastern Caribbean.

SKIING & SNOWSPORTS

Canada, Greenland and the USA are blessed with an incredible amount of winter snow-play possibilities. Canada's main alpine ski centres are in Ontario, Québec, Alberta and around Whistler in British Columbia. In the USA, the Rocky Mountain states (Colorado in particular) host the most popular slopes, including Aspen, Vail, Big Sky and Jackson Hole. Mammoth and Lake Tahoe in the Sierra Nevada are California's major downhill destinations.

Dog-sledging is all the rage in Alaska, Canada and Greenland. Trips can last for a few hours or a few weeks. After home-brewing, beer drinking, curling (did we mention drinking?) and ice fishing, hockey and ice-skating are the most popular Canadian pastimes, ey.

SURFING & WINDSURFING

There's more groovy surf than you can shake a wetsuit at along the US coastlines. Surfing is king in Hawaii. Waves reach monstrous proportions, mostly on Oahu's north shore, between November and February; beginners can learn the basics at gentle Waikiki and then go gawk at the world-class big-wave pros. Maui attracts top international windsurfers like moths to a candle. California also boasts plenty of killer breaks – Malibu, Rincon, Trestles and Mavericks among them.

Canada has some chilly surfing off Nova Scotia and in the warmer waters off Melmerby and Caribou near New Glasgow.

There are a few surf spots in Cuba and some *super-bueno* secret breaks along the north and east coasts of the Dominican Republic.

TREKKING, MOUNTAINEERING & CLIMBING

Alaska is pretty out-there when it comes to trekking, climbing and mountaineering. Even in summer the weather can quickly turn harsh and cold. Epic tracks include the Chilkoot Trail near Skagway, the Resurrection Pass Trail on the Kenai Peninsula and the alpine Chena Dome Trail west of Fairbanks.

Trekking in Greenland is equally extreme. Trips onto the ice cap are increasingly popular. Intrepid hikers can enjoy spectacular scenery while serious mountaineers can conquer a lifetime's supply of rock and ice.

In Canada, Ontario's Killarney Park has a long-distance trail around the tops of its rounded mountains. Other vertically oriented regions include Gaspésie Park and Mont Tremblant Park (Québec), Gros Morne National Park in Newfoundland and Cape Breton National Park in Nova Scotia. More hard-core trekking can be had in Pukaskwa National Park and the Trans Canada Trail (can you spare 750 days?), slated to be the world's longest recreational trail upon completion.

The USA has even more long-distance trekking options, ranging from the alpine meadows along the Pacific Crest Trail in northern California's High Sierra to the forested byways of the Appalachian Trail. Especially in winter, don't overlook desert trails and canyoneering in the southwest (it's possible to trek a mile down into the depths of the Grand Canyon). Further afield, Hawaii boasts unique lava-filled tramps in Haleakala and Volcanoes National Parks, plus a stunning cliffhanger of a trek along Kauai's Na Pali coast.

The Caribbean is not renowned for trekking but Cuba has some good options, such as the three-day trek over the Sierra Maestra via the 2000m-high Pico Turquino. Other interesting possibilities include the national parks and central highlands in the Dominican Republic; embryonic trails in the Blue Mountains in Jamaica; the rainforest of El Yunque in the Karst region of Río Camuy Cave Park in Puerto Rico; and cloud forests, alpine meadows and complex limestone cave systems of Macaya and La Visite National Parks in Haiti.

Rock-climbing and mountaineering are popular in California's Yosemite National Park (El Capitan and Half Dome are legendary big-wall climbs), the Sierra Nevada and the Rockies. Canadian climbing meccas include Collingwood, Sault Ste Marie and Thunder Bay in Ontario, Banff and Jasper in Alberta, and Squamish in British Colombia. In Alaska, Mt McKinley (6096m), the highest peak in North America, is the preserve of organised expeditions in late spring and early summer.

WATERSPORTS

In the USA explore the subtropical wetlands of Florida, Georgia and Louisiana by airboat or take a cruise to check out the bioluminescence at Esperanza and Phosphorescent Bay in Puerto Rico. Alaska overflows with amazing kayaking at Misty Fjords, Glacier Bay and Katmai National Parks. In Canada, you can't go wrong in Nova Scotia's Kejimkujik National Park.

Sea kayakers will never look back after paddling Muir Inlet in Glacier Bay National Park or Tracy Arm Fjord, south of Juneau in Alaska. British Columbia and Vancouver Island in Canada and the Pacific Northwest and Maine Atlantic coast in the USA, are similarly blessed. In Greenland 'yaking trips benefit from the added chilly thrill of icebergs.

Idaho's Salmon and Colorado Rivers are just two among many Class-V white-water locations in the Rockies, Sierra Nevada and Appalachian Mountains. 'Tubing' (floating downriver in an old truck tyre), kayaking and canyoneering are all popular in the USA and there's white-water rafting on Canada's Ottawa River.

WILDLIFE WATCHING

Whale-watching is popular in New England and in numerous places along the California coast and around the Caribbean. Killer whales are often spotted spyhopping off Vancouver Island and numerous other spots in western Canada. Manatees can be seen in Florida, which is also a good place to dive with sharks (if there is such a thing). Baby seals await your cooing adoration on the Magdalen Islands of Québec.

Bears rule the roost in northern Canada (beware the polar bears in Churchill, Manitoba). Wolves, mountain lions and grizzly bears flourish in famous North American national parks such as Glacier and Yellowstone, which harbours the greatest unfenced concentration of charismatic (and photogenic) megafauna in the Lower 48 states.

OTHER ACTIVITIES

Fantastic deep-sea fishing is found off Hawaii and various ports around the USA and Cuba. Most anglers come to North America to fish for native rainbow and cutthroat trout, Dolly Varden, Arctic char and grayling in the remote lakes, rivers and streams of Alaska and Canada. Float planes deposit anglers at the top spots. Bountiful trout streams are also found in the Rockies, on both sides of the border.

Horse riding in Cuba takes place at tourist ranches at Baconao and Trinidad. In the wide-open expanses of Montana, Wyoming and Colorado horse riding is cowboy style on huge working cattle (aka 'dude') ranches. Horse riding is a great way to explore Jamaica, and most resorts have stables.

The Caribbean is a first-rate sailing destination between November and May, outside the hurricane season. New England, North Carolina, Florida and San Francisco are popular sailing locales in the USA.

Got the extreme itch? The USA is a cheap place to give adrenaline-charged sports such as flying, kite-boarding, hang-gliding, parachuting and parasailing a try.

Work a Little

Securing a work visa for any country in North America is very difficult unless you join a student work program such as those run by BUNAC (British Universities North America Club; see p337). There are loads of opportunities at summer camps, ski resorts, national parks, dude ranches and for au pairing, which is booming in the USA. Canada lacks an official au pair scheme, but runs something called the Live-In Caregiver Program (see www .cic.gc.ca/english/pub/caregiver), which sounds suspiciously similar. Working illegally is a sketchy option – the pay is awful and you'll be in big trouble and get deported *tout de suite* if busted. Whatever you do, when you enter North America don't carry anything in your luggage related to job-hunting.

Crewing on yachts in southern USA and the Caribbean is a real possibility (rich folks regularly need deck hands). For more information see p388.

For a comprehensive, up-to-date page of reference links regarding the volatile, ever-changing US visa requirements for foreign job-seekers see http://coolworks.com/foreign -applicant.asp.

Travel Around

Air travel in North America is not as cheap as many people believe, but given the vast network and distances involved this is not surprising. When you consider dollars per kilometre, winging it is not bad value. Book as far in advance as possible and try one of the following no-frills domestic carriers:

AirTran (☎ 00 1 800-247 8726; www.airtran.com) Based in the south in Atlanta, Georgia; focuses on the eastern third of the USA, with a few direct flights to Las Vegas and the west coast.

America West Airlines (☎ 00 1 800-235 9292; www.americawest.com) Based in the southwest in Phoenix, Arizona; serves 35 destinations non-stop nationwide from Las Vegas, plus a couple of non-stop cross-country routes.

ATA (☎ 00 1 800-435 282; www.ata.com) Based in the midwest in Chicago, Illinois; besides a few big east coast cities, serves mostly sunny vacation destinations.

Frontier Airlines (☎ 00 1 800-432 1359; www.flyfrontier.com) Links all four corners of the country with a limited network of flights that all stop at its Rocky Mountains hub in Denver, Colorado.

JetBlue (☎ 00 1 800-538 2583; www.jetblue.com) Has made waves with its direct New York City to Long Beach (near LA) route, good service and free in-flight satellite radio and TV at every seat. It also wings it frequently to Florida and the Caribbean.

Song (☎ 00 1 800-359 7664; www.flysong.com) Delta's cut-rate regional carrier features 24 channels of digital audio and satellite TV in the back of each seat, optional gourmet meals and in-flight fitness; it links the northeast, Las Vegas, LA, Florida and the Bahamas.

Southwest Airlines (☎ 00 1 800-435 9792; www.iflyswa.com) Invented no-frills flying three decades ago and offers the most extensive network (60 airports); links everywhere in the USA except the upper midwest and Rocky Mountain states.

Spirit Airlines (☎ 00 1 800-772 7117; www.spiritair.com) Serves Florida, Cancun and the Caribbean from the northeast, with a couple of flights to LA and Las Vegas via Detroit.

Ted (☎ 00 1 800-538 2583; www.flyted.com) United's answer to Song; from its hub in Denver it has an expanding network of short hops to LA, San Francisco, Florida and Mexican beaches.

Zoom Airlines (☎ 00 1 866-359 9666; www.flyzoom.com) Takes a thrifty, low-frills approach to flying, with flexible open-jaw options and minimal restrictions. The Ottawa-based carrier claims to offer the lowest scheduled transatlantic fares on their daily Manchester–Toronto route. Charters link six Canadian cities with Florida and the Caribbean.

Soaring around Greenland, northern Canada and Alaska can be a real budget-buster, but it's often the only way to access remote places. Canadian tour companies fly to Greenland in the summer months (July–August). From the USA the cheapest Caribbean flights are into Puerto Rico or the Bahamas. There are no direct scheduled flights between the USA and Cuba – go via Canada or the Yucatán in Mexico. Within the Caribbean, flights are costly but a number of air passes are available. For air travel within North America, ask your travel agent about Visit USA (VUSA) and Visit North America (VNA) air passes; note that these are only available for purchase outside the continent in conjunction with an intercontinental ticket.

North America's limited train network is a super (if rather expensive) way to see the countryside. Two classic rail journeys are Toronto to Vancouver and the *California Zephyr*, which runs through the whole gamut of US environments between Chicago and San

Francisco. Toronto is linked by train to New York and Chicago, as are Montreal and New York. Joint USA-Canada rail passes (which can be bought in either country) open up all sorts of horizons.

North America's bus network is much maligned but extensive. Greyhound (www.greyhound.com or www.discoverypass.com for its bus pass) is the biggest player. The bus is derided by many (wealthier) Americans but 'riding the dog' provides an unvarnished view of life in relative comfort. Bus passes are often good value but give some thought to how much public transit your bum can stand. Near national parks and in rural areas local bus services are often inadequate or nonexistent.

The alternative travel company Green Tortoise (www.greentortoise.com) provides bus transport around the USA but their long-haul services are more like a group-orientated tour. Moose Travel (www.moosenetwork.com) runs a hop-on, hop-off bus service in Canada.

In the Caribbean, buses and minibuses are hit and miss, ranging from air-conditioned luxury to crowded squalor. Jamaica's bus 'system' is the epitome of chaos.

Driving in the USA is a cultural and sensual experience as well as the best way to get off the beaten track. However, if you're under 25 hiring a car is often impossible and insuring your own car can be expensive for under-21s.

Driveaways are an option for over-21s (see p396). Basically you deliver someone's vehicle – sometimes stylish low-mileage, late-model machines – across some vast distance within a set time frame; stipends are sometimes offered to cover petrol costs.

Car shares are rather casual in the USA (check out hostel notice boards) and more official in Québec, thanks to the ride-sharing organisation Allo Stop (www.allostop.com).

Hitching is never entirely safe and not recommended (especially in the Lower 48 US states). However, many travellers happily hitch around Canada and Alaska. If you do hitch, don't overstretch yourself – distances between towns are often massive. Hitching in Cuba is pretty common and government vehicles are legally required to pick up hitchhikers if they have the room.

Ferries operate along the Pacific coast of Canada and Alaska. Ferries from Bellingham, Washington, take 2½ to 4 days to complete the stunning, tranquil trip to Juneau, Alaska. Sailing is an essential part of the Greenland experience; a fleet of coastal ferries plies the west coast from Aappilattoq in the south to Uummannaq in the north.

Jamaica is an easy yachters' hop from neighbouring islands and the eastern seaboard of North America. Many Eastern Caribbean islands are linked by ferry and freighter services to other islands in the group and beyond.

CLASSIC ROUTES

In the USA your route is a matter of taste. If you've got at least a month, you could make a huge loop around the country, sampling your favourite flavour of hotspots. One option is snaking up California's west coast from LA to San Francisco, with a detour to Death Valley or Yosemite National Park, en route north to Portland, Seattle and Vancouver. From the Pacific Northwest, you can cruise east over the Rockies via Chicago and the Great Lakes to New England. From big, bad New York City, you could make your way across the open plains of the midwest to the magnificent desert landscapes of the southwest. Alternatively, you could head down the Atlantic coast to tropical Florida, before looping around the Gulf of Mexico to the Rocky Mountains via a couple iconic must-sees – Las Vegas and the Grand Canyon.

If you've got less than a month (you poor thing), you'll want to restrict yourself a little and explore one region more completely: the parks and deserts of the southwest; the Rockies, their foothills and nearby national parks; or the bucolic rivers and forests of New England.

Heck, you can do anything, but as fans of American movies know, the best Americana is discovered by hitting the open road. Classic US byways include:

Pacific Coast
The meandering two-lane Hwy 1 hugs the stunning central California coast as it links LA to San Francisco. The route continues north as the equally dramatic US-101 through Oregon to Seattle and the Olympic Peninsula. To do it right, you need at least two or three weeks.

Eastern Seaboard
You can either zip 2400km along the industrial I-95 corridor from Boston to Miami in a couple of weeks, or escape the urban sprawl and take it easy along the coastal route. Extend your trip with a detour to Everglades National Park, ending up in paradise at tropical, kick-back Key West.

Cross-Country Options
Several epic east-west routes crisscross the USA. Less than a week is pushing it. Give yourself at least a couple of weeks, if not a month, to allow for exploration beyond rest stops and detours. A popular northern route begins in Boston and heads east via I-90 across New York to Niagara Falls. The Great Lakes, Cleveland's Rock & Roll Hall of Fame and brawny Chicago are all-American highlights of the midwest. Next up are the Black Hills, the Rockies and a detour to must-see Yellowstone National Park. The home stretch hits Montana's wide-open big-sky country and Idaho's Wild West before rolling into urbane Seattle. To escape the interstate's hustle-bustle, cruise rural stretches of two-lane US-20.

Hwys 163 & 261
These are two relatively short but magnificently scenic roads through the sandstone monoliths of Utah's mythic Monument Valley and Valley of the Gods. They are easily done as day trips, but deserve a couple of nights camping to appreciate the surroundings.

Route 66
From Chicago to LA, the nostalgic 'Main Street USA' traverses a fascinating variety of landscapes: the Great Plains, vast deserts, the Rocky Mountains and old frontier towns. Heaps of quirky roadside Americana awaits, but since modern interstate routes have superseded much of the original route the Mother Road struggles to live up to the significant hype. Allow around a week to traverse the 3540km.

The Caribbean
Routes through the Caribbean are smooth sailing outside of hurricane season, if you've got cash – head down to southern Florida, across to the Bahamas and then south. Obviously a yacht comes in handy, but hopping between islands in the Eastern Caribbean is pretty easy via a combination of yachts, catamarans and ferries.

Trans-Canada Highway
The classic Canadian route follows the Trans-Canada Hwy (www.transcanadahighway.com; with convenient camp sites along the way) from Newfoundland to the Rocky Mountains of Alberta and British Columbia, where more adventurous options open up. These include the epic Alaska Hwy (the Alcan), the Top-of-the-World Hwy up north into Alaska, or a thorough exploration of British Columbia that takes in the natural wonders of Vancouver Island.

WHEN TO GO?

The clement days of June to August are when most tourists flock to Alaska, northern Canada and Greenland. At this time the tundra is a riot of wild flowers and ripe berries but plagues of mosquitoes and insects are a major nuisance until September. The 24-hour daylight of high summer brings a wave of slightly unhinged behaviour and loads of festivals in the far north. The more remote roads in Alaska and Canada can be safely navigated between May and September. October brings the aurora borealis (northern lights) and the beginning of dog sledging and cross-country skiing.

For the rest of North America, it's best to be a bit more selective about when to visit, ideally hitting the road in spring or autumn. During this 'shoulder season' (cheap times to travel are May and September) the summer mobs that descend upon the national parks and other family-oriented attractions are absent and off-season discounts are yours for the asking. Autumn is an especially good time to visit New England and the upper Great Lakes because of the spectacular colours of fall foliage. Winter and spring are ideal for exploring the Rockies' ski slopes and the southwest's arid deserts.

The Caribbean, Hawaii and tropical southern USA are pleasant places to visit in winter and autumn – which also happens to be when millions of tourists turn up.

Climate

Most of North America has four distinct seasons, the same as Britain, though their time of arrival varies. Summers and winters are most extreme in the middle third of the continent.

East of the Rockies, the USA can be nastily hot and humid during summer, especially in the south. North America's western and eastern coasts are sopping wet, though much of the precipitation falls during winter. The great North American prairies – lying in the midwest between the Rocky Mountains and eastern seaboard – are fairly dry year-round and stay well below freezing in winter. Florida enjoys a tropical climate and California's southern coast is comfortable year-round. Hawaii's balmy weather is near perfect, with northeasterly breezes – the rainiest period is between December and March. Alaska's climate is not known for its consistency (if you don't like the weather, just wait five minutes) but, like northern Canada, temperatures of minus 45°C aren't uncommon in midwinter. High rainfall and moderate temperatures (15–21°C) dominate summer and there's an unpleasant thaw in May.

George Washington, the USA's first president, referred to the Bahamas as the 'Isles of Perpetual June', which pretty much sums up the climate of most of the Caribbean – warm and humid. Generally, the rainy season runs from May to November, when the Caribbean and southern USA gets a battering from the occasional anthropomorphised hurricane – Florida suffered wicked visits from Alex, Bonnie, Charley, Ivan and Jeanne in the summer of 2004.

Festivals

Festivals and events in small towns and big cities are common across North America. Most Caribbean villages fete various saints and hold colourful, vibrant carnivals. Check out www .whatsonwhen.com for details on the following celebrations:

Québec City Winter Carnival (Canada; www.carnaval.qc.ca) Features parades, ice sculptures, live music and dogsled racing. Held in February.

New Orleans Mardi Gras (USA; www.mardigrasneworleans.com) A rowdy, touristy, bacchanalian, take-no-prisoners knees-up held in February/March.

Caribbean carnivals (www.caribseek.com) Rampant throughout the region – there are parades and much merriment in Havana (Cuba) during late February/early March. Santiago de Cuba's carnival is in late July. Santo Domingo's (Dominican Republic) raucous carnival straddles Independence Day (27 February). A second carnival in Santo Domingo begins 15 August.

Arctic Circle Race (Greenland; www.greenland-guide.gl/acr) A three-day, 160km extreme cross-country ski race that takes places 65km north of the polar circle. Word has it that it's more painful to spectate than participate. Held in late March.

Spring Break (USA; www.springbreakworld.com) Students let loose for a week around Easter. Most descend on beach towns like migratory birds, to drink, dance and engage in ravenous mating rituals. Held in April.

Summer Solstice (Alaska) Almost continuous daylight and midnight baseball, log-chopping, axe-tossing and tree-climbing competitions across the state. Held on 21 June.

Moose Dropping Festival (Alaska) A high-class poo chucking held in Talkeetna in early July. Don't miss the burly Mountain Mother Contest.

Vodou Pilgrimages (Haiti) A pilgrimage to the sacred waters of Saut d'Eau in Ville-Bonheur on 16 July and another one to Plaine du Nord around 25 July. The next day many pilgrims move to the town of Limonade, where the feast day of St Anne doubles as a day of respect for the Vodou spirit Erzulie.

Merengue Festival (Dominican Republic) Held in Santo Domingo in late July, the epicentre of the sultry Haitian and Dominican dance form.

Reggae Sunsplash and **Reggae Sumfest** (Jamaica; www.reggaesumfest.com) Held about one week apart (in July/August) in Ocho Rios and Montego Bay respectively, they are the island's biggest beach parties.

Antigua Sailing Week (Antigua; www.sailingweek.com) A massive yachting festival and a highlight of the Caribbean. Held in late August.

Burning Man (USA; www.burningman.com) A massive, arty alternative happening held in the Black Rock Desert of northwestern Nevada in late August.

Halloween (USA & Canada) The time to dress up in an over-the-top costume and act out your alter-ego at wild parties in big cities such as New York, New Orleans and San Francisco. Held on 31 October.

Thanksgiving (USA & Canada) One of the year's busiest travel periods and a time of feasting and family get-togethers, much more so than Christmas. There are also highly commercialised parades and American football games. Held on the last Thursday in November, with a long holiday weekend afterwards.

New Year's Eve (USA & Canada) New Year's Eve (31 December) is celebrated continent-wide with fancy-dress parties, champagne toasts, fireworks and/or watching festivities on TV.

WHAT TO EXPECT?
Travellers

Your travel mates are just as likely to be locals as other visitors but a fair number of Northeast Asian, European and antipodean travellers go to North America. You'll see very few backpackers in the Eastern Caribbean (unless you're very selective, it's just too expensive). There are more travellers in Jamaica and the Dominican Republic, plus many package tourists.

Back in North America, coastal California attracts loads of foreign and domestic visitors looking for a place to chill by the beach. Austin and San Antonio lure honky-tonk types, Haight-Ashbury in San Francisco attracts a drifting, alternative crowd, and Venice Beach in LA draws all sorts of freaky folks. Certainly San Francisco features heavily in many a gapper's plans and with good reason. New Orleans, Seattle and Vancouver attract many travellers as well, while Alaska and northern Canada tempt those interested in peaceful outdoor pastimes. For a cheap, easy-going time trek around any of the national parks or make a beeline for the free camp sites in the west's myriad national forests.

Locals

North Americans suffer from some cracking stereotypes. Sure, you're likely to encounter your share of portly, car-obsessed, parochial folks who've never been outside of their country, bub. But you'll also encounter kindred spirits in the most unlikely places and you'll struggle to find a more polite, friendly and helpful people (handy when you're presented with 50 choices of bread and coffee in a café).

Immigration (forced or otherwise) is a defining characteristic of America's national identity. In the well-organised society that is the USA, the eastern seaboard is more formal than the west and many people in the east hold strong Christian beliefs. Don't underestimate the scale of flag-waving, red-white-and-blue patriotism, which has grown considerably since September 11. Afro-American culture is strongest in the south, just as Mexican and Latin American culture is increasingly influential in California, Texas, Colorado and the southwest.

Canadian national identity has been shaped by the harsh realities of life on the northern frontier. Canucks (Canadians) are still discovering their modern identity but for sure it's distinctly different from the character of the USA. Some people see them as a little more reserved, more laid-back, amazingly hospitable, more sensible – and far from boring.

You may not meet any native peoples travelling randomly through North America but if you make the effort to visit a reservation or tribal lands be polite and respectful. Whatever you do, never snap photographs without permission.

True to stereotypes, the Caribbean is relaxed and laid-back, mon, a place of many influences. Caribbean society and family structures are to some extent still shaped by Africa, a legacy of the region's population by the descendants of African slaves. The region also exhibits the flavours of France, Britain and the USA and, thanks to off-shore financial opportunities, is home to a large and growing contingent of expats.

Language

English is the lingua franca across North America but it can be difficult to understand the Creole patois in the USA's Deep South and in the Caribbean. French and English are duelling official languages in Canada but in Québec you'll need to rely on French, which is also spoken around Louisiana in the USA. Spanish is spoken in Cuba, the Dominican Republic and Puerto Rico. Thanks to immigration from Latin America, 'Españglish' is increasingly spoken in El Norte (aka the USA).

See p244 for information about Lonely Planet's handy phrasebooks.

Health Risks

North America is a pretty healthy place, which is just as well since being ill costs a fortune. Gappers should be aware of the small risk of tick-borne diseases (such as Rocky Mountain fever and Lyme disease), giardiasis (known locally as 'beaver fever') caught by drinking contaminated water and the odd case of rabies in the northern wilderness. Sharks are an occasional health risk to surfers and swimmers in Florida and northern California.

In the Caribbean a few more travel precautions and vaccinations are required. Some fresh water is contaminated with schistosomiasis (bilharzia) or leptospirosis, and mosquitoes in some areas carry dengue fever.

Consult the Health chapter (p59) and seek professional medical advice for more travel health information.

Time & Flight Time

The USA is divided into five time zones: Eastern Standard Time (EST), which is Greenwich Mean Time (GMT) minus five hours; Central Standard Time (CST; GMT minus six hours), Mountain Standard Time (MST; GMT minus seven hours) and Pacific Standard Time (PST; GMT minus eight hours). Alaska is nine hours behind GMT. Time in Canada starts 3½ hours behind GMT in Newfoundland and stretches to US Pacific Standard Time in the west. Clocks leap forward an hour during Daylight Saving Time (DST; April to October). Greenland is three hours behind GMT and most of the Caribbean is four hours behind.

Montreal is the closest hub to London (a seven-hour flight, since the demise of the Concorde), followed smartly by Boston and New York. LA is 11¼ hours away, St Lucia 8½ hours and Montego Bay (Jamaica) 10½ hours.

Issues

Borders are pretty easy-going throughout the region, although upon arrival gappers should be prepared for a thorough shakedown by the beefed-up US Department of Homeland Security. If anything is out of order or they suspect you of intending to work illegally they'll send you straight back to Blighty. Strict new US biometric and machine-readable passport requirements (scheduled to take effect in October 2005) promise to create some extra immigration hassles.

You need to jump through an increasing number of hoops to get a US visa, but since the UK is party to the USA's Visa Waiver Program, short-stay visas of up to 90 days are issued upon arrival. Note that you must clear US immigration even if you are only transiting through a US port of entry for a few hours en route to Mexico, Canada or the Caribbean.

Guns and violent crime in the USA scare off a few potential gappers but once you've been there a while you'll realise that these are pretty well localised to 'bad neighbourhoods' and that rural America is very safe. Before you land in a big US city it's advisable to find out which areas are too dangerous to venture into (even during the day) by asking locals or posting a question on Lonely Planet's Thorn Tree (http://thorntree.lonelyplanet.com).

In the wake of 2004's Hurricane Jeanne, the environmental and political situation in Haiti remains troubled. Since kidnapping of foreign nationals (for ransom money) is not uncommon, it's difficult to advise spending your hard-earned gap year there.

The vast majority of visits to Jamaica are trouble free but gappers should be aware that there are high levels of crime and violence, particularly in Kingston.

For further information on travel hotspots, general safety issues and governmental travel advice see Safety (p79).

Internet & Communications

Internet cafés and wi-fi (wireless) hotspots are commonplace in the USA and Canada – access is cheapest (often free) in public libraries.

The North American mobile-phone system lags a few years behind Britain but is finally jumping on the GSM bandwagon. Service can be patchy outside of big cities and typically only tri-band phones can be used. Pay-as-you-go (prepaid) mobile (known as 'cellular') phones are available from most of the major carriers.

DAILY SPEND

If you want to do North America in style, welcome to the world of credit and consumerism. You're not going to get much change from £30 a day (more like £60 if you're living it up in the city). The US Bureau of Land Management (BLM) and national forests often have very basic free camp sites (which sometimes cost if you have a car). A similar system of camp/picnic sites operates in Canada and discrete campers will have no problem in rural areas. More organised, full-facility camping costs £7–10 per tent. Hostels are £7–17 a night and dirt-cheap motel rooms start around £20 per couple. In Hawaii you can squeeze by on £20 a day if you're camping and self-catering. Costs in Canada can be up to 25% less than the USA, but hefty taxes can nullify any savings. In Alaska and Greenland, expect to spend more like £40 a day, perhaps £30 if you're entirely self-sufficient.

Cars and fuel are cheap in North America but insurance for gappers under 21 can be expensive in the USA, less so in Canada (Vancouver is the cheapest state to get insured).

Cars are cheaper in California and have less rust and are therefore more valuable if you unload them in New York.

Be aware that taxes, surcharges and tips (a minimum of 15%, when service warrants it) can tack more than 20% on to advertised costs. Thankfully, a number of air, train and bus passes help reduce costs.

Cuba is pretty cheap for the Caribbean but you're still looking at £30 a day to have fun in Havana (many tourist-oriented businesses demand US dollars but using pesos is much cheaper). Jamaica is a bit cheaper (from £20 a day) but Puerto Rico and the Dominican Republic are tricky propositions for independent travellers. In the rest of the Caribbean, accommodation can be prohibitively expensive. Trinidad and Tobago is not bad cost-wise but forget about visiting yachtie-friendly places like the US and British Virgin Islands on a shoestring.

GETTING THERE

Unless you're an ace transatlantic sailor or are keen to swim the Bering Strait you'll be flying to North America and the Caribbean.

Air

Chicago, LA, New York, Miami, San Francisco and Washington, DC, are the USA's major international hubs but flights into other cities are rarely frighteningly more expensive. Toronto, Montreal and Vancouver are the major Canadian air hubs. From London, flying direct to New York is almost always the cheapest option for reaching North America.

Getting to Greenland is expensive from Britain (less so from Canada) and most flights go via Denmark or Iceland.

There are direct flights from London to a few former British colonies in the Caribbean and flights from Paris to Guadeloupe and Martinique. The cheapest way to visit the Caribbean is often as part of a package deal, at least initially.

Transatlantic alliances and code-share agreements mean that reaching many major Caribbean and far-flung North American destinations such as Hawaii and Alaska often require at least one change of planes (in order to get the cheapest deal). Ask about the possibility of free stopovers on these routes.

Air India and Air New Zealand were offering some of the best deals into New York and LA at the time of writing. American Airlines, British Airways (BA), Continental Airlines, Delta Airlines, Kuwait Airways, United Airlines and Virgin Atlantic are reliable but tend to be a bit more expensive. A raft of no-frills domestic US airlines (see p235) offer the best deals to destinations elsewhere in the country. Within the USA, American and United often deliver the best open-jaw deals.

Low-cost transatlantic carriers such as Aer Lingus are pushing the low-fare envelope by simplifying their economy-class fare structures and eliminating minimum-stay, round-trip and advance-purchase requirements. Going forward, watch to see if other transatlantic carriers follow suit with similar cut-rate offerings.

If you're flexible with your travel dates, another option is flying stand-by with last-minute, space-available specialists such as Airhitch (www.airhitch.org) and AirTech (www.airtech.com), which can shuttle you from Western Europe to the eastern USA for as little as £115 each way, even during peak periods.

TICKET COSTS

What are you waiting for? Transatlantic fares are at an all-time low. The best available student/under-26 fares are quoted here. See Passports, Visa, Tickets & Insurance (p28) for details on how to get the best, most flexible deals. Also check out special North American air passes only available for purchase outside the continent in conjunction with an international ticket (see p217) – these are a cheaper alternative to buying separate domestic tickets once you arrive.

The cheapest way into North America from London is to wing it to New York (from £169 return), Washington, DC (£199), or Boston (£209). For a seat to San Francisco or LA you're looking at £265, about the same as Miami fares. Toronto can be as cheap as New York, while fares to Vancouver hover around £300. In summer, return tickets to Anchorage, Alaska, fetch around £500, and free stopovers in the Lower 48 are often possible.

There are no direct flights from the UK to Greenland. However, there are flights from Copenhagen (£690; mostly western and southern Greenland) and Reykjavík (£300; mostly eastern Greenland). Both cities can, with a little cunning, be reached from the UK for under £120 (see p119).

Return flights to Montego Bay (£339), Jamaica, are the best Caribbean deal. Shoulder-season specials to islands such as St Lucia are comparable. Port of Spain (Trinidad) is among the region's most expensive gateways (£600).

Open-jaw tickets often make a lot of sense. Into LA and out of New York starts around £175, or £330 if you fly into Anchorage, Alaska (with the possibility of a free stopover). If you'd like to see some of Central America, too, then a ticket into New York and out of Mexico City or San José (Costa Rica) can cost as little as £300 or £400 respectively, though peak-season fares are often £100 higher.

Sea

Sailing might be loads more fun, but any seafaring journey will likely cost more than a flight. With some pluck and luck you can work your passage across the Atlantic on a yacht or cruise ship (see p388). Ferrying it to Iceland from the Shetlands, and then hoping for a passage to Greenland is another optimistic notion.

Specialist Tour Operators

There are hundreds of tour operators running sightseeing and activity-based tours in North America. Of particular interest to sea-worthy gappers are the numerous sailing operators in the southern USA and Caribbean. Two specialists are:

Green Tortoise Adventure Travel (☎ 00 1 415-956 7500, 1 800-867 8647 within USA & Canada; www .greentortoise.com; 494 Broadway, San Francisco, CA 94133, USA) Offers a wide range of budget-minded itineraries for independent travellers. Utilising customised ex-Greyhound sleeper coaches, they explore national parks and seldom-surfed beaches and run party-hearty charters to big events such as Mardi Gras and Burning Man. You (try to) sleep by night, wake up every morning in a beautiful new spot and everyone lends a hand with communal meals. The Alaska trips, Mexico migrations and cross-country routes are fun alternatives to long hauls on Greyhound.

TrekAmerica (☎ 0870 444 8735; fax 0870 444 8728; www.trekamerica.co.uk; Grange Mills, Weir Rd, London SW12 0NE) Caters to adventurous souls aged 18 to 38 with lodging, camping and trekking tours in 12- to 14-seater vans. Trips take in a combination of big cities, national parks, out-of-the-way towns and remote beaches.

NORTH AMERICA, THE CARIBBEAN & BEYOND

With some patience, you can get from the Eastern Caribbean to Güiria in Venezuela by ferry and then the whole of South America is before you.

Occasionally it's possible to catch a boat from Jamaica and other Caribbean islands to Central America (normally Belize, Honduras or Panama). Hitching a berth on a yacht is another option and might transport you through the Panama Canal to the Pacific. May is the turnaround time in the Caribbean – sailors skedaddle before the hurricanes arrive.

Border crossings between Canada, the USA and Mexico are busy but relatively efficient, though post-September 11 security concerns sometimes slow things down. From southern Mexico, the whole of Central America can be explored by land via the Pan-American Hwy.

From Greenland you can travel to Copenhagen and Reykjavík, and continue on to the rest of Europe.

FURTHER INFORMATION
Reading Material

Lonely Planet publishes a range of guidebooks to countries, regions and cities in North America, as well as to Cuba, Jamaica and the Eastern Caribbean. Trekkers are spoilt for choice with *Hiking in Alaska, Hiking in the Rocky Mountains, Hiking in the Sierra Nevada* and *Hiking in the USA*. If you're checking out the national parks, Lonely Planet has all the classics covered: *Banff, Jasper & Glacier; Grand Canyon; Yellowstone & Grand Teton;* and *Yosemite. Cycling Cuba, Cycling USA: West Coast,* a couple of food guides, and phrasebooks round out the comprehensive coverage.

North America's literary history is as rich as the country is powerful. Fiction is often as insightful as travelogue, but if you're happy with random recommendations try *Coming into the Country*, by John McPhee (about Alaska); *Native Peoples & Cultures of Canada*, by Allan Macmillan; *Dread: The Rastafarians of Jamaica*, by Joseph Owens; *Che Guevara: A Revolutionary Life*, by Jon Lee Anderson; Peter Matthiessen's *Indian Country*; Dee Brown's seminal *Bury My Heart at Wounded Knee;* and *The Autobiography of Malcolm X*.

Zora Neale Hurston's classic *Tell My Horse: Voodoo and Life in Haiti and Jamaica* is well worth a look, as is Pico Iyer's *Cuba and the Night;* Peter Stark's *Driving to Greenland;* Tete-Michele Kpomassie's *An African in Greenland*; Mark Twain's *Roughing It;* Jack Kerouac's *On the Road* and *Dharma Bums*; and Edward Abbey's *Desert Solitaire* (the last three are real classics). Jon Krakauer's *Into the Wild* is a tale of wilderness misadventure; also try Bill Bryson's *The Lost Continent*, VS Naipaul's *A Turn in the South*, Jonathan Raban's *Old Glory*, Sean Condon's *Drive Thru America* and Richard Grant's *Ghost Riders: Travels with American Nomads*.

Useful Information Sources

For specific country overviews, the lowdown on travel in the region and hundreds of useful links surf Lonely Planet's website (www.lonelyplanet.com).

The portals listed here provide a different slant on the region:

Canoe (www.canoe.ca) Canadian news and culture portal.

caribbean-on-line.com (www.caribbean-on-line.com) Caribbean travel portal.

Caribseek (www.caribseek.com) Popular portal into all things Caribbean.

Google Directory (http://directory.google.com/Top/Regional/North_America/Travel_and_Tourism) Google's well-organised gateway is chock-full of intriguing North American links.

Road Trip USA (www.roadtripusa.com) Ace guide to the USA's best off-the-beaten blacktop road trips.

Roadfood.com (www.roadfood.com) Drool-inducing guide to the USA's best roadside eats…yum!

Roadside America (www.roadsideamerica.com) Wacky one-stop guide to offbeat all-American attractions.

Travel.org (www.travel.org/na.html) Huge North American travel directory.

US Survival Tips for Aussies (www.uqconnect.net/~zzdonsi/us_tips.html) Heaps of helpful travel-survival tips from an Aussie living in the USA.

BEEN THERE, DONE THAT

Bicycling across the USA had been a dream of mine ever since I ditched my training wheels and gashed up my knees in a memorable (and scar-filled) jaunt around the block at the tender age of five.

I'd consulted many maps and guidebooks – and even took a part-time job as a bicycle messenger – but wasn't ready to undertake the 5635km journey solo. That's when I came across an advertisement for a charity ride called Bike Aid. If you were willing to raise several thousand dollars that would go to support grass-roots community-development organisations, then you could join a group of volunteers for a summer-long cross-country ride, which mixed sightseeing with community service. Best of all, you wouldn't have to schlep all your gear because the group was supported by a van.

I worried that raising the money would be more difficult than getting in shape for the ride, but it turned out to be just the opposite. I received overwhelming support from friends and family after soliciting donations in exchange for the promise of a weekly newsletter from the road. To raise the remaining funds, I collected donated goods and organised a massive yard sale.

Our group of 20 convened in early June in Seattle, Washington, and headed out east across the Rocky Mountains for Washington, DC. Besides raising money for charity and promoting community service, the trip's mission was to foment cross-cultural exchange. We were lucky enough to have riders and community activists join us from Brazil, Ghana and the Philippines. We got in shape as we went, by riding for six days a week and averaged 105km per day. A couple of the riders were experienced cyclists but most of us were rank amateurs. On our rest days, we volunteered with community-service projects organised by our hosts, which consisted of local churches, environmental organisations, community groups and other non-profit organisations.

Experiencing America on two wheels can't be beat. Having a purpose for the journey really helped to get below the surface and provided insight into what really makes America tick.

See the weblog www.rideforjustice.org for inspiration and www.globalexchange.org/get Involved/bikeaid for schedules and details about upcoming Bike Aid opportunities.

Andrew Dean Nystrom

MEXICO, CENTRAL & SOUTH AMERICA

JOLYON ATTWOOLL
Jolyon fled office life in Hammersmith for a stint as a volunteer in Guatemala, where he quickly developed a healthy fear of bus drivers, and an abiding love for a beautiful country and its people. Bitten by the dreaded Latin America-itis bug, he then journeyed via Peru to Chile, where he stumbled upon gainful employment as a journalist for the Santiago Times, *the local English-language newspaper. His time there confirmed his fear of bus drivers but introduced him to the delights of pisco sours and tango (although never at the same time). Despite being drenched by Patagonian downpours and engulfed by Santiago smog, the Latin America-itis still shows no sign of remission...*

INTRODUCTION

UK life may seem pedestrian and grey after a trip to this region. Once you experience its majestic scope and mingle with the vibrant, colourful residents – well, your local city centre just won't seem the same. The area stretches from the arid northern border of Mexico to the windswept, glacial southerly tip of Patagonia in South America. Between those distant frontiers lies a staggering array of landscapes and people. Idyllic beaches, lush jungles, pristine lakes, pulsating cities and towering mountains all grace the region – sometimes all within the same country! Add the voices of remarkable ancient Aztec, Mayan and Incan civilisations, which still echo down to the present day despite the ravages of the Spanish conquest, and you have a fascinating brew that has many people vowing to come back for more.

WHY MEXICO, CENTRAL & SOUTH AMERICA?

If continents had their own ecosystem of gap-year opportunities, then this region would probably have the richest, most abundant and varied of them all. The epic scale of the area, the extraordinary variety of its terrain, and the history of its inhabitants lend themselves perfectly to the adventurous traveller.

Mexico's magnificent Aztec heritage draws many visitors, who can also kickback on the white-sand beaches of the country's resorts or sample the cultural highlights of its sophisticated (and crowded) capital city. Southern Mexico, Guatemala, Belize and Honduras form the heartlands of the complex and learned culture of the Maya, whose cities stood proud when Britain's were languishing in the Dark Ages. Many of the sites lie deep in jungles that teem with wildlife, including howler monkeys who screech each sunset.

Although Costa Rica is known as the area's most ecofriendly destination, other Central American nations have just as many spectacular landscapes and amazing creatures – and fewer tourists. The underwater vistas can be stunning too – the Honduran Bay Islands and Belize in particular are prized for their diving and snorkelling.

Other Central American charms include perfectly formed volcanoes, picturesque old colonial towns, colourful religious festivals and tranquil volcanic lakes. On a gap year here you will inevitably hone your bartering skills in the region's kaleidoscopic markets. Be prepared also for the exhilarating, if slightly nerve-racking, thrill of bus travel, most probably to a whiny *merengue* or salsa soundtrack!

In South America, the Andes mountain range stretches from Colombia to the tip of Patagonia like a continental backbone. The sweeping majesty of the slopes attracts an ever-growing number of climbers, trekkers and skiers. In the Peruvian lowlands trekkers can uncover the breathtaking beauty of Machu Picchu at the heart of the former Incan empire. On the west coast the tapering mountains are greeted by a variety of terrains, from coastal desert in southern Peru, to steamy equatorial tropics in Ecuador and thousand-year-old rainforests in the south of Chile.

The lungs of the continent are, of course, the lush, fertile Amazon jungle that carpets much of the interior. Few places fill the senses so completely, and the wealth of wildlife is beyond description, ranging from pink dolphins to toucans. An altogether different ecosystem, but one so striking that it inspired Darwin, populates the Galápagos Islands, which belong to Ecuador. And to the far south, off the Patagonian coast, boatloads of tourists stand enthralled by the cataclysmic cracking of giant glaciers in the ice fields.

The list of stunning vistas and ecosystems goes on. The salt plains of Bolivia leave many onlookers spellbound; the wetlands of Argentina are arguably one of the best places on the continent to spot wildlife; and towering waterfalls – Angel Falls in Venezuela (the world's highest), and the Iguaçu Falls on the Brazilian, Paraguayan and Argentinean borders – reel in crowds of awed spectators.

People lose their hearts to South American cities too. Buenos Aires' wide, grand boulevards, and the sensual melancholy melody of its tango, have cast a spell on many a visitor. Chile's Santiago is less outwardly grand but has a lot of charm for those who know where to look, while Quito in Ecuador is perhaps the ultimate in colonial South American cities. And the *joie de vivre* and sights of Río de Janeiro and Brazil's legendary Carnaval are known the world over.

Of course, in an area so vast and varied, transport is not always easy. Infrastructure is poor in many areas, as are some of the people, and travelling is often more fraught and unpredictable than in Europe. But, with the exception of far-flung outposts such as the Falkland Islands, the area is still a relative bargain for travellers, and the rewards for a little effort are enormous.

WHAT TO DO?

With so many highlights to uncover, and such an array of breathtaking sights, you could easily amble round the region for many months and never tire of it. And the backpacker trail is a sure-fire way to meet like-minded gappers.

However, spending a bit more time in one place could help you gain a much deeper understanding of the area. There are many ways to do this. Volunteering opportunities abound in many different fields and learning the lingo is another favourite. And this is paradise for outdoor types – there is a huge variety of activities, often considerably cheaper than on the old continent.

Volunteering

The region is awash with volunteer positions, with something to suit almost everyone. You could work with street kids in Lima, build houses in Honduras, teach orphans in Buenos

Aires, conserve sea turtles in Costa Rica, support women's groups in Chile – the range of options is simply huge. Many prefer to sort out their volunteer work through an organisation in their home country, which is good for peace of mind. These groups usually arrange projects before you arrive, and provide back-up and support in case things go wrong. See the Volunteering, Conservation & Expeditions chapter (p19) for comprehensive listings. Don't rule out, however, the possibility of finding volunteer work once you are in the region. It's often cheaper and you can get a feel for a project before you agree to join in.

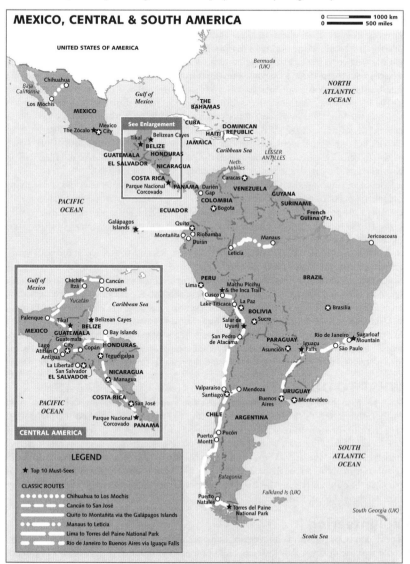

Learning Spanish

As a way of getting more out of your travels – and making your CV look even more impressive – few things beat learning the local lingo. Get beyond *una cerveza por favor* and you will dig a lot deeper into the local culture – and that, surely, is what it is all about. You may want lessons just to help you get by; or you may be altogether more serious about learning a language. In the first case, the language schools in the popular tourist towns – Antigua in Guatemala, Mexico City or Buenos Aires – are just the job. If you're a would-be linguist, however, try somewhere slightly more off the beaten track where you are less likely to be sharing a beer each night with 10 other gringos and speaking in English. Homestays are good for this. Ultimately, however, language-learning is like anything else. You'll have to work at it even if you are in a Spanish-speaking country.

Get Active

The region offers loads of activities – just remember to check the Climate section (p255) if yours is affected by the weather.

CAVING

Central America has a labyrinth of caves, many of which were used as ceremonial sites by the Maya. Lanquín is the most well known in Guatemala and has a spectacular exodus of bats each dusk. Mexico's Cuetzalan cave system is renowned among cavers as is Sótano de las Golondrinas, which is reputedly the world's second-deepest cave entrance. In South America, Venezuela is riddled with cave systems – Cueva del Guácharo (inland from Cumaná) is definitely up there on the speleology must-do list. In the northeast of Brazil, around 200 deep underground caves are known to exist in the Terra Ronca region, one of the largest networks in Latin America, where many caves are still unexplored.

CYCLING & MOUNTAIN-BIKING

In Central America, Costa Rica is best geared to the two-wheeled traveller. One recent visitor reported that the only hazard was a giant sloth that fell from a tree over the road he was travelling on! Potholes in other parts of the region can put off some pedalling fans – but, with a bit of patience, successful journeys can be made. Extreme mountain-bikers might fancy biking down 'Death Road' in Bolivia. Statistically the most dangerous road in the world, its sweeping downhill run still attracts many a saddled daredevil. An increasingly popular biking

---

TOP 10 MUST-SEES

Tikal (Guatemala) Hidden in the depths of the jungle, this is one of the great wonders of the Mayan world.
Belizean Cayes (Belize) Fantastic diving and snorkelling amongst pristine coral.
Parque Nacional Corcovado (Costa Rica) Captivating place where you can witness virgin coastal rainforest, stunning beaches and loads of wildlife.
Sugarloaf Mountain (Río de Janeiro, Brazil) Quintessential sight within one of the world's most spectacularly located cities.
Galápagos Islands (Ecuador) Darwin was fascinated by the teeming wildlife. You will be too.
Torres del Paine National Park (Chile) Turquoise lakes, towering granite pillars, glaciers and God's own trekking country.
Salar de Uyuni (Bolivia) Enter another world when you drive on the world's largest salt flats.
Machu Picchu & the Inca Trail (Peru) Classic trek to one of the wonders of the ancient world.
The Zócalo (Mexico) Mexico City's main square, blending magnificent colonial architecture with Aztec ruins.
Iguaçu Falls (Argentina, Paraguay, Brazil) Awesome waterfalls, more than 2km wide.

option is to cycle the spectacular forests and lakes of southern Chile and Argentina – but be sure to bring your waterproofs for this trip. Chile's Carretera Austral is particularly unspoilt. Some gappers opt to spend their entire time on two wheels and there are few finer ways to appreciate the breadth of the region's landscapes.

DIVING & SNORKELLING
Belize has the planet's second-largest barrier reef, some crystal-clear waters, and breathtaking dive sites. Cozumel in Mexico is also known as a great destination for lovers of underwater life. If you're on a tight budget, you could head to the Honduran Bay Islands. Utila is particularly geared to cheap open-water Padi courses. You can shadow angel fish or swim with whale sharks as you please. Don't ignore the Pacific coast – there is still some memorable diving here, including off Panama's Coiba Island. Down in South America, the best diving is off Venezuela and the Galápagos Islands. Only experienced divers take the plunge here, but they get a privileged glimpse into a world of sea lions, hammerhead sharks and eagle rays.

SKIING & SNOWBOARDING
Some world-class slopes are located in Argentina and Chile. The most renowned resort is Chile's Portillo, just over an hour and a half away from Santiago, where off-season training and competitions are often run for northern-hemisphere downhillers. El Colorado, La Parca and Valle Nevado are also not far away from the Chilean capital city – and all of them have decent facilities. Termas de Chillán is the main destination for slope junkies in the south of Chile. Across the Andes in Argentina, Las Leñas, Chapelco and Cerro Catedral all have decent powder from June to September.

Less developed, but worth going just to say you've been, is Chacaltaya in Bolivia, the world's highest ski resort (operating from October to June). The altitude (over 5000m) may leave you gasping if you go up straight from sea level.

SURFING & WINDSURFING
The Pacific Ocean off Central America has some great surfing. The Red Hot Chili Peppers are regular pilgrims to the surf hotspots of Costa Rica, where you can choose from two oceans. The Pacific has more consistent waves, but the swells on the Caribbean coast can be more impressive during the right season. El Salvador is often overlooked but its beaches have some great breaks – mainly in the La Libertad region. The powerful Mexican Pipeline break at Puerto Escondido in Baja California is also a big draw for wave fans. But do be wary of some ripping Pacific currents, even paddling close to the shore – fatalities are not unknown here.

In South America, try the Chilean town of Pichilemu for low-key (and colder!) surf, while Brazil's coastline is almost one uninterrupted line of surfing nirvana. Perhaps the best breaks are found near Florianópolis in Santa Caterina state to the south of São Paulo. On a cautionary note, some local surfers, particularly on beaches near Río, can get unpleasantly territorial.

Windsurfers are also well catered for in Brazil, particularly around Búzios, while Los Barriles is Mexico's windsurfing capital. For an alternative, you could try the waters of French Guiana, but be ready to spend more.

TREKKING & MOUNTAINEERING
Pick any spot in Central America and the chances are there will be a mountain looming nearby. Many are active volcanoes that rumble and belch out steam at regular intervals. One of the most accessible is Volcán Pacaya near Antigua, Guatemala. A stream of tourists

makes the relatively easy trek to the summit for a noxious waft of sulphur and the chance to stride on the volcanic ash. Volcán Masaya in Nicaragua, just a few kilometres outside of Managua, is another easy one to get to.

If you prefer your mountains dormant, again the choice is huge. Guatemala's Tajumulco (Central America's highest peak at 4220m) is a challenging trek, while El Salvador has 25 extinct volcanoes. Going with guides is recommended for most climbs in the region.

In northwest Mexico, trekking trails in the stunning Copper Canyon (Barranca del Cobre) cater to all different walking abilities.

A very different kind of trekking can be experienced within the thick layers of jungle that carpet vast swathes of Latin America. Ruins from old Mayan civilisations tend to be hidden deep in tropical rainforest (especially in Guatemala and Belize) and these are often superb destinations for the more adventurous trekker. Other interesting Central American jungle hikes include the Montecristo cloud forest in El Salvador, Selva Negra in Nicaragua, or the Parque Nacional Pico Bonito in Honduras. The Monteverde cloud-forest reserve in Costa Rica is but one of that country's excellent walking grounds.

South America's Andes mountain chain is magnificent. And, if the Andes look awesome from below, they are even more breathtaking once you are in amongst them. Among the cognoscenti, the peaks in Peru are thought to provide the best climbing opportunities. The Cordillera Huayhuash (home to Siula Grande, the notorious peak of *Touching the Void* fame) is one for hard-core climbers, while the Cordillera Blanca includes some of the more popular peaks around the town of Cusco. A good chunk of Bolivia lies at head-spinning altitudes – at 4000m, La Paz is the world's highest capital city. There are some mind-blowing climbs following old Inca trails just beyond the city towards the dramatic Yungas region. The Cordillera Real is also rightfully lauded for its beautiful peaks. In Ecuador, too, the capital Quito is a great trekking base, as is the charming Venezuelan city of Merída. Of course, a jaunt into the jungle has got to be done in at least one of South America's Amazonian countries. Key jumping-off points are Iquítos in Peru, and Rurrenabaque in Bolivia, while Puerto Ayacucho is the main point for organising a jungle trip in Venezuela.

In the north of Chile, San Pedro de Atacama is a popular launching point for treks. Further down, many 'andinistas' (as opposed to alpinists) get tempted by the mountains that encircle Santiago. Los Leones is a good one for the enthusiastic but inexperienced climber. Argentina's Mt Aconcagua (6962m) is the highest summit in the western hemisphere and should not be undertaken lightly – most people need several days simply to acclimatise to the thin air.

The less hard core are often lured to the pristine charm of the trails around Chile's forested lakes, many of which are easily accessible from the attractive tourist town of Pucón.

WHITE-WATER RAFTING & OTHER WATERSPORTS

When it comes to watersports, Costa Rica, once again, got there first in Central America. The Reventazón and Pacuare rivers in Costa Rica are in a stunning virgin forest setting. However, other countries are now getting in on the white-water action. Both Honduras and Guatemala have some decent rafting opportunities with varying levels of difficulty. In Mexico, visit Veracruz state for the best of that country's white-water rafting.

Chile arguably has the best (and most challenging) rapids in South America with exhilarating runs for both rafters and kayakers on the Maipó, Trancura and Futaleufú rivers. Just across the Andes in Argentina, Mendoza offers plenty of scope to satisfy white-water thrill seekers. There's also rafting just outside of Cusco in Peru, and Ecuador's many rivers bubble with possibilities.

In Venezuela, get down to the Delta del Orinoco for the best in river and boating excursions. Sea kayaking in the Gulf of California (Mar de Cortés) off Mexico's Baja California is very popular, and is increasingly so off Chilean Patagonia – although the climate is somewhat less forgiving.

WILDLIFE WATCHING
Latin America hogs more than its fair share of all creatures great and small. It isn't for nothing that the continent sparked Charles Darwin's thoughts on evolution. In Central America, you can banter with spider monkeys in Nicaragua, recoil from tarantulas in El Salvador, and view a kaleidoscopic range of birds, from macaws to the elusive quetzal in Guatemala. Costa Rica, with its rainforest-canopy walkways, is the most developed nation for wildlife spotters, but the ecosystem is equally broad in most of its neighbours. Panama has around 940 different types of bird to spot, for example.

In South America you are even more spoilt for choice. The Amazon has an estimated 15,000 animal species, with around 1800 species of butterflies alone! Manaus in Brazil is one of the most common entry points to the jungle.

Less fêted, but with far more visible wildlife, the Pantanal wetlands in the west of Brazil teem with pumas, anacondas, giant river otters and a myriad of other exotic creatures. The same accessibility is also available in the Esteros del Iberá marshlands in Corrientes (Argentina), while the Peninsula de Valdés in the same country is a great place to watch whales. Then, of course, there are the legendary Galápagos Islands, where a couple of the giant tortoises may even have been around to welcome Darwin ashore back in the old days.

OTHER ACTIVITIES
Wherever you go in Latin America, football fever bubbles close to the surface. If you're up for an impromptu kick-about, you'll never have a shortage of friends. Watch out, too, for the international matches, or one of the highly charged local derbies (Boca versus River Plate in Buenos Aires is perhaps the most famous). Sheer rock faces attract gravity-defying climbers near to Río de Janeiro, while horse riding is popular throughout much of Latin America. Paragliding and hang-gliding are popular in Mérida state (Venezuela) and gliders also catch the aerial currents around Pedra Bonita (close to Río). Stop at Búzios (Brazil) or the larger resorts along the Brazilian coast if you want to go sailing. The serious adrenaline-addict can even organise base jumps (parachuting from a stationary start) from Venezuela's Angel Falls, the world's highest waterfall.

Work a Little
Note that speaking English as a first language is no longer the guaranteed ticket to employment it once was. Many language schools no longer take on teachers without a degree or a TEFL qualification – so go armed with one or the other, or have an alternative plan to make ends meet. The big cities are your best bet here – Santiago, Buenos Aires and Quito. Sometimes big multinationals will take on English teachers for their local staff. Possibilities exist for crewing on foreign yachts that stop along the Pacific, especially on the Guatemalan, Costa Rican, Venezuelan, Ecuadorian and Peruvian coasts. Deck hands are occasionally taken on by yachts at either end of the Panama Canal. In popular tourist areas, jobs for tour leaders, trekking guides, hostel managers, bar hands or shop workers do crop up – but don't expect to make much more than *cerveza* money from these.

Most countries require some sort of work visa, but these are not always strictly enforced for transient gringo casual workers. Plenty of travellers opt to avoid the paperwork.

Travel Around

How many people can you get onto a Central American bus? Answer: Two more. Not the funniest joke perhaps, but the punch line has a point – travelling on the cheap in much of Central America is not for the nervous or claustrophobic! However, a ride on the 'chicken buses' of Guatemala and Nicaragua is an essential part of the travelling experience in the area – you'll often find yourself sandwiched between two locals (and maybe their infants too) in a space designed to accommodate two school children. Get a little off the beaten track, and you won't see paved road for dust – quite literally. Buses get more infrequent in these parts too – often the only way to get about is in the back of a pick-up truck. Drivers usually charge a nominal fee.

If you're heading to the Honduras Bay Islands, consider a flight over from La Ceiba. It's cheap and a lot faster than the ferry.

As for travelling between Central American countries, unless you're on a tight schedule, the longer-distance buses are a reasonable option (and might even be blessed with air-conditioning – not something you'll find on most local buses). It's a compact little isthmus, and the roads between the capital cities are usually less potholed than others, but you should always expect a journey to take longer than it looks on the map. In Mexico, it's a different story. Distances here are huge, and an internal flight can save many hours' sweating on an uncomfortable bus. The bus system is regular though.

In South America, the distances are also so vast that, unless you have endless patience or insist on shoestring travel, you will probably need a flight at some point. You can get some good deals. Air passes do exist for different sub-regions within this massive area, and they are well worth considering. Most need to be purchased in advance and outside of participating countries – consult a travel agent who's a Latin America specialist for information about the different passes available and their conditions and restrictions.

Some parts of South America are blessed with a developed road network, especially the southern-cone countries of Chile, Argentina and Uruguay. Bus travel here is generally efficient and comfortable, and relatively good value compared to Europe. However, the highland roads of Bolivia, Peru and Ecuador can get badly affected by the weather and are subject to flooding and mudslides as well as poor surfacing. On the flip side, bus travel does tend to be cheap. Pick-up trucks and minibuses often cater to travellers at the margins of the normal bus networks. Note that night-time bus travel can be a security risk in the region, so seek reliable advice before you book your ticket.

Latin America's rail networks, much depleted in recent years, can offer some spectacular sightseeing – although, in many countries, it is not worth bothering if you're in a hurry. Train networks in Argentina are generally modern and comfortable, but improbably difficult terrain stops the railways reaching some of the more isolated spots.

CLASSIC ROUTES
Chihuahua to Los Mochis
Riding the legendary Copper Canyon railway, this route is rightfully renowned for some stunning views as it cuts through canyons and winds around dizzyingly high cliffs on its way from Chihuahua to the Pacific.

Cancún to San José
Many visitors to Mexico want to combine some quality beach time with visits to the spectacular ruins. The Yucatán peninsula handily blends the two. A few nights in party-friendly Cozumel and Cancún could be followed by a healthy dose of visits to pre-Columbian sites,

including the stunning cliff-top ruins at Tulum and the famous Mayan sites of Uxmal and Chichén Itzá. Continue on the same theme, and you should make it to the Indiana Jones-esque lost jungle city of Palenque, before heading on to Guatemala's Tikal, the crown jewel of the old Mayan cities.

Then head down the Panamericana in Central America, taking a few diversions here and there. One has to be at the classic travellers' hang-out in the lovely setting of Lago Atitlán. Pretty much every traveller and their dog stops off at the beautiful volcano-ringed old city of Antigua, Guatemala, before rapidly skipping through Guatemala City on their way down to the Copán ruins just within Honduras. A jaunt out to the Bay Islands for a spot of diving or snorkelling is an understandably popular diversion. In this narrow waist of the Americas, it's not difficult to make rapid headway down through Honduras or El Salvador (surfers favour the El Salvador route), and through to the potholed but fascinating environs of Nicaragua, where it would be rude not to take time out to dip in a volcanic lake or a climb up a smouldering peak. For many, the Central American Gringo Trail stops at the eco-haven of Costa Rica, but those who continue south to Panama are richly rewarded. Mixing the metropolis of its canal city with an extraordinary breadth of wildlife, this country remains bewilderingly underexplored.

Some intrepid folk skirt around the dangerous no-man's land of the Darién Gap by freighter or yacht, but it's far safer to get a flight if you're continuing down to South America.

Quito to Montañita via the Galápagos Islands
Many travellers, lured by the Galápagos Islands, pick up the Gringo Trail in Ecuador. Ecuador's capital, Quito, is a stunning city more than worthy of its World Heritage status. There is also a memorable Devil's Nose (El Nariz del Diablo) train journey leading from Riobamba to Durán on the coast, which is worth working into your jaunt around Ecuador (often referred to as South America in miniature).

Manaus to Leticia
Sample the feverish swirling life of the Amazon with this unforgettable river trip from the jungle city of Manaus in Brazil to Leticia in Colombia.

Lima to Torres del Paine National Park
Almost all travellers in Peru will pass through Lima (once one of the most glorious colonial cities, now fallen on harder times) on their way to the Inca Trail. The Southern Railway to Cusco provides a wonderful rickety ride close to Machu Picchu itself. From there, the laid-back, altitudinous climes of Lake Titicaca draw in a lot of gappers, as do the breathtaking Bolivian Salar de Uyuni salt plains and Chile's laid-back San Pedro de Atacama.

Most travellers to Chile arrive in Santiago, either by bus or by plane, at some point. It's a short hop to the charming, faded grandeur of the port city of Valparaíso, and a pivot for the exhilarating trans-Andean bus ride over to the colonial Argentinean city of Mendoza. More and more travellers are venturing to the very tip of the continent to see the majestic Torres del Paine, often taking in mighty glaciers on the Puerto Montt to Puerto Natales ferry. Of course, many gappers come here from the Atlantic coast and sweep up the Pacific side in reverse of the above.

Río de Janeiro to Buenos Aires via Iguaçu Falls
To the east, a sort of Gringo Trail triangle has formed around Río de Janeiro, through the populous and cultured São Paolo to the awesome Iguaçu Falls and Buenos Aires, the

capital of Argentina. Of course, there are many diversions and possibilities within this area. Island-hopping off the coast of Río is one option, and a trip into the unsung but interesting nation of Uruguay is another.

Brazil is almost like a continent unto itself, with a whole network of mini routes within its borders, including in the northeast where there are clusters of colonial ruins.

WHEN TO GO?

The busiest time for tourism tends to last from December to March, when many gringos seek shelter from cold, northerly climes. July and August are also popular. In such a vast region with such geographical extremes, there is, unsurprisingly, a huge variety in climate. And the best time to go will hang largely on what you plan to do. There are no seasonal patterns that apply everywhere in Latin America, so be careful to check the weather cycles for each of your destinations when you are planning your trip.

Climate

Central America sits firmly in the tropics. However, the region still has real variations in its climate, which are mainly determined by the different altitudes. High-altitude areas are sometimes billed by tourist boards as 'lands of eternal spring' and there is some truth in that – between 1500m and 2000m the climate is often idyllic (about 25°C). Above 2000m, things get cold at night. Inland mountain temperatures can approach freezing in Mexico and the Central American highlands from December to February.

In the lowland coastal regions, heat (around 30°C) and humidity rule, although by the coast at least you have the refreshing sea breezes and the ocean to cool you down. No such luck in the jungle – unless you have ice in your bloodstream, prepare to swelter when the sun is up.

There is also a rainy season, generally known as *invierno* (winter), which is a far cry from the northern hemisphere's idea of winter. The downpours generally start around May and run through to October. However, the rains are not a reason to put you off. Often showers only happen for a short period in the afternoon (although they can be heavy), leaving bright sunshine for the rest of the day. One area where you will be affected by the rains, however, is the jungle. Such is the strength of the downpours that many paths are left either impassable or very difficult until January or February. Hurricanes can hit Central America, especially from August to October, but such extreme conditions are rare.

Most of South America lies in a tropical or subtropical climate zone, which means visitors can go year-round. Around the tropic of Capricorn, temperatures rarely dip below 20°C, and in much of the tropics the maximum daily temperature is consistently around 30°C. However, altitude has a major bearing. The vertiginous rise of the Andes affects the weather in more ways than simply getting colder the further you go up; it also creates some unique climatic conditions. Rain-bearing winds are blocked by the peaks, creating the world's driest desert in northern Chile. In some parts, rain has been a stranger for some 10,000 years!

The best ski resorts, all found in Argentina and Chile, have snow from June through to September. Don't expect to do too much trekking if you head down to Patagonia at this time of year – the weather is unforgiving. January and February are the best (but busiest) times to head down to the end of the earth.

Festivals

From sacred indigenous ceremonies in Peru to Carnaval in Río, Latin Americans are never ones to shirk an opportunity for a full-blooded celebration. Try to fit as many of the following into your trip as possible:

New Year's Eve (Chile) Not, strictly speaking, a festival, but the spectacular fireworks extravaganza and New Year's celebration at Valparaíso is one of the finest of its kind anywhere.

Carnaval (Brazil) The February carnivals in Río, Olinda, Recife and Salvador are some of the most spectacular festivals on earth. Parades, dancing, music and song combine for the most hedonistic of celebrations.

Oruro Carnaval (Bolivia) Tub-thumping raucous festival where costume parades and hedonistic festivities enthral thousands of visitors in February each year.

Semana Santa (Guatemala) The Easter celebrations in the delightful colonial town of Antigua include colourful parades, elaborate ceremonies and beautiful yet fragile decorations.

Los Diablos Danzantes (Venezuela) Held on Corpus Christi (usually the ninth Thursday after Easter) in San Francisco de Yare; a fiery parade and devil-dancers cap off the festivities.

Inti Raymi (Peru) The 'sun festival' of Cusco (24 June) culminates with a re-enactment of the Inca winter solstice observance at Sacsayhuamán.

Festival of Yamor (Ecuador) Otavalo's biggest shindig (early September) has fireworks, parades and an all-round party atmosphere. The Queen of the Fiesta procession is a highlight.

Día de los Muertos (Day of the Dead; Mexico) Mexicans welcome the souls of their dead back to earth across the country (Pátzcuaro is especially colourful) on 2 November.

Día del Tango (Argentina) Informal celebration of the birthday of tango great Carlos Gardel (11 December) and a good time to hit Buenos Aires to see tango, an integral part of that city's character.

Día de Nuestra Señora de Guadalupe (Mexico) The day (12 December) of Mexico's patron saint, Guadalupe. Festivities culminate with a huge procession and party at the Basilica de Guadalupe in Mexico City.

WHAT TO EXPECT?
Travellers

In Mexico and Central America, there is a large North American travelling contingent, while in South America, the backpacker balance is slightly more European. Central America has strong historical links with Germany. Plenty of Aussies and Kiwis frequent most of the Gringo Trail in Latin America, and there are a growing number of Korean and Japanese visitors. Surprisingly, given the language, there are not so many Spanish people travelling in Latin America.

In Central America, you will rarely be joined on the backpacker trail by locals, but this is much more common in the richer countries of South America. Hitching around the country is almost a rite of passage for many Chilean students, for example. Expect to meet a diverse range of characters on your travels. Fellow gappers will be plentiful, but you will also find a reasonable sprinkling of retirees, 'career' travellers, preachers, and people on short adventurous holidays. Although you'll find travellers all over the continent, here are some of the most legendary of the backpacker hangouts:

Antigua (Guatemala) Ringed by volcanoes, buzzing with nightlife and steeped in history, this is a delightful place to relax.

Cusco (Peru) The former Inca capital is not only the gateway to Machu Picchu but is also a happening town in its own right.

Isla Montecristo (El Salvador) Tranquil community on the Pacific peninsula.

Jericoacoara (Brazil) This is the latest off-the-beaten track beach to get popular with the laid-back travelling crowd.

Lago Atitlán (Guatemala) One of the most gorgeous settings imaginable. No place for stress here.

Lake Titicaca (Bolivia & Peru) A massive high-altitude lake with accessible islands in the middle and colourful locals.

Montañita (Ecuador) Bohemian little place with the best surf in the country.

Pucón (Chile) One for action fans, this picturesque town also has plenty of sedate trekking options on offer.

San Cristóbal de las Casas (Mexico) Charming colonial town with a distinct bohemian vibe, perched in the invigorating air of the Chiapas highlands.

San Juan del Sur (Nicaragua) Magnificent Pacific bay and party town.

San Pedro de Atacama (Chile) Sleepy, laid-back stopoff for travellers to the moonlike surroundings of the Chilean desert.

Locals

The Latin Americans' reputation for being extroverted, warm and always up for a fiesta is well deserved, although you may find isolated indigenous communities are more reserved.

The majority of Latin Americans are *mestizos* (of mixed indigenous and European descent), although the ethnic influences vary widely depending on the country. More than half the population of Bolivia and Guatemala is indigenous, for example, while in Argentina and Chile most people have European ancestry.

The legacy of the slave trade has led to a strong African influence in parts of South America, particularly in Brazil, Ecuador and the Caribbean areas of Colombia and Venezuela.

And there are also surprising little pockets of people dotted about the continent. In Venezuela, Colonia Tovar is an old German settlement where the inhabitants did not even learn Spanish until the 1940s; in Argentinean Patagonia there is a community of Welsh speakers; and in São Paolo, Brazil, there is the largest Japanese population outside Japan.

Some countries still rely heavily on agriculture, but there has been a huge drift of people to the big cities. The majority of the population is now thoroughly urbanised. Sadly, however, there is still a big divide between the haves and the have-nots in much of Latin America.

Religion is much more noticeable in these parts. Most countries are strongly Catholic, though evangelism is on the rise, especially in Central America. Partly through this religious influence, you will find many nations are quite conservative in their outlook (Chile, for example, has only just passed a law permitting divorce).

Female travellers should be aware that a machismo attitude is widespread in Latin America (although not universal), meaning attention from the opposite sex is much more obvious than in the UK. While this can be annoying, it is rarely threatening. The best way of dealing with unwanted catcalls is to ignore them.

Language

Spanish is the official language in every Latin American country with the exceptions of Brazil, where Portuguese is spoken, and Belize, where English is the official language. English is on the rise and often spoken in big cities and tourist areas, but learning the rudiments of the Spanish and/or Portuguese is strongly advised.

The type of Spanish differs noticeably from country to country. A Chilean speaking to a Costa Rican is bit like a Glaswegian having a conversation with a Texan!

Generally, Central Americans tend to speak slower than their South American counterparts. Argentineans, and especially Chileans, speak very quickly and pepper their phrases with slang. Peruvian Spanish is known as the clearest variety of Spanish in South America.

Brazilian Portuguese has distinct differences in pronunciation from the language in Portugal but does not vary much within its huge borders.

There are hundreds of indigenous languages still being used in Latin America, although the number of speakers is dwindling. However, inhabitants in some isolated regions only speak their native tongue – neither Spanish nor Portuguese will be much use. You can learn indigenous languages in the areas where they are most widely used.

For more information on language courses see p420.

Health Risks

If you're going to a tropical region of Latin America, the list of recommended vaccinations can seem intimidating. Don't let this faze you. Even if you're headed deep into the jungle, the most serious condition you're likely to encounter is a dose of diarrhoea. If you've got the runs, the most important thing to do is keep hydrated.

Malaria is a risk, especially in lowland, tropical areas, while yellow fever is endemic in Panama and most of the top half of South America. If you are going on a jungle trip, do take proper precautions. Dengue fever, Chagas disease and typhus can all strike here.

Climbers should be wary of altitude sickness, which can be fatal. If you start feeling its effects, go down the mountain immediately. In the desert, the tropics or on a mountain, the sun can be dangerous. Make sure your skin is properly protected.

On the beach, you should be aware of dangerous riptides, especially on the Pacific coast. These can be deadly.

Consult the Health chapter (p59) and seek professional medical advice for more travel health information.

Time & Flight Time

All of Central America is six hours behind Greenwich Mean Time (GMT), with the exception of Panama (which is five hours behind GMT). South America is divided into zones that are three, four and five hours behind GMT. Brazil has two zones, which are three and four hours behind GMT.

There are direct flights to the region from London, including to Mexico City (an 11½-hour flight), Rio de Janeiro (12 hours) and Buenos Aires (12 hours). Most flights to Central America pass through the USA.

Issues

While Latin America is no longer the hotbed of civil unrest that it once was, some countries still have fairly shaky political situations.

Colombia in particular is noted for the armed conflict between its government and FARC (the Revolutionary Armed Forces of Colombia) rebels. Kidnappings, murders, paramilitary reprisals and counter-reprisals are still depressingly common. That needn't put you off altogether, as there are some parts of the country that are relatively trouble-free. Check the latest Foreign and Commonwealth Office (FCO; www.fco.gov.uk) advice carefully before you go.

Unfortunately, Colombian tensions have spread to the Ecuador border, which should generally be avoided, although the rest of Ecuador remains unaffected.

Venezuela, too, has teetered dangerously towards civil unrest following a frosty stand-off between the government and opposition. The situation is potentially volatile, so keep up with the latest developments if this country is on your wish list. The same applies to Bolivia, which has seen some nasty uprisings over the past few years, and, to a lesser extent, Peru. The economic crash in Argentina caused a well of resentment that still simmers today, although this is directed towards the government and banks rather than foreigners. Elsewhere there is still tension in parts of the Mexican state of Chiapas. Again, check the latest on the FCO website.

If you find yourself in a country where unrest is brewing, avoid political demonstrations as far as possible. Tourists are unlikely to be targeted intentionally.

In some countries, the police and military are not entirely trustworthy. A clean-cut, neat appearance can help. In Central America, you will almost inevitably face a corrupt border official at some point. If you go in armed with exact knowledge of what you are supposed to pay, that can help. If you're not with a local friend who can help out, however, it is often easier to simply pay up.

Serious sexual assaults against women do occur. They are still relatively rare, but there are some precautionary measures you can take. Dressing modestly certainly helps, and, in isolated areas, you should avoid travelling alone or in pairs. If you're sensible, the chances of anything bad happening are slim.

Petty and violent crime are issues in some cities, and even some tourist areas. Be vigilant, don't keep any more money than is necessary with you, and stick to tried and trusted routes and areas.

Credit-card fraud is also a known problem. Maker sure you retain your transaction slips and carbon paper.

For further information on travel hotspots, general safety issues and governmental travel advice see the Safety chapter (p79).

Internet & Communications

Internet cafés are springing up like mushrooms in all the tourist areas, and the prices have come tumbling down, while the speed of connection has accelerated. Mobile-phone technology is also spreading. Calls in some countries (especially in Central America) are surprisingly cheap – worth looking into if you're sticking around in the one place for a while.

Those on the move often find net phones in the well-frequented hostels along the Gringo Trail. With a good connection, these are a cheap and effective way of keeping in touch – see p87 for more details.

DAILY SPEND

Although Latin America is generally still very good value for travellers, it is not always quite as cheap as some expect – and unfavourable exchange rates have upped the costs too. The amount you need to spend will fluctuate a lot within the region, and, obviously, will depend on how many cervezas you plan to consume, and how comfortable you want to make yourself. Some places, in fact, may hit your wallet harder than a night on the town in London. French Guiana, the Falklands and the Galápagos Islands are three such destinations – expect to fork out at least £50 a day just to get by. The Falklands and the Galápagos are also expensive to fly to. Belize is easily the most expensive place in Central America, draining around £30 a day for a bed and three square meals.

Although the economic crisis of 2001 massively devalued Argentina's currency (and, to a lesser extent, Uruguay's), prices are creeping back up in this area again. Go soon if you want to get a good deal.

The biggest bargains in the region are still Guatemala, Honduras, and Bolivia, where transport is cheap and you can still find *hospedajes* (lodgings) for under £5. If you're frugal, you can get away with spending less than £20 a day.

Bear in mind, however, that these figures don't take into account the extras that might tempt you. In sophisticated Buenos Aires, for example, you may want to take in a show. Car hire, a foray into the jungle or a scuba dive are other things that could really make your trip memorable. Make sure you take account of these when organising your travelling coffers.

GETTING THERE

You'll need to fly. It is of course possible to fly to the USA and then go overland into Latin America. Some travellers even buy cars before hitting the open road, but you'll really need to be confident you know your stuff, both mechanically and driving-wise to even contemplate this option. Also, be sure to check that your travel insurance covers you for driving.

Air

South America is covered by many round-the-world (RTW) tickets. Some tickets to the region also allow stopovers in the USA, but do make sure you are up on all the latest visa requirements if you plan to do this.

US carriers such as American Airlines and United Airlines often offer the cheapest deals into Central America, though you'll have to be ready for longer flight times. Iberia, Lufthansa and Air France can offer some good deals and quicker journeys into both Central and South America.

TICKET COSTS

The best available student/under-26 fares are quoted here. See the Passports, Visas, Tickets & Insurance chapter (p19) for more information on how to get the best, most flexible deal.

The cheapest cities to fly into are Mexico City (around £440) and Caracas (£440). The most expensive destinations are Lima, San José and Guatemala City, where a return ticket is likely to set you back at least £550, even when you travel off-peak. There are some good-value open-jaw options for the region, namely into Mexico City and out of Panama City for around £540; into Caracas and out of Lima, Santiago or Buenos Aires for around £530; and Mexico City and out of São Paulo for £450. UK travel agents can book you short-hop flights, including between Panama City and Quito in Ecuador for about £130.

Specialist Tour Operators

Latin America is very well served by specialist tour operators, and this can be a great way to get around. You have the reassurance of a group around you – as well as people who really know their stuff. Established operators include Exodus, Encounter and Dragoman, which organise overland trips to Patagonia and boat journeys by the spectacular glaciers off the coast of Chile or even all the way to the Antarctic. Some region-specific operators include:

Journey Latin America (☎ 020 8747 3108; www.journeylatinamerica.co.uk; fax 020 8742 1312; 12–13 Heathfield Terrace, Chiswick, London W4 4JE) Runs tours across the continent using public transport and private vehicles. It also offers cruises to Antarctica.

South American Experience (☎ 020 7976 5511; www.southamericanexperience.co.uk; info@south americanexperience.co.uk; fax 020 7976 6908; 47 Causton St, Pimlico, London SW1P 4AT) Organises tours, flights and accommodation.

MEXICO, CENTRAL & SOUTH AMERICA & BEYOND

There are plenty of flights to Australia and New Zealand from Chile, Brazil and Argentina. You may get a stopoff in the South Pacific en route but obviously the cheapest way to arrange this is with a RTW ticket. Flights up to North America (Miami is the cheapest destination) are frequent and often good value.

In São Paulo and Buenos Aires there are also some cheap deals to Johannesburg. It could even be worth getting a return ticket if you fancy a quick blast in a different continent. Note that RTW tickets no longer offer Easter Island as a stopover, making travel to the world's most isolated inhabited island considerably more expensive for the gapper.

FURTHER INFORMATION
Reading Material

Lonely Planet publishes guides to numerous countries, regions and cities in Latin America. *Healthy Travel: Central & South America*, *World Food Mexico*, *Trekking in the Patagonian Andes*, and diving guides to Belize, Baja California and Honduras' Bay Islands provide excellent background. The *Brazilian, Costa Rica Spanish, Latin American Spanish* and *Quechua* phrasebooks offer practical, no-nonsense linguistic support for all sorts of travelling scenarios.

Latin America itself has a rich literary tradition. Perhaps the most famous of its authors is Gabriel García Márquez, whose dazzling novels (including *One Hundred Years of Solitude* and

Love in the Time of Cholera) have rightfully found a global audience. Also try Isabel Allende's *House of Spirits* or *My Invented Country* for her impressions of her native Chile. Rigoberta Menchú was the author behind *I, Rigoberta Menchú*, a book that brought the world's attention to the plight of her oppressed Mayan people in Guatemala – and won her a Nobel prize to boot. And, of course, don't forget revolutionary Che Guevara's *The Motorcycle Diaries*, his own amusing and moving account of his youthful travels around South America.

Other portraits of the region include *The Old Patagonian Express* by travel-writing veteran Paul Theroux, who tells of a train journey from Boston to Patagonia in his inimitably cantankerous but evocative style. Joe Simpson's *Touching the Void* brilliantly captures the drama of an Andes mountaineering disaster. For a highly readable historical account of the bloody formative years of the region, try *Liberators* by Robert Harvey. Charles Darwin's *Voyage of the Beagle* describes the trip that stirred the English scientist to form his theory of evolution.

Useful Information Sources

For specific country overviews, the lowdown on travel in the region and hundreds of useful links head first to Lonely Planet's website (www.lonelyplanet.com).

The websites below are also very useful resources, whether you're planning your trip, or simply want to feed your appetite for all things Latin American.

www.buenosairesherald.com The most established English-language daily in the region.

www.gosouthamerica.about.com Portal with a range of links to Latin America–related sites.

www.lanic.utexas.edu One of the best resources for Latin America.

www.larutamayaonline.com Concentrates on Guatemala and Central America.

www.latinamericapress.org News on political and human-rights issues from across the region.

www.saexplorers.org Travel-club site with bulletin board and volunteer information.

www.santiagotimes.cl Daily English-language update on Chilean current affairs, with a broader South American perspective too.

www.southamericadaily.com Good place for a lowdown on the region's news.

www.ticotimes.net News source relied upon heavily by ex-pats in Costa Rica.

BEEN THERE, DONE THAT

The jaguars didn't bother me much during the day. Adonis, our local guide who was leading us deep into the Guatemalan jungle, assured us they were elusive, shy creatures. The most recent time he had seen one was more than a year ago when he had surprised a pair in the act of jaguar love. Last week, he had spotted some jaguar spoor, which was probably about as close to the animals as we would get, he said.

But his reassurance meant little that night as I cowered in my hammock under the Central American stars. Now my mind turned every rustle into a prowling big cat full of murderous intent (probably to get back at the rude human who had interrupted a moment of feline passion). And, if it wasn't a jaguar poised to spring, it was a poisonous fer-de-lance viper, picking which of my buttocks to sink its fangs into.

Tiredness calmed my over-active imagination, and I dozed. Next day, big surprise: no death by either snakebite or jaguar mauling. We packed up our stuff and continued towards our destination, El Mirador, the site of the tallest temple in the Mayan world, and two days' trekking from the small village of Carmelita at the end of the road.

Although we may have questioned why we had left a perfectly nice Honduran beach to come here, that night no doubts remained. Just before sunset we took our places at the top of the unexcavated temple mound. A Mayan astrology priest had probably sat in the same place

2000 years before and honed his knowledge of the galaxy. Tonight, as with every night, the howler monkeys screeched their farewells to the setting sun as spectacular pink shades streaked the western skyline. The sky darkened, and, one by one, the stars shimmered into life.

Then the howler monkeys hushed, and we too were quiet, the purest silence I have ever known. Maybe it was this tranquillity that made me forget about jaguars for the whole walk back to our hammocks. Or maybe I was just too worried by the tarantulas at the edge of the path…

Jolyon Attwooll

Part III

VOLUNTEERING, CONSERVATION & EXPEDITIONS

WHY VOLUNTEER?

One in three gappers volunteer at some point during their gap year, whether it be for one week or the whole 12 months. Reasons for volunteering are as varied as the opportunities, although many are driven by the desire and rewards of 'giving something back'. For Amanda Akass this was important. She explains:

I definitely wanted to volunteer during my gap year, otherwise it would just have been a holiday. I felt my life had always been fairly privileged and insular and there are many world issues that concern me and I wanted to do something to help. I have always been interested in conservation and as Quest Overseas offered working for a conservation charity (www.intiwarayassi.org) for a month as part of their program it seemed the ideal opportunity.

For Tabitha Cook this was important too but so were other considerations:

I volunteered as an English teacher in Ja-Ela, Sri Lanka, and at Pinnawala Elephant Orphanage in Sri Lanka. I chose volunteering as I wanted to feel like I was putting something back into the countries I went to. I also wanted to have a base and friends and be involved in the local life and culture more than visiting allowed. I loved my teaching, and playing with the elephants was an experience of a lifetime.

As Tabitha says, another good reason to volunteer is to get a better insight into the country you're visiting. You do this because you're actually living in the country as opposed to travelling through it and you're often working and playing alongside local people.

Claire Loseby also had a variety of reasons for volunteering. She says:

I decided to teach in China because I thought it'd be a really worthwhile experience for both me and the children but I also wanted to do something out of the ordinary that I could get really enthusiastic about. I've always loved travel and had been thinking about teaching as a future career for a while and so volunteering in such an interesting country seemed like a once in a lifetime experience.

Claire makes a really valuable point here: volunteering is an excellent way of gaining work experience. In addition, there are so many volunteering options out there that finding one that complements your future career or gives you experience relevant to a future college or university course is a doddle. Whatever you choose to do, though, will give you new skills and look great on your CV.

Jack Ray's reason for volunteering was short, sweet and highly topical. He says:

Call me superficial but I was inspired by the year 2005 being Year of the Volunteer.

So, what can you do? Well, er, almost anything that takes your fancy. If you are interested in helping children you might work with the street kids of Brazil, in an orphanage in Romania, or teach children drama in Ghana. If you want to work with the sick then you might provide support for HIV/AIDS sufferers in Tanzania or work in a health clinic in India. If you are interested in animals, you might help repatriate wild horses in Mongolia, protect the turtles in Madagascar, work with an anti-poaching patrol in a South African game reserve or do what Amanda Akass did in Bolivia:

The reserve cared for native animals who had been hunted so they could be sold as pets or to circuses. The reserve looked after them until they could be released back into the wild or, if this wasn't possible, they'd give them as natural a life as possible in captivity. We built a large enclosure for a jaguar, which was extremely tiring. We spent all day carrying sacks of rocks and sand through the jungle to the building site, digging trenches and mixing cement (I'm now a dab hand at that). It was tremendously rewarding when we released the jaguar into his new home.

Living in the park itself was a fantastic experience. We were literally living in a hut in the middle of the jungle, playing with baby jaguars and ocelots who were too tame to be released, with parrots on our shoulders and monkeys sleeping around our necks. I do not exaggerate, it was unbelievable. Next up I was a surrogate mother to a three-month-old puma cub called Sonko. We walked for about four to six hours every day on his trails through the jungle, stopping for him to sleep occasionally or attempt to climb trees. It was a humbling and unique experience to help him grow and develop. Top Tip: if you're going to volunteer in the jungle, take loads of insect repellent.

If it's conservation that really turns you on then you could work to save the rainforest in Costa Rica, survey coral reefs in the Philippines or monitor climate change in the Arctic circle. If you are interested in the media, you could work on an English newspaper in Bolivia, Mongolia or Ghana. Otherwise, why not get your hands really dirty and help build a school or a community centre almost anywhere in the world. And the list doesn't stop there. It is pretty much endless. Ask yourself what you really want to do and chances are you'll not only find an organisation that offers that type of placement but, most importantly, a community or region of the world that needs that type of help.

Most gappers who decide to volunteer in their gap year do so at the beginning. There are three main reasons for this:

- In the run-up to your time off it gives you something really concrete to focus on and to aim for.
- If arranged through an organisation that gives good support and back-up, a period of time volunteering abroad can provide a useful stepping-stone between life at home and life on the road. This is particularly the case if you haven't done much independent travelling before.
- Ahhhhh, the price tag. There's no real nice way of saying this. Volunteering costs. Don't be put off right here and now (read p42), but one month's volunteering can cost around £945 (excluding flights & travel insurance), depending on who you go with, what you do, where you go and for how long. As such, most gappers spend (bad word, don't spend, you need to save) a year or more saving up and so it makes sense to volunteer at the beginning of your time out when you've still got the money rather than at the end when you might have blown it all on partying and wardrobe therapy.

ARRANGING A PLACEMENT

Once you have made the decision to volunteer you have the awesome task of deciding what to do and how to arrange it. The variety of volunteering options are seemingly endless and so too is the list of organisations that can arrange your voluntary work.

So, how do you decide who to go with? Well, that really depends on the type of experience you want. The following section looks at the different categories of organisation, what they offer and why you might want to volunteer with them.

Gap-Year Organisations

First up, a category of volunteer organisation specifically catering for the gap-year market with hundreds of cool placement, project and program options. Sounds great, doesn't it?

Often these groups have grown out of youth-development activities and have recognised that gappers want to take on a challenge but need a far greater degree of support and direction than you get volunteering with a standard charity or 'sending agency' (see p275). Gap-year organisations offer a structured expedition program or volunteer placement, lots of pre-departure and in-country help. They will usually arrange your accommodation (eg living with host families, in a hostel or in a purpose-built camp), food, travel insurance, visas and sometimes your flights. Cultural visits, lectures and language courses often come as part of the deal too.

However, that is where the similarities end. The key to understanding this sector is to recognise that all gap-year organisations are different and that these differences will directly impact on whether you're happy or sad with your particular volunteer project. Some gap-year organisations are large, such as i-to-i and Teaching & Projects Abroad, offering almost any volunteer opportunity under the sun. Others are smaller and more specialised such as Quest Overseas or Project Trust. Some offer placements in conservation work only, such as African Conservation Experience, and others, such as Gap Challenge offer both conservation or development and humanitarian work. A few offer voluntary programs which are very much geared towards your own personal development, such as Raleigh International.

Although all gap-year organisations offer a very different genre of volunteering experience, the types of trips they run can roughly be divided into two groups: expeditions and placements.

EXPEDITIONS

This is not to be confused with the sort of expedition where you're slashing your way through the jungle with a machete getting from A to B in search of a lost city. This type of volunteering describes an experience that is very team-based. You usually live and travel with a group of around 10 to 16 volunteers on a structured program accompanied by qualified staff. Often these expeditions are combined with an outward-bound adventure such as trekking, climbing, or rafting. Gap-year organisations offering this type of experience include Adventureworks, Madventurer, Quest Overseas and Raleigh International. Personal development is usually a key component of expedition-style volunteering. Laurence Gale travelled to Ghana with Raleigh and says:

I did a 10-week expedition. As soon as we arrived in Accra we went to base camp. We were immediately put into groups. The first week was spent doing ice breakers and basic first aid and camping skills. Then we had three projects to work on: community, adventure, and environmental. My community phase was spent on the border with Burkina Faso building pit latrines in a most primitive village. The adventure phase involved doing 260km over land and lake in two and a half weeks. It was an awesome challenge and great fun for someone like me who loves running around outdoors. We also spent a lot of time in the schools of each village we came to teaching about HIV/AIDS awareness. In my final phase (environmental) I spent my nights combing a sandy beach for olive Ridley/giant leatherback turtles. By the way, we slept in big army tents with various bugs, snakes and grass rats, woohoo!

Often, volunteering on an aid project is combined not only with an adventure element but also a language- or cultural-learning segment. This is what attracted Sarah Collinson to her choice of gap-year organisation. She says:

It was quite difficult trying to choose the company to go with but in the end I settled with VentureCo, as they did a cross section of activities: a Spanish course, an aid project and then a two-month overlanding trip.

PLACEMENTS
This is when a gap-year organisation acts more like a temping agency or traditional 'sending agency', matching your requirements with any number of worldwide placements they know need volunteers. This means you could be on your own, but more usually with one or two other gap-year volunteers, although there'll often be others in the immediate vicinity. In addition, you are often left to your own devices to make what you will of your placement. You still get a good standard of in-country support and backup. For instance, there'll usually be a local staff member who is looking after a number of gap-year volunteers in your area and a UK representative from your organisation will probably fly out to make sure that everything is OK. Organisations that arrange these sorts of volunteering experiences include: GAP Activity Projects, i-to-i, the Leap, Teaching & Projects Abroad and Travellers Worldwide. Some gap-year organisations working in this way allow you to combine a set of different placements either on the same or on different continents, as with the Global Adventures Project (see p289). Louise Ellerton travelled with Teaching & Projects Abroad to Ghana and had this to say:

I did voluntary work in a veterinary practice as this is the field that I will be going into. You have to be prepared for the differences and sometimes accept that it's not always how you expected. I found the people so very laid back and a lot of the day is spent sleeping. At first this frustrated me as I was there to gain experience but you learn that this is how they are and you make the most of the times when you do get to see a case or an operation.

I went alone but with the knowledge that I was going with a gap-year company who would be there for me when I arrived and had sorted out my placement and my accommodation for the year. Via the company it was then very easy to meet other volunteers doing the same thing and you had immediate friends who knew the country a little better.

There are pros and cons of volunteering with a gap-year organisation and these are looked at in detail next. However, anyone with an ear to the ground will know that recently some gap-year organisations have come in for a bit of criticism. This has mostly been directed at one or two of the larger organisations where the sheer number of volunteering options they now offer has resulted in some lowering of standards. To ensure you don't end up more pissed than kissed with your choice, make sure that you thoroughly check out any organisation you're considering (see p273 for advice). Also, take advice from the Year Out Group website – see p271.

PROS & CONS
Pros
A structured & packaged volunteering experience
As a rule, gap-year organisations offer a packaged program that takes care of almost everything. You pay a flat fee and won't need to spend months trying to arrange everything in an unknown country from afar (see p270 for further information). Your travel, accommodation, food, local support and the project itself will all usually be arranged for you.

If you take this route you'll get a structured experience while abroad and there will be plenty of help provided so that you don't feel as if you're being chucked in at the deep end. Some gappers may be leaving home for the first time or might never have lived abroad and so there's plenty of value in getting a leg up.

A challenging yet safe environment with high standards of in-country support
Safety will probably be your parents' number one priority when you tell them you're taking a gap year. It's probably quite high on your list of requirements too. OK, no-one can guarantee that something won't go wrong but most gap-year organisations do their utmost to ensure it doesn't or, if it does, a crisis doesn't turn into a tragedy. If you're thinking about going on a volunteering expedition then you'll be accompanied by experienced team leaders and, if necessary, a doctor or a nurse. If you're on a volunteering placement then there'll be in-country reps who will provide support in an unfamiliar culture and there will be established procedures in case of an emergency. Damien Rickwood travelled to Belize with Trekforce and says:

We had two trained medics on each expedition so I felt completely safe living in a jungle environment. Also, the whole group went through a thorough jungle training week before being sent to our projects. However, some things are unavoidable and when one of my friends contracted an unknown tropical disease, she was swiftly evacuated by plane to the nearest hospital where she recovered quickly.

Thorough pre-departure training & briefings about your project
Many gap-year organisations pride themselves on how they prepare volunteers for their expeditions or placements. Lucy King, Managing Director of Quest Overseas, says:

We place enormous importance in the preparation and training of our students before they head off overseas on one of our projects and/or expeditions. Our training weekends encompass workshops on culture awareness, language training, risk assessment, kit and equipment talks, project expectations and health and safety issues whilst on expedition. Without a doubt we have found that students who attend these training weekends are better prepared when they arrive in a country and make the most of their experience from day one. This is one of the key benefits of going overseas with a gap-year company.

Information on local culture and courses in the language are particularly important if you are to interact positively with the local people. They can be invaluable if you are intending to live with a local family or work on a community project such as in an orphanage or school.

In addition, as many volunteers end up in the developing world where living conditions are, well, developing, it is important that you understand what to expect. Some volunteer opportunities may exist in villages without electricity or running water and it's best if this doesn't come as a shock to you, as it did to Claire Loseby who volunteered in China. She says:

Everything seemed a bit daunting at first because I had never expected to live in such horrible conditions (no toilets for example) but you soon adapt to it.

And if you undertake an expedition with someone such as Raleigh, for instance, you could be camping in the jungle and sleeping in hammocks. This is a fantastic experience on the one level but you could feel like you're living on the film set of either *A Bug's Life* or *Ants*.

Experience working with gappers & local communities on an ongoing basis

Gap-year organisations usually have years of experience and enjoy good working relationships with countries and local communities. Interestingly, a gap-year organisation cannot become a member of the Year Out Group until they have been operating for three years (see p271).

Another advantage of using a gap-year specialist is that you'll be around other gappers at the same stage in life, either school leavers or postgrads, who will become new friends and a surrogate family while you're far from home. Tabitha Cook really appreciated being around like-minded people of her own age and says:

If you're thinking of volunteering look at who you live with, whether it is a homestay or with other volunteers. I chose to live with other volunteers because I wanted to be around people that I could moan to if it all got on top of me and so that if I made a cultural boo-boo, I wouldn't offend those I was living with. It was the best decision I have ever made. I made so many friends and learnt a lot, plus we had some great house parties.

Volunteer programs geared towards 'personal development'

Nearly every gap-year organisation will have your personal development in mind when it puts together a project. However, some organisations are stronger on this aspect of your experience than others. For Raleigh International, for instance, developing your own skills, whether it be in team-work or leadership, is a key component of their projects. With Global Adventures Project you get the chance to complete a City and Guilds Professional Development Award as a part of all programs. And, at the end of the day, the definition of a successful volunteering gap-year experience is probably one which is both challenging and educational.

A contact for your parents

Gap-year organisations are used to dealing with paranoid parents and good at reassuring them while you're away. Some, such as Global Adventures, go to extreme lengths to ensure that you and your parents are kept happy while you're away. Their director, Heather Thompson, says:

We have a facility on our website whereby travelling students can upload diary entries onto their own personal (secure) page so that family and friends can easily track how they are doing and what they are up to. This page also contains their itinerary and information they might like access to when they travel.

Costs

You might think that the cost of volunteering is a con, not a pro, and you'd be right, costs appear in both sections. However, there are two issues here. Firstly, some gap-year programs are bloody expensive to run properly and you don't want to volunteer with an organisation that can't afford to have first-class equipment, whether this be proper tents, comprehensive first-aid kits, satellite phones or GPSs (global positioning systems). Secondly, all overseas aid or conservation projects need funding in order to exist and a good proportion of the money you pay to a gap-year organisation should go towards supporting these projects. See p270 for more information.

Cons
Cost may seem excessive
If you've been online and checked out how much some volunteer programs cost then you've probably already emailed the site's web master to tell them about the typos on the site. The bad news is that those zeros are supposed to be there. The good news is that almost all gap-year organisations offer help with fund-raising and that year after year gappers do manage to save that sort of money. This is what Louise Ellerton had to say on the subject:

It may cost a little extra to go with a gap-year organisation but it reassures you before going, and it reassures your parents.

For more information about costs see p270.

You're locked into a pre-paid commitment for a certain period of time
It is important to think about how long you want to be away for. Most gap-year organisations offer programs of varying length. However, once you've thought about your timing it is often difficult to shorten or extend your stay. In addition, if you leave early then it is very unlikely you'll get any of your money back. Some organisations like you to volunteer for a longish period of time. For instance, Project Trust asks for a commitment of one year.

In addition, coming out of school or college, you might feel that going away with a gap-year organisation is too managed and institutional. For the more independent, particularly postgrads with previous experience of life abroad, there might also be too much 'hand-holding'.

Not enough interaction with local culture and people
Sometimes a group-based volunteer experience might not provide you with enough exposure to the local culture. Are you sure you want to be surrounded by mostly other British people when you go abroad? A good way to ensure that you do have local interaction is to live with a host family, so check if this is an option with the program you are considering. Otherwise, a placement where you're working on your own or in pairs might be more your cup of tea.

No respect for the staff managing the projects
Mmm, it can happen. Like any situation where you find yourself rubbing up against authority you'll probably just have to like it or lump it.

Too much emphasis on personal development
If you're serious about helping a charity in a poorer part of the world, you might be better off volunteering with an organisation that's totally focussed on world development rather than your own personal development (see p275).

COSTS
When looking at the prices of volunteer programs, you'll notice that you're rarely comparing apples with apples. Each volunteering experience is different. Price will be affected by how long your project lasts (are you going for one week or one year?) and what sort of experience you want (are you just volunteering, or doing an adventure-based activity and perhaps a language course too?). Where you're going will affect price – some destinations are cheap, such as

India, and some more expensive, such as Japan. What you choose to do will also affect what you pay (some volunteer work is more expensive to finance than others – marine conservation, for instance, does not come cheap). In addition, some gap-year organisations quote an all-inclusive cost and others expect you to pay extra for flights, food, travel insurance and visas (always check to see what exactly is included in your program). Finally, the amount of money that is donated to your volunteer project will vary from organisation to organisation too (more on this later). This all means that putting figures into a spreadsheet to compare and contrast them is more difficult than you'd expect. And, of course, you're not necessarily looking for the cheapest option – isn't it said that if you pay peanuts you get monkeys?

OK, the bottom line is this. The minimum you'll usually pay for one month's volunteering with a gap-year organisation is around £945, excluding flights and travel insurance. Many three-month volunteer programs come in at around £2000 to £3000 all-inclusive. In general, the longer your placement, the less you pay per month. This is definitely the case with Project Trust whose year-long program costs £3950 for everything, including a small wage. And, just to show that you really can't generalise where cost is concerned, you've then got GAP Activity Projects (GAP) who charge a flat fee of £900, excluding flights and a few extras, regardless of whether you volunteer for 12 months or for three.

YEAR OUT GROUP

Year Out Group (☎ 07980-395789; www.yearoutgroup.org; info@yearoutgroup.org; Queensfield, 28 Kings Rd, Easterton, Wiltshire SN10 4PX) was formed in 1998 to promote the concept and benefits of well-structured gap-year programs and to ensure good practice among its members. It is a not-for-profit organisation. All members have to sign up to the following code:

Accurate Literature Brochures and briefing packs have to be clear and accurately describe what is on offer.
Ethical Considerations Sensitivity to social, environmental and local issues has to be shown, particularly in the programs' host countries.
Financial Security Compliance with UK statutory financial regulations, including systems in place to protect payments from clients.
Membership All new members must agree to these criteria.
Professional Support and Welfare Programs are vetted and monitored by member organisations to make sure that security and safety procedures are followed. This includes good briefing of participants before they embark on their trip and in-country support once they're there. Companies also have to ensure that their staff are well trained.
Standards Programs must be continually evaluated and improvements made where necessary.

The Year Out Group came about because founding members got fed up with operating in an unregulated environment. This doesn't mean that if you decide to go with a company not in the group that you're stuffed, because there are plenty of good gap-year companies out there who haven't joined up. However, it does give you another layer of protection and guarantees. Whatever, do check out their website (www.yearoutgroup.org) because there's some useful information and suggestions on it in terms of all your gap-year options.

Current Year Out Group members are Africa & Asia Venture, African Conservation Experience, Art History Abroad, BSES Expeditions, BUNAC, CESA Languages Abroad, Changing Worlds, Coral Cay Conservation, Council on International Educational Exchange, CSV (Community Service Volunteers), Flying Fish, Frontier Conservation, GAP Activity Projects, Gap Challenge/World Challenge Expeditions, Greenforce, i-to-i, Outreach International, Project Trust, Quest Overseas, Raleigh International, SPW (Students Partnership Worldwide), St James's & Lucie Clayton College, Tante Marie School of Cookery, Teaching & Projects Abroad, Travellers, Trekforce Expeditions, The International Academy, The Year in Industry, Wind, Sand & Stars, Year Out Drama, VentureCo.

Whatever you end up paying, there's no denying that volunteering can be costly. Gap-year organisations recognise this and will often give you plenty of advice and help to raise the funds. Indeed, many organisations, such as Raleigh International, Project Trust and Gap Challenge, see the fundraising aspect of the programs as an integral part of your experience. Raising the money can be hard. You need to be inventive, organised and committed – see p42. When you finally get there you feel exhausted, but remember, this whole process is, er, good for your personal development. Seriously, though, many gappers enjoy raising the money and come back from their trips claiming to have had the time of their lives.

In addition, there are a number of gap-year/year-out organisations that have bursaries or grants available to those students who come from a background where this sort of money is only dreamed of and who might not have supportive family and friends. These include GAP Activity Projects (GAP), Raleigh International and Experiment in International Living (EIL) – see p287 for other organisations that help with funding.

When you are looking at costs, there is another important factor to take into consideration. Some gap-year organisations are registered charities or not-for-profit organisations while others are running a business. Having said that, the situation isn't black and white. It is not that charities are good and companies are bad – plenty of ethical gap-year companies donate excellent sums of money to fund worthwhile volunteer projects. However, do find out where *exactly* your money is going. The best way of doing this is to ask for a break-down of costs. Some organisations will give this to you automatically when you start enquiring about a program, some, such as Quest Overseas, publish this information on their websites, and others need to be asked.

You, of course, also need to know exactly what the fee covers in terms of your own costs. Ensure you know who is picking up the tab for international return flights, accommodation, food, in-country travel, travel insurance, visas, cultural activities, and vaccinations. On top of that, are you expecting your fee to cover a language tuition component or an adventure-based activity with specialist equipment? Remember, any adventure segment in a gap-year program, such as an overland expedition, jungle trekking, mountaineering or rafting will push the price of your program up as it'll need more supervision and first-class equipment.

After you've done your research and found a volunteer program that fits your exact requirements, draw up a budget for this segment of your gap year. You know from the start that you have to raise the fee but what is more difficult to estimate is how much cash you may need for day-to-day living expenses. Most placements will provide food and lodging but you will need some spending money for drinks, phone calls, internet cafés and additional travel. The cost of all this is quite tricky to establish in advance, but you can get a good idea by talking to returned volunteers and to the organisation's staff. Don't forget to set aside some money for an emergency or on-the-spot temptation. For instance, you might need to buy a set of clothes if your backpack is lost or stolen, or you might want a few more weekends away than you'd anticipated.

Whether you think the funds needed for the volunteering project you choose is good value or not very much depends on you. Ultimately, it's a question of priorities. What else could you do with this money? You could buy a gaggle of MP3s or, to put it into a travel context, most gappers travel around the world for 12 months on a shoestring budget of between £5000 and £6000.

TIMING & APPLICATIONS
Timing is a crucial aspect of joining an organised gap-year project. Places fill up fast and it's first come first served. Africa & Asia Venture says that places in Kenya are so popular

they start filling a year ahead and sometimes individuals apply two years before they plan to go. This can sometimes be the case with the expeditions run by Quest Overseas too. Project Trust requires you to apply giving at least 18 months' notice and some gappers apply to Raleigh International up to a year in advance. This means that if you plan to take a gap year after school start thinking about organisations in the lower sixth.

If this all seems a rather daunting and your crystal ball is a tad cloudy, don't despair. There's more flexibility with many gap-year organisations. Most *do* like you to give three months' notice (particularly if there are complicated visas to get) but all of them will do their best to accommodate late-bookers. If things don't go according to the plan and you end up taking a gap year at the last minute then chances are you will still be able to find a volunteer placement, particularly with one of the larger organisations such as i-to-i.

Most gap-year organisations require you to apply online to receive an information pack. Each then has its own selection procedures. For most this is a face-to-face interview (although some are by phone), followed by briefing and training days. There are a number of reasons for an interview. Firstly, the gap-year organisation needs to know more about you so they can place you on the right project. Secondly, they'll be checking you out to see if you have the right 'attitude' to work in a different culture – after all, when you're abroad you will be acting as their ambassador. Thirdly, this interview offers an excellent opportunity for you to check them out. Applicants are rarely turned down but if they are they'll be encouraged to reapply.

The selection process for some organisations is more rigorous. With Project Trust, for instance, all applicants attend a four-day selection course on the island of Coll in Scotland. During your stay you're set a number of tasks to discover your strengths and weaknesses, which helps match applicants to suitable projects. As Project Trust programs run for a whole year, it is really important that you are matched with the right project.

CHECKING THEM OUT

Whether you decide to volunteer with a gap-year organisation or not, you will need to spend time checking them out. Standards *do* vary. Your first step should be to read all the information on their website – most gap-year organisations have excellent sites.

While you're online, check out what other gappers are saying about various organisations. There's always a lively debate about the specific pros and cons of volunteer organisations on Lonely Planet's bulletin board called the Thorn Tree (http://thorntree.lonelyplanet.com) – go onto the Gap Year & RTW Travel branch. This is also the case on www.gapyear.com. If what you're looking for isn't being discussed on these two sites, why not post your own question and see what responses you get?

Of course, there's nothing like meeting the organisations face-to-face and this should be your next step. There are a number of ways of doing this. Many gap-year and year-out organisations take stands at the annual travel shows such as the *Daily Telegraph's* Adventure Travel & Sports Show (www.adventureshow.co.uk) and Destinations Holiday & Travel Show (www.destinationsshow.com). These usually take place in London from January to March. Gap-year and year-out organisations also take stands at various gap-year fairs. Many of these are held throughout the year all over the country and are organised either by ISCO (Independent Schools Careers Organisations; www.isco.org.uk) or by UCAS (www.ucas.com).

Best of all is to attend an open-day or open-evening. Most organisations hold these on a regular basis and promote them on their websites. They provide an excellent opportunity to meet staff members, returned volunteers and to find out more about the organisation's objectives and programs. Many of these open-sessions involve talks and slide shows and are really fun. Plus, of course, you get to meet and gossip with other gappers.

If you can't get along in person to any of these events then at least pick up the phone and talk everything through with a staff member. These groups welcome inquiries and are used to being quizzed about themselves and what they offer.

So, what do you need to find out and what should you ask?

Organisation What are the organisation's goals? How long have you been established? Are you a charity, not-for-profit organisation, private or public company? Are you a member of the Year Out Group?

Selection What is the application and selection procedure? What is the average age of your volunteers?

Project What choice do I have? How are your programs or placements chosen? How will I know that I'm working on a worthwhile, sustainable project that is needed by a local community (ie no-one wants to build a bridge where no bridge is needed)? What specifically will I be doing on a day-to-day basis (if you're teaching, ask how many hours per day you will be working)? Will I be working on my own or with other volunteers? If so, how many are usually in a group? Where will I be living? Is there a choice of accommodation (ie homestay, hostel, camp). What will the conditions be like (ie are they really basic)? What will the food be like? How will I benefit from this project? What happens if I'm not happy with my placement or program when I'm there? How can I get in contact with past volunteers to talk to them about their experiences? How will I keep in contact with friends and family while away?

Costs Exactly what is included in the costs (particularly remember to check about visas and travel insurance)? Can I see a break-down of where my money is going? How much of what I pay is donated to the project I'm working on? How much pocket-money will I need? Do you help with fundraising? When do you need payment by? Is my deposit refundable? What are your cancellation terms?

Pre-departure What briefing, training and/or cultural orientation days are there? What exactly is needed from me pre-departure? Do you give advice on medical requirements? What kit do I need to take with me?

Safety What safety and emergency procedures do you have in place? Are there staff members on site all the time or a local representative looking after a number of volunteers in one region? How are your leaders or in-country support representatives chosen and what experience and training do they have? What medical care is available? Will they speak English?

Debriefing Is there any support and debriefing procedure for when I get home? How can I stay in touch with the organisation if I want to? You won't be putting my name forward to talk to a pesky Lonely Planet author about the next edition of *The Gap Year Book*, will you?

Phew, that's about it – if you're asking these questions by phone, better not make it a mobile – you don't want to start your fundraising in debt to Orange or Vodafone. And if you don't get around to all of them, whatever you do, don't miss out on asking to talk to returned volunteers. This is really crucial. If you speak to several people who've had positive experiences in the recent past then the organisation you're checking out must be doing something right. Remember, do all of this before making any financial commitment to anyone.

Most gap-year and year-out organisations are professional at selecting, placing and supporting their volunteers while overseas. However, occasionally things go wrong – usually with larger organisations who run so many programs that not all the placements are vetted as well as they could be. Difficulties usually arise because expectation doesn't match reality and because individuals find themselves out of their normal comfort zone. This is why it is so important to know exactly what you're signing up for before handing over your hard-earned cash. Do remember that working in many developing countries might be uncomfortable at times but if you know what to expect before you arrive then you're less likely to be disappointed.

Of course, you might sometimes feel frustrated, unwell or homesick – you'd be an android if you didn't feel some of these feelings some of the time. But, most eventualities can be treated as an adventure and a time to learn. With the right attitude you can make the most of many tricky situations.

However, don't put up with anything that makes you feel persistently uncomfortable and unhappy. The point of going on an organised placement, of having in-country reps and leaders, and of choosing a gap-year organisation staffed by experienced people, is that serious problems with your placement or program can and should be sorted out immediately.

FURTHER INFORMATION

Try to visit one of the travel fairs mentioned in the previous section. Not only can you meet a number of gap year groups all at once but you can also attend their program of talks, slide shows and panel discussions. Rarely is there a travel fair that doesn't have at least one gap-year lecture or session. Of course, these fairs offer an excellent opportunity to check out anything to do with travel, whether it be clothing, equipment, tour operators, tourist boards, guidebook publishers etc.

On the internet there's a mass of information about volunteer organisations for gappers. As well as www.lonelyplanet.com and www.gapyear.com, try http://education.independent .co.uk/gap_year, www.yearoutgroup.org, www.gapwork.com, www.findagap.com and www .gap-year.com. Many of them have message boards, news, views, advice and case studies.

Year-Out Organisations

Year-out organisations operate in a similar way to gap-year groups but have one main difference – they cater for volunteers of all ages and market themselves more broadly. This means that the average age of volunteers is usually nearer 30 than 20. However, many gappers *do* choose to volunteer with these organisations, particularly those post-university or college. And there's nothing to stop a school-leaver from going with them too – it could be that they are the only organisation offering the type of program you are looking for. Molly Bird was 19 when she travelled with MondoChallenge and has this to say:

I worked with children in a school in India, teaching them English. Teaching can be exhausting but it is so exciting!!! I don't think I have ever laughed so much as I did in India with those kids. And when I left I turned around and realised that they knew something, I'd actually taught them something. Volunteering was without a doubt the best part of my gap year and probably the best thing I've ever done.

Like gap-year organisations, year-out groups offer a wide variety of programs of varying length and charge similar prices. For instance, you could teach drama in Ghana with the Tema Theatre Company or volunteer with the Task Brasil Trust and work among the street children of Brazil. Otherwise, Experiment in International Living (EIL) promotes a greater cultural understanding and awareness between the volunteer and the host country by emphasising the importance of homestays.

The year-out tag is one that can be applied to many conservation organisations such as African Conservation Experience, Coral Cay Conservation or Frontier. For a discussion of volunteering opportunities with these groups, see p281.

Charities, NGOs & Sending Agencies

However, what happens if you don't fancy volunteering with an organisation that arranges everything for you? Perhaps you don't want so much hand-holding, or cotton-wool wrapping. Maybe you desire an experience that is more direct – less whistles and bells and more grit. If this is the case then there are alternatives. There are hundreds of charities and NGOs (non-governmental organisations) all over the world working with local people suffering from poverty or a lack of resources such as healthcare or education. Many of these recruit young and enthusiastic volunteers to donate their labour and abilities. This is done in one of two ways. Either they'll have their own office in the UK who is responsible for supplying volunteers for on-the-ground work abroad, or they'll go through a 'sending agency'. Both routes are very similar, both act like temping agencies, matching volunteers of all ages to placements according to their skills. What charities and NGOs don't want, however, is for you just to turn up unannounced and trying to clock on for the next shift.

Enthusiasm and dedication are always appreciated by these organisations. You might even have a favourite cause you want to help. But your volunteering experience will probably be tougher. Sometimes you might be living and working in a village without running water or electricity. You might also be working alone without other volunteers from the UK or with volunteers much older than yourself. You will still have in-country support, although you'll be expected to be fairly resilient and self-sufficient. There is some overlap with gap-year or year-out volunteering but a charity, NGO or sending agency will always put their work and the people it serves first.

Sending agencies, charities and NGOs are normally small organisations that recruit by word of mouth, as they are often run on a shoestring. Most require between three- to six-months' notice and have some form of selection or interview process. A number have a minimum age restriction and might prefer you to be aged 21, or for you to be a postgrad. Others will take school-leavers but you'll need to convince the recruiters that you are sufficiently dedicated to its work and that you have the maturity to cope with the challenges. So try to do some research about any charity you approach.

These organisations usually charge a fee to volunteer but not always, as long as the volunteer is totally self-funding (ie will pay for all flights, accommodation, food, in-country travel). This is the case with Casa Alianza UK and L'Arche. However, you might pay anything up to £2000 for three months – in this case you can expect at least your accommodation and food to be thrown in. Often the volunteering program fee is a valuable source of income for the charity. Sometimes an organisation will pay you a small stipend or pocket-money. This is the case with L'Arche and ATD Fourth World, for example. So, yes, on the whole the costs are significantly lower than volunteering with a gap-year or year-out organisation, but your experience is a totally different one too.

You can volunteer with charities, NGOs and sending agencies for any period of time from two weeks to two years. The choice of what to do and where to go is enormous. Tom Law from the Sudan Volunteer Programme, for instance, chose to teach in a destination that isn't necessarily at the top of everyone's must see list:

Forget what you see in the media. The majority of Sudanese are the most friendly people on earth, I haven't paid for a single thing yet. For every bus journey, meal and drink I try to pay but someone always gets there first 'No, no you are our guest'. Paying for things individually is rude, 'English pocket' they call it. Everything is like buying rounds. Just it is never anyone's turn. People fight over who gets to pay. It's crazy.

Men who are friends walk down the street holding hands, totally un-homophobic. A refreshing change from our culture. You ask for directions and they take you by the hand and guide you. I have lost count of how often within an hour of talking to someone you have been invited to stay with them, meet their family, take dinner. Always before you are comfortable in your seat, tea, coffee or Pepsi appears.

I went to Neilin uni for the first time two days ago with my flatmate Paul to sit in on one of his classes. 'Mr Paul, how are you?' 'New teacher? You are ever so welcome here in Sudan, You teach us English, we teach you Arabic. You most welcome'. I ended up standing at the front of the class while they guessed where I was from, my age, hobbies, family. They thought I was French, 26, married with children and that I like football but not fish!

Otherwise, you could work with disadvantaged Anglo-Indian children in Madras (the Batemans Trust), work alongside the Belize government in engineering consultancy (Challenges Worldwide) or with the Karen Hilltribes of northwest Thailand (the Karen Hilltribes Trust, funnily enough).

EUROPEAN VOLUNTARY SERVICE (EVS)

Q: What has the EU ever done for me?
A: Quite a lot, actually, if you wish to volunteer in Europe.

If you've ever asked this question then you need to know about the EVS scheme. EVS is funded by the EU and, put crudely, will pay you to volunteer in another European country. Placements are normally for between six to 12 months but shorter placements of three weeks to six months are available for those with special needs. There's a wide variety of placements available in the social, environmental, cultural and sports sector. For instance, you might be working with children in an Estonian orphanage, working with a marine research organisation in Greece, or volunteering with handicapped people in Poland. In return you will receive an allowance of approximately £100 per month (depending on the country), plus accommodation, food, medical insurance and some language training. International travel costs are also covered. In order to qualify you need to be aged between 18 and 25 (though it might be going up to 30 in the future) and live in an eligible program country. This means all members of the EU, plus Iceland, Liechtenstein, Norway, Romania, Bulgaria and Turkey. In addition, some EVS projects can take place in partner regions of the EU such as Eastern Europe and the Caucasus, southeastern Europe and Latin America.

The scheme is administered by **Connect Youth** (☎ 020 7389 4030; c/o the British Council, 10 Spring Gardens, London SW1A 2BN; www.connectyouthinternational.com; connectyouth.enquiries@britishcouncil.org) but organised through specific EVS-affiliated sending organisations (ie you need to apply through them). There's a list of these on the Connect Youth website and on p287. If you want to apply from Northern Ireland then you can go through IVS Northern Ireland (www.ivsni.org). There are five deadlines for submitting applications – 1 February, 1 April (don't be a fool, go for it), 1 June, 1 September and 1 November.

As you can imagine, this is a very popular program. There's around 600 places per year and a tough selection process is applied. To have a real chance of being successful you need to apply nine months in advance, preferably have some language skills (or at least show an interest in learning the language of your chosen country) and demonstrate you are really 'into' your volunteer project. For more information contact Connect Youth. There's also a website for current and ex-EVS volunteers (www.evs-uk.org), which is worth having a look at.

This program also allows all volunteers who have completed their EVS placement to apply for a Future Capital Grant of up to £3480 to devise and manage their own individual project in program countries. You need to apply within two years of completing the EVS scheme.

VOLUNTARY SERVICE OVERSEAS (VSO)

VSO is an international development charity that works through volunteers to alleviate poverty. It is the largest independent volunteer-sending agency in the world. In 2004 it was voted top international development charity in the International Aid and Development category at the annual Charity Awards. VSO does not send food or money to disadvantaged areas, but men and women from a wide range of professions. These volunteers pass on their expertise to the local people so that skills remain in a society long after the volunteers have left. Volunteers are aged between 20 and 75 years and are skilled professionals in areas such as medicine, engineering, small businesses, social work, health, management consultancy, marine biology, accountancy and farming. VSO pays the airfares and insurance of its volunteers, provides accommodation and awards them a small local wage. The average age of most volunteers is 38 and postings are usually for two years.

Yes, you're right, this often means that there aren't a lot of gappers on VSO's main program but, don't worry, VSO has two volunteering programs for those aged between 17 and 25. There's the Youth for Development (YfD) and World Youth (WY) programs.

YOUTH FOR DEVELOPMENT PROGRAM (YFD)
Under this scheme, volunteers spend between 10 to 12 months abroad working in one of six areas: education, HIV and AIDS, disability, health and social well-being, secure livelihoods, participation and governance. For example, if you were working in education then you might be sent to Kathmandu to help run workshops and activities for the street children. If you were working in secure livelihoods you could be working in Mongolia helping out with small scale farming projects. You will also be expected to develop a global education project before, during and after your placement – for examples of these, see VSO's website (www.vso.org.uk).

To qualify for this scheme you need to be:
- A UK resident;
- Aged between 18 and 25;
- Have one year's volunteering and/or community work experience under your belt.

Placements start in August, September and October each year and you will be expected to raise £700 towards your placement costs. Apart from that, all other costs, such as airfare, accommodation, food etc, are paid by VSO. There is a highly competitive assessment procedure for this program. If you're successful six days of training are given. You need to apply giving at least 10 months' notice. Alice Tedd was successful at getting on this scheme and tells us:

I went to the Philippines and after three weeks of training (language/culture/customs etc) the six of us youth volunteers were let loose. I was working with a small NGO in Manila, which implemented renewable energy projects in remote communities: just simple electricity can make a huge difference to people's lives. I was lucky – being able to travel around to the different project sites – dotted all around the country – and then get back and relax in the relative luxury of the house in Manila. I really felt that I got to know the country and the people very well. I learnt about the differences that exist in Filipino culture – from the very wealthy people in the capital frequenting the plush malls to the poorest of the poor in the remote villages with nothing to their name but a small patch of land to feed a large family. It was fun and supportive having the VSO network in the country – especially at holiday times when our group of YfDs met up to travel around.

For more information ring ☎ 020 8780 7500 or email yfd@vso.org.uk.

WORLD YOUTH PROGRAM (WY)
This program aims to bring together young people from different cultures and backgrounds. Twice a year nine individuals are paired with nine overseas visitors to spend three months in the UK and three months abroad working on a practical project. In either country you could be working on education projects as care assistants with older people or people with physical and mental disabilities, with children, or on building and renovation projects. On each leg of the exchange the pair live with a host family.

To qualify for this program you need to be:
- A resident of the European Economic Area, Norway, Liechtenstein or Iceland;
- Aged between 17 and 25;
- Have a good grasp of English and life in the UK.

Placements start in spring and summer and you need to raise at least £600. VSO then pays for your medical costs, training, international travel, accommodation, food, visas and basic allowance. Again, competition for places is keen and the selection process rigorous – look on the website (www.vso.org.uk) to get an idea of what tasks you'll be set. You need to apply giving at least four months' notice. If you are accepted you'll need to attend two compulsory training courses. Then you have the choice of working with visitors from Ghana, Nigeria, Sri Lanka, South Africa, India, Indonesia, Kazakhstan and Uzbekistan. Justin Ward took part in this scheme and writes:

I spent three months in a community in Britain (High Wycombe) and three months in India (Garwhal). Each participant lived with a counterpart from the exchange country. In the UK phase I worked on environmentally-focused placements. I assisted with teaching and policy research at Amersham Field Studies Centre and I helped to develop a website and coordinated a community workshop on sustainable transport systems for the Environment Centre in High Wycombe. In India the whole team was involved in a project to encourage young people to participate in the village community. Some team members and I made a documentary film about the project. I am really glad I had the opportunity to take part in this program: the people, communities, work placements and projects have, and will continue to, provide rewarding experiences and learning for me. I would recommend this program to anyone who wants to experience and positively influence the lives of two communities: one in the developed world and one in the developing world.

For more information ring ☎ 020 8780 7500 or email enquiry@vso.org.uk.

Kibbutzim

Due to political and civil unrest, Israel might not be top of the pops for gap-year travel right now. However, if you're aged between 18 and 40 you could work as a volunteer on an Israeli kibbutz. These co-operatives are famous for their pursuit of a communal ideal where all members jointly work the land and own everything in common. Similarly, all the members act as an assembly to make the governing rules.

Volunteers from all backgrounds (provided their country of origin has diplomatic relations with Israel) are welcomed to join the community. A kibbutz has on average about 600 people living on it and there are about 270 of these communities spread throughout the country. The kibbutz movement is non-religious and pluralistic. While you are living in the community everything is shared with you but in return you will be expected to pull your weight and make a proper contribution to the communal life.

The work is physically hard and volunteers might be expected to work up to eight hours per day, six days per week. Work is usually divided into three areas: agriculture, tourism and services. In the agriculture area you might be picking citrus fruits, avocados, bananas, dates, melons etc; maintaining irrigation systems; or working with chickens and eggs (which came first?) or farmed fish. Some kibbutzim derive income from tourism so you might work in a guesthouse, restaurant, health spa or shop. The third branch of work is on the service side, helping in the kitchen, laundry or in a factory.

It's not all hard work and no play. Volunteers are welcomed into the social life of the community and are free to use the cinema, swimming pool and join the sports teams. The weekend in Israel is Friday and Saturday, while Sunday is a normal working day. Every three weeks volunteers are given an extra day's holiday, which is often used to travel within the country.

In the UK you apply through Kibbutz Reps (see p298). A minimum commitment of two months is expected, but you can live and work in a kibbutz for up to eight months. You can apply all year-round giving two weeks' notice. A fee of approximately £410 includes your return flight, accommodation, food, insurance, laundry facilities and pocket-money.

To volunteer on a Moshav or village farm see p374.

Religious Organisations

Traditionally, bringing relief and aid to the world's poorest people is the work of religious or faith-based organisations. In Britain, volunteer programs are mostly run by Christian-based groups; neither Muslim Aid (www.muslimaid.org) nor the Islamic Relief Fund (www .islamic-relief.org.uk) send volunteers abroad.

Most faith-based charities and NGOs describe themselves as non- or inter-denominational, meaning that it doesn't matter if you're Greek Orthodox or Baptist provided that you support the Christian basis of faith. However, some of these charities are affiliated to particular churches in Latin America, Africa and Asia so it's best to learn more about the distinct religious culture of each organisation. Some will have an evangelistic mission meaning the promotion of faith is important, for instance you might be teaching in Sunday schools, while others focus more on specific development projects.

Some of these organisations run specific programs for gap-year students. For instance, BMS World Mission offers a 10-month placement where you are trained in the UK for one month, spend six months volunteering in countries such as Uganda, Brazil or Trinidad, and follow up with a further two months back in the UK. Christian Aid has a similar 10-month program except you spend most of your time in the UK with a two-week trip overseas to visit Christian Aid partner organisations. World Vision runs shorter summer gap-year programs of between four and six weeks where you might find yourself volunteering in countries such as Armenia, Ghana or Zambia.

The kind of work you might be doing with a faith-based organisation resembles that of other charities or NGOs working in humanitarian aid and development (ie there's no cute, furry animals involved in this sector). For instance, you could be teaching in schools, working in a medical centre, helping out in a soup kitchen or building a community resource (anything from a bridge to a school). Some organisations send you out in teams and others require you to work alone. Some will pair you up with another gap-year student, as is the case with Katy Bray and Anna Priestley who worked together with the street children of Guatemala City. Anna told us:

I am a Christian and had been wanting to volunteer with Toybox for quite a few years. Whilst in Guatemala City, we helped out in all areas of the project, from the first point of contact on the streets, to the school and the homes. The street team was the most challenging part of the work, but also very rewarding. The team goes onto the streets in the afternoon and evenings and spends time with the children. Most of them live in gangs and know the charity well so as soon as they see the van they all come swarming. We spent a lot of time on the streets, just talking to the children and playing with them. We also did some basic education – teaching them to write and do maths. The street kids love to play football and we'd play with them. In effect, most of the time on the streets is spent getting to know the children so that they begin to trust you, as they have been let down by adults so many times before.

And, without looking at what Anna said, Katy wrote:

I volunteered to work with Toybox because, being a Christian, I wanted to serve God in this way. It was fantastic to have the privilege of working in Guatemala City for four months. I worked with the street team but also spent time in the family-style homes. In the homes we got to help the house parents by playing with the children, cleaning up and even cooking for over 10 hungry mouths. I also spent a lot of time playing football, which was a fantastic way of getting to know the children, since my Spanish isn't great.

If you're unsure about where to apply but want to work in a faith-based environment you could contact Christians Abroad, which acts as a sending agency, recruiting volunteers to work on faith-based grass roots projects, mainly in Africa.

Much like other charities or NGOs working in world development, volunteers are expected to be self-funding. Likewise you will be charged a program fee, which contributes to the development work. These fees are wide-ranging but can range from £700 to £5,600 for a one-year placement. However, most charge in the region of £1500 to £1850 for six or seven weeks' of volunteering abroad. These costs are all-inclusive (ie include your flights, accommodation, food) as most faith-based groups organise all-inclusive volunteering packages. Fundraising can often be slightly easier if you choose this option as many churches will help potential volunteers with collections and back sponsored activities. In return, the minimum time you can volunteer for is usually in the region of four to six weeks. Most religious organisations need around three-months' notice to arrange a placement and if you want to get onto one of the specific gap-year programs there are application deadlines – see p287 for details.

Conservation & Scientific Programs Abroad

Prince Charles hugs trees and thousands of us talk to plants everyday. Luckily these two facts have no connection to the adventure and down-to-earth science that you'll encounter on an international conservation holiday or expedition.

There's a huge range of environmental and wildlife conservation projects worldwide and many gap-year students are keen to donate muscle in return for the experience of living in some of the most untouched areas of the world. You could help save turtles in Mexico, work in the rainforests of Costa Rica, survey pristine coral reefs in the Philippines or help save orang-utans in Kalimantan. This is what Claire Webber did in her gap year. She writes:

I chose to volunteer with the Orang-utan Foundation as I had always had a specific interest in these animals but also, on a more practical level, the program costs were reasonable and the placement length suited me. Camp Leakey, in the Tanjng Putting National Park, is spectacularly beautiful and an ex-release site for rehabilitated orang-utans. To walk to breakfast in the morning and be surrounded by these enigmatic creatures is a breathtaking experience. They may break into your sleeping quarters or steal your sarong whilst you are washing but that is all part of the charm. Don't get me wrong – the program was also one of the most challenging things I have done. Our main project was to build an anti-logging patrol post on the banks of the river. This involved spending three weeks working in waist-deep swamp and living on a wooden platform in extremely close proximity to the other volunteers.

Caron Heath volunteered with Azafady and her experiences emphasize one of the most important parts of conservation work – winning the support and cooperation of the local people. She says:

I spent 10 weeks working as a pioneer in Madagascar. I was working in the remote villages outside the southeastern hub of Tolangnaro, more affectionately known as Fort Dauphin. Our daily activities were extremely diverse and included locating some of the world's most critically endangered species of palm tree, constructing wells and latrines, consulting with villagers on sustainable livelihood initiatives such as beekeeping and community vegetable gardens, as well as conducting health education days for local children on issues such as malaria, nutrition and the importance of hand-washing. I had a fantastic experience in Madagascar and I have remained friends with my fellow pioneers. Since returning I have remained devoted to Madagascar and a year later am now volunteering in Azafady's London office.

Not all conservation projects are land-based. Lucy Misch volunteered on a marine project with Coral Cay Conservation where she was surveying the coral reefs of Fiji. She tells us:

I was descending into the 'blue' on my first deep survey of the day. I was about half way down when a large stingray came swooping out of nowhere, circled us once and then took off. It was a stunning moment as I watched this massive creature majestically move through the water…After a hard week of surveying and putting all our skills into practice, came our recreational day. On Saturdays we would dive for fun in different locations around the many islands. We saw rays, massive groupers, trigger fish, sharks, barracuda and morays. You never forget when you're being circled by 16 grey reef sharks and a shoal of barracuda swim by.

Volunteering with a wildlife or environmental conservation program is not, however, a nice green holiday with animals and trees. Many groups working in this field recruit volunteers because they genuinely need extra help to gather scientific data. The science is taken seriously. You'll be trained to identify plant and animal species and record your observations and you will become an integral part of any scientific program. Biosphere Expeditions makes a point of telling volunteers that they will also receive a written report after a project is finished outlining the findings or results of the project. Lucy Misch explains about the two weeks of training she received with Coral Cay:

Phew! That's the only thing I can say about 'science weeks'. There was a lot of information to absorb, three lectures a day, 'pointies' (where the old volunteers took us out on dives to 'point out' things we had just learnt and write them down on our slates) and then in the final week the tests. The tests are not to be feared, if failed the first time you can repeat them as many times as you need. We were also taught how to boat marshal (look after the boat whilst dives are occurring), and the survey techniques used in the actual surveys. It was fascinating. After our two weeks of instruction the surveying began.

In addition to project-specific training, some wildlife and conservation organisations offer instruction in related qualifications. For instance, many marine conservation groups take on beginner divers and train them up, eg Coral Cay Conservation and Blue Ventures (who runs one of the remotest dive operations in Africa and the Indian Ocean). With Frontier you can gain a BTEC Advanced Diploma in Tropical Habitat Conservation during your expedition. This is the equivalent of an A-Level and takes 10 weeks to complete (see p313-18 for details).

Most wildlife or environment conservation programs tend to be based in one place, such as a rainforest camp or beside a coral reef, however some volunteering programs move around. What they all have in common is that you'll usually be living and working with a team of people in quite tough conditions, such as high humidity, extreme cold, out at sea or among lots of creepy-crawlies, far from the creature comforts of home. Initially, this can be a shock, as Lucy Misch explains:

It was then that I found out about the toilet and shower situation. Two showers of two minutes long only, and no flushing of toilets in a week. Needless to say the little rhyme 'if it's yellow let it mellow, if it's brown flush it down' sprang to mind. But worse was when the time came to 'flush' as you had to take a bucket down to the sea, fill it up and flush the toilet. Ah, the shame and horror of everyone knowing what you just did! To begin with we all tried our best 'not to go' for the first couple of weeks. But by then we had settled into the flow of things and realised that everyone else was in the same boat, or island (excuse the pun) so it became a very normal thing.

You'll need the right kit for the conditions you'll encounter and a dossier outlining what equipment to bring will be sent to you when you sign up with an organisation. Take note of what you're expected to bring and what your organisation says it will provide.

If all of this sounds exhilarating, exciting and lots of other adjectives beginning with 'e', don't rush out and book your trip until you've considered the costs. Conservation groups recruit volunteers not only to help with collecting data but because they need your money to fund their research. In addition, costs can be high because the programs you join are often quite remote. Trips range from one week to one year and prices start from around £550 for two weeks excluding flights and rise to around £3900 for 12 weeks all-inclusive. Any courses, such as PADI diving certificates etc, cost extra (or are built into an all-inclusive price). However, there are some cheaper option, such as volunteering in Tenerife with the Atlantic Whale Foundation (see p313).

Selection for a conservation program is pretty basic. Before joining a team you will need to produce a medical certificate confirming that you're in good health, reasonably fit and have had the relevant vaccinations. That's it, off you go then.

Do-It-Yourself

Do you have to sign up with any of the preceding organisations, charities, NGOs or sending agencies or can you cut out the middle person and arrange a placement direct? The answer is yes, you can. Listed in the Contacts (p318) section of this chapter are a number of online organisations that list volunteering opportunities abroad. These all work in slightly different ways but basically you send them your criteria (dates, destinations, volunteering interests etc) and they'll act like a dating agency, matching your requirements with those of an overseas project. It is then up to you to contact the project directly and arrange a placement. Some do this through an online database such as Worldwide Volunteering and Timebank, others, such as Working Abroad, have ex-volunteers assessing and selecting your projects. You can access the Timebank database for free but Working Abroad and Worldwide Volunteering costs between £10 and £36. Otherwise, World Service Enquiry (the sister organisation of Christians Abroad) publishes an annual guide to working and volunteering overseas and a monthly list of volunteering vacancies called Opportunities Abroad. See p318 for full details.

There are pros and cons of finding a volunteering opportunity this way. The main advantage is price – going down this route will save you money as you're basically doing all the work. In addition, there will be projects on these databases that are real one-offs and might offer an extraordinary opportunity that would otherwise be very difficult to find. But, there are risks, especially if you're a volunteer-virgin. However up-to-date and comprehensive these online facilities might be, you can never be sure of what you're getting (until you get there, that is). In addition, very few, if any, of these placements will have been personally vetted by the online organisations – this is not part of what they are offering. As such, if there are problems when you get there then it is up to you to sort them out. The bottom line is this: if you've had some experience of volunteering before, know how it all works, and are a university-leaver or postgrad, then DIY might be for you. However, if this is your first experience and you're a school leaver then a more 'guided' experience might be better. It's up to you.

DO YOU HAVE WHAT IT TAKES?

Do you scream when you see a spider in the house or get on with the process of releasing it back to the wild? When camping, do you hate getting up in the middle of the night to tramp across a wet field to the toilet block? These are just some of the questions you might ask yourself when thinking about whether to volunteer overseas. Other questions include:

- Are you adaptable and willing to learn?
- Are you interested in humanitarian volunteering (ie people-based) or wildlife and environment conservation?
- Are you looking for a single volunteer experience or something combined with another activity (such as a course) or an adventure (such as an overland expedition)?
- Are you sensitive to other cultures and tolerant of difference?
- Can you make the most of difficult situations or circumstances?
- Do you have a good sense of humour?
- Do you want to work in a team or on your own?
- How much time can you give?
- How much tolerance do you have to limited facilities, eg running water or electricity?
- What is your budget?
- What level of in-country support do you require?
- What skills can you put to good use? What skills do you want to learn?
- What sort of accommodation do you want (eg homestay, camp, hostel)?
- What sort of organisation will you go with?
- Where do you want to volunteer? Is it in one country or in a number of destinations?

VOLUNTEERING & CONSERVATION IN THE UK

You don't need to travel to the ends of the earth in order to volunteer. After all, we all know that 'charity begins at home'. If you plan to stay nearby during your gap year to earn money for university, to resit exams or just because you want to, there's no better use of your time and skills. Plus, volunteering is excellent experience and looks great on your CV whether you do it in Wigan (UK) or Wagga Wagga (Oz).

Even the government has woken up to the idea that encouraging young people to volunteer in their community makes sense. In 2004 this culminated in the Russell Commission (www.russellcommission.org), which will make recommendations to the government's National Youth Volunteering Strategy. Watch this space – no-one knows what they'll come up with yet but there's talk of funding students who spend time in the UK doing voluntary work.

One of the best places to start researching volunteer options is your local volunteer centre. To find the one nearest to you see www.volunteering.org.uk or look in the local *Yellow Pages*. There are about 400 individual volunteer centres throughout the UK with loads of information on organisations or projects looking for help in your area. Even if you have no clear idea what you'd like to do, an adviser can make suggestions by assessing your interests and abilities. Then the centre will come up with as many suitable matches as possible.

To search from the comfort of your armchair, try plugging your interests into the Youth-Net-UK website (www.do-it.org.uk), which has a comprehensive database of UK volunteering options. It will also give you an immediate result which, like doing the washing-up, is always a gratifying experience. While you're online, check out Millennium Volunteers (www.mvonline.gov.uk) and TimeBank (www.timebank.org.uk). For details on how these volunteer schemes work see p318.

Humanitarian Projects in the UK

If you want to work with people in your local community there are tons of challenging experiences. For instance, you could volunteer with recovering drug addicts, the homeless, the disabled, the elderly, youth groups, women's groups, the mentally ill, hospitals and hospices, children and families, prisoners and ex-offenders, human rights, refugees and literacy. The list is almost endless; take your pick.

Some charities and organisations may offer formal training and qualifications such as a National Vocational Qualification (NVQ). Millennium Volunteers gives you certificates if you complete 100 or 200 hours of voluntary work. At the very least you should be able to obtain a reference outlining what you did and, with luck, what a valuable contribution you made. If you're doing something entirely motivated by the need to raise cash, such as working in a call centre or supermarket, finding an interesting volunteering project might provide relief for part of the week.

A postgraduate might be thinking of a career in social work or medicine, so time spent volunteering in a hospital or prison might help steer professional choices.

If you are looking for a structured assignment in your gap year, which resembles an international placement, then contact Community Service Volunteers (CSV). This charity attaches volunteers to residential projects for four to 12 months, largely in social services for young offenders, the homeless, children in care and the disabled. CSV particularly welcomes interest from gap-year students. Food, travel and accommodation are provided and an allowance of £29 paid per week. See p319 for more details.

If you're not already drowning in a) UK volunteering options and b) where to find out about them, read on. Other places to look out for volunteering options include the reference library, where you'll find a copy of *The Voluntary Agencies Directory*, and your local library and community groups where you'll find requests for help pinned to the notice boards. In addition, there are usually some interesting paid and unpaid volunteering opportunities listed in the jobs section of Tuesday's *Times* and Wednesday's *Guardian*.

Conservation Programs in the UK

If you're going to be a home-bird during your gap year, there are some cool long-term conservation volunteer programs on offer. And, unlike the foreign ones, the majority are free to join and usually include accommodation and some out-of-pocket expenses.

You could become a Volunteer Officer with the British Trust for Conservation Volunteers (BTCV) and spend six months or more working in UK National Parks, coasts, urban parks or wildlife parks. BTCV even offers an NVQ in environmental management. This work experience and training can be used as a first step to a career in conservation. You could also take a conservation holiday either in the UK or abroad with BTCV and try your hand at dry stone walling, hedging, or sand-dune restoration.

A similar scheme is run by the National Trust (NT) where placements of around six months are available helping property managers, wardens, gardeners and educational officers. The NT also runs a number of working holidays where teams of up to 12 people go away for a weekend or a week to plant trees, clean up beaches or paint a lighthouse.

If you want to work with wildlife then the Royal Society for the Protection of Birds (RSPB) is a good place to start because it runs a voluntary warden scheme for up to 100 people at its 39 reserves around the country. You'll help to run the bird sanctuaries and in return receive professional training in bird conservation.

Although most of the programs highlighted here are long-term and residential, almost all conservation organisations stress that you can help out for as little or as much time as you can afford. The majority of their volunteers live at home and help out at the weekends or summer evenings.

EXPLORERS & EXPEDITIONS

The term 'expedition' is commonly used by gap-year, year-out and conservation organisations to cover all kinds of adventure travel, volunteer work or scientific research. In this section, it refers to a team of people journeying through challenging landscapes with a set purpose or aim in the spirit of traditional exploration.

While these expeditions can be physically demanding, the sense of achievement is often exhilarating. Tom Murray told us of his experience with British Schools Exploring Society (BSES) expeditions:

I was selected for the three-month BSES 'Footsteps of Shackleton Expedition' 2003/4, taking in Patagonia, the Falkland Islands and the Antarctic island of South Georgia; three remote and very different places. I chose to apply for this venture because I wanted a physical and mental challenge. Plus, in my opinion, BSES offers more serious expeditions than gap-year organisations. The expedition involved quite a bit of physical preparation before we left to ensure we were all fit enough for the three months of trekking and climbing in unusual environments. The expedition was better than I could ever have hoped, mainly due to the fantastic and inaccessible landscapes we were in and the awesome military and logistical support we were given. Living in tents for three months, eating military rations and walking or skiing many miles a day, often in horrible weather, might not sound like fun but it was definitely the best three months of my life. And, I now have 21 of the most fantastic friends I could ever have hoped for and some of the most amazing photos and memories imaginable.

BSES is just one of several companies that arrange scheduled expeditions specifically for young people. Others include the Brathay Exploration Group, the Dorset Expeditionary Society and World Challenge Expeditions. Most run up to eight expeditions a year, mainly departing in the summer. The aims and destinations of these expeditions vary annually but on many you can qualify for sections of the Duke of Edinburgh Gold Award. Depending on the location, expeditioners are taught about ice work, camping, hill walking and living outdoors. If you're a postuniversity gapper then you might qualify as an assistant team leader on some of these trips.

As you'd imagine, these expeditions do not come cheap. Depending on the location, you can pay anything from £300 for one week, excluding flights, to £4000 for three months, all included. Despite this, competition for places is fierce and there's often a tough selection process. To ensure you're not disappointed, apply nine to 12 months before an expedition departs.

As well as the organisations that target the under 25s (and often younger), there are those that run scheduled expeditions catering to all ages. Jagged Globe, for example, specialises in mountaineering, combining both rock climbing and trekking. There's even the chance to climb Mt Everest, but you'll have to raise a sky-high £28,000 to achieve that.

If you're feeling really adventurous, have some experience and a lot of cash, you could organise your own expedition with a group of friends. The Royal Geographical Society (RGS) gives help and advice to over 500 expeditions a year and has a special expedition advisory centre. Each November there's a weekend expedition planners' seminar where you can find contacts, listen to talks and get fired up about DIY expeditions. In addition, RGS publishes a host of useful publications such as the *Expedition Planners Handbook* by Shane Winser.

If you don't feel up to leading and organising your own expedition, the centre publishes a bulletin of expedition vacancies listing trips that are looking for team members.

CONTACTS

Gap-Year Organisations

Adventureworks

The Foundry Studios, 45 Mowbray St, Sheffield S3 8EN
☎ 0845 345 8850
fax 0114 275 5740
info@adventurworks.co.uk
www.adventureworks.co.uk
Adventureworks (youth arm of mountaineering company Jagged Globe) runs a gap-year program combining a three-week adventure in the mountains with a community-based project. Adventure activities include climbing, trekking, mountain biking and rafting. You then have the option to help a community conservation or social project, which largely involves teaching in schools. Training is given to all expeditioners. The program fulfils the expedition requirements of the Duke of Edinburgh's Gold Award and the Queen's Scout and Guide Awards.
Timing & Length of Placements: Three-week adventures with the option to join a community project with a one- to three-month commitment. Applications should be sent six to 12 months in advance of departure. Expeditions to Ecuador and Tanzania leave in July/August (and December for Tanzania), and to Nepal in April/May or October/November.
Destinations: The mountainous regions of Ecuador, Nepal and Tanzania.
Costs: The adventure phase costs between £1500 and £2000, flights and all in-country costs included. The volunteering phase costs roughly an additional £200 per month.
Eligibility: Aged 18 plus, but most applicants are school leavers.

Africa & Asia Venture

10 Market Place, Devizes, Wiltshire SN10 1HT
☎ 01380 729009
fax 01380 720060
av@aventure.co.uk
www.aventure.co.uk
For motivated students and graduates who want to teach in the developing world. Comprehensive training is provided in local language, religion, culture and history. Throughout the placement local staff give full support and backup.
Timing & Length of Placements: Apply as early as possible; places in Kenya start to fill up a year in advance. Departures take place in September, January and May. Placements are for four to six months, but some are only five weeks.
Destinations: Botswana, Kenya, India, Malawi, Mexico, Nepal, Tanzania and Uganda.
Costs: Four-month placements cost £2590, including accommodation, food and an allowance. International flights etc are extra.
Eligibility: Applicants must be aged 18 to 24.

AFS Intercultural Programmes UK

Leeming House, Vicar Lane, Leeds LS2 7JF
☎ 0113 242 6136
fax 0113 243 0631
info-unitedkingdom@afs.org
www.afs.org
With over 90 years of experience in volunteering and community work around the world, AFS offers a large variety of opportunities. For instance, you could work with street children in Brazil, rebuild communities in Honduras or work in an orphanage in Peru. There is on-site support for volunteers. Cultural exchange and immersion are as important as the development work itself. All volunteers live with a local family.

Timing & Length of Placements: Placements range from four and a half months to six months with departures in January/February and July/August. Apply six to seven months in advance.

Destinations: There are over 50 different member countries of the AFS network around the world.

Costs: A six-month program costs from £3300 including everything except pocket-money and visa fees.

Eligibility: Most applicants must be aged 18 to 29 but some countries accept older volunteers.

BUNAC (British Universities North America Club)

16 Bowling Green Lane, London EC1R 0QH
☎ 020 7251 3472
fax 020 7251 0215
volunteer@bunac.org.uk
www.bunac.org

Better known for their working holiday and camp counselling programs (see p363), BUNAC also offers four volunteer programs. You can, for instance, help out on a school-based project in Ghana, work in rainforest conservation in Costa Rica or work with poor communities in South Africa.

Timing & Length of Placements: Placements last from eight weeks to 12 months and run all year-round (there are monthly group departures). Apply at least eight weeks before departure.

Destinations: Costa Rica, Ghana, Peru and South Africa.

Costs: Eight weeks from £1500, which usually includes all international flights, program literature, travel insurance, an arrival orientation course, UK and in-country support, accommodation and food (check with BUNAC for full details). Pocket money is extra.

Eligibility: Minimum age is 18 and some programs require you to be a student or recent graduate. With the exception of Ghana, programs are only open to British nationals. With the Peru and Costa Rica placements you need to speak conversational Spanish.

Changing Worlds

Hodore Farm, Hartfield, East Sussex TN7 4AR
☎ 01892 770 000
fax 0870 990 9665
ask@changingworlds.co.uk
www.changingworlds.co.uk

Changing Worlds offers a wide variety of volunteering experiences for a gap year across the globe. Opportunities include teaching or working in an orphanage.

Timing & Length of Placements: Placements are usually for three or six months but can be extended at no extra cost. There are departures all year-round. Apply a minimum of four months in advance.

Destinations: Chile, India, Latvia, Nepal, Romania and Tanzania.

Costs: Costs for a six-month placement are from £1665 including flights, insurance, food, accommodation, in-country briefing and support from in-country managers.

Eligibility: Minimum age is 17 and most volunteers are school and university leavers.

Cultural Destination Nepal

GPO Box 11535, Dhapasi, Kathmandu, Nepal
☎ 00 977 1- 437 7623
fax 00 977 1-437 7696
cdnnepal@wlink.com.np
www.volunteernepal.org.np

Cultural Destination runs a program called 'Volunteer Nepal'. This is for volunteers who want to contribute their time and skills to benefit the community while, at the same time, learning about Nepalese culture and customs by living as a member of a Nepali family. The voluntary work usually involves placements in schools teaching English. A placement also includes two weeks of pre-service training (including the do's & don'ts of Nepalese culture), sightseeing tours, lectures on topics such as religion and politics, meditation, some trekking, a jungle safari and white-water rafting.

Timing & Length of Placements: Placements last from two to four months and depart in February, April, June, August and October, but there is a certain amount of flexibility with these dates. Apply giving three months' notice.

Destination: Nepal.

Costs: A placement costs £490 regardless of whether you go for two or four months. This includes food and lodging (half board), in-country transport and the above activities. Your airfare, visas, entrance fees, insurance etc are extra.

Eligibility: Applicants should be aged 18 to 65, have a high school diploma or A- Levels, be able to communicate well in English, be flexible, physically fit and willing to immerse themselves in another culture.

GAP Activity Projects (GAP)

44 Queen's Rd, Reading, Berkshire RG1 4BB
☎ 0118 959 4914
fax 0118 957 6634
volunteer@gap.org.uk
www.gap.org.uk

With over 30 years of experience, GAP is a well-established name in the gap-year market. Experiences offered include Teach English as a Foreign Language (TEFL) placements, caring for the disadvantaged, working in medical clinics and environmental work. GAP prides itself on offering good-value placements and runs a bursary scheme for those in-dividuals who need help with the fees. Preparation for your placement is important and courses are arranged including teaching skills, language skills and orientation. There is also a business partnership scheme, where a number of large UK businesses have access to the GAP volunteer database and target former volunteers with information on summer jobs while at university or graduate recruitment.

Timing & Length of Placements: Placements can be found year-round but most start September, January and March. Placements last from three to 12 months. Applica-tions and interviews are year-round too, but you must apply two months in advance.

Destinations: 32 different countries.

Costs: There's a flat fee of £900 for most of your costs except international flights. This fee applies whether you're going for three or 12 months.

Eligibility: Applicants must be aged 17 to 19.

Gap Challenge

World Challenge Expeditions, Black Arrow House, 2 Chandos Rd, London NW10 6NF
☎ 020 8728 7200
fax 020 8961 1551
welcome@world-challenge.co.uk
www.world-challenge.co.uk

Gap Challenge runs expeditions and gap projects around the world intended to educate and develop skills among young people. The organisation sees raising the cost of an expedi-tion as an integral part of the gap experience. Gap-year placements include medical support, conservation, teaching and care work. Travel is encouraged with 12-month return air tickets. In-country support is provided. See p322 for information on the company's World Challenge Expeditions.

Timing & Length of Placements: There are no official deadlines as applications can be approved and arranged in nine days, but earlier applications lead to greater choice. Three-, six- and nine-month gap challenge placements leave in September, January and April.

Destinations: The 12 different destinations include Australia, Canada, Costa Rica, Galápagos Islands and Peru.

Costs: Prices start at £2000 with 12-month date-changeable return flights included. Board and lodging are sometimes

part of the deal too (depending on the program). Travel insurance needs to be bought separately.

Eligibility: Applicants must be aged 17 to 24.

Gap Sports Abroad

Willowbank House, 84 Station Rd, Buckinghamshire SL7 1NX
☎ 0870 837 9797
fax 01494 76 9090
info@gapsportsabroad.co.uk
www.gapsports.com

Volunteering opportunities include coaching underprivileged children in football, rugby, cricket, tennis, basketball, hockey and boxing. There are also non-sports-related volunteering where you can teach abroad, work in a hospital, teach art and design, volunteer in the journalism sector or work with athletes overseas in sports psychology and physiotherapy.

Timing & Length of Placements: There are four depar-tures a year: January, April, July and October. Placements last five weeks or three months. Apply six weeks before you want to travel.

Destinations: Costa Rica, Ghana and South Africa.

Costs: A five-week placement starts at £1190 and three months start from £1495. This includes all your costs except international flights and travel insurance.

Eligibility: Minimum age 18.

Global Adventures Project

38 Queen's Gate, London SW7 5HR
☎ 0800 0854197
fax 020 7590 7444
info@globaladventures.co.uk
www.globaladventures.co.uk

Global Adventures Project is a division of the American Institute for Foreign Study (AIFS), more commonly known for its Camp America program (see p409). Global Adventures Project combines a choice of placement options with a 12-month round-the-world (RTW) ticket. Placements range from working with street children in India and reforestation projects in Brazil to rebuilding homes in rural South African townships (the South African placement includes a course on politics and culture at Stellenbosch University). There's a two-day orientation course four to six weeks before de-parture. The RTW ticket allows up to 10 stops, which means students can travel independently between placements. You also have the chance to complete a City and Guilds Profes-sional Development Award as part of the program.

Timing & Length of Placements: Each placement lasts three months and participants choose between two to four placements. Departures are in January, June and September. Applications should be sent three to 12 months in advance.

Destinations: Brazil, India and South Africa.

Costs: Program fees start from £3195 and include a minimum of two placements and a RTW ticket. Accommodation and food is included in all placements except South Africa where only accommodation is included. All other costs including travel insurance are extra.

Eligibility: Minimum age 18.

i-to-i

England: Woodside House, 261 Low Lane, Leeds LS18 5NY
☎ 0870 333 2332
fax 0113 205 4619
Ireland: Exploration House, 26 Main St, Dungarvan,
Co Waterford
☎ 00 353 58 40050
info@i-to-i.com
www.i-to-i.com

i-to-i specialises in international volunteer and teaching placements. There are over 300 placements in 24 countries. Placements are available teaching English, in conservation, health and other professions. An online TEFL course is included for those hoping to teach English. Alternatively, you can pay to attend one of the weekend courses held in 16 cities around the country. It's also possible just to take the TEFL course alone and arrange independent travel.

Timing & Length of Placements: Placements can be arranged in four weeks but it is recommended that you apply three months in advance. Placements last from between one week to 52 weeks and run all year.

Destinations: Include Australia, Bolivia, China, Costa Rica, Ecuador, Ghana, Honduras, India, Ireland, Mongolia, Nepal, South Africa, Sri Lanka and Thailand.

Costs: Many placements are for eight weeks and cost around £1295. This price includes insurance, sometimes food and accommodation, but not international flights. TEFL courses taken alone cost £245.

Eligibility: Open to anyone aged 18 to 80.

Inter-Cultural Youth Exchange (ICYE) UK

Latin America House, Kingsgate Place, London NW6 4TA
☎ 0870 774 3486
fax 020 7681 0983
info@icye.co.uk
www.icye.co.uk

ICYE-UK is a user-led charity working in the field of personal, social and community development. It is a member of an international federation, recognised by the UN as an international peace messenger with consultative status with UNESCO. Volunteer placements include: working in HIV clinics and in orphanages, working with disabled people or teaching in primary schools. If you're interested in volunteering in Europe, ICYE-UK is an EVS-affiliated sending organisation (see p277 for details).

Timing & Length of Placements: Placements last from two weeks to 12 months. The shorter ones run all year-round but the longer ones (six months or 12 months) depart January and August. Apply giving three months' notice.

Destinations: Many around the world including Bolivia, Brazil, Colombia, Costa Rica, Europe, Ghana, Kenya, Mozambique, Nepal, New Zealand and Thailand.

Costs: A six-month placement costs from £2900 and a 12 month one from £3300 including international flights, living costs, insurance, pocket money, language course and on-arrival training seminars. If you're 18 to 25 and going to Europe then your trip could be funded by the EVS.

Eligibility: Long term international placements are open to those aged 18 to 30; EVS open to 18 to 25 year olds; and shorter term placements to 18 years plus.

Jubilee Ventures

Main Office: PO Box 2242-00100, GPO, Nairobi, Kenya
☎ 00 254-721-646624
Tanzanian Office: PO Box 767 Mbeya, Tanzania
☎ 00 255-74-843 4491
jubilee@jubileeventures.org
www.jubileeventures.org

Jubilee Ventures offers gap-year students opportunities to volunteer in schools, orphanages, health clinics or to work in animal welfare. You might be working in HIV education or helping local women make baskets. You can also take part in a two-week language and culture program, or go on a jungle adventure safari.

Timing & Length of Placements: Projects run from one week to one year. There are two start dates per month – see the website for details. Apply at least one month in advance.

Destinations: Kenya and Tanzania but expanding to other African countries and into Asia during 2005.

Costs: A placement costs £430 for the first two weeks and £54 per week thereafter. This includes pick-up and drop-off from the airport, in-country transport, accommodation, food, language tuition and park fees for the safari.

Eligibility: Applicants must be aged over 16.

Kwa Madwala

PO Box 192, Hectorspruit, 1330, Mpumalang Province,
South Africa
☎ 00 27 13-792 4526
fax 00 27 13 792 4534
gapyear@kwamadwala.co.za
www.kwamadwalagapyear.com

This gap-year organisation is based in South Africa. Their objective is to give gappers a broader outlook on conservation,
wildlife and life in general. The 12-week gap experience will
appeal to the 'all-rounder' seeking a challenging adventure
and a unique holiday in the bush. A shorter option of 25 days
is also on offer. You'll learn how to track lions, identify snakes
and survive in the bush. At the end of the experience you'll
receive a certificate in conservation competency. The email
address is the best means of contact.

Timing & Length of Placements: The 12-week placements start mid-January, mid-May and mid-September.
Those lasting 25 days start mid-April, mid-August and
mid- December. Apply one month in advance.

Destinations: Kwa Madwala Private Game Reserve in
South Africa, located south of Kruger National Park.

Costs: 12 weeks cost roughly £3460 and 25 days cost
roughly £1626. This includes accommodation, meals, all
activities, entry fees, specialised courses and transfers from
KMIA International Airport. It excludes international flights,
travel insurance or airport transfers from Johannesburg.

Eligibility: Open to anyone aged over 17. You need to be fit,
healthy and able to work in a team; 'not for the faint hearted'.

The Leap

1st fl, 121 High St, Marlborough, Wiltshire SN8 1LZ
☎ 0870 240 4187
fax 01672-519944
info@theleap.co.uk
www.theleap.co.uk

The Leap specialises in ecotourism that combines conservation and community projects and has a choice of placements
in different types of environment, such as game parks,
ranches, deserts, rainforests, mountains, beaches and coral
reefs. Seventy-five per cent of volunteers are on a gap year.

Timing & Length of Placements: Placements are for
six, 10 or 12 weeks. Some departures are flexible while
others take place in January, April, July and September.
You need to apply at least a month before you leave.

Destinations: Botswana, Kenya, Malawi, Mozambique,
South Africa and Zambia. The Leap are also hoping to move
into Argentina, Asia, Australia, Costa Rica and Swaziland.

Costs: Placements cost from £1600 to £2500, depending on
whether you're on the six-week or 12-week program. The
price is also influenced by where you go and what you choose
to do. All costs except international flights are included.

Eligibility: You must be aged at least 18 at time of departure.

Link Overseas Exchange

25 Perth Rd, Dundee DD1 4LN
☎ 01382 203192
fax 01382 226087
info@linkoverseas.org.uk
www.linkoverseas.org.uk

Volunteers mainly teach conversational English to children
in schools, girls' or boys' homes, and orphanages. Other
options include teaching English in Tibetan monasteries
or helping out in community projects such as a women's
development centre. These experiences are intended as a
prelude to knowledgeable and culturally sensitive travel at
the end of the placement. As a registered charity, Link can
provide you with a charity number to help fundraise.

Timing & Length of Placements: Placements are for
six months (including up to six weeks holiday), which can
sometimes be extended to 12 months. Applications are
taken year-round but departures are limited to February
and August. You are advised to apply three months in
advance of departure.

Destinations: China, India and Sri Lanka.

Costs: The six-month package costs £2520, which includes
all your needs (including international flights).

Eligibility: Applicants must be aged 17 to 25.

Madventurer

Hawthorn House, fourth banks, Newcastle upon Tyne NE1 3sG
☎ 0845 121 1996
team@madventuer.com
www.madventurer.com

Madventurer combines volunteering activities with a travel
adventure. You choose how long you want to volunteer
for and how long you want to travel to create a bespoke,
individual experience. Projects range from building schools
and teaching in rural communities to coaching sports and
working on specialist conservation initiatives. Normally
you're part of a group of five to 12 people working on a
project. Some adventure travel opportunities include travelling the entire length of Africa or visiting the mountain
gorillas of central Africa. If you're a university student then
you can opt for one of the summer programs, which allows
you to volunteer and travel during the summer holiday.

Timing & Length of Placements: You need to apply between three and nine months in advance of travel but late applications can sometimes be accommodated. Projects last anything from two weeks to 12 months and run all year-round. Adventure travel is from 15 to 77 days.

Destinations: Australia, Brazil, Costa Rica, Ghana, India, Kenya, Peru, Tanzania, Thailand, Togo, Trinidad & Tobago and Uganda.

Costs: A two-week volunteering project costs from £690, five weeks from £980 and 12 weeks from £1480 including all food and accommodation overseas, a donation to the communities that you'll be supporting, full-time overseas crew project support and in-country travel (flights, visas, insurance and personal kit are not included). A 21-day adventure trip to Timbuktu costs £550 (same things included as above).

Eligibility: Open to those aged 17 and upwards.

Personal Overseas Development (PoD)

Linden Cottage, The Burgage, Prestbury, Cheltenham GL52 3DJ
☎ 01242 250 901
info@thepodsite.co.uk
www.thepodsite.co.uk

PoD specialises in gap-year placements, mini-gap placements (in your summer holiday) and career-break placements. There are three programs: teaching English in Thailand, Tanzania or Peru; working in an orphanage in Peru; and working in an animal rescue centre in Thailand. The programs all include a training weekend in the UK, local training in-country and adventure activities such as a safari, diving or trekking. Four to 12 gappers live together on one site and are supervised at a distance, unlike some gap-year placements where you tend to work with team leaders all day.

Timing & Length of Placements: Gap-year programs last from two to six months. Ideally you should apply at least two months in advance of departure but last minute applications are catered for. Departure dates are January, April, May, July, September and October. The mini-gap program lasts for two months with a departure early July so you can get back in time for university.

Destinations: Africa, Asia and South America.

Costs: A two-month gap year program starts at £1400 and includes all costs apart from international flights and food.

Eligibility: Minimum age is 17.

Project Trust

Hebridean Centre, Isle of Coll, Argyll, Scotland PA78 6TE
☎ 01879 230444
fax 01879 230357

info@projecttrust.org.uk
www.projecttrust.org.uk

The philosophy of Project Trust is to provide young people with an opportunity to understand an overseas community by immersing themselves in it by living and working there for a full year. Two hundred placements are made every year. All volunteers attend a five-day selection course on the Hebridean island of Coll, those that are successful will attend a five-day briefing and training course specifically for their country group. Project Trust will provide advice and administrative help in fundraising. Opportunities exist in fields such as teaching, social/care work, outdoor education and development. Project Trust is a member of the ASDAN (award scheme, development and accreditation network) university awards scheme so if you complete your ASDAN workbooks while overseas then this can count towards extra UCAS points.

Timing & Length of Placements: Gappers are usually sent abroad for one year, but there is also a small eight-month winter program. Departures are August/September (January for the winter program). Applications start 18 months prior to departure so get your application in quickly. Training courses are in July for autumn placements.

Destinations: 24 different destinations including Bolivia, Chile, China and Malawi.

Costs: The price of £3950 includes all your costs for a year, including international flights, a small local wage and accommodation.

Eligibility: Applicants must be aged between 17 and 19.

Quest Overseas

North West Stables, Borde Hill Estate, Balcombe Rd, Haywards Heath, West Sussex RH16 1XP
☎ 01444 474744
fax 01444 474799
emailingyou@questoverseas.com
www.questoverseas.com

Quest Overseas specialises in volunteer projects and expeditions in South America and Africa. Volunteers have the opportunity to join any one of three different types of trip: the gap year quest, which runs for three months and combines a worthwhile project and an expedition; the project quest, which runs for five to eight weeks where volunteers work in the community on construction or conservation projects; and the expedition quest, which is a six week 'adventure' through South America or Africa. Projects include helping to rehabilitate wild animals in the Amazon, working on a children's project in a Peruvian shanty town or helping to provide essential infrastructure to villages in Tanzania.

Timing & Length of Placements: The gap year quest program runs for three months, the project quest for five to eight weeks and the expedition quest for six weeks. Applications are processed up to 18 months in advance. Departures are between December and July.

Destinations: Africa and South America.

Costs: Prices range from £1150 to £4460 for a three-month expedition or project (including food, board, activities and a contribution to the project). International flights and insurance are excluded.

Eligibility: School leavers, undergraduates and graduates aged 18 to 25.

Raleigh International

27 Parsons Green Lane, London SW6 4HZ
☎ 020 7371 8585
fax 020 7371 5852
info@raleigh.org.uk
www.raleigh.org.uk

Raleigh International is an established youth development and expeditions charity. The programs incorporate conservation and community work such as diving to carry out marine surveys and building schools and clinics. All projects are sourced with the local communities and NGOs to ensure they are worthwhile and sustainable. Volunteers choose from three programs: the Raleigh expedition, which lasts for 10 weeks, the Raleigh explorer, which lasts for four or seven weeks and the Raleigh adventure, which runs for two or three weeks and is for those over 21. Those on a 10-week expedition will experience the diversity of three projects – environmental, community and adventure. Those on shorter trips will choose the type of project they want to work on. Each new project sees the volunteers placed with a new project group. Uniquely, Raleigh runs two programs for young disadvantaged people in the UK and for local young people in the host country. In the UK this means that people who have been unemployed for a long time, have suffered problems with drug addiction or have been homeless can go abroad and participate in some of the projects under the Motivate8 program. The host country program also allows young people from the country you're working in to participate in the expeditions. This mix of cultures is very important to any Raleigh volunteer program. All volunteers are given training and introduced to the wider global issues of development and sustainability.

Timing & Length of Placements: There are usually 10 expeditions per year. The Raleigh expedition is for 10 weeks, the Raleigh explorer lasts from four to seven weeks, and the Raleigh adventure for two or three weeks. Programs run throughout the year. You need to apply four to 12 months in advance.

Destinations: Chile, Costa Rica, Fiji, Ghana, Malaysia, Namibia and Nicaragua.

Costs: A 10-week expedition program (three projects) costs from £2995, a four-week explorer program (one project) costs from £1500, a seven-week explorer program (two projects) from £2350 and the adventure program from £1500. This includes all training, flights, food, accommodation and in-country support.

Eligibility: Open to those aged 17 to 25, except for the adventures program which has a minimum age of 21. Raleigh also look for volunteer staff who are over 25 and can offer skills.

Teaching & Projects Abroad

Aldsworth Pde, Goring, Sussex BN12 4TX
☎ 01903 708 300
fax 01903 501 026
info@teaching-abroad.co.uk
www.teaching-abroad.co.uk

With Teaching & Projects Abroad you can volunteer as an English teacher in China, work to save the rainforests in Peru, save turtles in Mexico, gain experience as a journalist in Romania or gain medical experience in India. These are just some of the hundreds of placements available. In each destination there are paid and trained staff to provide support to volunteers. For every three months of voluntary work it's possible to take two weeks off for travel. Alternatively, it's possible to travel independently either before or after a placement.

Timing & Length of Placements: Placements can be anything from one to 12 months and you can move from placement to placement, if you wish. There are programs all year-round and placement departure dates are flexible. Try to give at least three months' notice.

Destinations: Many countries around the world including Bolivia, China, India, Mexico, Mongolia, Nepal, Peru, Russia, Swaziland and Thailand.

Costs: A one-month placement will cost from £945, which includes food, accommodation, comprehensive insurance and in-country back-up. International flights are extra.

Eligibility: For those aged over 17 to 70.

Travellers Worldwide

7 Mulberry Close, Ferring, W Sussex BN12 5HY
☎ 01903 502595
fax 01903 500364

info@travellersworldwide.com
www.travellersworldwide.com
Travellers Worldwide offers placements including teaching English or sports (cricket and football), working in conservation (lion breeding in South Africa, orang-utan rehabilitation in Malaysia or working with elephants in Sri Lanka) or gaining work experience abroad (law, journalism, tourism and medical placements).

Timing & Length of Placements: One- to three-month placements with the possibility of an extension or taking more than one placement. Some placements can be arranged with only four weeks notice but the most popular need to be booked between six to 12 months in advance. Programs run throughout the year with flexible start dates.

Destinations: Argentina, Brazil, Brunei, China, Cuba, Ghana, Guatemala, India, Kenya, Malaysia, Nepal, Russia, South Africa, Sri Lanka, Ukraine, Vietnam and Zimbabwe.

Costs: A one-month placement costs from £945 for everything except international flights and travel insurance. Extra months cost roughly £295.

Eligibility: Open to those aged 17 to 70 with many volunteers aged between 17 to 25.

Trekforce Expeditions

34 Buckingham Palace Rd, London SW1W 0RE
☎ 020 7828 2275
fax 020 7828 2276
info@trekforce.org.uk
www.trekforce.org.uk

Trekforce Expeditions organises conservation, scientific research and community projects to the rainforests of Central and South America and Southeast Asia. Volunteers complete an entire project (eg building a ranger station or working on a bio-diversity study) while living and working in the jungle. They then take part in a week-long jungle trek. Each expedition team is accompanied by an experienced expedition leader, assistant leader and two medics. Volunteers are a good mix of gappers and career-breakers. Trekforce also offers extended programs incorporating optional phases of learning new languages and teaching in rural communities.

Timing & Length of Placements: Each expedition lasts two months with an option to extend to five months. Expeditions depart all year. There's no official deadline for applications but apply at least three months before you want to travel.

Destinations: Belize, East Malaysia, Guatemala, Guyana and Venezuela.

Costs: Volunteers are required to fundraise £2590 for the basic two-month expedition. This includes all costs except international flights. The five-month combination placement (two-month expedition plus intensive language course and teaching) costs from £3900 for all but international flights.

Eligibility: For those aged 18 to 38.

Ventureco Worldwide

Ironyard, 64–66 the Market Place, Warwick CV34 4SD
☎ 01926 411122
fax 01926 411133
mail@ventureco-worldwide.com
www.ventureco-worldwide.com

VentureCo offers volunteering experiences in three phases on a gap-year venture program. Part one is a language and cultural orientation course to learn about your host community. Part two is the aid project where you work alongside local people. Part three is the expedition where you and your team explore the back country and neighbouring lands including jungles, deserts and mountains. Aid projects include: orphanage work in Ecuador, conservation in the Amazon, ebony-tree conservation on the foothills of Mt Kilimanjaro (the wood that you plant is harvested to make clarinets) and teaching local children about road-signs in Rajasthan. VentureCo makes the distinction between school leavers and graduates on gap years. There is some flexibility with the travel arrangements of placements as they can be fitted into your own RTW ticket (if you have one).

Timing & Length of Placements: The placements are for a group of sixteen people and last for four months. There are departures throughout the year. The shortest notice period is two weeks in advance.

Destinations: Central and South America, East Africa, India, Indo China and Nepal.

Costs: Prices from £4200 for four months, including flights, travel insurance, airport taxes, all in-country costs and a contribution to the aid project. Some pocket money is recommended on top.

Eligibility: Gap-year ventures are for school leavers aged between 17 and 19; career gap ventures are for those taking a career break or sabbatical from work or university.

Work & Travel Company

45 High St, Tunbridge Wells, Kent TN1 1XL
☎ 01892 516164
fax 01892 523172
info@worktravelcompany.co.uk
www.worktravelcompany.co.uk

This company arranges gap years and career breaks for those interested in discovering the world. For instance, you can volunteer in an animal rehabilitation centre in Namibia called Noah's Ark, which is a secure home for neglected or orphaned wild animals, and help feed the animals, learn about their environment and build and repair camps. You could work at a research and breeding facility for cheetahs in South Africa where you'd assist in the feeding of baby, juvenile and adult cheetahs, help the vets and rangers where needed, and see animals in the wild in bush sleep-outs. Volunteers can go as individuals or in groups. There's extensive pre-departure material so you'll know what to expect.

Timing and Length of Placement: Programs are from two weeks to 12 months and run all year-round. Try to apply two months in advance, but there is late availability.

Destinations: Africa, Australia, India, eight countries in South America and Thailand.

Costs: A four-week placement ranges from £499 to £1600, depending on where you go. This includes everything except flights.

Eligibility: From ages 18 to 70.

Year-Out Organisations

Cross-Cultural Solutions
Tower Point 44, North Rd, Brighton BN1 1YR
☎ 0845 458 2781/2782
fax 0845 458 2783
infouk@crossculturalsolutions.org
www.crossculturalsolutions.org
Cross-Cultural Solutions offers volunteer programs in 16 regions of the world. Placements are based on the individual's skills and interests and the needs of the local community. All work is with locally designed and driven projects, usually in the fields of education, healthcare and social services. Strong emphasis is put on the cultural exchange aspect so you'll have the chance to immerse yourself in the culture through travel, activities and seminars as well as having time to yourself.

Timing & Length of Placements: Placements are from one week to 12 weeks and can be extended. There are start dates throughout the year. Apply 60 days in advance.

Destinations: Africa, Asia, Central America, South America and Russia.

Costs: The cost of a two-week program is approx £1250 and each additional week comes in at approx £140. This includes lodging, meals, in-country transportation, airport transfers, full staff support, medical insurance, language training and cultural trips (but not international flights).

Eligibility: Everyone under 18 needs parental permission, 16- to 18-year-olds can travel independently to some programs if granted permission. No upper age limit.

Daneford Trust
45–47 Blythe St, London E2 6LN
☎ /fax 020 7729 1928
dfdtrust@aol.com
www.danefordtrust.org
The Daneford Trust is a listed charity that promotes youth development through international exchange. There is a small volunteer program where volunteers work as teaching assistants, youth workers and on children's projects. There are about 30 places a year. This volunteering opportunity is only open to young people in the London boroughs. There are monthly briefings and seminars before you go.

Timing & Length of Placements: Placements last from three to 12 months and depart all year-round. Apply nine months in advance.

Destinations: Bangladesh, Barbados, Botswana, Ghana, Grenada, India, Jamaica, Namibia, Nepal, St Lucia, St Vincent and Zimbabwe.

Costs: A three-month placement costs from £2000 and 12 months from £5000. The Daneford Trust will work closely with you to get this money – they are supported by many charitable trusts who will help you financially. The Daneford Trust believes that commitment is more important than the money. These costs include everything, even international flights and pocket money.

Eligibility: Restricted to residents of the London boroughs aged 18 to 30. Multicultural applications encouraged.

Experiment in International Living (EIL)
287 Worcester Rd, Malvern, Worcestershire WR14 1AB
☎ 0800 018 4015/01684 562577
fax 01684 562212
info@eiluk.org
www.eiluk.org
EIL is a registered charity and specialises in bringing people from different parts of the world together. Many programs involve homestays for all or part of the projects. This is so a volunteer gets a much better understanding of the culture that they are visiting. EIL programs include: English language teaching, working with street children, bush clearance and recreating national parks, and working in community centres with disabled people. On some programs you might learn the language for one month before you start volunteering.

Volunteers travel alone but can join teams of international volunteers. EIL is the largest sending organisation in the UK for the EVS program. You can apply through them if you're based in England or Scotland.

Timing & Length of Placements: A minimum placement is six weeks and the maximum one year. Some programs have specific departure times and others are flexible (check the website for details). Applications are needed eight weeks in advance.

Destinations: Africa, Asia and 12 countries in Latin America.

Costs: A six-week placement in Thailand costs £555 for a familiarisation week and five weeks of volunteering. This includes accommodation and food. International flights and all other in-country costs are extra. Three months in Argentina costs from £1166. If you require help towards funding for an EIL project then you can apply to the EIL Trust (TEIL).

Eligibility: Applicants must be 18 and over. A willingness to work in a team and get involved with the local community is important. A knowledge of languages is an asset, especially Spanish if you're going to that part of the world. If you're on the EVS scheme then you need to be aged between 18 and 25.

Global Vision International (GVI)

Amwell Farmhouse, Nomansland, Wheathampstead, Hertfordshire AL4 8EJ

☎ 0870 608 8898

fax 01582 834002

info@gvi.co.uk

www.gvi.co.uk

GVI offers conservation expeditions and volunteer community programs in 20 countries worldwide. Projects include: wildlife research in South Africa and Costa Rica, marine conservation in Mexico and the Seychelles, and teaching English in Nepal and Guatemala. GVI provides bi-monthly volunteer workshops to give prospective volunteers an idea of what they will be doing, plus full training upon arrival at the host project.

Timing & Length of Placements: Participate for as little as two weeks or commit to up to two years. There are departures throughout the year. Apply at least one month in advance.

Destinations: Twenty countries including Namibia, Ecuador, Honduras, Panama and Sri Lanka.

Costs: A four-week volunteer placement costs from £695 and includes everything apart from international flights and insurance. A 10-week diving conservation expedition costs from £2395 including everything but flights and insurance.

Eligibility: Anyone from 18 to 65 is welcome to apply. No experience needed.

Marlborough Brandt Group (MBG)

Upper Office, the Dutch Barn, Elmtree Park, Manton, Marlborough, Wiltshire SN8 1PS

☎ 01672 861116

fax 01672 861211

info@mbg.org

www.mbg.org

Named after the Brandt Commission Report advocating support for the developing world, MBG runs an aid and education project in the Gambia. Younger volunteers leave in groups of four to stay with local families and work as teaching assistants in secondary schools. Postgrads with skills can find a placement according to their expertise. Volunteers should apply in writing and they will receive an information pack.

Timing & Length of Placements: Placements are for three months but some skilled volunteers can stay longer. Most volunteers depart March but you can go out at other times. Apply six months in advance.

Destination: Gunjur in the Gambia.

Costs: A three-month placement costs £1500, which covers your training, airfare, insurance and living expenses. Advice and help can be given to help fundraise.

Eligibility: Applicants must be 18 or over.

MondoChallenge

Galliford Bldg, Gayton Rd, Milton Malsor, Northampton NN7 3AB

☎ 01604 858225

fax 01604 859323

info@mondochallenge.org

www.mondochallenge.org

MondoChallenge sends volunteers to work on educational and business development projects in the developing world. There are also opportunities to get involved with environmental projects and healthcare projects (HIV/AIDS). You might teach English in the Himalayan foothills, provide support to HIV/AIDS sufferers in Tanzania or bee-keep in the Gambia. Two to three volunteers normally work on a project and training days are run at the UK office prior to departure. There are managers in each country and they give an induction to all volunteers and offer support throughout the placement. There's also the 'MondoCombo', which means you can combine two projects in different countries or continents.

Timing & Length of Placements: Stays are normally from two to six months. You can travel out at any time of the year and there's no deadline for applications.
Destinations: Bolivia, Chile, Ecuador, Gambia, India, Kenya, Nepal, Sri Lanka and Tanzania.
Costs: Volunteers pay £900 for three months, which does not include international flights, accommodation or food. MondoChallenge arranges board and lodging with local families at approximately £15 to £20 per week. Part of this fee is channelled into local development work.
Eligibility: Minimum age is 18 but MondoChallenge appeals to the older gapper.

Student Partnerships Worldwide (SPW)

17 Dean's Yard, London SW1P 3PB
☎ 020 7222 0138
fax 020 7233 0008
spwuk@gn.apc.org
www.spw.org
SPW is an international development charity. SPW offers the chance to work with African and Asian volunteers in rural communities, developing young peoples' life skills and changing attitudes to health and environmental issues. There are two programs: health education and a community resource program (environment issues). For instance, you could be running HIV/AIDS workshops in South Africa, setting up sustainable organic farming initiatives in Uganda or working with a green club in Nepal. Volunteers from the UK are paired with a volunteer from the host country. There are information days every two months in London – see the website for details.
Timing & Length of Placements: Volunteers leave every September and January. The assignments are from four to nine months, depending on the country and program. Apply two months in advance.
Destinations: India, Nepal, South Africa, Tanzania, Uganda and Zambia.
Costs: Fees range from £3000 to £3500, regardless of how long you spend volunteering. This fee covers all your costs including your international airfare.
Eligibility: Applicants should be aged 18 to 28 and open to living in a different culture.

Tanzed

80 Edleston Rd, Crewe, Cheshire CW2 7HD
☎ 01270 509994
enquiries@tanzed.org
www.tanzed.org

Tanzed is a registered charity. It recruits voluntary teachers to work alongside Tanzanian primary school teachers in the Morogoro region of Tanzania. You'll live in pairs within a village. There may be electricity but certainly no running water – although you'll be within reach of a well. After you're interviewed there's a short induction in the UK and a two-week induction on arrival. There's a UK coordinator, a Tanzanian coordinator and a Tanzed UK trustee in-country.
Timing & Length of Placements: You need to commit to a 12-month period, which can be extended by agreement. Departures are in January and September. Applications should be made six months in advance.
Destination: Tanzania.
Costs: A donation of £2000 is required. This covers international flights, insurance, training, accommodation and all other living expenses. Any travel you do during the academic school holidays is extra.
Eligibility: Applicants must be postgrads aged 21 to 60 plus with either a TEFL or Professional Graduate Certificate in Education (PGCE) certificate.

Task Brasil Trust

PO Box 4901, London SE16 3PP
☎ 020 7735 5545
fax 020 7735 5675
info@taskbrasil.org.uk
www.taskbrasil.org.uk
Task Brasil works with the street children of Río de Janeiro, where it runs a shelter and several outreach projects. Volunteers are encouraged to use all of their skills to help out with teaching, cooking, cleaning and generally caring for the children. Task Brasil is hoping to accommodate 10 children on an organic farm in the country (this is called Epsom College Farm, after Epsom College in the UK who fundraises for it) to take children out of the harsh urban environment and teach them agricultural skills. Volunteers can spend alternating weeks in the city and the farm or choose to remain on just one project. Epsom College Farm also runs ecotours three times a year (see the website for more details).
Timing & Length of Placements: Placements run from one month to one year. You can join Task Brasil year-round but do need to apply three months in advance.
Destinations: Río de Janeiro and the surrounding countryside (the farm is 90km from Río).
Costs: A one month placement costs £800 and 12 months from £2500. This includes international flights, basic accommodation, food and airport transfers.
Eligibility: Applicants must be 21 plus.

Tema Theatre Company

A1 Value Office, 225-229 Church St, Blackpool, Lancashire
FY1 3PB
☎ 01253 299988
clare@tematema.com
www.tematema.com
Tema is a small theatre company offering the chance to teach
drama in Ghana. You have your own small class of children
around 10 years old. It is hoped that in your final week they
will perform a small show that you have all devised together
in front of the local community. You might want to perform
yourself too. Accommodation is provided in a residential
house in Sakumono, which is within walking distance of the
schools. A vehicle is available for volunteers at weekends
and in the evenings. At any one time there are six volunteers
living in the house and working in the village schools.
Timing & Length of Placements: All placements are
for four weeks, departing every six weeks year-round.
Apply giving six weeks notice.
Destinations: Sakumono in Ghana.
Costs: A four-week placement is £695 and this covers accommodation, orientation, airport pick-ups and drop-offs.
Eligibility: Minimum age 16. You don't need to have
qualifications or experience in drama, but you do need to
have an interest in the theatre.

Volunteer Africa

PO Box 24, Bakewell, Derbyshire DE45 1YP
support@volunteerafrica.org
www.volunteerafrica.org
Volunteer Africa is a registered charity. Volunteers work
with local people in Tanzania to build community resources
such as schools or health centres, which is '...hard work
and hard living but fun'. You could be breaking rocks,
bricklaying, painting, sanding or undertaking any number
of practical, hands-on duties. Volunteers live together in
groups of between four and 12 in camp conditions. There's
full pre-departure and overseas support. Anyone interested
is asked to contact Volunteer Africa through the online
application form or via email. After the placement, many
volunteers head off on safari in the Serengeti.
Timing & Length of Placements: There are placements for four, seven or 10 weeks departing between May
and November. Ideally you should apply six months in
advance, particularly if you need help fundraising.
Destination: Singida Region, Tanzania.
Costs: The four-week program costs from £950, seven
weeks from £1330 and 10 weeks costs from £1710. This

includes everything but your international flights, insurance
and kit.
Eligibility: For anyone over 18.

Charities, NGOs & Sending Agencies

Africatrust Networks

Africatrust Chambers, PO Box 551, Portsmouth PO5 1ZN
☎ 01873 812453
info@africatrust.gi
www.africatrust.gi
This loose partnership of NGOs in Africa working closely
with its UK sister organisation called Africa Bridge Club
(www.africabridgeclub.org) provides scholarship funding for
young African students. ATNs offers topical work experience,
particularly relevant if you're looking to a career in Oxfam,
British Council, UN etc. Volunteers work with disadvantaged
young people in African rural and urban communities.
Teams of six to 12 travel out and work together.
Timing & Length of Placements: There are three
and/or six month placements. Departures are in September
and January. The earliest you can apply is 18 months ahead
of departure.
Destinations: Cameroon, Ghana and Morocco.
Costs: Volunteers are invited to raise donations of £500
for a three-month placement and £750 for longer. All other
costs (around £2000/3000 for air travel, food, accommodation, in-country induction course and tours of the country)
are picked up by the volunteers, as set out on the online
application form. ATN assists with raising these funds and
knows the best sources to approach.
Eligibility: Minimum age is 18, but life experience needed.

AidCamps International

5 Simone Court, Dartmouth Rd, London SE26 4RP
☎ 020 8291 6181
info@aidcamps.org
www.aidcamps.org
AidCamps International is a charity founded by overseas
volunteers and run on a voluntary basis. No-one who works
at Aid Camps receives any financial incentive and there
are no expensive offices to run. In addition, its website is
fantastic and everything you could possibly need to know
is on there. ACI runs short-term voluntary work for groups
of between 10 and 20 volunteers. Most projects involve the
financing and building of schools.
Timing & Length of Placements: Projects run for two

or three weeks and depart at set times – these are posted on the website when they become available. Apply by post giving as much notice as you can.

Destinations: Cameroon, India, Nepal and Sri Lanka.

Costs: A two-week placement costs £500 and three weeks £600. This includes all accommodation, food (while working), ground transport, and some organised excursions. Your international flights, travel insurance, visa costs, food (when not at the project base), and pocket money is extra. Fifty percent of your participation fee goes on implementing the aid project.

Eligibility: For those aged 18 and over. No skills/experience needed.

L'Arche

10 Briggate, Silsden, Keighley, W Yorkshire BD20 9JT

☎ 01535 656186

fax 01535 656426

info@larche.org.uk

www.larche.org.uk

L'Arche is an international network of 130 residential communities for adults with learning disabilities. Volunteers are needed at its overseas communities (and in the UK) to live with the residents and share their lives. You'll be asked to accompany residents to college, to assisted workplaces or therapeutic workshops. L'Arche in the UK does not arrange international placements but will handle inquiries and can provide a list of international L'Arche contacts.

Timing & Length of Placements: Volunteers are asked to devote at least a year and there are no set departure dates – volunteers are needed all the time. Apply giving three months' notice if possible.

Destinations: Australia, Canada, Europe, New Zealand and the USA.

Costs: There's no fee from L'Arche. In general, you'll have your own room and earn some pocket money but have to cover all other costs (such as international flights etc).

Eligibility: Assistants must be at least 18.

ATD Fourth World

48 Addington Square, London SE5 7LB

☎ 020 7703 3231

fax 020 7252 4276

atd@atd-uk.org

www.atd-uk.org

ATD sends volunteers to support human rights and alleviate extreme poverty around the world. It asks for a high level of commitment both in terms of training and time spent abroad. Assignments are drawn up according to interests and

skills but you could be working in policy development, family support or working with young people. You need to train for at least three months in the UK before going abroad.

Timing & Length of Placements: One to two years are spent abroad. International volunteers depart in September as long as you've completed the three months in the UK. Apply giving at least one month's notice.

Destinations: 25 countries on five continents.

Costs: Accommodation is provided in the UK for the three months training and a stipend is paid at the end of the second month. International volunteers receive £220 per month for their first year and £345 for all subsequent years. International flights, and accommodation is provided by ATD but you need to pick up all other costs.

Eligibility: Volunteers must be 18 and over.

Batemans Trust

Stocks Lane Farm, Steventon, Abingdon, Oxon OX13 6SS

☎ /fax 01235 832077

info@batemanstrust.org

www.batemanstrust.org

The Batemans Trust was set up to help educate Anglo-Indian children and descendants of former Anglo-Indian marriages over several generations. This substantial community continues to be socially disadvantaged and the families suffer many problems including poverty. Volunteers who can teach English or extra-curricular activities such as music, drama and art are sent out to help. Trained medical staff such as nurses are also needed. There is constant in-country support and all placements are at St George's School and Orphanage.

Timing & Length of Placements: Commitment is needed for at least one of the school terms, which run June to September, October to December and January to April. Apply giving six months' notice.

Destinations: Chennai (Madras).

Costs: Volunteers need to cover their own flights and insurance and either raise £500 or pay a weekly charge for their food and lodging.

Eligibility: For postgrads aged over 23 with TEFL, PGCE or medical/nursing training.

British-Romanian Connections

PO Box 86, Birkenhead, CH41 8FU

☎ /fax 0151 512 3355

brc@pascu-tulbure.freeserve.co.uk

BRC is a charity registered in Romania. Each term one or two volunteers are sent to teach English at a children's

English club in the town of Pitra-Neamt. Charity staff work at the school and there's in-country support.

Timing & Length of Placements: Volunteers are expected to stay at least three months, which is the length of a school term. However, you can stay for more terms. Terms start mid-September, early January and Mid-April. You need to apply at least two months in advance.

Destination: Pitra-Neamt in northeast Romania.

Costs: Volunteers need to cover their airfare but accommodation and food is provided.

Eligibility: School leavers, students and postgrads welcome.

Casa Alianza UK

Unit 2, the Business Exchange, Rockingham Rd, Kettering, Northamptonshire NN16 8JX

☎ 01536 526447

fax 01536 526448

casalnza@gn.apc.org

www.casa-alianza.co.uk

Casa Alianza provides care and support for Central American street children. If you work directly with the children, you could be organising activities, doing sports or helping to teach English at the group homes. Obviously, this work is challenging and often emotionally difficult. However, there is a head office in San José and you could volunteer to work there on administration tasks. There are also administrative jobs at the group homes. The charity picks applicants who can demonstrate a serious and mature commitment.

Timing & Length of Placements: Volunteers must commit for a minimum of six months upwards. Volunteers are needed all year-round.

Destinations: Guatemala, Honduras, Mexico and Nicaragua.

Costs: There's no fixed fee but you'll need to be self-funding. The coordinator at Casa Alianza's head office will help you find accommodation – this might be with a family, hotels, hostels or flats.

Eligibility: For university students and postgrads with a high level of dedication. You must speak fluent Spanish.

Casa Guatemala

☎ 0151 606 0729

pete_rachel@lineone.net

www.casa-guatemala.org

Volunteers are needed to help out in a large orphanage teaching and caring for the children. Other types of work may include working on the orphanage farm or at Hotel Backpackers, which raises income for the children. For an information pack or to volunteer, contact Pete or Rachel, two ex-volunteers who live in England.

Timing & Length of Placements: If you want to work with the children then you need to stay for three months, but you can volunteer indefinitely. You can work at the hotel for as little as one week and what is really needed on the farm is an agronomist willing to work for one year (do you know any?). Placements are ongoing and no great notice is needed.

Destination: Rio Dulce, Guatemala.

Costs: Volunteers need to pay £97 regardless of how long they volunteer for. Accommodation and food (mostly rice and beans) is provided but you have to cover all other costs such as international flights etc.

Eligibility: Applicants must be over 18.

Challenges Worldwide (CW)

13 Hamilton Place, Edinburgh EH3 5BA

☎ /fax 0131 332 7372

Helen@challengesworldwide.com

www.challengesworldwide.com

CW is a registered charity that matches skilled individual volunteers with local host organisations in four countries. For instance, you might be an engineer doing consultancy work for the Belize government, a marketing graduate working with an environmental charity in Ecuador or a teacher working on vocational training with students in Antigua. Volunteers usually live with host families.

Timing & Length of Placements: There are year-round opportunities for placements of three to six months. You need to apply at least three months in advance.

Destinations: Antigua, Bangladesh, Belize and Ecuador.

Costs: From £1950 for three months, which includes help with preparation and training, food, accommodation, insurance and airport transfers. Post-placement advice and support is also included in the cost. International flights are extra.

Eligibility: Minimum age of 18.

Children on the Edge

60 East St, Chichester, W Sussex PO19 1HL

☎ 01243 538530, 0845 458 1656

fax 01243 538532, 0845 458 1657

office@childrenontheedge.org

www.childrenontheedge.org

Children on the Edge works with orphaned and vulnerable children around the world. Volunteers are needed to be part of play schemes for these children. Volunteers go out in groups of 10 to 15 people. Play schemes vary each year, depending on needs, so contact the office for further details.

Timing & Length of Placements: Placements last from two to six weeks. There are set departure dates, which vary each year (contact the office for up-to-date information). Apply six months in advance.
Destinations: East Timor and Romania, subject to change.
Costs: From £1200 all inclusive, regardless of whether you're going for two or six weeks.
Eligibility: Applicants must be 18 or over. Experience of working with children an advantage.

Concordia
2nd fl, Heversham House, 20–22 Boundary Rd, Hove, E Sussex BN3 4ET
☎ 01273 422218
fax 01273 421182
info@concordia-iye.org.uk
www.concordia-iye.org.uk
Concordia is a not-for-profit charity committed to international youth exchange. The international volunteer program offers the opportunity to join international teams working on a community-based project. Project types include conservation, renovation, archaeology, construction, youth work, special needs, arts and culture.
Timing & Length of Placements: Two to four weeks throughout the year but most placements are between June and September. Concordia does not stipulate a minimum notice period for applications.
Destinations: Over 60 different countries worldwide.
Costs: There's a registration fee of £80 to £125. Volunteers need to pay all their travel costs, but accommodation and food is provided.
Eligibility: Anyone aged 16 to 30 can apply.

Cuba Solidarity Campaign (CSC)
Red Rose Club, 129 Seven Sisters Rd, London N7 7QG
☎ 020 7263 6452
fax 020 7561 0191
office@cuba-solidarity.org.uk
www.cuba-solidarity.org.uk
CSC organises volunteers for the International Work Brigade camps near Havana. British contingents (or 'Brigadistas', as they are called) work alongside Cubans and groups from other countries. Volunteers carry out light agricultural work (such as picking oranges on a local cooperative farm) or construction work. There is a full program of activities including visits to factories, hospitals, trade unions, schools and educational or political events. A preparation weekend takes place two months before you leave.

Timing & Length of Placements: These camps run for three weeks and are organised twice a year in summer and winter. Apply four months in advance.
Destination: Cuba.
Costs: The cost of the trip will be around £900, which includes flights, accommodation and food.
Eligibility: There are no age limits.

Development in Action (DiA); formerly Student Action India; SAI
c/o Voluntary Services Unit, University College London, 25 Gordon St, London WC1H 0AY
☎ 07813 395957
info@developmentinaction.org
www.developmentinaction.org
DiA runs volunteer placements in social development. Volunteers are involved in both formal and non-formal education, working with street children or children with disabilities, environmental projects, women's credit unions, fundraising, and the day-to-day running and administration of local Indian NGOs.
Timing & Length of Placements: A two-month summer program runs from July to August and a five-month winter placement from September to February. Apply in January for the summer program and in April for the winter one, although there is some flexibility.
Destinations: Bangalore, Delhi, Indore, Mumbai and Pondicherry.
Costs: Two months cost from £550 and five months from £1000, including training in the UK, an orientation course in India and accommodation while on placement. The price excludes flights, food and insurance. Budget for roughly £70 to £100 per month living expenses.
Eligibility: Applicants must be 18 plus. Volunteers should try to demonstrate an awareness of development and an interest in India, although first-time visitors are welcome.

Ecologia Trust
The Park, Forres, Moray, Scotland IV36 3TZ
☎ /fax 01309 690995
all@ecologia.org.uk
www.ecologia.org.uk
Ecologia sends volunteers on gap years to Kitezh (Russia), an ecovillage where orphaned children are cared for. You'll live with a Russian family, teach English and help with the pioneering play therapy.
Timing & Length of Placements: Volunteers can go for two to 12 months year-round, but August and New Year

are popular times. You'll need to apply a minimum of two months in advance so that visas can be arranged.
Destinations: Kitezh (300km south of Moscow).
Costs: Volunteers pay £710 for two months, which covers accommodation, food, visa support and Moscow transfers. International flights are extra.
Eligibility: Applicants must be 16 or over.

Habitat for Humanity
11 Parsons St, Banbury OX16 5LW
☎ 01295 220188
fax 01295 264230
globalvillage@hfhgb.org
www.habitatforhumanity.org.uk
HFH is an international house-building charity. Each year teams of 10 to 15 volunteers travel overseas to help build simple, decent houses alongside local people in desperate need of shelter.
Timing & Length of Placements: Each trip lasts for two weeks and there are 10 departure dates throughout the year. This is a popular option so try to apply at least six months in advance.
Destinations: Africa, Asia/Pacific, Europe and South America.
Costs: The cost depends on where you are going but the minimum price is £700 for two weeks in Portugal, which includes international flights, accommodation, food, in-country transport, insurance, first-aid provision and activities. On top of that you need to commit to raise a minimum sponsorship of £300. The most expensive trip (to New Zealand) is £1500 (all inclusive), plus the £300 sponsorship minimum.
Eligibility: Volunteers must be 18 and upwards.

Hands Around the World
PO Box 25, Coleford, Glocestershire GL16 7YL
☎ /fax 01594 560223
info@handsaroundtheworld.org.uk
www.handsaroundtheworld.org.uk
Hands Around the World is a registered charity that sends UK-based short-term volunteers to work in developing countries. Skilled volunteers are needed to train local professionals working in hospitals, clinics and community centres. You could, for instance, be a physiotherapist, an accountant or a maintenance engineer.
Timing & Length of Placements: Projects last from three to six months and volunteers are needed all year-round. Apply at least three months in advance.
Destinations: Africa.

Costs: You are asked to give a £200 commitment fee and to raise £1500. HATW then meets your other expenses including accommodation, food, insurance and international flights.
Eligibility: Minimum age is 25 with two years of post-qualification experience. You need to be UK-based.

HiPACT
PO Box 770, York House, Empire Way, Wembley, Middlesex HA9 0RP
☎ 020 8900 1221
fax 020 8900 0330
hipact@hipact.ac.uk
www.hipact.ac.uk
HiPACT is an association of British universities working to develop educational resources in the UK and abroad. Each year it sends volunteers to work in Nigeria. Volunteering ranges from peer tutoring in village schools, running a basic computer training course or organising a summer school. Volunteers usually go out as a group and training is given before departure in the UK in the form of a summer school.
Timing & Length of Placements: You can volunteer for between four and six weeks but sometimes you can extend your stay. Most departures take place in July. Apply six months in advance.
Destination: Various states in Nigeria.
Costs: There's no fee but you'll have to pay for your international flights, visas and all other travel costs. Sometimes you'll be asked to contribute towards food and accommodation.
Eligibility: You must be an undergrad or a postgrad.

India Development Group (IDG)
Navigator House, 60 High St, Hampton Wick, Surrey KT1 4DB
☎ 020 8973 3773
fax 020 8973 3993
indiadevelopment@btconnect.com
www.idguk.org
IDG works for the revitalisation of village communities in rural India, through the dissemination of appropriate knowledge in the context of community development projects. Volunteers who can contribute to this process – whether in the field of shelter, water, village democracy, entrepreneurship etc – are welcome to apply. IDG's work is based on the teaching of EF Schumacher (author of *Small Is Beautiful*) and there is in-country support from Schumacher Centre in Delhi.
Timing & Length of Placements: Placements are from one month to six months, depending on the area in which the volunteer can contribute. Placements run all year-round. There's no set deadline for applications.

Destination: India.
Costs: Volunteers pay for travel and living costs. Half-board lodging will be found for you at around £8 a day.
Eligibility: For those aged over 21. Any applicant needs to understand the responsibilities and expectations arising from their involvement. Only those willing to commit to high standards of personal conduct and the values of Schumacher need apply.

International Voluntary Service (IVS)

Old Hall, East Bergholt, Colchester CO7 6TQ
☎ 01206 298215
fax 01206 299043
ivs@ivsgbsouth.demon.co.uk
www.ivs-gb.org.uk

IVS is a registered charity. It sends volunteers to short-term work camps, which assist conservation, inner-city children, orphanages, community arts and people with disabilities. You'll be joining teams made up of six to 20 volunteers from around the world. Volunteers live and work on the project. There are over 700 placements to choose from every year. There are a small number of EVS projects each year.
Timing & Length of Placements: Placements are for two to four weeks but you can join a couple of different work camps back-to-back. A booklet comes out on 1 April detailing all the summer month opportunities. Ninety percent of the projects run from the June to September period, but there other projects that run all year-round. Give as much notice as possible.
Destinations: Mainly Eastern, central and Western Europe.
Costs: The registration/membership fee is £120, food and accommodation provided. Volunteers cover their own travel costs.
Eligibility: Volunteers need to be at least 18.

Karen Hilltribes Trust

Midgley House, Heslington, York YO10 5DX
☎ 01904 411891
fax 01904 430580
penelope@karenhilltribes.org.uk
www.karenhilltribes.org.uk

The work of this trust helps the Karen Hilltribes to develop their own social, educational and economic infrastructure. KHT sends pairs of volunteers to live in the Karen villages and to teach English at primary and secondary level. Help is also needed to install a water system. There is a Karen Hilltribes manager (he's a local) who personally vets all the families. Training is given before you depart.

Timing & Length of Placements: It is preferred that you commit for between six to 12 months. You can go all year-round but the best period is from October to March because of the climate. Apply three to six months in advance, but you can sometimes be lucky at short notice.
Destination: Northwest Thailand.
Costs: There's a fee of £1500 for a six-month placement (shorter periods are negotiable). This fee goes towards the work of the charity. You need to raise a further £1500 to cover all your costs such as international flights, visas, accommodation, food and pocket money. You will live with a host family.
Eligibility: For anyone aged 18 and over but graduates preferred. Dedication to the work of the charity is important. You'll also need to make the effort to learn both the Thai and Karen languages while you're there.

Kibbutz Reps

16 Accommodation Rd, London NW11 8EP
☎ 020 8458 9235
fax 020 8455 7930
inquiry@kibbutz.org.uk

This is the official representative of the Kibbutz movement in the UK. Register with them and they'll arrange your volunteering placement in Israel.
Timing & Length of Placements: It's recommended that you apply at least two weeks in advance, but last-minute arrangements are sometimes possible. Volunteers are asked to make a minimum two-month commitment and can stay for up to eight months.
Destinations: Israel.
Costs: The fee is roughly £410 including administration, insurance and the return flight to Israel. Accommodation, food and laundry is provided on the kibbutzim. Spending money of approximately £50 per month is paid to volunteers.
Eligibility: For those aged 18 to 40 in good health and willing to work hard.

Muirs Tours

Nepal House, 97a Swansea Rd, Reading, Berkshire RG1 8HA
☎ 0118 950 2281
info@nkf-mt.org.uk
www.nkf-mt.org.uk

Muirs Tours is a UK-based non-profit tour operator that specialises in sustainable travel. It also arranges five main volunteer projects: working with Tibetan communities in northern India; tourism development in Tanzania; teaching English in Peru; teaching English in Thailand; and helping repatriate wild horses in Mongolia. Local partner support and training is given while abroad.

Timing & Length of Placements: Placements start from one month upwards (there's no maximum limit). The exception is Mongolia where three weeks is the minimum and six months the maximum. There are departure dates all year-round except for the Mongolian project, which only operates between March and October. Apply giving two months' notice.

Destinations: India, Peru, Thailand, Mongolia and Tanzania.

Costs: There's a registration fee of £120 and volunteers have to pick up all other costs. However, board and lodging is arranged by Muirs Tours and will cost about £5 to £7 per day. The exception is Mongolia where there's an approximate £900 cost on top of the registration fee, which covers all in-country facilities (ie accommodation, food, use of domesticated horses and some transport). This is for a three-week placement.

Eligibility: Minimum age 18, fluent in English, physically fit and ideally possessing some specialist skills.

Muyal Liang Trust

53 Blenheim Crescent, London W11 2EG
☎ 020 7229 4774
jjulesstewart@aol.com
Volunteers are needed to teach English at a school in Sikkim (India) run by the trust. Four to five teachers are needed from March to December (the local school year). It's best to register your interest by email then you'll receive a fact sheet explaining the project in detail.

Timing & Length of Placements: You need to commit to two months and volunteers are needed at anytime during the school year. Apply two months in advance.

Destination: India.

Costs: No fee required and full board and lodging is given. All other costs are borne by the volunteer.

Eligibility: For those aged 18 and above, but older postgrad volunteers preferred. A school leaver would need to demonstrate enough maturity.

Nepal Kingdom Foundation

Nepal House, 97a Swansea Rd, Reading, Berkshire RG1 8HA
☎ 0118 950 2281
info@nkf-mt.org.uk
www.nkf-mt.org.uk
The Nepal Kingdom Foundation is a UK-registered charity and the trustees are the owners of Muirs Tours, a UK-based non-profit tour operator. The foundation sends about 320 volunteers a year to Nepal. They are needed to teach

English, to take part in projects to equip local people to help themselves (eg the sale of carpets and craftwork) and there are also projects involving the building of schools and health centres. Some projects are also of a specialised nature such as the provision of water supplies. Some projects are group-based and some are just for individuals. Training and in-country support is provided by resident staff in Nepal.

Timing & Length of Placements: Placements start from one month; there's no maximum length of time. Many volunteers go between October and December and March and May, although you can go at other times. Apply giving two months' notice.

Destination: Four or five different areas in Nepal.

Costs: There's a registration fee of £120 and volunteers have to pick up all other costs. Board and lodging is arranged by the foundation and will cost about £5 to £7 per day.

Eligibility: For those aged 18 and over.

Nicaragua Solidarity Campaign (NSC)

129 Seven Sisters Rd, London N7 7QG
☎ 020 7272 9619
fax 020 7272 5476
nsc@nicaraguasc.org.uk
www.nicaraguasc.org.uk
NSC operates short trips to help Fair Trade agricultural co-operatives grow and harvest coffee, sesame oil and vegetables. If a volunteer wants to stay longer than the usual three weeks, NSC will help provide a 'tailor-made' placement for several months. Volunteers live with host families.

Timing & Length of Placements: Trips are usually for three weeks. For departure dates and deadlines, contact NSC as this varies from year to year.

Destination: Nicaragua.

Costs: The approximate cost is £1000, which covers everything except spending money.

Eligibility: For those aged 18 and over.

Outreach International

Bartlett's Farm, Hayes Rd, Compton Dundon, Somerset TA11 6PF
☎ /fax 01458 274957
info@outreachinternational.co.uk
www.outreachinternational.co.uk
Outreach International specialises in sending committed volunteers to small grass roots projects overseas. Most of the programs involve conservation, education, social and humanitarian issues.

Timing & Length of Placements: Projects are for three to six months. Departures are in January, April, July and September. You should apply at least three months before, although last-minute applications can still fill any empty places.

Destinations: Cambodia, Ecuador and Mexico.

Costs: Placements cost £3250 for three months plus £400 for each additional month, including flights, full insurance, local travel, food, accommodation, in-country support, language training, weekend trips (and free Lonely Planet guides!).

Eligibility: Minimum age 18, average age is 18 to 25, but some projects are suitable for older volunteers.

Rokpa UK Overseas Projects

Kagyu Samye Ling, Eskdalemuir, Langholm, Dumfriesshire DG13 0QL

☎ 01387 373232 Extension 3

fax 01387 373223

charity@rokpauk.org

www.rokpauk.org

'Rokpa' means 'to help' or 'to serve' in Tibetan. This is a worldwide humanitarian charity that helps communities in need. It is non-political and run almost entirely by volunteers. The majority of activities focus on providing education and training, though health and training in healthcare are also important. There are two main volunteer programs: you could work in a Nepalese soup kitchen for the destitute in Kathmandu or teach English in Tibet.

Timing & Length of Placements: If you want to work in Nepal you could volunteer for any period of time between mid-December and mid-March (ie when the soup kitchen is open). If you want to teach it is for a minimum of six months, usually from March. Apply six months ahead.

Destinations: Nepal and Tibet.

Costs: Both schemes require total self-funding. In Tibet food and accommodation are provided but in Nepal volunteers are asked to find local lodging.

Eligibility: Rokpa prefer you to be aged 20 or over to work in Nepal and 25 or over to work in Tibet teaching. Plus, if you're teaching, you need a TEFL qualification and experience.

Rural Centre for Human Interests (RUCHI)

Bandh, Bhaguri 173233, Solan district, Himachal Pradesh, India

☎ 00 91 1792 82454

fax 00 911792 82516

totem_volunteer_India@yahoo.com

www.ruchin.org

RUCHI is a grass roots organisation working in villages in the colourful foothills of the Himalayas. RUCHI's Totem Volunteer Program gives volunteers a real experience of Indian village life. You can choose to work in social development, environmental management or on improving water facilities. There is space for 20 volunteers at any one time.

Timing & Length of Placements: You can travel out year-round. Volunteers usually come for three weeks but it's possible to stay longer by arrangement with the charity. Only six weeks notice is required.

Destination: India.

Costs: Volunteers pay £600, which covers transfers, food, board and program costs for three weeks. Flights are extra.

Eligibility: For those aged 18 plus.

Save the Earth Network

PO Box CT 3635, Cantonments, Accra, Ghana

☎ /fax 00 233 21-667791

ebensten@yahoo.com

This is an organisation dedicated to promoting environmental preservation, sustainable development, international cultural exchange, solidarity and friendship through voluntary work placements and host family homestays in Ghana. Volunteers help teach children English or maths, care for orphans or abandoned children, educate people about AIDS, help with reforestation or work in healthcare clinics and hospitals. You work four days per week.

Timing & Length of Placements: Placements are from one week to four months. You can join year-round. At least two months' notice is required to arrange a placement.

Destination: Ghana.

Costs: Prices start at £320 for one to four weeks. A 12-week stay costs £1020. Prices include accommodation and food.

Eligibility: Applicants must be 18 plus.

Sudan Volunteer Programme (SVP)

34 Estelle Rd, London NW3 2JY

☎ 020 7485 8619

davidsvp@blueyonder.co.uk

www.svp-uk.com

SVP is a registered charity, largely run by Sudanese expats. SVP recruits 20 to 30 native English speakers a year as teachers of the language, preferably with a TEFL qualification. Most teaching takes place in universities or cultural centres. You can go out as an individual or as a small group. There's on-site training and orientation given by local staff. During recess, volunteers often travel back with Sudanese students to their villages. The people of

Sudan are very welcoming and hospitable, volunteers only teach in the safest of areas.

Timing & Length of Placements: SVP likes people to volunteer for at least six months. If you specialise in a certain area you can go for a shorter period of time. Volunteers mainly leave in September, January and July. Apply giving at least one month's notice.

Destination: Northern Sudan.

Costs: There's a £5 application fee and you need to pay £60 for insurance. Otherwise you pay all other costs except accommodation, which is provided. You are also paid a monthly stipend equivalent to £54.

Eligibility: For undergraduates upwards.

Trade Aid

Burgate Court, Burgate, Fordingbridge, Hants SP6 1LX
☎ 01425 657774
fax 01425 656684
info@tradeaiduk.org
www.tradeaiduk.org

The Trade Aid project is based in Mikindani, Tanzania. In February and September each year Trade Aid takes four gap-year students to work in the community. Each group is set a specific project that necessitates special research and training before leaving the UK. In 2004, for instance, one group established a school's resource centre in the village.

Timing & Length of Placements: Placements are for 22 weeks, leaving twice a year in February and September. You should apply at least six months in advance.

Destination: Tanzania.

Costs: There's no placement fee but food and lodging are provided. Volunteers need to pay for all travel (international and in-country), insurance and medical costs. A small local wage is paid each week.

Eligibility: Those aged 17 to 20 can apply for gap-year placements but older professionals are also taken.

2WayDevelopment

PO Box 51413, London N17 8WW
☎ /fax 020 8801 9541
Volunteer@2way.org.uk:
www.2way.org.uk

2WayDevelopment is an independent organisation specialising in creating unique voluntary placements in a variety of development NGOs and grass roots charities overseas. You could, for instance, be in Mexico working on a community health project, in India working in wildlife research or in Malawi working in a hospital. You could also work in development media (ie helping to establish a newspaper) in Africa, India or South America. Volunteers most travel out on their own but can become part of a local social network of volunteers and expats. All volunteers receive a handbook guiding them through the whole pre-departure and arrival process. In-country support is provided by the host organisation.

Timing & Length of Placements: All placements are for between three and 24 months and are on-going. Apply at least four months in advance.

Destinations: Africa, Asia and the Pacific, India, Latin America and the Middle East.

Costs: Regardless of the placement length, the costs are between £695 and £795. This includes all the literature, a personal consultation, arrangement of placement, greeting at airport and in-country accommodation. Food and international flights are extra.

Eligibility: Minimum age is 21, a formal education or previous experience in a sector of work is required.

UNA Exchange

Temple of Peace and Health, Cathays Park, Cardiff CF10 3AP
☎ 029 2022 3088
fax 029 2022 2540
info@unaexchange.org
www.unaexchange.org

UNA Exchange is a registered charity. It works with a network of not-for-profit local community organisations worldwide. These partners contact UNA Exchange with specific volunteering projects. These could be environmental or social projects such as monitoring turtle populations in Mexico or providing activities in a Romanian orphanage. Some projects require an orientation weekend. UNA is also a sending agency for the EVS scheme (see p277 for details). Apply through them if you live in Wales.

Timing & Length of Placements: Projects are from two weeks to 12 months throughout the year. There's no real notice period for your application.

Destinations: Over 50 countries worldwide.

Costs: There's a registration fee of £130 for non-members (£110 for members). This fee includes all board and lodging during your project regardless of how long it lasts. Some projects will require an additional fee. Unless you're on the EVS scheme, you need to cover your own travel costs.

Eligibility: There are projects from two weeks to six months for all ages. Projects lasting six to 12 months are for 18- to 25-year-olds through the EVS scheme.

VAE Volunteer Teachers Kenya

Bell Lane Cottage, Pudleston, Nr Leominster, Herefordshire HR6 0RE

☎ 01568 750329

fax 01568 750636

harris@vaekenya.co.uk

www.vaekenya.co.uk

A gap-year teaching program designed to assist poor primary and secondary schools in the central highlands area of Kenya, overlooking the Great Rift Valley. Volunteers are sent in pairs and live with the Kenyan people in a rural setting where houses have no water or electricity. On average 20 volunteers are sent out each year, but demand for help is huge so there is some flexibility on numbers.

Timing & Length of Placements: Volunteers have the option of either a three- or six-month placement. Departure is usually in January. Apply at least one month in advance.

Destination: Kenya.

Costs: A fee of £3300 includes flights, insurance and accommodation. Volunteers earn a small local salary. Part of the cost pays for local support staff and a program for street kids.

Eligibility: Most volunteers are school or university leavers.

Village Education Project (Kilimanjaro)

Mint Cottage, Prospect Rd, Sevenoaks, Kent TN13 3UA

☎ 01732 459799

info@kiliproject.org

www.kiliproject.org

VEP is a charity dedicated to improving education in the Kili-majaro region of Tanzania. Each year 10 volunteers go out to teach in village primary schools 1500m up the slopes of Mt Kilimanjaro. You teach English to the children and organise extra-curricular activities such as football, netball, music, drama etc. You also accompany pupils on school outings to national parks and the Indian Ocean. Volunteers live in rented accommodation in one village. In-country support is provided by UK and local staff members. There's a two-week pre-departure training course in Sevenoaks in November.

Timing & Length of Placements: Teaching assignments last eight months and a group departure takes place in January. Apply by October.

Destination: Mshiri village on the slopes of Mt Kiliman-jaro, Tanzania.

Costs: From £2250 including flights and accommodation. Your food and all other costs are excluded.

Eligibility: For those aged 18 and over.

Voluntary Service Overseas (VSO)

317 Putney Bridge Rd, London SW15 2PN

☎ 020 8780 7500

fax 020 8780 7652

enquiry@vso.org.uk

www.vso.org.uk

See the VSO section (p277) for detailed information.

Timing & Length of Placements: The YfD program lasts for 10 to 12 months with departures in August, September and October. The WY program runs for six months starting in the spring and summer. Apply at least 10 months in advance for the former and four months in advance for the latter. VSO's main placement programs usually run for two years, all year-round. Apply giving between four to nine months' notice.

Destinations: VSO works in over 40 countries worldwide. On the YfD program you could be sent anywhere. The WY program runs in Ghana, India, Nigeria, Sri Lanka and South Africa.

Costs: You'll need to raise at least £700 for the YfD program and at least £600 for the WY program. VSO will then cover your other costs. If you participate in VSO's main volunteer program then all your costs are paid, including a small monthly stipend and a small resettlement grant upon return to the UK.

Eligibility: Both youth programs are open to anyone aged 17 to 25. VSO's main volunteer program is open to anyone aged 20 to 75.

Volunthai

1739 Soi Mookmontree 13, Korat 30000, Thailand

☎ 00 66 999 50881

volunthai@yahoo.com

www.volunthai.com

This grass roots teaching project in northeast Thailand is ideal for people who are already planning to travel to Thailand. Volunteers teach English to rural students for three to four hours a day and stay with local families.

Timing & Length of Placements: Placements last one to three months throughout the year. Apply at least two months in advance.

Destinations: Korat, Thailand.

Costs: There is no cost for volunteering and meals and homestay accommodation is provided with local families, but volunteers must make their own transport arrangements to Korat and cover their expenses on days off.

Eligibility: For those aged 20 to 28. Must have a good grasp of English, but formal teaching qualifications are not required.

Winant Clayton Volunteer Association (WCVA)

St Margaret's House, 21 Old Ford Rd, Bethnal Green, London E2 9PL

☎ 020 8983 3834

wcva@dircon.co.uk

www.winantclayton.com

For more than 50 years this charity has placed British volunteers in social projects such as working with the homeless, inner-city children, HIV sufferers and the elderly. There are about 12 to 15 places each year. You have two weeks of independent travel at the end of your placement.

Timing & Length of Placements: Placements are for two months from late June to August. Applications should be in by the end of January.

Destination: Most projects are in New York, USA.

Costs: There's a £15 registration fee. WCVA arranges group flights and visas but you need to pay for them. Your accommodation is provided and there's a stipend for food, essential transport and pocket money. There are limited bursaries available for Irish passport holders and for applicants living and/or working in the east end of London.

Eligibility: For British and Irish passport holders aged 18 and over.

Youth Action for Peace (YAP)

8 Golden Ridge, Freshwater, Isle of Wight PO40 9LE

☎ 08701 657927

fax 01983 756900

action@yap-uk.org

www.yap-uk.org

YAP-UK is part of an international movement promoting human rights, sustainable development and youth exchanges. It has information on hundreds of projects and work camps looking for short-term volunteers. You'll be sent out to work with a team of international volunteers on any number of projects. You might build schools and clinics, refurbish community facilities, construct footpaths, assist social, cultural or arts projects or undertake archaeological or ecological work.

Timing & Length of Placements: Most camps last two to three weeks but it's possible to do a series of camps for up to a year. There's no deadline but most of the camps take place in summer. It's best to join in March when the website is updated with all the latest project programs worldwide.

Destinations: Africa, Europe, Latin America, Southeast Asia, Turkey and the USA.

Costs: There's a registration fee of £110 per project. This includes accommodation and food but you must pay all

other costs. There are additional preparation and hosting fees in developing countries.

Eligibility: Applicants must be 18 or over.

Religious Organisations

Africa Inland Mission (AIM)

Halifax Place, Nottingham NG1 1QN

☎ 0115 983 8131

fax 0115 941 7338

synergy@aimeurope.net

www.aimeurope.net

AIM is an interdenominational evangelical mission agency working in many locations across Africa. You can volunteer as part of a team, individually or in pairs. Placements include teaching in local schools, teaching missionaries' children, youth work, sports and music.

Timing & Length of Placements: The summer program lasts for six weeks departing July and August. Other placements range from three to 12 months departing September and January. If you wish to depart in January you need to have applied by 1 September; departures in September need to be applied for by 1 February.

Destinations: Chad, Kenya, Lesotho, Madagascar, Mozambique, South Africa, Tanzania and Uganda.

Costs: Summer volunteers need to raise £1500 (six weeks), which covers all your costs, including international airfare. Three- to 12-month placements range from £1500 to £5000, all inclusive.

Eligibility: You need to be at least 18 and a committed Christian.

Assumption Lay Volunteer Programme (ALVP)

23 Kensington Sq, London W8 5HN

☎ 020 7361 4752

fax 020 7361 4757

cburns@rayouth.freeserve.co.uk

www.alvp.org.uk

ALVP is for individuals willing to take up the challenge of living and working in a culture that is very different from their own. ALVP is for those whose faith calls them to share in the lives of the poor, the young and the marginalised. Volunteers are mostly involved in education in its broadest sense, ranging from teaching in the class room to working with street children to pastoral based activities.

Timing & Length of Placements: All placements are for a minimum of one year. Departures are in September.

You need to apply at least six months in advance to join the part-time training course.

Destinations: Mexico, Philippines, Rwanda, Thailand and the USA. You can volunteer in the UK too.

Costs: Volunteers are asked to raise £700 covering the training program, return flights, insurance and living expenses and a small resettlement grant upon return. The balance for the full cost is covered by the organisation.

Eligibility: Professional skills aren't essential but a willingness to do anything is important. You must be aged 22 to 40.

BMS World Mission

PO Box 49, 129 Broadway, Didcot, Oxfordshire OX11 8XA
☎ 01235 517700
fax 01235 517601
shortterm@bmsworldmission.org
www.bmsworldmission.org

This Christian mission organisation works in partnership with Baptist churches and other organisations in around 40 countries around the world. Its gap-year program is called 'BMS Action Teams' and is in three phases: a month of training in the UK during September; six months volunteering alongside mission staff or a local partner organisation overseas; then back to the UK for a two-month tour of Baptist churches, talking about the overseas experience and encouraging other people to get involved. Volunteers work in teams of four and are matched to an overseas placement according to their skills and experience. Overseas projects may involve street children, teaching English, evangelism, music, drama, youth and children's work.

Timing & Length of Placements: The program lasts for 10 months from early September to late June. You need to apply by the end of February.

Destinations: The UK, with a six-month placement in a different country each year. Countries may include: Bangladesh, Brazil, India, Italy, Malta, Sri Lanka, Thailand, Trinidad and Uganda.

Costs: The whole gap-year program (10 months) costs from £3400 per person. This includes just about everything except vaccinations, minor medical costs and personal spending money.

Eligibility: You must be aged 18 to 25 and have a living and active Christian faith – but you don't have to be a Baptist.

Christian Aid

PO Box 100, London, SE1 7RT
☎ 020 7960 2703
fax 020 7620 0719

gapyear@christian-aid.org
www.christian-aid.org/gapyear

Each year 12 people volunteer 10 months of their time and energy to Christian Aid's gap-year scheme. You join one of 40 teams in the UK and get people fired up about poverty and injustice through events, workshops, worship and campaigns. Previous volunteers have worked in Christian Aid offices in Glasgow, Leeds, Bangor, Belfast or Southampton. You then get first-hand experience of what Christian Aid's work is all about by going overseas for two weeks to visit some of the organisations Christian Aid works with. Internship programs are also available in the international department and the schools and youth Team. Internship posts are advertised in the jobs pages of the website when they arise.

Timing & Length of Placements: Placements run for 10 months from September to June. You can apply anytime but interviews are from March to July.

Destinations: Based in one of Christian Aid's area offices in the UK and Ireland with a two-week trip to visit Christian Aid partner organisations overseas.

Costs: Volunteers are asked to raise £1800. Christian Aid covers food, accommodation and the overseas trip, as well as £28 per week spending money.

Eligibility: Open to those aged 18 to 25 from the UK and Ireland. Non-denominational, but practising Christians are preferred because much work takes place in church groups.

Christians Abroad

237 Bon Marché Centre, 241–251 Ferndale Rd, London SW9 8BJ
☎ 0870 770 7990
fax 0870 770 7991
recruitment@cabroad.org.uk
www.cabroad.org.uk

Christians Abroad recruits for volunteer and paid posts on behalf of church projects in the developing world. Most opportunities are in education, health and social care but not all need professional qualifications. For instance, you could be nursing in the Cameroon, working in an AIDS hospice in South Africa or helping out at a rural school in Nigeria. Applicants need to show a connection to a UK church but denomination is not relevant. All volunteers need to attend an interview, show they can adapt to possible isolation and cross-cultural living, and attend a briefing and debriefing session. Volunteering vacancies, medical electives, short- and long term professional possibilities are all listed on the website.

Timing & Length of Placements: Placements last from two months to over one year. Placements arise year-round. Applicants normally give three months' notice.
Destinations: Mostly in Africa: Cameroon, Kenya, Nigeria, South Africa and Tanzania.
Costs: There's a £150 administration fee. Volunteers then need to meet all their other costs, although Christians Abroad can arrange travel and health insurance. Some opportunities (ie those working with children) will require criminal records bureau clearance. Fees do not apply to paid posts.
Eligibility: Applicants must be aged 18 and over.

Church Mission Society
157 Waterloo Rd, London SE1 8UU
☎ 020 7928 8681
fax 020 7401 3215
info@cms-uk.org
www.cms-uk.org
The Church Mission Society is a voluntary society within the Church of England. It welcomes Christian volunteers of all denominations. The 'Make A Difference', 'Encounter', and the 'Praxis' programs operate around the world in cross-cultural missions. You could be working alongside local people helping in refugee centres, schools, hospitals and rural development work.
Timing & Length of Placements: The 'Make a Difference' program runs for six to 18 months and there are set departure dates (see the website for details). The 'Encounter' program is for three to four weeks between July and September. The 'Praxis' program is two to three weeks throughout the year. Apply giving at least two months' notice.
Destinations: 21 different countries in Africa, Asia and Eastern Europe.
Costs: All placements are self-funding and there is fundraising advice. A year-long placement will cost around £3000 all included.
Eligibility: Applicants must be aged 18 to 30 unless you're on the 'Make a Difference' program and going to Africa or Asia, in which case you need to be aged 21 to 30.

Experience Exchange Programme (EEP)
USPG/Methodist church, 157 Waterloo Rd, London SE1 8XG
☎ 020 7928 8681
fax 020 7928 2371
habibn@uspg.org.uk
www.uspg.org.uk
EEP is self-funding volunteering program that enables residents of Britain and Ireland to volunteer abroad. EEP

is jointly run by the United Society for the Propagation of the Gospel (USPG) and the Methodist Church. It provides opportunities for volunteers to work on social projects alongside local people. There are no set programs, but EEP will find a placement matching your requirements in terms of what you want to do, when you want to go, where you want to go and for how long. Twelve-day training programs take place in July and December.
Timing & Length of Placements: Placements are for six to 12 months. Placement start dates are flexible. Apply at least three months in advance.
Destinations: All over the world.
Costs: Volunteers need to raise around £1800 (depending on your destination) to cover living expenses and health insurance. EEP offers a grant to help with international airfares.
Eligibility: Applicants must be at least 18.

Jesuit Volunteer Community (JVC)
23 New Mount St, Manchester M4 4DE
☎ 0161 832 6888
fax 0161 832 6958
staff@jvc.u-net.com
www.jesuitvolunteers-uk.org
JVC mainly runs a gap-year scheme in the UK but it also places individuals within sister projects in Europe. Volunteers live in communal houses and work on inner-city projects following four guiding principles: spirituality, simple living, social justice and community. You will be working with people who are marginalised within European countries. For instance, in Germany you could be working with refugees and the homeless or in Slovakia with people who have physical or learning disabilities.
Timing & Length of Placements: You need to apply by the end of April in order to qualify for the scheme, which takes place from September to July. Contact JVC to find out the European application deadline.
Destinations: France, Germany, Ireland, Poland and Slovakia.
Costs: The in-country programs will cover accommodation and basic living costs. You need to pay for international flights, in-country travel etc.
Eligibility: Applicants must be aged 18 to 35. You must be fluent in the language of the country where you are going.

Latin Link
175 Tower Bridge Rd, London SE1 2AB
☎ 020 7939 9000
fax 020 7939 9015

step.uk@latinlink.org
www.stepteams.org
Latin Link is a Christian organisation that sends teams
of young people called step teams out to Latin America.
They work on social projects such as building community
resources, helping with street children or working in soup
kitchens. The step teams often work alongside a Latin
American church. Volunteers work in a non-denominational
Christian ethos. Volunteers work in teams of between 10
and 12 people.
Timing & Length of Placements: Spring programs last
four months and leave mid-March. Summer programs are
for seven weeks and leave mid-July. These can be taken
back-to-back. Application deadlines are November for the
spring teams and April for the summer teams.
Destinations: Argentina, Brazil, Bolivia, Cuba, Ecuador,
Peru and Spain.
Costs: Fees start from £2450 for the spring program,
which includes all your costs except pocket money. The
summer program is £1850. Spending money is usually
estimated at around £400 or more.
Eligibility: For those aged 17 and over. Most volunteers
are 18 to 30 years old.

Oasis Trust

The Oasis Centre, 115 Southwark Bridge Rd, London SE1 0AX
☎ 020 7450 9000
fax 020 7450 9001
enquiries@aoasistrust.org
www.oasistrust.org
Oasis Trust is a Christian charity. Oasis runs several different
programs for volunteers to work in 'social action' around
the world, helping to provide shelter, food and education
for the vulnerable and socially excluded. For instance, you
could be building a school, working with street children,
teaching English or working on farming projects. A team
of four or five people travel out and work together. There's
training in the UK before you leave and a debrief when you
return. There's good in-country support.
Timing & Length of Placements: Placements range
from one month to 12 months. Most volunteers go on the
global action teams scheme which lasts for six to seven
months. There are two departure dates for the global action
teams – September and March. Most other placements
depart in September. There's also a round the world team,
which departs September and lasts for eleven months. Volunteers work in Australia, India and Zimbabwe. Applications
need to be sent in at least three months in advance.

Destinations: 24 countries on five continents.
Costs: If you're part of a global action team the cost will
be from £3500 all inclusive for six to seven months. A
round-the-world team placement is from £5600 inclusive
of all costs (11 months). Taking additional spending money
is recommended.
Eligibility: For those aged 18 or over. Anyone younger
can apply for under a month's work.

Time for God (TFG)

Chester House, Pages Lane, Muswell Hill, London N10 1PR
☎ 020 8883 1504
fax 020 8365 2471
recruit@timeforgod.org
www.timeforgod.org
TFG is about enabling people to grow through full-time
volunteering both internationally and nationally. The
core activity is a program for young adults who are sent
abroad to work in people-based community projects. For
instance, you could be taking care of the elderly, working
with adults who have learning difficulties or special needs,
working in activity centres or working in rehabilitation
centres (substance abuse or alcoholism).
Timing & Length of Placements: You can volunteer
for between 10 and 12 months. There are two start dates:
September and January. Applications should be in at least
two months beforehand.
Destinations: Africa, America, Australia, Europe and
New Zealand.
Costs: Volunteers need to raise approximately £1500 to
£2000 depending on the destination. This covers accommodation, food and pocket money. International flights are
extra. Contact the office for help and advice on fundraising.
Eligibility: Applicants must be aged 18 to 25.

Toybox Charity

PO Box 660, Amersham, Buckinghamshire HP6 5YT
☎ 01494 432591
fax 01494 432593
info@toybox.org
www.toybox.org
Toybox is a small charity that offers four to six places each
year working with street children in Guatemala. Volunteers
work in pairs with local Guatemalan teams. They work
on the streets, in the day-centre, in a hostel, in children's
homes and also with families at high risk. There's a week's
training in the UK before you go and a month's Spanish
training before you start.

Timing & Length of Placements: There are two gap programs. The 12 month scheme runs from September to August and the nine-month program from January to August. Apply giving three months' notice.

Destination: Guatemala City.

Costs: You need to raise £3000 for a year's placement, which covers all your costs, including international flights.

Eligibility: For those aged 18.

Transform (Tearfund)

100 Church Rd, Teddington, Middlesex TW11 8QE
☎ 020 8943 7777
fax 020 8943 3594
transform@tearfund.org
www.tearfund.org/transform

Tearfund is a Christian charity working for relief and development among the world's poor. Transform is the short-term missions program for this charity. There are approximately 200 places for volunteers to work with children in areas such as AIDS, disability and teaching English. Otherwise there are practical placements such as painting, decorating and building a school, health centre or orphanage. Work is with Christian partners and volunteers are expected to be committed Christians. Training and orientation in the UK is provided.

Timing & Length of Placements: Most placements are in the summer and teams volunteer for between four and six weeks. Apply in January for the summer program, which departs July. There are also placements lasting four months, which depart in March. Apply by September for these.

Destinations: Destinations can change every year but include Africa, Asia, Central Asia, Latin America and Mexico. (See the website for details.)

Costs: The summer program costs between £1400 and £1700. This includes everything. The four-month placements cost between £2600 and £2900 all-inclusive. Spending money is extra.

Eligibility: For those aged 18 plus.

World Exchange

St Colm's International House, 23 Inverleith Terrace, Edinburgh EH3 5NS
☎ 0131 315 4444
fax 0131 315 2222
we@stcolms.org
www.worldexchange.org.uk

World Exchange is an ecumenical development education organisation. It offers educational opportunities for volunteers to work in schools, community projects, administration and health care. Volunteers live and work alongside the local community, adapting their skills and experience to what is required. Gap-year volunteers can stay for six months and have full support from a host and the UK office. Recruits are sent abroad in pairs.

Timing & Length of Placements: Projects normally last from six to 12 months but shorter visits will be arranged if requested. Most departures are in August with a second set of departures in January.

Destinations: Cuba, India, Kiribati, Malawi and Pakistan.

Costs: A six-month placement costs around £2000. It's around £3000 for the full year. This includes international travel, insurance, accommodation, food and a modest living allowance.

Eligibility: You need to be a British citizen aged 17 to 75.

World Vision UK

World Vision House, Opal Drive, Fox Milne, Milton Keynes MK15 0ZR
☎ 01908 841000
fax 01908 841025
studentchallenge@worldvision.org.uk
www.worldvision.org.uk

World Vision is a relief and development charity working in over 100 countries worldwide. The student challenge program puts small teams (between six and 10) of highly motivated Christians to work in one of World Vision's long-term development programs for the summer. World Vision works with poor communities for up to 15 years at a time. Volunteers help out in these communities and the work varies from year to year depending on what needs to be done. You could, for instance, help out in a local school, help out with local healthcare, construct schools or bridges. World Vision staff live in the communities full-time so the in-country support is excellent. There are orientation and debriefing sessions before and after your placement.

Timing & Length of Placements: Applications must be received by 20 February. Interviews take place in March/April. Placements last from four to six weeks during July and August – this varies slightly from year to year.

Destinations: Varies from year to year but could be countries such as Armenia, Ghana and Zambia.

Costs: The summer placements cost in the region of £900 to £1500, which includes flights, food, in-country transport and accommodation. Visas and vaccinations are extra.

Eligibility: For supporters of the Christian faith aged 18 to 30.

Conservation & Scientific Programs Abroad

African Conservation Experience
PO Box 206, Faversham, Kent ME13 8WZ
☎ /fax 0870 241 5816
info@conservationafrica.net
www.conservationafrica.net
Offers conservation placements in game and nature reserves in southern Africa. These are ideally suited to anyone interested in botany, biology, environmental sciences and veterinary science, especially school leavers and students considering a career in conservation and the environment. Postgrads are able to carry out specific field research.
Timing & Length of Placements: Placements are available all year and usually last from one to three months. You need to apply three to four months in advance.
Destinations: Southern Africa.
Costs: From £2700 for four weeks to £3900 for 12 weeks, including international flights, in-country transfers, accommodation, food and all project-related costs.
Eligibility: Anyone with an enthusiasm for conservation. Minimum age 18.

African Conservation Trust
PO Box 310, Linkhills, South Africa 3652
☎ /fax 00 27-31-2016180
info@projectafrica.com
www.projectafrica.com
The African Conservation Trust provides a way for conservation projects to become self-funding through the active participation of volunteers. Projects that need volunteers vary each year. From 2003 to 2005 African Conservation Trust worked on a rock art mapping project in KwaZulu-Natal (South Africa) and in 2005 on a bushmen community game farm project in the Kalahari Desert (Botswana).
Timing & Length of Placements: Placements range from two weeks to three months and are on-going. Apply three months in advance, but short notice can usually be accommodated.
Destinations: Botswana and South Africa.
Costs: There's a fee of £450 per month with a £50 once-off payment for airport pick-up and drop-off. This fee includes accommodation, food, training and in-country travel. All other costs are extra.
Eligibility: No skills are needed as training is given, but you do need to be fit and healthy and aged 18 or above.

Archaeology Abroad
31–34 Gordon Square, London WC1H 0PY
☎ /fax 020 8537 0849
arch.abroad@ucl.ac.uk
www.britarch.ac.uk/archabroad
This is an organisation based at University College London. It provides information about excavation opportunities both for experienced and inexperienced diggers. It has a twice-yearly (April and November) magazine called *Archaeology Abroad* where around 1000 archaeological opportunities are listed. Most excavations need volunteers for a minimum of two weeks and most digs take place in the summer or early autumn. Basic accommodation and food is normally provided, but volunteers pick up all other costs. Fieldwork awards are available to help subscribers with their excavation expenses.

Atlantic Whale Foundation
59 St Martins Lane, London WC2N 4JS
☎ /fax 0116 2404566
edb@whalenation.org
www.whalefoundation.org.uk
The Atlantic Whale Foundation has collaborated with Tenerife's whale-watching industry for 10 years with the objective of establishing the industry as a global example of best practice. There are programs in education, research, conservation and ecotourism. Volunteers can participate in each of these areas. For instance, you might carry out research on tour boats or run children's workshops on the boats. Otherwise, you could be help organise the European Festival of the Whale, which takes place each July and August.
Timing & Length of Placements: You can stay as long as you wish but there's a minimum of two weeks. You can volunteer year-round. There are limited places so apply as soon as possible.
Destinations: Tenerife (Canary Islands).
Costs: Two weeks costs from £150 to £350 per week, depending on the program. If you're staying six weeks the cost is from £68 to £175 per week. Your fees fund the cost of the projects and also include basic half-board accommodation and training.
Eligibility: For those aged 16 and over.

Azafady
Studio 7, 1a Beethoven St, London W10 4LG
☎ 020 8960 6629
fax 020 8962 0126
mark@azafady.org
www.azafady.org

'Azafady' is a Malagasy word meaning 'please'. This registered charity sends volunteers to help with grass roots conservation and sustainable development in Madagascar. You could help protect lemurs and turtles, set up income-generating schemes for the villagers or build wells in local villages. There's permanent in-country support and cultural visits are arranged at the weekends.

Timing & Length of Placements: Assignments last for 10 weeks and start in January, April, July and October. Apply giving at least one month's notice.

Destination: Southeast corner of Madagascar.

Costs: The fee is £2000, excluding flights, vaccinations and visa.

Eligibility: For those aged 18 and over.

Biosphere Expeditions

Sprat's Water, Nr Carlton Colville, Broads National Park, Suffolk NR33 8BP

☎ 01502 583085

fax 01502 587414

info@biosphere-expeditions.org

www.biosphere-expeditions.org

Biosphere Expeditions is a not-for-profit organisation specialising in wildlife conservation. It emphasises the genuinely scientific nature of its expeditions and discourages any impression that they are 'tours'. The programs are not specifically aimed at gap-year students, but school leavers and post-university graduates are welcome to join. Expeditions in 2005 and 2006 include researching the movements of snow leopards, cheetahs, monkeys, macaws, elephants, whales, dolphins, chamois wolves and bears.

Timing & Length of Placements: Places go very fast so apply at least eight months in advance. Expeditions range from two weeks to three months.

Destinations: Altai Republic (Central Asia), the Azores, Honduras, Namibia, Oman, Peru, Slovakia and Sri Lanka.

Costs: Two weeks start from £990 including everything but flights. Three months will cost from £3500 all-inclusive, but flights are extra.

Eligibility: Open to all.

Blue Ventures

52 Avenue Rd, London N6 5DR

☎ 020 8341 9819

fax 020 8341 4821

enquiries@blueventures.org

www.blueventures.org

Blue Ventures is a not-for-profit organisation dedicated to facilitating projects that enhance global marine conservation and research. Volunteers work alongside teams of marine scientists and local communities whose livelihoods depend on marine ecosystems. As a volunteer you could carry out underwater ecological research on coral reefs, teach marine environmental awareness in local schools, or study the sustainability of coral reef fisheries within local communities. There's three to four weeks of extensive and intensive training on site in scuba-diving and marine science. You need to show real commitment to the conservation aims of the project. Blue Ventures runs one of the remotest dive operations in Africa and the Indian Ocean.

Timing & Length of Placements: Placements last from six weeks upwards (there's no maximum time limit). Groups of up to 12 volunteers depart every six weeks throughout the year. Apply giving six weeks notice.

Destinations: Madagascar.

Costs: A qualified diver will pay from £1580 for six weeks, this includes everything except international flights and insurance. It costs an extra £200 for a beginner diver. There's a scholarship program (one per expedition) for those without the financial resources.

Eligibility: Minimum age 18, enthusiasm, competent swimmer, commitment to the project.

BTCV International Conservation Holidays

Conservation Centre, 163 Balby Rd, Doncaster, South Yorkshire DN4 0RH

☎ 01302 572244

fax 01302 310167

information@btcv.org.uk

www.btcv.org

This not-for-profit organisation offers working holidays on conservation projects. Among the many options, you can help monitor sea turtle populations in Thailand, maintain trails in the Grand Canyon or carry out research at national parks in South Africa. Normally you join groups of up to 15 holiday-makers.

Timing & Length of Placements: Most holidays last from two to eight weeks and run all year-round. Book two months in advance.

Destinations: Worldwide but many holidays take place in Europe.

Costs: The price of these holidays depends on where you go and what you're doing. For instance, for £800 you could spend eight weeks in Thailand (excluding flights but

including everything else) or £575 for two weeks in Japan (all-inclusive except flights).
Eligibility: Minimum age 18.

Conservation Volunteers Australia
c/o The Work and Travel Company, 45 High St, Tunbridge Wells, Kent TN1 1XL
☎ 01892 516164
fax 01892 523172
info@worktravelcompany.co.uk
www.worktravelcompany.co.uk
Conservation Volunteers Australia offers you the opportunity to contribute in a practical way to the conservation of the Australian environment. Projects include tree planting; erosion and salinity control; seed collection; construction and maintenance of walking tracks; endangered flora and fauna surveys and monitoring; weed control; habitat restoration; and heritage restoration. A visitor's visa for Australia is appropriate because you are regarded as simply being on holiday and covering all your own costs. You'll be joining a team of six to 10 other volunteers. The agent for Conservation Volunteers Australia in the UK is The Work and Travel Company.
Timing & Length of Placements: There are two-, four- and six-week programs, but extensions are possible. There are volunteering opportunities all year-round and you can start any Friday.
Destination: Australia.
Costs: Two weeks costs from £299 and four weeks from £499 (including meals, travel insurance, accommodation, project-related transport, Conservation Volunteers Australia membership and T-shirt!). You'll need to arrange your own international flights and you can do this through The Work and Travel Company.
Eligibility: For anyone aged 15 to 70.

Coral Cay Conservation (CCC)
The Tower, 13th fl, 125 High St, London SW19 2JG
☎ 0870 750 0668
fax 0870 750 0667
info@coralcay.org
www.coralcay.org
Coral Cay is a not-for-profit organisation that sends international volunteers to survey some of the world's most endangered coral reefs and tropical forests. Volunteers play a crucial role in the conservation of threatened tropical environments through the collection of scientific data. For instance, you could be surveying coral in the pristine waters of the Philippines, recording butterflies in the

Malaysian jungle, or diving with whale sharks in Honduras. You can either travel as a group or individually. Each placement is prefaced by one or two weeks of scientific training.
Timing & Length of Placements: Expeditions range from two weeks to one year. You need to apply three months before an expedition is set to leave. There are monthly start dates throughout the year.
Destinations: Fiji, Honduras, Malaysia and the Philippines.
Costs: A two-week forest expedition starts from £550 and a two-week marine expedition from £700. This includes accommodation, food, full science training and expedition equipment. Everything else, such as international flights, insurance and in-country travel, is extra. There's a handy online calculator to help give you an idea of how much each expedition will cost.
Eligibility: All ages from 16 upwards.

Earthwatch Institute (Europe)
267 Banbury Rd, Oxford OX2 7HT
☎ 01865 318838
fax 01865 311383
info@earthwatch.org.uk
www.earthwatch.org/europe
Earthwatch is an international environmental organisation. It supports more than 140 research expeditions in 50 countries, sending volunteers to work alongside expert scientists. You could be monitoring climate change in the Arctic Circle, investigating the fragile ecosystems of Brazil's Pantanal region, or uncovering the mysterious past on the East Island World Heritage Site. No formal qualifications or experience are required – you will be taught everything you need to know.
Timing & Length of Placements: Placements range from two days to three weeks. There are programs throughout the year. There are no application deadlines.
Destinations: Fifty countries across six continents including Australia, Botswana, Cuba, Iceland, Mongolia, New Zealand and Spain.
Costs: Placements vary from £150 (two days) to £2100 (this is the most expensive project). This includes all the costs of running the project, accommodation, food and transport in the field. International flights etc are extra.
Eligibility: Expeditions are restricted to individuals aged 16 years and over (18 years on some projects). There is no maximum age limit.

Eco Africa Experience
Guardian House, Borough Rd, Godalming, Surrey GU7 2AE
☎ 01483 860560

fax 01483 860391
info@ecoafricaexperience.com
www.ecoafricaexperience.com
Eco Africa is a tour operator who places volunteers on some of South Africa's premier game reserves or leading marine ocean research projects. You may be involved in conservation projects such as anti-poaching patrols, monitoring and counting wildlife, bush rehabilitation and the day-to-day maintenance of the reserve. You can also divide your time by volunteering at different reserves. Some placements include an option to take a field guide training course.
Timing & Length of Placements: Placements range from one to 12 weeks throughout the year. There are departure dates at the beginning of each month. Apply giving one month's notice.
Destinations: Eight different locations in South Africa and sometimes other parts of Southern Africa.
Costs: One week placements cost from £1850 and 12 weeks from £4195 all inclusive (including international flights). Some of your money goes to the Born Free Foundation, The Wilderness Trust and Save The Rhino.
Eligibility: Minimum age 17.

Ecovolunteer

c/o WildWings, 1st fl, 577/579 Fishponds Rd, Bristol BS16 3AF
☎ 0117 965 8333
fax 0117 937 5681
wildinfo@wildwings.co.uk
www.ecovolunteer.org.uk
Ecovolunteer provides holidays working with endangered or mistreated animals and birds worldwide. These are often run by research scientists. You work hands-on to collect information and help out in animal and bird sanctuaries. Some of the choices include working with elephants in Thailand, wolves in Russia, rhinos in Swaziland, river otters in Brazil and vultures in Croatia (if you feel up to it). Ecovolunteer is based in the Netherlands, but bookings are taken through the WildWings travel agency.
Timing & Length of Placements: Volunteering can last from one week to six months. Some places are year-round but others are seasonal – look on the website for full details. Apply several weeks in advance; certain popular programs such working with horses in Mongolia or elephants in Thailand require at least four months' notice.
Destinations: Africa, South America, Asia, North America, Europe.
Costs: A one-week placement in Croatia costs from £95 and a six-month placement in Brazil costs from £3060. This includes

accommodation, food and in-country transport. Some projects do not include food and none include your international flight.
Eligibility: You need to be aged over 18 to participate.

Frontier

50–52 Rivington St, London EC2A 3QP
☎ 020 7613 2422
fax 020 7613 2992
info@frontier.ac.uk
www.frontier.ac.uk
Frontier is a not-for-profit organisation. It offers keen volunteers the opportunity to make an effective contribution to global conservation by working on research projects in remote tropical environments. You could, for instance, dive in the Indian Ocean mapping coral reefs, observe lemurs in Madagascar or work on a forest program in Cambodia. Frontier also offers the opportunity to gain a BTEC Advanced Diploma in Tropical Habitat Conservation during an expedition, equivalent to an A-level. It takes 10 weeks to do this.
Timing & Length of Placements: Trips are for four to eight weeks departing January, April, July and October. Apply two months in advance.
Destinations: Cambodia, Madagascar, Nicaragua and Tanzania.
Costs: A four-week expedition costs from £1400 and eight weeks from £1900. This includes visas, insurance, accommodation, food, training, in-country travel. International flights are extra.
Eligibility: For those aged 17 and over.

Greenforce

11–15 Betterton St, London WC2H 9BP
☎ 0870 770 2646
fax 0870 770 2647
info@greenforce.org
www.greenforce.org
Greenforce is a registered charity. It runs a series of environmental projects around the globe, focusing on wildlife conservation. The work ranges from tracking elephants in Africa or collecting scientific information in the Amazon rainforest (Ecuador) to monitoring species on coral reefs in Borneo. All training is provided, including scuba diving for marine volunteers. Open evenings are held once a month in London and there are pre-departure training days. Teams comprise 16 people. Greenforce staff live and work on location to give support to volunteers.
Timing & Length of Placements: Programs last from four weeks to six months. There are four or five departures

spread throughout the year. Apply six months in advance so that you don't miss out on pre-departure training.

Destinations: Marine expeditions in the Bahamas, Borneo and Fiji. Terrestrial expeditions to Africa, Ecuador and Nepal.

Costs: All expeditions cost £2300 for 10 weeks. Additional weeks cost £150. This includes everything except international flights. Also, there's a £200 charge if you are a beginner diver to train you up to an advanced diving qualification.

Eligibility: For those aged 18 to 70.

Orangutan Foundation

7 Kent Terrace, London NW1 4RP
☎ 020 7724 2912
fax 020 7706 2613
info@orangutan.org.uk
www.orangutan.org.uk

Prompted by the popularity of visits and offers of help, the Orangutan Foundation now runs a program for volunteers to help save this rare Asian ape. Skills are not required because volunteers are not used for research work. Volunteers participate in activities such as clearing trails and maintaining the education centre.

Timing & Length of Placements: Places are very popular so try to apply eight months in advance. Volunteers stay for six weeks and owing to visa restrictions this cannot be extended. Teams of 12 volunteers leave four times a year in May, June, August and October.

Destination: Kalimantan (Borneo).

Costs: The fee of £500 covers all your expenses except international flights and in-country travel.

Eligibility: For anyone aged 18 to 70.

Nautical Archaeology Society (NAS)

Fort Cumberland, Fort Cumberland Rd, Eastney, Portsmouth PO4 9LD
☎ /fax 023 9281 8419
nas@nasportsmouth.org.uk
www.nasportsmouth.org.uk

NAS can provide contacts and information about nautical archaeology at home and abroad. Diving is not essential because some excavations take place on the foreshore or in tidal waters. NAS also provides training courses ranging from diving to IT for archaeology.

Rainforest Concern

27 Landsdowne Crescent, London W11 2NS
☎ 020 7229 2093
fax 020 7221 4094
info@rainforestconcern.org
www.rainforestconcern.org

Rainforest Concern is a non-political charity dedicated to the conservation of vulnerable rainforests and their biodiversity. Rainforest Concern runs two long-term projects. One is called Yachana in the Amazon Basin of Ecuador and teaches the local people to make a living from the land. The second project is called Namuncahue and involves working in a monkey puzzle forest (one of the last such forests in the world) in the Lake District of Chile. Volunteers for these projects are recruited and trained by Quest Overseas (see entry on p292) and are part of their gap-year quest and project quest programs.

Scientific Exploration Society (SES)

Expedition Base, Motcombe, Shaftesbury, Dorset SP7 9PB
☎ 01747 853353
fax 01747 851351
base@ses-explore.org
www.ses-explore.org

SES shares the same ethos as Raleigh: to take up a challenge and build teamwork. Expeditions have a scientific purpose, for example, mapping reefs or conducting an archaeological survey. Volunteers work in teams of around 14 people. Often SES is invited in by host governments and local communities to achieve a specific goal. All teams have an expert related to the project and a doctor.

Timing & Length of Placements: Expeditions leave throughout the year and generally last for three weeks. Applications need to be in at least two to three months before departure so volunteers can attend a briefing weekend six weeks before departure.

Destinations: Bolivia, Botswana, Guyana, India, Madagascar, Tibet and many more.

Costs: A three-week expedition costs approximately £3000 and everything is included (even international flights).

Eligibility: No skills required. Applications welcomed from anyone aged 18 and over. For fit, healthy individuals who are happy working in a team.

Sunseed Desert Technology

SDT, Apdo 9, 04270 Sorbas, Almeria, Spain
☎ 00 34 950 525770
sunseedspain@arrakis.es
www.sunseed.org.uk

Sunseed Desert Technology is a British/Spanish not-for-profit organisation that aims to develop accessible, low-tech methods of living sustainably in a semi-arid environment. Work is done on appropriate technology, renewable energy, organic growing, dryland management, construction and maintenance, education and much more. Volunteers are needed to help and are also welcome to develop their own projects that can be used as part of a course of study or self-development.

Timing & Length of Placements: Volunteers can come for periods of one to two weeks or stay for up to one year. Longer-stay, full-time volunteers can develop their own research project. There are places all year-round but you must book in advance.

Destination: Almeria (Spain).

Costs: Volunteers pay a contribution to cover their room and board. This is anything from £34 to £96 per week, depending on the time of year, your length of stay and any concessions.

Eligibility: There is no age limit but those aged 16 and 17 need their parents' permission.

Do-It-Yourself

TimeBank

3/Downstream Bld, 1 London Bridge SE1 9BG
☎ 0845 456 1668
fax 0845 456 1669
feedback@timebank.org.uk
www.timebank.org.uk
TimeBank is a registered charity set up in 1999 to inspire a new generation of volunteers using media and web technologies to make it as easy as possible to volunteer. It has a web-driven database for anyone looking to volunteer overseas. It lists more than 500 British and indigenous aid and development projects that recruit volunteers. Submit an online profile and the database will match you with suitable placements anywhere in the world. There is no fee.

WorkingAbroad

France: 'La Rasseque', Cuxac Cabardes, France
England: PO Box 454, Flat 1, Brighton, East Sussex BN1 3ZS
☎ /fax 00 33 4 68 26 41 79
info@workingabroad.com
www.workingabroad.com
Set up by two ex-volunteers in 1997, WorkingAbroad is a referral service linking volunteers to small-scale indigenous projects in 150 countries worldwide. For a fee, WorkingAbroad will do a personalised search of volunteering opportunities based on your requirements, as outlined in the application form. Your personalised report will contain a minimum of 20 different organisations who are all looking

for volunteers. You could, for instance, assist scientists in an Indonesian tropical forest, undertake conservation work in Iceland, help protect turtles in the Caribbean or work with street children in Mexico. The fee is £29 for a report to be emailed to you and £36 for it to be sent by post. Personalised reports are produced within two weeks.

World Service Enquiry

237 Bon Marché Centre, 241–251 Ferndale Rd, London SW9 8BJ
☎ 0870 770 3274
fax 0870 770 7991
wse@cabroad.org.uk
www.wse.org.uk
This agency provides guidance for individuals hoping to volunteer abroad. It publishes the annual *Guide to Volunteering and Working Overseas* and a monthly list of vacancies called *Opportunities Abroad*. World Service Enquiry also offers 'One to One', a vocational guidance service for people thinking of a career in international development. The *Guide to Volunteering and Working Overseas* costs £4 for a printed edition (plus an A5 SAE 60p) and £3 to access the PDF file online. The guide for the previous year can be accessed online for free. Subscriptions for *Opportunities Abroad* start from £15. There's a £95 fee for 'One to One', which includes research, a 90-minute interview and a report outlining the best course of action for each individual.

WorldWide Volunteering

☎ 01935 825588
fax 01935 825775
worldvol@worldvol.co.uk
www.wwv.org.uk
Worldwide volunteering has a search and match database to help you find your ideal project either in the UK or worldwide. Over 1000 organisations are listed with over 350,000 projects. Every organisation is contacted every six months to ensure currency of information. It costs £10 to search the online database on three separate occasions during one calendar month.

Volunteering & Conservation in the UK

Millennium Volunteers (MV)

Youth Volunteering Team, Department for Education and Skills, Room E4c, Moorfoot, Sheffield, S1 4PQ
Millennium.volunteers@dfes.gsi.gov.uk
www.mvonline.gov.uk

Millennium Volunteers is a UK-wide initiative to encourage young people to volunteer their time for the benefit of others. Millennium Volunteers allows young people to get involved in an activity that involves issues that they care about, using their interests or hobbies as a starting point. For instance, you could find yourself coaching a local school football team, working at a community radio station or helping to create a garden for local residents. Volunteers who complete 100 or 200 hours of work earn certificates recognising their achievement. Log onto the website, select a location and an area in which you'd like to volunteer and, hey presto, a list of local volunteering opportunities will come up. Volunteers need to be aged between 16 to 24. There is no fee. The scheme is run separately in Scotland (www.mvscotland.org.uk), Wales (www.wcva.org.uk) and Northern Ireland (www.volunteering -ni.org). Contact to be by post or email.

Timebank

3/Downstream Bld, 1 London Bridge SE1 9BG
☎ 0845 456 1668
fax 0845 456 1669
feedback@timebank.org.uk
www.timebank.org.uk
TimeBank is a registered charity and was set up in 1999 to inspire a new generation of volunteers using media and web technologies to make it as easy as possible to volunteer. TimeBank's web-driven directory offers thousands of diverse opportunities to help out in your community. First register your interests and then you will be matched with a local volunteer centre who will give you all the info you need on volunteering in your area. There's no fee.

Volunteering England

Regents Wharf, 8 All Saints St, London N1 9RL
☎ 0845 305 6979
fax 020 7520 8910
volunteering@volunteeringengland.org
www.volunteering.org.uk
Launched on 1 April 2004, Volunteering England is the new national volunteer development agency for England. It maintains a large and well-organised website covering all aspects of volunteering in the UK, including detailed listings of long- and short-term options and organisations that place volunteers abroad. There is no fee. If you are based in Wales, contact Wales Council for Voluntary Action (www.wcva.org. uk), in Northern Ireland contact the Volunteer Development Agency (www.volunteering-ni.org) and for Scotland contact Volunteer Development Scotland (www.vds.org.uk).

Youthnet-UK

3rd fl, 2–3 Upper St, Islington, London N1 0PQ
☎ 020 7226 8008
fax 020 7226 8118
info@do-it.org.uk
www.do-it.org.uk
This youth-orientated organisation has a database of UK volunteering opportunities and pages of links to volunteer opportunities worldwide. It is very easy to use and will give you a range of options and opportunities immediately.

Humanitarian Projects in the UK

Independent Living Alternatives (ILA)

Trafalgar House, Grenville Place, London NW7 3SA
☎ /fax 020 8906 9265
enquiry@ilanet.co.uk
www.ilanet.co.uk
ILA is a non-profit company that promotes independence for people with disabilities. ILA needs full-time volunteers to work as personal assistants providing physical support, such as helping someone get out of bed, get dressed, and do practical things such as cooking, shopping and housework. Personal assistants work on average four days per week and all placements are live-in. This is an ideal gap-year opportunity if you want to live in London, Nottingham or Cumbria. Applicants need two references and a medical reference plus a criminal records check and will attend two interviews, which can be by telephone or online if the applicant is overseas.
Timing & Length of Placements: All placements are for four months. Placements are available year-round; applicants should apply three to four months in advance.
Destinations: Cumbria, London and Nottingham.
Costs: You get free accommodation and an allowance of £63.50 per week for pocket-money, travel expenses and food.
Eligibility: Minimum age 18, no experience necessary as all training is given. A driving licence is useful though not essential. You must have an empathy with the disability movement and with the philosophy of ILA.

Community Service Volunteers (CSV)

5th fl, Scala House, 36 Holloway Circus, Queensway, Birmingham B1 1EQ
☎ 0121 643 7690
fax 0121 643 7582
volunteer@csv.org.uk
www.csv.org.uk

CSV is a registered charity. Its national network challenges young people to volunteer away from home. There are over 600 varied projects to choose from. The emphasis of CSV placements is on social work such as working with the homeless, young offenders and at-risk youth, children with learning disabilities or children in care. CSV runs one of the UK's largest programs, with 2500 full-time volunteers.

Timing & Length of Placements: There are placements for between four and 12 months. You can start anytime. CSV can place you quite quickly on a project but if you can, try to apply giving at least one month's notice.

Destinations: Anywhere within the UK – you will be placed where the need is greatest.

Costs: Accommodation, food and all travel is provided. In addition, there's a weekly allowance of £29.

Eligibility: For anyone aged 16 plus.

Samaritans

The Upper Mill, Kingston Rd, Ewell, Surrey KT17 2AF
☎ 08705 627282
fax 020 8394 8301
volres@samaritans.org
www.samaritans.org

Samaritans offers confidential emotional support 24 hours per day via phone, email and face-to-face in the UK and Ireland. Samaritan's volunteers provide emotional support to people experiencing feelings of distress or despair. Most volunteers commit to at least one four-hour session per week as well as a night shift every six weeks. Eight weeks of full training is provided covering topics such as active listening, communication skills, self-awareness and suicide awareness. Their national Helpline is ☎ 0845 790 9090.

Conservation Programs in the UK

British Trust for Conservation Volunteers (BTCV)

Conservation Centre, 163 Balby Rd, Doncaster DN4 0RH
☎ 01302 572244
fax 0302 310167
information@btcv.org.uk
www.btcv.org.uk

BTCV is the UK's largest practical conservation charity, annually involving 10,000 volunteers in projects to protect and enhance the environment. The organisation offers millennium volunteer placements and volunteer officer posts, which combine leadership training with work experience.

These fall into two categories: practical conservation and marketing and administration. Some volunteer officers can work towards NVQs in environmental management. BTCV doesn't organise international placements but it can put you in touch with sister NGOs such as the Australian Trust for Conservation Volunteers. BTCV also organises conservation holidays both in the UK and abroad, which involve work such as drystone walling, hedging and sand-dune restoration.

Timing & Length of Placements: Volunteer officers are asked to commit to approximately six months or more to justify the cost of training. UK conservation holidays run from two to six weeks.

Destinations: National parks, coasts, urban parks, wildlife parks.

Costs: Volunteer officers don't need to pay anything. Conservation weekends in the UK cost from £40 and weeks start from £80, including instruction, food and accommodation. International holidays start from £275 for two weeks, all-inclusive, except for flights.

Eligibility: Volunteer officers need to be 18 and over. UK conservation holidays are for those aged 16 and above. International holidays are those aged 18 and above.

Centre for Alternative Technology (CAT)

Machynlleth, Powys SY20 9AZ, Wales
☎ 01654 705950
fax 01654 702782
info@cat.org.uk
www.cat.org.uk

CAT is Europe's leading ecocentre, which inspires, informs and enables people to live more sustainably. Key areas of work are renewable energy, environmental building, energy efficiency, organic growing and alternative sewage systems. There are two volunteer schemes. One is for long-term volunteers who come for six months and work in a specific area or department. This could be in biology, building, engineering, gardening, information, media, publications or visitor centre management. The second program is for short-term volunteers who come for a week or two and help with general outdoor, practical work (mostly gardening). The volunteer coordinator is Rick Dance.

Timing & Length of Placements: The short-term program is for one or two weeks and these run during particular weeks in the spring or summer (contact Rick Dance for more information). The long-term six-month placements begin either in spring or autumn. Apply six months in advance.

Destination: Powys (Wales).

Costs: Short-term volunteers pay £5.50 per day for full-board. Long-term volunteers pay £105 per month if they are staying on site and an additional £110 per month for food, laundry, fuel etc. Some long-term volunteers cannot be accommodated on site so there's no fee payable to CAT (although you obviously need to pay rent to someone else).

Eligibility: For those aged 18 and over.

Friends of the Earth (FOE)

26–28 Underwood St, London N1 7JQ
☎ 020 7490 1555
fax 020 7490 0881
info@foe.co.uk
www.foe.co.uk

FOE campaigns for the protection of the environment. There's a national office, regional offices and a network of over 200 local groups, all of which rely on volunteer help. At the London HQ there are roughly 30 volunteers at any time. Contact your local group or go online for an application form. Volunteers might be working with a campaigner, helping out with administration tasks or assisting with research. There are some interesting volunteer case studies on the website.

Timing & Length of Placements: Volunteers can work for as little or as long as they wish and volunteers are needed most of the time.

Destinations: London and regional offices.

Costs: Travel expenses up to £5 per day are paid and there's also a lunch allowance of £4 a day.

Eligibility: Open to anyone.

National Trust (NT)

Rowan, Kembrey Park, Swindon SN2 8YL
☎ 0870 609 5383
fax 01793 496815
volunteers@nationaltrust.org.uk
www.nationaltrust.org.uk

The NT conserves many of Britain's historical buildings and landscapes, from Roman sites to contemporary houses, and industrial architecture, mountains, woodland and coast. There are hundreds of volunteering opportunities. You could help out for a few hours a week as a room guide, assist the gardeners, help with special events or help conserve the countryside (ie creating a wildflower meadow, footpath construction, rare tree planting). There are also full-time volunteering opportunities in conservation or heritage that could help you career-wise. These opportunities include assisting property managers, wardens, gardeners and educational officers. There are also NT working holidays in the UK where you can go away for a week or weekend. On these you might be painting lighthouses, herding goats, planting trees or cleaning beaches – this usually takes place in teams of up to 12 people (☎ 0870 429 2429 for more information).

Timing & Length of Placements: You can volunteer for a few hours a week to six months full-time. Positions are updated constantly on the website and there's no deadline for applications. Working holidays are from a weekend to a week all year-round.

Destinations: England, Northern Ireland and Wales (contact National Trust Scotland for Scottish opportunities).

Costs: The NT will pay agreed out-of-pocket expenses for general volunteering on a part-time basis. Full-time volunteering can also offer on-site accommodation plus out-of-pocket expenses. You might also be eligible for Job Seeker Allowance. Working holidays cost from £60 for a week and from £32 for a weekend, including accommodation and food.

Eligibility: Minimum age 16.

Royal Society for the Protection of Birds (RSPB)

The Lodge, Sandy, Bedfordshire SG19 2DL
☎ 01767 680551
fax 01767 683262
volunteers@rspb.org.uk
www.rspb.org.uk

The RSPB runs a voluntary warden scheme on 39 of its reserves around the UK. There are over 100 places each year. For an application form see the website. As a residential volunteer there are a variety of tasks such as ditch digging, fence mending, nest box maintenance or working with visitors. See the website for the brochure/application form, which details all the locations and gives a snapshot of what you may expect. It is possible that you might be a lone volunteer in a remote location.

Timing & Length of Placements: Volunteers can stay on a reserve from one week to six months, depending on location. Start dates are flexible. Apply four to six weeks beforehand.

Destinations: Around the UK – from the tip of Scotland to the toe of Cornwall (and in Northern Ireland).

Costs: Accommodation is provided free of charge. Training is provided if appropriate. Volunteers need to pick up all other costs.

Eligibility: Volunteers must be aged 16 (18 on some reserves).

Wildlife Trusts

The Kiln, Waterside, Mather Rd, Newark NG24 1WT
☎ 0870 036 7711
fax 0870 036 0101
volunteer@wildlife-trusts.cix.co.uk
www.wildlifetrusts.org

The WT partnership is the UK's leading conservation charity dedicated to all wildlife. There's a network of 47 local wildlife trusts and to volunteer you need to contact your local one (see the website). Volunteers help care for over 2400 reserves from rugged coastline to urban wildlife havens. Volunteers help with a range of projects: you might do some community gardening, species surveying, help in the office or help run wildlife watch groups. The only trust that can accommodate volunteers for residential placements is in the Isles of Scilly.

Timing & Length of Placements: This varies but usually ranges from a couple of days to 12 months. You can volunteer at any time and there's no real notice period.
Destinations: 2400 reserves across the UK.
Costs: This varies from trust to trust but out-of-pocket expenses are normally covered.
Eligibility: Minimum age 18.

Explorers & Expeditions

Brathay Exploration Group

Brathay Hall, Ambleside, Cumbria LA22 0HP
☎ 015394 33942
admin@brathayexploration.org.uk
www.brathayexploration.org.uk

Brathay Exploration Group was set up in 1947. It is a charitable trust. It runs educational and challenging overseas expeditions for young people. Some expeditions focus on fieldwork, others on trekking. One expedition in 2004 went to Belize and worked with a branch of the British Museum in the rainforests. The average size is 15 people. Parts of the Duke of Edinburgh award can be completed on these expeditions.

Timing & Length of Expedition: Expeditions are for one to five weeks, all departing late July to early September. Apply as soon as the programs are advertised on the website.
Destinations: These vary each year but may include the Channel Islands, China, the French Alps, Italy, the Lake District, Morocco, Mull (Scotland), South Africa and Tanzania.
Costs: Expedition costs range from around £300 to £2000, excluding international flights. This includes comprehensive insurance, all accommodation, food, group equipment and in-country travel.
Eligibility: Expeditioners are aged 15 to early 20s.

British Schools Exploring Society (BSES) Expeditions

The Royal Geographical Society, 1 Kensington Gore, London SW7 2AR
☎ 020 7591 3141
fax 020 7591 3140
info@bses.org.uk
www.bses.org.uk

BSES was founded in 1932 by a surviving member of Scott's Antarctic expedition. It aims to provide opportunities for young explorers to join exploratory projects in remote areas of the world. There are four expeditions a year – three summer ones and one gap-year expedition. There are between 20 and 60 places on each expedition, depending on where you are going and what you are doing. Explorers work within groups of 12 on a variety of environmental and research projects. For instance, 2006 expeditions will include projects in the Peruvian Amazon (bat studies, flora and fauna counts etc), the Arctic (glaciological and geological projects) and the High Andes in South America (botanical and ecological projects). All explorers go on a briefing weekend three months prior to departure to learn camp and navigation skills. A qualified doctor accompanies every expedition, there's also a chief mountaineer, chief scientist, base camp manager and two leaders for every group of 12. Regional introduction days are held in London, Bristol, Manchester, Newcastle and Edinburgh throughout the year.

Timing & Length of Expedition: The gap-year expedition is for three months and departure dates vary – check the website for details. The four- to six-week summer expeditions depart mid-July. Apply nine to 12 months in advance.
Destinations: Varies year to year. Traditionally expeditions were to Arctic and sub-Arctic destinations, but over the last 16 years BSES expeditions have expanded to include India, Kenya, Morocco, Papua New Guinea and the Peruvian Amazon.
Costs: A three-month gap-year expedition will cost between £3500 and £4000, depending on destination. The shorter expeditions of four to six weeks cost between £2500 and £3000. This covers all your costs including international airfare.
Eligibility: Applicants must be aged 16 to 23. Recent college graduates aged 21 to 24 can apply to be assistant team leaders and anyone from 18 years of age with extensive outdoor skills can apply as a young leader. Some experience of camping, hill walking and outdoor activities is recommended.

Dorset Expeditionary Society (DES)

Lupins Business Centre, 1–3 Greenhill, Weymouth DT4 7SP

☎ /fax 01305 775599

dorsetexp@wdi.co.uk

www.dorsetexp.co.uk

DES is a registered charity promoting up to six adventurous overseas expeditions each year to remote parts of the world. Expeditions are open to anyone in the UK and can usually qualify for two sections of the Duke of Edinburgh's Gold Award. Leaders and helpers are all volunteers. Training/team building weekends take place in the UK before departure. Skills such as rock/ice climbing, canoeing, white-water rafting, mountain trekking will be learnt. The society also has a training grants scheme to help fund formal courses.

Timing & Length of Expedition: Applications begin in September. Expeditions last three to five weeks, and most leave in July and return in August.

Destinations: Alaska, Ecuador, India, Italy, Kenya, Nepal and Scotland.

Costs: From £500 to £2200 all-inclusive. Pocket money should be taken.

Eligibility: Generally 15 to 21 years but some expeditions may have specific age requirements within that range. Expeditioners must first win a place during a selection weekend where they need to demonstrate a capacity for teamwork.

Expedition Advisory Centre

The Royal Geographical Society, 1 Kensington Gore, London SW7 2AR

☎ 020 7591 3030

fax 020 7591 3031

eac@rgs.org

www.rgs.org/eac

The Royal Geographical Society expedition advisory centre provides training and advice to anyone embarking on an expedition. This is a free service. The centre is open Monday to Friday 10am to 5pm – you need an appointment.

Jagged Globe

Foundry Studios, 45 Mowbray St, Sheffield, South Yorkshire S3 8EN

☎ 0845 345 8848

fax 0114 275 5740

climb@jagged-globe.co.uk

www.jagged-globe.co.uk

Jagged Globe offers tailor-made or scheduled group mountaineering expeditions. If tailor-made you can choose whether to go with a Jagged Globe leader or be self-led (as long as you have the necessary experience). Introductory to advanced climbing courses are also held in the Alps and on the Via Ferrata.

Timing & Length of Expedition: Around 30 expeditions a year ranging from two weeks to 70 days (eg climbing Mt Everest). Most last for around three weeks. Expeditions are scheduled all year-round – see the website for details.

Destinations: Expeditions take place in every continent (including Antarctica). There are six programs: the seven summits (each of the highest points on each continent); the cold regions; the mountains of Asia; the mountains of the Americas (Alaska to South America); the 8000m peaks (eg Everest, G2); and the Africa region (Atlas Mountains of Morocco and Mt Kilimanjaro).

Costs: From £1095 to £28,000 (Mt Everest) all-inclusive except for travel insurance, airport taxes and main meals in the big cities. You can buy mountaineering travel insurance from Jagged Globe.

Eligibility: No age restriction but you must have relevant experience for your chosen trip (if you don't then you can do the courses you need to achieve this).

Wind, Sand, Stars

6 Tyndale Terrace, London N1 2AT

☎ 020 7359 7551

fax 020 7359 4936

office@windsandstars.co.uk

www.windsandstars.co.uk

This tour operator runs an annual summer expedition in the desert and mountains of the Sinai to develop desert survival skills while working with the local Bedouin people. The first part of the expedition involves trekking in the high mountain region of the Sinai with time to swim in mountain rock pools and sleep under the stars at night. The second part of the expedition involves working on various projects to help the Bedouin communities such as painting schools, digging dams, regenerating gardens and medical projects.

Timing & Length of Expedition: The expedition is for four weeks in July/August. Apply giving eight weeks notice.

Destination: The Sinai desert (Egypt).

Costs: The cost is £1400, including everything except flights.

Eligibility: Applicants must be aged 16 to 25.

World Challenge Expeditions

World Challenge Expeditions, Black Arrow House, 2 Chandos Rd, London NW10 6NF

☎ 020 8728 7200

fax 020 8961 1551

welcome@world-challenge.co.uk

www.world-challenge.co.uk

World Challenge Expeditions runs expeditions and gap projects (see p289) around the world intended to educate and develop skills among young people. The organisation sees raising the cost of an expedition as an integral part of the gap experience. Shorter than most gap-year placements, their expeditions are designed to promote team building and personal development. The teams all have an experienced leader and participants are all assigned a specific role with responsibilities such as looking after the food or the budget.

Timing & Length of Expedition: All expeditions leave in July and last for four weeks. Application deadlines are flexible because expeditions are conditional upon demand. Call for an application pack or use the online form.

Destinations: The Amazon, the Andes, Borneo, Central America, East Africa and the Himalaya.

Costs: The average price is £2900, which include flights and all in-country costs.

Eligibility: Applicants must be aged 16 to 22.

PROPER JOBS

WHAT KIND OF WORK?

There are as many kinds of gap year as there are kinds of people. While some gappers dream of scuba diving on a coral atoll, others are just as happy boosting their finances to cover their university tuition fees or working towards a dream job. Although it's not as glamorous as hiking across the Serengeti, working in your gap year will demonstrate to future employers that you are a mature, forward-thinking individual, which could win you valuable Brownie points when you apply for a proper job further down the line.

There are brilliant opportunities out there for budding entrepreneurs. You might think about doing work experience with a local company. Or why not earn while you travel with temp work in Australia? Or how about embarking on a fully paid work placement in Europe or America? A lot will depend on how much time and money you have at your disposal.

Of course, you could always apply for a proper long-term job and leave at the end of the year but few companies will be impressed if they invest time and training in you and you leave and take those skills elsewhere. Among other things, you'll be writing off your chances of a good reference and you'll also have to come up with a creative answer if anyone asks you why you left your last job.

Fortunately there are loads of ways to work in a temporary position and get paid without damaging your career prospects. If you do decide to spend a year working in the UK or overseas, this chapter covers some of the choices that lie ahead.

Work Placements Abroad

Given the choice, most gappers would prefer to work overseas. As well as the interesting experience of living in a foreign city, you'll learn new ways of doing things and end up with a cracking bit of work experience to put down on your CV. You can imagine how the job interviews will go already. 'Ah, I see you worked for a year at an investment bank in New York. Good, very good…'

By far the easiest way to work abroad is to take a work experience or training placement. These short-term positions are available all over the world – in Europe they are usually known as *stages* or *traineeships*; in the US they're almost always called *internships*. Most foreign schemes pay a salary or a monthly allowance and some organisations will also pay for your initial travel to the placement.

There are also unpaid placements in many countries, but you must find an alternative way to cover your living expenses. The Leonardo da Vinci program (www.leonardo.org.uk) provides funding for vocational training in more than 30 countries but you must apply through your school or university – inquire at your careers service.

Even if the placement is unpaid, you may still require a work permit, which makes things a little tricky once you leave the European Economic Area (EEA). Fortunately, a whole industry has sprung up sponsoring foreign gappers on traineeships around the world. For a fee, the British Universities North America Club (BUNAC) and a host of similar organisations will sponsor your J1 visa, which allows you to take a work-placement in America for up to 18 months (note there are two types of J1 visa - the J1 for students allows you to work for only four months) – see Rules & Regulations (p334) for details.

Most programs restrict you to certain types of job – usually management, business, finance and commerce – and you normally have to arrange your own placement in advance. However, foreign companies are often happy to offer you a place if they know there's a big organisation behind you; see opposite) for some useful tips. You can work in paid or unpaid internships, but you must show evidence of sufficient funds to support yourself for unpaid positions.

The length of time you can work for varies with the program and some schemes are restricted to graduates or people with relevant work experience. Contacts (p336) lists several of the most popular intern schemes in America. Andrew Douglas sent us this appraisal of the Mountbatten Internship Programme, which allows you to work in New York for a year:

The Mountbatten Internship Programme was one of the best years I've had. It's a great opportunity to continue the University experience, make more lifelong friends, live and work in New York and gain some excellent work experience that will set you up for life. I worked as a Trade Analyst for P&O Nedlloyd, where I gained experience in the North–South American Trade Department. This internship – and the experience as a whole – ultimately helped me to find a good job as a Business Analyst when I returned to London.

Whatever you end up doing, you usually need to be studying a subject that directly relates to the internship you apply for and you must complete a detailed training plan, explaining what you hope to get out of your traineeship. A wishy-washy plan is going to go straight into the 'return to sender' pile so it's worth thinking about this when you start looking for an internship.

Some organisations can also arrange work placements in Australia, South Africa and Brazil but these tend to be shorter and most are unpaid – see p336 for some suggestions. Another good source of overseas traineeships is the European Union (EU). Many organisations in Europe take on paid interns *(stagiares)* every year. Conducting a *stage* is a great way to learn about international economics and politics, and working in a foreign-language environment will really beef up your CV come graduation.

Most *stages* last around five months. You can work in fields such as translating, journalism, finance, politics, economics, human rights and engineering. To apply for these positions, however, you usually need to be able to speak at least one other EU language apart from English, and it helps if your degree relates to the position you are applying for. Note that some programs are only open to people who have never taken a *stage* at an EU institution before.

Most European organisations offer a monthly cash allowance to cover your living and travelling expenses, and you'll be asked to produce a report or research project during your *stage*. The main centres of European politics – and therefore the best places to find placements – are Brussels (Belgium), Geneva (Switzerland), Frankfurt (Germany) and Luxembourg. See opposite for some tips on finding a *stage* in Europe.

FORTRESS AMERICA?

Working in the USA became much more difficult after 9/11. People applying for a visa to work in the USA must now attend a face-to-face interview at the US embassy in London or Belfast. There's a £65 application fee which is non-refundable, even if the embassy rejects your application.

People visiting the USA on a J1 visa must pay a further US$100 fee to register with SEVIS (www .sevis.net), which allows the US government to keep tabs on you while you are in the USA. You *must* register with SEVIS within 30 days of arrival in the USA, and you must also inform them every time you change address. Unfortunately, there's no way around this, so you'll either have to accept these intrusions or get your work experience somewhere else.

Some gap-year companies offer voluntary work placements in the developing world, including Teaching & Projects Abroad (p293; www.teaching-abroad.co.uk), Travellers Worldwide (p293; www.travellersworldwide.com) and i-to-i (p290; www.i-to-i.com); most of the opportunities are in business or journalism.

A few of the big international language schools offer short unpaid internships with European companies as part of a language course overseas. You pay for the language course and your living expenses so this is more like volunteering than proper work. However, it will provide 'work experience in a foreign language environment' which can add sparkle to your CV.

The main schools offering these programs are Càlédöñià Languages Abroad (p421; www.caledonialanguages.co.uk), Don Quijote (p422; www.donquijote.org) and Euro Academy (p422; www.euroacademy.co.uk).

FINDING A WORK PLACEMENT

The USA is the most popular destination for work placements and a year working for an American company is likely to bowl over employers back home. There are thousands of internships available every year and many are published in annual lists, which you can buy over the internet or in bookshops.

Two of the most useful publications are *The Internship Bible* (Princeton Review; £13.50) and *Peterson's Internships* (Peterson's; £19.99). Both publications are updated annually and list thousands of internships in all sorts of professional fields. The websites listed on p328 also are invaluable tools for finding an internship across the pond.

For a European *stage* or traineeship, the best place to start your search is the web. The website www.eurodesk.org/euinfo/euenbody.htm has links to internship programs at dozens of European institutions, and you can find more listings at www.eu-careers-gateway.gov.uk/finding/stage.htm.

Some international organisations outside Europe offer similar programs. The website www.missions.itu.int/~italy/vacancies/vaclinks.htm lists internships as far afield as Tanzania and the Philippines. Some gap-year organisations can also fix you up with a paid or unpaid internship in other exotic locations.

Self-starters may be able to find internships in foreign countries by approaching companies on spec – see Work Placements in the UK (p328) for some tips. Miriam Raphael found a placement at a radio station in Israel:

I was doing a study-abroad program at the Hebrew University and I managed to arrange an internship with Jerusalem Post Radio – the radio news component of the newspaper. I happily dropped out of the study program and took on a full-time journalist's work-load for a weekly bus pass and the odd free lunch.

In the Middle East you're always thrown in the deep end and this was no exception. Mornings I might be interviewing protestors outside the Prime Minister's house. Afternoons would be spent at funerals, in hospitals, and once, shockingly, at the scene of a suicide bombing.

It was dynamic, challenging, emotionally exhausting work for anyone, let alone a 19-year-old fresh out of school. But the team of reporters was incredibly supportive and they pushed me to do things most journalists never have the chance to cover.

People hoping to study medicine or nursing can gain work experience on thousands of voluntary health-care programs in the developing world – see p264 for some suggestions.

If you're a qualified nurse you can easily find temporary, paid work overseas. The website www.nursingnetuk.com has excellent advice on nursing in the UK and overseas. There's a global nursing shortage and countries such as Australia and the USA have special immigration programs to entice nurses from abroad. See the websites www.bluchip.com and www.australiannursingsolutions.com.au for some ideas of what's out there.

Business-minded gappers can find placements at businesses and corporations across Europe at www.careersineurope.hobsons.com. Another fantastic resource for business internships is the job site Monster (www.monster.co.uk). You can search for placements in dozens of countries around the world by visiting the local Monster website and typing 'internships' into the job search engine.

Other useful websites:

http:\\internships.wetfeet.com US internship search engine.

www.internationaljobs.org Publishes listings of internships worldwide.

www.internjobs.com Member of the AboutJobs.com group, with a huge database of internships worldwide.

www.internships.com Publishes guides to US internships, broken down by city or subject.

www.internships-usa.com Publishes guides to over 3000 internships in the USA.

www.internweb.com Search engine for internships in the USA.

www.rsinternships.com US site with subject by subject search engine for internships.

www.traveltree.co.uk Has a search engine for volunteer and paid internships.

Work Placements in the UK

Sure, it may not be as glamorous as working in New York, but plenty of people do work placements in the UK during their year out. There are also some excellent industrial placement schemes that pay a perfectly respectable salary, but you usually have to sign up for the whole year. Loads of companies offer shorter paid and unpaid work experience, which will allow you to earn some CV beans and still see a bit of the world before you start your degree.

Industrial placement schemes are usually aimed at students taking a gap year during their degree, such as students on sandwich courses. There are, however, a handful of schemes specifically targeted at pre-university gappers and graduates. The best opportunities are in engineering, IT and business but if you look around you can find placements in almost any field. Some of the some of the larger schemes that offer paid placements are listed on p336.

Paid placements tend to last one whole year, or a few months over the summer and pay is based on an entry-level salary – typically £10,000 to £13,000 for the year. Office-based placements are usually open to people studying for any degree but industry-related placements require specific subjects. Competition can be fierce and you usually need at least 300 UCAS points to apply (24 points in the old system).

The Year in Industry program (YINI; www.yini.org.uk) is the main scheme for school leavers who want to do paid work experience before university. Placements can be found for aspiring engineers, scientists, IT professionals and businesspeople. If a company takes a shine to you, it may offer you future vacation work or even sponsorship through university. YINI has an arrangement with the gap-year organisation Raleigh International (see p293 for more information), allowing you to combine working in industry with travel – contact YINI (p347) for more details.

Another interesting option is to arrange a work placement at a local government office (see the website www.lgjobs.com/workplacements.cfm).

As well as these gold-dust paying programs, there are thousands of British companies that offer unpaid work experience. Try contacting the human resources or personnel department of any company you want to work for to see if they can offer you a placement. Most companies will cover the cost of your lunch and reasonable work-related travel expenses. Aspiring doctors and nurses often volunteer at local hospitals.

The website www.prospects.ac.uk is the official site for graduate careers advice in the UK and is an excellent place to start looking for work placements. The website has a search engine for work placements, managed by the National Council for Work Experience (NCWE). The website www.doctorjob.com/workexperience/search.asp also has great listings. Another good place to get information is your school or university careers service.

Recruitment Agencies

Although you can sometimes find a job by just turning up and explaining how great you are, most positions are filled through recruitment agencies or adverts in the national press. There are thousands of recruitment agencies around the world that can find work for foreign workers, but remember that you probably need a work permit to work outside Europe – see Red Tape (p332).

Agencies tend to specialise in certain types of jobs – engineering, IT, hospitality, sales or secretarial work for example – and almost all offer permanent and temporary positions. For gap-year work or work overseas you'll probably be looking at temporary work rather than a permanent job, though it is possible to start off temping and move to a permanent position.

In theory, agencies will match you with a job that matches your skills, but sometimes it's just a case of taking what is available. It's a good idea to carry a digital copy of your CV and the addresses of some references when you travel so you can print them out or email them in when you start applying for work.

For jobs in Europe, the website www.europa.eu.int/eures has links to government-run job centres across the EU. The Australian equivalent is jobsearch.gov.au, and the New Zealand version is job-bank.winz.govt.nz. America's Jobs Bank (www.ajb.dni.us) is the state-run jobs agency in the US and Jobs Etc (www.jobsetc.ca) serves the same function in Canada.

Job Centres in the UK offer everything from cleaning jobs to management positions at glossy corporations, but they tend to be rather gloomy places (remember *The Full Monty*?). You can search for jobs countrywide without leaving the house on the official Job Centres website www.jobcentreplus.gov.uk.

Private recruitment agencies tend to be more upbeat and have a reputation for providing better-paid, more skilled jobs. There are links to loads of private agencies in Europe on the website www.jobs-in-europe.net. Australian agencies are listed on employment.byron.com.au/agencies and UK agencies can be found on www.rec.uk.com and www.agencycentral.co.uk. The leading international job agencies are covered in Work Placements Abroad (p336).

There are also hundreds of job-search sites where you can hunt for jobs abroad from the comfort of your own PC. Try some of the following.

WORLDWIDE JOBS
www.escapeartist.com Has extensive global jobs links and a free online magazine.
www.hotrecruit.com Recruitment website focussed on young people.
www.jobsabroad.com Extensive American site with international listings.
www.jobware.com Search engine for international jobs.
www.planetrecruit.com Global job search site.

UK & EUROPE
www.eurojobs.com Extensive jobsite for European jobs.
www.expatica.com/jobs Western European site with job search engine.
www.jobs.co.uk UK jobsite with a search engine for specialist job agencies.
www.jobsite.co.uk Search engine for jobs in the UK and Europe.

AUSTRALIA & NEW ZEALAND
careerone.com.au Jobs listings from major newspapers in Australia and New Zealand.
seek.com.au & **www.seek.co.nz** Search sites for jobs in Australia and New Zealand.
www.mycareer.com.au Australia and New Zealand job search site.
www.workingin-newzealand.com Foreign-oriented jobsite for New Zealand.

NORTH AMERICA
hotjobs.yahoo.com American and Canada job search site.
www.aboutjobs.com Umbrella site for several US job sites targeting young people.
www.careerbuilder.com State by state search engine for the US and Canada.
www.careersusa.com US jobsite with state by state search.

Temping
When people think of temping, they imagine the original 'Kelly Girls' – ie prim secretaries with horn-rimmed glasses. These days, however, you can temp in almost any field, from engineering to web design, and there are just as many 'Kelly Guys' out there. Some people even make a full-time living moving from temp job to temp job.

Loads of people use temp agencies to find work overseas. You can often register with a recruitment agency in the UK before you leave and it will pass on your details to one of its branches abroad. Reed, Hays Personnel and Adecco all have offices around the world – see p348 for details.

Once you find a suitable agency you'll have to register and attend an interview, which will be followed by a series of aptitude tests. For general office work this usually involves a typing test (40 words per minute or above is preferred) and an assessment of how good you are at using computers.

Temporary staff are employed directly by the agency rather than individual companies and wages are typically paid a week in arrears with tax deducted. Temping used to get a bad rap for long hours and poor pay, but these days temps in many countries are entitled to a decent hourly rate, reasonable working hours and paid holidays.

As a rough indication, wages for office temps start at around £7 an hour in the UK, £5 an hour in America and £7 an hour in Australia. You can earn more if you can touch-type or have a specific skill, such as web design or computer programming.

The downside of temping is that you often end up doing tedious, repetitive jobs such as data entry and photocopying. If you have specific skills or experience you can often find something a bit more challenging but even skilled staff sometimes end up doing jobs that are far beneath their abilities, giving rise to the popular temp joke:

Temp to Agent: 'I want to complain – I'm a trained secretary but a monkey could do this job!'
Agent to Temp: 'That's why we're paying you peanuts.'

Most temp jobs are nine-to-five positions but you can work over the weekend or only on specific days if this suits you better. Lots of people use office temping as a way to pay the rent while they establish careers in all sorts of unrelated fields.

Alex Banks sent us the following tale of working as an office temp in Australia:

I wound up in Sydney early one summer out of cash and had to get a job fast. I could type fast and had switchboard experience so being an office temp seemed ideal. I sent my CV to 10 agencies and sat back waiting for a phone call. Two weeks later and I was still waiting for that call, so I went into pest mode and called each agency first thing in the morning every day asking for work. I didn't know that in summer the city goes slow for two months and work is scarce!

In the end, it took 10 days before one girl got fed up and gave me something to shut me up. The bad news – office temping is always unexciting and badly paid. The good news is that it's much more bearable when gazing all day at a stunning opera house and bridge from 42 floors up!

Our advice is to approach things with a positive attitude. Even if an assignment is boring, you won't be doing it forever, and if you seem keen employers will often try to find you something more interesting to do and may ask for you for future assignments. If you're working for more than a few weeks you may also get some vocational training which you can plonk straight down on your CV.

Freelancing

If you have a skill such as writing, editing, photography, translating or web design, you might consider freelancing during your year out. However, don't expect to make a fortune – even experienced freelancers sometimes struggle to cover their expenses.

Journalism is probably the best-known freelance occupation and if you've got a good idea for a story you have as much chance of selling it as the next freelancer. When you call a magazine or newspaper, pitch your idea directly to the editor of the specific section where you think the article might go.

Pay rates for freelance writers, editors and photographers depend on the publication – national newspapers and glossy magazines usually pay more than local papers, the free press or websites. Writers usually get around £200 per 1000 words, photographers get around £100 to £200 for a day or £150 per photo, and editors get £60 to £100 per day. For more information, see Lonely Planet's *Travel Writing* book.

A press card can open doors (literally – it's a similar size to a credit card) but you normally need to earn a certain amount of your income from journalism to qualify. In the UK, press cards are issued by the National Union of Journalists (NUJ; www.nuj.org.uk), which can provide more information. The phoney press cards available in places such as Bangkok really aren't worth the paper they're printed on.

For some ideas of publications to approach, there are listings of newspapers, magazines and news websites around the world at www.world-newspapers.com. Many English-language newspapers overseas are desperate for writers and editors so it may be worth dropping into their offices with some examples of your work. If you're heading somewhere exotic you could always try contacting editors at travel magazines and websites and offering to file reports back home while you travel.

Journalism isn't the only way to freelance. Translating is another skill you can use almost anywhere and you can charge around £50 per 1000 words translated. Teaching is another skill you can freelance almost anywhere in the world – see p350 for details. Many web designers and IT professionals also fund their travels by taking on short computer jobs. Mady MacDonald put her IT skills to work in Nepal and sent us this report:

In Kathmandu, I simply helped those around me and word quickly spread that I 'knew computers.' However, my knowledge of computers pales compared to many people's; it was my attitude that made the difference. I'm now well advanced in my communications career, but the ready availability of internet cafés allows me to freelance whenever I travel. I don't make thousands per month while travelling but I do have a steady dribble of money being dumped into my account.

Whatever your field, people need to be able to reach you. A roaming email account and a mobile phone are essential. A digital copy of your CV and some examples of past work will also come in handy. You might also think about setting up your own website, listing your skills and contact details. Having your own business cards will also add a touch of professionalism.

As a freelancer you technically require a work permit to work outside Europe but many people get around this by only working for clients back home or arranging to be paid electronically into a UK bank account. You still have to pay tax on these earnings, however, unless you're registered as a nonresident (see p334 for more information).

Useful resources for journalists and other freelancers:

www.allfreelancework.com Site for desktop publishers and designers.

www.aquarius.net Agency that links freelance translators with translating jobs worldwide.

www.freelance.com American site for freelance IT professionals.

www.freelance-proofreaders.co.uk UK jobs site for freelance proofreaders, editors and translators.

www.freelancers.net Listing service for freelance IT professionals.

www.freelanceworkexchange.com US site with listings of media, consultancy, design and programming jobs.

www.freelancewriting.com Portal for information on freelance writing.

www.journalism.co.uk Leading UK site for journalists.

www.journalism.org US site with extensive tools for journalists.

www.proz.com Site with extensive jobs listings for freelance translators.

www.translationdirectory.com Portal for freelance translators.

www.translatortips.com US site with advice for freelance translators.

Working for a Gap-Year Organisation

If you're thinking of a career in the development or charity fields, consider joining a volunteering project or expedition overseas. Loads of ex-participants end up working for the companies they spent their gap year with, so this can be the first step towards a career as an overland driver or aid worker.

All of the organisations that take volunteers or adventurers overseas need team leaders and support staff. There is a huge turnover within the industry so new jobs come up all the time. Assuming you have the necessary skills, it's possible to work for a single contract or turn this into the kind of career that people in offices only dream about.

For team leader and project manager positions, you normally need a degree plus expedition experience and a Mountain Leader (Summer) certificate, which puts these positions out of the reach of most gappers. There are, however, also opportunities for qualified HGV drivers, engineers, dive instructors and other expedition support staff.

Most gap-year organisation jobs require a current certificate in first-aid, preferably with a focus on wilderness or expedition medicine – see p444 for details. There are also openings for qualified doctors and nurses – experience in Accident and Emergency or tropical medicine is preferred.

Frontier (p316; www.frontierprojects.ac.uk), Raleigh International (p293; www.raleigh international.org) and Trekforce (p294; www.trekforce.org.uk) have special schemes for volunteer or trainee staff. However, be aware that you usually have to pay a fee for these programs. It's also worth contacting the other volunteering and expedition organisations listed in Volunteering, Conservation & Expeditions (p264).

RED TAPE

Working overseas is easy! You can go wherever you want to go and do whatever you want to do! Okay, back to reality. Working in a foreign country is much, much harder than visiting on holiday. You'll have to jump through all sorts of legal hoops before the authorities will grant you permission to work overseas.

Due to the harmonisation of labour rules across the EU, Europe is by far the easiest place to work – citizens of countries in the European Economic Area can work in any other member country without restrictions. To work anywhere else you usually need to be sponsored by an overseas employer, and they must prove that they couldn't find a local person to do the job.

Fortunately many countries have special immigration programs that allow graduates or professionals from Britain to visit and take paid training positions with local companies. Most of these programs must be arranged through a sponsoring organisation such as BUNAC and you typically have to be a graduate or have relevant work experience to qualify.

Wherever you are going, speaking the local language will increase your chances of finding work. In countries such as France and Germany, this is essential. No French company is going to hire you if you don't know the difference between a *classeur* (filing cabinet) and a *broyeur à papier* (paper shredder).

Computer skills are also desirable, particularly if you want to work in any industry that relies on a particular kind of software. Make sure you mention on your CV if you have experience with any relevant computer applications – eg Quark, Photoshop and HTML for desktop publishing.

The exact skills you need will depend on the job, but it always pays to be enthusiastic, flexible and open-minded. Foreign employers are looking for people who can adjust quickly to a different way of doing things and are happy working with new people.

Rules & Regulations

Back in the days of the British Empire, doing anything overseas required a stamped form, filled out in triplicate. Things haven't improved much since then. To work in most countries outside Europe, you need to obtain a work permit, which will affect how long you can stay and the kinds of things you can do when you arrive.

The easiest option for gappers is to join an organised work-abroad program. Dozens of organisations will sponsor you for a temporary permit to work in the USA or Canada and you can apply independently for working-holiday visas for Australia, New Zealand and Japan – see p363 for details.

Applying for permission to work, however, takes longer than applying for a tourist visa and it usually costs more. You may have to find a job or work placement before you leave and there may be an interview at the relevant embassy. If you have a criminal record (particularly a drugs conviction) your application is probably dead in the water. The authorities may also ask to see proof of private health insurance or personal funds.

The point of all this is to ensure that:
- you aren't working illegally;
- you aren't taking jobs away from the locals;
- you aren't going to start claiming benefits and free healthcare;
- you won't stay longer than you are entitled to; and
- you will pay your taxes.

Permits are generally issued at the same time as your visa, and most prohibit you from doing certain kinds of jobs – for example, tobacco-picking in Canada or working as a pilot in the USA. Things have gotten even tougher since the events of September 2001 – see Fortress America? (p326) for more information.

Work Permits

The essential piece of paper that you need to work abroad is a work permit. Unfortunately, persuading the governments of some countries to give you one can be like asking a Rottweiler to give up a sausage. To work outside Europe, you normally need sponsorship from a foreign company, and they must be able to prove that they couldn't find a local person to do the job.

Fortunately, citizens of countries in the EEA – ie Austria, Belgium, Denmark, Finland, France, Germany, Greece, Ireland, Italy, Luxembourg, the Netherlands, Portugal, Spain, Sweden and the UK (the nations of the EU), plus Iceland, Norway and Liechtenstein – can work in each other's countries without restrictions. EU citizens can also work without restrictions in the new EU member states of Cyprus, Czech Republic, Estonia, Hungary, Latvia, Lithuania, Poland, Malta, Slovakia and Slovenia. Citizens of these countries, however, will have to wait a few years before they can enjoy the same freedom to work in the UK.

Generally, you can visit and look for work in any of the aforementioned countries for up to three months. After this time you must apply for a residence permit, which usually involves taking your passport and job contract down to the local town hall. Most EU countries require you to take out medical insurance before you start working. The rules and regulations vary slightly from country to country – the website europa.eu.int/eures provides information on working conditions for every country in the EEA and the new EU member states.

In contrast, America can be harder to get into than Fort Knox. Luckily, you can get around most of the red tape if you join an educational exchange program with an organisation such as BUNAC (see p337). For a fee, these organisations will sponsor you for a J1 visa – which will allow you to take a paid work placement in the USA for up to 18 months. However, you can't use these programs for just any job – the focus has to be on learning new professional skills that will help you in your future career.

To apply you must be a university student or graduate, or have two years of work experience and there's a £65 visa fee and US$100 (£52) SEVIS fee (p326) on top of the program costs. You must also attend an interview with the local US embassy – for residents of the British Isles, this will take place in London or Belfast. You can only work for the company you were placed with but you're allowed to travel for about a month at the end of your placement.

For some jobs you may need to have a medical examination, which usually has to be carried out by a doctor approved by the immigration authorities. You may also need to show a clean criminal record. In the UK this information resides with the Criminal Records Bureau. You can apply for a certificate (the fee is £12) of your criminal record (known as a 'disclosure') on the website www.disclosure.gov.uk.

Australia, New Zealand and Japan offer useful working-holiday visas that allow you to work and travel for up to a year. These schemes are really designed for people who want to take on casual work while they travel, but plenty of people use them to get a proper job. Canada also offers a one-year working-holiday visa, but you must apply through a sponsoring organisation – see p363 for more on working-holiday visas.

Up-to-date information about work permits and visa restrictions can be found on the websites of many embassies in London, eg www.usembassy.org.uk, www.australia.org.uk or www.nzembassy.com. Handy guides to international working conditions are published by the website www.goinglobal.com.

Taxation

As Benjamin Franklin said, 'only two things in life are certain, death and taxes.' Students are generally exempt from paying tax, but as soon as you get a proper job you must start contributing to the running costs of the nation. Every country has its own rules, but both foreign workers and local workers must pay income tax and chip in to the local health-insurance scheme.

In the UK, tax is collected by the Inland Revenue (www.inlandrevenue.gov.uk). Before you can start working, you need to obtain a National Insurance number from the Department of Work & Pensions (www.dwp.gov.uk). Single people can then earn up to £4745 a year tax-free; after that you have to pay tax at the prevailing rate for your income level. Under the Pay As You Earn (PAYE) scheme, tax and national insurance contributions are deducted by the Inland Revenue at source. If you are self-employed, you should set aside some money to pay your tax bill at the end of the year.

The UK tax year runs from 6 April to 5 April and you must file a tax return at the end of the year (see the Inland Revenue website www.inlandrevenue.gov.uk for more information). If you've paid tax too much you can claim a refund at the end of the year, or use this money as credit against your tax bill for the next year.

If you work overseas you'll be liable for local income tax, and you may also have to pay local government taxes and make health insurance contributions. In most countries, you must register with the tax authorities before you can start working.

In Australia, you should apply to the Australian Taxation Office (ATO) for a Tax File Number (TFN)– you can do this online at www.ato.gov.uk. In New Zealand, you should apply to the local Inland Revenue Department office (see www.ird.govt.nz for listings).

In America, exchange visitors only pay federal and state taxes and not Social Security. However, you still need to apply for a Social Security card from the Inland Revenue Service (www.irs.gov) – the sponsoring organisation will usually help with this. In Canada, you should apply for a Social Insurance Number at the Canada Revenue Agency (www.ccra-adrc.gc.ca).

Rules within Europe vary from country to country – the websites europa.eu.int/eures and europa.eu.int/citizensrights provide information on tax and employment rules for every country in the EEA. Details of the tax laws in many other countries can be found on the website www.taxsites.com/international.html#countries.

If you're working overseas for a whole year you can declare yourself nonresident in the UK to avoid paying tax twice. Some countries have specific tax deals with Britain to make this easier – more information is on the Inland Revenue website.

Red tape can also work in your favour, particularly if you've paid too much tax while working overseas. Exchange organisations such as BUNAC (p337) have well-established schemes where you can claim back any overpayments before you leave. Alternatively the company ESS Tax Refunds (www.taxback.com) can, for a fee, help you reclaim tax you've overpaid.

SPEC LETTERS & APPLICATIONS

If you sit around waiting for the perfect career opportunity it may never knock. Many companies are impressed by people who take the initiative and approach them on spec.

However, this won't work for every company. Large corporations often insist that people only apply for advertised jobs. Trying to wow them by parachuting into the boardroom probably won't work. Your careers service can give you advice on whether or not to speculatively approach specific companies.

Almost all employers prefer you to approach them first by phone. Once you've established that they accept speculative applications you can then write a letter asking for an interview. Try to address the letter to a specific person (and make sure you spell their name correctly!) and tailor the letter to the company you are approaching. You want to grab their attention – try an opening such as:

Dear (name of the person you're writing to),

I am very interested in finding out how I could come and work for your organisation. I'm currently studying for a business studies degree at Southampton University and I will be graduating in June 2005. In my final year I have specialised in investment banking in the new member states of the EU. As Bancorp is one of the pioneers in this area I feel the research I have carried out would make me an asset to your organisation...

Aim to make the letter short and punchy and say when you are available for an interview. Make sure you include your contact details in the letter and attach a copy of your CV; your careers service can advise you on how to write a good covering letter.

If you apply for a job in a country that requires a work permit, find out what the foreign company needs to do in order to employ you and explain this in your covering letter. However, you probably stand a better chance of success if you stick to companies in Europe.

There are all sorts of cultural nuances when it comes to applying for jobs in different parts of the world. Most importantly, the letter should be in the local language of the country where the company you are applying to is based. More practical information about working in Europe can be found on the European Job Mobility Portal EURES (http://europa .eu.int/eures).

Expertise in Labour Mobility (www.labourmobility.com) publishes guides to job application procedures in 33 countries worldwide. These handy guides cost €20 (£14) and provide plenty of helpful advice on applying for jobs overseas, including pointers for culturally appropriate CVs and tips on local letter-writing etiquette.

If you apply for advertised jobs you generally need to apply using the official application form; this can often be downloaded from the internet and returned by email with a digital copy of your CV. Once you've filled it out it's a good idea to take a copy so you can remember what you said come interview time. Many companies now use online application forms and you can often revise what you've written before you decide to officially submit.

CONTACTS

Work Placements Abroad

PLACEMENTS IN THE USA

The following organisations offer work placements in North America. Note that you cannot take part on American work experience schemes if you have previously held a J1 trainee visa for the USA. Applicants must complete a training plan for all J1 visa programs and wages will depend on the work placement.

Alliance Abroad

1221 South Mopac Expressway, Austin, Texas 78746, USA
☎ 00 1 512-457 8062
fax 00 1 512-457 8132
inbound@allianceabroad.com

www.allianceabroad.com

Alliance Abroad organises paid and unpaid internships in America based on a J1 visa. You can either find your own internship or take a pre-arranged placement. For seasonal work programs in the USA and Australia see p376.

Types of Work: Hospitality, management, finance, business and IT.

Timing & Length of Work: US internships last six to 18 months, beginning at any time.

Destination: USA.

Costs/Pay: Fees include insurance but not flights or visa fees – contact Alliance Abroad directly for the latest rates.

Eligibility: Applicants must be aged 18 to 30 and be university graduates.

How to Apply: Download an application pack from the website; you must provide four passport photos and a reference and there's a phone interview.

Association for International Practical Training (AIPT)

10400 Little Patuxent Parkway, Suite 250, Columbia, Maryland 21044-3519, USA

☎ 00 1 410-997 2886

fax 00 1 410-992 3924

cd@aipt.org

www.aipt.org

AIPT has been facilitating work placements in the USA since 1950. You must find your own placement and AIPT will then provide you with sponsorship for a J1 visa. See p376 for information on short, summer work exchanges.

Types of Work: Work placements must be in a field that relates to your studies or future career plans.

Timing & Length of Work: Six to 18 months.

Destination: USA.

Costs/Pay: Fees range from £800 for six months to £2250 for 18 months, including insurance but excluding flights and visa fees. Pay varies with the placement.

Eligibility: Applicants must be aged at least 18 and must either be a full-time university student or have at least two years' work experience in the relevant field. You must not have been unemployed in the last six months.

How to Apply: Download an application from the website; once you register for a program you must sign up for a presentation and attend an interview.

BUNAC (British Universities North America Club)

16 Bowling Green Lane, London EC1R 0QH

☎ 020 7251 3472

fax 020 7251 0215

enquiries@bunac.org.uk

www.bunac.org/uk

This popular working-abroad organisation offers an Overseas Practical Training Programme that allows you to work on paid or unpaid internships in the USA on a J1 visa. You must find your own internship and up to 30 days' travel is permitted at the end of your training. For details of casual work and summer-camp programs see p376 and p411.

Types of Work: Internships should be in business, management, finance, commerce, education, social science, library science, counselling, social services, health (excluding nursing or medical internships) and arts and culture (within a gallery or museum).

Timing & Length of Work: Traineeships in the USA can last three to 18 months starting at any time.

Destination: USA.

Costs/Pay: Registration fees for the US program for students/nonstudents range from £300 to £334 (for three months) to £881 to £785 (for 18 months), including compulsory insurance. Flights and visa fees cost extra.

Eligibility: Applicants must be aged at least 19 for programs in the USA. Students and nonstudents are accepted and you need a degree or relevant work experience.

How to Apply: Download an application form from the website; applicants must arrange a full-time traineeship before they apply – BUNAC can provide assistance.

CCUSA

1st floor North, Devon House, 171/177 Great Portland St, London, W1W 5PQ

☎ 020 7637 0779

fax 020 7580 6209

info@ccusa.co.uk

www.ccusa.com

CCUSA offers a Practical Training Scheme that allows you to work on paid or unpaid traineeships in the USA. You must find your own traineeship and have it approved by CCUSA, who then arranges the paperwork. For seasonal work programs and summer-camp jobs see p377 and p412.

Types of Work: Management, finance, commerce or business.

Timing & Length of Work: Traineeships can last up to 12 months and can start at any time of year.

Destination: USA.

Costs/Pay: Registration costs £390, plus £300 for compulsory insurance. Visa fees, flights and accommodation are extra.

Eligibility: Applicants must be at least 20 and have two years' college/university study or work experience in the same field as the proposed training program.

How to Apply: Applicants must find a traineeship and have it approved by CCUSA. Application forms can be downloaded from the website; apply at least two months before you want to start work.

CDS International

871 United Nations Plaza, New York, NY 10017-1814, USA

☎ 00 1 212-497 3500

fax 00 1 212-497 3535

info@cdsintl.org

www.cdsintl.org

CDS offers a Professional Development Programme that lets you visit the USA on a career-related internship. You have to arrange your own placement but CDS will handle the paperwork and provide an orientation on arrival in the USA.

Types of Work: Placements in business, at technical and engineering companies, and in hotel administration.
Timing & Length of Work: Programs can start at any time and placements should last two to 18 months.
Destination: USA.
Costs/Pay: The fee for the program is US$1100 (£585) (US$750 [£400] for less than four months) and you must then cover your flights, insurance and visa fees.
Eligibility: Applicants must be aged 21 to 35 and have completed at least two years of a university degree. One year of work experience is an asset.
How to Apply: Download an application form from the website. Applicants must provide a US-style resume (CV), photo, copy of passport identity pages and evidence of qualifications or student status.

English-Speaking Union

Dartmouth House, 37 Charles St, London W1J 5ED
☎ 020 7529 1550
fax 020 7495 6108
esu@esu.org
www.esu.org
This registered charity offers unpaid internships for around 10 students per year in the offices of the US Congress as part of the Capitol Hill program – former participants have worked in the offices of Edward Kennedy and on Bill Clinton's re-election campaign. There's also a smaller program at the Assemblée Nationale in France.
Types of Work: Administrative work in the offices of politicians.
Timing & Length of Work: June to August.
Destination: Washington, DC (USA).
Costs/Pay: Application is free but successful applicants pay a £200 administration fee and £1200 for accommodation. You cover your own flights, insurance and living expenses.
Eligibility: Candidates must be in the penultimate or final year of their degree (any discipline) when they apply.
How to Apply: Send a detailed CV and 250-word statement by post explaining how the internship will benefit your future career by 26 November. Interviews are held in December. Political experience is a definite advantage.

InterExchange

161 Sixth Ave, New York, NY 10013, USA
☎ 00 1 212-924 0446
fax 00 1 212-924 0575
training@interexchange.org
www.interexchange.org

InterExchange is another organisation that sponsors people on training placements in the USA on the J1 visa scheme. You can either find your own internship or take a pre-arranged placement. See the website for details of internships in other countries. There are also work and travel schemes in the USA; these schemes are covered on p378.
Types of Work: Internships can be in any career-related field.
Timing & Length of Work: Six, 12 or 18 months.
Destination: USA.
Costs/Pay: Most internships are paid and the program fee starts at US$425 (£226) for six months. It costs extra for flights and compulsory insurance (about US$40 (£21) per month.
Eligibility: Age range 20 to 38 and must be a graduate or have relevant professional training or experience.
How to Apply: Download an application pack from the website to start the application process.

International Employment & Training (IET)

45 High St, Tunbridge Wells, Kent TN1 1XL
☎ 01892 516164
fax 01892 523172
info@jobsamerica.co.uk
www.jobsamerica.co.uk
Part of the Work & Travel Company group, IET offers internship schemes in the USA. It provides J1 visa sponsorship but you must arrange your own training placement. See p379 for details of casual-work programs in the USA.
Types of Work: Internships can be in agriculture, hospitality, engineering, finance, IT, law, fashion, HR, insurance, architecture and marketing/sales.
Timing & Length of Work: Six, 12 or 18 months – apply at least two months in advance.
Destination: USA.
Costs/Pay: Most internships are paid and fees start from £868 for six months, including visa fees and compulsory insurance. Flights are extra.
Eligibility: Age range is 18 to 28. Must have a degree or appropriate professional qualifications and preferably a year or more of workplace experience.
How to Apply: Register on the website to start the application process.

International Exchange Centre (IEC)

89 Fleet St, London EC4Y 1DH
☎ 020 7583 9116
fax 020 7583 9117

isecinfo@btconnect.com
www.isecworld.co.uk
The IEC is another major J1 visa sponsor. You can either arrange your own internship or take an organised work placement with a US company. There are also short internships in France – see the website for details. Seasonal work and summer-camp programs are covered on p378 and p413.
Types of Work: Internships can be in any career-related field.
Timing & Length of Work: Internships last four to 18 months and can start at any time. Organised placements start in June or December.
Destination: USA.
Costs/Pay: American internships cost from £520 for four months if you arrange your own internship, or from £1190 if you take an organised work placement. Transport and visa costs are extra.
Eligibility: Applicants must be aged between 20 and 28, and you must be a graduate or have relevant work experience.
How to Apply: Email or phone for an application form three months before you want to start. For organised placements, you should apply by 5 February for a June start and by 5 August for a December start.

IST Plus

Rosedale House, Rosedale Rd, Richmond, Surrey TW9 2SZ
☎ 020 8939 9057
fax 020 8332 7858
info@istplus.com
www.istplus.com
IST Plus runs work programs in the USA on behalf of CIEE/ Council Exchanges. The Internship USA program is for students and the Professional Career Training Programme is for graduates and professionals. You can work on any paid traineeship in the USA but you find your own placement.
Types of Work: Any career-related traineeship is allowed, subject to approval – see the website www.internshipusa.org/trainee for some examples.
Timing & Length of Work: Traineeships may last for up to 18 months.
Destination: USA.
Costs/Pay: Program fees start at £340 (£350 for graduates and professionals) for two months. Flights, visa fees and compulsory insurance are extra.
Eligibility: Applicants for the student program should be undergraduate or postgraduate students. Applicants for the Professional Career Training program should be aged

between 20 and 40 and have a university degree or two or more years of relevant work experience.
How to Apply: Download the application pack from the website to start the application process.

Mountbatten Internship Programme

5th floor, Abbey House, 74–76 St John St, London EC1M 4DZ
☎ 020 7253 7759
fax 020 7831 7018
info-uk@mountbatten.org
www.mountbatten.org
Mountbatten offers around 180 business-focussed internships with companies in New York City every year. Participants are awarded a Certificate in International Business Practice. After you apply, you will be matched with an internship and make all the visa, insurance and accommodation arrangements.
Types of Work: Clerical or administrative work at financial firms or other city businesses.
Timing & Length of Work: One year from January, April/May or September. Apply by 15 March for the September program, by 31 July for the January program or by 31 October for the April/May program.
Destination: USA.
Costs/Pay: The total cost is £1745, plus air fares, rising to £1955 in September 2005. Participants are paid about £460 per month, with a possible £260 bonus.
Eligibility: Applicants must be university or college graduates aged between 21 and 28. A typing speed of 45 words per minute and experience with common desktop computer applications is preferred.
How to Apply: Download an application pack from the website. Applicants must provide a digital copy of their CV, a personal statement giving their reasons for applying and at least two references, then there's an interview.

USIT

19-21 Aston Quay, O'Connell Bridge, Dublin 2, Ireland
☎ 00 353 1-602 1600
fax 00 353 1-679 2124
internshipsusa@usit.ie
www.usit.ie
USIT is Ireland's leading student travel company and it administers internship programs in the USA for Irish citizens. You must find your own internship, but USIT will sponsor you for a J1 visa. There's also a working holiday in Canada program for Irish citizens – see p379 for details.
Types of Work: Any career-related traineeship is allowed, subject to approval.

Timing & Length of Work: In the USA, internships can be for up to 18 months, starting at any time.
Destination: USA.
Costs/Pay: Internships can be paid or unpaid and costs vary with the duration of the internship – a two-month-long position costs €489 (£345), while an 18-month placement costs €1319 (£930).
Eligibility: The US scheme is open to people aged 20 to 40, and you need a university degree or at least two years of relevant work experience.
How to Apply: Apply at least eight weeks before you want to start.

PLACEMENTS IN EUROPE
The following organisations offer work placements at businesses and political institutions in Europe.

Civil Service EU Recruitment
EU Staffing, Room G6, Admiralty Arch, The Mall, London SW1A 2WH
☎ 020 7276 1609
fax 020 7276 1652
eustaffing@cabinet-office.x.gsi.gov.uk
www.eu-careers-gateway.gov.uk
This Civil Service department provides information on jobs at European institutions. You must register online to receive free information about *stages* (traineeships) at organisations such as the European Parliament (opposite) and European Commission (right).

Council of Europe
Temporary Unit (Traineeships), Directorate of Human Resources, Council of Europe, F-67075, Strasbourg, France
☎ 00 33 3 88 41 20 00
fax 00 33 3 88 41 27 10
recruitment@coe.int
www.coe.int/t/e/human_resources/jobs/10_traineeship
_opportunities
This large European institution offers unpaid traineeships for graduates with an interest in European politics. Trainees take an induction course and attend meetings of the European Parliament and European Assembly.
Types of Work: Administrative duties, eg taking minutes at meetings, drafting reports and carrying out research in council offices.
Timing & Length of Work: Three months from January, April or October.
Destination: Strasbourg (France).

Costs/Pay: Traineeships are unpaid and trainee must pay all transport and accommodation costs.
Eligibility: Applicants should be university graduates, preferably with intermediate or fluent French.
How to Apply: You can download from the website an application form; applications are accepted from April to 15 September.

European Central Bank
Recruitment & Staff Development Division, Postfach 16 03 19, D-60066 Frankfurt am Main, Germany
☎ 00 49 691 344 0 (switchboard)
fax 00 49 691 344 60 00
recruitment@ecb.int
www.ecb.int (follow the link 'Working for Europe')
Europe's leading financial institution offers a wide range of internships at its headquarters in Frankfurt for university students studying economics, finance, law, translation and other fields related to the work of the bank. Current vacancies are listed on the website.
Types of Work: Auditing, translation and financial services.
Timing & Length of Work: Internships last three to six months.
Destination: Frankfurt (Germany).
Costs/Pay: Interns get a monthly allowance, accommodation is provided and travel costs to/from Frankfurt will be reimbursed.
Eligibility: Applicants must have an excellent academic background and be fluent in English and at least one other European language. You should also have strong computer skills. Translators need a university degree in a relevant language.
How to Apply: See the website for current vacancies. Apply online or by post with at least two references, a covering letter and CV in English, and evidence of qualifications. Then there's an interview in Frankfurt or by phone (travel costs will be reimbursed).

European Commission
Traineeships Office, B100 1/7, European Commission, B-1049 Brussels, Belgium
☎ 00 32 2-29 911 11
Email using the form on the website.
europa.eu.int/comm/stages
The European Commission is the largest *stage*-offering organisation in Europe and about 600 administrative placements are offered every year. Applicants should apply to be included in the so-called 'Blue Book'. Successful applicants must then

'lobby' individual departments for a position. There's a similar scheme for translators – see the website for details.

Types of Work: Administrative work, taking minutes of meetings, researching and assessing projects etc.

Timing & Length of Work: Five months from March and October.

Destinations: Belgium (Brussels) & Luxembourg.

Costs/Pay: *Stagiares* get around £500 per month and pay for their own food, accommodation and transport. Initial transport to Brussels or Luxembourg may be reimbursed.

Eligibility: Applicants must be aged under 30, have a first- or second-class honours degree, be fluent in one EU language and competent at another.

How to Apply: Apply by 31 August for the March *stage* or by 1 March for the October *stage*. Apply through the website; you must then send in evidence of qualifications and a signed paper application.

European Parliament

Bureau des Stages, KAD O2C007, L – 2929 Luxembourg
☎ /fax 00 352 4300 248 82
stages@europarl.eu.int
www.europarl.eu.int/stages

The European Parliament offers a variety of paid and unpaid traineeships at its Luxembourg headquarters – useful for people hoping to work in politics or international business – but you need to demonstrate an interest in European politics. Different rules apply for translating traineeships – see the website for details.

Types of Work: Administrative jobs in economics, law, political science, journalism and translating.

Timing & Length of Work: Five months from February or September for paid traineeships; one to four months from January, May or September for unpaid traineeships.

Destinations: Brussels (Belgium) & Luxembourg.

Costs/Pay: Paid interns earn around £600 per month; accommodation is extra. All interns are reimbursed for the cost of travelling to internships.

Eligibility: Applicants must be aged 18 to 45, university graduates, fluent in one EU language and competent in another. This must be your first EU internship. University students can apply for unpaid internships.

How to Apply: Read the application guidelines on the website, then download the application forms. You must provide a reference and proof of qualifications – see the website for application deadlines.

ESA (European Space Agency)

ESA Education Office, Personnel Department, 8–10 rue Mario Nikis, 75738 Paris Cedex 15, France
☎ 00 33 1 53 69 76 54
fax 00 33 1 53 69 75 60
maileduc@hq.esa.fr
www.esa.int/hr/educational/index.htm

As well as training astronauts and building space craft, ESA has a paid Young Graduate Trainee Scheme (YGTS) for science and technology graduates. You can work at the European Space & Technology Center in the Netherlands, the European Space Operations Center in Germany, the ESA Center in Italy or the ESA Headquarters in Paris.

Types of Work: Interns do hands-on technical work relating to their field of study.

Timing & Length of Work: The YGTS lasts for one year. End-of-studies training of one to six months is also available. Selection takes place in June and December – application deadlines are on the website.

Destinations: France, Germany, Italy & the Netherlands.

Costs/Pay: Trainees get a monthly stipend for living expenses. End-of-studies trainees are unpaid.

Eligibility: Applicants for the YGTS must be recent graduates from a science or technology degree.

How to Apply: See the website for current vacancies and apply online. There's an interview and you have to take a medical examination. Apply at any time for sandwich traineeships by submitting a CV and covering letter to the relevant department (see the website for addresses).

Grampus Heritage & Training

Ashgill, Threapland, Wigton, Cumbria CA7 2EL
☎ 016973 21516
fax 016972 23040
grampus@clark-mactavish.co.uk
www.grampus.co.uk

This educational organisation offers work-experience placements in Europe for art students as part of the Leonardo da Vinci program (www.leonard.org.uk). Projects have a heritage or environmental focus – one scheme focuses on preserving traditional crafts.

Types of Work: Placements on art, heritage, archaeology and environmental projects.

Timing & Length of Work: Projects last five to nine weeks and are available year-round.

Destinations: Bulgaria, Czech Republic, Germany, Hungary, Iceland, Ireland, Italy, Latvia, Poland, Slovakia & Spain.

Costs/Pay: Costs are covered by a Leonardo da Vinci grant; travel, accommodation, meals and insurance are included.
Eligibility: Applicants must be at least 18, have a current passport and demonstrate interest in the project applied for.
How to Apply: Download an application from the website; you'll need to provide two references.

Interspeak

Stretton Lower Hall, Stretton, nr Malpas, Cheshire SY14 7HS
☎ 01829 250641
fax 01829 250596
enquiries@interspeak.co.uk
www.interspeak.co.uk
Interspeak has been arranging unpaid work placements or *stages* in Europe since 1981. Traineeships are tailor-made to match your interests and you stay with a host family.
Types of Work: Categories include law, IT, journalism, tourism and marketing.
Timing & Length of Work: Mini-*stages* last one to three weeks; maxi-*stages* last one to six months.
Destinations: France, Germany, Spain & the UK.
Costs/Pay: There's an £80 registration fee for both mini- and maxi-*stages*. Placement fees start at £320 for one week, including accommodation and meals.
Eligibility: Applicants must be aged 16 to 18 for mini-stages and 18 or older for maxi-*stages*, with some knowledge of the local language.
How to Apply: See the website or call for an application form; applications are accepted year round.

Office of the United Nations High Commissioner for Human Rights (OHCHR)

Palais des Nations, CH-1211 Geneva 10, Switzerland
☎ 00 41 22-917 90 00
fax 00 41 22-917 90 24
personnel@ohchr.org
www.ohchr.org/english
Europe's leading human rights institution offers unpaid internships at its headquarters in Geneva. Graduates in international law, political science, history and social sciences are preferred and applicants must demonstrate an interest in human rights and current affairs.
Types of Work: Research, drafting reports and other administrative tasks.
Timing & Length of Work: Three to six months from May/June or November/December.
Destination: Geneva (Switzerland).

Costs/Pay: Positions are unpaid and you must make your own travel arrangements.
Eligibility: Applicants must be university graduates in a relevant field and speak two of the following languages: English, French, Spanish, Arabic, Russian and Chinese.
How to Apply: Print off the application form from the website. You must provide three references and obtain sponsorship from an academic institution (contact the office for details). Apply by 30 April for May/June internships or by 31 October for November/December internships.

Smallpeice Trust

Holly House, 74 Upper Holly Walk, Leamington Spa, Warwickshire CV32 4JL
☎ 01926 333200
fax 01926 333202
info@smallpeicetrust.org.uk
www.smallpeicetrust.org.uk
Partly funded by the EU, this independent educational trust offers a gap-year program of engineering training at a UK university, followed by a language course at a European university and an unpaid work-experience placement with a European engineering company.
Types of Work: Engineering.
Timing & Length of Work: Programs run from September to May. Engineering training and work placements last for three months; the language course lasts one month.
Destinations: Training is at a UK university; the language-study and work-placement sectors can take place in one of five European nations.
Costs/Pay: The program costs £4950, including tuition, full-board accommodation and flights.
Eligibility: Applicants must be aged at least 18 and need to have just finished secondary education and to have a deferred place at university to study engineering.
How to Apply: Send a SAE to the office or go online to get an application form. There will be an interview as part of the selection process.

PLACEMENTS IN OTHER COUNTRIES

Try the following organisations for other placements around the globe.

Earthwise Living Foundation (ELF)

PO Box 108, Thames 2815, New Zealand
☎ /fax 00 64 9-353 1558
info@elfnz.com
www.elfnz.com

ELF organises custom-made internships and work-experience programs in New Zealand. Accommodation is provided with a host family or in an apartment. You can arrange a placement to match whatever you are studying.

Types of Work: Internships include marketing, finance, law and conservation.

Timing & Length of Work: Placements are for one month to one year.

Destination: New Zealand.

Costs/Pay: Fees start from £1430 for six weeks, including accommodation. Flights and insurance cost extra. Most positions are unpaid.

Eligibility: Applicants must be aged between 16 and 50, and paid interns must have a Working Holiday visa.

How to Apply: Download the application from the website. There's a phone interview and you should provide two references and a CV. Apply three months before you want to start.

International Association for Students of Economics and Management (AIESEC)

2nd floor, 29–31 Cowper St, London EC2A 4AT
☎ 020 7549 1800
fax 020 7336 7971
national@uk.aiesec.org
www.workabroad.org.uk

AIESEC is the world's largest student organisation and arranges overseas work-exchange programs for around 100 students a year from member universities – see the website for a list. It provides an orientation before you go and a debriefing session when you get home. Introductory meetings take place at member universities several times every year.

Types of Work: Management, technical, development and education traineeships.

Timing & Length of Work: Placements are for three to 18 months, depending on the field of work.

Destinations: Placements are possible in 86 countries.

Costs/Pay: The registration fee for successful applicants is £200. Most placements pay a small stipend towards your expenses. You must pay for your own transport, insurance and living costs.

Eligibility: Applicants must have graduated within one year or be an undergraduate at an AIESEC member university. Candidates aged under 27 are preferred.

How to Apply: Apply online or through your university, then there's an assessment and interview. See the website for application deadlines.

International Association for the Exchange of Students for Technical Experience (IAESTE)

Education & Training, British Council, 10 Spring Gardens, London SW1A 2BN
☎ 020 7389 4771
fax 020 7389 4426
iaeste@britishcouncil.org
www.iaeste.org.uk

Run in conjunction with the British Council, IAESTE has provided engineering and industrial placements overseas for more than 300,000 students. You must apply on spec, and a list of available placements is sent out to successful candidates. There is stiff competition for places and you must provide a strong written statement explaining why you are interested in each placement you apply for.

Types of Work: Placements are mainly at technical and engineering companies.

Timing & Length of Work: Eight to 12 weeks from June.

Destinations: Placements are possible in 80 countries.

Costs/Pay: Participants get an allowance for accommodation, food and work-related travel; flights cost extra. There's a £60 IAESTE administration fee.

Eligibility: Applicants must be full-time university students studying for an engineering, science, agriculture or architecture degree, and you must have completed at least two years of your studies.

How to Apply: Download the application from the website and apply by 10 December. A list of placements is sent to registered students in January and you have until 18 February to apply for placements on the list.

International Student Placement Centre (ISPC)

Suite 804, Level 8, 32 York St, Sydney NSW 2000, Australia
☎ 00 61 2-9279 0100
fax 00 61 2-9279 1028
info@ispc.com.au
www.ispc.com.au

This Australian organisation places recent graduates and professionals on internships with more than 1000 Australian companies. In exchange, Australians get to take work placements in other countries.

Timing & Length of Placements: From one week to one year, starting at any time.

Destination: Australia.

Costs/Pay: Most internships are unpaid, though some provide a living allowance. The fee for applicants ranges from AUS$1100 (£448) for one to six weeks to AUS$2500 (£1017) for a year, not including flights, insurance or visa fees.

Eligibility: Minimum age is 16. Most nationalities are accepted providing you can get the appropriate visa (normally a working-holiday visa – see p364 for details).

How to Apply: Download an application form and supply a CV and covering letter about eight weeks before you want to start.

Internships Australia

Level 3, 80 Stamford Rd, Indooroopilly, Queensland 4068, Australia

☎ 00 61 7-3720 2244

fax 00 61 7-3720 2255

info@internships.com.au

www.internships.com.au

Australia's largest internship sponsoring organisation, Internships Australia provides unpaid internships in most business fields. Placements are arranged to match your field of study or work experience. For shorter internships, you can usually work on a Working Holiday visa. Internships Australia will assist you with work permits for longer internships.

Timing & Length of Placements: One week to one year, starting at any time.

Destination: Australia.

Costs/Pay: Most placements are unpaid, but some provide an allowance for living expenses. Fees range from A$1390 (£566) for up to six weeks to A$3200 (£1302) for a year, not including flights, insurance or visa fees.

Eligibility: You should be a university graduate and you must provide evidence of your academic qualifications, full travel insurance and proof of sufficient funds to support yourself.

How to Apply: Apply using the online form.

Work Placements in the UK

The following organisations provide work experience placements for students and graduates in the UK.

ABN AMRO

Graduate Recruitment Dept, 250 Bishopsgate, London EC2M 4AA

☎ 020-7553 9118

fax 020-7678 2588

www.graduate.abnamro.com

This international bank accepts large numbers of interns at its European offices.

Types of Work: Management and global finance.

Timing & Length of Work: Ten weeks, from July.

Destinations: Amsterdam, London & Paris.

Costs/Pay: Wages are based on entry-level salary.

Eligibility: Applicants should be in their penultimate year of university with 300 UCAS points (24 in the old system) and a predicted 2:1 degree.

How to Apply: Apply online using the forms on the website, which also has the application deadlines.

BBC

All inquiries are handled through the website.

www.bbc.co.uk/jobs

The BBC offers short unpaid internships in various different disciplines relating to TV and radio. Some positions are in regional centres, such as Birmingham, Bristol and Manchester.

Types of Work: Journalism, program making, sound engineering, lighting, costumes and business support.

Timing & Length of Work: Internships last one to four weeks and can start any time.

Destination: UK.

Costs/Pay: Placements are unpaid.

Eligibility: The minimum age varies from 15 to 18 years.

How to Apply: See the website for upcoming vacancies and apply online.

Blackwell Publishing

Graduate Work Experience, Blackwell Publishing Ltd, 9600 Garsington Rd, Oxford OX4 2DQ

☎ 01865 776868

fax 01865 714591

freshchallenge@oxon.blackwellpublishing.com

www.blackwellpublishing.com/graduate

This large publishing house offers work experience for people interested in a career in publishing.

Types of Work: Marketing, production and editing.

Timing & Length of Work: Varies with the placement.

Destination: Oxford (UK).

Costs/Pay: An allowance is provided for travel and food expenses.

Eligibility: The scheme is open to graduates and university undergraduates.

How to Apply: Program details are on the website but speculative applications are also possible; see the website for closing dates.

Civil Service

All inquires are handled through the website.
www.careers.civil-service.gov.uk
The Civil Service offers large numbers of paid and unpaid
work-experience placements every year in government
departments all over the country, from the Scottish Executive
to the Ministry of Defence.
Types of Work: Most positions involve administrative
tasks in government offices.
Timing & Length of Work: Placements vary from
short summer placements to long-term sandwich
placements.
Destination: UK.
Costs/Pay: Paid placements earn either a stipend for
living expenses or a full wage of around £12,000 per year,
depending on the role and placement.
Eligibility: Applicants should be graduates or undergraduates studying for a relevant degree.
How to Apply: See the website for current vacancies and
then apply to the relevant department.

Deloitte Scholars

London, 180 The Strand, London WC2R 1BL
☎ 020 7303 7019
fax 020 7583 1198
hmanthorpe@deloitte.co.uk
scholars.deloitte.co.uk
Deloitte is a major provider of tax, finance, consulting
and auditing services for the corporate sector and it
offers an incredibly generous scheme for pre-university
gappers who may be interested in working in the industry. Placements are available at nine offices around the
UK and you don't have to commit to working for Deloitte
on graduation.
Types of Work: Various types of business and finance
positions.
Timing & Length of Work: Placements last 30 weeks.
Destinations: Birmingham, Bristol, Leeds, London,
Manchester, Reading and St Albans (England); Edinburgh &
Glasgow (Scotland).
Costs/Pay: Deloitte scholars get a 30-week placement,
a £1500 bursary to pay for travel after the scheme and
before university, plus a £1000 bursary and four weeks of
paid placement work each academic year.
Eligibility: Must be a pre-university gapper with an interest
in corporate business.
How to Apply: Apply online or phone for paper applica-
tions; apply from July for August positions.

Euromoney Institutional Investor PLC

Nestor House, Playhouse Yard, London EC4V 5EX
☎ 020 7779 8888
fax 020 7779 8842
graduates@euromoneyplc.com
www.euromoneyplc.com
This financial publisher offers work-experience placements
and graduate training courses in journalism, which can
potentially lead to full-time work with the company.
Types of Work: Journalism, sales and marketing.
Timing & Length of Work: Work-experience placements
last three months and graduate placements last six months.
Both kinds of placements are available year-round.
Destination: UK.
Costs/Pay: Varies with the program – wages are around
£1000 per month on the graduate program.
Eligibility: The graduate scheme is open to graduates
from any university degree, while the work experience
is open to people with a keen interest in journalism and
relevant qualifications or experience.
How to Apply: Download an application from the
website and submit it by email with your CV; there will
then be an interview.

FreshMinds

125 High Holborn, London, WC1V 6QA
☎ 020 7692 4300
fax 0870 460 1596
info@freshminds.co.uk
www.freshminds.co.uk
This innovative organisation recruits high-performing graduates (only) for paid work on corporate research projects.
Types of Work: Participants work on a variety of projects
for leading international companies and learn various
aspects of international business in the process.
Timing & Length of Work: Individual projects can
range from a few days to six months, but most people
work with FreshMinds for six months to a year.
Destinations: UK and some projects overseas.
Costs/Pay: Projects pay a competitive industry salary.
Eligibility: Should have a minimum 1st or 2:1 degree from
a top ten university and A and B grades at A level/GCSE.
How to Apply: Apply online with a CV, then there is a
formal interview and training.

IBM UK

Student Employment Officer, Recruitment Dept, PO Box 41,
North Harbour, Portsmouth, Hants PO5 3AU

☎ 02392 564104
student_pgms@uk.ibm.com
www-5.ibm.com/employment/uk/students
This computer giant offers a variety of trainee schemes for students. You can do short summer placements or longer schemes for up to a year. The Pre-University Employment program is specifically targeted at gap-year students.
Types of Work: IT design, software development, marketing, administration, finance, HR, sales etc.
Timing & Length of Work: Pre-university placements last 12 months from August. Summer and sandwich traineeships last three to 12 months from July.
Destinations: North Harbour (near Portsmouth, UK); Hursley (near Winchester, UK); Basingstoke, South Bank and Warwick (Central London, UK); Bedfont & Sunbury (Greater London, UK).
Costs/Pay: Wages are based on an entry-level salary (around £12,000 per year).
Eligibility: Varies with the program, but generally, you need 340 UCAS points (28 in the old system) and English and Maths to GCSE grade C. The pre-university scheme also requires a deferred place at university.
How to Apply: Apply using the online form to begin the assessment process. Apply October to February for pre-university placements, or October to January for summer/sandwich placements.

KPMG

All recruitment inquiries should be made through the website or by phone.
☎ 0500 664665
www.kpmgcareers.co.uk
This large accountancy multinational offers paid work-experience placements across the UK and special gap-year placements for pre-university gappers.
Types of Work: Placements are in various financial and accountancy sectors.
Timing & Length of Work: Gap placements last six to nine months from October. There are also summer and sandwich placements if you are studying a relevant degree.
Destination: UK.
Costs/Pay: All positions are paid based on approximately £12,500 per year.
Eligibility: Varies with the program – for the gap program applicants must have A-grade GCSE maths and 300 predicted UCAS points (24 in the old system).
How to Apply: See the website for vacancies and apply online.

PricewaterhouseCoopers (PwC)

The Graduate Recruitment Centre, PO Box 5885, Birmingham B4 6FB
☎ 0808 100 1500
e-recruitment.processing@uk.pwc.com
www.pwcglobal.com/uk/eng/careers/main/index.html
This leading management consultancy offers summer and long-term internships at its offices around the UK. There's also a specific scheme for pre-university gap-year students.
Types of Work: Business advice, tax, law and finance.
Timing & Length of Work: Summer internships last for six weeks from July. The gap-year program lasts six months from October. Six-month sandwich placements start September/August.
Destination: UK (the gap program is in London and the southeast of the UK only).
Costs/Pay: Pay is based on an entry-level salary.
Eligibility: Applicants for internships must be in their penultimate year of university study. Gap-year applicants should have good A-Level prospects and be interested in the financial world.
How to Apply: See the website for current vacancies. Apply on the website (preferred) or call for an application form.

Royal Opera House

Covent Garden, London WC2E 9DD
☎ 020 7212 9410
fax 020 7212 9441
education@roh.org.uk
info.royaloperahouse.org/education/Index.cfm
The Royal Opera House offers work experience in most of its departments, including the press, costume and technical departments.
Types of Work: Mostly technical and costume-related roles, plus some administrative jobs.
Timing & Length of Work: Placements are available year-round except August/September. Most people stay for two weeks to a month.
Destination: UK.
Costs/Pay: Positions are unpaid.
Eligibility: Applicants should be aged over 18. Students or graduates from a theatre or art-management background, or people with previous theatre work experience are preferred.
How to Apply: Apply with a CV and covering letter by post or email.

STEP Enterprise

2nd floor, 11–13 Goldsmith St, Nottingham NG1 5JS
☎ 0870 036 5450
fax 0115 950 8321
info@step.org.uk
www.step.org.uk

STEP offers more than 1500 paid summer placements for students at British businesses and technology companies. The main STEP program runs in the summer but sandwich students can do placements for up to a year. See the website for your local STEP representatives and projects.

Types of Work: Accounting, business, community work, engineering, education, health, IT, law, media, manufacturing, retail, tourism and web design.

Timing & Length of Work: The STEP program lasts eight weeks; specialised industrial placements can last up to a year.

Destination: UK.

Costs/Pay: Students on STEP programs get a weekly tax-free stipend of £175. The stipend varies for longer projects.

Eligibility: Applicants must be second- or penultimate-year students on full-time degree courses at university or final-year HND students planning to continue studying at university.

How to Apply: Fill in an online application form (applications are accepted year-round).

Year in Industry (YINI)

www.yini.org.uk

Run in conjunction with the Engineering Development Trust, this annual scheme provides paid industrial work placements for thousands of school leavers and university undergraduates every year. The work should relate to your studies, but formal training is provided during the year. Many companies offer jobs or final-year sponsorship to students who finish the scheme. See the website for your nearest YINI representative.

Types of Work: Placements are mostly in engineering, science, IT and business.

Timing & Length of Work: Placements usually start in September and usually finish the following July or August.

Destination: UK.

Pay: The annual salary varies from £8000 to £12,000 (£9000 to £14,000 for undergraduates).

Eligibility: Applicants should have a confirmed offer at university for the following year or be taking a gap year as part of an undergraduate degree.

How to Apply: Apply online or download the application form from the website. There's a £25 application fee and an interview with YINI.

Working for a Gap-Year Organisation

If your career ambitions lie in the development or travel fields, try the following organisations.

Frontier

50–52 Rivington St, London EC2A 3QP
☎ 020 7613 2422
fax 020 7613 2992
info@frontier.ac.uk
www.frontierprojects.ac.uk

Frontier offers a variety of conservation-based expeditions in rainforest and coral reef environments throughout the tropics.

Types of Work: There are often openings for assistant staff to help with research, which can be a route to a paid position.

Timing & Length: Research positions last up to a year – see the 'Careers' section of the website for individual opportunities.

Destinations: Cambodia, Madagascar & Tanzania.

Costs: Self-funding volunteers cover all their own costs, including airfares and participation fees, but may be eligible for a career-development loan to help with costs. There are also positions for experienced researchers where the airfare is covered and a small stipend is paid at the end of the project.

Eligibility: Paid projects are generally for postgraduates or graduates with scientific research experience. Unpaid projects are open to people with a relevant degree.

How to Apply: See the website for individual opportunities and download an application.

Raleigh International

Staff Office, Raleigh House, 27 Parsons Green Lane, London SW6 4HZ
☎ 020 7371 8585
fax 020 7371 5116
staff@raleigh.org.uk
www.raleighinternational.org

One of the original gap-year organisations, Raleigh recruits around 400 volunteer staff members for its expeditions every year. Volunteer staff assist with the day-to-day running of the expeditions, which include conservation, volunteering placements and adventure activities.

Types of Work: There are openings for adventure activity instructors, nurses, doctors, drivers, press officers, youth workers, photographers, health staff and logisticians – see the website for a full list.

Timing & Length: From 12 weeks (no maximum). Projects start on set dates from January to June or in September.

Destinations: Chile, Costa Rica, Fiji, Ghana, Malaysia, Namibia & Nicaragua.

Costs: Applicants must fundraise £1100 (this can be reduced if you take advantage of the UK government Gift Aid scheme) and the cost of flights. All meals, accommodation, transport and insurance are then provided. Bursaries are available for some positions.

Eligibility: Volunteer staff must be aged 25 or over with relevant skills for the position.

How to Apply: Follow the instructions on the website; there's an interview and an assessment weekend in the UK.

Trekforce Expeditions

34 Buckingham Palace Rd, London SW1W 0RE

☎ 020 7828 2275

fax 020 7828 2276

info@trekforce.org.uk

www.trekforce.org.uk

This registered charity organises expeditions that involve voluntary work on rainforest conservation projects and teaching programs in rural communities.

Types of Work: There are regular short-term opportunities for medics and qualified team leaders.

Timing & Length: Two to five months. Expeditions start on set dates from January to July.

Destinations: Belize, Guatemala, Guyana, Malaysia & Venezuela.

Costs: Medics cover their own flights, then all other costs are covered. Team leaders get a small salary and Trekforce covers all costs.

Eligibility: Age range is 18 to 38. Doctors and nurses need post-qualification experience in Accident and Emergency; team leaders require a first-aid qualification and Mountain Leader (Summer) certificate.

How to Apply: See the website for individual opportunities and download an application.

Recruitment Agencies

The following are the leading agencies for temp and permanent jobs. Visit the websites to find local branches in the country where you want to work.

Adecco

www.adecco.com

This international recruitment agency has more than 5000 offices in 62 countries and specialises in temp and permanent jobs in business, education, engineering, health and construction.

Drake Employment

www.drakeintl.com

Drake has offices in the UK, USA, Canada, Australia, New Zealand, South Africa, Hong Kong, Singapore, Malaysia and Switzerland and covers most professions.

Hays Personnel

www.hays-ap.co.uk

This leading recruitment agency specialises in office, IT, education, engineering and construction jobs and it has offices throughout the UK, Europe, Canada and Australia. You can register and do a virtual interview over the web.

Kelly Services

www.kellyservices.com

The original temp agency, Kelly has offices in the UK, Europe, the US, Canada, Asia, Australia and New Zealand. There are temp and permanent office, technical, engineering, IT, and education jobs available around the world.

Manpower Services

www.manpower.co.uk

This huge international agency offers temp and permanent jobs and has offices in the USA, Canada, Latin America, Europe, the UK and Asia.

Monster

www.monster.com

This truly global company has offices almost everywhere, including the UK, USA, Canada, Australia, New Zealand, most European countries and most of Asia. You can register, create a digital CV and contact job experts on the website.

Reed Executive PLC

www.reed.co.uk

Another recruitment multinational, with hundreds of offices in the UK, Europe, Canada, South Africa, Australia and New Zealand. Reed specialises in temporary and permanent office and engineering/construction jobs.

TMP/Hudson Global Resources

www.hudsonresourcing.com

TMP/Hudson has 101 offices in 28 countries and offers mainly permanent and contract jobs. Staff can provide visa advice and conduct interviews on behalf of overseas companies.

TEACHING

Congratulations! You've opened this book, and presumably you understand what you're reading, so you already possess the prime qualification needed to become an English-language teacher. From Addis Ababa to Ostende, proficiency in English is seen as the key to a better future and there are thousands of schools around the world where you can pick up work as an English-language teacher. If you play your cards right, you might even come home with some cash in your pocket at the end of the year.

The phenomenal popularity of the English language is partly a consequence of globalisation – English is, after all, the language of international business and the World Wide Web, and of Britney Spears, Bart Simpson and *Buffy the Vampire Slayer*. Armed with a few easy-to-obtain qualifications, you can teach English almost anywhere in the world. Quite a few gappers go on to make a full-time career out of English-language teaching (ELT), travelling from school to school and clocking up teaching experience around the globe.

It is possible to teach other subjects apart from English, but you usually need to be fluent in the local language. After all, no-one is going to hire you if you can't get your message across to the class. In some developing countries, a degree in the subject you want to teach may be enough, but more often, foreign schools want to see formal teaching qualifications and teaching experience.

The following sections cover the pros, cons and logistics of teaching overseas.

WHY TEACH?

One of the main attractions of teaching is that it can actually be your ticket to travel, unlike the majority of casual work overseas, which requires you to obtain a work permit before you travel and then look for work when you arrive. Demand for English teachers is so great that most language schools will take care of all the paperwork and even cover your airfare – typically half upfront, and half when you finish your contract. Of course, if you apply to a school within the EU, work permits won't be an issue!

English teaching can also pay surprisingly well, at least compared to most casual jobs that gappers do overseas. Stories of teachers in Tokyo earning hundreds of thousands of pounds are probably exaggerated, but you can easily make £18,000 a year teaching in Japan or South Korea, which is more than many people earn in their first year of full-time employment in the UK. Living in these countries, however, can be an expensive business.

Most language schools are affiliated with dozens of other language schools around the globe, which makes English-teaching the perfect globetrotting profession. Once you've proven your worth at one school, it's easy to find work at a partner school in another country. As you gain experience, you'll be able to take on more responsibility and earn more dosh. Quite a few gappers take several gap years back to back, and use English-teaching to hopscotch around the globe – nice work if you can get it!

However, there is an art to teaching English overseas. The days when you could turn up in a foreign country and walk straight into an English-teaching job just by talking slowly and loudly in English are gone. Most language schools want to see evidence of formal teacher training, which usually means a certificate in teaching English as a foreign language (TEFL) – see opposite for more information.

In exchange, most schools provide free flights, a work permit (if you need one), and assistance finding accommodation, either with a local host family or in a shared flat with other teachers. Teachers usually have to pay something for rent and board, but levels of pay are pretty good, and most people manage to maintain quite a comfortable lifestyle.

Schools typically employ teachers from a variety of countries and backgrounds, which can make for an interesting social mix. A staff room full of like-minded travellers is a welcome discovery when you have just arrived alone in a new country.

Of course, teaching isn't for everyone. The work can be tedious and frustrating, requiring superhuman levels of patience, especially if the students are absolute beginners and have to learn everything from scratch. Bettina Shzu has this cautionary tale from her time teaching English on the Indian Ocean island of Réunion.

One of the worst classes I had was at a school where I wasn't wanted. Because I came late and wasn't expected, I was assigned a class notorious for apathy. Many students were smart and creative but were too lazy to work. I had to keep on going back to basic sentence structure, even though all of them had been learning English since primary school.

I experimented with different lesson plans. I shared jokes. I asked students to suggest songs for translation. I asked for group work and made up creative make-believe scenarios. Eventually I gave up. I dreaded going to class and the students could tell. For the rest of the year, it was just two hours a week of torturous clock-watching.

Teaching can also be very demanding on your time. For every hour in the classroom, you'll probably spend at least half an hour preparing for lessons; being pinned down to a five- or six-day week doesn't leave much time for travelling around either.

However, it isn't all work, work, work. Schedules are often split between morning and evening classes and at least one day of the weekend will be free, so you'll have some time to explore the local area. As long as you are self-reliant, gregarious and don't take life too seriously, you should have a whale of a time.

TEACHING ENGLISH AS A FOREIGN LANGUAGE (TEFL)

Gone are the days when being able to speak English fluently was the only qualification required to become an English-language teacher. Increasingly, language schools are asking for cold, hard qualifications.

In fact, there are two main certificates that qualify you to teach English overseas – TEFL (pronounced teffle) and TESOL (Teachers of English to Speakers of Other Languages). Both qualifications are accepted as proof of teaching competence by schools all over the world.

There are a handful of places where you can teach English without qualifications – specifically China, Japan and Korea – but you generally need to be a university graduate. People with formal teacher training can also find work overseas without a TEFL or TESOL certificate – both these options are covered in detail in Teaching for Graduates (p355).

Training

Speaking English is the bottom-line entry requirement for English teachers, but the vast majority of schools ask for a recognised English-language teaching qualification. With so many people jumping on the English-language teaching bandwagon, a TEFL or TESOL certificate really is the minimum requirement if you want to find a teaching job with decent working conditions and a respectable salary.

You can study for both these qualifications at dozens of teacher training centres around the UK and worldwide. However, not all TEFL and TESOL certificates carry the same weight with employers, so it's worth paying a bit extra for a certificate that is backed by a big international organisation.

The most widely recognised TEFL certificate is CELTA (Certificate in English-Language Teaching to Adults), which is administered by the University of Cambridge ESOL (English for Speakers of Other Languages) department. Training centres that offer the qualification are listed on the university website at www.cambridgeesol.org.

The main rival to CELTA is CertTESOL (Certificate in Teaching English to Speakers of Other Languages), administered by Trinity College London; there are listings of approved centres on the Trinity College website at www.trinitycollege.co.uk.

Most courses combine lessons on teaching methods with live teaching sessions where you get to practise what you've learned. Toby Stanier sent us this description of a typical day on a TEFL course:

You spend the morning getting lessons on teaching and the afternoon actually teaching yourself, which is useful as you gain experience of actually getting up and talking to a class. However, you then have to watch everyone else on the course do the same, which can be a bit dull and repetitive.

Applicants to CELTA or CertTESOL courses must be educated up to the level for university entrance and the minimum age is from 18 to 21. Full-time courses last four to five weeks and cost anything from £650 to £1250 depending on where you study. You can also study part-time over nine or 10 weeks, but this will cost more – typically £1300 to £1900.

Studying overseas is usually the cheapest way to obtain a TEFL/TESOL certificate, particularly in Eastern Europe (where the costs of accommodation and beer are also attractively low). Course fees can be a fraction of what they are in the UK but you must cover your flights and accommodation.

As well as the University of Cambridge ESOL and Trinity College certificates, many large international language schools run their own TEFL and TESOL courses. Although these don't have quite the same international clout as CELTA or CertTESOL, the schools generally give graduates of their courses preferential treatment when it comes to finding a job. Some schools even offer reduced fees if you agree to work for a partner school at the end of the course.

The language school International House (www.ihworld.com) operates schools in 40 countries, with a particular focus on Italy, Portugal, Spain, Poland and the UK. The head office in London (see p358 for contact details) offers CELTA training or a special International House TEFL certificate, with the option of working at an affiliated school overseas on completion.

If you are fluent in another European language, you can also take a Language Teaching to Adults (LTA) course, which qualifies you to teach French, German, Italian or Spanish overseas. You can also study for the certificates at International House schools overseas.

One unusual option is the TEFL Bus (www.tefl-bus.com), run by the language school Via Lingua (see p359 for contact details), which combines TEFL training with an overland bus tour through Europe and North Africa. Along the way, you study for a TEFL certificate at four partner schools around Europe.

As a general rule, you should be sceptical of any course that offers less than 100 hours of tuition and less than six hours of classroom practice. However, there are some shorter online study courses – such as the course offered by the volunteer organisation i-to-i (see p359) – that provide a basic introduction to TEFL teaching and may be useful for people who want to work as a volunteer teacher.

Most training centres have a screening process for applicants to make sure you have the necessary qualities for teaching. This usually begins with a test of vocabulary and grammar, followed by a face-to-face discussion, which will enable the school to assess how well you stand up to the pressures of teaching to a group of strangers.

Even after you are accepted, you must still work hard throughout the course to pass, though reassuringly, only about 5% of candidates fail or drop out of TEFL/TESOL courses worldwide.

FINDING A TEFL/TESOL COURSE

The logical starting point for finding a TEFL/TESOL course is to visit the websites of University of Cambridge ESOL and Trinity College. The organisation Cactus TEFL (p358; www .cactustefl.com) acts as a central admissions centre for TEFL and TESOL courses worldwide – the website is a good place to gauge the prices of courses in different countries.

You can also find listings of courses on the following websites.

Europa Pages (www.europa-pages.com)
TEFL.net (www.tefl.net/tcd)
TESALL (www.tesall.com)

Jobs for TEFL Teachers

Once you have a TEFL or TESOL certificate in your hand, you can start looking for a teaching job. If you studied for a course that came with a guaranteed job offer, this may already be taken care of, but if not, you will have to start contacting schools and agencies and offering your services.

Teaching positions in high-profile cities such as Paris, Rome or Barcelona get snapped up quickly, so it pays to be a little bit flexible about where you get posted. The school that finally offers you a job could easily be somewhere less glamorous such as Wroclaw in Poland or Odessa in Ukraine. In practice, most people manage to find a job in their first choice of country, but if you are dead set on working in a specific city, start looking for a job as early as possible.

It also pays to time your job search to coincide with the annual recruitment drive from May to August, when schools take on new staff for the academic year beginning in September. Contracts typically last for one full year, but some schools have a second recruitment drive in January or February for short three-month summer contracts starting in June or July.

Some people manage to find a contract starting immediately, but more often, you'll have to allow a lead time of around three months. However, a word of warning: if you break your contract before the year is up you normally forfeit the return flight and may have to pay back the cost of the outbound journey, too.

Before you start your job search, give some thought to the kind of teaching you want to do. Would you prefer to work in a big city or out in the countryside? Do you want to teach children or adults? Big cities provide more distractions outside class hours, but the costs of living are higher, and teachers at rural schools usually manage to save more money (there are fewer things to spend it on!). Children can be enthusiastic and fun to teach, but they are also easily distracted and prone to mucking about. Adults tend to be more focussed and willing to learn.

Simone Manegre spent a year teaching English to children in Japan and has the following advice for new teachers:

Before you accept a job overseas, make sure it meets all your requirements in terms of location and size of city, type of school, whether students are children or adults, whether you teach conversational English or English grammar, if textbooks are provided or if you are solely responsible for planning lessons, how many hours of teaching are required per week etc.

The school I worked for was privately owned and run by one woman who had spent a couple of years in Canada as a student. She was the sweetest boss I have ever had in my life and I was the only teacher, so it was a very intimate setting. I taught conversational English with textbooks, so I didn't have to spend much time preparing lessons. The job was super cushy for the amount of work I had to put in and I made enough money to live comfortably and still save.

It is sometimes possible to get a job teaching English without a TEFL qualification, but you may find yourself stuck at a dubious cowboy school, with little job security and wages that barely cover your living costs. Nevertheless, once you've worked at one language school, you'll have the required experience to apply for work at other, better schools, so this isn't necessarily a wasted enterprise.

Lara Day got lucky when she applied for a job at a French-language school after finishing her English degree:

I thought I'd be able to find work teaching English with an English degree from Oxford under my belt, but I had trouble getting interviews because I was younger than most of the French graduates and I lacked a TEFL qualification (the French tend to be sticklers for diplômes*).*

When I was invited for an interview by a private language school I was thrilled, but instead of a teaching job, they offered me a position as a receptionist. Despite some misgivings, I took the job and at the end of the summer, the school asked me to stay on. I said yes on the condition that I could stay on to teach afterwards. The school agreed, so I began a year-long career as a TEFL teacher.

However, the transition from receptionist to teacher wasn't a natural one. Although I got on well with the students, being sweet on the telephone was very different from having to instruct people, some of whom were much older than me. But with the support of the school and a bit of bluffing, I managed to settle into my new role without too much difficulty.

As a rule, there are usually more opportunities in the developing world. Private schools in Thailand and Cambodia have a good record for taking on unqualified teachers. Job adverts are often posted on hostel and hotel noticeboards in Bangkok and Phnom Penh, or you could try posting a message on Lonely Planet's online travellers forum Thorntree (http://thorntree.lonelyplanet.com) asking for recommendations.

Regardless of where you want to work, the arrival of the Internet has made finding a teaching job overseas so much easier. These days, there are hundreds of websites that list ELT jobs and many will link you straight through to pages where you can apply for jobs online. Note that North American websites may refer to English-language teaching as ESL (English as a Second Language) or EFL (English as a Foreign Language).

Top websites for teaching jobs:

Dave's ESL Cafe (www.eslcafe.com) Dave Sperling's long-running ESL site has jobs listings, teaching advice and teachers' forums.

Edufind Jobs (www.jobs.edunet.com) International teaching site with a country-by-country search engine for TEFL jobs.

EFL Web (www.eflweb.com) Good TEFL site for beginners with advice on teaching and TEFL courses and job vacancies.

EL Gazette (www.elgazette.com) Online TEFL magazine with teaching news and jobs listings.

ELT News (www.eltnews.com) Japanese teaching site with jobs listings and a message board.

ESL Guide (www.esl-guide.com) US site with worldwide listings of jobs and English-language schools.

Europa Pages (www.europa-pages.com/jobs) Europe-focussed site with information on TEFL courses in Europe and teaching jobs worldwide.

Guardian TEFL News (http://education.guardian.co.uk/tefl) Part of the *Guardian* newspaper, with TEFL news, advice and jobs.

TEFL Asia (www.teflasia.com) Extensive listings of teaching jobs across Asia.

TEFL Professional Network (www.tefl.com) Huge jobs site with TEFL jobs listings worldwide.

TEFL.Net (www.tefl.net) International TEFL site with listings of jobs and courses and a forum for teachers.

TESOL Job Finder (www.vv-vv.com/tesol) Search engine for English teaching jobs run by the US governing body for English-language teaching.

Another option is to contact language schools directly. Some of the biggest schools are covered in Contacts (p358), or you can find more listings in the *EL Gazette Guide to English Language Teaching around the World* (Short Books, £13.95) or Susan Griffith's comprehensive *Teaching English Abroad* (Vacation Work, £12.95).

TEACHING FOR GRADUATES

With university behind you and a brand new qualification in your hand, you can take advantage of several graduate teaching programs. Many of the most lucrative opportunities for graduates are in Asia, where language schools employ English-speaking university graduates as English-language teachers without any requirement for a TEFL/TESOL certificate or previous teaching experience.

Most of these schools offer high salaries, guaranteed work permits and free flights, as well as discounted accommodation, but you must have completed a university degree. Contracts typically last for one year, with the option to extend if you form a good relationship with the host school.

The most famous teaching project in Asia is the Japanese government's Japan Exchange and Teaching (JET) scheme – covered in detail on p356 – but there are similar schemes at private schools in Japan, South Korea and China (see p360 for some examples). In fact, China has seen a massive explosion in English-language teaching in the run-up to the 2008 Olympics in Beijing.

The following websites provide useful information on teaching in Asia.

Ohayo Sensei (www.ohayosensei.com) Bimonthly newsletter for foreign teachers in Japan, with extensive jobs listings.

Teach in China (www.teach-in-china.net) Online classifieds site with teaching jobs across China.

Teach Korea (www.teachkorea.com) Useful site with jobs listings and general tips about teaching in Korea.

Teaching in Japan (www.teachinginjapan.com) Useful website with information on all aspects of teaching in Japan.

If the teaching is more important than the money, Voluntary Service Overseas (VSO; www.vso.org.uk) offers a huge range of two-year volunteering opportunities worldwide for graduates, including teaching placements. However, bear in mind that the focus of VSO placements is on helping people rather than making money. VSO will cover your expenses but placements don't come with a salary.

Many of the big gap year organisations offer voluntary teaching opportunities in the developing world, but you normally have to make a financial contribution to join the projects. BUNAC (p337; www.bunac.org.uk), Travellers Worldwide (p293; www.travellersworldwide.com), i-to-i (p290; www.i-to-i.com) and IST Plus (p339; www.istplus.com; part of CIEE/

Council Exchanges) offer teaching placements in Asia that come with a small local salary, but these are mainly for university graduates. Volunteering, Conservation & Expeditions (p264) has more information on teaching as a volunteer.

If you have formal teaching qualifications, you may be able to find work at an international school overseas. These upmarket private schools teach the UK curriculum to children of wealthy locals and expats. There are opportunities for teachers of most subjects and wages can be quite generous. You generally need a teaching degree or a PGCE (one-year-long teaching conversion course) plus a TEFL/TESOL qualification and some schools ask for one or two years of teaching experience.

The following websites list international schools.

Association for the Advancement of International Education (www.aaie.org)
Council of International Schools (www.cois.org)
Mediterranean Association of International Schools (www.mais-web.org)

The British Council

One of the best options for people with teaching qualifications is the British Council (www .britishcouncil.org) – see p360 for more contact details. To work as a fully-fledged British Council teacher you generally need a TEFL or TESOL diploma, rather than a certificate, and two years of TEFL teaching experience. Graduates with language degrees, however, can work as English Language Assistants at affiliated schools in 20 countries worldwide, including Russia, China, Canada and most nations in Western Europe.

To qualify, you must be a native English speaker (preferably a British citizen) with a full secondary education (up to the age of 18) and at least two years of higher education, which usually means a university degree in the language of the host country. Placements in China are open to graduates of any discipline.

Contracts are for one year or a single six-month semester and assistants work 12 to 18 hours per week. The salary varies depending on where you get posted: in Canada, you can earn £1000 per month but you must cover your own living costs, while in Russia, the salary drops to just £175 per month, but accommodation and meals are provided. All teaching assistants must cover their own flights and insurance.

There is also a special program in Germany for pre-university gap-year students, but only eight to 10 places are offered each year. The scheme is open to students aged 18 to 20, and you must have a German A-level to qualify. Successful applicants work in a rural German school for a year and earn a salary of around £120 per month, and receive free room and board.

To apply for any of these positions, download an application form from the website www .britishcouncil.org/languageassistants.htm. All applicants must have a medical examination and there's usually a face-to-face interview. The deadline for applications varies for each country (most are from December to March), and positions start the following September – the website has full details.

JET (Japan Exchange & Teaching)

One of the most popular schemes that allows graduates to teach overseas is JET. This government program invites huge numbers of university graduates from overseas to teach in Belgium. Just joking. Japan. To apply, you must be aged 39 or younger and a university graduate, but you don't need a TEFL certificate. This is a generous program – JET offers a year of work at full pay, flights are free and there is no fee to take part in the scheme.

There are two jobs you can apply for – Language Assistants teach English in Japanese schools while Coordinators for International Relations (CIR) assist in the day to day running of local government departments (you must be fluent in Japanese for this position).

Participants work a 35-hour week from Monday to Friday and earn an annual salary of around £18,400. However, you must pay for accommodation and compulsory health insurance. Living in Japan is notoriously expensive, particularly if you develop a taste for sashimi, karaoke and the latest consumer electronics. However, with a little self-control, you should be able to live quite comfortably and even save money.

In the UK, JET is administered by the Japanese embassy in London (see p361 for contact details) – around 400 teachers and 10 CIRs from the UK took part in JET in 2004. The official UK website for the JET program is www.jet-uk.org, but you can also find detailed information on the international JET website www.jetprogram.org.

Applications are accepted from late September and the interviews take place from November. There's an orientation for successful applicants in July, shortly before you leave for Japan. If the school is impressed with your work, you may be able to extend the program to three or even five years.

However, you must have lived outside Japan for six or more of the last eight years when you apply and you must wait 10 years before you can repeat the program. You can express a preference about where you are placed, but schools in big cities such as Tokyo and Osaka fill up quickly and many people end up teaching in rural schools.

It's a good idea to talk to former participants to find out more about the experience of being a foreign worker in Japan. The website of the Japan Exchange & Teaching Alumni Association (JETAA; www.jet.org) lists websites run by past and current participants.

Tom Luff gave us this appraisal of his time on the JET program:

I taught English in two state schools to students aged 15 to 18 and though I was officially an assistant language teacher, I often led the classes myself. I spent three or four hours per day teaching, plus about an hour for lesson planning and marking. This left plenty of time for extracurricular activities, and to chat with the teachers and study Japanese.

The language barrier and cultural misunderstandings were sometimes overwhelming. But the JET program offered a unique insight into Japan and its way of life, and to use a nice, well-worn cliché, it's what you make of it.

OTHER KINDS OF TEACHING

It is possible to find other teaching jobs abroad aside from teaching languages, but this will generally depend on you having desirable skills that you can pass on to others. The ability to whistle the theme tune to *Mission Impossible* probably won't cut it. One popular option is to teach adventure sports at foreign resorts – see Activity Holidays (p372) for more information.

Some people manage to find work teaching computer skills or alternative therapies overseas, but these kinds of jobs generally come about as a result of living in a foreign country and spotting an opportunity. If you have a particular gift for desktop computing, yoga, t'ai chi, massage or martial arts, you could try advertising your services as a freelance instructor in backpacker haunts such as Ko Samui in Thailand or Byron Bay in Australia.

Musicians may be able to pick up work teaching other people to play their instruments – you can always fall back on busking if your teaching ambitions come to naught. However, bear in mind that the immigration authorities tend to frown on foreign visitors who work without a permit. If you get caught working illegally, you could find yourself on the next plane home.

CONTACTS
TEFL & TESOL Courses

The following organisations offer training for English-language teachers and most provide jobs at schools overseas at the end of the course.

Bell Language School
Hillcross, 1 Red Cross Lane, Cambridge CB2 2QX
☎ 01223 212333
fax 01223 410282
info@bell-centres.com
www.bell-centres.com
This UK-based school runs CELTA programs in Cambridge and Norwich. Bell has affiliated English-language schools in Bulgaria, China, Czech Republic, Latvia, Malta, Poland, Spain, Switzerland and Thailand, which offer employment opportunities once you are qualified.
Type of Course: CELTA.
Timing & Length of Course: Four weeks for CELTA, starting on set dates monthly.
Destination: UK.
Costs: The CELTA course costs £962, plus an £85 candidate entry fee. Accommodation can be arranged.
Eligibility: Minimum age is 20 and you must have academic qualifications up to university entrance level.

Cactus TEFL
4 Clarence House, 30–31 North St, Brighton BN1 1EB
☎ 0845 130 4775
fax 01273 775686
suzanne@cactustefl.com
www.cactustefl.com
Cactus offers language courses worldwide and also acts as an admissions service for internationally recognised TEFL/TESOL certificate courses – see the website for listings of courses worldwide.

EF English First
Arthur House, Chorlton St, Manchester M1 3EJ
☎ 0161 236 7494, 0161 236 5521 (recruitment)
fax 0161 236 0949
recruitment.uk@englishfirst.com
www.englishfirst.com
This international English-language school has branches worldwide and offers TEFL and TESOL courses in Manchester and in Hove (near Brighton, UK). As well as Trinity College–certified courses, the school has its own TEFL course. Prices are significantly reduced if you work at an EF school overseas after the course.
Types of Courses: Trinity CertTESOL or the EF TEFL Certificate (equivalent to CELTA).
Timing & Length of Courses: Four weeks for CertTESOL (eight weeks part time), approximately monthly. The EF TEFL course lasts four weeks, starting on set dates around four times a year.
Destinations: Currently, the Trinity course is only available in Manchester, but you can take the TEFL course in Manchester or Hove (UK), and some other overseas locations. Once you complete the course, there are job opportunities at 170 affiliated schools worldwide, particularly in China and Indonesia.
Costs: Vary with the training centre – in Manchester, the EF TEFL and CertTESOL courses costs £800. If you agree to work for EF after the course, prices drop to £400.
Eligibility: Minimum age is 19 and you must be educated to the level for university entrance.

Inlingua International
Rodney Lodge, Rodney Rd, Cheltenham, Gloucestershire GL50 1HX
☎ 01242 250493
fax 01242 250495
info@inlingua-cheltenham.co.uk
www.inlingua-cheltenham.co.uk
Inlingua has 300 member schools worldwide and offers TESOL training at its UK centre in Cheltenham, with the option to work at Inlingua schools at the end of the course. There's also an optional one-week-long business-English course that you can take in conjunction with your TESOL certificate.
Type of Course: Trinity CertTESOL.
Timing & Length of Course: Five weeks for CertTESOL, starting monthly.
Destination: Cheltenham (UK).
Costs: CertTESOL costs £995 and the business-English course costs £298 (less if you also book the CertTESOL course).
Eligibility: You need university entry-level qualifications for CertTESOL.

International House London
106 Piccadilly, London W1J 7NL
☎ 020 7518 6999
fax 020 7518 6998

info@ihlondon.co.uk

www.ihlondon.co.uk

This leading London language institute offers a variety of teacher training courses, including CELTA and an International House–certified TEFL course. There are also International House Language Teaching to Adults (LTA) certificates for French, German, Italian and Spanish. Jobs are then available at International House partner schools in 38 countries.

Types of Courses: Various TEFL courses, plus courses in teaching other European languages.

Timing & Length of Courses: CELTA and IH TEFL courses last four weeks; LTA courses last four or eight weeks.

Destinations: Courses run year-round in London (UK), then there are job opportunities at 120 partner schools in Europe, the Americas, Africa, Asia and the Middle East – see the website www.ihworld.com for a full list.

Costs: Fees vary with the course – for example, the standard CELTA course costs £1110 including the International House registration fee.

Eligibility: Minimum age is 21 (18 for CELTA and IH TEFL courses) and you must be a native speaker or completely fluent in the appropriate language.

i-to-i

Woodside House, 261 Low Lane, Leeds, LS18 5NY

☎ 0870 787 2375

fax 0113 205 4619

info@i-to-i.com

www.onlinetefl.com

This popular year-out organisation offers an online TEFL course, accredited by the Open and Distance Learning Quality Council, which oversees distance learning courses in the UK. The course is popular with volunteer teachers and training is conducted using the Internet and an interactive CD.

Type of Course: Online TEFL.

Timing & Length of Courses: Courses last 40 or 60 hours and you can work to your own timetable.

Destination: Online.

Costs: The 40-/60-hour courses cost £245/275.

Eligibility: The courses are open to fluent English speakers aged 17 or older.

Language Link

181 Earl's Court Rd, London SW5 9RB

☎ 020 7370 4755

fax 020 7370 1123

teachertraining@languagelink.co.uk

www.languagelink.co.uk

Language Link has 30 years' experience of English-language teaching. On completion, teachers can apply for placements at 50 affiliated schools.

Type of Course: CELTA.

Timing & Length of Course: The standard CELTA course lasts four weeks and starts monthly.

Destinations: CELTA training takes place in London (UK), Beijing (China) or Hanoi (Vietnam), then there are jobs in China, Slovakia, Russia or Vietnam.

Costs: Varies with the location; in the UK, the full-time CELTA course is £695.

Eligibility: Minimum age is 20 and you should be a university graduate.

Saxoncourt UK

59 South Molton St, London W1K 5SN

☎ 020 7499 8533

fax 020 7499 9374

tt@saxoncourt.com

www.saxoncourt.com

Saxoncourt offers CELTA training in London (UK), Cape Town (South Africa) and Honolulu (Hawaii), with the option to go on to work at private language schools in 20 countries worldwide. The Trinity CertTESOL course is sometimes available in Auckland.

Type of Courses: CELTA and Trinity CertTESOL.

Timing & Length of Courses: Vary with the course – the four-week CELTA course involves 100 training hours and six classroom hours. In London (UK), courses start on set dates monthly.

Destinations: There are training centres in Auckland (New Zealand), Cape Town (South Africa), London (UK), and in the USA. There are teaching placements worldwide.

Costs: Vary with the training centre – CELTA courses in the UK cost £695.

Eligibility: Minimum age is 18 (20 in South Africa and Hawaii) and you must have education to level for university entry.

Via Lingua

FAO Rufus Vaughan-Spruce, Via Lingua EPE, K Hiotaki 7, Hania 73134, Crete, Greece

☎ 00 30 28210 55577

info@vialingua.org

www.vialingua.org

The large international ESL teacher-training school provides TEFL certificate training in 10 European countries and provides help with finding a job on completion of the

course. It also offers the unusual TEFL Bus (www.tefl-bus
.com), which combines TEFL training with an overland bus
tour through Europe and North Africa.

Type of Course: Via Lingua TEFL Certificate.
Timing & Length of Course: Four weeks, with 120
hours tuition and 10 hours teaching practice. Dates vary
with the location – see the website for details. The TEFL
Bus tour lasts 11 weeks, with a week of tuition in four dif-
ferent European cities. There are two departures a year.
Destinations: Australia, Crete, Czech Republic, Germany,
Greece, Hungary, Italy, Mexico, Spain, Portugal, Russia
and Turkey.
Costs: Vary with the location – in Rome the course costs
£1040, plus around £175 for accommodation. The TEFL
Bus costs £2055, which includes meals, lodging, transport
and tuition.
Eligibility: Minimum age is 20 and you must be fluent in
English and educated to the level for university entry.

Windsor TEFL

21 Osborne Rd, Windsor, Berkshire SL4 3EG
☎ 01753 858995
fax 01753 831726
info@windsorschools.co.uk
www.windsorschools.co.uk
This UK-based training centre offers the chance to study
for a Trinity College–accredited TESOL certificate in the UK,
Spain or the Czech Republic.
Type of Course: Trinity CertTESOL.
Timing & Length of Course: One month beginning on
set dates monthly (see the website for details).
Destinations: London, Oxford and Windsor (UK); Barcelona and Madrid (Spain); Prague (Czech Republic).
Costs: UK courses start at £799, plus £99 to cover the
course admin fees charged by Trinity College. Courses in
mainland Europe cost £749 plus a £169 moderation fee.
Accommodation can be arranged for an extra fee.
Eligibility: Minimum age is 18 and you must have two
A-levels or equivalent (eg matriculation in the USA).

TEFL & TESOL Jobs Abroad

The following organisations offer jobs for English-language
teachers overseas.

Berlitz

Lincoln House, 296–302 High Holborn, London WC1 7JH
☎ 020 7611 9640
fax 020 7611 9656

europe.careers@berlitz.com
www.berlitz.co.uk
Berlitz is a huge international ELT employer and it has more
that 400 schools worldwide – use the search engine on
the website to see where you are eligible to work. There
are also teaching opportunities for fluent speakers of other
European languages (particularly French and German).
Timing & Length of Work: Minimum of one year.
Destinations: Worldwide.
Costs/Pay: Wages vary with the destination.
Eligibility: Minimum age is 21 and you must have a
university degree and be a native speaker of the language
you want to teach.
TEFL Requirement: Teacher training is provided by
Berlitz and you can then work anywhere that you can
obtain a visa for.

British Council

Language Assistants Team, Education and Training Group,
British Council, 10 Spring Gardens, London SW1A 2BN
☎ 020 7389 4596
assistants@britishcouncil.org
www.britishcouncil.org/languageassistants.htm
The British Council is the largest employer of ESL teachers
in the world. Most formal teaching positions require ESL
teaching experience, but gappers with a university language
degree can work as language assistants – see p356 for details.

China Education Exchange

Asian Games Garden, Building No 2-6A, No12 Xiaoying Lu,
Chao Yang District, Beijing 100101, China
☎ 00 86 10 8463 4451
fax 00 86 10 8463 4872
teaching@cbwchina.com or cex@chinaeducationexchange.org
www.chinaeducationexchange.org
This is the only ESL teaching program officially approved
by the government of the People's Republic of China. There
are opportunities all over China and teachers are recruited
from most English-speaking countries.
Timing & Length of Work: Contracts last six months
to a year.
Destination: China.
Costs/Pay: You can apply to schools directly via the website
or sign up for an organised placement through China Education Exchange for an application fee of £44. Accommodation,
work permits and visas are provided and most schools
reimburse the cost of your plane ticket at the end of your
contract. Wages range from £155 to £310 per month.

Eligibility: Minimum age is 21 and you should be native English speaker. A university degree is preferred.
TEFL Requirement: A TEFL/TESOL certificate is required for some positions.

China TEFL Network

16th fl, Blue Sky Business Center, 18 Moganshan Rd, Hangzhou, Zhejiang 310005, China
☎ /fax 00 86 571 8823 4517
helen@chinatefl.com
www.chinatefl.com
This Chinese organisation acts as an agency, linking qualified English-language teachers to schools and universities across China. Around 20,000 teachers find jobs through the site each year and you can post your CV online.
Timing & Length of Work: One or two years.
Destination: China.
Costs/Pay: There is no charge for job seekers to search the database and all teaching positions are paid.
Eligibility: Open to teachers of all nationalities.
TEFL Requirement: TEFL or equivalent certification required.

ECC Foreign Language Institute

EEC UK, c/o AIL International Ltd, Pardix House, Cadmore Lane, Cheshunt, Hertfordshire EN8 9LQ
☎ 01992 642677
fax 01992 642675
ail@orbix.co.uk
www.japanbound.com
This Japanese organisation runs language schools across Japan and hires large numbers of English-language teachers from overseas. The website has details of recruitment offices around the world and applications are also accepted from people who are already in Japan.
Timing & Length of Work: Minimum of one year, with the option to renew annually.
Destination: Japan.
Costs/Pay: Wages are around £1250 per month before tax. Flights, visa fees, accommodation etc are extra.
Eligibility: Minimum requirement is a degree and native English – there are interviewing offices in Canada, the USA, the UK and Australia.
TEFL Requirement: No formal TEFL/TESOL requirement.

International Department of Liaoning Union of Degree & Graduate Education

Room 1108, A, No 20, Beiling St, Shenyang City 110032, China
☎ /fax 00 86 24 6223 1958

teachers@ludge.org or teach@ludge.org
www.teach-in-china.cn
This Chinese government program recruits English-language teachers to work in the northeastern Chinese province of Liaoning. There are places in schools, colleges and universities and teachers get free accommodation and a local salary.
Timing & Length of Work: Contracts last six months from September or February, or one year from September.
Destination: China.
Pay: Teachers earn around £200 per month and you get a one-way/return plane ticket to China if you work six/twelve months.
Eligibility: Applicants should be university graduates with fluent English.
TEFL Requirement: TEFL/TESOL qualifications are an advantage.

Japan Exchange & Teaching (JET)

Embassy of Japan, 101–104 Piccadilly, London W1J 7JT
☎ 020 7465 6668/6670
fax 020 7491 9347
info@jet-uk.org
www.jet-uk.org
This is the UK office of the popular JET exchange program, which allows university graduates to work in Japan as teachers or international relations coordinators for a year or more – see p356 for details.

Linguarama

Moorgate Hall, 155 Moorgate, London EC2M 6XB
☎ 020 7382 1800
fax 020 7374 0507
personnel@linguarama.com
www.linguarama.com
Linguarama runs numerous English-language schools in Western Europe and has regular openings for qualified teachers to teach English to business clients.
Timing & Length of Work: Contracts generally last nine months from September, but you can extend this by teaching English to foreign students in the UK over the summer.
Destinations: You can work across 21 schools in France, Germany, Italy, the Netherlands, Spain and the UK.
Costs/Pay: Wages are proportional to the local cost of living and flights and accommodation are provided.
Eligibility: Must have a university degree and EU citizenship. Teaching and business experience is an advantage.
TEFL Requirement: A recognised TEFL or TESOL certificate is required.

Nova Group

Carrington House, 126–130 Regents St, London W1B 5SE

☎ 020 734 2727

fax 020 734 3001

applications@novagroupuk.com

www.teachinjapan.com

Nova is Japan's largest private language school, with 580 branches throughout the country. There are opportunities for English, Spanish and German university graduates and no previous teaching experience is required.

Timing & Length of Work: Contracts last one year.

Destination: Japan.

Costs/Pay: Flights, accommodation and work permits are provided and you can earn £870 to £1360 per month, depending on the school and number of weekly teaching hours.

Eligibility: Must have a university degree and teach in your native tongue. There is no requirement to speak Japanese, but teaching experience can be an advantage.

TEFL Requirement: No TEFL or TESOL certification required.

YBM Education

7th fl, YBM Education Center, 56-15 Chongno 2-ga, Chongno-gu, Seoul 110-122, Korea

☎ 00 82 2-2267 0532

eccmain@ybmsisa.co.kr

www.ybmecc.co.kr

YBM operates a series of franchised English schools across Korea and it accepts large numbers of foreign English-language teachers on sponsored work permits.

Timing & Length of Work: One year.

Destination: Republic of Korea.

Pay: The monthly salary starts from £780 per month and YBM covers your flights, national-holiday and health-insurance costs and shared teacher accommodation.

Eligibility: The program is open to native English speakers with a university degree from the UK, USA, Canada, Australia, or New Zealand. Experience of ESL teaching or working with children is preferred.

TEFL Requirement: TEFL/TESOL training is useful but not essential.

CASUAL & SEASONAL WORK

If you want to make a bit of money without signing your whole gap year away, then casual work is the way to go. Working on a casual basis has loads of advantages. You can start and leave whenever you want. You can do almost any job that takes your fancy. And on top of this, you'll walk away with spending money at the end of the day.

Lots of people take on casual jobs to earn a bit of cash before embarking on a gap-year project overseas, but there are loads of exciting ways to travel and do casual work at the same time. The only real obstacle is getting a visa that will allow you to work in the country where you want to work.

Luckily for gappers, Britain has special immigration agreements with various countries that allow young Brits to travel and work in casual jobs for a summer or even a whole year. We'll cover these upfront, as you can do any job you like once you have the official seal of approval.

With a work permit, a whole world of casual work opens up. You could do bar work in Athens or New York. Or maybe spend the winter as a ski instructor in the Rocky Mountains. Or how about picking bananas on the coast of Australia? Whatever you feel like doing, this chapter should give you some pointers.

CASUAL WORK PERMITS

If you're young, able and willing to work overseas, the world is your oyster, well almost. First you need to get permission to work overseas, which isn't quite as easy as it sounds. British citizens can work wherever they want within the European Economic Area (EEA), including the new member states of the EU (see p332), but to work outside Europe you need a work permit. Fortunately, students and young people are eligible for special treatment.

The UK has special arrangements with a number of countries that allow people of a certain age to visit each other's countries to work. Currently gappers from the UK can use these schemes to visit the USA, Canada, Australia, New Zealand, South Africa and Japan. The website www.liveworkplay.com.au/visa.html is primarily set up for Australians but also provides information on working holidays for Brits around the world. The following sections cover the nuts and bolts of the main working-holiday programs.

We generally don't recommend working without a work permit. If you work illegally and get caught, you'll probably be deported at your own expense and you may never be able to visit that country again, even for a holiday!

Working in the USA

People with American relatives or dual British-American nationality may be able to apply for a residents permit which allows you to do any job in the USA. Everyone else will need to obtain a work permit. The easiest way to go about this is to apply for sponsorship from an educational exchange organisation such as the British Universities North America Club (BUNAC), which will arrange the paperwork for a J1 visa. This lets you work for up to four months over the summer and travel for up to a month after you finish work. You normally need a confirmed job offer before you start but you can change jobs once you reach America.

The total cost of the program is around £745, including flights, visa fees and insurance, and you must provide evidence of £210 in emergency funds (£420 if you don't have a job offer in advance). You must also attend an interview at the US embassy in London or Belfast (£65) and register on the SEVIS (Student and Exchange Visitor Information System) scheme (US$100) – see p326.

Most of the job opportunities are at resorts, theme parks and other places that employ seasonal workers. Work in health care, however, is prohibited. The same organisations can also place you in a support role (eg cleaning, cooking) at children's summer camps in the US with free flights and a guaranteed job placement. However, you need a clean criminal record and a medical to make sure you aren't carrying anything noxious from Europe that might affect clean-living American children!

This used to be a great option for gappers, but sadly the US immigration authorities are putting the squeeze on foreign casual workers. To qualify for the J1 visa, you must now be a student aged 18 or over on a degree course (or equivalent) *and* be returning to university after the summer.

A more practical way for gappers to work in the US is on an H2B visa. The company that hires you must apply on your behalf and you have to work in the same job for your entire stay. The visa is initially granted for up to a year but can be extended, providing you stay with the same company. Several of the big working-holiday organisations can arrange H2B visas with a guaranteed job offer for a fee, which is usually the easiest way to go about things – see p376. Some of the larger ski resorts (p384) also sponsor gappers on H2B visas.

Working in Canada

Students and non-students aged 18 to 35 can work for up to a year in Canada in any job, apart from camp counselling and – curiously – tobacco picking. British citizens should apply through BUNAC or one of the other organisations listed in Contacts (p376). Irish citizens should apply through the Irish travel company USIT.

There's an application fee of about £160 and you must cover the costs of your travel insurance and flights, and bring a minimum of £500 in funds. To work in health or child-care, you need a Canadian-government approved medical, which can be arranged by the sponsoring organisation for around £150. Most companies ask you to attend a scheduled orientation in Toronto, Montreal or Vancouver.

There's an annual quota, which can be filled as early as May – apply early in January to avoid disappointment. You can leave and re-enter Canada during the year, but you can only participate in the scheme once; if you have previously visited Canada with a visa, you must wait 12 months before you can apply. For more details, visit the website www.canada.org.uk.

Working in Australia, New Zealand & South America

Working in Australia, New Zealand or Japan is a much more relaxed affair. You can apply for a year-long working-holiday visa yourself at the appropriate embassy and then do whatever job you like when you arrive for up to a year.

The working-holiday schemes in Australia and New Zealand are open to anyone aged 18 to 30 but you can only participate in the scheme once for each country, so make sure this is the time when you will get the most out of the experience. The Australian visa restricts you to a limit of three months' work for any particular employer but you can work for as many people as you want to during the year. Some people manage to change departments within the same company to get around this restriction.

The visa fee is £70 for Australia and £50 for New Zealand. You must show evidence of a return plane ticket (or the money to pay for one) and savings of £1500 to £2000. The annual quota of working-holiday visas for British citizens is around 35,000 for Australia and 10,000 for New Zealand. More information can be found on the websites www.immi .gov.au (for Australia) and www.immigration.govt.nz (for New Zealand).

You can apply online for the Australian visa, but you must visit an office of the Department of Immigration and Multicultural and Indigenous Affairs (DIMIA) on arrival in Australia to get a hard copy of the visa stamped into your passport. For New Zealand, you should apply directly to the New Zealand embassy in London.

Many of the working-holiday organisations listed in Contacts can also arrange working-holiday visas in Australia and New Zealand for a fee. Most offer packages that include assistance with job hunting, insurance, orientation sessions, membership cards for useful organisations and support for the whole of your trip, which is useful if you find the idea of spending a year on the other side of the world a bit daunting.

There are also opportunities in Brazil and South Africa for current university students aged 18 to 30 – see p376 for more information.

Working in Japan

Japan issues about 400 year-long working-holiday visas annually to Brits aged between 18 and 25. You must have a return plane ticket (or money to pay for one) and £1500 in savings; the visa fee is £6. Most of the work available is TEFL teaching, but Japanese speakers can also find hospitality and office jobs. See the website www.uk.emb-japan.go.jp for more information. The Japanese Association of Working Holiday Makers (see Contacts for details) provides job-hunting assistance to working holiday-makers.

FINDING A JOB OVERSEAS

Once you've got your work permit or visa, the next step is finding a job. Many working-holiday organisations can set you up with work overseas before you leave, but if you need to find a job independently you can speed things up by starting your job hunt on the web. There are hundreds of job-search and recruitment websites that specialise in seasonal jobs, allowing you to arrange a job almost anywhere in the world from the comfort of your own living room.

Websites that advertise resorts and construction jobs are listed in those sections, but some of the better general job sites include:

www.aboutjobs.com – umbrella site for several American job sites, including www.sum merjobs.com, www.overseasjobs.com and www.resortjobs.com

www.abroadnaway.com – useful for people wanting to work in the USA, with listings of seasonal jobs

www.anyworkanywhere.com – another good work-abroad site with worldwide job listings and an email job bulletin

www.jobpilot.co.uk – Europe-wide job-search site

www.jobsabroad.com – decent American job-listings site

www.jobs-in-europe.net – listings of jobs across Europe, broken down by country

www.nzjobs.go.to – specialises in jobs for working holiday-makers in New Zealand

www.payaway.co.uk – an excellent website with jobs for gappers and an email jobs bulletin

www.voovs.com – has sites devoted to ski and snowboard jobs, hospitality jobs and leisure jobs worldwide

Employment agencies are useful weapons in your job-search arsenal. Many of the agencies listed in the Proper Jobs chapter (p329) also provide seasonal jobs. Alternatively, look in the phone book for the town or city where you want to work – you should be able to find a local recruitment agency who can point you in the direction of some gainful employment.

Most casual jobs overseas involve hospitality, resort or farm work, but there are opportunities to work as an office temp – covered on p330 – or a door-to-door salesperson. Some gappers make a fortune selling vacuum cleaners and encyclopaedias, but it takes a real get-up-and-go personality to make a success of door-to-door selling and you only get paid according to what you sell.

In Australia several backpacker organisations run job searches specifically for people on working-holiday visas. Worldwide Workers (www.worldwideworkers.com) runs recruitment centres in Sydney and Auckland and provides work for thousands of travellers a year at bars, restaurants, hotels, shops, offices and farms.

HOSPITALITY

Hotels, restaurants and bars are huge employers and there is usually loads of work to do over the summer and winter holiday seasons. The best time to apply is about a month before the start of the season, though new openings come up once the season starts as people drop out. Keep an eye out for any new restaurants that look like they might be opening soon.

Tourists always need places to stay and eat, so holiday resorts are great places to pick up hospitality jobs. Places to think about include the Greek Islands and Cyprus; the Spanish Costa Brava and Ibiza; the French Alps; the east coast of Australia; New Zealand (both the North and South Islands); the Rocky Mountains (in Canada and the USA); and the east coast of the US. Note that European companies usually prefer you to speak the local language.

You can often pick up hospitality work by responding to signs in restaurant windows or local ads, or by walking in and asking if they have any work. Some working-holiday organisations can fix you up with a hospitality job in the USA or Canada. Tour operators also take on loads of hospitality staff every season. See the websites at the end of this section for places to start looking for a hospitality job on the net.

Previous experience is helpful but not essential – after all, flipping burgers isn't exactly rocket science. The local minimum-wage laws usually cover hospitality jobs. In the UK, workers aged 18 to 21 must be paid at least £4.10 an hour and workers aged 22 or over earn £4.85. It is also possible to work part-time in exchange for free accommodation, as Andrew Nystrom discovered while backpacking through Ireland:

I was running short on funds and I noticed a flyer on a bulletin board advertising free room and board at a rural farmhouse B&B. I called the woman up and, since she sounded cheery and reasonable I got myself there by hitchhiking across the country. In exchange for vacuuming, cleaning, making beds, and helping out with dinner at night, I got my own (tiny) room, all the great food that was left over and a bit of free time to roam the countryside around the farm. However, I left after a few weeks when the woman refused to let me take a day off to have a pint with some folks who had given me a ride there. Be wary of far-flung situations where you might get stuck and not be able to leave!

HelpExchange.net (www.helpx.net) provides listings of host families, farms, hotels and B&Bs in Europe, Australasia and the Americas that provide free accommodation and food in exchange for unpaid labour (usually from two weeks to a month).

The following websites are useful for hospitality jobs:
www.alseasonsagency.com – hospitality recruitment agency in Australia that provides work for working holiday-makers at certain times of year
www.berkeley-scott.co.uk – UK recruitment agency for temporary hospitality, leisure and office jobs

www.caterer.com – a huge catering website with a worldwide job search for chefs, waiters, kitchen and bar staff
www.wineandhospitalityjobs.com – large US hospitality recruitment site
www.seek.com.au - huge Australian job search engine with lots of catering and hospitality jobs

Hotels & Restaurants

Hotel and restaurant jobs are normally easy to find in seaside resorts, tourist towns and big cities. However, competition for jobs is often fierce so you may have better luck in a quiet, out-of-the-way place. If you don't already have experience, you may get stuck doing jobs such as dishwashing, cleaning or working in the kitchen.

Hotel work typically involves working in reception or cleaning rooms and making beds. Some more upmarket hotels also have jobs for lift operators and old-fashioned bellboys. You generally need computer and typing skills to work on reception but anyone can be a maid, and that includes you guys out there. Wages reflect the unskilled nature of the work – you can earn around £3.50 to £5 per hour in the UK, £3 to £4.50 in the USA and £3.50 to £4.50 in Australia.

A fun – though less well paid – option is to work in a backpacker hostel. Accommodation is usually thrown in and there's often a chance to lead local sightseeing tours and pub crawls. Backpacker hostels can be found all over Europe, Australia, New Zealand, Canada and the USA – try searching on the website www.hostels.com. In Britain, the YHA (www.yha.org .uk) takes on around 400 staff every year for its hostels around the UK.

Restaurants may be looking for waiters, kitchen assistants, chefs (if you have catering qualifications), short-order cooks (if you don't), door staff to greet diners and bus boys to clear away the plates and food. And if you want hands that are soft as your face, there are always openings for people to wash dishes.

Typical hourly wages start at £3.50 to £5 in the UK and £3 to £4.50 in Australia, plus tips. US wages are usually lower – typically £2 to £3 an hour – but you earn loads of tips on top of this. In fact, not tipping is a huge taboo in America – if you leave less than 15% don't be surprised if staff follow you out into the street asking what they did wrong!

Darren Miller provided this story of working as a waiter in Chicago:

I worked on a summer program in the US and ended up taking a job at a Croatian pastry shop in Belmont, the big gay district in Chicago. The work itself was horrible – the boss would sit around all day drinking coffee, moaning to his friends about the staff and making disparaging comments about the clientele – but the tips were fabulous. The gay couples who came to the café tipped really well, and I'd often make US$40 a night in tips. Of course, being a politely spoken Englishman seemed to be a huge asset!

The 'Gap Packs' published by www.gapwork.com have useful listings of hotels and restaurants that employ backpackers around the world. If you don't mind lowering your standards, Ronald MacDonald, Colonel Saunders and friends are invariably on the lookout for fast-food staff.

Bars & Clubs

Bar work is a great way to earn money while you travel, whether you end up pulling pints in a village pub or mixing cocktails – Tom Cruise–style – in a trendy bar downtown. But while the work is easy and very sociable, the pay isn't great and the hours don't suit everyone (though late risers will feel right at home).

These days many places expect you to have some experience behind the bar (this is where that Saturday job at the Crown & Anchor comes into its own). As well as serving drinks

HOW TO GET AHEAD IN BARTENDING

Bar work is the job that most people fantasise about when they head to Australia on a working-holiday visa. However, competition for jobs can be cutthroat and there is never enough work to go around. Fortunately, there are a few steps you can take to make yourself more desirable to foreign publicans.

The first – and most important – is to get some bar experience before you go away. That way, you won't be left scratching your head when your new employer asks you to change a barrel or check the gas. Another way to gain some extra clout is to take a course in mixology (bartending and cocktail-making). You'll learn the difference between a Tom Collins and a Shirley Temple and get some live bartending experience into the bargain. Shaker UK (www.shakerbartending.co.uk) is a recommended course provider – see p429.

To do bar work in Australia, you'll need a Responsible Service of Alcohol (RSA) certificate, which guarantees that you won't serve liquor to underage or intoxicated drinkers. You can get this at the end of a one-day course for around £35. There are listings of approved courses on the website of the Restaurant & Catering Association – follow the links for individual states on www.restaurantcater.asn.au.

And remember, there's no point applying for bar work if you aren't old enough to drink yourself – the minimum legal drinking age is 18 in the UK, Australia, New Zealand, Canada and parts of Europe, and 21 in the USA.

you'll have to change barrels of beer, clean up spilt drinks and persuade people to go home at the end of the night. It's amazing how many people forget they have homes to go to.

The kind of bar work you do will partly depend on where you are. Rural pubs can be pleasantly chilled-out but the time can crawl by. At the other end of the scale, nightclubs and bars often have a great vibe but you can end up knackered by the end of the night. There are some daytime bar jobs but most places will ask you to work at least a few nights. There is always more competition for jobs at trendy nightspots, so it may be easier to pick up work at a local drinking hole in the suburbs.

As far as wages go, you can earn £4 to £7 an hour in the UK and Europe and £3 to £6 in Australia. American bar wages are quite low – typically £2 to £4.50 – but most people tip at least a dollar every time they buy a round. Bar work is much sought-after in the US – it's often easier to find a job on the door or as a glass clearer.

The best places to find bar work are big cities and coastal resorts. Pubs regularly put up notices in their windows or in backpacker hostels, but you can often find a job just by walking in and asking if they are hiring. There are also specialist recruitment agencies for hospitality and bar jobs. Women can often find work in promotional sampling, which involves roaming bars and handing out complimentary drinks or other freebies. The male equivalent – handing out fliers for clubs and bars – is also popular, though not well paid.

Special Events

Conferences, exhibitions, sporting events and festivals are all great sources of temporary work. Staff at special events are usually supplied by agencies, but you can sometimes get a job by approaching the organisers directly. Many businesses that have nothing to do with the event need extra staff to deal with all the extra people in town.

Sporting events provide some great opportunities. You might want to consider the Melbourne Grand Prix (www.grandprix.com.au), the Australian Indy Car World Series (www.indy.com.au), the Wimbledon tennis championships in London (www.wimbledon .org) and the Super Bowl in America (www.superbowl.com), plus any summer or winter Olympic event. Most people work as gate staff, hospitality workers and cleaners, but there are always openings for people in giant animal costumes to hand out fliers – a dirty job, but someone has to do it.

Big music events such as the Glastonbury Festival (www.glastonburyfestivals.co.uk) in the UK take on staff every year to clean up the site in exchange for free tickets, but paid staff tend to be supplied by agencies. Cultural festivals are a better bet. The Edinburgh International Festival (www.eif.co.uk) takes on lots of temporary staff every August. Listings of major festivals around the world can be found on the website www.festivals.com. Exhibitions and conferences also employ huge numbers of people. Try contacting art galleries and museums directly to see if they have any openings.

If you want to go down the agency route, you'll need to find a local company, as few agencies supply staff for overseas events. Try searching on the web for 'event staff' or 'promotional personnel' and the name of the country you want to work in. The agencies Event Staff (www.event-staff.co.uk) and Recruit Event Services (www.recruiteventservices.co.uk) provide staff for concerts and sporting events across the UK.

TOUR OPERATORS

The holiday trade is the most seasonal business of all. Almost all tour operators take on extra staff during the holiday season and gappers make up a sizable proportion of the intake. Holiday companies usually specialise in either summer sun or winter snow but quite a few cover both seasons and have jobs year round.

The most common job openings at holiday companies are for reps and couriers. Basically, reps are the people who greet holiday-makers at the airport and rush around organising activities, while couriers work on the resort, taking care of people's day-to-day needs. This often involves looking after children while the adults are off having fun.

The minimum age for couriers is 18 but you usually need to be over 21 to be a rep. If you work for a camping holiday company you'll also have to help with *montage* and *démontage* – putting up and taking down tents.

Because of the difficulty of obtaining work permits for casual workers, many tour operators will only employ people who already have the right to work in Europe, ie European citizens. However, there are resorts around the Mediterranean and North Africa that are itching to employ gappers, as Danielle Ades found when she went to work at a plush resort on the coast of Turkey:

I found a job through a resort recruitment website, working in a five-star resort on the Aegean Coast as a Guest Relations Officer. While the pay wasn't great, I was close to the beach, I got to play volleyball on my time off and my accommodation and meals were all taken care of.

One of my 'responsibilities' was to perform in the nightly shows, so I geared up in zombie outfits for a Michael Jackson 'Thriller' show and even did a turn as an Arabian Belly Dancer! I was pretty apprehensive about shaking my booty in front of so many people, but suddenly there I was, shimmying my way across the dance floor!

Summer resorts are great fun and you meet some awesome people, but keep in mind that you work long hours and in searing heat. Always check your contract thoroughly, and clarify in writing anything you don't understand. That way you're sure to have a great working-holiday experience!

If you want to work at resorts in the USA or Canada, you'll need to join a working-holiday program – see p363 for details. Some of the larger resorts also recruit seasonal workers directly using the H2B visa system.

Other possible jobs include adventure-activity instructors (watersports and skiing instructors are most in demand), entertainers, bar and restaurant staff, and domestic staff and cleaners for hotels and ski chalets. The main jobs that people do at holiday resorts are covered in this section.

Wages for resort work can seem a bit stingy at first – typically £50 to £150 per week – but accommodation is included and you also get free transport to and from the resort and free or subsidised meals. Winter resorts usually throw in a ski-pass and free ski hire. Most companies hold back a portion of your wages until you finish your contract to dissuade you from bailing out mid-season.

The easiest way to find resort jobs is to apply directly to big holiday companies – see the listings for PGL, Holidaybreak, Club Med and others (p380). You can also find resort jobs on the following websites:

www.adventurejobs.co.uk – excellent UK site listing adventure, winter and watersports jobs, including holiday-company jobs

www.backdoorjobs.com – excellent US site with listings of outdoor, artistic and adventure jobs

www.coolworks.com – listings for all kinds of seasonal, resort and sporting jobs worldwide

www.jobmonkey.com – US site with excellent listings of outdoor jobs, ski work and other casual jobs

www.leisureopportunities.co.uk – good for leisure jobs in the UK and Europe

www.hotrecruit.com – UK site with all sorts of seasonal and adventure jobs for young people

www.payaway.co.uk – extensive work-abroad site with resort-job listings

www.resortjobs.com – part of the AboutJobs group with listings of resort opportunities worldwide

www.themeparkjobs.com – search engine for work at US theme parks

Ski Resorts

Try saying 'Awesome!' and '360!' in front of the mirror. If you like how it looks, you probably have what it takes to be a ski or snowboard instructor. There are loads of opportunities for work at ski resorts around the world and you could end up skiing all day and partying all night for your whole gap year – working on a ski resort is less a job than a lifestyle decision!

France is the most popular destination for British skiers, followed by Austria, Switzerland and Italy, but there are also opportunities – albeit less well paid – in the mountains of Eastern Europe. Skiing in the USA and Canada is concentrated in the Rocky Mountains. More unusual places to ski include Australia, New Zealand, Japan and South America.

Ski-resort work is usually available from November to April in mainland Europe, North America and Japan, and from June to October in Australia, New Zealand and South America. In the summer many ski resorts reinvent themselves as 'mountain and lake' resorts, so there may be summer vacancies as well. For most jobs you work one shift in the morning and another in the early evening, so you can squeeze in a few hours on the slopes every afternoon.

Kirsty Sneddon went to work at the Blackcomb ski resort in Canada and sent us this report:

I left Scotland, along with my boyfriend, to go and live in Canada, having never skied or snowboarded in my life. We applied for jobs at the resort online before we left (we were both on working-holiday visas) and had interviews set up for a few days after we arrived. Luckily

we both passed our interviews and were offered full-time employment, which gave us a lift pass for the entire season.

The season itself was fantastic. The snow was great, I got free lessons as I worked for the resort, and we got to wake up every day in one of the most beautiful places in the world! I met some amazing people and made lifelong friends. You meet a lot of like-minded people as you're all there for the same thing – the mountain and the partying! However, it's not all rosy. The working hours can be pretty unpredictable – I was employed 'full-time' but I often only worked 20 hours a week if there were no tourists.

A useful source of ski information is the **Ski Club of Great Britain** (☎ 0845 458 0782; www.skiclub.co.uk). It costs £16 a year to join if you are under 24, or £49 otherwise and membership entitles you to all sorts of perks, including special ski trips and training courses.

WORKING ON THE SLOPES

If you have the right qualifications, working as a ski instructor or ski guide will maximise your time on the slopes and provide an excuse to wear sunglasses right through the day. There are also plenty of openings for ski couriers – basically baby-sitters on skis – and staff at ski shops up on the slopes.

Although these jobs are undeniably cool, the wages are not as high as you might expect. Instructors in Europe tend to earn £60 to £100 per week, including all meals, accommodation, ski gear and ski pass. In the USA and Canada, you can earn £5 to £6.50 per hour but accommodation is extra. You may be able to make extra cash offering private lessons in your time off.

Ski staff usually stay with other workers in resort chalets which cuts down on food bills – unfortunately, it also increases the chances of blowing your pay check on a night of partying!

To work as a ski or snowboard instructor or guide you need international instructor qualifications. Skiing and snowboarding courses are licensed by national governing bodies such as the British Association of Snowsport Instructors (BASI; www.basi.org.uk). Links to governing bodies around the world can be found on the International Ski Instructors Association website (www.isiaski.org).

There are three grades of qualification but you usually only need the lowest grade (Grade III) for seasonal instructing or guiding jobs. Schools offering ski-instructor courses are listed on p442). Other jobs you might end up doing out on the slopes include working on a snow-making machine, operating ski lifts or working in a ski-repair clinic.

CHALET STAFF

Obviously, given the choice, you'd rather be a ski instructor. But if your skiing skills aren't quite there yet, you can do plenty of other jobs at ski resorts. Probably the easiest work to find is behind the scenes in a ski chalet. Chalets operate like mini-hotels and the same kinds of jobs need to be done every day – changing the sheets, cleaning, cooking meals etc.

The majority of chalets rely on 'chalet boys' and 'chalet girls' to do the cooking and cleaning. If there is any cooking involved, the company will test your skills before signing you up. Many UK cookery schools (see p429) offer specialist cooking courses just for chalet chefs. Lots of people prefer to stick to cleaning; the pay is lower but so are the responsibilities!

Chalet staff work long hours and usually have to share accommodation with other workers. On the other hand, the sense of camaraderie can be great and you can spend all your free time out on the slopes. In most chalets, every night ends up being party night.

The majority of chalet jobs are arranged through agencies or big holiday companies – see p384. Transport to the resort and accommodation and meals are usually free, plus ski and boot hire and a ski pass are often thrown in. Wages range from £60 to £165 per week.

APPLYING FOR SKI JOBS

Competition for jobs on the pistes can be fierce. If you're serious about ski or chalet work you should start your job hunt as early as possible. The big recruitment push usually begins in the summer but jobs sometimes come up later in the year as people drop out due to injury or après-ski related exhaustion. You might consider taking a ski-instructor course over the summer to improve your chances of finding work when the snow starts to fall – see p442 for some recommendations.

To work at ski resorts in Europe, you usually just need to be an EU passport-holder; working-holiday visas are fine for Australia, New Zealand and Canada. For the US you normally need to apply for your work permit or visa through BUNAC or another sponsoring organisation. However, some big US ski resorts sponsor international ski and snowboard instructors on H2B visas – Aspen Snowmass (www.aspensnowmass.com) and Steamboat Ski & Resort (www.steamboat.com) are two reliable companies.

The best place to start your search for ski work is the web. The agency Ski Staff (p385) recruits for over 100 companies in the Alps. There are hundreds of other great ski websites out there – point your browser towards:

www.coolworks.com – listings of ski-resort work worldwide

www.freeradicals.co.uk – recruits for ski companies all over Europe and America

www.natives.co.uk – online recruitment agency with listings of ski and resort work year round

www.payaway.co.uk – excellent listings for ski jobs

www.skiconnection.co.uk – a huge database of ski jobs worldwide

www.voovs.com – an excellent ski site with listings of current ski jobs around the world

Activity Holidays

While some people want to chill out on holiday, others are looking for a bit of a thrill. Companies such as Sunsail, Acorn Adventure and the Kingswood Group offer activity holidays around the world and almost all take on seasonal instructors for watersports and other adventure activities – see p380) for their details. Most companies ask for formal instructor qualifications but some companies will let you train up while you work. Instructor courses for watersports and other activities are covered on p440.

Ned Lloyd worked for Acorn Adventures for a season and liked it so much he made it a full-time career:

I started working in the outdoor industry thinking it would be a nice summer job. The hours were long but I saw I made a positive difference to lives of the children I was working with. Thirteen years later I'm still doing it (a world record I think?). I've worked in support roles, cooking and cleaning, and worked as an instructor in France, Italy and Spain. You have to sleep in tents and work hard but the benefits are amazing – on my days off I can go rafting in the Alps or rock-climbing in the Valle d'Aosta.

Coastal resorts may have openings for windsurfing, sailing, water-skiing, jet-skiing, scuba diving or traditional surfing instructors. At holiday centres inland you might be able to teach canoeing and kayaking, rock-climbing, bungee jumping, skydiving…the list goes on and on.

The easiest way to get work is to apply directly to a tour operator – various companies that take on adventure-activity staff – see p380. Some industries – scuba diving in particular – have a huge turnover of staff and you may be able to find work by just turning up and offering your services. Dive schools in Australia and Asia often provide free training to dive master or instructor level if you promise to work on their dive boats when you qualify. However, check the school out carefully – we've heard from several people who have worked a season then been let go before obtaining their qualifications.

Companies that train watersports instructors can often find work around the world for their graduates – see p440 and talk to Flying Fish (www.flyingfishonline.com) or the International Academy (www.international-academy.com).

Theme parks and other big tourist attractions take on thousands of staff every summer. Accommodation is usually provided and you can ride on roller coasters till you're green in the face on your days off. Disneyland Resort Paris (p382) is the most obvious choice in Europe. The Star Parks (www.sixflagseurope.com) group runs parks across Western Europe, and Alton Towers in Staffordshire (www.alton-towers.com) takes on 1500 staff every year in the UK.

America invented the theme park, and Six Flags (www.sixflags.com) runs more than 30 parks across the USA. Another good place to pick up theme-park work is the Gold Coast of Australia. Theme parks around the world are listed on the website www.themeparkcity.com.

DOWN & DIRTY

If you don't mind getting your hands dirty there are loads of jobs out there that let you work outdoors in the summer sun and improve your tan while you work. Some gappers earn money to go travelling by working on a fruit farm or building site in the UK. Others pack their bags and pick up farm work on the road – grape picking in France is a legendary year-out activity.

You don't need any particular skills to do most casual building and farm jobs but previous experience will increase your chances of finding work in either field. In all cases, expect long hours and hard physical work. Training is required for potentially dangerous jobs such as operating heavy machinery or working with power tools.

Farm wages are generally low but accommodation is often thrown in and you'll have few opportunities to fritter away your earnings out in the sticks. In most places you should be able to earn at least £150 per week. Building sites often pay better, and skilled jobs such as laying concrete floors can pay more than office work.

Fruit Picking

As a casual job, fruit picking has tons of advantages. You can work outside, you don't need any previous experience and the work is often cash in hand. However, it can be back-breaking work and you usually have to get up at the crack of dawn to get the fruit to market on time.

Depending on where you are in the world, you might end up picking apples, grapes, strawberries, lettuces or even bananas. There are even opportunities for harvesting *fruits de mer* (shellfish)! You can find harvest timetables for various countries around the world on the website www.anyworkanywhere.com/jg_farms.html.

Pickers usually get paid according to the amount of fruit they pick – most people manage to take home £30 to £40 per day. Many farms will let you camp on the grounds or provide free accommodation, which can cut down your expenses.

If you just want to earn a bit of quick cash to fund your gap year, fruit and vegetable farms in Kent and East Anglia take on pickers between March and October. Jobs are often advertised in Job Centres, or try calling the farms direct. However, there is lots of competition for work from migrant workers from Eastern Europe.

France's *vendange* (grape harvest) is probably the best-known fruit-picking job in Europe. The two-month season kicks off in September but may be delayed after rainy summers. This is one of the cushier fruit-picking jobs as most vineyards lay on a huge French lunch with copious quantities of wine for their workers. The largest grape-growing centre in France is the Beaujolais region in Burgundy, just north of Lyon. The organisation Appellation Contrôlée can arrange grape picking in France – see p386.

New Zealand and the east coast of Australia are also good places to find fruit-picking work. The Australian government provides comprehensive harvest-job information through the website www.jobsearch.gov.au/harvesttrail.

Benjamin Smart sent us this report on fruit picking in New Zealand:

Picking fruit in New Zealand is a quick way to earn a few dollars. Within an hour of my arrival in Napier, the manager of the hostel I was staying at had found me a job picking apples. At 6.30am the next day I found myself in an apple orchard trying to fill a bin as large as a small car with fruit. We worked 11 hours a day and only had an hour to eat our lunch – which comprised a handful of apples! – but after work all the fruit pickers chipped in to buy a few slabs of beer and we fired up the barbecue!

Another good place to look for picking work is around Cape Town in South Africa. The website www.pickingjobs.com has a search page where you can find fruit- and vegetable-picking jobs around the world. See p386 for some companies that specialise in picking work.

Farm Work

Fruit picking is just one of a thousand jobs that need doing on a farm. Seasonal workers are hired to plant crops, repair fences, drive tractors, shear sheep and do a host of other farming chores. The work is hard but you'll be out in the open air and it's easy to save money. There are lots of specialist companies who can place you in a farm job overseas for a fee. See p386 for some examples. Wages typically start at around £150 per week.

Much of the work on Australian farms is done on horseback or off-road motorcycles, so working as a jackeroo or jilleroo can be a fabulous way to spend a season. The Visitoz scheme (see p387) will equip you with the skills you need to work as an Aussie farm hand and provide you with a guaranteed job at the end of it.

Many travellers used to work on moshavim (community farms) in Israel but most of the volunteer offices have closed due to the current security situation. Try contacting the **Moshav Movement** (☎ 00 972 3 695 8473; 19 Leonardo da Vinci St, Tel Aviv 64733, Israel) to see if things have changed by the time you read this. For information on working on a kibbutz see the Volunteering, Conservation & Expeditions chapter (p279).

Building Work

The construction industry has always relied on contractors, so short-term building work is easy to find in most countries. It can also pay surprisingly well, particularly if you have experience working with heavy machinery. There are openings around the world for labourers, steelworkers, heavy-vehicle drivers, electricians, plumbers, carpenters, furniture makers, civil engineers and surveyors.

The easiest way to find work is to go through one of the established recruitment agencies. Kelly Services, Adecco and Hays Personnel all recruit construction staff and have offices

HARVEST SEASONS

Eager pickers can find fruit-picking jobs all over the world at different times of year. Harvest seasons in different countries include:

UK
- apples and pears – August to October
- soft fruit – June to October
- vegetables – May to October
- hops – August to October

France
- grapes – September to October
- soft fruit – May to September
- apples and pears – July to October
- vegetables – July to October
- olives – November to December

Southern Mediterranean
- grapes – June to October
- oranges – November to April
- olives – November to April
- apples and pears – June to October

Australia
- grapes – January to March
- bananas – July to August
- apples and pears – January to September
- soft fruit – August to December
- vegetables – year round
- shellfish – year round

New Zealand
- grapes – January to April
- apples – January to May
- kiwi fruit – May to July
- soft fruit – November to December
- vegetables – July to October

South Africa
- grapes – December to March
- other fruit – January to April

worldwide (see p348). One recommended agency is Hill McGlynn (www.hillmcglynn.com .au), which has offices in London and Australia and welcomes working holiday-makers with construction experience. Construction is usually union-controlled so there isn't much point approaching building sites directly.

Building work can range from completely unskilled jobs such as labouring, to highly skilled jobs such as structural engineering. As well as big construction sites, many small businesses take on unskilled labourers for short-term projects such as site clearing.

Useful resources for anyone thinking about building or construction work include:

www.constructor.co.uk – good construction and civil engineering site with lots of UK jobs
www.ukconstruction.com – extensive listings of UK jobs and other construction resources
www.buildersplanet.com – worldwide resources for working in construction
www.constructionjobs.com – US site with lots of job listings

CONTACTS

Working-Holiday Organisations

The following organisations arrange working holidays around the world. Unless otherwise stated, wages will depend on what kind of job you can find. For summer work programs in the US, you must be returning to university

in the autumn. Working-holiday visa conditions apply for Australia and New Zealand programs.

Alliance Abroad
1221 South Mopac Expressway, Austin, Texas 78746, USA
☎ 00 1 512-457 8062
fax 00 1 512-457 8132
email using the online form
www.allianceabroad.com

Alliance Abroad offers a Work & Travel Program in the USA over the summer for continuing university students, and a more useful Seasonal Work Programme on a H2B visa that is open to students and non-students. Work placements are provided or you can find your own job. There's also a working-holiday program in Australia, which includes job-hunting assistance. See p336 for details of work-placement programs.

Types of Work: Participants on all programs mainly work in unskilled jobs, particularly in hospitality and catering or at resorts.

Timing & Length of Programs: The Work & Travel Program runs for four months from mid-May. The Seasonal Work Program runs for three to 10 months from March or November.

Destination: USA.

Costs/Pay: Fees and wages vary – call or email for the latest rates. Insurance is included but flights are extra.

Eligibility: For the Work & Travel Program you must be aged 18 to 28 and be a current university/college student returning to university after the summer. For the Seasonal Work Program you can be 18 to 40. The Australia program is open to people aged 18 to 30.

How to Apply: Download the application form from the website, then there's a telephone interview. Apply about four months in advance.

Association for International Practical Training (AIPT)

10400 Little Patuxent Parkway, Suite 250, Columbia, Maryland 21044-3519, USA
☎ 00 1 410-997 2200
fax 00 1 410-992 3924
swt@aipt.org
www.aipt.org

This well-established operator offers a work-placement program in the USA for continuing university students. They handle the paperwork, arrange a job placement and provide insurance, and there's an orientation before and after you fly. See p337 for its career-related work programs.

Types of Work: Jobs placements are in hospitality, shops, sports camps and offices.

Timing & Length of Programs: Four months from June.

Destination: USA.

Costs/Pay: Contact AIPT directly for the latest fees.

Eligibility: Applicants must be at least 18 and full-time university students returning to university after the program.

How to Apply: Download an application form from the website and apply by January. Once you register for the program, you can sign up for a presentation where you'll have an interview.

BUNAC (British Universities North America Club)

16 Bowling Green Lane, London EC1R 0QH
☎ 020 7251 3472
fax 020 7251 0215
enquiries@bunac.org.uk
www.bunac.org/uk

BUNAC runs various work schemes in North America. The summer camp and Work America schemes are only for continuing university students, but there are working-holiday programs in Canada, Australia, New Zealand and South Africa for other gappers. Orientation sessions are held before departure and when you arrive, and they'll help you find a job on most programs. For information on working with children or professional work programs in the USA, see p406 and p337.

Types of Work: US programs involve resort work, casual jobs or support roles on summer camps. Participants on other schemes can do most kinds of jobs.

Timing & Length of Programs: US programs last eight to nine weeks from early to mid-June. Other programs last 12 months and start on set dates throughout the year.

Destinations: USA, Canada, Australia, New Zealand & South Africa.

Costs/Pay: Fees vary with the program – the Work America program costs £745, including flights and insurance but not visas. Work Canada scheme costs £156, and flights, visas and insurance are extra. See the website for fees for other programs.

Eligibility: For US programs, you must be aged at least 18 and be a student on a full-time course returning to university that autumn. For Work Canada you must be 18 to 35, and students and non-students are accepted. See the website for details of other programs.

How to Apply: Apply from September for US programs, then there's an interview (and medical for summer camp jobs). Apply a few months in advance for other programs. Application packs for all programs can be downloaded from the website.

Camp America

American Institute for Foreign Study (AIFS), 37a Queen's Gate, London SW7 5HR
☎ 020 7581 7373

fax 020 7581 7377
enquiries@campamerica.co.uk
www.campamerica.co.uk
Camp America offers various work packages in the USA but only for students who are returning to university. Visas, travel and work placements are arranged by Camp America. Countrywide job fairs and interview sessions are held in February. For information on working as a camp counsellor see p412.

Types of Work: Camp America offers catering, maintenance and administrative work at resorts, theme parks, hotels and country clubs.

Timing & Length of Programs: Placements are typically for nine to 12 weeks from May or June.

Destination:USA.

Costs/Pay: Programs cost from £300, including flights, insurance accommodation, in-country transport and food (but not visa fees).

Eligibility: Applicants must be aged at least 18 by 1 June. You must be a full-time student returning to study.

How to Apply: Apply from September. Download the application form or apply online. There's an interview, medical and criminal-record check.

CCUSA

1st floor north, Devon House, 171/177 Great Portland St, London, W1W 5PQ
☎ 020 7637 0779
fax 020 7580 6209
info@ccusa.co.uk
www.ccusa.com
CCUSA offers support jobs at American summer camps and working-holiday programs in Australia, New Zealand and Brazil. For camp work (continuing university students only) all visas, paperwork and flights are organised by CCUSA. For other programs, CCUSA will help you with job hunting or provide a job placement. For information on professional work programs and working as a camp counsellor see p337 and p412.

Types of Work: Summer-camp jobs include kitchen, cleaning and office work. Jobs in Brazil include office work, hotel work and teaching beach sports. Participants on other work programs can do any kind of job.

Timing & Length of Programs: US programs run for nine to 11 weeks from May or June. Brazil programs last for three or six months and begin on set dates in January, April, July, October and November. Australia and New Zealand programs start monthly and last up to 12 months.

Destinations: Australia, Brazil, New Zealand & USA.

Costs/Pay: The US summer-camp program costs £315, including flights, visas and accommodation; support staff earn around £640 for the season. Fees and wages vary for other programs – see the website for details.

Eligibility: Applicants must be aged at least 18, and maximum ages apply for some programs. For US programs you must be a full-time student returning to university after the summer. Portuguese and Spanish speakers are preferred for the Brazil program.

How to Apply: Download an application form from the website. Apply by March for US programs; then there's an interview and group orientation. Apply at least two months in advance for other programs.

Changing Worlds

Hodore Farm, Hartfield, East Sussex TN7 4AR
☎ 01892 770000
fax 0870 990 9665
welcome@changingworlds.co.uk
www.changingworlds.co.uk
Changing Worlds organises work placements in Australia and New Zealand based on a working-holiday visa. You can work in hotels, on farms or in zoos or do unpaid crewing on an old-fashioned tall ship in New Zealand. Accommodation is provided for all placements, and prices include visas, flights and an orientation on arrival.

Types of Work: Hospitality workers work as receptionists, maids or waiters in hotels, while workers on tall ships assist with rigging and maintanence. Zoo workers deal with zoo visitors and help feed and care for animals.

Timing & Length of Programs: Placements are for three to six months from September or January (also from March for Australia).

Destinations: Australia & New Zealand.

Costs/Pay: Fees are £2395 for Australia and £2495 for New Zealand, including flights but not insurance or visa fees. All jobs are paid local wages, except for work on ships and in zoos, which is unpaid.

Eligibility: Applicants must be aged 18 to 30. A clean driving licence is useful for farm work and sailing experience is needed to work on the tall ships.

How to Apply: Apply via the website or call for an application form, then there's an interview.

IST Plus

Rosedale House, Rosedale Road, Richmond, Surrey TW9 2SZ
☎ 020 8939 9057
fax 020 8332 7858

info@istplus.com
www.istplus.com
IST Plus runs work programs in the US on behalf of CIEE
(Council on International Educational Exchange)/Council
Exchanges. The summer work scheme in America is only
for continuing university students. For gappers, there are
working-holiday programs in Australia and New Zealand
that include job-hunting assistance. See p339 for details of
professional work programs.
Types of Work: You can do any job you want for the
time period specified on your visa.
Timing & Length of Programs: US programs last
for four months from June. Australia and New Zealand
programs last up to a year and can start any time.
Destinations: Australia, New Zealand & USA.
Costs/Pay: Work & Travel USA costs £365, plus a £67 visa
fee and £50 SEVIS fee. Australia and New Zealand programs cost from £320, plus visa fees. Flights and insurance
are extra for all programs.
Eligibility: For the US program, applicants must be aged
18 to 30 and be full-time university students returning
to university after the summer. For Australia and New
Zealand, applicants must simply be aged 18 to 30.
How to Apply: Download the application pack from the
website to start the application process.

InterExchange

161 Sixth Ave, New York, NY 10013, USA
☎ 00 1 212-924 0446
fax 00 1 212-924 0575
see the website for email addresses of different programs
www.interexchange.org
InterExchange arranges numerous work-exchange
programs in the US. As well as J1 visa summer schemes for
university students, there's a useful H2B visa scheme that
allows you to work in seasonal jobs at resorts, theme parks
etc. You can either take a prearranged placement or find
your own job. Professional training schemes in the US are
covered on p338.
Types of Work: Casual and seasonal jobs, mainly at resorts.
Timing & Length of Programs: The US summer program
lasts four months from June. The H2B program usually last six
months over the summer or winter tourist seasons.
Destinations: USA.
Costs/Pay: Varies with the program – the H2B program
costs from £250, plus flights, insurance and visa fees.
Most programs offer a discount if you find your own job
in America.

Eligibility: For the summer program, the age range is
18 to 28 and you must be university student returning to
university in the autumn. For the H2B scheme, the age
range is 18 to 40 and you don't have to be a student.
How to Apply: Download an application pack from the
website to start the application process.

International Exchange Centre (IEC)

89 Fleet St, London EC4Y 1DH
☎ 020 7583-9116
fax 020 7583 9117
isecinfo@btconnect.com
www.isecworld.co.uk
The IEC organises work placements all over the world.
Gappers can work and study in Russia (with four weeks of
Russian lessons in Moscow) or South Africa, and continuing
university students can work in America. For information
on internship programs or working as a camp counsellor
see p338 and p413.
Types of Work: You can do hospitality work in Russia, and
casual jobs (plus support jobs on summer camps) in the US.
Participants on other work programs can do most jobs.
Timing & Length of Programs: US programs last for
up to four months from June. Programs in South Africa and
Russia last 12 months and can start at any time.
Destinations: Russia, South Africa & USA.
Costs/Pay: Camp placements in the USA cost £115,
including flights, meals and accommodation; total wages
for the season vary from £266 to £365. If you work in other
casual jobs, the fee is £280, air fares are extra. See the
website for costs of other programs.
Eligibility: Applicants must be at least 18 (19 for South
Africa). For US and South Africa programs you must be
a full-time student (returning to university for the US
program). Russian speakers are preferred for the Russia
program, or you can take an additional language course at
the start of the program for £495.
How to Apply: Email or phone for an application form
three months in advance. Apply before end of April for US
programs. Following your application there will be a phone
interview. People on US programs must provide a clean
criminal record and take a medical.

Japan Association of Working Holiday Makers (JAWHM)

Sun Plaza 7f, 4-1-1 Nakano, Nakano-ku, Tokyo, Japan
164-8512
☎ 00 81 3-3389 0181

fax +81 (0)3-3389 1563
www.jawhm.or.jp
JAWHM offers a job-referral service and support for people visiting Japan on working-holiday visas. There are branches in Tokyo, Osaka and Fukuoka. Visit the offices with your passport and two passport photos to register. You then have an orientation and can apply for the positions on their jobs list. Most jobs last three months or more.

USIT

19–21 Aston Quay, O'Connell Bridge, Dublin 2, Ireland
☎ 00 353 1 602 1600
fax 00 353 1 679 2124
programmes@usit.ie
www.usit.ie
USIT administers the J1 summer jobs program for Irish students who are returning to university, and a more useful H2B visa program – open to gappers – which comes with a confirmed seasonal job in the US. The Work Canada program lets you work in almost any job in Canada for up to a year. There are also Australia and New Zealand programs for working holiday-makers – see the website for details. The Proper Jobs chapter (p339) has details of work placements in the USA.
Types of Work: Jobs in the US are mainly casual roles at resorts. You can do any job in Canada, apart from summer camp work and tobacco picking.
Timing & Length of Programs: In the US, the H2B program lasts four to five months, usually beginning in March, June or October. You can work in Canada for a maximum of one year starting at any time.
Destinations: Canada & USA.
Costs/Pay: The US scheme comes with a confirmed job placement; it cost €599 (£422) in 2004. You can work in most paid jobs in Canada; the fee for students in 2004 was €349 (£246) with a meet-and-greet package on arrival. Non-students pay €269 (£190) without the extras. Flights, visas and insurance are extra for both programs. Contact USIT for current prices.
Eligibility: The minimum age is 18 for the H2B program. The Work Canada program is open to students and non-students aged 18 to 35. Apply at least eight weeks before you want to start for either program.
How to Apply: For the H2B program, apply for a specific position on the website by email with your CV. For the Work Canada Student Programme, apply using the online forms for www.canada.usit.ie. See the website for the application process for other programs.

Village Camps

Recruitment Office, 14 Rue de la Morâche, 1260 Nyon, Switzerland
☎ 00 41 22 990 9405
fax 00 41 22 990 9494
personnel@villagecamps.ch
www.villagecamps.com
Village Camps has openings for support staff at summer camps across Europe but you must apply for specific job openings – see the website for a list. For information on becoming a camp counsellor see p414.
Types of Work: Positions exist for chefs, kitchen workers, bar staff, receptionists and drivers.
Timing & Length of Programs: Placements are from April/May to June, June to August or August to October.
Destinations: Austria, France, Holland, Switzerland & UK.
Costs/Pay: Wages vary with the position and location – contact Village Camps directly for details. Participants pay for transport to camp, but room and board is provided.
Eligibility: The minimum age varies from 21 to 25, depending on the job. All staff need a first-aid certificate, and a driving licence is preferred. Some jobs need language skills, instructor qualifications, catering qualifications etc.
How to Apply: Download the application forms from the website and return by mail or fax.

Work & Travel Company

45 High St, Tunbridge Wells, Kent TN1 1XL
☎ 01892 516164
fax 01892 523172
info@worktravelcompany.co.uk
www.worktravelcompany.co.uk
This reliable working-holiday organisation arranges working holidays around the world. The US program is just for continuing university students, but there are also working-holiday programs in Australia and New Zealand. You can take an all-inclusive package with a visa, guaranteed job, local support and an orientation on arrival, or go for a bare-bones package with job-hunting assistance and travel insurance. See p338 for details of work experience placements in the US.
Types of Work: Participants on all the programs can do most casual jobs, but working-holiday visa conditions apply in Australia and New Zealand.
Timing & Length of Programs: Four months from June in the USA. Up to 12 months starting anytime in Australia and New Zealand.

Destinations: Australia, New Zealand & USA.

Costs/Pay: The US program costs from £349, including insurance. For the Australia program, you'll pay £699 for the all-inclusive option and £369 for the bare-bones package. Fees for the same deal in New Zealand are £499 and £359 respectively. Flights are extra for all programs.

Eligibility: You must be over 18 and be a full-time university student returning to university for the US program. For the Australia and New Zealand programs, you should be 18 to 30.

How to Apply: Apply by February for prearranged positions in the US, or by April for self-arranged positions. Apply around two months in advance for other programs. Application forms are on the website.

WorldNetUK

Avondale House, 63 Sydney Rd, Haywards Heath, West Sussex RH16 1QD

☎ 0845 458 1551

fax 01444 441160

info@worldnetuk.com

www.worldnetuk.com

WorldNetUK offers support jobs on US summer camps for returning university students – it handles all visas and paperwork, and flights, transport etc are included in the cost. There are also ski nanny and childcare jobs at resorts in Europe that are more useful for gappers. For details on working as a camp counsellor see p415.

Types of Work: Catering, domestic and general maintenance work at US summer camps; childcare at winter and summer resorts in Europe.

Timing & Length of Programs: US placements are for eight to 10 weeks from June. European resort placements run from June at summer resorts and from October at winter resorts.

Destinations: USA & resorts in Europe.

Costs/Pay: Fees vary with the program – the US summer program is around £300, including flights, medical insurance and administration costs, and workers earn approximately £550 for the season. Contact WorldNetUK for details of other programs.

Eligibility: For the US program, applicants must be at least 18 by 1 June and a full-time university student, returning to university after the summer.

How to Apply: Call or email for a brochure. There will be an interview and a medical and criminal-record check. Apply from January.

Tour Operators, Ski Resorts & Activity Holidays

3D Education & Adventure

Osmington Bay Centre, Shortlake Lane, Weymouth, Dorset DT3 6EG

☎ 01305 836226

fax 01305 834070

admin@3d-jobs.co.uk

www.3d.co.uk/jobs

3D hires instructors in adventure sports and camp monitors (ie couriers) on summer camps for its centres on the south coast of England and the Isle of Wight. It also places staff at Pontin's resorts around Britain. It takes on around 500 instructors and 750 camp staff annually. Staff have the option to train for adventure-sport qualifications for free.

Types of Work: Roles include watersports instructors, IT instructors, activity-sport instructors, lifeguards and camp monitors.

Timing & Length of Programs: Camp monitors work for six weeks from July. Instructors work from January or February to November.

Destination: UK.

Costs/Pay: Wages start at £75 per week for camp monitors, including food and accommodation. Wages are higher for instructors and skilled positions.

Eligibility: Applicants must be at least 18. You need to have relevant qualifications for instructor jobs.

How to Apply: Apply online or download the application form. You must provide three references. Successful applicants are invited on a six-day assessment. For summer camp jobs, there's a training course in July.

Acorn Adventure

Acorn House, Prospect Rd, Halesowen, Birmingham B62 8DU

☎ 08701 219951

fax 0121 5042058

jobs@acornadventure.co.uk

www.acorn-jobs.co.uk

Acorn is one of Britain's leading adventure-holiday companies and has seasonal openings for around 300 staff every year at centres around Europe. A one- or two-week training course is held in April, and you have the option of studying for adventure-sport teaching qualifications at the end of the season.

Types of Work: Positions are available for instructors in adventure sports (eg canoeing, rock-climbing, sailing, windsurfing), camp reps, catering staff and drivers.

Timing & Length of Programs: April to September.

Destinations: France, Italy, Spain & UK.
Costs/Pay: Wages start are above the minimum wage, and food, accommodation and transport to the centres are provided.
Eligibility: Watersports and other instructors will benefit from relevant qualifications (see the website for details), and drivers need a clean driving licence and experience of driving abroad. Minimum age varies from 18 to 21, depending on the position.
How to Apply: Apply on the website. You must provide two references and evidence of qualifications. Apply from November for April positions.

Camp Beaumont
West Runton Centre, West Runton, Cromer, NR27 9NF
☎ 01263 835151
fax 01263 835192
apply using online form
www.campbeaumont.com
Part of the Kingswood Group (see p382), Camp Beaumont organises summer camps for kids around the UK and takes on loads of seasonal staff every year.
Types of Work: Group leaders look after children and help with sport and activity sessions.
Timing & Length of Programs: Positions run from June to August.
Destinations: London & southeast England.
Pay: Varies with the position – group leaders earn £780 per month, minus £65 per week for food and accommodation.
Eligibility: Minimum age is 19, and leadership or childcare experience is an advantage. Arts and sports experience is useful but not essential.
How to Apply: Apply online with two references. Then there's an interview and compulsory training session.

Canvas Holidays
East Port House, Dunfermline, Scotland KY12 7JG
☎ 01383 629018
fax 01383 629071
recruitment@canvasholidays.co.uk
www.canvasholidays.co.uk
Canvas Holidays takes on seasonal couriers at around 100 holiday camps across Europe. Work includes looking after campers and children and setting up tents for campers. Transport from a UK port and accommodation in shared permanent tents are provided.
Types of Work: Camp Couriers do rep work and put up and take down tents.

Timing & Length of Programs: Positions run from March to October.
Destinations: Austria, France, Germany, Holland, Italy, Spain & Switzerland.
Costs/Pay: Salaries start at £437 per month, with accommodation and transport included; meals are extra.
Eligibility: Applicants must be at least 18 (19 for France) and have a clean criminal record.
How to Apply: Fill in the online application form on the website. Successful applicants are invited to an interview.

Club Med
Club Med Recrutement, 11–12 Place Jules Ferry, 69458 Lyon Cedex 06, France
☎ 0845 367 6767
recruit.uk@clubmed.com
www.clubmed-jobs.com
This huge holiday company has 120 holiday villages around Europe and the Mediterranean, including North Africa, and takes on large numbers of seasonal staff in all sorts of positions, from watersports teachers to bartenders. Jobs are available for both the summer and winter seasons.
Types of Work: Work includes sports coaching, entertainment, childcare and hospitality work.
Timing & Length of Programs: Positions run for three to eight months from April to October (summer resorts) or December to April (winter resorts).
Destinations: France, Italy, Morocco, Portugal, Spain, Tunisia & Turkey.
Costs/Pay: Wages vary with the job but you can earn around €800 (£564) per month. Room, board and transport to resorts are provided.
Eligibility: Applicants must be aged 20 to 35. French speakers are preferred and good people skills are essential.
How to Apply: You must include a CV, covering letter and photo. Following your application there will be an interview in London.

Disneyland Resort Paris
Service net Recrutement, BP 110, 77777 Marne La Vallée Cedex 4, France
☎ 00 33 1 64 74 61 01
fax 00 33 1 64 74 61 61
dlp.casting.fr@disney.com
www.disneylandparis.com/uk/employment
This huge theme park just outside Paris employs huge numbers of seasonal staff, from professional cartoon characters

to waiters and office staff. Actors, circus staff and performers should check the website for casting details.

Types of Work: Seasonal staff are employed as receptionists, sales and public-relations staff, ride attendants, business support staff and entertainers.

Timing & Length of Programs: Seasonal contracts run from March to October.

Destination: France.

Costs/Pay: Contact Disney for salary information on specific positions – the starting salary is €1179 (£820) per month. Accommodation costs €230 (£160) per month.

Eligibility: Applicants must be aged at least 18.

How to Apply: Apply by email or post well in advance with a CV and covering letter. Previous experience is required for waiting jobs but not for other positions and you should have a working knowledge of French.

Haven Europe

Haven Europe HR, Byranstone House, Seldon Hill, Hemel Hempstead, Hertfordshire HP2 4TN

☎ 01442 203970

fax 01442 241473

lynn.garwood@bourne-leisure.co.uk

www.haveneurope.com/www.siblu.com

Part of the Siblu group, Haven Europe operates around 30 holiday camps in Europe and takes on large numbers of seasonal staff. Family members can visit on discounted Haven holidays.

Types of Work: Seasonal staff are taken on as bar, hospitality, maintenance and reception staff, and as entertainers, reps and lifeguards.

Timing & Length of Programs: Positions are available from March to October.

Destinations: France, Italy & Spain.

Costs/Pay: Contact Haven directly for current wages. Accommodation and transport to resorts is provided but workers take care of their own food.

Eligibility: Applicants must be aged at least 18. Previous experience and conversational French, Spanish or Italian is preferred. Lifeguards need relevant qualifications.

How to Apply: See the website or call for an application form, then there's an interview.

Holidaybreak

Hartford Manor, Greenbank Lane, Northwich CW8 1HW

☎ 01606 787522

fax 01606 787040

overseasplacements@holidaybreak.com

www.holidaybreakjobs.com

Holidaybreak is the owner of the Eurocamp and Keycamp holiday companies. It employs around 2000 staff per year for its holiday camps in Europe. Most people work as couriers or reps or in hospitality positions. For some jobs there's a training session before you go off to camp.

Types of Work: Jobs are available for couriers, reps, tent erectors and guides.

Timing & Length of Programs: Placements are from May to September.

Destinations: Austria, Croatia, France, Germany, Holland, Italy, Luxembourg, Spain & Switzerland.

Costs/Pay: Wages start at £114 per week, including accommodation; meals are subsidised.

Eligibility: Applicants must be at least 18 (21 for some jobs). Language skills and a clean driving licence are preferred.

How to Apply: Apply from October using the online application form or call for an application pack. There will be an interview and orientation; some jobs require a clean criminal record.

Kingswood Group

Operations HQ, Kingswood Centres, West Runton, Cromer, Norfolk NR27 9NF

☎ 01263 835151

fax 01263 835192

jobs@kingswood.co.uk

www.kingswoodjobs.co.uk

Kingswood organises educational camps for kids around the UK and takes on activity instructors and general staff every season. As part of the job, staff are trained for National Governing Body (NGB) qualifications in activities such as fencing, climbing, archery and lifeguarding.

Types of Work: Sports instructors, teachers of IT and environmental subjects, catering and maintenance staff.

Timing & Length of Programs: Positions run from September to June.

Destination: UK.

Costs/Pay: Wages vary with the position and your experience (wages increase for repeat seasons). Accommodation and meals are included.

Eligibility: Applicants must be aged 18 to 24.

How to Apply: Apply online with two references. Assessment weekends take place in January.

PGL Recruitment Team

Alton Court, Penyard Lane, Ross-on-Wye, Herefordshire HR9 5GL

☎ 0870 401 4411
fax 0870 401 4444
pglpeople@pgl.co.uk
www.pgl.co.uk/gapyear
PGL is the UK's leading provider of residential activity holidays for children. There are opportunities to train for NGB qualifications while you work and wages increase every season you work. For information on working with children on PGL camps see p414.
Types of Work: PGL employs seasonal support staff (hospitality staff, administrators and maintenance), as well as instructors and children's reps.
Timing & Length of Programs: Positions are available for a minimum of eight weeks from February to November.
Destinations: France, Spain & UK.
Costs/Pay: Jobs pay £60 to £80 per week, and meals, accommodation and transport to your centre from a UK port are included.
Eligibility: Applicants must be at least 18 and enthusiastic about working outdoors with children. Priority is given to applicants who can start before May.
How to Apply: You can apply year round. Download the application form from the website. You need to provide three referees and show a clean criminal record.

Solaire Holidays
1158 Stratford Rd, Hall Green, Birmingham B28 8AF
☎ 0870 054 0202
fax 0121 778 5065
holidays@solaire.co.uk
www.solaire.co.uk
This small camping-holiday company hires summer staff at its European holiday camps. Transport to the resorts and accommodation is free, but you must pay for your own food.
Types of Work: Solaire employs seasonal camp couriers, and bar, cleaning and maintenance staff.
Timing & Length of Programs: Positions run from May to September.
Destinations: France & Spain.
Costs/Pay: Wages start at around £100 per week; travel and accommodation are free.
Eligibility: Applicants must be aged at least 18.
How to Apply: Send in your CV with a covering letter stating when you are free to work. There will then be an interview.

Specialist Holidays Group (SHG)
Overseas Recruitment, Specialist Holidays Group, King's Place, Wood St, Kingston-upon-Thames, Surrey KT1 1FH
☎ 020 7420 2081
fax 020 8541 2492
overseasrecruitment@s-h-g.co.uk
www.shgjobs.co.uk
SHG is part of the group that includes Thomson, Lunn Poly and TUI. There are numerous seasonal jobs for waiting and hotel staff, reps, couriers, child carers, sports instructors etc. See p385 later for ski and chalet jobs.
Timing & Length of Programs: Summer jobs run from April/May to September/October.
Destinations: Summer jobs are mainly in countries around the Mediterranean, including Corsica and Turkey.
Pay: Wages vary but are standard for the industry. Transport, accommodation and food are provided.
Eligibility: Minimum age is 18 to 21, depending on the position, and you should speak the language of the destination for some positions.
How to Apply: Apply using the form on the website.

Sunsail
Human Resources, the Port House, Port Solent, Hampshire PO6 4TH
☎ 02392 222322
fax 02392 224280
hr@sunsail.com
www.sunsail.com
Sunsail employs around 1700 assorted staff on its yacht and beach resorts around the world. There are opportunities for qualified sailors and sailing instructors and general resort support staff, mostly in the Mediterranean.
Timing & Length of Programs: Most jobs run from April/May to November, but there are short contracts in the high season (June to September).
Destinations: Croatia, Greece & Turkey, but there are occasional opportunities for repeat staff in the Caribbean.
Pay: Wages start from £50 for land-based jobs and £105 for yacht-based jobs, and workers get a weekly bonus, paid at the end of the contract. Accommodation, meals and transport are provided.
Eligibility: The minimum age is 19 to 21 for yacht staff and you must have relevant skills or qualifications for the job (eg RYA or equivalent yachting qualifications).
How to Apply: Apply for specific vacancies using the application form on the website.

Ski Resorts

Changing Worlds

See Working-Holiday Organisations (p377) for contact details. This big gap-year operator offers a Work Canada program with placements at ski resorts in the Canadian Rockies. Most people work as chalet staff, but you have the option of taking a ski-instructor course during the placements.

Types of Work: Ski chalet and hospitality jobs at resorts.

Timing & Length of Programs: Six months from November to March.

Destinations: Canada (Banff & Whistler).

Costs/Pay: Most resorts pay around £4.50 per hour and you pay for your own accommodation and some meals. Participation costs £1875 for Banff and £1935 for Whistler, including flights and visa fees but not insurance.

Eligibility: You should be a current university student or within a year of starting or finishing university. Minimum age is 18.

How to Apply: Request an application pack on the website. Candidates are then invited to an interview and assessment.

Inghams Travel

Overseas Reps Department, Inghams Travel, 10–18 Putney Hill, London SW15 6AX

☎ 020 8780 4400

☎ 020 8780 8803 (for chalet/hospitality jobs)

fax 020-8780 8805

travel@inghams.com

www.inghams.co.uk

Inghams is a highly regarded ski company and has openings for staff at its ski resorts in Europe every winter. It also has openings for hotel staff at some of its summer resorts in Europe.

Types of Work: Chalet and hotel staff, bar and waiting staff, managers, reps etc.

Timing & Length of Programs: Winter positions run from December to April.

Destinations: Austria, France, Italy, Lapland & Switzerland.

Costs/Pay: Wages vary depending on your age and the level of skills required, but accommodation, meals and transport to the resorts are provided.

Eligibility: Applicants must be at least 18 (23 for rep and management jobs). Reps should ideally speak French, German, Italian or Spanish.

How to Apply: Download the application form from the website, then there's an interview. Applications are accepted from June.

Jobs in the Alps

All inquiries through the website www.jobs-in-the-alps.co.uk

Jobs in the Alps provides around 100 ski and chalet jobs every winter and around 80 hospitality jobs every summer, all in the Alps.

Types of Work: Chalet and hotel jobs.

Timing & Length of Programs: Positions run from December to April and mid-June to mid-September.

Destinations: France & Switzerland.

Costs/Pay: There's no fee to take part, but gappers can become a Jobs in the Alps member, which provides perks such as travel assistance and insurance – contact Jobs in the Alps for latest details. Most workers earn about €1000 per month with free board and food, but travel costs are extra.

Eligibility: Applicants must be EU citizens aged at least 18 and should have studied A-level French or German.

How to Apply: Apply through the website for an application pack and list of vacancies.

Mark Warner

Resorts Recruitment Department, George House, 61–65 Kensington Church St, London W8 4BA

☎ 0870 330750

fax 0870 330751

recruitment@markwarner.co.uk

www.markwarner-recruitment.co.uk

Mark Warner is a major tour operator with 27 years of experience. Winter jobs are available at seven ski resorts in the Alps, including jobs as chalet and ski hosts (ie ski couriers). Summer positions are available in the Mediterranean and Aegean. Transport, meals and accommodation are provided for all jobs.

Types of Work: Catering, housekeeping and ski/snowboard hosting (courier work) are available in winter. Hotel, restaurant and waterfront positions are available in summer.

Timing & Length of Programs: Winter jobs are for six to seven months from November and summer jobs are for six to seven months from April.

Destinations: Austria, France & Italy (winter); Corsica, Greece, Italy (including Sardinia) & Turkey, (summer) & Egypt (year round).

Costs/Pay: Rates of pay depend on the position and are competitive for the industry.

Eligibility: Applicants must be aged at least 19 (you must be older for jobs with more responsibility). Ski/snowboarding staff and watersports instructors must have relevant qualifications.

How to Apply: You can apply year round. Download the application form from the website. Successful applicants are called for an interview.

PGL Ski

Ski Personnel Dept, Alton Court, Penyard Lane, Ross-on-Wye, Herefordshire HR9 5GL
☎ 01989 767311
fax 0870 403 4433
skipersonnel@pgl.co.uk
www.pgl.co.uk/people
PGL specialises in holidays for children and offers around 100 short-term seasonal winter jobs at resorts around Europe. For information on working with children see p411. For summer jobs see Tour Operators & Activity Holidays (p380).
Types of Work: Short-term jobs as instructors, ski reps and ski group couriers (working with small groups of children).
Timing & Length of Programs: Positions are for one to six weeks around February or the Easter holidays.
Destinations: Austria, France, Italy & Switzerland.
Costs/Pay: All jobs pay around £175 per week. Board, lodging, travel, lift pass and insurance are all free.
Eligibility: Applicants must be aged at least 20 (18 for instructors) and be able to speak conversational French, Italian or German.
How to Apply: Recruitment for the following year starts in July. Download the application form from the website. You'll need to provide two referees and show a clean criminal record.

Ski Staff

Farm View House, 45 Farm View, Yateley, Hampshire GU46 6HU
☎ 0870 432 8030
fax 0870 011 0719
work@skistaff.co.uk
www.skistaff.co.uk
Ski Staff is a recruitment agency that provides staff for over 100 British ski companies operating in the French, Swiss, Austrian and Italian Alps. Jobs can be found for instructors, ski hosts and chalet workers and there are specialist cookery courses for chalet staff – see the website for details.

Specialist Holidays Group (SHG)

See Tour Operators & Activity Holidays (p383) for contact details. As well as summer resort work, SHG offers a wide range of winter resort jobs for ski escorts, instructors and chalet staff. They can also arrange cooking courses for chalet staff. Ski

recruitment road shows take place around the country – see the website for details.
Timing & Length of Programs: Winter jobs from November to May.
Destinations: Ski jobs are mainly in Austria, Andorra, France & Italy.
Pay: Wages vary but are standard for the industry. Transport, accommodation and food is provided and there's a free ski pass.
Eligibility: The minimum age is 18 to 21, depending on the position, and you must speak the language of the destination for some positions.
How to Apply: Apply using the form on the website.

Total Holidays

185 Fleet Rd, Fleet, Hampshire GU51 3BL
☎ 01252 618309
fax 01252 618328
recruitment@skitotal.com
www.skitotal.com
Ski Total has been running ski holidays in Europe for 20 years and has winter jobs for instructors, reps and chalet and catering staff. Positions in Canada require a working-holiday visa and tend to be reserved for people who have already done a season in Europe. This office also recruits for Esprit holidays (www.esprit-holidays.co.uk).
Timing & Length of Programs: From mid November to end of April (apply from March).
Destinations: Austria, Canada, France, Italy & Switzerland.
Pay: Weekly wages vary with the position but start at around £70, including transport, meals, accommodation, lift passes, ski or snowboard hire and insurance. Participants pay a refundable commitment bond of £100, which is returned at the end of the season.
Eligibility: The minimum age varies from 19 to 23, depending on the job. Instructors, reps, chefs, nannies and managers require qualifications and experience.
How to Apply: Download an application pack from the website.

World Challenge Expeditions (WCE)

Black Arrow House, 2 Chandos Rd, London NW10 6NF
☎ 020 8728 7200
fax 020 8961 1551
individuals@world-challenge.co.uk
www.world-challenge.co.uk
WCE's Gap Challenge offers paid work placements at hotels and ski resorts in Canada. They arrange the work permit,

flights and job placement, and orientation sessions and workers receive a free ski pass. WCE also offers working-holiday programs in Australia and New Zealand with a guaranteed job offer – see the website for details.

Types of Work: Canada placements are in hotels and ski resorts, and jobs range from housekeeping to lift operating.

Timing & Length of Programs: Positions run for six months from November (hotel work is also available in March and September).

Destination: Canada (Banff).

Costs/Pay: The total fee is £1700, including flights and a ski pass. Insurance and accommodation are extra (estimated cost £75 to £150 per month). Participants earn £60 to £150 per week.

Eligibility: Applicants must be aged 19 to 24. You must be a full-time student or have graduated within the last year, or be a gap-year student with a confirmed offer of a university place.

How to Apply: Download the information pack and application form from the website, then there's an interview and selection day.

Fruit Picking & Farm Work

AgriVenture

Speedwell Farm Bungalow, Nettle Bank, Wisbech, Cambridge-shire PE14 0SA

☎ /fax 01945 450999

uk@agriventure.com

www.agriventure.com

AgriVenture arranges paid work exchanges for aspiring farmers in five different countries. It arranges all the paperwork and provides a guaranteed farm job, transport and visas, plus support in the host country. The host farm provides board and lodging.

Types of Work: Work is on arable or mixed farms.

Timing & Length of Programs: Placements are for four to 14 months. Work in the USA, Canada and Japan starts between February and June. Work in Australia and New Zealand can start year round.

Destinations: Australia, Canada, Europe, Japan, New Zealand & USA.

Costs/Pay: Fees start from £1900, including flights, visa fees and insurance. Wages vary depending on the job and host country. Contact AgriVenture for prices of individual programs.

Eligibility: Applicants must be aged 18 to 30 and have practical farming or horticultural experience.

How to Apply: Request an information pack online to start the application process.

Appellation Contrôlée (APCON)

Ulgersmaweg 26c, 9731 BT, Groningen, Holland

☎ 00 31 50-549 2434

fax 00 31 50-549 2428

project2@bart.nl

www.apcon.nl

This Dutch organisation places seasonal workers on the annual grape harvest in France. You make your own way to the farms.

Types of Work: The main option is grape picking in France.

Timing & Length of Programs: Grape picking in France starts in September or October, depending on the weather.

Destination: France.

Costs/Pay: Registration costs from £60. Workers are paid around £28 per day, and food and accommodation are usually included.

Eligibility: Applicants must be aged at least 18.

How to Apply: Fill in the online form and send in the payment.

Fruitfuljobs.com

c/o AMS, Unit 3, Honeybourne Industrial Estate, Evesham, Worcestershire WR11 7QF

☎ 01386 832555

fax 01386 833960

info@fruitfuljobs.com

www.fruitfuljobs.com

This is a recruitment service for jobs in the British soft-fruit industry. It can put you in contact with farms needing workers throughout the harvest season. Most jobs involve supervising and managing the crop rather than actually picking fruit.

Types of Work: Jobs can be found as field supervisors, packing supervisors, tractor drivers, and in crop management (laying plastic sheeting for strawberries etc).

Timing & Length of Programs: Harvesting jobs run from April to October.

Destination: UK.

Costs/Pay: Workers earn around £5 per hour. Accommodation is normally provided on the farms for a small supplement.

Eligibility: Applicants must be aged at least 18.

How to Apply: Fill in the online registration form. You will then be contacted to discuss matching you with a grower.

International Exchange Centre (IEC)

89 Fleet St, London EC4Y 1DH
☎ 020 7583 9116
fax 020 7583 9117
isecinfo@btconnect.com
www.isecworld.co.uk

The IEC organises a variety of work placements around the world, including farm placements. Casual options include strawberry picking in Denmark, farm work in Norway and paid training programs for agricultural students in Finland, New Zealand and the USA.

Types of Work: Fruit picking, planting, harvesting and other agricultural jobs.

Timing & Length of Programs: Varies with the program. Some placements are related to the harvest season, others start year round – see the website for details. Traineeships last up to 12 months.

Destinations: Denmark, Finland, New Zealand, Norway & the USA.

Costs/Pay: Program fees range from £150 for Denmark to £640 for agricultural training in the USA. Wages vary from country to country.

Eligibility: Applicants must be aged at least 18. You must be an agricultural student or have two years' practical experience for the agricultural training programs.

How to Apply: Email or phone for an application form three months in advance.

Visitoz

Chapel House, 6a Shipton Rd, Ascott-under-Wychwood, Oxon OX7 6AY
☎ 01993 831972
will@visitoz.org
www.visitoz.org

This popular family-run organisation offers training in the essential skills needed to work on an Australian farm, including horse riding, driving a tractor and managing livestock. Work placements are then provided on outback farms across Australia. You have the option of just taking the training course or taking an introductory package that also includes a three-day orientation at Rainbow Beach near Brisbane and a job placement.

Types of Work: Work is on arable and livestock farms. Jobs include mustering cattle, harvesting or planting crops and building fences.

Timing & Length of Programs: The training course lasts four days. Farm work is then available in three-month blocks for up to a year. The orientation begins on Friday, and most people aim to arrive in Australia on Thursday.

Destination: Australia.

Costs/Pay: The fee is AU$1680 (£670), including the training course and orientation. The host farms provide accommodation and food, and wages start at around £150 a week. Flights, insurance and visa fees are extra.

Eligibility: Applicants must be aged 18 to 30. A tidy appearance is required as workers stay with farming families.

How to Apply: Call or email for an application pack. There will then be an interview in person or by phone.

World-Wide Opportunities on Organic Farms (WWOOF)

PO Box 2675, Lewes, East Sussex BN7 1RB
☎ /fax 01273 476286
hello@wwoof.org
www.wwoof.org.uk

WWOOF arranges unpaid farm work at organic farms around the world. You stay with a host family and do about six hours' work a day in exchange for room and board. You must make all your own travel arrangements.

Types of Work: Volunteer farm work on organic arable and mixed farms.

Timing & Length of Programs: Placements can range from a few days to a year.

Destinations: WWOOF represents host farms in dozens of countries around the world – see the website for a list of WWOOF partners.

Costs/Pay: Work is unpaid but room and board are provided.

Eligibility: The minimum age at most farms is 18.

How to Apply: Join the local WWOOF organisation where you want to work (see the website for contact details); it costs £15 to join and members get a regularly updated list of WWOOF host farms.

WORK YOUR ROUTE

Travel, the actual process of getting from A to B, can be one of the most expensive elements of any gap year, but some people travel the world for free and others even get paid for it. Sound interesting? Some of the options here are great for gap-year travel, like crewing a yacht or doing a summer season as a tour leader. Others require more than one year's commitment, plus more experience, and are better suited to a post-university gap year.

CREWING A YACHT

Ever thought of working your passage? The world is full of water and flying over it quickly is the expensive option. On a yacht the world really opens up and you get to see so much more than is possible by public transport (and wind in your sails is really far more exotic than chewing gum on your bus seat). Many gappers say it's the only way to experience the islands of the Aegean, the Pacific, the Indian Ocean and the Caribbean. And they're right – you get to places in a private boat that the rest of us only dream about.

As well as getting you cheaply from land to land, crewing a yacht also looks good on your CV. Many of the skills you need at sea are also needed in business – teamwork, preparation, attention to detail, anticipation, keeping cool in a crisis and working efficiently under pressure.

Competition for crewing jobs is fierce, so the more sailing experience you've got the easier it'll be to get that first job. To maximise your chances, why not do a competent crew course in the UK before you leave (see p440)? A first-aid course is also a good idea, as anyone with any medical training is always useful at sea. Oli Byles, who crossed the Bay of Biscay on his first crewing position, adds:

Skills such as rope splicing and whipping can prove invaluable, along with engine and electrical maintenance. You should also know a few useful knots.

If you only have limited experience then the job you're most likely to get is deckhand, right at the bottom of the heap. Gareth Granville, who's done a lot of crewing in the South Pacific, explains:

Depending on the boat, what you do as a deckhand can change dramatically. On a big stinkpot (power superyacht) you could be one of four or five deckies taking orders from a bosun or a mate. On a smaller sailing yacht, it could be just you and the skipper and your responsibilities would stretch to more areas of running the boat, like engine maintenance and keeping all the systems going (aircon, fresh water/salt water/grey water/black water pluming systems, refrigeration, all the sails and rigging, the gas systems, the list is endless). The hours can be long but the lifestyle is good.

If you're working your passage as a deckhand then you'll probably be asked to contribute a little towards your upkeep. Skippers/owners often ask for up to £10 a day towards costs – but not always.

Before running away to sea, though, it's worth considering whether this is a lifestyle that will suit you. A private yacht is a very small place to live and you need to get on with everyone. When you're at sea you're together 24 hours a day. Gareth Granville agrees:

The big thing about boats, whether large or small, is that you're living in a very limited amount of space. There's an irony at work, where on the one hand you can be out in the middle of the ocean with a sense of almost infinite space all around you, but your real available space is slightly bigger than a shoebox. Moreover, there are other people in your shoebox.

In addition, your sleep is disrupted because of night watches, meal times are shifted to fit in with your watch, you'll encounter bad weather (and possibly life and death situations), you'll be seasick and you'll never feel really clean. Oli Byles explains:

As far as washing goes there are usually two attitudes – 'We all stink; so who cares?' or, for those who worry about it, very sparing use of fresh water with a flannel and a sea-water rinse. Or just go for a swim. The dishes usually take priority over personal hygiene.

Your skipper is always in absolute charge. Oli Byles again:

Decisions are made on a day-to-day basis by the skipper, so the crew have to be totally accommodating of that and remember that his or her word is the law on board.

If you like a drink and a smoke it's worth sounding out the skipper's views on these habits, particularly when at sea.

If you want to tee up a crewing position before leaving the UK then yacht delivery is a great way to go (see p396). You sail to some amazing places, it costs you nothing and you notch up some valuable sailing experience. Then there are the specialist crewing agencies where, for a small fee, your requirements are matched with those of a skipper – see p396. Otherwise, try the classified ads in magazines such as *Yachting Monthly* (www.yachtingmonthly.com) and *Yachting World* (www.yachting-world.com). Women should watch out, though, as lonely old sea dogs are sometimes sniffing around for company rather than crew.

Most gappers are usually on the road when they decide to try a little crewing. Although there are usually crewing agencies wherever there's a decent-sized marina, many gappers are better off finding their own jobs. Gareth Granville advises:

A good way of getting your foot in the door is through day work. Lots of yachts find themselves overwhelmed with work before guests arrive or before they put to sea. During these times they will hire extra hands to help do whatever needs to be done. Often the work is menial, like sanding and polishing. But the money comes in handy and day-working is a good way to meet people and prove your ability to work.

Also, pretty much every yacht club I've been to has a notice board with posted notes looking for crew. The boats are generally small and privately owned.

Getting a crewing job is all about who you meet, who you know and who will recommend you. Looking for work in the yachtie bars can be fruitful. This was how Gareth got his first job:

My very first job was on a yacht going from Antigua to St Thomas, long before I had any qualifications or real experience. I got the job just by hitting it off with the skipper while playing pool and having a few beers. So basically, there are plenty of short-term and quite casual jobs around, but you have to be at the right place at the right time and you simply have to be honest and hard-working. Never overstate your abilities and always ask questions if you're not sure about something.

A word of warning though: while the captain is checking you out, make sure you check out the captain. Take heed from yachtie-gapper Gareth:

Make sure you trust the person in charge. Safety should always be the main concern. It's all a lot of fun when things are going well, but the sea has a will of her own, and short of being prepared we have little or nothing in our power to stop her.

Yachting is totally seasonal. This means that if you're in the right place at the right time then getting a job will be much easier (see table below).

Months	From	To
January-March	Cape Town (South Africa)	the Caribbean, the Mediterranean, South America
March-April	Gibraltar	Greece, Turkey
March-May	the Caribbean	East Coast (USA), the Mediterranean, Panama Canal
March-June	West Coast (USA)	South Pacific (particularly Tahiti)
March-May	Northern Europe	the Mediterranean
April	New Zealand	Australia, West Coast (USA) via Pacific Islands
April-June	East Coast (USA)	the Mediterranean
May-July	Durban (South Africa)	Islands of the Indian Ocean
June-August	Darwin (Australia)	Indonesia, Indian Ocean
August-September	Fiji	New Zealand
September-October	Greece, Turkey	Gibraltar
October-November	Gibraltar	the Caribbean via the Canary Islands
October-November	West Coast (USA)	Mexico
November	Islands of the Indian Ocean	Durban (South Africa)
November	East Coast (USA)	the Caribbean
November- December	the Canary Islands	the Caribbean

The two main sailing seasons are from April to October in the Mediterranean and from October to May in the Caribbean. In the Mediterranean, boats usually sail west to east in the spring, ending up in the Greek islands or the Turkish coast. In October they all head back to Gibraltar before congregating in the Canary Islands for a November/December Atlantic crossing to catch the season in the Caribbean.

If you want to crew in the Mediterranean then good yachting centres are the French Riviera, Gibraltar, the Balearics or the Greek islands. In the Caribbean, try Antigua. In the southern hemisphere, Kiwis are always sailing from Auckland to Tonga or Fiji, and in Australia try the Whitsunday Island group.

Another good bet are the hundreds of worldwide amateur long-distance races or regattas. The most famous is the Atlantic Rally for Cruisers (ARC; www.worldcruising.com), which starts in November from Las Palmas in the Canaries and finishes in St Lucia in the Caribbean. Another big yachting event is Antigua Sailing Week (www.sailingweek.com) at the end of April. Yacht owners are often looking for crew at these times either to be an extra pair of eyes and hands or to help contribute to costs.

When crewing you need a passport with more than a year left on it, and either a ticket home from your final destination or enough money to buy that ticket plus additional funds. Basically, immigration authorities want to ensure that you're not going to stay in their country and that you're definitely not going to be a drain on their resources. When you join a boat you'll be signed on as crew and you can only be signed off, or assigned to another boat, if you can fulfil these requirements.

Finally, drugs are a huge no-no on boats. Skippers are really big on this because they stand to lose almost everything if drugs are found on their ship. And, as you can imagine, US coast-guards are very hot on this when boats arrive in American waters from the Caribbean.

CRUISE SHIPS

Cruising is a year-round business and cruise lines are constantly looking to fill vacancies. Some of the larger ships have up to 1000 crew, and the turnover of staff is high.

Most people choose to work on cruise ships to see the world. The Mediterranean and the Caribbean are the main stomping grounds, but the Far East is also popular. Many people then stay on because it's a good way to save money as you get free board and lodging. It's also a real opportunity to make international friends – cruise ships hire from all over the world and some ships will have over 50 nationalities working on board. The leading supply is from the Philippines, India (particularly Goa) and the countries of the former Soviet Union (particularly Ukraine). Suzi Dona, who worked as a purser, agrees:

There are many positive aspects about working on a cruise ship – obviously travelling, the opportunity to meet new friends, free accommodation, tax-free salaries and duty-free shopping.

Most cruise ships are like floating towns with every convenience you'd expect on a trendy high street. This means that the variety of jobs on board is enormous: there are casinos needing dealers, retail outlets needing sales assistants, gyms needing fitness trainers and masseurs, offices needing secretaries, and ship newspapers needing journalists. For the stage-struck, some of the best jobs on board are as entertainers – singers, musicians, dancers etc – but the standards are as high as the kicks in a can-can. In contrast, you don't have to be David Bailey to become a ship's photographer. You can just be a beginner because all training is normally given on board – see p397 for details. Nigel Deayton did this and says:

I would say that being a photographer is probably one of the most interesting and active jobs aboard. We basically come up with a plan of the best photo opportunity moments like formal evenings and the captain's parties. We photograph the guests at their table in the restaurant, at the parties and on studio backdrops. I've also been on some fantastic tours to photograph the guests at exotic locations. So far I've been on a camel riding tour to the Pyramids in Egypt, ice climbing on glaciers in Norway, helicopter flights over Montserrat, and 4WD truck rides up the side of Mt Etna.

Plus, in the land of the midnight buffet, there are always loads of jobs for catering and waiting staff. In all there are between 150 and 200 different positions on board a decent-sized cruise ship.

The top jobs pay anything from £20,000 per annum upwards, but the majority of positions pay around £1000 a month. If you're in the service front-line then you'll get less, because most of your income will come from tips – some waiters, bar or cabin staff make more than £300 a week from the paying guests. Don't forget, you don't stump up for the rent or weekly shop and, on top of this, most cruise employees are classed as self-employed, which means that wages are paid tax free.

However, it's not all plain sailing. Suzi Dona explains:

The jobs are very demanding. The hours are long with no days off during a working period of between six and eight months and passengers always assume that wherever you're on the ship or ashore in your free time (possibly relaxing on a lovely white sandy beach) that you're always on duty and at their service.

And Nigel Deayton says:

As for life on board, well, we work every day of the week and do an average of 50 to 60 hours a week (depending on the season). It's like 'life intensified' because you're living in this big floating steel village, with loads of people literally on top of each other, most cabins are small with bunk beds. Lots of nationalities have to work together to serve the guests (who can be very demanding). It can be a fast pace of life on board, we work hard, party hard, make friends quickly, eat quickly, sleep quickly, fall in love quickly and fall out of love even quicker.

In addition, a cruise ship is very hierarchical, there are more classes aboard than you ever took at school. Many of the lowliest and worst-paid positions are taken by crew from developing countries and so racism is often an element of life aboard. In September 2002 the charity War on Want and the International Transport Workers' Federation wrote a report called *Sweatships – what it's really like to work on board cruise ships* highlighting the situation of these workers. It can be downloaded from www.waronwant.org.

If you're thinking of working on a cruise ship during your gap year then there are a couple of things to bear in mind. Firstly, working on a cruise ship is like having a 'proper job'. Cruise lines hire professionals with good communication skills, often with a minimum of two years' relevant experience and qualifications in their field. As a result, most jobs are advertised with a minimum age of between 20 or 23, with 21 being the norm. Many positions with passenger contact also prefer you to speak at least one other language. These requirements can be a stumbling block if you're a pre-university gapper, but there's no reason why you might not be qualified if you're taking a gap year after higher education. Needless to say, the selection process is rigorous and usually only those with the right attitude win through.

It's unusual for cruise lines to hire direct. Recruitment is mostly handled by agencies or 'concessionaires' – companies who own and run their own facilities on a ship (eg shops, gyms, hairdressers). A lot of recruitment agencies or concessionaires are based in the USA, but they interview and hire worldwide, so it's definitely worth applying to them. Those listed on p397 all have UK offices.

Start applying at least two months before you want to depart. The best time for a newcomer to get their first job is around Christmas and New Year when experienced crew want to be at home (they also know what hell festive cruises can be to work). Most contracts last from between four to 10 months, but six months is the most usual. You then get two months' unpaid leave (or you quit altogether). When you're at the contractual stage it's important to understand what you'll be paying for and what the cruise line or concessionaire will pick up. For instance, most ships won't depart from or arrive at Britain; so who's going to pay your air fare? Steer clear of agencies that charge upfront fees or internet sites trying to sell you a list of current vacancies – both are usually an expensive waste of time.

To work at sea you'll need a passport with more than a year left on it, a clear criminal record (you can even run into trouble with a jaywalking fine) and travel insurance. This is also a good time to get your yellow fever vaccination. If you intend to work in US waters, where so much of the cruise industry is based, you will also need a C1/D visa (see www.usembassy.org .uk/cons_web/visa/niv/cdvisas.htm for details). If any other visas are needed once you're on board then the crew purser will sort this for you. Sometimes agencies or concessionaires require other bits from you like a basic sea survival certificate and a medical examination (you'll have to jump through several medical hoops to work for an American cruise company). When you're offered a job the cruise line will help you sort all of these out and will pay for them.

There are lots of websites about working on cruise ships, often written by those who've been there and done that. Two good ones are www.cruiseman.com/cruiseshipjobs.htm and www.cruise-community.com.

TOUR LEADING

Independent travel isn't everyone's cup of yak butter tea (ugh). Plenty of people prefer to see the world as part of an organised tour. Some are run on a shoestring where you sleep in tents and cook your own food; others stay in top-class hotels and eat in Michelin-starred restaurants. Some cater for school children, others for groups of 20- and 30-somethings, and many are for older people. The type of customer and their expectations are very different in all these cases and it's important to work for the company that best suits your personality and style of travelling. You also have to decide how long you want to spend doing this sort of job. Many tour operators want you to sign up for a minimum of two seasons or more. This is because training costs are high and they want a decent return on their investment. In addition, you often need to be aged 21 or more (sometimes 23 to 25) to work your route in this way. As such, this option is more suited to a post-university gapper than a school leaver.

What is initially attractive about tour leading is being paid to sightsee in a foreign country. What you get out of it, though, is much deeper than that. You get under the skin of the countries where you lead. The experience of working day-to-day with the local people means you form relationships and understandings that simply aren't possible as a traveller or tourist. Working as a tour leader also looks great on your CV due to the job's high levels of responsibility and pressure.

As a tour leader you're responsible for the smooth running of a trip and the overall satisfaction of your group. This means that you're not only a leader and motivator but also a facilitator and manager, ensuring that all hotel and restaurant reservations, sightseeing opportunities, and group needs and requests are met. You also look after company funds, keep expense accounts, handle a string of stressful events from stolen passports to serious illnesses, and write tour reports. Some tour companies will expect you to spout educational commentary, some will use local guides for this, or there'll be a good mixture of the two. At the end of the trip your performance will be assessed by the group when they fill in feedback forms – so you'll even have to be nice to the loudmouth know-it-all (it's the law: there'll be one per group).

Catherine McCormack worked for the American Council of International Studies (ACIS) in Italy:

It was like nothing else I've ever done before, which made the whole experience all the more rewarding. You're given an itinerary for seven to eight days, which has been pre-arranged and includes details of all hotels and restaurants, which have been booked in advance. It's then your job to make sure everyone gets to these places at the right time, in the right order and learns about the country you're touring along the way. You're responsible for facilitating their experience through your cultural knowledge and communication skills. You decide the day-to-day schedule and with the help of a driver make sure a good time is had by all on the road. Aside from injecting the tour with a good dose of fun and education, it's also up to you to sort out any mishaps, from missing luggage to accident and illness and try and accommodate the unpredictable nature of touring with 40 people and a bus with professionalism and panache. The unpredictability and varied nature of each tour, however, is also one of the most exciting aspects of the job.

Quite often trips run back-to-back, which means that as one group goes home the next one arrives. It also means that you could be working abroad, with very little time off, doing a succession of tours for up to six months. Being with new people all the time gives great variety but also means you constantly have to prove yourself.

To work as a tour leader, Catherine says:

You must be a naturally outgoing person who's confident with your language skills, very diplomatic, copes well under stress and loves meeting people and sharing what you know and who you are with them.

Don't expect a holiday. The early starts and often late nights are one of the biggest challenges of the job and the ability to remain energetic when utterly exhausted is probably the toughest aspect. I fell asleep on the bus once and slipped off my seat – very embarrassing.

Tour companies often require their leaders to speak a foreign language. Excellent communication skills are essential, as well as a love of public speaking.

You won't be doing this job for the pay, but whatever you do get is often on top of free accommodation, return air fare and sometimes free meals – see p398 for details. In addition, many tour leaders earn good tips. You should share these with your driver (if you have one). Also, it's traditional for tour leaders to make a little bit on the side by getting free meals at the restaurants where you take the group or commission at some of the shops the group visits. Obviously, these tactics need to be used with discretion and in moderation.

In terms of work visas, you'll be expected to have a passport from one of the EU countries allowing you to work in Europe. The tour operator will arrange work visas for outside of Europe.

Jobs are often advertised in the free London magazine *TNT* (www.tntmagazine.com/uk), or the independent travel magazine *Wanderlust* (www.wanderlust.co.uk). They are also pinned on notice boards in the languages department of universities, or the careers office. Sometimes, they turn up on www.payaway.co.uk. Otherwise, many are advertised on the tour operator's website and on notice boards at travel fairs.

BEHIND THE WHEEL
Coach and overland companies estimate that 90% of their drivers are male. This ratio reflects the proportion of applications, not the selection process; all companies would love to hire more female drivers. So girls, how about seeing the world this way?

Insurance cover requires drivers to be aged at least 23 (and often 25) years old.

Overland Companies
Practically all drivers who work for overland companies lead the tours too, so there's a lot of 'tour leading' in their job description – see the preceding section for more information. This makes the job twice as difficult, or twice as rewarding, depending on whether you see your billycan as half empty or half full.

It's got to be said that the overland companies would really prefer gap-year students as paying customers rather than paid employees. It often takes between six and 18 months to become a fully qualified overland driver/tour leader and so they want you to stay in the job for at least a couple of years. The minimum age of 25 also means that this is probably a post- rather than pre-university option.

Overland drivers will always tell you they have the best job in the world. They love travelling in challenging environments, seeing extraordinary things every day, being their own boss, having high levels of responsibility, making a difference to the developing countries they visit, and being on the road for much of the year.

The 4WD trucks that overland companies use are pretty sophisticated. They're rough and tough but more comfortable than they look, with padded seats, stereo, safe, camp oven, retractable awnings, reference libraries, roof racks, lighting and sometimes a fridge/freezer. They seat around 25 passengers. As tour leader your main job is to look after the vehicle, know the routes and drive safely through them. You'll also have to fix the truck if it breaks down. Many of the overland routes run through Africa, Asia or South America, and sod's law dictates you always break down in the middle of nowhere – sound mechanical knowledge has to be matched by the wily thinking of a bush mechanic.

The other important part of the job is the leading and tour guiding. One moment you're a driver and mechanic and the next you're a cultural and wildlife expert, crew manager, local fixer, social secretary, medical doctor, love counsellor and international peacemaker (not all groups exist in perfect harmony). For these reasons on most overland trips there are two drivers/tour leaders, and often a cook, who can share the responsibility of keeping the group safe, happy and well.

The roads on many overland trips are better than they used to be. Many are now sealed, although they all still compete in the pothole Olympics. Importantly, there's no night driving when you're overlanding (unless there's an emergency) and rare are the days when you're driving for nine hours at a stretch.

To drive for overland companies you need a LGV (Large Goods Vehicle)/HGV (Heavy Goods Vehicle) or PCV (Passenger Carrying Vehicle) licence. It takes between five and eight days to train for this at around £135 a day – see p446. Often you'll also need to be a mechanic.

Overland drivers/tour leaders don't do it for the pay – as you'll see on p401, many companies are a little cagey about salary. But, your pay does increase with seniority, and all your day-to-day costs are met, as well as flights to and from the UK. In addition, there's not much time to spend what you do earn and so much of your wages can go into savings.

The overland company sorts your visas and immigration documents, but you do need to know how to get yourself and your group through some dodgy border crossings where petty bribery and corruption is often part of everyday life.

Coach-Touring Companies

Driving for a coach company is a very different ball game. For starters the minimum age is 23. You'll also concentrate just on the driving, as there'll be an on-board guide – this is just as well in places like Italy where their national dish (pasta) rhymes with their national speed limit (fasta).

You'll also need a PCV, which is like the LGV/HGV but concentrates more on passenger comfort. Mechanical knowledge isn't so crucial because garages in Europe are everywhere.

In many cases, coach drivers are paid better than the tour leaders/on-board guides. This is because they have less opportunity to earn any unofficial extras, although good tour leaders (or those savvy enough to realise they need to get on with you) will share their passenger tips.

Other Work

Drivers are always needed. With a LGV/HGV or PCV licence under your belt you'll be able to pick up driving work abroad. Good bets are the local temp agencies for drivers; otherwise a short contract or full-time job with one of the freight-forwarding or road-haulage companies is quite possible.

Driveaway Cars

Hey, here's a driving opportunity that doesn't require you to be at the older end of the gap-year market. If you're in America and want to get around cheaply then think about registering with one of the many driveaway car companies who need drivers to move cars from one place to another.

You need to over 21 and have a valid driving licence, personal references and around £162 in cash as a deposit that's refundable when you deliver the car safely. You pay nothing for the use of the car and the company stumps up for insurance, but you have to cover the petrol. The car's got to be delivered to its destination at a specified time – six to eight hours of driving per day is usually allotted. Maximum mileage is also stipulated, so you have to follow the shortest route. Obviously, availability depends on demand, but coast-to-coast routes come up a lot and at the start of winter many cars need delivering to Florida.

Driveaway car companies are listed in the *Yellow Pages* under 'Automotive Transport and Driveaway Companies' (phone a week or two before you want to travel), otherwise try Auto Driveaway Company (www.autodriveaway.com).

CONTACTS

Crewing a Yacht

Blue Water

La Galerie du Port, Bldg d'Aguillon, Antibes 06600, France
☎ 020 7829 8446/00 33 4 93 34 34 13 (UK number is redirected to France at local rate)
fax 00 33 4 93 34 35 93
crew@bluewateryachting.com
www.bluewateryachting.com
This is a training school and crew placement centre that places a variety of crew on yachts worldwide, from captains, engineers, stewards and deckhands. Most vacancies occur from March to May for the Mediterranean season and October to November for the Caribbean season. Crew are able to register via the website where there's a one-off registration fee of £13. Once registered, crew are asked to contact the agency by phone or email twice a week to check in. Most crew using this service are experienced, but not always. In addition, you can do RYA (Royal Yachting Association) or MCA (Maritime Coastguard Agency) training here.

Crewseekers

Hawthorn House, Hawthorn Lane, Sarisbury Green, Southampton SO31 7BD
☎ /fax 01489 578319
info@crewseekers.co.uk
www.crewseekers.co.uk
This is the largest crewing agency in Europe. A six-month membership costs £60 and 12 months is £85. There are three levels of crew: leisure sailing, where crew fund their return fare to the boat and usually pay up to £10 a day towards costs; boat delivery for more experienced crew, where expenses are paid but there's no salary; and professional crew where all positions are paid. Vacancies occur year round if you're prepared to travel; the late availability section on the website is particularly useful. To register, go online.

Cruising Association

CA House, 1 Northey St, Limehouse Basin, London E14 8BT
☎ 020 7537 2828
fax 020 7537 2266
office@cruising.org.uk
www.cruising.org.uk
The Cruising Association was founded in 1908. It has a large nautical library, a cruise planning section, and a crewing service that runs from February to June. During these months five lists are published of skippers looking for crew and crew looking for a berth. On the first Wednesday of each month between February and June there's a meeting for skippers and crew. If you're not a member of the Cruising Association,

the crewing service fee is £34 for skippers and £24 for crew. Many skippers will take novice crew.

Global Crew Network

23 Old Mill Gardens, Berkhampstead, Hertfordshire HP4 2NZ
☎ 0870 9101 888
fax 0870 9101 887
john@globalcrewnetwork.com
www.globalcrewnetwork.com

Global Crew Network is a crew recruitment service for professional and novice crew members. You can apply to work on the tall ships, traditional boats, motor and sailing yachts worldwide. Normally there's a £35 registration fee for one year. If you're a novice contact Global Crew Network online so the company can best advise you on the types of positions most suitable for you. This service is good for those seeking working holidays/working passages.

Professional Yacht Deliveries Worldwide

Witherslack, Grange-over-Sands, Cumbria LA11 6RQ
☎ 01539 552140
fax 01539 552131
crew@pydww.com
www.pydww.com

Professional Yacht Deliveries Worldwide is one of the largest UK yacht deliverers, in need of hundreds of crew a year.

Type of Work: Deckhands and mates.
Timing & Length of Work: Boats are delivered all year round; journey times depend on route.
Destinations: Worldwide.
Pay: No registration fee. Crew are unpaid but all on-board expenses are covered. Travel to the boat is sometimes included, dependent on experience and qualifications.
Eligibility: Minimum age 17. They'll take relative beginners but expect some experience or Competent Crew certificate.
How to Apply: Send in CV and the contact name of someone who has sailed with you to vouch for character and ability.

Reliance Yacht Management

1st fl, 127 Lynchford Rd, Farnborough, Hampshire GU14 6ET
☎ 01252 378239
fax 01252 521736
crew@reliance-yachts.com
www.reliance-yachts.com

Reliance Yacht Management is one of the largest yacht deliverers in the world. It recruits a minimum of 400 crew a

year. Current vacancies are on the website. The office keeps in regular touch with the boats.

Type of Work: Deckhands and mates.
Timing & Length of Work: Boats are delivered all year round; journey times depend on route.
Destinations: Mostly from Europe or South Africa to the Caribbean, North America, Central America, Mexico, South Pacific, Seychelles, New Zealand and Australia.
Pay: There's a registration fee of £35 for one year. If you don't get any work during this time, the fee will be returned. Crew are unpaid but all on-board expenses are covered.
Eligibility: Minimum age 17. They'll take relative beginners but expect some experience or Competent Crew certificate.
How to Apply: Download registration form from the website or ring the office.

Cruise Ships

Agency Excellent Entertainment

Suite 2, the Business Centre, 120 West Heath Rd, London NW3 7TU
☎ 020 8458 4212
fax 020 8458 4572
theagency@excellententertainment.biz
www.excellententertainment.biz

This agency supplies entertainers and entertainment staff to the cruise line industry worldwide. The company is the sole UK supplier to Disney Cruise Line and 12 other cruise lines. Send your CV with a photo. If you get through this stage then you will be invited to an audition. Minimum ages from 18 to 21, depending on cruise line.

Berkeley Scott Group

11–13 Ockford Rd, Godalming, Surrey GU7 1QU
☎ 01483 791291
fax 0870 1372169
cruise@bsgplc.com
www.berkeley-scott.co.uk

Berkeley Scott recruits hotel positions including assistant waiter, hotel director, chef de partie, restaurant manager, cabin steward, housekeeping manager. It recruits for all the major international cruise lines, including Carnival, Celebrity, Costa, Cunard, Disney, Residensea, Holland America, Princess Cruises, P&O, Royal Caribbean and Silversea. It also recruits sales staff for retail outlets, entertainers, health and beauty staff, and casino staff. Most positions require one year's experience in a similar role in four- or five-star standard establishments.

Crew's People International

c/o Harding Bros, Avonmouth Way, Avonmouth, Bristol
BS11 8DD
☎ 0117 982 5961
fax 0117 982 7276
info@hardingbros.co.uk
www.hardingbros.co.uk
Concessionaire for around 25 ships covering all the major
cruise lines and supplying gift-shop staff, fitness instructors, spa consultants, beauticians and hairdressers. Retail
staff must be aged at least 21, with three years' full-time
retail experience. The minimum age for other positions is
also 21 and you must have relevant qualifications. If you're
offered a job you'll need to obtain a number of safety and
medical certificates before taking up the post.

Ocean Images UK

7 Home Farm Business Centre, Lockerley, Romsey, Hampshire
SO51 0JT
☎ 01794 341818
fax 01794 341415
jobs@ocean-images.com
www.ocean-images.com
Ocean Images works with 40 cruise ships across all the
main cruise lines and has openings for over 180 ship
photographers. All levels are considered and beginners are
trained on board. Personality and sales skills are important,
as all pay is commission-based. To apply, download the
application form from the website.

VIP International

17 Charing Cross Rd, London WC2H 0QW
☎ 020 7930 0541
fax 020 7930 2860
cruise@vipinternational.co.uk
www.vipinternational.co.uk
VIP supplies housekeeping, food and beverage, pursers'
office, culinary department and hotel operations staff to 10
leading cruise lines. You'll need at least three years' experience in a similar position with either a four-star or five-star
international hotel or equivalent on a cruise liner.

Tour Leading

Adventure Company

15 Turk St, Alton, Hampshire GU34 1AG
☎ 01420 541007
fax 01420 541022
jobs@adventurecompany.co.uk
www.adventurecompany.co.uk
This adventure tour operator has a worldwide program of small
group tours. Recruitment happens all year round. Office-based
training takes place over a long weekend followed by a one or
two week training tour with an experienced tour leader. Tour
leaders are employed on short fixed-term contracts.
Type of Work: Tour leaders.
Timing & Length of Work: Trips last from one to three
weeks. Back-to-back trips mean you could be out in one
country for up to six months. Trips run all year round but
there's less work in winter. Due to the growth in the 'family
adventures program' there's an increasing demand for leaders
taking one-off trips abroad during UK school holidays.
Destinations: Argentina, Brazil, Chile, China, Ethiopia,
France, Greece, India, Italy, Japan, Libya, Mexico, Spain
and Uganda.
Pay: You're a self-employed subcontractor on a basic day
rate depending on experience (the Adventure Company
will not disclose more than this). Accommodation and
meals provided as per the group itinerary (ie if your tour is
B&B, then you get B&B only).
Eligibility: Minimum age 25, university degree preferable,
travel knowledge essential, languages – especially Spanish
or Italian – preferable, previous first-aid training and outdoor
experience/certificate useful.
How to Apply: Happy to receive on-spec CVs. Usually
advertises in *Wanderlust* magazine.

American Council for International Studies (ACIS)

TM Department (Recruitment), AIFS (UK) Ltd, 38 Queen's
Gate, London SW7 5HR
☎ 020 7590 7474
fax 020 7590 7475
tm_dept@acis.com
www.acis.com
ACIS is an educational travel company which works in
partnership with US teachers to provide educational tours
for them and their students. Most of the students are first-
time travellers. Recruitment starts each autumn for the
spring season and in spring for the summer season. There's
a weekend training course and extensive back-up while on
the road (24-hour emergency line).
Type of Work: Tour managers.
Timing & Length of Work: Tours last between one
week and 10 days, and the seasons run from February to
May (busiest at Easter) and early June to the end of July.

Destinations: Either one European country, one European city or all over Europe, depending on the tour.
Pay: Daily rates are discussed at interview. On top there are tips, plus ACIS pays for in-country expenses and return travel.
Eligibility: The minimum age is 21. Applicants must be graduates or students who can speak a second European language (French, Italian, German or Spanish preferred).
How to Apply: Apply online. There will then be a panel interview.

Busabout

258 Vauxhall Bridge Rd, London SW1V 1BS
☎ 020 7950 1661
fax 020 7950 1662
recruitment@busabout.co.uk
www.busabout.com/recruitment
This is a hop-on-hop-off style coach transportation service for independent travellers in Europe. Recruitment starts December/January for the summer season. If you're successful you'll get a four-week training course around Europe. You will be expected to work more than one full season.
Type of Work: On-board guides.
Timing & Length of Work: Summer season runs from May to October.
Destinations: Thirty-six cities in 12 European countries.
Pay: A £200 training bond is refundable after working two full consecutive seasons. First-year pay is around £150 gross per week, including all accommodation. There's commission on top of this.
Eligibility: Minimum age 24, familiarity with Europe important, a second European language helpful.
How to Apply: Download application form from website, send in with colour photo. There's a group interview, where you give a short talk to the panel, followed by a longer private one.

Casterbridge Tours

Salcombe House, Long St, Sherbourne, Dorset DT9 3BU
☎ 01935 810810
fax 01935 815815
tourops@casterbridge-tours.co.uk
www.casterbridgetours.com
Casterbridge runs educational and cultural tours for US and UK schools, colleges and adult groups, mostly in the UK and Europe. The trekking division has tours worldwide. Training takes place over a weekend.
Type of Work: Tour guides.

Timing & Length of Work: Tours of around 10 days run year round. The busiest time is from March to June.
Destinations: Worldwide.
Pay: The daily fee depends on experience and the number of languages you speak. The rate is negotiated at interview.
Eligibility: Applicants must be aged at least 21.
How to Apply: Positions are advertised in national newspapers but you can also phone or email the office.

Contiki Holidays for 18–35s

Wells House, 15 Elmfield Rd, Bromley, Kent BR1 1LS
☎ 020 8290 6777
fax 020 8225 4246
jobs@contiki.co.uk
www.contiki.com
Contiki is a tour operator offering 'soft adventure' coach holidays in Australia, Canada, Europe, New Zealand, the UK and the USA for those aged 18 to 35. Offices recruit regionally; this office deals with Europe and recruits from October to March for the following summer and winter. Six weeks of on-the-road training is given during February, March and April.
Type of Work: Tour managers.
Timing & Length of Work: Trips range from five to 46 days and run year round. Tour managers usually work from April to October.
Destinations: Europe.
Pay: Wages and benefits will be discussed at interview but accommodation, meals and transport are provided.
Eligibility: The minimum age is 23.
How to Apply: Download the application pack from the website.

Exodus Travels

9 Weir Rd, London SW12 0LT
☎ 020 8675 5550
fax 020 8673 0779
info@exodus.co.uk
www.exodus.co.uk
Exodus runs biking, walking, trekking and snow tours in Europe and elsewhere. Recruitment takes place in February. Training takes around three weeks and usually includes a first-aid course, a summer mountain leadership course, and an overseas training trip shadowing an experienced tour leader.
Type of Work: Tour leaders.
Timing & Length of Work: You can be away working from between six weeks to three months. Busiest times are Easter, May to October and Christmas. There's usually six to seven months of work a year.

Destinations: Africa, the Americas, Antarctica, Asia, Australasia and Europe.

Pay: On average around £200 a week, plus tips, accommodation and food. You're not paid when you're not leading.

Eligibility: Minimum age 25, independent travel experience, language skills, strong interest in outdoor pursuits and people skills are required.

How to Apply: Job vacancies are placed on the website year round. Advertisements are placed in *TNT* and *Wanderlust*. Please apply for specific positions, although CVs sent on spec will be looked at.

Explore Worldwide

1 Frederick St, Aldershot, Hampshire GU11 1LQ
☎ 01252 760200
fax 01252 760201
ops@exploreworldwide.com
www.explore.co.uk

This small-group adventure travel company accepts job applications all year round, but most recruitment takes place between January and April for the summer season and occasionally late summer for the winter season. Vacancies are advertised on the website. You're given a four-day training course and a two-day wilderness first-aid course, followed by on-the-road training with an experienced tour leader. Requires a minimum commitment of one year but ideally more.

Type of Work: Tour leaders.

Timing & Length of Work: Trips last from a weekend to one month. A leader can be overseas working on back-to-back tours for up to six months.

Destinations: One hundred countries worldwide.

Pay: There's a £200 training bond, refundable after the first season. A basic starting salary is around £25 a day, including accommodation and most meals. Tips can be a good bonus on top of this if you do your job well.

Eligibility: Minimum age 24, independent travel essential, customer service, walking/outdoors experience and second language preferable.

How to Apply: The application form is eight pages long and has problem-solving sections on it. You can download the application form from the website. Candidates are then invited to Aldershot for an interview.

High Places

Globe Centre, Penistone Rd, Sheffield S6 3AE
☎ 0114 275 7500
fax 0114 275 3870
treks@highplaces.co.uk

www.highplaces.co.uk

High Places is a small independent tour operator specialising in treks and mountaineering worldwide. It recruits year round. Training consists of shadowing an experienced leader on an overseas trip. It is expected you'll do at least two consecutive seasons.

Type of Work: Tour leaders.

Timing & Length of Work: Trips are for 18 to 27 days. A leader would normally do two or three back-to-back trips, which comprises an average year's work.

Destinations: Africa, Bolivia, Canada, Eastern Europe, Ecuador, the Himalaya, Iceland, New Zealand, Patagonia and Peru.

Pay: The daily rate depends on experience and the nature of the trip. Accommodation, meals and transport are included.

Eligibility: The minimum age is 21. You'll need a Summer & Winter Mountain Leadership Certificate (see p439) and a current first-aid certificate.

Imaginative Traveller

1 Betts Ave, Martlesham Heath, Suffolk IP5 3RH
☎ 01473 636066
fax 01473 636016
tljobs@imtrav.net
www.imaginative-traveller.com

The Imaginative Traveller is an adventure travel operator specialising in small-group travel to worldwide destinations. Recruitment is year round but main times are January and May. There's three to five days of training in the UK followed by three to four weeks overseas. Most tour leaders do their first contract in Egypt, China or Southeast Asia. Initial contract is for 10 to 12 months, subsequent contracts may be shorter.

Type of Work: Tour leaders.

Timing & Length of Work: One-week to four-week trips run all year round.

Destinations: Worldwide.

Pay: Up to £18 a day plus meals, accommodation, living allowance and bonuses.

Eligibility: Minimum age 22, travel experience essential.

How to Apply: Application form on website.

Kumuka Worldwide

40 Earls Court Rd, London W8 6EJ
☎ 020 7937 8855
fax 020 7937 6664
humanresources@kumuka.com
www.kumuka.com

Kumuka is a specialist in adventure holidays and overland travel. It recruits year round. Tour leaders are usually employed on annual contracts, although there's seasonal work in Europe between April and October. Four to six weeks of training takes place in London and overseas.

Type of Work: Tour leaders.

Timing & Length of Work: Trips last from four days to 15 weeks. Tour leaders are based overseas for a minimum of 12 months.

Destinations: Africa, Asia, Central America, Europe, the Middle East and South America.

Pay: Depends on experience and the area in which you work. Accommodation, food and excursions are normally included.

Eligibility: The minimum age is 23. A second language is preferred, and you must have travelled in at least two continents. Applicants should have great communication skills and be outgoing, positive, energetic and friendly.

How to Apply: Apply via the website or email the office.

Top Deck Tours

William House, 14 Worple Rd, London SW19 4DD
☎ 020 8879 6789
fax 020 8944 9474
ops@topdecktravel.co.uk
www.topdecktravel.co.uk

This is a budget adventure travel company, travelling by coach. Recruitment details are on the website. Interviews are held from October to March. Training trips last six weeks, starting early April. Crew are expected to work with the company for at least two summer seasons.

Type of Work: Tour leaders (although there is also work for drivers and cooks).

Timing & Length of Work: Trips run all year round but almost all the work is April to October. The trips range from weekends to 48 days.

Destinations: Europe, Russia and Turkey.

Pay: Your training trip costs £350, £150 of it is refundable at the end of your third season. Pay for tour leaders starts from £165 per week (including a performance-related bonus). Pay for cooks starts at £150 per week. Accommodation and food is included while working.

Eligibility: Minimum age 23, travel experience preferable.

How to Apply: Download application from website and return with photo. Group interviews, where you have to give a speech, are followed by individual interviews.

Venture Abroad

Rayburn House, Parcel Terrace, Derby DE1 1LY
☎ 01332 342050
fax 01332 224960

tours@ventureabroad.co.uk
www.ventureabroad.co.uk

Venture Abroad's tours are aimed at scouts and guides. You're based at one of two centres in Europe and accompany the groups on day excursions. Recruitment takes place in February for the summer season. One or two training days take place in the office then the rest takes place in the overseas resort around Easter or early June.

Type of Work: Tour leaders.

Timing & Length of Work: Trips are between 10 to 12 days. Tour leaders live in the destination from July to August.

Destinations: Belgium and Kandersteg or Adelboden in Switzerland.

Pay: Pay is from £180 per week, accommodation and all transport provided.

Eligibility: Applicants must be undergraduates or postgraduates aged at least 18. German-language skills preferred. Scouting or guiding experience preferred.

How to Apply: Ads are placed in careers' offices or language departments of universities. Otherwise ring or email the office.

Behind the Wheel

Busabout

258 Vauxhall Bridge Rd, London SW1V 1BS
☎ 020 7950 1661
fax 020 7950 1662
recruitment@busabout.co.uk
www.busabout.com/recruitment

Busabout has 18 buses in Europe during the summer. Drivers are expected to work more than one summer season. There's a five-week training course, most of which takes place in Europe where you learn the routes.

Type of Work: Drivers.

Pay: The £200 training bond is refundable after the first training trip. Pay is approximately £300 gross a week, reviewed annually.

Eligibility: Minimum age 23, you need a PCV licence and either a UK work permit or an EU passport.

How to Apply: Download application form from website and mail with copy of licence and current photograph. There are usually two interviews.

Contiki Holidays for 18–35s

Wells House, 15 Elmfield Rd, Bromley, Kent BR1 1LS
☎ 020 8290 6777
fax 020 8225 4246

jobs@contiki.co.uk
www.contiki.com
All information for tour managers is the same for tour drivers except the following:
Type of Work: Drivers.
Pay: The package is available on request and is dependent on experience.
Eligibility: The minimum age is 23. You'll need a PCV licence plus on-the-road experience.

Dragoman Overseas Travel
Camp Green, Kenton Rd, Debenham, Suffolk IP14 6LA
☎ 01728 861133
fax 01728 861127
info@dragoman.co.uk
www.dragoman.com
The largest overland company in the UK, Dragoman offers a slightly more upmarket experience. Recruitment takes place all year round – vacancies are advertised on the website. There are 12- to 14-week training courses at Camp Green and then you're a trainee for the first six months on the road. There are always two drivers on a trip. They work as tour leaders/guides too.
Type of Work: Leader drivers, co-drivers, leader mechanics, co-driver mechanics and trainees.
Timing & Length of Work: The trips are from two to 47 weeks and run all year round. Crew are expected to work for a minimum of 12 to 18 months at a time.
Destinations: Central America, Central Asia, China, Hong Kong, Middle East to Indian Subcontinent, South America and the USA.
Pay: A daily rate, which increases annually. Pay also depends on experience and skills. Accommodation, meals and transport included. There's also a bonus scheme.
Eligibility: Minimum age 25, PCV or LGV/HGV licence and first-aid certificate essential.
How to Apply: Contact office for application form.

Encounter Overland
Camp Green, Kenton Rd, Debenham, Suffolk IP14 6LA
☎ 01728 861133
fax 01728 861127
info@encounter.co.uk
www.encounter.co.uk
This is a budget overland company aimed squarely at the student market. All recruitment details are the same as for Dragoman (Encounter is owned by Dragoman). One big difference is that there's only one driver/tour leader.

All Encounter crew are experienced Dragoman crew so the way you get work is through Dragoman.
Type of Work: Leader mechanics.

Exodus Travels
9 Weir Rd, London SW12 0LT
☎ 020 8675 5550
fax 020 8673 0779
info@exodus.co.uk
www.exodus.co.uk
Exodus also recruits people to lead and drive overland expeditions. This is full time and leaders spend most of the year overseas, so it isn't suitable for anyone with commitments at home. You are expected to work for a minimum of two years.
Type of Work: Expedition leaders.
Timing & Length of Work: Trips run all year round and last from three to 30 weeks.
Destinations: The Americas and Asia.
Pay: According to Exodus, there's competitive rates of pay as well as accident and sickness insurance.
Eligibility: Minimum age is 25. You need a PCV or LGV/HGV licence, an immaculate driving record, the right to work in the UK, mechanical skills, travel experience and people skills.
How to Apply: Job vacancies are placed on the website year round. Apply for specific positions rather than sending in your CV speculatively.

Kumuka Worldwide
S40 Earls Court Rd, London W8 6EJ
☎ 020 7937 8855
fax 020 7937-6664
humanresources@kumuka.com
www.kumuka.com
Kumuka recruits year round. Drivers are usually employed on annual contracts. Overland trips have a separate driver and tour guide/leader.
Type of Work: Overland driver.
Timing & Length of Work: Trips last from four days to 15 weeks. Drivers are based overseas for a minimum of 12 months.
Pay: Pay depends on experience and the area in which you work. Accommodation, food and excursions are normally included.
Destinations: Africa, Asia, the Middle East and South America.
Eligibility: Minimum age 25, LGV/HGV or PCV licence and sound mechanical knowledge required. You must have travelled around at least two continents. Applicants

should have great communications skills and be outgoing, positive, energetic and friendly.

How to Apply: Apply via the website or email the office.

Top Deck Tours

William House, 14 Worple Rd, London SW19 4DD
☎ 020 8879 6789
fax 020 8944 9474
ops@topdecktravel.co.uk

www.topdecktravel.co.uk

All information for tour leading is the same for drivers except the following:

Pay: The training trip costs £350, £150 of which is refundable at the end of your third season. Pay starts at £220 per week (including a performance-related bonus). Accommodation and food is included whilst you're working.

Eligibility: The minimum age is 23 and you need an EU, NZ or Australian coach licence.

AU PAIRING & WORKING WITH KIDS

Working with children during your gap year means spending anything from two to 12 months in one country. This is a great opportunity to get to know a foreign culture and people really well, especially if you're an au pair and living with a family. It can also be a fabulous opportunity to master a language – which is why most au pairs are language students (the pay may be poor but fluency is priceless).

Other people's children – you either love them or hate them! Before you decide to spend either part of your gap year or the whole thing working with them, it'd be wise to know which category you fall into. Get some experience working with kids either at a local nursery or school, or spend time with your relatives' children when they're awake (very important: baby-sitting the little terror(s) when sleeping doesn't count). Does the time go quickly, with everyone having fun, or does every minute seem like an hour and every missed poo in the potty a drag to clean up?

You'll have to show that you've spent varying amounts of time spent caring for children when you apply for these types of jobs. The programs in America are particularly hot on this – and good for them. Working with youngsters is one of the most responsible jobs you could ever do in your gap year.

This chapter looks at working abroad as an au pair, au pair plus, mother's help and with children on holiday camps in return for pocket money. It doesn't cover voluntary work with children in orphanages or on the streets – see the Volunteering, Conservation & Expeditions chapter for this.

WORKING AS AN AU PAIR

An au pair can work in any country in the European Economic Area (EEA) and in the countries included in the official au pair scheme. There's an up-to-date list on the Home Office website (www.workingintheuk.gov.uk) of these countries but, at present, they're: Andorra, Bosnia and Hercegovina, Bulgaria, Croatia, Faroe Islands, Greenland, Macedonia, Monaco, Romania, San Marino and Turkey.

You can also au pair in Australia and New Zealand for three months on a working holiday visa. Au pairing in America is popular – see p406 for more details. In general you don't need a visa for most countries where you can au pair, but do check with the embassy or your agency before departure.

The au pair scheme states that you should be single, have no dependents, and be aged between 17 and 27. As an au pair you can stay in one country for up to two years. In practice, individual countries participating in the scheme sometimes have a few rules and regulations of their own, so check with your agency or with the relevant consulate website.

You pay to travel out to your host family. Once there you'll be expected to work around 25 hours a week (often five hours a day over five days) and baby-sit two nights a week. If you work more than 30 hours a week then you should get paid for this. Usually an au pair will stay with a family for a year (September to June), although contracts can be anything from three months to two years. Both sides are usually entitled to end the contract by giving at least a week's notice. In return you get pocket money of around £55 a week – this can vary slightly depending on the generosity of your family and also the country you're working in. You should also expect your own room, three meals a day, two days off a week plus time to attend classes (most au pairs are language students and take a language course). It's also usual to get one week off for every six months worked.

The words 'au pair' mean 'on an equal footing'. This means that au pairs should live and be treated like a member of the family. Because of this, it's a good idea to sit down with your family when you arrive and work out exactly what they'll expect from you and vice versa. Au pair duties vary but include either some or all of the following:

- Waking the children and getting them dressed.
- Preparing or helping to prepare breakfast.
- Clearing up the children's rooms.
- Picking up and tidying away toys from every room in the house...constantly. (Remember that other people pay personal trainers to devise this type of exercise.)
- Taking and/or picking the children up from nursery or school.
- Some shopping.
- Playing with the children.
- Helping to prepare the children's tea.
- Bathing the children and putting them to bed.
- Sweeping up – there's enough mess under a toddler's high chair after meals to top a family-sized pizza – plus vacuuming, or ironing the children's clothes.
- Accompanying the family on outings or on holiday.

If you want to earn a little more money, then there's the option of being an au pair plus. This is similar to being an au pair except that you work more hours – usually seven hours a day, five days a week or longer, depending on family requirements. For this you should be paid the normal £55 for your core 25 hours and then around £2.20 to £3 for any extra hours. Or you could work even longer, as a mother's help or nanny: both are full-time positions. A mother's help is expected to work between 45 and 50 hours a week, and does a lot more housework and cooking. You need to have a little more experience in childcare but no professional qualifications. The pay is around £170 to £200 per week. Nannying isn't an option for your gap year unless you've got proper qualifications and experience. The pay, though, can be good at around £220 to £400 a week plus perks, depending on your previous experience and the location. Nannies are also in demand by holiday resorts and companies.

The best and safest way to get a job as an au pair abroad is to go through a UK agency. Although there are lots of agencies specialising in matching foreign au pairs with British families, there are fewer doing it the other way around. This is because an agency cannot charge more than £40 for finding you a job, and this fee is only charged once you've accepted a family. So you could register with lots of agencies and they'd all find you work but only one of them will be paid. In addition, £40 doesn't really cover the time and effort needed to place you with a suitable family. Having said this, most of the agencies listed under Contacts (p409) are members of the International Au Pair Association (IAPA; www.iapa.org) and will definitely help you find a family through their partner agencies.

Surprisingly, the au pair industry is unregulated. Many of the good agencies are members of IAPA, the Recruitment & Employment Confederation (REC; www.rec.uk.com) or the British Au Pair Agencies Association (BAPAA; www.bapaa.org.uk). All three have lists of their members online.

If you want to get a job through an agency, then it's best to apply two or three months before you want to travel. If you're a bloke it could take longer because, sorry to say it, you're not in such demand. Most families also prefer a nonsmoker and often want a car

---

IS IT A MAN'S WORLD?

For the reserved British male, working as an au pair in Europe requires something of an adjustment. I had no experience of childcare and was surprised by the hands-on nature of the job; not only was I expected to bathe and dress the children, but I also found myself in the unenviable position of having to insert suppositories and clean up vomit and diarrhoea. I also discovered that children in France are generally much more affectionate than they are in the UK and the constant kissing and cuddling they expect of you can take some getting used to.

In the family, I was shocked to discover that some sexist attitudes still prevail. Unlike their previous au pairs, I wasn't expected to do the ironing – instead I was responsible for the suitably manly task of chopping wood for the log fire.

The two young boys wanted to build dens, go for long bike rides and play rough and tumble. I came to enjoy endless afternoons running around the forest restaging epic battles using branches and sticks for guns.

When my year was over I was immensely sad to leave the children; my year with them had not only improved my French but it had also taught me important lessons about myself. And I'm sure the wood-chopping and suppository-inserting skills I learned will come in handy one day!

Matt Cain

---

driver. Agencies will also need you to provide at least two character references, two childcare references, a criminal records bureau check and sometimes a medical. You'll then be given a telephone interview.

You can, of course, fix up an au pair placement yourself. There are ads for au pairs in the *Lady* magazine (www.lady.co.uk) – top tip: if reading it in public, wrap it inside a copy of *Heat* magazine. Try London's ads paper *Loot* (www.loot.com) or www.payaway.com. In addition, there are internet sites such as Au Pair Job Match (www.aupairs.co.uk), where au pairs and families can go online to find each other. These options all have risks attached to them on both sides – no-one has vetted you and no-one has properly vetted the families. If you don't want to go through a UK agency then you can always register direct with a foreign one, either in the UK or when abroad (refer to IAPA's listing of overseas agencies on their website).

WORKING IN NORTH AMERICA AS AN AU PAIR

Au pairing in America is big business. Each year thousands of British gappers go to the USA to au pair on US government-sponsored programs. The deal is so different to au pairing in Europe or elsewhere that it really needs covering separately.

These programs are represented through any UK agency that can place you in the USA – see Contacts (p409). All of the programs are much of a muchness but the biggest is run by Au Pair in America, part of the American Institute for Foreign Studies – see p409. The options and requirements for this program are as follows and will be similar for any program you go on:

Age 18 to 26.

When to Apply Usually three months before departure, but that depends on how long it's taking the American embassy to process J1 Visitor Exchange visas.

Selection Process This is rigorous. You'll be interviewed in person and need to have three written references (two childcare and one character). You'll need to show a clear police record, submit a medical form and be psychometrically tested. It's good to know that the selection process for the host families is just as rigorous.

Duration of Stay One year. There are up to four departure dates a month.

Visas A J1 Visitor Exchange visa is valid for 12 months, but includes a one-month grace period after the visa has finished.

This means that if your visa expires on August 28 then you don't need to leave the country until September 28, allowing you one month's travel in the USA. Due to security concerns, J1 visas are currently taking longer to process and a personal interview in London or Belfast is now part of the process. You also have the option to extend the J1 visa by a further six, nine or 12 months. This is done while you're in the USA, and needs the recommendation of your host family.

Orientation & Training Before you join your family there's a four-day orientation program, which includes basic first aid, 24 hours of child-development training and eight hours of child-safety training. After settling in the home, au pairs are also encouraged to complete an infant/child CPR and first aid certification program, paid for by Au Pair America and run with the American Red Cross.

In-Country Support A community counsellor is allocated to every au pair and he/she will either see or call you within 48 hours of your arrival. There are then monthly 'cluster' meetings, where all the au pairs in the area get together to bond and chat.

Standard Program Up to 45 hours of work a week at around £85 per week. There's also a study allowance of £300 provided by the host family, because under the rules of your visa you need to study for a minimum of three hours a week. If you complete your one year then your flights to/from the USA are free; if you don't, then you need to pay your own homeward airfare. You'll need to show proof of 200 hours recent childcare for nonfamily members, and you must have had a driving licence for at least six months. There's a £45 non-refundable placement fee, a £60 contribution towards insurance, and a £245 'good faith' payment returnable upon completion of your one year.

Au Pair Extraordinaire Up to 45 hours of work a week at around £122 per week. You need to have completed a full-time two-year academic course in childcare or be 19 and have two years' full-time experience as a nanny, childcare provider or nursery school teacher. You also need to have had a driving licence for around six months. All the fees are the same as on the Standard Program.

EduCare Up to 30 hours of care a week at around £65 per week. This program is mostly for families with school-age children and au pairs who want to do more studying. Students usually arrive in late July/August or December. The study allowance is £612 and you're placed in areas where you can attend a good college or university. You'll be expected to study for at least six hours a week. You need a minimum of 200 hours childcare experience and to be an experienced car driver. Your fees include £45 for placement, £460 for the program and £153 for comprehensive insurance. All the other conditions are the same as for the Standard Program.

What Else You Can Expect A private room, three meals a day, time off to attend classes, one weekend off per month and one weekend per month holiday.

Going to the USA to au pair is really popular, perhaps because you hear so many good reports back from gappers who've taken this option, such as Mandy-Lee Trew:

I was an au pair for an amazing 10-year-old girl in Lexington, Kentucky. Our schedule was pretty hectic as she was very sporty. I'd be up at 6am. At 6.40am I'd wake her up for breakfast. At 7am we needed to get ready for school and by 7.30am we were in the car. From 8.30am to 2.30pm I had free time. School finished at 3pm and we'd come home, have a snack and attack homework, after which we'd go to swimming, soccer, Girl Scouts, horse-riding or basketball. We'd then come home have dinner and get ready for bed. My day usually ended around 8.30pm to 9.30pm after I'd put her to bed. The bad thing was the long hours, but the good thing was I didn't work weekends. We built up an amazing relationship, one that'll certainly last. I know I had a very positive impact on her life and she did on mine. I've come away from my American experience feeling as though I've gained a whole family. We are in constant communication and the family visited me in 2005.

On the other hand, au pairing in Canada isn't easy. Canada's version of the au pair scheme is the Live-in Caregiver Program regulated by the Canadian Government. To qualify you'll need to have completed six months' full-time training in a field related to your job in Canada or 12 months of full-time paid employment in a related field.

CHILDREN'S HOLIDAYS

An integral part of American life is families sending their kids to camp. There are over 12,000 summer camps in the USA for children aged between six and 16. They spend from one to eight weeks at these residential centres, following a packed multi-activity agenda during the day and sleeping in tents or cabins at night. Most camps are in the countryside, beside a lake or in the mountains, so the emphasis is on outdoor life. For many American children camp is heaven on a stick.

These camps are run by thousands of adults who come from all over the world. Most jobs are as a general or specialist counsellor. Both involve looking after the children's welfare, being mother, father, sister, brother and friend to them, as well as helping out with morning, afternoon and evening activities. As a specialist counsellor, though, you'll be instructing them in your speciality, whether it's drama or water sports. Ramone Param was a counsellor at the Trade Winds Lake Camp near Windsor in New York State. This was his typical day:

7.30am: Wake up.
8am: Breakfast.
9am: Cabin clean up – you just try getting kids to clean up when they don't want to.
10am: Activities – I would lead activities in soccer, tennis, the farm and nature. This was good fun, especially nature activities, where I could improvise hikes along different routes in the wood.
12 noon: Lunch.
1pm: Cabin time-out – this would mean an hour of letter writing home, diaries, folder work from the activities or cabin meetings.
2pm: Activities again.
4pm: Free swim – during this hour everyone would be at the lake and could swim or play football.
5pm: Shower hour – this was very intense. Everyone was supposed to have two minutes of showering and then get ready for dinner.
6pm: Dinner.
7pm to 9pm: Evening activities organised by the head counsellors, like camp games.
9pm: Light snack.
10pm: Lights out.
After lights out a few counsellors would be on duty till midnight, checking the cabins, making sure everyone was asleep etc, until all the camp counsellors were back in their allotted cabins.

Apart from the activities that Ramone led, the list of activities at many camps is endless. There's all sorts of team sports (eg basketball), water sports (eg water-skiing, sailing), arts and crafts (eg pottery, painting), entertainment (eg drama, singing), outdoor pursuits (eg horse riding, orienteering), music, science and IT.

Life at camp for adults isn't all fun and games though. You practically spend 24 hours a day with the kids, living and sleeping in the same tent or cabin. The days are long and physically demanding. Being responsible for a group of children, particularly for their safety, is also very tiring. And you can't relax at the end of the day with a ciggy or a beer because smoking and drinking are usually prohibited. In addition, you'll only get around six days off during your nine-week stint. On the plus side, though, this means you'll be able to save all your pay to go towards your free travel time afterwards.

In terms of money, some camps and some programs pay better than others, but that has to be weighed up against their costs – see Contacts (p409) for full details. Once you've done the sums you'll usually still end up in credit, but as pocket money often depends on your age (you get more if you're older), school-leavers may only have as little as £50 left over. But don't forget that this is on top of free flights, accommodation and food.

To work at a camp, get in touch with the companies listed in the following Contacts (p409) section. Many ask you to apply in the autumn before you want to go and competition for jobs can be fierce.

Although many gappers will be after the American experience of camp, many of the camps in Europe, Russia or the UK are modelled on the American type. In Russia, though, they're more basic and less organised. The pay is also atrocious (you'll be lucky to earn £1 a day) and sometimes you also pay for your return flights. But, hey, you're not doing it for the money – the opportunity to work in this part of the world is very unusual.

Contact details for European and Russian opportunities follow. In the UK, try contacting **Barracudas** (☎ 0845 123 5299; www.barracudas.co.uk) or **Kids Klub** (☎ 01449 742700; www.kidsklub.co.uk).

CONTACTS

Working as an Au Pair

A-One Au Pairs & Nannies
Top floor, Union House, Union St, Andover, Hampshire SP10 1PA
☎ 01264 332500
fax 01264 362050
info@aupairsetc.co.uk
www.aupairsetc.co.uk
Founded in 1997, A-One places au pairs in the UK and abroad. It's southern England's regional coordinator for Au Pair in America, covering Hampshire, Dorset, Devon, Cornwall and parts of Wiltshire.
Type of Work: Au pairs, au pairs plus, mother's helps and nannies.
Timing & Length of Work: Placements are available year round, for a maximum of one to two years. There are also some summer-holiday placements.
Destinations: All EU countries, Australia, Canada, New Zealand, South Africa, Switzerland, Turkey and the USA.
Costs: There's no agency fee.
Organisation Memberships: IAPA, founding member of BAPAA.

Almondbury Au Pair & Nanny Agency
4 Napier Rd, Holland Park, London W14 8LQ
☎ /fax 01288 359159
admin@aupair-agency.com or admin@nanny-agency.com
www.aupair-agency.com or www.nanny-agency.com
This is one of Europe's largest Internet-based agencies for au pairs and nannies. There's full agency backup if things go wrong.

Type of Work: Au pairs, nannies and mother's helps.
Timing & Length of Work: Placements of between six to 12 months are available year round.
Destinations: Worldwide including Australia, Canada, Europe, New Zealand and the USA.
Costs: There's no agency fee.
Organisation Memberships: Universal Au Pair Association.

Anderson Au-Pairs & Nannies
58 Sweet Bay Crescent, Ashford, Kent TN23 3QA
☎ 01233 668336
sarah@andersonau-pairs.com
www.childcare-europe.com
Founded in 1996; au pairs are provided with contact lists, emergency telephone numbers and full support through their international partner agencies.
Type of Work: Au pairs, au pairs plus and mother's helps.
Timing & Length of Work: Placements of three months to two years are available year round.
Destinations: Canada, Western Europe and the USA.
Costs: There's an agency fee of £40.
Organisation Memberships: IAPA, founding member of BAPAA.

Au Pair in America
American Institute for Foreign Studies
37 Queen's Gate, London SW7 5HR
☎ 020 7581 7311
fax 020 7581 7355
info@aupairamerica.co.uk
www.aupairamerica.co.uk
Au Pair in America has placed over 48,000 au pairs since 1986 and is the largest program of its kind. See p406 for full details.
Organisation Memberships: IAPA.

Au Pairs Direct
7 Little Meadow Rd, Bowdon, Cheshire WA14 3PG
☎ 0161 941 5356
enquiries@aupairsdirect.co.uk
www.aupairsdirect.co.uk
Founded in 1989, this is northwest England's regional coordinator for Au Pair in America.
Type of Work: Au pairs, au pair extraordinaires and nannies.
Timing & Length of Work: Placements are available year round for one year in the USA and a minimum of six months in Europe.
Destinations: France, Spain and the USA.
Costs: There's a fee of £40 for European placements.
Organisation Memberships: IAPA, founding member of BAPAA.

Bunters
The Old Malt House, 6 Church St, Pattishall, Nr Towcester, Northampton NN12 8NB
☎ 01327 831144/99
fax 01327 831155
office@aupairsnannies.com
www.aupairsnannies.com
Founded in 1994, this is a hands-on, owner-run business with good contacts abroad.
Type of Work: Au pairs, mother's helps and nannies.
Timing & Length of Work: Placements are available year round. There are some summer-holiday placements; otherwise the maximum stay is one to two years.
Destinations: All EU countries.
Costs: There's no agency fee.
Organisation Memberships: IAPA, founding member of BAPAA.

Childcare International
Trafalgar House, Grenville Place, London NW7 3SA
☎ 020 8906 3116
fax 020 8906 3461
office@childint.co.uk
www.childint.co.uk
Founded in 1986, over 600 au pairs per year are placed in in-bound and out-bound programs.
Type of Work: Au pairs, au pairs plus, mother's helps and nannies.
Timing & Length of Work: Placements are available year round. There are some summer-holiday placements; otherwise the maximum stay is one to two years.
Destinations: Australia, Canada, Europe and the USA.

Costs: There's a placement fee of £40 for Australia, Canada and Europe.
Organisation Memberships: IAPA, FIYTO, Recruitment & Employment Confederation (REC), founding member of BAPAA.

ChildCare Solution
Avondale House, 63 Sydney Rd, Haywards Heath, West Sussex RH16 1QD
☎ 01444 453566/0845 458 1550
fax 01444 440445
southernoffice@thechildcaresolution.com
www.thechildcaresolution.com
Founded in 1989, this is one of the largest UK agencies. It also recruits nannies and nursery nurses for the ski resorts and summer beach resorts, but you've got to be qualified.
Type of Work: Au pairs, au pairs plus, mother's helps and nannies.
Timing & Length of Work: Placements are available year round. There are some summer-holiday placements; otherwise the maximum stay is one to two years.
Destinations: Europe and the USA.
Costs: There's no agency fee.
Organisation Memberships: IAPA, REC, founding member of BAPAA.

Just Au Pairs
35 The Grove, Edgware, Middlesex HA8 9QA
☎ 020 8905 3355
fax 020 8905 3838
hill@aupairs.freeserve.co.uk
www.justaupairs.co.uk
Founded in 1996, this is a family-run business with multilingual staff.
Type of Work: Au pairs, au pairs plus, mother's helps and nannies.
Timing & Length of Work: Placements are available year round. There are some summer-holiday placements of three months; otherwise stays are for six, 12 or 24 months.
Destinations: All over Europe and the USA.
Costs: There's no agency fee.
Organisation Memberships: IAPA, founding member of BAPAA.

Matchmaker Au Pair Agency (MMAPA)
Rosewood, Leigh Gardens, Chelford Rd, Knutsford, Cheshire WA16 8PU
☎ 01565 651703

fax 01565 631726
mmaupair@aol.com
www.matchmakeraupairs.co.uk
Founded in 1996, MMAPA is a small owner-run agency.
Type of Work: Au pairs, au pairs plus and mother's helps.
Timing & Length of Work: Placements are available year round. There are some summer-holiday placements; otherwise the maximum stay is one to two years.
Destinations: Europe.
Costs: There's no agency fee.
Organisation Memberships: IAPA, founding member of BAPAA.

Quickhelp Agency

307a Finchley Rd, London NW3 6EH
☎ 020 7794 8666
fax 020 7433 1993
mailbox@quickhelp.freeserve.co.uk
www.quickhelp.co.uk
Founded in 1975, Quickhelp is an owner-run agency with experienced staff.
Type of Work: Au pairs, au pair plus, mother's helps and nannies.
Timing & Length of Work: Placements are available year round. There are some summer-holiday placements of at least three months; otherwise six to 12 months is preferred.
Destinations: France, Germany and Spain.
Costs: There's no agency fee.
Organisation Memberships: IAPA, founding member of BAPAA.

Children's Holidays

Boy Scouts of America (BSA)

The Scout Association, Gilwell Park, Bury Rd, Chingford, London E4 7QW
☎ 0845 300 1818
fax 020 8433 7114
international@scout.org.uk
www.scoutbase.org.uk/inter/jambo/campusa/ics.htm
BSA runs the International Camp Staff Program (ICSP) in conjunction with the Scout Association. It's a program recognised by the US State Department. You can work in one of the 400 US boy-scout camps, allocated by the BSA. One week's training is given. You're responsible for arranging your own visa with support from the Scout Association.
Type of Work: Counsellors (the work is constant and the hours long, but it's challenging and rewarding).

Timing & Length of Work: Placements are for six to 12 weeks from mid-June.
Destination: The USA.
Costs/Pay: You pay a £30 application fee. You also pay for the visa cost, travel insurance, flights and transport to and from camp. Accommodation and food are free. The salary totals on average £430, depending on your experience.
Eligibility: Applicants are aged between 18 and 30 and must be members of the Scout Association.
How to Apply: Applications are processed from September to February. There'll be a local interview and a medical.

BUNAC (British Universities North America Club)

16 Bowling Green Lane, London EC1R 0QH
☎ 020 7251 3472
fax 020 7251 0215
enquiries@bunac.org.uk
www.bunac.org
BUNAC has run work/travel programs worldwide since 1962. Over 3500 students go on its Summer Camp USA program each year. Orientation programs are held before departure and upon arrival at camp. BUNAC will guide you through the visa process and handle the rest of your paperwork and travel arrangements. You get up to six weeks of free travel time after camp. Participants on soccer-coaching programs can also apply through BUNAC and are placed on summer soccer camps. For information on the other programs it runs and jobs at camps not directly related to children, see the Proper Jobs (p337) and Casual & Seasonal Work (p376) chapters.
Type of Work: Camp counsellor, also activity staff for waterfront (sailing, swimming etc), entertainment (dance, stage performances etc), music, arts and crafts, pioneering (outdoor pursuits), science and sports coaching (football, golf, tennis, horse riding).
Timing & Length of Work: Placements are for eight to nine weeks from early/mid-June to mid-August.
Destination: Canada and the USA.
Costs/Pay: The application fee is £72, insurance costs £127 and the visa fee is around £67 (payable to the US embassy). In-country transport costs, food and lodging are free. Return airfares are loaned to you by BUNAC and deducted from your final salary. The in-hand pay ranges from £440 for under-21s to £473 if you're over 21. You usually get paid at the end of the camp.
Eligibility: Applicants must be between 18 and 35, and have experience of working in a leadership capacity with children.

How to Apply: Contact the office in September for a brochure and then book yourself an interview. These are held nationally from November to April. You'll need two character references, one childcare one, a clear criminal record and sometimes a medical.

Camp America

American Institute For Foreign Study (AIFS), 37a Queen's Gate, London SW7 5HR
☎ 020 7581 7373
fax 020 7581 7377
enquiries@campamerica.co.uk
www.campamerica.co.uk
Around 10,000 young people from all over the world travel with Camp America each year. Country-wide recruitment fairs and road shows are held in February and March – check the website for details. Camp America will guide you through the visa process, but all other paperwork and travel is handled by them directly. There's predeparture and arrival orientation, training days and a free 24-hour emergency phone number for you to call at anytime during your stay in the USA. You can travel for 10 weeks after the camp. For information on jobs at camp not directly related to children see p377.

Type of Work: Camp counsellors, special needs counsellors and Christian counsellors.

Timing & Length of Work: Placements last for nine weeks from May or June.

Destination: The USA.

Costs/Pay: There's a visa arrangement down payment of between £20 and £66 (the earlier you apply the cheaper the visa), £234 for your medical insurance and visa-sponsorship administration fee (to be paid upon acceptance of a place), European airport tax of £35, and £67 payable to the US embassy for the visa. Flights, accommodation, in-country transport and food are then free. Pay ranges from £322 to £857 depending on your age and the job you're doing. There are higher rates if you've already done a season.

Eligibility: Applicants must be aged at least 18 by June 1 and have some childcare experience.

How to Apply: Apply from October. Download the application form from the website. At the interview you'll need to undertake a criminal record bureau check and two references (one character and one childcare).

CCUSA

1st floor North, Devon House, 171/177 Great Portland St, London W1W 5PQ
☎ 020 7637 0779

fax 020 7580 6209
info@ccusa.co.uk
www.ccusa.com
CCUSA has been a summer-camp specialist since 1986. You can choose from eight different types of camp. Job fairs are held in March and April – see the website for details. Group orientation sessions are held in the UK during April and May and training is given when you arrive at camp; waterfront staff take the American Red Cross Lifeguard Course (for those aged 19 or over). You're guided through the visa process by CCUSA and they handle the rest of your paperwork and travel arrangements. After camp you can travel for up to 30 days. There's also a 24-hour emergency telephone hotline for your time in America. For information on jobs at camp not directly related to children see the Proper Jobs (p325) and Casual & Seasonal Work (p363) chapters.

Type of Work: General counsellors, specialist counsellors, rope-course instructors (training given), waterfront staff and, in the Russian camps, English/American culture instructors.

Timing & Length of Work: Placements in the USA are from nine to 11 weeks from early June. In Russia it's four or eight weeks from June or July.

Destinations: Russia (Black Sea, Lake Baikal, St Petersburg, Siberia and around Moscow) and the USA.

Costs/Pay: The total cost of the US program is from £299. The Russian four-week and eight-week programs both cost £795. Pay in the Russian camps is £20 a month and in America it's from £363 to £524, depending on your age. Flights, board and lodging are free.

Eligibility: Applicants must be over 18 by June 1 and be enthusiastic about working with children.

How to Apply: Apply in October. Download the application from the website. There's then an interview where you'll need to provide two references, show a clean criminal record and take a medical.

French Encounters

63 Fordhouse Rd, Bromsgrove, Worcestershire B60 2LU
☎ 01527 873645
fax 01527 832794
admin@frenchencounters.com
www.frenchencounters.com
French Encounters is a small company employing eight gap-year students a year to work with school children aged between 10 and 13 on language and education field trips. There's two weeks of training, including first aid and presentation skills.

Type of Work: Animateurs (ie children's entertainers, commentators, supervisors and organisers).

Timing & Length of Work: The four-month season is from mid-February to mid-June.

Destinations: Two chateaux in Normandy, France.

Pay: Pay is from £70 a week, including all accommodation, food, travel and insurance.

Eligibility: Applicants must be aged at least 18 and have A-level French.

How to Apply: Contact the office for an application form. Interviews are held from August.

International Exchange Centre (IEC)

89 Fleet St, London EC4Y 1DH

☎ 020 7583 9116

fax 020 7583 9117

isecinfo@btconnect.com

www.isecworld.co.uk

IEC organises work placements worldwide (see p338). It also offers work with children on various camps. All paperwork to apply for the visas will be provided. With the American program you can travel for at least one month after your placement. Travel after camp can be arranged for the other destinations.

Type of Work: General and special counsellors (a special counsellor teaches something such as swimming or music).

Timing & Length of Work: Placements run from June and are for one, two or three months in Eastern Europe and Russia. American placements run from mid-June and last nine weeks.

Destinations: Belarus, Latvia, Lithuania, Russia, Ukraine and the USA.

Costs/Pay: The placement fee for Eastern Europe and Russia is £85, plus you pay for your visa and return flights. The placement fee for American camps is £115, with free flights. You also pay for your visa on this program. The salary in Eastern European and Russian camps is between £6 and £30 a month; in America it's from £310 to £425 depending on your age. Accommodation and meals are free.

Eligibility: For Eastern European and Russian camps, applicants must be aged 18 to 30. A basic knowledge of Russian is helpful but not required. For American camps you need to be aged 18 to 28.

How to Apply: Email or phone for an application form. Apply in April for the Russian camp program and before 15 January for the American one. Interviews are usually over the phone. You have to show two to four references and have a clean criminal record, plus some camps require a medical.

King's Foundation

The Manor House, Ecclesall Rd South, Sheffield S11 9PS

☎ 0870 345 0782

fax 0870 345 0783

staff@kcjobs.org

www.kingscamp.org

The King's Foundation runs King's Camps – nonresidential sport and activity camps for children aged four to 14 years old in the UK. There are over 300 staff vacancies in the UK. The King's Foundation also recruits for a leading holiday company and there are 100 vacancies annually in France and Spain for staff to lead children's activities on campsites. (There are also a few voluntary positions for gap-year students each year to teach multi-sports activities to children in Africa. If you're interested call for more information.)

Type of Work: In the UK there are group carers, group coaches, senior coaches and managers. In Europe there are children's couriers (working with children aged 10 to 16), base couriers (working with children aged 13 to 16), football coaches (with children from six years upwards) and team leaders (with children from six years upwards).

Timing & Length of Work: In the UK, positions are available during the Easter and summer holidays. In Europe, positions start on 1 May or mid-June and run until the beginning of September.

Destinations: Thirty venues in the UK. There are around 50 campsites in France and Spain.

Pay: This is discussed at interview. All European positions come with free accommodation and travel to and from the site. All UK positions are non-residential.

Eligibility: Applicants must be over 17 for UK positions and over 18 for European ones. A strong interest in working with children is essential.

How to Apply: Applications are accepted all year round. However, if you want a summer position abroad, it's best to apply by March.

MLS Camps (UK)

Malmarc House, 116 Dewsbury Rd, Leeds LS11 6XD

☎ 0113 272 0616

fax 0113 277 1100

employment@mlscamps.com

www.mlscamps.com

MLS Camps represents the professional soccer league of the USA. It provides football coaches to USA day camps. The children are aged from two to 18 years. In the summer, coaches move from camp to camp each week. In the spring and autumn you work as a player development officer in one location for a youth soccer club. MLS Camps sorts out your visa, paperwork and travel arrangements. Coaching assessment days are held in various national locations and there's a three-day induction held before you leave the UK.

Type of Work: Soccer coaches.

Timing & Length of Work: Contracts range from four weeks to 10 months. Short contracts start in June or July; longer ones start in spring.

Destinations: Every US state, including Alaska and Hawaii.

Costs/Pay: There's a £340 membership fee, which includes your background check, visa processing, flights, accommodation, training, car hire and kit (three sets). You also have to pay £110 insurance. You'll be paid while you're working. The amount depends on your hours, age, qualifications and experience. Accommodation is usually with host families; meals are sometimes provided.

Eligibility: Applicants must be aged at least 19, have attained a football-coaching qualification (contact MLS camps if you don't have this and they can point you in the right direction) and be a competent player. A driving licence is preferred.

How to Apply: Apply five or six months before you want to travel. Recruitment takes place year round. Apply online. You'll then have to attend a recruitment day, fill in a medical form and hand over all the info needed for a background check.

PGL Travel

Alton Court, Penyard Lane, Ross-on-Wye, Herefordshire HR9 5GL

☎ 0870 401 4411

fax 0870 401 4444

pglpeople@pgl.co.uk

www.pgl.co.uk/people

Over 100,000 children aged between six and 18 take a PGL holiday each year, and 2500 staff are needed annually. There are 16 residential centres in the UK, eight in France and one in Spain.

Type of Work: Group leaders (pastoral and social welfare), instructors (water sports, climbing, multi-activity, pony-trekking, surfing) and support staff (administrators, catering and maintenance).

Timing & Length of Work: Positions are available for between eight weeks and 10 months. The season in the UK and northern France runs from February to November, and in southern France and Spain from April to September.

Destinations: France, Spain and the UK.

Pay: Rates of pay start from £65 a week but depend on your job and the location. All board and lodging is paid for, plus your travel from Dover if you're working in France or Spain.

Eligibility: Applicants must be at least 18.

How to Apply: Recruitment starts in October. Download the application form from the website. You'll need to provide three referees and show a clean criminal record. There's no interview.

Village Camps

Personnel Office, Dept.1000, 1260 Nyon, Switzerland

☎ 00 41 22 990 9405

fax 00 41 22 990 9494

personnel@villagecamps.ch

www.villagecamps.com

This is a Swiss company that has been operating European residential and day camps for children from spring to autumn since 1972. For details on facilities and administrative positions see p379.

Type of Work: All sorts of counsellors – activity, house, assistant, junior, outdoor education, specialist plus language teachers.

Timing & Length of Work: Placements are from five to eight weeks beginning April/May, June/July and August/September.

Destinations: Austria, England, France, Holland and Switzerland.

Pay: A weekly allowance is paid in local currency and varies depending on your skills, languages spoken and experience. On top of pocket money, your meals, accommodation and accident/liability insurance are provided. Travel allowance to camp and medical insurance aren't provided.

Eligibility: The minimum age requirement for most positions is 21 years. House, junior and assistant counsellors are 18 to 20 years of age. All counsellors need experience of caring for children, a first aid and CPR certificate and relevant skills/experience/qualifications to lead activity sessions.

How to Apply: Recruitment begins in January for the spring and summer, and June for the fall. You may download the application from the website or request one by email. Complete and mail it along with photocopies of relevant qualifications/certificates, two passport-sized photos, two references, a photocopy of your passport and CV. Successful applicants are selected and interviewed by phone.

WorldNetUK

Avondale House, 63 Sydney Rd, Haywards Heath, West
Sussex RH16 1QD

☎ 01444 457676

fax 01444 440445

info@worldnetuk.com

www.worldnetuk.com

This is the UK representative for InterExchange/Camp
USA, placing young people in American summer camps. It
handles all visas and paperwork. Training is given on camp.
You can travel for up to a month afterwards on your visa.
For details of support staff positions see p380.

Type of Work: Camp counsellors.

Timing & Length of Work: Placements are for seven to
nine weeks from June.

Destination: The USA.

Costs/Pay: Programs cost from around £250, including
flights, medical insurance and administration. Pay starts at
£400 and increases with age and experience.

Eligibility: Applicants must be at least 18 and have
experience in sports, arts and crafts, drama, IT etc.

How to Apply: Call/email for brochure. Apply from
October. There will be an interview, medical and criminal-
record check.

COURSES

Taking a course is usually only one component of a gap year. Often it's combined with travelling or working abroad. If you want to combine a course with volunteering, there are lots of gap-year organisations offering courses, usually language-learning, as part of their program (see p287). Sarah Bruce told us:

Part of my five-month placement with Trekforce involved a one-month Spanish course in Guatemala, which was amazing. It was one-on-two tuition for four hours a day, five days a week and I learnt so much.

A course can last anything from a few days to 12 months, although most gappers go for one lasting between two and three months. A year-long course is a big commitment (both in time and money) but there are some fabulous ones out there such as 'Introduction to Film and Television Production' at the Film School in Wellington, New Zealand, or the safari field guide course run by Global Vision International in South Africa.

There are millions of courses out there – you can learn French in France, belly-dancing in Turkey, jewellery-making in Italy, photography in Cuba or do a mountain-bike instructor's course in Canada's Rocky Mountains. Many courses are either taught by multilingual instructors or in English (apart from the language courses). Many are run by UK-based organisations with group departures and robust in-country support, which is reassuring, if this is going to be your first big sortie abroad.

WHY DO A COURSE?

You've just finished studying at school or university and now you're ready for a break. Why on earth would you sign up for another course? That's easy: an investment in yourself, your skills and your knowledge is always worth your time and money. Ramone Param says:

Although I have a grade A at GCSE French, my Spanish, which I learnt from scratch for three weeks in Ecuador, is far superior.

And, if you have the opportunity to do this abroad then your experience will be a hundred times more rewarding. When you do a course in a foreign country what you learn in the classroom is only half of what you learn overall. You can really get to grips with the country's culture and people. Kate Wilkinson did a Spanish course in Cuba and agrees:

I got right into the culture by living with a Cuban family enabling me to see a side of the country that I wouldn't have if I had not done the course.

You meet a lot of like-minded students from around the world and often make lifelong international friends. Living and studying abroad also engages other parts of your brain; having to integrate yourself into a new social environment in a different country does wonders for your self-reliance, independence, maturity and self-confidence.

Let's also not forget that the more you know, the more valuable you'll be to a prospective employer. That course on your CV could help you stand out in a big pile of job applications and secure an interview. It will certainly be looked upon favourably by a university, particularly if it is linked to your undergraduate course. Rebecca Udy took a six-week course in Italy with Art History Abroad:

As an English literature student, I saw the course as a rite of passage before embarking on an arts degree – I really felt I should make some attempt to understand the culture and history that stood behind some of the texts I would be studying.

Your gap year is the ideal time to learn new things, precisely because you *do* have the time. When you start working and progressing in your career it's harder to take a proper break and justify a ski and snowboarding instructor course in New Zealand or that PADI dive master course in the Seychelles. And, although it might be the furthest thing from your mind right now, even a course in time-management won't tell you how to find a window in your diary when/if you have kids.

WHAT COURSE?

Now all you have to do is decide what you want to study.

It could be that you want to indulge a passion or an interest you've always had and learn circus skills in Australia or how to play flamenco guitar in Spain. Rebecca Udy writes:

I wasn't sure what I wanted to do in my gap year. All my friends were off trekking in Nepal, helping in schools in Africa, inter-railing around Europe or travelling across Australia, and I knew I didn't want to do anything like that. I wanted to learn something, I wanted to do something I was passionate about, and I wanted it to be fun, as I had booked a one-term secretarial course for the autumn term. That was my 'serious, get some qualifications that will help you find temp work' part of my gap year.

You might choose a lifestyle course and learn Tai Chi in Thailand or meditation in Greece. The relaxation and stress-busting skills you learn on courses like these you'll put to good use in a year or two, either at university or at work.

A smart choice is to do a course that helps you get a job abroad during the rest of your gap year. You could train as a jackaroo or jillaroo in Australia and work on a farm, take a cookery course leading to work in a ski chalet or become a watersports instructor and work anywhere around the world where there are deep puddles. Emily Koch writes:

I chose to do a course with Flying Fish because I wanted to spend part of my gap year training to become a watersports instructor, so that I could use these qualifications in my uni holidays to earn some money. Flying Fish's course looked particularly inviting because it was in sunny Greece. I learnt how to sail dinghies and windsurf, and I then trained to be a dinghy sailing and windsurf Level 1 instructor. I also did first aid and powerboat training.

Many gappers decide to take a course that will help with their university study or enhance their future career prospects. For most this means learning a new language or brushing up on an old one. These days the most popular language to learn is Spanish. As Kate Wilkinson says:

I wanted to learn Spanish as it is one of the most spoken languages in the world.

As language courses are so popular, you can often find them combined with a cultural activity. Amanda Akass studied Spanish in Sucre, Bolivia, and found:

The school also offered lots of extra-curricular activities, such as local cooking and salsa lessons.

Another way to immerse yourself in the culture of a foreign country and experience its way of life is to live abroad with a family in a homestay or study at a secondary school in the USA or Canada – see p429.

Researching all your possible course options would almost fill a gap year by itself. Apart from this book, the internet is obviously a great resource and the following organisations can give you loads more information about courses in their own country:

Canning House Education and Cultural Department (☎ 020 7235 2303; www.canninghouse.com; 2 Belgrave Sq, London SW1X 8PJ) This is the UK's largest library for all things Spanish, Portuguese and Latin American. There's lots of information on courses here, some of which can be mailed to you.

DAAD German Academic Exchange Service (☎ 020 7235 1736; http://london.daad.de; 34 Belgrave Sq, London SW1X 8QB) Ask for their book on summer courses in Germany.

Italian Cultural Institute (☎ 020 7235 1461; www.italcultur.org.uk; 39 Belgrave Sq, London SW1X 8NX; 🕙 10am-1pm & 2-5pm Mon-Fri) Try to visit in person. It offers loads of leaflets on various courses all over Italy.

It is also worth logging on to Studyzone (www.hothousemedia.com/studyzone), a continually updated online magazine for students wanting to learn a language or study overseas.

And, for potential language students, there's the annual London Language Show (www.language-show.com) that's held on the second weekend in November. It's free to get in.

Whatever your course, you need to know what the accommodation options are. Usually there's three: living with a host family; halls of residence (often on site); and shared apartments or houses. The cheapest option is to live with a host family. This is also one of the best and fastest ways to assimilate the local culture and language, as Sarah Collinson, who learned Spanish in Cusco found:

I lived with a Peruvian family, which meant when I went home in the evening I had to speak Spanish to them too, so I improved very quickly. Since I have come back from my gap year I have decided to do Spanish at university, as I love the language so much.

Last but not least, think about whether you want a recognised qualification at the end of your course. This will often mean taking an exam. Most gappers aren't that keen on more exams during a gap year, but if you feel you can bear it then it will look good on your CV.

WHERE?

Once you know what you want to study, you need to decide where you want to go, which school to attend and how you're going to book.

If you're doing a language course then the first bit is a no-brainer – you'll want to study in the countries that speak the language you want to learn. If that's Spanish and you're up for some real adventure as well as good schools then think about studying in Latin America. Argentina, Costa Rica and Peru can be cheaper than Spain (even with the air fare). Bolivia, Ecuador and Guatemala are slightly pricier. If you can't decide then what about attending a 'travelling' language school in Costa Rica where you're taught around the country in rainforests, cloud forests, beaches and volcanoes (see p424). If your heart is set on Spain then Seville is the most popular destination for gap-year language students. There are thousands of places to study Spanish in the USA, of course, but getting a student visa is more difficult than it once was, plus you're surrounded by English-speakers so your progress is slower. If it's French, Italian or German that turns you on, don't forget about Switzerland, if you can afford it.

Language students also need to decide whether to book a school direct or through an agency. An agency is usually based in the UK and so is easy to contact and talk to about your requirements. They also only work with the best schools, frequently visiting them to make sure they're up to scratch. An agency can book your course and your accommodation, and help with visas and any problems when you're abroad. On the downside, going through a third party can sometimes cost more, but according to gapper Nadia Karavias it's worthwhile:

Booking with a reputable agency might be more expensive but it is worth it because you are looked after in the case of any mishaps. It wasn't such an issue for me when I was studying in France but when I was in Ecuador, somewhere totally different to Europe, the agency really gave me a helping hand. In the end it's just one less thing for yourself or your parents to be worrying about.

If you bypass the language agencies you run the risk of booking a dodgy school in a seedy part of town. To avoid this, look for schools that belong to one of the national or international associations that monitor standards. There's a list of them at www.language-learning.net. Most language schools recommended in this chapter belong to the International Association of Language Centres (IALC; www.ialc.org) or International House (IH; www.ihworld.com). Otherwise, find ones that are recognised by the country's ministry of education.

If you fancy choosing your school and booking it all on the web then visit www.language course.net. You also get a 5% discount on the tuition fees charged by the language school.

Wherever you decide to go and whatever you study, you'll need to ask the following basic questions:

- Are there any exams and are they optional?
- How large are the classes?
- How many hours of teaching are there a week?
- Is the course academic or more recreational?
- Is there any one-to-one tuition?
- What activities do you organise outside of lessons and do they cost extra?
- What age group do you usually attract?
- What exactly is included in the price?
- Where do most of your students come from?

For many courses there are often 'centres of excellence', such as Italy: Florence for art courses and Milan for fashion and jewellery-making. Rebecca Udy, who studied art history in Italy, says:

I had never been to Italy before. I was really excited at the opportunity to study the culture and the history that it had to offer with a group of people my own age, guided by tutors committed to making it fun. It was not just a boring lecture course – we were always taught in front of the paintings and the course involved travelling all over Italy so you built up an intricate picture of the progression of art both through the ages and across the different regions.

There are also particular schools that have an outstanding reputation for certain subjects, such as the New York Film Academy for filmmaking or the Arvon Foundation for writing. Otherwise, you might make your choice on cost – if the course you want is run in several parts of the world, where is the cheapest location (this will often come down to the cost of living in different countries)? Sometimes your choice will depend on where the company you go with holds its courses. For instance, there's no point in wanting a European ski and snowboarding instructor course in the summer – even bottom-shufflers can tell you there ain't no snow. Cunningly, however, many course providers run summer ski and snowboarding instructor courses in the southern hemisphere (usually New Zealand) so you're fully-qualified to work a winter season on the Continent when the course finishes.

FUNDING

There's no denying it – many courses are expensive. You fork out for tuition fees and also flights, accommodation, meals, general living expenses and sometimes equipment. In general, most gappers spend around £2500 all up on a course lasting three months, but you can spend much less and also much more. See Contacts (p421) for specific details on course costs.

Although there are quite a few grants, funds and scholarships for postgraduate research or study abroad, there isn't much for pre-university students except the following:

Arvon Foundation See p436 for contact details. The foundation's writing courses are subsidised by the Arts Council of England and the Scottish Arts Council; grants are available to anyone who can't afford the fees.

Association of Sea Training Organisations (ASTO; www.asto.org.uk) This is the umbrella organisation for the tall ship charities. Around £200,000 each year is distributed to the individual charities to help fund students who can't afford to sail. For a full list of tall ship charities see the ASTO website; a few are detailed on p440.

Career Development Loan See p42 for full details. It may be possible to get one of these loans to help fund your course.

DAAD German Academic Exchange Service See p417 for details. Each year 80 grants are available to do summer courses in German. The catch is that they're not for pre-university students but those in the middle of a university course that has German as a component. You need to apply in the autumn of the previous year via your German department.

English-Speaking Union See p429 for contact details. This registered charity has around 30 scholarships each year for their secondary school exchange program where you attend a boarding school in the USA or Canada.

Lions Clubs International Contact your local club (get the address from www.lions.org.uk or call ☎ 0121 441 4544) to see if they participate in the youth exchange program for those aged 15 to 21.

Peter Kirk Scholarships For full details see p446.

Rotary International in Great Britain and Ireland Contact your local club (get the address from www.ribi.org) to see if they participate in Rotary's youth activities.

Unless you've managed to get rich quick, you'll have to save up for your course so start as early as possible. There are loads of good tips on p42, and saving up should be seen as part of your gap-year challenge. Otherwise, if your course trains you to do a paid job during the rest of your gap year, you could borrow the money up front and then pay it back as you earn. Whatever you do, though, it's a bad idea to start university or a proper job with a gap-year debt hanging over your head.

UK LEARNING

There are thousands of courses on every possible subject at colleges, universities and adult-education centres all over the UK. A useful resource for finding out what's available in your area is **Learndirect** (☎ 0800 101 901; www.learndirect.co.uk), a government scheme, which has details on 700,000 courses nationwide. If you live in London then the official booklets to part-time and full-time study in Greater London are: *Part-time Floodlight*, *Summertime Floodlight* and *Full-time Floodlight*. These are available at almost every London newsagent or you can look for a course at www.floodlight.co.uk.

For more detailed advice about UK gap-year study (as well as help with university, a gap year abroad and postgraduate career options) there's **Gabbitas Educational Consultants** (☎ 020 7734 0161; www.gabbitas.co.uk; consult@gabbitas.co.uk). Initial phone advice is free, or you can book a phone consultation at £60 for 20 minutes. Don't waste time: this works out at 5p per second.

Two useful courses to do in the UK are business studies or business administration and secretarial skills. Apart from anything else, touch-typing (it only takes 40 hours to learn) is an invaluable skill at university, in temp work, or a future career. These courses are offered at almost all local education centres or local business schools.

Other good courses to do in the UK are those that train you for a job abroad during the rest of your gap year. For instance, an international cocktail bartenders' course sets you up to work almost anywhere in the world. Otherwise, getting your competent crew certificate in the UK is wise if you intend to work your passage on a yacht (see p388).

A good UK course to ask your parents to pay for as a birthday or Christmas present is one of the gap-year safety and awareness courses. See p444 for details.

CONTACTS

Language Agencies

Cactus Language
4 Clarence House, 30–31 North St, Brighton, East Sussex BN1 1EB
☎ 0845 130 4775
fax 01273 775868
enquiry@cactuslanguage.com
www.cactuslanguage.com
Cactus offers tailor-made language holidays worldwide, which can combine a language course with activities such as salsa dancing, diving, cooking and volunteer work.
Types of Course: All standards of Western European and Middle Eastern languages, Chinese, Greek, Japanese, Russian and Turkish.
Timing & Length of Course: Courses are from one week to 12 months long; most start weekly.
Destinations: Asia, the Caribbean, Central and South America, Europe, the Middle East & Russia.
Costs: One month costs from £299, 12 months from £2500, tuition only.
Eligibility: The minimum age is 18.
Accommodation: Courses can be booked with or without accommodation. You can stay with a host family, in a shared or private student apartment, or at a student residence or hotel.
How to Apply: If you apply and pay online you get a £10 discount.

Càlédöñiâ Languages Abroad
The Clockhouse, Bonnington Mill, 72 Newhaven Rd, Edinburgh EH6 5QG
☎ 0131 621 7721/2
fax 0131 621 7723
courses@caledonialanguages.co.uk
www.caledonialanguages.co.uk
Càlédöñiâ offers a large range of straight language courses, as well as language and volunteering, or language combined with a cultural interest. See p435 for more details.
Types of Course: All standards of Arabic, French, German, Italian, Portuguese, Russian and Spanish. Some Spanish courses in Latin America are combined with volunteer work.
Timing & Length of Course: Courses are from one to nine months long; most start every Monday but more specialist courses start at specific times.
Destinations: Central and South America, Egypt, France, Germany, Italy, Portugal, Russia & Spain.
Costs: One-month courses range from £350 to £750, three months from £925, tuition only.
Eligibility: Applicants must be aged at least 17.
Accommodation: You can book your course with or without accommodation.

CESA Languages Abroad
CESA House, Pennance Rd, Lanner, Cornwall TR16 5TQ
☎ 01209 211800
fax 01209 211830
info@cesalanguages.com
www.cesalanguages.com
CESA is a booking agency with courses in more unusual languages and destinations.
Types of Course: All standards of Chinese, Japanese, Latin American Spanish (including Cuban), Moroccan, Russian and Western European.
Timing & Length of Course: Courses are from two to 24 weeks long, with extensions if required. Beginner courses have set start dates but anyone else can begin any Monday.

Destinations: Central and South America, China, Cuba, Dominican Republic, Guadeloupe, Japan, Mexico, Morocco, Russia & Western Europe.
Costs: Two weeks cost from £357, 24 weeks from £3645 with accommodation.
Eligibility: There's a minimum age of 16.
Accommodation: Mostly flat-share, student apartments or college residences.

Don Quijote

2/4 Stoneleigh Park Rd, Epsom, Surrey KT19 0QT
☎ 020 8786 8081
fax 020 8786 8086
info@donquijote.co.uk
www.donquijote.org
Don Quijote specialises in Spanish language courses. In Cuba you can also learn to salsa and in Tenerife you can learn to scuba-dive.
Types of Course: All levels of Spanish.
Timing & Length of Course: Courses are from one to 40 weeks, with weekly start dates for all except beginners who have prescribed start dates.
Destinations: Cuba, Mexico, Peru, mainland Spain & Tenerife.
Costs: One month costs from £479, 40 weeks from £3505, tuition only.
Eligibility: The minimum age is 17 (as long as you're staying with a host family).
Accommodation: Courses can be booked with or without accommodation. Options are homestay, or student flats and residences.

EF International Language Schools

Dudley House, 36-38 Southampton St, London WC2E 7HF
☎ 08707 200735
fax 08707 200767
gapyear@ef.com
www.ef.com
EF offers upmarket language courses, which can sometimes be combined with a Teaching English as a Foreign Language (TEFL) course and teaching placement.
Types of Course: All standards of Chinese, French, German, Italian, Russian and Spanish.
Timing & Length of Course: There are two start dates a month except in July and August when courses begin weekly. Courses are from two weeks to nine months.
Destinations: China, Ecuador, Russia & Western Europe.
Costs: Two weeks with half-board costs from £680, nine months from £5750, excluding flights.

Eligibility: There's a minimum age of 16.
Accommodation: Host-family or university-residence accommodation comes with each course.

Euro Academy

67–71 Lewisham High St, London SE13 5JX
☎ 020 8297 0505
fax 020 8297 0984
enquiries@euroacademy.co.uk
www.euroacademy.co.uk
Euro Academy offers language courses abroad, sometimes combined with cookery, dance and unpaid work placements.
Types of Course: All levels of French, German, Greek, Italian, Portuguese, Spanish and Russian.
Timing & Length of Course: Courses are from one week to one year, and most have weekly start dates.
Destinations: France, Germany, Greece, Italy, Portugal, Russia & Spain.
Costs: Two weeks costs from £300, 16 weeks from £1500, tuition only.
Eligibility: The minimum age is 15.
Accommodation: This is most often with host families or in university residences but hotels or apartments can be re-quested. Courses are offered with or without accommodation.

Gala Spanish in Spain

Woodcote House, 8 Leigh Lane, Farnham, Surrey GU9 8HP
☎ /fax 01252 715319
Gala specialises in sending students to Spain. There are also language courses plus internships available in Barcelona (ask for details).
Types of Course: All levels of Spanish.
Timing & Length of Course: Courses are from two weeks to nine months and start at two-weekly intervals.
Destinations: Nine cities in Spain & Ecuador.
Costs: Two weeks costs from £430, 12 weeks from £2100, including half-board accommodation. If you want to self-cater then the price drops to £400 for two weeks and £1500 for 12 weeks.
Eligibility: The minimum age is 16.
Accommodation: Courses usually come with half- or full-board accommodation with a host family, or in a student flat or residence.
How to Apply: Gala prefers telephone inquiries.

Goethe Institut

50 Princes Gate, London SW7 2PH
☎ 020 7596 4004

fax 020 7594 0210
german@london.goethe.org
www.goethe.de
Goethe is a worldwide organisation promoting German language and culture. There are institutes all over Germany where you can learn the language.
Types of Course: All levels of German including intensive, super-intensive and business.
Timing & Length of Course: Courses are from two to 12 weeks and run year-round at one or another of its locations.
Destinations: 16 centres in Germany.
Costs: Four-week intensive courses cost from £664, 12 weeks from £1750, tuition only.
Eligibility: The minimum age is 18.
Accommodation: Goethe can arrange accommodation, usually in student halls of residence or with a family.

IST Plus
Rosedale House, Rosedale Rd, Richmond, Surrey TW9 2SZ
☎ 020 8939 9057
fax 020 8332 7858
info@istplus.com
www.istplus.com
IST Plus is an international work and language study organisation. There are different work and cultural programs, including language study abroad courses.
Types of Course: All levels of French, German, Italian and Spanish.
Timing & Length of Course: Courses are from two to 36 weeks, starting every couple of weeks.
Destinations: Europe, Mexico & Latin America (including Cuba).
Costs: Courses cost from £350 for two weeks, including accommodation.
Eligibility: There's a minimum age of 16.
Accommodation: Courses can be booked with or without accommodation. Options include staying with a host family, in a self-catering apartment, at a hotel or student residence.

Language Courses Abroad/ Spanish Study Holidays
67 Ashby Rd, Loughborough, Leicestershire LE11 3AA
☎ 01509 211612
fax 01509 260037
info@languagesabroad.co.uk or
info@spanishstudyholidays.com
www.languagesabroad.co.uk or www.spanishstudy holidays.com

Offers language courses, volunteer and work-experience programs. Some courses are combined with cookery, wine courses or dancing lessons etc.
Types of Course: All levels of Spanish, Russian and Western European.
Timing & Length of Course: Courses are for one week to nine months; most start weekly, depending on the location.
Destinations: Central and South America (including Cuba), Russia & Western Europe.
Costs: Two weeks costs from £241, 40 weeks from £2290, tuition only.
Eligibility: The minimum age ranges from 11 to 18, depending on the course.
Accommodation: You can stay with a host family, in a shared apartment, private studio apartment, student residence or hotel.

Language Studies International (LSI)
19–21 Ridgmount St, London WC1E 7AH
☎ 020 7467 6506
fax 020 7323 1736
fl@lsi.edu
www.lsi.edu
LSI specialises in language courses abroad and also offers work-experience programs.
Types of Course: All levels of Chinese, French, German, Italian, Japanese, Russian and Spanish.
Timing & Length of Course: Courses are for one week to one year. They usually start every Monday but beginners' courses are monthly.
Destinations: Central and South America, China, Europe & Russia.
Costs: Two weeks cost from £200, 34 weeks from £2565, tuition only.
Eligibility: The minimum age is 16, except for courses in Latin America and China where it's 18.
Accommodation: This is normally with a host family, although other options are available.

OISE Intensive Language Schools
OISE House, Binsey Lane, Oxford OX2 0EY
☎ 01865 258300
fax 01865 244696
info@oise.com
www.oise.com
OISE is a specialist in intensive-language training, teaching either one-to-one or in groups of four and eight.
Types of Course: All levels of French, German and Spanish.

Timing & Length of Course: Courses are from one week to 36 weeks and start weekly.

Destinations: Heidelberg, Madrid & Paris.

Costs: Two weeks cost from £1085, 36 weeks from £19,365 (!), including half-board accommodation.

Eligibility: The minimum age is 17.

Accommodation: OISE always sells courses with half-board host-family accommodation.

SIBS

Beech House, Commercial Rd, Uffculme, Collompton, Devon EX15 3EB

☎ 01884 841330

fax 01884 841377

trish@sibs.co.uk

www.sibs.co.uk

SIBS offers language courses abroad, often combined with art, cookery or work experience.

Types of Course: Japanese, all levels of Russian, Western European languages including Dutch, Greek and Swedish.

Timing & Length of Course: Courses are from one week to one year; most start weekly but some start monthly.

Destinations: Japan, Mexico, Russia, South America & Western Europe.

Costs: Courses cost from £200 per week, including accommodation.

Eligibility: All welcome

Accommodation: All accommodation options are offered but students can opt for tuition only.

Society for Co-operation in Russian and Soviet Studies (SCRSS)

320 Brixton Rd, London SW9 6AB

☎ 020 7274 2282

fax 020 7274 3230

ruslibrary@scrss.org.uk

www.scrss.org.uk

SCRSS is a charity and offers language courses in Russia, as well as an information service and library. It can arrange visas if required.

Types of Course: All levels of Russian.

Timing & Length of Course: Courses are from one week to one year and usually start weekly.

Destinations: Moscow & St Petersburg.

Costs: One week costs from £370 for tuition, visa support, transfers and hostel accommodation.

Eligibility: The minimum age is 16.

Accommodation: Hostel or family accommodation can be booked if required.

How to Apply: Two months' notice must be given.

STA Travel UK

The Global Language Programme

St George House, 56 Peter St, Manchester M2 3NQ

☎ 0870 160 6070

fax 0161 830 8550

global.languages@statravel.co.uk

www.statravel.co.uk/c_yearout/globallanguages.asp

STA Travel has developed a language program offering courses at 65 schools in 29 countries all over the world. Sometimes you can study a language in the morning and do a cultural activity in the afternoon. For instance, you could learn Spanish in Santiago (Chile) and spend the afternoon skiing the Andes. Or there's a travelling language school in Costa Rica where you travel around the country seeing the sights but also learning the language.

Types of Course: French, German, Italian, Japanese, Portuguese, Russian and Spanish.

Timing & Length of Course: From one week to one year, all year-round.

Destinations: Twenty-nine countries including Brazil, Cuba & the Dominican Republic.

Costs: One week in Guatemala from £114 and three months in Guatemala from £1140, including airport transfers and accommodation.

Eligibility: Minimum age 16.

Accommodation: Hostel, university halls and homestays with a local family.

How to book: It is easy to book online.

Vis-à-Vis

2–4 Stoneleigh Park Rd, Epsom, Surrey KT19 0QT

☎ 020 8786 8021

fax 020 8786 8086

info@visavis.org

www.visavis.org

The French-language partner of Don Quijote offers French-language courses in Europe and Canada.

Types of Course: All levels of French.

Timing & Length of Course: Courses are from one to 40 weeks and start weekly.

Destinations: Belgium, Canada & France.

Costs: Two weeks cost from £193, 12 weeks from £797, tuition only.

Eligibility: The minimum age is 16.

Accommodation: A homestay or student flats and residences are all options.

Language Schools Abroad

AUSTRIA
Actilingua Academy
Gloriettegasse 8, A-1130 Vienna
☎ 00 43 1-877 6701
fax 00 43 1-877 6703
info@actilingua.com
www.actilingua.com
Actilingua is situated in central Vienna. Courses for beginners start once a month, intermediary level courses start weekly.
Accreditation/Organisation Memberships: IALC.

CANADA
LSC Language Studies Canada
Suite 401, 1610 St Catherine St West, Montreal, Québec H3H 2S2
☎ 00 1 514-939 9911
fax 00 1 514-939 2223
marketing@lsc-canada.com
www.lsc-canada.com
Established in 1962, LSC teaches seven levels of French. There are 13 start dates a year and there's a good range of excursions and cultural visits.
Accreditation/Organisation Memberships: IALC, Canadian Association of Private Language Schools.

CENTRAL & SOUTH AMERICA
Latin Immersion, Buenos Aires
Amenabar 3065, Buenos Aires, Argentina
☎ 00 54 11-4544 3217
fax 00 1-866 726 5705
info@latinimmersion.com
www.latinimmersion.com
Study Spanish in the 'Paris of South America'. Argentina is one of the world's cheaper cities. The school is situated on a tree-lined, middle-class neighbourhood, close to bars and restaurants. Classes usually start every third Monday with special start dates for beginners. Latin Immersion also has a school in Chile.
Accreditations/Organisation Memberships: IALC.

Estudio Internacional Sampere, Cuenca
3–43 Hermano Miguel, Escalinata, Cuenca, Ecuador
☎ 00 593 7-82 3960
fax 00 593 7-84 1986
cuenca@sampere.es
www.sampere.com
The school overlooks the Barranco River in Cuenca, Ecuador's third largest city and cultural capital. Most courses start on Mondays throughout the year. All standards welcome.
Accreditations/Organisation Memberships: IALC.

Excel Spanish Language Center
Cruz Verde 336, Cusco, Peru
☎ 00 51 84-235298
fax 00 51 84-232272
info@excelinspanish.com
www.excel-spanishlanguageprograms-peru.org
The school is a five-minute walk from Cusco's main plaza. It has a beautiful courtyard. Courses at all levels start weekly on Mondays. Courses can be combined with volunteering. There are Excel schools in other parts of Peru.
Accreditations/Organisation Memberships: Recognised and accredited by the Ministry of Education of Peru.

Latin Immersion, Santiago
Roman Diaz 297, Providencia, Santiago, Chile
☎ 00 56 2-264 2659
fax 00 1 866 726 5705
info@latinimmersion.com
www.latinimmersion.com
The school is found on a quiet side street of a residential part of Santiago. Classes usually start every third Monday with special start dates for beginners. Latin Immersion also has a school in Argentina.
Accreditations/Organisation Memberships: IALC.

Academia Tica
PO Box 1294, San José, Costa Rica
☎ 00 506 229 0013
fax 00 506 292 7136
actica@racsa.co.cr
www.academiatica.com
Founded in 1986, this is one of the oldest Spanish schools in Cost Rica. The school is situated in a tropical garden six miles from the capital (there's a bus stop right outside). Classes start every Monday except for beginners who have two start dates a month.
Accreditations/Organisation Memberships: Among others, IALC and member of the Costa Rican National Chamber of Tourism.

FRANCE
BLS Bordeaux
42 rue Lafaurie de Monbadon, 33000 Bordeaux
☎ 00 33 5 56 51 00 76
fax 00 33 5 56 51 76 15
info@bls-frenchcourses.com
www.bls-frenchcourses.com
BLS is housed in a 19th-century building set in the heart
of town. Classes for beginners start monthly and for other
levels weekly. There are also schools in Biarritz and Toulon.
Accreditations/Organisation Memberships: IALC,
Maison de la France, Groupement Professionnel des
Organismes d'Enseignement du Français Langue Étrangér
(SOUFFLE).

ELFE Paris
8 Villa Ballu, 75009, Paris
☎ 00 33 1 48 78 73 00
fax 00 33 1 40 82 91 92
contact@elfe-paris.com
www.elfe-paris.com
In a mansion house close to the Arc de Triomphe, ELFE
courses start weekly except for beginners who start monthly.
You can also combine language with a civilization course.
Accreditations/Organisation Memberships: IALC,
SOUFFLE.

France Langue
22 Av Notre Dame, 06000, Nice
☎ 00 33 4 93 13 78 88
fax 00 33 4 93 13 78 89
nice@france-langue.fr
www.france-langue.fr
Six blocks from the Mediterranean, courses for all levels
run year-round. There is also a school in Paris, not far from
the Arc de Triomphe.
Accreditations/Organisation Memberships: Among
others, FIYTO (Federation of International Youth Travel
Organisations), IALC, Maison de la France.

GERMANY
BWS Germanlingua
Bayerstrasse 13, D-80335 Munich
☎ 00 49 89-599 89200
fax 00 49 89-599 89201
info@bws-germanlingua.de
www.bws-germanlingua.de
Established in 1984, courses at all levels start weekly

except for beginners where there are set dates (see the
website). Classes get booked up quickly around Oktoberfest, which begins mid-September. There is also a BWS
school in Berlin.
Accreditations/Organisation Memberships: IALC.

Colón Language Center
Colonnaden 96, 20354 Hamburg
☎ 00 49 40-34 58 50
fax 00 49 40-34 68 54
info@colon.de
www.colon.de
This old school, founded in 1952, is in the middle of
Hamburg and has its own foreign-language bookshop.
Beginner courses start monthly and all others weekly. You
get a discount when you book online.
Accreditations/Organisation Memberships: IALC.

GLS Sprachenzentrum Berlin
Kolonnenstrasse 26, 10829 Berlin
☎ 00 49 30-78 00 89
fax 00 49 30-787 41 92
germancourses@gls-berlin.com
www.german-courses.com
In the school opposite Marlene Dietrich's former home, beginner courses start monthly and other courses every Monday.
Accreditations/Organisation Memberships: Among
others, IALC, European Association for Quality Language
Services (EAQUALS).

GREECE
Athens Centre
48 Archimidous St, Athens 11636
☎ 00 30 210-7012268
fax 00 30 210-7018603
info@athenscentre.gr
www.athenscentre.gr
Established in 1969, this is one of the leading places to
study Greek. New classes start monthly and there's also a
three-week summer course on the island of Spetses each
year. All levels are welcome.
Accreditations/Organisation Memberships:
Recognised by Greek Ministry of Education.

IRELAND
National University of Ireland, Galway
University Road, Galway
☎ 00 353 91-595101/595038

fax 353 91-595041
treasa.uilorcain@nuigalway.ie
www.mis.nuigalway.ie
Situated in an Irish-speaking area of the country, this
school has courses for more advanced students from Easter
to September. For complete beginners a four-week course
starts mid-July. Lonely Planet author Steve Fallon did a
course here and recommends it.
Accreditations/Organisation Memberships: Part of
the National University of Ireland, Galway.

ITALY
Istituto Italiano, Centro di Lingua e Cultura
Via Machiavelli 33, 00185, Rome
☎ 00 39 06-704 52 138
fax 00 39 06-700 85 122
istital@uni.net
www.istitoitaliano.com
Ten minutes' walk from the Colosseum, beginner courses
start monthly and other courses each Monday.
Accreditation/Organisation Memberships: IALC,
Association of Schools teaching Italian as a Second
Language (ASILS).

Linguaviva
Via Fiume 17, 50123, Florence
☎ 00 39 055-294 359
fax 00 39 055-283 667
info@linguaviva.it
www.linguaviva.it
Housed in a 19th century building, close to the main
railway station, most classes start any Monday. You can
also study cookery, art history and fine art along with your
language course.
Accreditation/Organisation Memberships: Among
others, FIYTO, IALC.

Linguadue
Corso Buenos Aires 43, 20124, Milan
☎ 00 39 02-2951 9972
fax 00 39 02-2951 9973
info@linguadue.com
www.linguadue.com
In a beautiful Art Nouveau building in the centre of town,
most courses start weekly. The school has its own garden.
Accreditations/Organisation Memberships: Among
others, FIYTO, IALC.

JAPAN
WorldLink Education
Academy of Japanese Language and Culture
Yotsuya TS Building, 4-31 Yotsuya Shinjuku-ku, Tokyo
160-0004
☎ 00 81 3-5366 3304
fax 00 81 3-5366 3305
info@wle-japan.com
www.wle-japan.com
The school is in the heart of Tokyo. Most classes start each
Monday throughout the year but some have a specified start
date. There are also art, culture and cooking workshops.
Accreditations/Organisation Memberships:
Licensed by the Association for Promotion of Japanese
Language Education.

MEXICO
Solexico, Oaxaca
Calle Abasolo #217, Esquina con Av Juarez, Oaxaca, OAX 68000
☎ 00 52 951-516 5680
fax 00 52 951-516 5680
info@solexico.com
www.solexico.com
The school is housed in a beautiful, colonial building in the
centre of Oaxaca's historical quarter. Courses start every
Monday. Their other school is in Playa del Carmen, six
blocks from the ocean.
Accreditations/Organisation Memberships: FIYTO,
IALC.

PORTUGAL
CIAL Centro de Linguas, Lisbon
Avenida da República 41-80, 1050, Lisbon
☎ 00 351 21-7940 448
fax 00 351 21-7960 783
Portuguese@cial.pt
www.cial.pt
Courses start monthly in Lisbon or Faro and lots of cultural
trips to museums, monuments and concerts are included.
Accreditations/Organisation Memberships: Among
others, IALC, recognised by the Portuguese Ministry of
Education, American Association of Teachers of Spanish and
Portuguese.

RUSSIA
Liden & Denz Language Centre
Transportny per. 11, 191119, St Petersburg
☎ 00 7 812-325 22 41

fax 00 7 812-325 12 84
lidenz@lidenz.ru
www.lidenz.ru
Situated in the heart of this beautiful city, most courses start twice a month. There is also a Liden & Denz Language school in Moscow.
Accreditations/Organisation Memberships: IALC, Russian Association for Teaching Russian Language and Literature.

SPAIN
ABC Language Center
Guillem Tell 27, 08006 Barcelona
☎ 00 34 93-415 5757
fax 00 34 93-218 2606
info@ambricol.es
www.ambricol.es
Located in a six-storey building with a penthouse terrace overlooking Barcelona, beginner classes start monthly and all other classes every Monday.
Accreditation/Organisation Memberships: IALC, accredited by the Instituto Cervantes, FIYTO.

Estudio Internacional Sampere
Lagasca 16, 28001, Madrid
☎ 00 34 91-431 4366
fax 00 34 91-575 9509
info@sampere.es
www.sampere.com
Founded in 1956, this is a large school located within walking distance of the Prado Museum and other great buildings. Classes start most Mondays except for beginners where there are special start dates. There are also schools in Salamanca, Alicante, El Puerto de Santa Maria and Cuenca in Ecuador.
Accreditation/Organisation Memberships: IALC.

Malaca Instituto
Cale Cortada 6, Cerrado de Calderon, 29018, Malaga
☎ 00 34 95-229 3242
fax 00 34 95-229 6316
espanol@malacainstituto.com
www.malacainstituto.com
The school is 15 minutes' walk from the beach. It has a cinema, two sun terraces, a dance studio and a swimming pool. The intensive Spanish course starts every two weeks. You can also study Spanish along with either dance or cookery.

Accreditation/Organisation Memberships: Among others, IALC, EAQUALS.

SWITZERLAND
ASC International House
72 rue de Lausanne, 1202 Geneva
☎ 00 41 22-731 85 20
fax 00 41 22-738 21 58
admin@asc-ih.ch
www.asc-ih.ch
ASC is four blocks from Lake Geneva, in the French-speaking part of Switzerland. You can learn French, German, Italian, Spanish and Russian here. Most courses start on Mondays except for beginners who have set start dates.
Accreditations/Organisation Memberships: Affiliated to International House World Organisation.

TAIWAN
Taipei Language Institute (TLI)
Taipei Roosevelt Center 4F, No 50 Roosevelt Rd, Sec 3, Taipei
☎ 00 886 2-2367 8228
fax 00 886 2-2363 4857
tli.Taipei@msa.hinet.net
www.tli.com.tw
Founded in 1956, TLI has five centres in Taiwan. You can transfer between them in order to see more of the country while you study. There are also 10 centres in mainland China, one in Tokyo and one in New York. Courses start four times a year.
Accreditations/Organisation Memberships: None, they used to be a member of the IALC, but they outgrew their membership. They have an excellent reputation.

UK
Language School
School of Oriental and African Studies, Thornhaugh St, Russell Sq, London WC1H 0XG
☎ 020 7898 4888
fax 020 7898 4889
languages@soas.ac.uk
www.soas.ac.uk/languagecentre
Unfortunately for travellers wanting to go abroad, this is the best place to study the more unusual languages of African, Near and Middle Eastern, East Asian, Southeast Asian and South Asian countries. There are courses for all standards.
Accreditations/Organisation Memberships: Part of London University.

Living Abroad/Educational Exchange Programs

En Famille Overseas

La Maison Jaune, Avenue du Stade, 34210, Siran, France
☎ /fax 00 33 468-914990
marylou.toms@wanadoo.fr
www.enfamilleoverseas.co.uk

Founded in 1945, students stay with families in Europe. Language tuition is optional.

Timing & Length of Stay: Stays are from one week to 12 months and are available year-round.

Destinations: France, Germany, Italy & Spain.

Costs: Usually from £350 a week full-board.

Eligibility: The minimum age is 14.

English-Speaking Union

Dartmouth House, 37 Charles St, London W1J 5ED
☎ 020 7529 1550
fax 020 7495 6108
education@esu.org
www.esu.org

A number of programs, scholarships and opportunities are offered worldwide by this registered charity that promotes international understanding through the use of English.

Types of Course: Secondary school exchange program at a boarding school in the USA or Canada.

Timing & Length of Course: Programs are for two or three academic terms: September to July or January to July.

Destinations: Canada & the USA.

Costs: There are around 30 scholarships available each year that are worth about £13,535 to £16,240 each and cover full-board accommodation and tuition. All other expenses such as flights, uniform and books have to be met by the student (around £2500).

Eligibility: You need to have done A-Levels or equivalent and intend to go to university. The maximum age is 19 years and six months at the time school starts.

How to Apply: Apply to the education officer by letter and an application form will be sent to you. There is a selection and interview process. Application closing dates are mid-January and early-September.

Experiment in International Living (EIL)

287 Worcester Rd, Malvern, Worcestershire WR14 1AB
☎ 0800 018 4015
fax 01684 562212
info@eiluk.org
www.eiluk.org

EIL is a registered charity that offers many gap-year programs (see p295) including homestays with urban or rural families, farms and ranches. One of the most popular destinations is Japan.

Timing & Length of Stay: Stays are from one week to four weeks.

Destinations: Twenty-five worldwide destinations in all continents, including Ghana, India, Nigeria & Thailand.

Costs: One week in Morocco costs from £153 and the most expensive stay is in France at £805 for four weeks. Four weeks in Japan is £663. All prices include full-board accommodation.

Eligibility: The minimum age is 18.

Cookery & Cocktail-Making in the UK

Cookery at the Grange

The Grange, Whatley, Frome, Somerset BA11 3JU
☎ /fax 01373 836579
info@cookeryatthegrange.co.uk
www.cookeryatthegrange.co.uk

This is a very popular place for gap-year students to study. The courses are residential, with 24 students living on site. The social life is good. The course gappers do is the essential cookery course, which equips you to work in chalets, or galleys (ie on boats) at home or abroad.

Types of Course: The essential cookery course.

Timing & Length of Course: The Essential Cookery Course runs for four weeks, nine times a year.

Costs: The course costs from £2520, including accommodation and food.

Eligibility: The minimum age is 18.

How to Apply: It's advisable to book at least one year in advance (particularly for the autumn courses).

Edinburgh School of Food & Wine

The Coach House, Newliston, Edinburgh EH29 9EB
☎ 0131 333 5001
fax 0131 335 3796
info@esfw.com
www.esfw.com

You can take courses in practical cookery, wine appreciation or basic food-handlers' hygiene, plus there's a six-month diploma course. The intensive certificate course is especially for gap-year students and will equip you to work in chalets, lodges and on yachts. The school works closely with ski company reps to help students gain employment once they have completed the course.

Types of Course: Survival course and intensive certificate course.

Timing & Length of Course: The survival course lasts for one week and runs twice a year (usually in August). The certificate course is a four-week course and runs four times a year (January, July, September and October).

Costs: The four-week certificate course costs from £2000, including your essential cook's kit. Accommodation is extra. The survival course costs from £395.

Eligibility: The minimum age is 17.

Leiths School of Food & Wine
21 St Alban's Grove, Kensington, London W8 5BP
☎ 020 7229 0177/020 7937 3366
fax 020 7937 5257
info@leiths.com
www.leiths.com
Founded in 1975, Leiths offers three main courses geared towards gap-year students.

Types of Course: The foundation course, basic certificate in practical cookery and beginners certificate in food and wine.

Timing & Length of Course: The foundation course lasts from two to four weeks and starts mid-July, the basic certificate runs for four weeks from the end of August and the beginners certificate is for 10 weeks and starts at the end of September.

Costs: The foundation course costs from £1030, the basic certificate from £2055 and the beginners certificate from £4600. All courses are non-residential.

Eligibility: The minimum age is 18.

Murray School of Cookery
Glenbervie House, Holt Pound, Farnham, Surrey GU10 4LE
☎ /fax 01420 23049
kmpmmsc@aol.com
www.cookeryschool.net
Murray's non-residential courses are for up to nine students at a time. The two courses below are of real interest to gap-year students. The school has contacts with ski companies and yachting agencies.

Types of Course: Certificate course and chalet chef course.

Timing & Length of Course: The certificate course lasts four weeks and runs seven times a year; the chalet chef course lasts one week and runs twice a year in October.

Costs: The certificate course costs from £1500, the chalet chef course from £395; accommodation is extra.

Eligibility: The minimum age is 18.

Shaker UK
Unit 213, Jubilee Trade Centre, 130 Pershore St, Birmingham B5 6ND
☎ 0121 6222 055
gapyear@shaker-uk.com
www.shaker-uk.com
Shaker offers practical courses for a durable and transferable skill in bartending and cocktail-making (mixology).

Types of Course: International cocktail bartenders course.

Timing & Length of Course: The course is for five days and runs monthly.

Costs: The course costs from £495, tuition only.

Eligibility: The minimum age is 16.

Tante Marie School of Cookery
Woodham House, Carlton Rd, Woking, Surrey GU21 4HF
☎ 01483 726957
fax 01483 724173
info@tantemarie.co.uk
www.tantemarie.co.uk
Founded in 1954; courses range from diploma standard to short courses for amateurs. Gap-year students usually do the two courses listed here. Most ski companies prefer you to have done the certificate course but often accept students who have completed the shorter course.

Types of Course: Cordon bleu certificate course and essential skills course.

Timing & Length of Course: The certificate course runs for three months, three times a year; the essential skills lasts one month and runs four times a year.

Costs: The certificate course costs from £4500, the essential skills from £1950; accommodation is excluded (and usually takes place with local host families).

Eligibility: The minimum age is 16.

Cookery Abroad

Apicius: The Culinary Institute of Florence
Via Guelfa, 85 50129 Florence, Italy
☎ 00 39 055-2658135
fax 00 39 055-2656689
info@apicius.it
www.apicius.it

As well as offering professional one- and three-year courses, this school has many different weekly and monthly courses plus a culinary program for amateurs where you can study five out of 15 possible subjects, from Italian vegetarian cooking to an introduction to Italian wines.

Types of Course: The culinary program for amateurs.
Timing & Length of Course: One-week, two-week, monthly and term-long courses run all year-round.
Destination: Florence.
Costs: Weekly courses start from £140 and term-long ones from £3660. This is tuition only and there's also a lab fee of £115.
Eligibility: Anyone over 18.

Ballymaloe Cookery School

Shanagarry, Co Cork, Republic of Ireland
☎ 00 353 21-4646 785
fax 00 353 21-4646 909
info@cookingisfun.ie
www.cookingisfun.ie

Set in the countryside close to the sea, this well-known Irish school runs short courses ranging from one day to one week, plus there are longer courses.

Types of Course: Certificate course and introduction course.
Timing & Length of Course: The certificate course is 12 weeks long and runs three times per year (January, April and September); the introduction course lasts one week and runs once each July.
Costs: The certificate course costs from £5585, the introduction course from £530, tuition only.
Eligibility: The minimum age is 16.
How to Apply: Online applications are preferred.

Flying Fish

25 Union Rd, Cowes, Isle of Wight PO31 7TW
☎ 01983 280641
fax 01983 281821
mail@flyingfishonline.com
www.flyingfishonline.com

Flying Fish is a training provider for watersports and snow sports staff (see p440). One course combines sailing and chefing, training students to cook on yachts. The cookery element of the course lasts six weeks and involves cooking both on dry land and at sea.

Types of Course: Crew/galley chef traineeship.
Timing & Length of Course: The course is for 13 weeks and runs twice a year in spring and autumn.

Destinations: UK (one week) & Australia (12 weeks).
Costs: The course costs from £8950, including accommodation and flights.
Eligibility: The minimum age is 18.

Laskarina Holidays

Bolney Place, Cowfold Rd, Bolney, West Sussex RH17 5QT
☎ 01444 880380
fax 01444 880387
info@laskarina.co.uk
www.laskarina.co.uk

Laskarina is a specialist holiday company offering courses in the Greek Islands, including a cookery course with the owner of the Mythos restaurant on the island of Symi.

Types of Course: Cooking with Stavros.
Timing & Length of Course: The course lasts five days and runs in May or October.
Destination: The island of Symi, Greece.
Costs: Tuition costs from £195, excluding accommodation, flights and transfers.
Eligibility: Everyone is welcome.

Mexican Home Cooking School

Apdo. 64, Tlaxcala 90000, Mexico
☎ 00 52 246-46 809 78
fax 00 52 246-46 809 78
info@mexicanhomecooking.com
www.mexicanhomecooking.com

On offer here is a hands-on cookery course with small classes of only four people. The mornings are spent in the kitchen and the afternoons are free for exploring.

Types of Course: Mexican home cookery.
Timing & Length of Course: The course is for five days and runs year-round, depending on bookings.
Costs: The course, six nights' full-board accommodation plus beer and wine costs from £650. There is a 10% discount for Lonely Planet readers.
Eligibility: All welcome.
How to Apply: There's usually a two-month waiting list so book early.

Tasting Places

Unit 108, Buspace Studios, Conlan St, London W10 5AP
☎ 020 7460 0077
fax 020 7460 0029
ss@tastingplaces.com
www.tastingplaces.com

Tasting Places offers cookery holidays in three main countries. It can also fix up bespoke courses for students anywhere in the world, at any time.

Timing & Length of Course: Holidays are for one week in spring or autumn.

Destinations: France, Italy & Thailand.

Costs: Tuition, full board and lodging costs from £1300; flights cost extra.

Eligibility: All welcome.

The Arts

ART & CRAFT
Art Workshops in Guatemala

4758 Lyndale Ave South, Minneapolis, Minnesota 55409-2304, USA

☎ 00 1 612-825 0747

fax 00 1 612-825 6637

info@artguat.org

www.artguat.org

This is an art program in Antigua set up and run by Liza Fourre, an American.

Types of Course: Backstrap weaving, beading, drawing and painting, Mayan culture lessons, photography and much more.

Timing & Length of Course: All courses are for eight days and usually run once a year from February to April, in July, and from the end of October to the beginning of November.

Destination: Guatemala.

Costs: Tuition, lodging, breakfast and transfer cost from £812, flights are extra.

Eligibility: The minimum age is 18.

Centro Dedalo Arte

Loc. Greppolungo 43-44, 55041 Camaiore (LU), Italy

☎ /fax 00 39 0584-984 258

info@dedaloarte.org

www.artcoursestuscany.com or www.dedaloarte.org

In a farmhouse near Pienza, southern Tuscany, this international association of artists runs residential art courses in all media. All courses are taught in English and Italian.

Types of Course: Lots of courses are available covering bronze casting, sculpture, clay, mixed-media painting and fresco work.

Timing & Length of Course: Courses are for two weeks but you can stay for longer or shorter periods; they run from June to October.

Destination: Tuscany (Italy).

Costs: Courses cost from £730 for two weeks, including half-board and lodging.

Eligibility: The minimum age is 16; you need to find out which courses are for beginners.

Scuola Orafa Ambrosiana

Via Tadino 30, 20124, Milan, Italy

☎ /fax 00 39 02-29405005

info@scuolaorafaambrosiana.com

www.scuolaorafaambrosiana.com

This is a famous goldsmith's school in the centre of Milan where students can learn the art of jewellery-making. Many courses are taught in English and beginners are welcome.

Types of Course: There are 12 different courses from jewellery design and necklace threading to all different levels of goldsmithing.

Timing & Length of Course: Courses last from six to 115 hours and run throughout the year. Some have specific start dates so see the website for details.

Destination: Milan (Italy).

Costs: Tuition only costs from £84 to £1190.

Eligibility: The minimum age is 15.

Verrocchio Arts Centre

119, Lynton Rd, Harrow, Middlesex HA2 9NJ

☎ 020 8869 1035

maureen.ruck@ukgateway.net

www.verrocchio.co.uk

Between Siena and Florence, this residential art school offers a range of fine-art courses with visiting tutors. All classes are taught in English.

Types of Course: There are 16 courses in painting and sculpture.

Timing & Length of Course: The two-week courses run fortnightly from mid-May to mid-September.

Destination: Tuscany (Italy).

Costs: Tuition and half-board accommodation costs from £780, flights are extra.

Eligibility: All welcome.

DRAMA
Year Out Drama Company

Stratford-upon-Avon College, the Willows North, Alcester Rd, Stratford-upon-Avon CV37 9QR

☎ 01789 266245

fax 01789 267524

yearoutdrama@Stratford.ac.uk

www.yearoutdrama.com

There are 24 places available each year at this college. It runs an intensive, broad-based drama course for gap-year students of all abilities. Subjects studied include acting, directing, script-writing, design, movement, music and costumes.

Types of Course: The year-out drama course.

Timing & Length of Course: The course runs for one year from September.

Destination: Stratford-upon-Avon (England).

Costs: The course costs from £4100, including all tuition, production costs and numerous theatre visits. You will be housed in halls of residence or flats at your own cost.

Eligibility: The minimum age is 18.

How to Apply: Application forms are processed year-round but it's best to give at least four months' notice. Successful candidates will then have an interview.

FASHION
Istituto di Moda Burgo

Piazza San Babila 5, 20122 Milan, Italy
☎ 00 39 02-3655 7600
fax 00 39 02-3655 7605
imb@imb.it
www.imb.it

This school of fashion and design has summer courses, shorter special courses for beginners and special courses for students with a degree in fashion. Lessons take place in Italian and English. You can preview the school on its website, thanks to the web cast.

Types of Course: Special courses include theatre costume, menswear, womenswear, childrenswear, underwear, wedding dresses, beachwear, pattern grading, jewellery, textile design, shoes, accessories and pattern making. There are summer courses in fashion design and pattern making.

Timing & Length of Course: Short special courses are from 50 to 80 hours and normal ones are between 300 and 450 hours. Summer courses range from 54 to 104 hours.

Destination: Milan (Italy).

Costs: Short special courses start at £312 and normal ones cost from £1375, tuition only. Summer courses cost from £562 and longer ones from £937. There is also an enrolment fee of £156.

Eligibility: The minimum age is 14. For some of the courses you need prior industry experience or a degree in fashion.

FILM
Film School

PO Box 27-044, Marion Sq, Wellington, New Zealand
☎ 00 64 4-380 1250

fax 00 64 4-939 2951
info@filmschool.org.nz
www.filmschool.org.nz

This school is rapidly gaining an excellent worldwide reputation – New Zealand is also a cheap place to study. There's one course designed to fast-track students for a working career in the screen-production industry, initially in a crew position.

Types of Course: A certificate course in introduction to film and television production.

Timing & Length of Course: The course is for 40 weeks and there are two intakes a year in February and July.

Destination: New Zealand.

Costs: The course costs from £7705, tuition only.

Eligibility: The minimum age is 18 and you'll have to apply for a student visa.

Freie Universität Berlin, International Summer University

Abteilung Aubenangelegenheiten, Kaiserwerther Strasse 16-18, D-14195 Berlin, Germany
☎ 00 49 30-83873 445
fax 00 49 30-83873 442
fusummer@fu-berlin.de
www.fu-berlin.de/summeruniversity

Types of Course: German cinema classics (taught in English).

Timing & Length of Course: The course runs for two days a week from mid-July to mid-August.

Destination: Berlin (Germany).

Costs: Tuition costs from £489 and there's a £70 application fee. Accommodation can be arranged for early bookers.

Eligibility: You must have completed at least one year of study at a university or college.

New York Film Academy

King's College, Drury Lane, London WC2B 5RL
☎ 020 7848 1523
fax 020 7848 1443
filmuk@nyfa.com
www.nyfa.com

This academy runs both long and short courses on film-making, acting for film, screen-writing, digital editing and digital filmmaking. These are very hands-on, practical courses.

Types of Course: Filmmaking.

Timing & Length of Course: Courses are from four weeks to one year. Short courses start every month and the year-long course starts four times a year.

Destinations: New York and Los Angeles, and other worldwide locations during the summer.

Costs: Four weeks' tuition (including equipment) costs from £1895, one year from £13,000. On top of this is the cost for film stock and processing.

Eligibility: The minimum age is 18.

How to Apply: Contact the London office or apply online. You'll need to get a student visa from the US embassy.

HISTORY OF ART & ARCHITECTURE
Art History Abroad

179C, New Kings Rd, London SW6 4SW
☎ 020 7731 2231
fax 020 7731 2456
info@arthistoryabroad.com
www.arthistoryabroad.com

Art History Abroad runs gap-year art-history trips to Italy, rather like a modern-day grand tour. There's up 24 students taught in small tutorials of eight in front of many of the masterpieces of European art.

Types of Course: Art history.

Timing & Length of Course: Six-week trips run once in spring, once early summer and once in autumn.

Destinations: Florence, Naples, Rome, Siena, Venice & Verona (you visit all of these).

Costs: The course costs from £5100, including tuition, flights, B&B accommodation, transport, museum entrance fees, basic Italian lessons, reading list and notes.

Eligibility: The minimum age is 18.

British Institute of Florence

Piazza Strozzi 2, 50123 Florence, Italy
☎ 00 39 055-2677 8200
fax 00 39 055-2677 8222
info@britishinstitute.it
www.britishinstitute.it

Established in 1917 to promote the cultures and language of Great Britain and Italy, the institute offers an extensive range of courses in Italian language, art history and Italian culture as well as teaching English to the local Italian population.

Types of Course: 'Living Italian' (three-month language course), history of art, life drawing, watercolour, Italian opera, cinema and film, Tuscan cooking and university credits available.

Timing & Length of Course: Courses are from two days to one year; most run monthly. There's a summer school in August.

Destinations: Florence & Massa Marittima near the Tuscan coast (Italy).

Costs: Tuition only costs from £63 for one week and from £206 for four weeks. Help is given to find and book accommodation. Students have the use of the library and free email and internet for the duration of their course.

Eligibility: The minimum age is 18.

John Hall Pre-University Course

12 Gainsborough Rd, Ipswich, Suffolk IP4 2UR
☎ 01473 251223
fax 01473 288009
info@johnhallpre-university.com
www.johnhallpre-university.com

Established in 1965, this company offers a course for gap-year students covering European civilisation, art history, architecture, music, literature, cinema, photography and life-drawing classes, with optional Italian-language courses. You also visit Ravenna and Padua, the villas and gardens outside of Venice and go to the opera. Thirty different lecturers are used during the course.

Types of Course: Pre-university course.

Timing & Length of Course: The course is from seven to nine weeks and starts at the end of January each year.

Destinations: One week is spent in London and six weeks in Venice, with an optional week in Florence and five days in Rome on top of that.

Costs: Seven weeks cost from £6100, including flights, half-board accommodation, lectures, visits, classes etc.

Eligibility: The minimum age is 18.

University of Sydney

Centre for Continuing Education (CCE), Locked Bag 20, Glebe, NSW 2037, Australia
☎ 00 61 2-9036 4789
fax 00 61 2-9036 4799
info@cce.usyd.edu.au
www.cce.usyd.edu.au

CCE is a not-for-profit centre of the University of Sydney. It runs 1200 non-accredited short courses per year covering a wide range of subjects.

Types of Course: History, culture (including Aboriginal art) and film with Australian and international themes.

Timing & Length of Course: There are four terms: summer, autumn, winter and spring (remember that summer in Australia means January to February). Courses vary in length from one day to 10 weeks (one session per week).

Destination: Sydney (Australia).
Costs: Tuition-only costs from £45.
Eligibility: The minimum age is 16.
How to Apply: Enrol online.

MUSIC & DANCE
Càlédöñiâ Languages Abroad
The Clockhouse, Bonnington Mill, 72 Newhaven Rd,
Edinburgh EH6 5QG
☎ 0131 621 7721/2
fax 0131 621 7723
courses@caledonialanguages.co.uk
www.caledonialanguages.co.uk
This company also offers a number of holidays with dance
instruction combined with a language element. It can also
fix up salsa lessons in Cuba any time of the year.
Types of Course: Salsa and Spanish language in Cuba,
flamenco or Sevillanas and Spanish language in Spain.
Timing & Length of Course: All courses run for between
two and four weeks. Cuba trips depart in spring, summer,
autumn, Christmas and New Year; the Spanish trips depart
in February, April, June, September and October.
Destinations: Santiago de Cuba and Havana (Cuba),
Vejer de la Frontera & Malaga (Spain).
Costs: A two-week course in Cuba costs from £725, including half-board accommodation, three evenings out to local
clubs, two cultural activities, a day trip, your dance tuition
and language course; flights are extra. A two-week Spanish
trip costs from £345, tuition only – everything else is extra.
Eligibility: The minimum age is 17.

David Hill
Calle del Pino, 17–11408, Jerez de la Frontera, Cadiz, Spain
☎ 00 34 956-34 09 74
bebitajoon@hotmail.com
www.geocities.com/jerezflamenco
David is an English-born flamenco guitar teacher based
full-time in Jerez. Classes at all levels are taught in English.
David can also put you in touch with flamenco dance
academies that will be open at the time you want to visit.
Types of Course: All forms of flamenco guitar.
Timing & Length of Course: You can have one lesson
or more year-round. If you're a beginner, 50 hours of tuition is advised to cover the basic forms.
Destination: Jerez de la Frontera (Spain).
Costs: Lessons cost from £15 per hour. There's a special
rate for more than 30 hours of tuition.
Eligibility: All welcome.

Kusun Study Tour to Ghana
c/o Jane Pentland, 8 Godfrey Ave, East St Kilda, Vic 3183,
Australia
☎ 00 61 3-9593 9598
fax 00 61 3-9225 4171
janepentland@xcel.net.au
www.ghanadrumschool.com
There are one or two study tours per year to the Kusun
Centre, in the village of Nungua, 15km from the capital
of Accra. It's an idyllic location, right on the ocean. The
courses are a combination of traditional drum, dance and
song taught by some of Ghana's finest musicians and
dancers. There are around 15 to 20 international students
on each study tour. Beginners welcome.
Types of Course: Four-week traditional Ghanaian drumming, dance and song.
Timing & Length of Course: Study tours last for four
weeks and there are one or two per year. They usually
depart in July/August and October/November.
Destination: Nungua village (Ghana).
Costs: The four-week course costs from £1360 for all tuition,
accommodation, meals, ground transport, special performances and demonstrations. Flights, visas, vaccinations etc
are extra.
Eligibility: None.

Susan French Belly Dancing Holidays
42 Sefton St, Putney, London SW15 1LZ
☎ 020 8789 4968
susandeniz@hotmail.com
www.bellydancingholidays.co.uk
Susan has been belly-dancing since 1992 and teaching
since 1997. She holds classes in Fulham, London. Two or
three times a year she takes groups abroad to teach.
Types of Course: Belly-dancing.
Timing & Length of Course: Trips abroad are for one to
two weeks and depart in May and October for Turkey.
Destinations: Marmaris & Istanbul (Turkey).
Costs: A one-week trip costs from £524, including tuition,
half-board accommodation, flights, transfers and a show.
Eligibility: All welcome.

Travellers Worldwide
7 Mulberry Close, Ferring, West Sussex BN12 5HY
☎ 01903 502595
fax 01903 500364
info@travellersworldwide.com
www.travellersworldwide.com

Travellers Worldwide runs two cultural courses where you learn to dance the tango and the salsa in Argentina. These are private lessons and so cater for all levels of experience.

Types of Course: Tango and salsa.

Timing & Length of Courses: Courses last from one month and can be arranged at anytime. Up to three months' notice is required.

Destination: Argentina.

Costs: One month costs from £995 including half-board accommodation, in-country support and backup and lessons. Extra months cost £295. International flights are extra.

Eligibility: All ages welcome. No experience required.

PHOTOGRAPHY
Steve Outram Travel Photography

D.Katsifarakis St, Galatas, Chania 73100, Crete, Greece

☎ /fax 00 30 2-8210 32220

mail@steveoutram.com

www.steveoutram.com

Steve is a British travel photographer living in Crete, supplying images to various agents and editorial clients. He runs three photography workshops and photo tours each year.

Type of Course: Travel photography that shows how to go behind the façade of a place and increase your visual awareness to give you more than just picture postcard type images on your travels.

Timing & Length of Course: The workshops/photo tours range from nine to 14 days and run in January, May and October.

Destinations: Lesvos (Greece), Western Crete (featuring Chania) & Zanzibar (Unesco World Heritage site of Stone Town).

Costs: Prices start from £1175 for nine days in Crete. This includes all tuition and B&B.

Eligibility: No minimum age. Beginners welcome but you must know how to work your camera.

Travellers Worldwide

7 Mulberry Close, Ferring, West Sussex BN12 5HY

☎ 01903 502595

fax 01903 500364

info@travellersworldwide.com

www.travellersworldwide.com

This gap-year organisation runs practical photography courses in Havana at the Institute of Superior Arts. It is advised that you need to speak some Spanish.

Types of course: Photography.

Timing & Length of Course: Courses last four, eight or 12 weeks. There are fixed start dates that change from year to year, so check with Travellers Worldwide. As the visas take a while to organise, apply at least three months in advance.

Destination: Cuba.

Costs: Four weeks cost from £1145 and 12 weeks from £1595. This includes only your course fees, accommodation and in-country support. All other costs are extra (eg international flights)

Eligibility: Minimum age 17, beginners welcome.

WRITING
The Arvon Foundation (National Administration Office)

2nd floor, 42a Buckingham Palace Rd, London SW1W 0RE

☎ 020 7931 7611

fax 020 7963 0961

london@arvonfoundation.org

www.arvonfoundation.org

Although these are all UK-based courses, this registered charity has some of the best writing courses you'll find. Courses cover writing for many genres, including poetry, fiction, stage drama and writing for TV and radio.

Types of Course: Over 30 different courses, from travel writing to song writing.

Timing & Length of Course: All courses are for 4½ days and run weekly between April and December.

Destinations: The Hurst (Shropshire), Lumb Bank (West Yorkshire), Moniack Mhor (Inverness-shire) & Totleigh Barton (Devon).

Costs: Courses cost from £455, including tuition, accommodation and food – some grants are available for those who cannot afford the fees.

Eligibility: The minimum age is 16.

How to Apply: Book through the centre that is running the course. All telephone details are online or in the brochure available from the national administration office.

Freie Universität Berlin, International Summer University

Abteilung Aubenangelegenheiten, Kaiserwerther Strasse 16-18, D-14195 Berlin, Germany

☎ 00 49 30-83873 445

fax 00 49 30-83873 442

fusummer@fu-berlin.de

www.fu-berlin.de/summeruniversity

Founded in 1948, the university runs an extensive summer-school program, with several courses conducted in English.

Types of Course: Creative writing: fiction and poetry workshops.

Timing & Length of Course: The course runs for two days a week from mid-July to mid-August.

Destination: Berlin.

Costs: Tuition costs from £489 and there's a £70 application fee. Accommodation can be arranged for early bookers.

Eligibility: Applicants must have completed at least one year of study at a university or college.

Skyros

92 Prince of Wales Rd, London NW5 3NE

☎ 020 7267 4424/020 7284 3065

fax 020 7284 3063

enquiries@skyros.com

www.skyros.com

Skyros is a specialist holistic holiday company offering courses that engage the mind, body and spirit. A variety of writing courses run nearly all year-round, often with well-known writers such as Steven Berkoff or Mavis Cheek. Skyros also runs courses on writing for theatre.

Types of Course: Anything from short story to theatre and screenplay writing.

Timing & Length of Course: Courses last from two weeks. A writing course runs at least every two weeks.

Destinations: Two centres on the island of Skyros (Greece) and one centre on the island of Koh Samed (Thailand).

Costs: Two weeks' tuition and half-board accommodation in Greece costs from £525; flights cost extra. Those under 25 get a 30% discount on the list price.

Eligibility: The minimum age is 15.

Alternative Health & Exercise

Karuna Yoga School

79 Clarendon Rd, Southampton SO16 4GD

☎ /fax 02380 773 987

paul.riddy@virgin.net

www.karunayoga.co.uk

The yoga school has a purpose-built house in Romania and has offered yoga lessons there for years. There's also a Lake District trip, which uses self-catering accommodation next to Lake Coniston, and a Spanish trip is being explored for 2005–06.

Types of Course: Yoga and walking (three to four hours of yoga per day).

Timing & Length of Course: Trips last one week and depart in June and August to Romania and in September to the Lake District (UK).

Destinations: Romania & Lake District (UK).

Costs: Trips cost from £320 for tuition and full-board accommodation. Flights are extra.

Eligibility: Minimum age 18.

Skyros

92 Prince of Wales Rd, London NW5 3NE

☎ 020-7267 4424/020 7284 3065

fax 020 7284 3063

enquiries@skyros.com

www.skyros.com

Skyros runs loads of 'alternative' lifestyle and curative courses.

Types of Course: Many types of yoga, reiki, massage, meditation, aromatherapy, reflexology, Tai Chi and a combination of several similar disciplines.

Timing & Length of Course: Two-week courses run at least every fortnight.

Destinations: There are two centres on the island of Skyros (Greece) and one on the island of Koh Samed (Thailand).

Costs: Two weeks costs from £525, including half-board accommodation, but not flights. Those under 25 get a 30% discount on the list price.

Eligibility: The minimum age is 15.

Tai Chi Chuan Center

Naisuan House, Room 201, 3/7 Doi Saket Kao (Rattanakosin), Soi 1, T.Watgate, A.Mung, Chiang Mai 50000, Thailand

☎ 00 66 017067406 (mobile)

keithtaichi@hotmail.com

www.taichithailand.com

There are morning, mid-day and evening practical sessions held here, combined with discussion on topics such as Tai Chi philosophy and theory, the I-Ching and the Tao Te Ching.

Types of Course: Intensive-training program on the essential postures of Tai Chi Chuan.

Timing & Length of Course: This is a 10-day course (60 hours) with year-round classes starting on the first and 16th of every month.

Destination: Chiang Mai (Thailand).

Costs: The program costs from £126, including accommodation (with hot shower) but no meals.

Eligibility: All welcome.

Sports & Outdoor Pursuits

Bear Creek Outdoor Centre

RR#3 Campbell's Bay, Québec J0X 1K0, Canada

☎ 00 1 819-453 2127 (summer)

info@bearcreekoutdoor.com
www.bearcreekoutdoor.com
Bear Creek is an outdoor centre in the Ottawa Valley, at the foothills of the Laurentian Mountains. Solar energy and gravity provide all electricity and running water. Courses are run in outdoor adventure leadership, with a bent towards watersports. There are over 10 different certificates you can gain during the course.

Types of Course: Gap-year program.

Timing & Length of Course: Courses last for 10 weeks from mid-June.

Destination: Canada.

Costs: Courses cost from £3700, including certification, full board and lodging, and all in-country transportation. Flights are extra.

Eligibility: The minimum age is 16. You must consider yourself in good health and be able to swim.

Gap Sports Academy

PO Box 1027, High Wycombe, Buckinghamshire HP13 7ZF
☎ 0870 837 9797
Fax 01494 76 9090
staff@gapsportsacademy.com
www.gapsports.com
If you're a budding rugby, cricket or golf player and fancy taking your game to the next level or want to gain international experience in your field then the Gap Sports Academy will send you to one of four different sports academies in South Africa to get professional training. Gap Sports Academy will also take beginning and intermediate scuba-divers.

Timing & Length of Course: All placements are from five to eight weeks. Departure dates are dependent on your program. Apply six to eight weeks before departure.

Destination: South Africa.

Costs: A five-week program starts at £1800 and the eight-week program from £2400. This covers all your costs except international flights and sports travel insurance.

Eligibility: Minimum age 18.

International Academy

St Hilary Court, Copthorne Way, Culverhouse Cross, Cardiff CF5 6ES
☎ 02920 672500
fax 02920 672510
info@theinternationalacademy.com
www.theinternationalacademy.com

The company runs quite a few courses, one of them is to become a mountain-bike instructor. There are free ride sessions, downhill sessions and orientation skills are also taught.

Types of Course: Mountain-bike instructor.

Timing & Length of Course: The course lasts five weeks and runs in June and July.

Destination: The Rocky Mountains (Canada).

Costs: The course costs from £4690 including flights, accommodation, food, transfers and examination fees.

Eligibility: The minimum age is 18. You need to be a fairly experienced mountain biker.

Killary Adventure

Leenane, Co Galway, Ireland
☎ 00 353 95 43411
fax 00 353 95 42314
mona@killary.com
www.killary.com
Killary is a family-based adventure centre in a remote but beautiful location. Their outdoor pursuits instructor course covers power boat level two, level two coach training (kayaking), canoe safety test (kayak), single pitch award training (rock climbing), high ropes site specific training, first aid, archery instruction and soft skills NVQ (the philosophy of being an instructor). At the end of your course you try out your skills abroad, either in Spain or Venezuela.

Types of Course: Outdoor pursuits instructor.

Timing & Length of Course: The course lasts for 14 weeks and runs twice a year (October and January). There's then an option for a further two weeks of work experience at no extra charge.

Destinations: Ireland & Spain or Venezuela.

Costs: Fourteen weeks cost from £3800 including accommodation, food, kit, in-country travel and Spanish holiday (if you go to Venezuela it might be more expensive). Travel insurance and flights to Ireland are extra.

Eligibility: Minimum age 18. Suitable for anyone with a keen interest in outdoor pursuits or someone who wants to get a job as an instructor.

Leconfield Jackaroo & Jillaroo School

Kootingal, NSW 2352, Australia
☎ /fax 00 61 2-6769 4230
jillaroojackaro@austarnet.com.au
www.leconfieldjackaroo.com
This school is a good 40-minute drive from the nearest shop, and students are taught from beginner level in

groups of 20 on the working property. Beginner horse-riders are welcome.

Types of Course: Jackaroo and jillaroo courses (cowboys and cowgirls).

Timing & Length of Course: Courses last 11 days and run about twice a month.

Destination: New South Wales (Australia).

Costs: Courses cost from £351, including full board and lodging.

Eligibility: Minimum age is 16.

Plas y Brenin

Capel Curig, Conwy LL24 0ET, Wales

☎ 01690 720214

fax 01690 720394

info@pyb.co.uk

www.pyb.co.uk

Plas y Brenin is a national mountaineering centre based in Snowdonia. A former hotel, the accommodation is excellent for residential courses. Many of the courses listed here can be condensed into a four-month fast-track instructor scheme.

Types of Course: Summer and winter mountain leadership certificate, single pitch award (rock climbing), European mountain leader award, mountain instructor award, mountain instructor certificate, British orienteering instructor award, rescue and emergency care (REC) mountain first aid award, REC high altitude first aid award, kayaking and canoeing qualifications: three-, four- and five-star award, level one to level five coach award (kayaking and canoeing), white-water safety and rescue.

Timing & Length of Course: From one weekend to four months, year-round.

Destinations: Summer courses take place in North Wales, winter courses in North Wales, Scotland and the Alps.

Costs: A weekend course costs from £140. The four-month fast-track instructor scheme, which costs from £8000, includes board and lodging, equipment and instruction.

Eligibility: The minimum age is 16. Each course has its own prerequisites, which are listed on the website.

Diving

Dive Centre Manly

10 Belgrave St, Manly, NSW 2095, Australia

☎ 00 61 2-9977 4355

fax 00 61 2-9977 3664

dcm@divesydney.com.au

www.divesydney.com

This is a PADI 5-star IDC (instructor development courses) centre offering courses for beginners through to instructor/dive-master training programs and shark dives. There's also a school in Bondi.

Types of Course: PADI open water diver course for beginners.

Timing & Length of Course: The full-time course takes place over four to five days and starts every Monday. Part-time courses start every Saturday and run over two weekends.

Destinations: Qualifying dives take place at Shelly Beach, Little Manly, Fairy Bower & Fairlight in Australia.

Costs: Tuition and all equipment costs from £145. A diving medical costs an extra £20.

Eligibility: The minimum age is 12. You must be able to swim for 200m and tread water for at least 10 minutes.

International Academy

St Hilary Court, Copthorne Way, Culverhouse Cross, Cardiff CF5 6ES

☎ 02920 672500

fax 02920 672510

info@theinternationalacademy.com

www.theinternationalacademy.com

This company runs two professional PADI diving courses designed to develop your leadership abilities and expand your knowledge to a professional level.

Types of Course: PADI dive master and PADI assistant instructor.

Timing & Length of Course: Courses are from five to six weeks with departures in March, July and October.

Destinations: The Seychelles.

Costs: The PADI dive master course costs from £5290 and the PADI assistant instructor course from £5990. This includes flights, accommodation, food, dive equipment and examination fees.

Eligibility: The minimum age is 18. Beginners welcome.

London Scuba Diving School

Rabys Barn, New Chapel Rd, Lingfield, Surrey RH7 6LE

☎ 07000 272822

fax 07000 348385

info@londonscuba.com

www.londonscuba.com

Based in London and Surrey, this PADI-registered dive school offers the full range of PADI courses. This includes the open water diver course with two days pool and theory with qualifying dives in the UK, Italy and the Red Sea.

Types of Course: PADI open water diver course for beginners to instructor.

Timing & Length of Course: The initial course runs for one or two days and there are courses midweek and every weekend.
Destinations: Europe, UK & worldwide.
Costs: The course costs from £99 and trips from £200 to £1000, including flights, transfers and B&B.
Eligibility: The minimum age is 10. You must be able to both swim 200m and tread water for 10 minutes. There's also a medical form to complete.

Watersports, Sailing & Crewing

Acorn Adventure
Acorn House, 22 Worcester St, Stourbridge, West Midlands DY8 1AN
☎ 01384 378827
fax 01384 378866
inquiries@acornadventure.co.uk
www.acornadventure.co.uk
Acorn has 10 centres in Europe offering training in all watersports, plus national governing body instructor qualifications and all levels within the dinghy scheme.
Types of Course: There are 14 watersports and dinghy sailing courses leading to nationally-recognised certification.
Timing & Length of Course: Courses are for one day to one week from April to September and start daily.
Destinations: France, Italy, Spain & the UK.
Costs: Courses cost from £50 to £400, including board and lodging but excluding flights.
Eligibility: The minimum age is 16 or 18, depending on the course.

Aussie Surf Adventures
PO Box 53, Pacific Palms, NSW 2428, Australia
☎ 00 61 2-4497 6113
surfadventurers@hotmail.com
www.surfadventures.com.au
Three Aussie mates, Kim, Nat and Dan, will take you on a five-day east coast adventure from Sydney to Byron Bay. They reckon they've got the best jobs in the world.
Types of Course: Learn to surf.
Timing & Length of course: Five-day surf trips run each week throughout the year.
Destinations: Surf beaches from Sydney to Byron Bay.
Costs: The trip costs from £249, including all meals, surf tuition, four nights' accommodation in beach cabins, equipment and transport.

Eligibility: None.
How to Book: Their agent in the UK is STA Travel.

Flying Fish
25 Union Rd, Cowes, Isle of Wight PO31 7TW
☎ 01983 280641
fax 01983 281821
mail@flyingfishonline.com
www.flyingfishonline.com
This company is a training provider for watersports and snow sports staff and arranges employment for sailors, dive, surf, kite surf, windsurf, snowboard and ski instructors, once qualified. Much of the training takes place abroad. Students are automatically registered for the Flying Fish careers advice and job placement service and gappers can take advantage of the company's 'three year plan' where you acquire qualifications that lead to jobs for your gap year and three years of future university vacations.
Types of Course: There are 65 different courses leading to professional qualifications as an action sports instructor or yacht skipper; some courses are for beginners, others require previous experience.
Timing & Length of Course: Most courses start eight times a year and last from two weeks to four months, depending on the course.
Destinations: Sydney (Australia), Whistler (Canada), Pissouri (Cyprus), Dahab (Egypt), Vassiliki (Greece) & Cowes (UK).
Costs: Courses cost from £1450 for two weeks to £11,740 for four months, including flights and accommodation.
Eligibility: The minimum age is 18.

International Academy
St Hilary Court, Copthorne Way, Culverhouse Cross, Cardiff CF5 6ES
☎ 02920 672500
fax 02920 672510
info@theinternationalacademy.com
www.theinternationalacademy.com
This company offers a number of courses, one of them is in white-water rafting. You practice on some of the best-known rivers in British Columbia's white-water playground.
Types of Course: White-water rafting course (swift-water rescue technician).
Timing & Length of Course: The course lasts for five weeks and runs in May each year.
Destination: Canada.

Costs: The course costs from £4600 including flights, accommodation, food, equipment, transfers and examination fees.
Eligibility: The minimum age is 18. No experience necessary.

Jubilee Sailing Trust

Hazel Rd, Woolston, Southampton, Hampshire SO19 7GB
☎ 0870 443 5781
fax 0870 443 5782
youth@jst.org.uk
www.jst.org.uk
Jubilee is a registered charity for able-bodied and disabled young people to crew a tall ship together. You can take part in the youth leadership at sea scheme. This could lead to sailing as bosun's mate or watch-leader on future voyages, either free of charge or at discounted rates.
Types of Course: Youth leadership at sea and informal sail training.
Timing & Length of Course: Courses are from five days to four weeks; a ship sets sail each week.
Destinations: The Mediterranean, Canary Islands and Caribbean in winter, and around the UK and wherever the tall ships race is held in summer.
Costs: Courses cost from £195 for five days and from £1600 for four weeks (you get a £300 discount for doing the youth leadership scheme).
Eligibility: The minimum age is 16.

Lymington Cruising School

24 Waterloo Rd, Lymington, Hampshire SO41 9DB
☎ 01590 677478
fax 01590 689210
lymingtoncruisin@aol.com
www.lymingtoncruising.co.uk
This Royal Yachting Association (RYA) training centre on the River Lym offers the whole range of RYA national cruising scheme courses, both shore-based and practical.
Types of Course: Competent crew practical course.
Timing & Length of Course: The course is for five days and runs weekly between March and October.
Destinations: From Lymington to the Solent & Poole.
Costs: Courses cost from £400 for five days, including board (on the boat), lodging, insurance and wet-weather gear.
Eligibility: The minimum age is 18.

Neilson Active Holidays

Locks View, Brighton Marina, Brighton, East Sussex BN2 5HA
☎ 0870 909 9099
fax 0870 909 9089
sales@neilson.com
www.neilson.com
Neilson is a holiday company offering RYA-recognised courses in windsurfing, yachting and dinghy sailing, plus PADI diving courses.
Types of Course: RYA levels one to four for windsurfing, levels one to three for dinghy sailing, levels one and two for keel boats.
Timing & Length of Course: Courses are from one to two weeks, or longer if required.
Destinations: The Caribbean, Croatia, Egypt, Greece, Spain & Turkey.
Costs: One week costs from £429, including flights, half-board accommodation and tuition.
Eligibility: The minimum age is 18.

Solent School of Yachting

Hamble Point Marina, School Lane, Hamble, Southampton, Hampshire SO31 4NB
☎ 023 8045 7733
fax 023 8045 6744
solent@boss-sail.co.uk
www.boss-sail.co.uk
A RYA-recognised sailing school on the River Hamble offering courses from competent crew through to ocean master. There's also an innovative fastrak course for keen sailors with 200 sea miles already logged.
Types of Course: Fastrak to yachtmaster.
Timing & Length of Course: The course lasts for 18 weeks and runs three times a year (usually January, May and August).
Destinations: From the Solent (UK) south coast to France, Spain & Ireland.
Costs: Fastrak costs from £8500 including board, lodging and mooring fees. There are also five-day competent crew courses from £510 including board and lodging.
Eligibility: Applicants for fastrak must be 18 years or over and have at least 200 sea miles already logged. Minimum age for competent crew is 16 and beginners are welcome.

Sunsail

The Port House, Port Solent, Portsmouth, Hampshire PO6 4TH
☎ 023 9222 2222
fax 023 9221 9827
sales@sunsail.com
www.sunsail.com

Sunsail is a holiday company that specialises in watersport activities and yacht charter. A number of sailing courses run for beginners to advanced students.

Types of Course: RYA competent crew, day skipper (shore-based and practical), yachtmaster (shore-based and practical) and coastal skipper (shore-based and practical).

Timing & Length of Course: Courses are from two to five days, throughout the year on demand.

Destinations: Australia, the Canaries, Malaysia, Thailand, the UK & the USA.

Costs: Courses cost from £350 for five days half-board (living aboard the boat) and tuition.

Eligibility: The minimum age is 18.

Tall Ships Youth Trust

2a the Hard, Portsmouth, Hampshire PO1 3PT
☎ 023 9283 2055
fax 023 9281 5769
info@tallships.org
www.tallships.org

This registered charity runs various sailing courses while at sea on the tall ships. You can move from being voyage crew to becoming volunteer crew and to sailing around the world for long periods of time for a nominal fee.

Types of Course: Competent crew practical course, Duke of Edinburgh gold award scheme (residential section), tall ships recommendation award.

Timing & Length of Course: Courses last from seven to 14 days.

Destinations: the Caribbean & Europe (including the Canaries).

Costs: Courses cost from £499 for seven days, including board, lodging and a berth. Some funding is available for people aged between 16 and 25 if needed.

Eligibility: You must be aged between 16 and 25, although there are some adult voyages that young people can join too.

How to Apply: Ring the office. If you're looking for funding there's an interview process.

Wildwind Holidays

2a Star St, Ware, Hertfordshire SG12 7AA
☎ 01920 484516
fax 01920 484704
wildwind@dial.pipex.com
www.wildwind.co.uk

Wildwind is a holiday company specialising in high-performance catamaran and dinghy sailing courses. It is a recognised RYA teaching establishment offering courses up to level five.

Types of Course: Fourteen courses from level one to five.

Timing & Length of Course: Courses last from two days to two weeks and run from May to October.

Destination: Vassiliki (Greece).

Costs: Courses cost from £399, including flights and accommodation.

Eligibility: The minimum age is 18.

Skiing & Snowboarding Instructor Courses

Basecamp Group

30 Baseline Business Studios, Whitchurch Rd, London W11 4AT
☎ /fax 020 7243 6222
contact@basecampgroup.com
www.basecampgroup.com

Basecamp runs a wide variety of courses that give you the chance to develop your all-round skiing and snowboarding abilities while learning to become an instructor. The courses can include racing, off-piste and freestyle training, work experience, first aid, avalanche/mountain awareness and French classes.

Types of Course: Ski and Snowboard instructor courses.

Timing & Length of Course: The courses last from four to 11 weeks and run all year (somewhere in the world).

Destination: Canada, France & New Zealand.

Costs: A four-week course costs from £2695 and an 11-week course from £5545, including tuition, accommodation and transfers but excluding flights.

Eligibility: The minimum age is 17.

British Association of Snow Sport Instructors (BASI)

Glenmore, Aviemore, Inverness-shire PH22 1QU
☎ 01479 861717
fax 01479 861 718
gap@basi.org.uk
www.basi.org.uk

BASI is the training and grading agency for all snowsport instructors in the UK on snow (ie real snow, not artificial slopes). BASI has a dedicated gap-year adviser who can advise on all aspects of your gap-year course and your options. The direct line for the gap-year advisor is ☎ 01479 861409.

Types of Course: Ski or snowboard instructor qualifications.

Timing & Length of Course: Ten-week courses start in January, June and December.

Destinations: Andorra, France, Italy, New Zealand, Switzerland & the USA.

Costs: Courses cost from £5500, including half-board accommodation, flights, transfers and training fees. You need to get your own travel insurance and bring your own equipment.

Eligibility: The minimum age is 17.

Gap Snow Sports

PO Box 1027, High Wycombe, Buckinghamshire HP13 7ZF
☎ 0870 837 9797
fax 01494 76 9090
team@gapsnowsports.com
www.gapsports.com

This company runs courses to become a snowboard or ski instructor and gain international qualifications. There are courses for beginners and intermediates. You also have French lessons and learn about mountain first aid, avalanche awareness, ski and snowboard maintenance, chef and bar training. There are also cultural trips to Montreal, Quebec City and Ottawa.

Timing & Length of Course: Departures are in January and the course lasts six or ten weeks. Apply six to eight weeks before travel.

Destination: Canada.

Costs: The six-week program costs from £3480 and the 10-week one from £5580 (including Canadian tax). This covers all your costs except international flights, snowsports equipment and winter sports insurance.

Eligibility: Minimum age 18.

International Academy

St Hilary Court, Copthorne Way, Culverhouse Cross, Cardiff CF5 6ES
☎ 02920 672500
fax 02920 672510
info@theinternationalacademy.com
www.theinternationalacademy.com

This company provides professional instructor training courses mainly in skiing and snowboarding. The national governing body of the country in which you train awards qualifications.

Types of Course: Snowboard instructor and skiing instructor courses.

Timing & Length of Course: Courses are from four weeks to 12 weeks in January, March and July.

Destinations: Canada, New Zealand, South America & the USA.

Costs: Courses cost from £4500 for four weeks, including flights, accommodation, food, tuition and examination fees.

Eligibility: The minimum age is 16. Applicants need to have some snow experience, but all levels can be catered for.

Peak Leaders

Mansfield, Strathmiglo, Fife KY14 7QE, Scotland
☎ 01337 860 079
fax 01337 868176
info@peakleaders.com
www.peakleaders.com

Peak Leaders offers gap-year and time-out programs in skiing and snowboarding, including mountain safety, avalanche awareness, first aid, skidoo driving, leadership and management skills. After your A-Levels you can get qualified as a ski or snowboard instructor in the southern hemisphere and Peak Leaders will then help you find employment during the winter of your gap year (typically in Canada or Europe).

Types of Course: Ski/snowboard instructor course.

Timing & Length of Course: Courses run for nine weeks and start in January and July. There are four courses per year.

Destinations: Argentina with a module in Chile, Whistler and Banff/Nakiska (Canada) & Queenstown (New Zealand).

Costs: Courses cost from £5850, including accommodation and flights. Equipment and travel insurance and some certification is extra.

Eligibility: The minimum age is 18.

Ski Le Gap

220 Chemin Wheeler St, Mont-Tremblant, Québec J8E 1V3, Canada
☎ 0800 328 0345
fax 00 1 819 425 7074
info@skilegap.com
www.skilegap.com

Catering particularly to British gap-year students, this school runs two instructor courses. Ski Le Gap can also help you get work visas and jobs after the courses.

Types of Course: CSIA (Canadian Ski Instructor's Association) ski and CASI (Canadian Association of Snowboard Instructors) snowboard instructor courses.

Timing & Length of Course: There's a four-week course and a three-month course. The four-week one runs from late November to late December and the three-month course from the beginning of January to mid-March.

Destination: Mont Tremblant resort, Québec (Canada).

Costs: Courses cost from £2600 for four weeks, including half-board accommodation but excluding flights. The

three-month course is from £6000, including half-board accommodation, flights, French lessons, first-aid course, city trips and an outdoor experience weekend.
Eligibility: The minimum age is 18. Intermediate level is needed for the four-week course but beginners can do the three-month one.

First Aid, Medical & Gap-year Safety

Planet Wise
10 Swan St, Eynsham, Oxford OX29 4HU
☎ 0870 200 0220
fax 01865-884213
info@planetwise.net
www.planetwise.net
This company offers one- and three-day courses for independent travellers and gap-year students about to undertake their big trip. Topics covered include first aid, safety advise, what to pack and how to get the best out of your trip.
Types of Course: Gap-year safety and awareness courses.
Timing & Length of Course: There's a one- or three-day course. Courses run weekly during the summer and fortnightly during the winter
Destinations: Oxford, Yorkshire & the south coast of England.
Costs: The one-day course costs from £160 and the three-day course from £445, including food, accommodation and first-aid certificate.
Eligibility: Minimum age 17.

Wilderness Medical Training
The Coach House, Thorney Bank, Skelsmergh, Kendal, Cumbria LA8 9AW
☎ /fax 01539 823183
info@wildernessmedicaltraining.co.uk
www.wildernessmedicaltraining.co.uk
This company is the longest established provider of expedition medical training in the UK for lay people and doctors. There are two levels of courses for the gap-year student. These are called far from help, which covers all medical conditions and use of drugs, and the advance medicine for remote foreign travel also covers suturing and IV cannulation covers.
Types of Course: Far from help and advance medicine for remote foreign travel.
Timing & Length of Course: Far from help is two or three days and runs three times per year (spring, autumn

and winter). Advanced medicine for remote foreign travel lasts five days and runs twice per year (spring and winter).
Destination: A number of destinations in England, ring for more details.
Costs: Far from help costs from £176, tuition-only. The advanced medicine for remote foreign travel costs from £500 including full-board accommodation.
Eligibility: All welcome. All courses are intensive and practical.

Conservation & Park Rangering

Frontier
50–52 Rivington St, London EC2A 3QP
☎ 020 7613 2422
fax 020 7613 2992
info@frontier.ac.uk
www.frontier.ac.uk
Frontier is an international conservation organisation that runs environmental-research expeditions for self-funding volunteers. The training you'll receive in the field can qualify you for two BTEC (Business Training and Education Council) awards.
Types of Course: BTEC advanced diploma in tropical habitat, conservation and/or BTEC certificate in expedition management (biodiversity research).
Timing & Length of Course: Expeditions run for four, eight, 10 and 20 weeks; they depart four times per year (January, April, July and October).
Destinations: Cambodia, Madagascar, Nicaragua & Tanzania.
Costs: Expeditions cost from £1220 for four weeks, £2100 for 10 weeks and £3400 for 20 weeks, including full board, lodging and all in-country costs; flights and the cost of BTEC assessment (£250) are extra.
Eligibility: The minimum age is 17.

International Academy
St Hilary Court, Copthorne Way, Culverhouse Cross, Cardiff CF5 6ES
☎ 02920 672500
fax 02920 672510
info@theinternationalacademy.com
www.theinternationalacademy.com
This company provides a number of courses, one of them is to become a qualified park ranger. Among other things you will learn conservation and wildlife management, animal and plant identification, spoor identification and tracking skills.

Types of Course: Park ranger.
Timing & Length of Course: The course lasts for 12 weeks and there are departure dates throughout the year.
Destination: South Africa.
Costs: The course costs from £4490 including flights, accommodation, food, uniforms, equipment and transfers and examination fees.
Eligibility: The minimum age is 18. No experience necessary.

Global Vision International (GVI)
Amwell Farm House, Nomansland, Wheathampstead, St Albans AL4 8EJ
☎ 0870 6088898
fax 01582 834002
info@gvi.co.uk
www.gvi.co.uk
GV runs expeditions and community projects in conjunction with registered charities worldwide. It also runs two courses. The shorter one will give you a taster of what it's like to be a professional field guide in one of South Africa's big game reserves. The longer one will train you up completely to become a fully-qualified FGASA (Field Guide's Association of South Africa) field guide and combines six months of study with a six-month placement in a game lodge. Topics cover ecology, botany, taxonomy, tracking, identification, weapons handling and bush driving.
Types of Course: Four-week safari field guide course and the one-year safari field guide course.
Timing & Length of Course: The short course lasts for four weeks and runs throughout the year, the one-year course runs in January and July.
Destination: Limpopo Province (South Africa).
Costs: The four-week course costs from £1275, including full board and lodging, transfers and project equipment, but excluding flights. The one-year course costs £3725, all-inclusive except flights.
Eligibility: The minimum age is 18 and applicants must have a driving licence.

Miscellaneous

Circus Oz
40 Bay St, Port Melbourne, Victoria 3207, Australia
☎ 00 61 3-9646 8899
fax 00 61 3-9646 9334
classes@circusoz.com.au
www.circusoz.com.au
This celebrated Australian circus has been going since 1978 and offers a series of workshops and courses for beginners or professionals.
Types of Course: Tumbling, aerials, hula hoops, acro-balance, juggling/manipulation, handstands, Chinese pole, clowning and flying trapeze (courses on offer may vary from term to term).
Timing & Length of Course: Most courses last for a school term, although some shorter courses are available. Circus Oz asks that you inquire about specific dates and course lengths when you apply.
Destination: Melbourne (Australia).
Costs: Tuition costs from £45 to £155.
How to Apply: Download the application form from the website.

Dennis Trott Alpine Flying Centre
799 route de la Grangeat, 74700 Domancy, France
☎ 00 33 450 54 59 63
fax 00 33 450 54 48 52
info@flyers-lodge.com
www.flyers-lodge.com
Close to the Chamonix Valley in the French Alps, this flying school offers paragliding for beginners, intermediate and advanced, plus thermalling and cross-country courses. The beginners course is an excellent introduction to paragliding flight and the new pilot will experience two to three hours of solo air-time whilst under supervision. The majority of new pilots require around three weeks of training before they feel confident to fly without supervision.
Types of Course: Paragliding – beginner to advanced. At the end of the beginners' course all successful students are awarded the internationally recognised French level 1, basic licence/log book. This licence can be taken to your own country and converted to the local basic licence.
Timing & Length of Course: The five-day beginners' paragliding course starts every Monday morning from early April to late September.
Destination: French Alps.
Costs: The beginners course costs between £279 and £308, depending on the time of year. This includes all tuition and all equipment. Accommodation is extra but B&B is available at the school's chalet at around £24 to £32 per person per double room.
Eligibility: Minimum age 14 and basically fit. For the training program insurance you need a doctor's letter stating that you are fit. This letter can be obtained in France.

Peter Kirk Memorial Scholarships

c/o Mrs Angela Pearson, 17 St Paul's Rise, Addingham,
Ilkley LS29 0QD
mail@kirkfund.org.uk
www.kirkfund.org.uk
Each year-round 10 scholarships of up to £1500 are
available to students who wish to live and study abroad
(usually in Europe) and undertake a project that increases
their understanding of modern Europe.

Types of Course: The project is up to you but examples
of recent ones include the Italian film industry, puppetry in
Spain and Middle-Easternisation in Berlin.

Timing & Length of Course: Study lasts from six weeks
to three months and takes place once a year.

Destinations: At least one country needs to be in Europe.

Costs: Students have to meet all costs in excess of the
scholarship amount.

Eligibility: Applicants must be citizens of a European
country and aged between 18 and 27.

How to Apply: You cannot ring or fax the office; visit
the website to download an application form. You'll have
to give a project outline. Candidates called for interview
have to bring a budget and an itinerary. The deadline for
applications is mid-February each year.

Wallace School of Transport

Unit 5a, Pop-in Building, South Way, Wembley, Middlesex
HA9 0HF
☎ 0845 602 9498
fax 020 8903 1376
info@wallaceschool.co.uk
www.wallaceschool.co.uk
Wallace is one of only seven DSA (Driving Standards
Agency) accredited training centres in the UK. An associate
company is Drivers on Demand, an employment agency,
meaning you can start earning money with your new
qualifications immediately.

Types of Course: All groups of Large Goods Vehicle
(LGV/HGV) and Passenger Carrying Vehicle (PCV) licences.

Timing & Length of Course: An intensive course takes
around five to eight days, depending on your experience and aptitude. You can start any day of the week by
arrangement.

Destination: Sunny Wembley, London.

Costs: It costs from £600 per licence. There's an assessment lesson costing £30 for training advice and a course
quotation.

Eligibility: The minimum age is 18 and you'll need a full
UK car licence.

GAPPER ITINERARIES

Name: Molly Bird
Age: 18/19
Favourite Country: India!!!!!!!!!!!!!

My Gap Year: During the first six months of my gap year I trained and worked as a cook in a small catering company. I had a really great time. I learnt a lot, laughed a lot and got to see London life, as opposed to school life. I also earned the money I needed for the big trip. My friend Jess and I travelled to India, Nepal, Vietnam, Singapore, Australia, New Zealand and Fiji in six months. I was absolutely intoxicated by India. It's so different, so beautiful, so smelly, so exciting, so never-on-time and absolutely bursting with life at every seam. I got so much from our 4½ months there and I'm desperate to go back. With a small charity I taught English in a primary school in a remote village in the foothills of the Himalaya. I lived with a family and we had no electricity, modest water facilities and there were no other Westerners in the village. Teaching was an experience which far exceeded my expectations. The three months whizzed by in a flurry of games, picnics, lessons, songs, homework and laughter. I found teaching much more rewarding than travelling. When you're living and working in a place you cease to be a tourist and that's when it really gets interesting. I absolutely loved India and the volunteering I did there.

Top Gap-Year Tip: Working and travelling are two different experiences; don't miss either.

Name: Jonathan Williams
Age: 18
Favourite Country: Fiji, in particular the islands of Taveuni, Tavewa and Ovalau.

My Gap Year: I decided to plan my year out so that I would be able to do a little bit of everything I wanted to do, rather than one particular activity in great depth. I began the year by setting off on a world trip immediately after receiving my exam results from school. My first stop was Fiji, where I taught in a primary and secondary school for four months. As it was my first international trip alone, I decided to go with an organisation who would offer the support unavailable to independent travellers during any arising emergencies. My eye-opening experience in Fiji was absolutely amazing, and I would recommend volunteering to anybody, particularly in a country where life is so different to that in the Western world. After Fiji, I joined the 'backpacker route', visiting the Cook Islands, New Zealand, Australia and Singapore over a two-month period. When I arrived back in the UK, I got a job working for a member of parliament at the House of Commons. The six months I spent in Westminster gave me a fascinating insight into the world of politics – which I later went on to study to degree-level at the University of Birmingham.

Top Gap-Year Tip: Make sure that you don't waste your gap year – have something planned from the beginning to the end. This will prevent you getting bored and consequently wishing that you hadn't taken a year out in the first place.

Name: Sarah Collinson
Age: 18
Favourite Country: Chile
My Gap Year: Once I had finished school I started work both as a waitress and doing temporary office work over the summer. In November I left to go to Peru with 10 others through the company VentureCo. Once we had arrived we spent a week travelling down from Lima to Cusco. Once in Cusco we lived with Peruvian families. During the week went to Spanish language school, while on the weekends we did mini-expeditions in the surrounding area. At the beginning of December we left for our aid project. We spent a couple of weeks living in tents while we finished building a community house. We then walked to our next aid project; an ecological survey on the endangered *polylepis* trees. The next two months of the group trip was spent travelling, sightseeing and trekking down through Bolivia, Chile and Argentina. One of the most challenging aspects of this was having to take it in turns to 'lead' the group. This meant that it was up to us where we stayed, how we got there and what we did when we were there. This gave us invaluable experience for when we were travelling by ourselves. Along the way many of us decided to change our flights and stay in South America longer. Once we had finished the group trip I travelled back up through Argentina, Brazil and then back to Buenos Aires via Uruguay with a couple of others from the group. I returned to the UK in April, and since then have been working so that I have money to go away again during university.

Top Gap-Year Tip: Never miss out on any experience offered to you.

Name: Damien Rickwood
Age: 18
Favourite Country: Belize – there is something for everyone here.
My Gap Year: Six months spent working in my mind-numbing local supermarket seemed like a distant memory when I eventually reached the exotic lands of Belize, Guatemala and Honduras on my Trekforce expedition. I soon realised that shelf-stacking was a justifiable means to realising the adventure of my dreams.

Here are some my indescribable experiences and accomplishments: jungle survival training, built a ranger station, logged an insane number of plants, trekked for weeks through dense jungle, acquired a Latin American Spanish accent, observed the best

Semana Santa celebrations in Central America, watched the sunrise from an ancient Mayan temple, been integrated into a remote indigenous community, spent four months washing in rivers, tried my hand at teaching, plunged through countless waterfalls, experienced many unforgettable parties, dived a coral reef, climbed an active volcano, explored the depths of bustling markets, spent days travelling in rickety buses, ate an unhealthy amount of tortillas and made some brilliant friends. I don't think there is a single word that could sum up my roller-coaster ride of senses and emotions.

Top Gap-Year Tip: Spending a lot of your time in the same country or area gives you a real insight into the culture and allows you to become part of the community.

Name: Amanda Akass
Age: 19
Favourite Country: Bolivia
My Gap Year: I spent the first six months of my gap year in a variety of non-exciting temping jobs, including five months in a city bank. I left for South America in March with a group from Quest Overseas, a gap-year organisation. We spent a month studying Spanish in the beautiful city of Sucre in Bolivia, which was invaluable, and then a month working in the jungle for a conservation charity called Inti Wara Yassi. As well as learning to be dab hands at cement mixing, we also looked after parrots, monkeys and jaguars in the charity's care. I spent two weeks walking through the jungle and swimming in rivers with a three-month-old puma, too tame to be released into the wild. We then travelled up through Peru and Bolivia, trekked in the mountains, explored ancient ruins and partied on beaches! After finishing my three months with Quest at Machu Picchu, I travelled on to Chile, Argentina and Brazil with friends from the group. On returning home, I volunteered at some youth camps, dazzled my poor family with my Spanish skills and dramatic anecdotes and went back to work for a bank to save up for university.

Top Gap-Year Tip: Don't worry if none of your friends are having gap years, I can guarantee you'll make friends for life travelling!

Name: Kate Wilkinson
Age: 19
Favourite Country: Ghana – the people are so friendly and the country is so unlike anywhere I have ever been before.
My Gap Year: I worked for most of the year in a geriatric ward, knowing that every moment I spent there was paying for three months of freedom. I started planning where to go and budgeting early on in the year, to maximise the amount of money that I could save for travelling. In April I left England and went to Cuba to learn Spanish for a month with a host family. That

was an awesome experience as the country was so different from capitalist Western Europe. After, I travelled around Costa Rica, which was more for fun than for experiencing anything different – it's pretty much Westernised. I moved on to the USA next and used the Greyhound bus to get up to Vancouver, where I saw old friends and revisited old places I used to go when I lived there. My gap year was for learning something new, and returning to some places I hadn't been for years. By working hard for six months, I could do that and it left me with a huge wealth of experience to take to university.

Top Gap-Year Tip: Keep your money in your bra. You know where it is and if someone is going for it!

Name: Phil Vintin
Age: 27
Favourite Country: New Zealand
My Gap Year: I travelled with my girlfriend for eight months in Australia, two months in Southeast Asia and two months in New Zealand. Most of this was pure laziness, beer-drinking and sight-seeing, but it did involve two months of actual working in Sydney. The work in Sydney was cold calling over the phone, trying to sell people credit card insurance. Although dull, it was a great way to meet fellow backpackers and earn a bit of extra cash.

Top Gap-Year Tip: If I was to do the whole thing again, I would have taken much more cash with me and done the work as early in the trip as possible – I met some great people and you never know when you might need a floor to sleep on.

Name: Graham MacPherson
Age: 25
Favourite Country: Botswana
My Gap Year: I spent a year teaching in a primary school in the southern suburbs of Cape Town, South Africa. My main duties were as a boarding house master and rugby coach and I also taught Maths and English to small groups of two or three to help with extra lessons. The rest of the work was completely varied: I drove school teams around, went as a supervisor on canoeing trips on the Orange River, played a hairy Ishmaelite in the school play *Joseph and his Technicolour Dreamcoat*. It was never boring, not always easy but very worth it.

Top Gap-Year Tip: I know everyone says have a sense of humour, keep an open mind or make a gap-year diary. These are useful, but really the best top tip available is save some time for travelling at the end of your trip to see a bit of the world.

Name: Rebecca Grossberg Joseph
Age: 29
Favourite Country: Poland
My Gap Year: After I finished university in the USA, I came to France and planned to stay for only three months to house-sit and help an American tour guide before returning home to a real job. I ended up spending the entire year in the south of France as an au pair. I then moved to Paris to look for a job, did a lot of babysitting and did an internship at a major news company. I also did a lot of travelling in France, Spain and Italy and around Europe.
Top Gap-Year Tip: The best advice I can give is to not be scared of being alone or going somewhere different. Listen to other travellers because the best advice comes from the people you meet in trains, bars, youth hostels etc.

Name: Lewis Webster
Age: 29
Favourite Country: Australia
My Gap Year: I spent the year in Australia on a one-year working holiday visa. I flew into Melbourne, bought a car and more or less followed the coast anticlockwise. My first big stop was Brisbane, where I spent about two months before continuing up the east coast. Then I worked as a dive master on a live-aboard dive boat on the Great Barrier Reef out of Cairns, for about three months, followed by a couple of months camping around the Northern Territory and Western Australia. I stopped off in Perth over Christmas and finally headed back to Melbourne to sell the car and fly home.
Top Gap-Year Tip: My 'top tip' would be to not plan too rigidly. Although a bit of structure is necessary for your trip, you'll have more fun if you value the unplanned and unexpected.

Gap Planner

Here are three blank Gap Planners that will help you map out your next year or so. You'll probably change your mind time and time again, and want to try out several itineraries, which is why we've printed three of them here.

July

August

September

October

November

December

January

February

March

April

May

June

July

August

September

July

August

September

October

November

December

January

February

March

April

May

June

July

August

September

July

August

September

October

November

December

January

February

March

April

May

June

July

August

September

Acknowledgments

This second edition of *The Gap Year Book* was written by a team of professional gappers led by Charlotte Hindle. Charlotte wrote all of Part I, and the Volunteering, Conservation & Expeditions, Work your Route, Au Pairing & Working with Kids and Courses chapters. Joe Bindloss wrote the Indian Subcontinent, Proper Jobs, Teaching and Casual/Seasonal Work chapters. The Part II chapters were all written by Lonely Planet regional experts.

The book was commissioned and developed in Lonely Planet's London office by Laetitia Clapton, and the project was managed by Bridget Blair and Andrew Weatherill. It was edited by Brigitte Barta and Martine Lleonart with assistance from Gina Tsarouhas, Adrienne Costanzo, Margedd Heliosz and Jodie Martire, and the index was prepared by Brigitte Barta. The book was designed by James Hardy and laid out by Adam Bextream. The cover was designed by Wendy Wright and James Hardy was responsible for the cover artwork. The maps were created by Wayne Murphy, Paul Piaia, Julie Sheridan and Herman So.

Thanks from the Authors
CHARLOTTE HINDLE
I would like to thank Paul and Jason Goodyer from Nomad Travel (www.nomad.co.uk), David Orkin, Jane Pringle from UCAS, Mark Restall from Volunteering England, Michelle Beresford, Rachel Day, Neil Mullane and Dawn Howell from STA Travel, John Masterson from Trailfinders, Peter Wilson from the UK Passport Service, Michelle Hawkins from Médecins du Monde, Paul from Crewseekers, Robert Weeks from the Berkeley Scott Group, John Stanford from the Royal Society for Disability and Rehabilitation (RADAR) and Phil Casey from Diabetes UK.

A special thanks must go to all the fabulous gappers who put so much time and effort into their interviews for this book. You were inspiring and really generous with your thoughts, comments, advice and tips. Thank you.

Last but not least, I'd like to thank Laetitia Clapton, my commissioning editor, and my husband, Simon, for proofreading and invaluable advice.

JOE BINDLOSS
My thanks to all the people who provided testimonials about their gap-year experiences and information about programs overseas. As always, thanks to my girlfriend Linda for her support and patience. Thanks to David McClymont at the Lonely Planet Thorn Tree for recruiting gappers to be interviewed and fielding off stalkers, and to Charlotte Hindle for solid support and advice.

Thanks from Lonely Planet
Lonely Planet would like to thank our fantastic team of authors on this book, helmed again by the wonderful coordinating author Charlotte Hindle. We would also like to thank the many people who talked to our authors so helpfully about their gap years for the book. We would love to hear from more gappers, so if you would like to tell us about your experiences and possibly be included in the next edition of this book please contact us at talk2us@lonelyplanet.com.au stating *The Gap Year Book* in the subject line.

456

Index

A

activities 229-32
adventure sports
    Indian Subcontinent 167-8
adventure travel 17
Africa 123-36
    activities 125-8
    attractions 126
    books 134-5
    border crossings 132
    classic routes 129
    climate 130
    costs 133
    festivals 130-1
    hangouts 127-8
    health 132
    language 131
    people 131
    safety 132
    time 132
    tours 134
    travel to/from 133-4
    travel within 128-9
    voluntary work 125
    wildlife watching 126
    work 128
air travel 24-9, 119-20
    air passes 26
    airlines 27-8
    circle fares 26
    discount return tickets 25
    e-tickets 27
    no-frills flights 27
    one-way tickets 26
    open-jaw tickets 26
    round-the-world tickets 25
    student & youth fares 27
    tickets 24-30
    to/from Africa 133-4
    to/from Australia, New Zealand &
        the Pacific 224, 225
    to/from Europe 119-20
    to/from Mexico, Central & South
        America 259-60
    to/from Middle East 146-7
    to/from North America & the
        Caribbean 242-3, 244
    to/from Northeast Asia 188
    to/from Russia, Central Asia & the
        Caucasus 159
    to/from the Indian Subcontinent 174
    within Africa 128
    within Australia, New Zealand &
        the Pacific 217
    within Indian Subcontinent 168

within Mexico, Central & South
    America 253
within Middle East 142
within North America & the
    Caribbean 235-7
within Northeast Asia 183
within Russia, Central Asia & the
    Caucasus 154
within Southeast Asia 198, 206-7
alcohol 73
Andalucía 109
arts courses 432-7
ashrams 165-6
au pairing 404-15
Australia, New Zealand & the Pacific
    210-27
    activities 211-19
    attractions 210-11
    books 225-6
    classic routes 218-19
    climate 219
    costs 223-4
    festivals 219-20
    hangouts 220-1
    health 222
    language 221-2
    people 221
    safety 223
    time 222-3
    tours 225
    travel to/from 224-5
    travel within 217-18
    work 216-17

B

bargaining 48
Berlin 109
bird-watching
    Northeast Asia 182
blogs 88
boat travel 29
    Africa 128
    to/from Africa 134
    to/from Australia, New Zealand &
        the Pacific 224
    to/from Europe 120-1
    to/from Middle East 147
    to/from North America & the
        Caribbean 243-5
    to/from Northeast Asia 189
    to/from Russia, Central Asia & the
        Caucasus 159
    to/from the Indian Subcontinent 174
    within Australia, New Zealand &
        the Pacific 218
    within Europe 114

within Indian Subcontinent 168
within Mexico, Central & South
    America 253, 254
within Middle East 142
within North America & the
    Caribbean 236, 237
within Northeast Asia 183
within Russia, Central Asia & the
    Caucasus 154
within Southeast Asia 197, 199, 207
books 18
    about Africa 134-5
    about Australia, New Zealand &
        the Pacific 225-6
    about Europe 121
    about Mexico, Central & South
        America 260-1
    about North America & the
        Caribbean 244
    about Northeast Asia 189-90
    about Russia, Central Asia & the
        Caucasus 160
    about Southeast Asia 207-8
    about the Indian Subcontinent 175
    about the Middle East 147-8
border crossings, see individual regions
boyfriend, see partner
British Council 356, 360
bungee jumping
    Australia, New Zealand & the
        Pacific 214
bus travel 30
    within Africa 128
    within Australia, New Zealand &
        the Pacific 217
    within Europe 114
    within Indian Subcontinent 168
    within Mexico, Central & South
        America 253
    within Middle East 142
    within North America & the
        Caribbean 236
    within Northeast Asia 183
    within Russia, Central Asia & the
        Caucasus 154
    within Southeast Asia 198

C

camel trekking
    Australia, New Zealand & the
        Pacific 216
    Indian Subcontinent 167
    Middle East 140
    Russia, Central Asia & the Caucasus
        151
cameras 56-7
canoeing, see watersports

CONTACTS